KAZAKHSTAN 2050

TOWARD A MODERN SOCIETY FOR ALL

KAZAKHSTAN 2050
TOWARD A MODERN SOCIETY FOR ALL

Editors

Aktoty Aitzhanova

Shigeo Katsu

Johannes F. Linn

Vladislav Yezhov

Oxford University Press is a department of the University of Oxford.
It furthers the University's objective of excellence in research, scholarship,
and education by publishing worldwide. Oxford is a registered trademark of
Oxford University Press in the UK and in certain other countries

Published in India by
Oxford University Press
YMCA Library Building, 1 Jai Singh Road, New Delhi 110001, India

National Analytical Center of Nazarbayev University
Astana, 010000, Kabanbay Batyr Avenue 17, Block A Floor 4, Kazakhstan

First edition published in 2014

ISBN-13: 978-0-19-945060-2
ISBN-10: 0-19-945060-9

Printed in India at Lustra Print Process Pvt Ltd., New Delhi

This report is part of a study commissioned by NAC of Nazarbayev University

The findings and recommendations of the report are solely the responsibility of the
authors and the Centennial Group International

Contents

Boxes, Figures, and Tables

Boxes

Figures

Tables

List of Abbreviations

ADB	Asian Development Bank
BAU	business-as-usual
BEEPS	Business Environment and Enterprise Performance Survey
BRICS	Brazil, Russia, India, China, South Africa
BRT	Bus Rapid Transit
BTI	Bertelsmann Transformation Index
CACO	Central Asian Cooperation Organization
CAREC	Central Asia Regional Economic Cooperation Program
CES	Common Economic Space
CIS	Commonwealth of Independent States
CPE	centrally planned economy
DB	Doing Business
EBRD	European Bank for Reconstruction and Development
ECO	Economic Cooperation Organization
EE	energy efficiency
EIA	US Energy Information Administration
EITI	Extractive Industries Transparency Initiative
ESCO	energy service company
EurAsEC	Eurasian Economic Community
FAO	Food and Agriculture Organization
FDI	foreign direct investment
FSU	Former Soviet Union
GATS	first agreement on trade in services
GCI	Global Competitiveness Index
GMO	Genetically Modified Organisms
GWh	gigawatt Hour
ICT	information and communications technology
IPCC	Intergovernmental Panel on Climate Change
KazREFF	Kazakhstan Renewable Energy Financing Facility
KMG	KazMunaiGas
KZT	Kazakhstan tenge
MOOC	massive open online course
MTOE	million tons of oil equivalent
OSCE	Organization for Security and Co-operation in Europe

n/a	not available
NAC	National Analytical Center of Nazarbayev University
NAFTA	North American Free Trade Area
NIS	Nazarbayev Intellectual Schools
NU	Nazarbayev University
OECD	Organisation for Economic Co-operation and Development
P4P	pay for performance
PAYG	pay-as-you-go
PIRLS	Progress in International Reading Literacy Study
PM	particulate matter
PPP	public-private partnership
PPP	purchasing power parity
PSP	private sector participation
RE	renewable energy
RTA	regional trade agreement
SCO	Shanghai Cooperation Organization
SER	State Energy Register
SEZ	Special Economic Zones
SGBP	State Guaranteed Benefit Package of services
SOE	state-owned enterprises
SPAIID	State Programs for Accelerated Innovation Development
SPECA	Special Programme for the Economies of Central Asia
TFP	total factor productivity
toe	tons of oil equivalent
TSA	Targeted Social Assistance program
TVET	Technical and Vocational Education and Training
TWh	terawatt hour
UES	United Economic Space
UNDP	United Nations Development Programme
UNEP	United Nations Environment Programme
UNT	Unified National Test
USD	US dollar
WEF	World Economic Forum
WGI	Worldwide Governance Indicators
WTO	World Trade Organization

Exchange Rate (September 2013)
1.00 Kazakhstani Tenge = .00653168 US Dollar
1.00 US Dollar = 153.100 Kazakhstani Tenge

Foreword

On December 16, 22 years ago a new state, the Republic of Kazakhstan was born. It was a difficult but decisive departure from the former Soviet Union. We subsequently went through a very trying period in the 1990s, but the country stayed true to the chosen course of sovereignty, of building a modern society, a market-oriented economy and a multi-ethnic society, and establishing good relations with all neighbors.

Since independence Kazakhstan's citizens have demonstrated time and again their willingness and ability to shape their own future. Whether dealing with regional crises or global crises, Kazakhstanis have found a way to keep their country on track.

As soon as the situation allowed, and even in the midst of major difficulties, we looked ahead and turned our attention to building for the future, for the next generations of Kazakhs.

We invested in education, including the creation of the Bolashak overseas scholarship program, because educated citizens form the foundation of a modern society;

We invested in modernizing the health care system as improvement in health status is a key measure of social progress;

We invested significant resources in modernization and expansion of infrastructure so as to provide better services to our citizens, enhance competitiveness of our economy and improve connectivity with our neighbors.

Our country is very fortunate to be endowed with oil, gas, and minerals; these sub-soil resources have facilitated our economic development. We have also established a National Fund to preserve the fruits of these resources for future generations.

We have always aimed to create a market based diversified economy built on sound macroeconomic management and on a supportive business environment, in order to generate high quality jobs for future generations of our citizens, to foster our international competitiveness, and to make the economy more resilient to external and internal shocks.

In the midst of our difficulties in 1997 we pulled together these and other strategic strands into the "Strategy 2030." By taking a long term view of nation-building we wanted to signal to our citizens that the sacrifices required during the early years of independence would be amply repaid by building shared long term prosperity.

Now at the mid-point of our endeavor toward 2030, we are comforted and feel validated. The ambitious "Strategy 2030" has indeed galvanized our society; and we are confident that the nation is ahead of schedule in achieving most of the goals laid out in this strategy. Our GDP has grown more than nine-fold and per capita income over eight-fold between 1997 and 2012. Kazakhstan is an upper middle-income country today and ranks among the top 50 most competitive economies. Population has rebounded to 17 million, 4 in 10 persons have tertiary education, life expectancy is back to almost 70 years, and we have been able to contain inequality. We have built credible economic institutions such as the National

Bank. Internationally we have no outstanding border issues, and our sovereignty is unchallenged.

As responsible global citizens, our country voluntarily decided to renounce nuclear arms and build a strong environmental platform. Our actions have helped to stake out a well-respected position in the international arena. Kazakhstan has become a regular venue for international dialogue.

However, this is not the time to rest on our laurels. Kazakhstan cannot afford to stand still. We are still far from where we want to be. At the same time, international competition is getting ever more intense and other successful economies continue to march forward even as we make progress at home. The world is seeing a number of emerging countries assuming a more prominent international role, buoyed by strong economic growth. We are not only witness to this seminal transformation of global economic and financial relations, but are determined to make Kazakhstan an important actor in this global transformation.

This is why, in December 2012, I announced the "Strategy 2050"; this is why we set out an ambitious new goal for Kazakhstan: to join the "Top Thirty Advanced Countries" by 2050. That is why on September 9, 2013, in a keynote address to the Eurasian Emerging Market Forum in Astana I presented my concepts of what it means to be a top thirty developed nation.

Of course economic well-being as reflected in per capita incomes is an important part of reaching this ambitious goal, and building an innovative knowledge-based economy that allows Kazakhstan to shed its dependence on natural resources is imperative. However, equally important will be "quality-of-life" with world class levels of education and science, health and environment, high quality jobs and housing, great cities and great outdoors, and great institutions including pubic administration and legal systems that rival the best in the world.

Together, we want to build a thoroughly modern inclusive society which upholds at the same time our traditional values of solidarity, loyalty, generosity, and tolerance.

Building this society that all citizens of Kazakhstan aspire to will neither be easy, nor will it be straightforward. But I want to challenge my fellow citizens to work with me to realize this vision, to take on this audacious project as we have taken on the challenge of our transformation since independence.

I have always maintained that it is always good to have someone else hold a mirror up to us to remind us of where we are today and what it takes to achieve our goals. This book, prepared by independent international experts with over 250 years of cumulative experience in international development, is meant to provide us with such a mirror. The authors present their sense of the path Kazakhstan needs to take to reach our vision by 2050. In my view, another fundamental contribution of their work is to provide a platform, jointly with other analytic work on the topic of Kazakhstan 2050, for a thoughtful debate and dialogue on the way forward for our society. I urge my fellow citizens to embrace the vision and participate in this open dialogue for our future.

I express my deep appreciation and thanks to the authors and reiterate our nation's determination to build a modern society with shared prosperity for all.

Nursultan Nazarbayev
President
Republic of Kazakhstan

Preface

Kazakhstan's ongoing efforts to create a modern state and become a top developed economy in less than two generations are of crucial importance not only to all Kazakhstanis, but also to the people throughout Asia and Europe.

A modern and affluent Kazakh society and a stable nation state will create a welcome and mutually beneficial land bridge between the best of two worlds: the fast-rising economies to its east and the most developed societies to its west, both of which seek Kazakhstan's abundant natural resources. On the other hand, a stagnant or weak Kazakhstan with many fragile states to its south could lead to instability throughout Central Asia — something neither Asia nor Europe desire. Kazakhstan's future economic and social trajectory would not only be watched by its former peers in the Soviet Union, by East Asia and Europe, but also by emerging market economies — particularly resource-rich countries — throughout the world.

The country has come a long way since it emerged as an independent state a mere twenty-two years ago, in 1991, on the dissolution of the Soviet Union. Despite its immense size and a long cultural history, it was widely regarded as the most fragile of the former states of the Soviet Union, and its per capita income at that time was lower than the average for these states. Like most new countries, its capacity as a nation state to succeed on its own was unproven and indeed doubted by many outside observers.

In the years immediately following its creation, the country's economy underwent a major and pro-longed decline as its economic role, trade and investment flows under the Soviet Union were broadly disrupted or even disbanded, without immediately being replaced by economic ties with other parts of the world. In other words, the country had to make do with its own human, physical and institutional resources.

In the past twenty plus years, Kazakhstan's citizens and leadership have demonstrated time and again their willingness and ability to shape their destiny. In dealing first with its own economic crisis and sub-sequently the 2008 global financial crisis, Kazakhstanis have found ways to overcome the challenges, while simultaneously moving the country forward. By now, Kazakhstan is universally recognized as a sovereign state, secure in its borders and respected by the international community; by most measures it is one of the most successful former Soviet republics.

Kazakhstan has created a market-oriented economy and a modern, multi-ethnic society, and has established good relations with its neighbors. It has also developed closer trade and investment relations with its neighbors to the East (China) and the West (Western Europe). Kazakhstan's macroeconomic management has proven effective. The economy has not only recovered fully from a severe economic depression in the 1990s and proved resilient after the global financial crisis in 2008, but has moved ahead of its peers in the former Soviet Union in terms of per capita income. The World Bank now classifies it as an upper middle income economy. And, Kazakhstan's rich natural resources have made it a magnet for foreign direct investments, while its exports have surged, aided of course by favorable international commodity markets. Given these positive developments on so many fronts since independence, Kazakhstanis would be justified in deriving great pride in their accomplishments and resting on their laurels.

It is therefore a great tribute to them and the country's leadership that they have instead chosen to set their sights much higher and adopted the very ambitious goal of joining the club of top thirty developed countries by 2050 in terms of not only per capita income levels, but also the quality of life as enjoyed in much of Europe, North America, and Japan today. The present book looks at how realistic these goals are and goes on to outline a strategy on how to realize them in less than two generations.

To me, the most impressive aspect of this endeavor is the fact that the Kazakh authorities tasked one of the country's top universities — the Nazarbayev University — to commission an independent study by a team of international experts with an impeccable reputation and over 250 years of development policy experience at the highest levels to carry out this work in collaboration with a local think tank.

The team has done an outstanding job in carrying out its mandate with integrity and has outlined a credible strategy. While not everyone may agree with each of its proposals and recommendations, I believe that, overall, the team has presented an excellent starting point for an open and broad discussion within the country on how to move forward.

Therefore I express my heartiest congratulations to the authors for a job well done.

Joseph Deiss
Co-chair, Eurasia Emerging Markets Forum,
Former President of the United Nations General Assembly,
Former Federal Councilor, and President of the Swiss Confederation

Acknowledgments

This report was prepared by a team of international experts consisting of William Y. Brown, Dennis de Tray, Harpaul Alberto Kohli, Johannes F. Linn, John Nellis, Richard Pomfret, Hossein Razavi, Michelle Riboud, and Shahid Yusuf. Staff of the National Analytical Center (NAC) of Nazarbayev University and of Centennial Group International provided research and editorial support. Johannes F. Linn served as project leader and principal coordinating editor. Shigeo Katsu, President of Nazarbayev University, Aktoty Aitzhanova and Vladislav Yezhov of the NAC, and Harinder S. Kohli of Centennial provided overall guidance.

• • • • • • • •

The editors owe a deep gratitude to the many individuals who contributed to making this book possible.

First and foremost, we thank the authorities of Kazakhstan for their support in making it possible for this independent research and analysis to be carried out. In particular we wish gratefully to acknowledge the overall interest of President Nursultan Nazarbayev in this work. Throughout our work the expert team benefited greatly from the guidance of Mr. Karim Massimov, Head of the Presidential Administration, and of Mr. Yerbol Orynbayev, Deputy Prime Minister. The expert team also had an opportunity to meet and discuss its analysis with many officials of the Government of Kazakhstan and benefited from access to many informative documents and to statistical information.

We are grateful to many experts from national and international institutions and to members of the diplomatic corps in Astana, whom the expert team was able to consult. Special thanks are due to the Asian Development Bank, the European Bank for Reconstruction and Development, UNDP, and the World Bank, whose in-depth analytical work was of great value to us.

We owe special thanks to the International Advisory Group consisting of Messrs. Michael Emerson, Peter Ho, and Christof Ruehl. They provided the team with important early feedback on its work.

We had an opportunity to present preliminary results of our analysis at the Second Eurasia Emerging Markets Forum in Astana on September 10-11, 2013. We are grateful to the participants for their many helpful comments and insights.

Finally we wish to thank the members of the expert team for their outstanding professional work and the members of NAC and of Centennial for their excellent analytical and editorial support. In particular, at NAC we wish to thank Dana Abiltayeva, Anastassiya Iskaliyeva, Daniyar Kaliyev, Azhar Khamidullina, Anara Makatova, Dmitriy Makauskas, Meryuert Shabakbayeva, Serik Tanirbergen, and Aida Urazaliyeva; and at Centennial, Hanzhi Jiang, Michael Lopesciolo, Anil Sood, Alex Tate, Ieva Vilkelyte, and Yanbei Yao.

• • • • • • • •

This project was funded by a grant from Nazarbayev University.

TOWARD A MODERN SOCIETY FOR ALL: OVERVIEW

Toward a Modern Society for All: Overview

Chapter 1

Aktoty Aitzhanova, Shigeo Katsu, Johannes F. Linn, and Vladislav Yezhov

A Confident Young Nation Looking at a Future of Opportunities

Kazakhstan is a vast country with 17 million inhabitants. Its massive size, equal to all of Western Europe, connects Europe and Asia. It is at once one of the cradles of modern human beings, with a rich history, and one of the youngest modern nations in the world, less than 22 years old.

The country has come a long way since independence on December 16, 1991 following the dissolution of the Soviet Union. Many observers considered Kazakhstan as perhaps the most vulnerable of the former Soviet republics. There were doubts about its viability as an independent nation and the security of its borders. The country's economy was fragile, and immediately after independence it entered free fall for a few years.

Since independence, Kazakhstan has made great progress with a sustained economic recovery since 1999 and significant improvements in the lives of Kazakhstani citizens. Today Kazakhstan is a sovereign state, secure in its borders and respected by the international community; by most measures, it is one of the most successful former Soviet republics.

Kazakhstan's Strategy 2030, launched in 1997, one of the most difficult years, has had a galvanizing effect on the country. Kazakhstan has created a market-oriented economy and a modern multi-ethnic society, and it has established good relations with its neighbors. It has also developed closer trade relations with its neighbors to the east (China) and the west (Western Europe).

Kazakhstan's macroeconomic management has proven effective. The economy recovered fully from a severe economic depression in the 1990s and proved resilient after the global financial crisis in 2008. High growth during the 2000s created jobs and brought down poverty (Figure 1.1). GDP has grown nine-fold and per capita income eight-fold between 1997 and 2012.

Kazakhstan is now an upper middle-income country and ranks among the top 50 most competitive economies in the world. Population has rebounded to 17 million, 4 in 100 persons have tertiary education, life expectancy is back to 70 years, and the country has been able to contain inequality. It has built some credible economic institutions, such as the National Bank.

The country has obviously benefited from strong international demand for petroleum, its main export. Fortunately, domestic oil and gas production surged just as the recent boom in international oil prices began. At the same time, prudent economic policies, a careful husbanding of oil revenues and decisive, forward-looking national leadership played a crucial role in the dramatic improvements in people's economic fortunes and well-being.

But, Kazakhstan cannot afford to be complacent. The country is far from where it can and wants to be. At the same time, international competition is getting ever more intense and other successful economies continue to march forward, even as Kazakhstan makes progress at home. Many emerging countries are assuming a more prominent international role, buoyed by strong economic growth. Based on the

1

1

foundation built during the past 20 years, Kazakhstan can also look forward to a promising future and become an important actor in this global transformation. It has a young and well-educated labor force. It has by now a proven track record of effective economic management. Revenues from natural resources should support future investments to create a diversified economy. The global economic environment is expected to be overall hospitable for the next few years. Last, Kazakhstan can benefit from its location at the center of Eurasia.

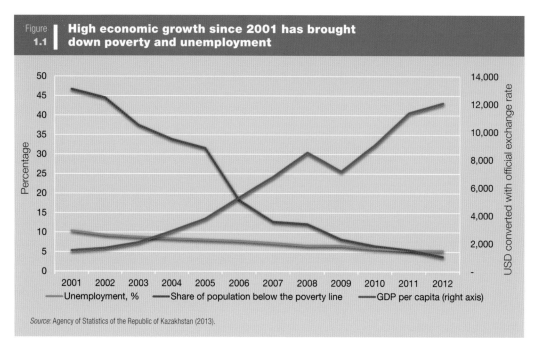

Figure 1.1 High economic growth since 2001 has brought down poverty and unemployment

Source: Agency of Statistics of the Republic of Kazakhstan (2013).

Kazakhstan's economy, like many others, also faces risks from the international environment, in addition to challenges at home. The global economy remains fragile. Important partners such as Russia, China, Europe, the US, and Japan may face economic stagnation. Oil and gas prices could soften. Unexpected technological developments could alter the direction of the global economy, including demand for oil and gas. There is also potential for conflict and political instability to Kazakhstan's south. And, over the longer term, climate change could adversely affect the Kazakh economy and people. More generally, Kazakhstan has to avoid pitfalls associated with the so-called "resource curse" that have held back progress in the majority of economies heavily dependent on exploitation of their natural resources, as well as avoid getting mired in the "middle-income trap," which has become the bane of so many countries at the same stage of development at which Kazakhstan is currently.

To manage these risks successfully and take advantage of opportunities, the country must continue to build a resilient, dynamic, and flexible economy. Also, to achieve the broad-based competitiveness and to provide the wide array of opportunities for its citizens associated with a developed country, Kazakhstan has to find ways to create a much more diversified and innovative economy with effective and credible institutions that rank amongst the best in the world.

Today, Kazakhstan ranks mostly in the middle of the global country rankings on many indexes of comparative performance. Looking ahead, Kazakhstan must move toward the top ranks of nations across the board. Special attention will need to be paid to the important areas of governance (particularly control of corruption), increase in accountability, promotion of transparency, development of civil society, and improvement of electoral participation. In implementing governance-related actions, it is helpful to keep in mind the international experience that high concentration of wealth can undermine such efforts.

The Ambitious Vision of Kazakhstan 2050

In December 2012, the President of the Republic of Kazakhstan announced the Strategy 2050, which sets forth a bold vision of the country joining the ranks of the top 30 developed countries by 2050. Becoming one of the top 30 developed countries in terms of per capita income is important, but as the President emphasized, what the 2050 vision really aims at most of all is to improve the quality of life of all Kazakhstani people.

Global experience confirms that, after a society reaches a basic threshold of income, qualitative aspects of life become increasingly more important to people than the acquisition of more material wealth: a clean environment (including air and water quality); personal safety; the rule of law; high-quality public services; universal education, health care, and social safety systems; credible and accountable institutions (civil service, courts, police, taxation authority, press, etc.), freedom of expression and freedom of choice; and peaceful relations with and ease of access to the rest of the world. To join the group of top 30 developed countries, Kazakhstan will require continuous progress over time in all these areas, in addition to significant improvements in per capita income and national wealth.

The Vision 2050 adopted by the country is unique in its ambition and scope. We are not aware of any other country where the leadership has publicly championed such a bold transformation extended over such a long period. This study indicates that it is a plausible goal for Kazakhstan to join the top 30 developed countries by 2050. But it is an extremely challenging goal, precisely because it not only means achieving a high per capita income, but because of the many other dimensions of achieving an outstanding quality of life. Perhaps the most important and the most difficult part of the vision is the achievement of the institutional dimension of the vision. In our work, therefore, we have focused equally on how to achieve the quantitative and qualitative goals to realize the 2050 vision.

Seven Priority Areas for Action

In line with the Vision 2050, the report discusses seven priority areas in which Kazakhstan faces great opportunities, as well as challenges, as it aims to achieve the goal of joining the ranks of the top 30 developed countries and creating a modern society for all Kazakhstanis:

- First, create a strong human resource base: value well-educated, healthy citizens who have meaningful jobs and are protected by a sound social safety net; build a modern education system from early childhood to post-doctoral research; and promote preventive medicine with patient responsibility;
- Second, effectively and sustainably manage Kazakhstan's energy resources: establish sound targets for energy extraction and efficiency, along with institutional structures that will help with their implementation;
- Third, achieve a green economy: preserve Kazakhstan's rich environment and enhance global competitiveness; explore carbon taxation; expand protection of natural reserves and biodiversity; and promote a resilient agriculture drawing on proven genetically modified organisms;

- Fourth, build balanced and efficient urban and regional economies: strengthen a decentralized, empowered, and accountable governmental structure; upgrade urban services; invest in information and communications technology (ICT) connectivity; expand local authorities' revenue and expenditure authority with clear oversight; and build strong local capacity for infrastructure and communal services management;
- Fifth, build a diversified, modern knowledge economy on the foundation of the aformentioned priority areas: promote competition in all economic activities; improve the business environment; support priority areas in a selective, transparent, and competitive manner; and develop world-class research universities and smart cities;
- Sixth, continue to be open to the rest of the world and ready to work with all neighbors: join the World Trade Organization (WTO); provide leadership on Central Asian cooperation; and develop transit infrastructure connecting its neighbors to the east and west; and
- Seventh, build a strong institutional capacity: implement policies in an effective, fair, and transparent manner; create more space for private entrepreneurship; control corruption; and pursue economic reforms while accelerating the pace of political reform, in line with repeated statements by the head of state.

As Figure 1.2 demonstrates, these seven priority areas constitute an interrelated package and should not be seen as stand-alone objectives. They interact with each other, reinforcing each other when they work well, but impeding each other when they do not. Effective human development is at the foundation of all economic and social development, and high-quality and effective institutions are crucial for timely implementation of policies and strategies adopted for all other areas. The other priority areas play

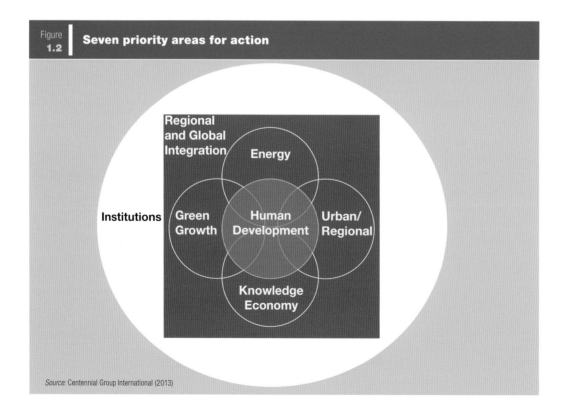

Figure 1.2 | **Seven priority areas for action**

Regional and Global Integration

Energy

Institutions

Green Growth

Human Development

Urban/ Regional

Knowledge Economy

Source: Centennial Group International (2013)

1

important roles in their own right and are supported by, and in turn support, human and institutional development. In other words, human and institutional development are like two book ends that hold the seven areas together; without them, actions in other areas will not work.

There are other priority areas that matter for Kazakhstan, including macroeconomic management, agriculture, and the financial sector, to mention just a few. We touch on these issues in various ways, but concluded that it is in the seven priority areas selected for this study that Kazakhstan faces the greatest challenges and opportunities in reaching for its long-term vision. We also did not explore the important area of cultural and ethnic roots of Kazakhstani society and its implications for contemporary economic, social, environmental, and institutional policy in Kazakhstan. We believe this deserves more attention and research, especially in connection with the institutional development agenda; however, it was beyond the scope of this study.

For each of the seven areas we take stock of the current situation in Kazakhstan and identify a vision consistent with the overall vision for Kazakhstan 2050. Based on Kazakhstan's experience to date and on lessons from international experience, the report then offers recommendations for actions phased in over the short, medium, and long term that in our view will help Kazakhstan achieve its ambitious vision. Among the many potential actions that we identify in these 7 areas, the 24 actions in Table 1.1 stand out.

Crosscutting Principles for Action

As we look across the seven priority areas we highlight as follows a number of important crosscutting issues and lessons taken from global experience that, in our view, should guide the formulation and implementation of strategies and policies in all areas, including the seven priority areas discussed. These key issues and lessons can be summarized best with a list of eight principles to be promoted with a sense of urgency: openness; resilience and flexibility; competition and competitiveness; cooperation; inclusiveness; sustainability; effective implementation; and accountability. These principles reinforce each other and play a critical role in designing the reforms. While the exact weight assigned to each principle in designing policies in specific areas may vary, in our view, most of them will be relevant in all policy areas. Figure 1.3 illustrates this framework.

1. *Openness*: All top 30 developed countries of today are open to the rest of the world in terms of trade, investment, and attraction of people with skills and ideas; in terms of transport and electronic connectivity; and in terms of linkages among individuals, firms, and cities. Openness together with other principles enunciated as follows is an essential prerequisite for innovation that has to drive the "new" economy. It also translates into transparent and accessible institutions.

2. *Resilience*: With openness comes inevitably exposure to external shocks, whether from fluctuating commodity prices, financial crises, conflicts in neighboring countries, or, in the longer term, the headwinds of global warming. The financial crisis of 2007-9 showed that resilience matters. Lessons from the experience of countries (including Kazakhstan) that performed well in the aftermath of the global financial crisis of 2007-9 include: the need to ensure that fundamental macroeconomic management remains prudent; the dangers of overextending the financial sector; the importance of ample fiscal and foreign exchange to make employing fiscal stimulus easier; and, most of all, the importance of strong and agile institutions.

3. *Competitiveness and competition*: To reap the opportunities that openness brings, Kazakhstan needs to attain a high degree of competitiveness in all seven priority areas (as well as in other elements of the economy and society). The creation of the modern knowledge economy will be critical to allow Kazakhstan to join the top-30 club. Competitiveness is built on competition—open and effective competition among the many actors (public and private) in the domestic economy and across the rest of the world.

Table 1.1	Major recommendations for Kazakhstan 2050		
Area	**Action**	**Area**	**Action**
1. Human Development	• Focus on quality improvement and implementation • Introduce targeted early childhood development program • Scale up school and university reforms • Promote preventive medicine, with patient responsibility	5. Knowledge Economy	• Selectivity in government support for priority areas • Attract/buy into foreign firms • Develop research universities
2. Energy	• Set energy sector targets aiming at efficiency and sustainability • Establish Super ESCOs • Establish renewable energy fund	6. Global and Regional Integration	• Join WTO and assure "open" Customs Union • Provide leadership on Central Asian cooperation • Develop hard and soft transit infrastructure
3. Green Growth	• Introduce carbon taxation and annual review of regulations • Expand and improve management of natural reserves and introduce "no-net-loss" provision of biodiversity generally • Allow Genetically Modified Organisms (GMOs) and advance industrial waste management	7. Institutions	• Reverse increasing trend of state involvement in the economy • Implement anti-corruption action • Promote accountability, transparency, civil society, and rule of law
4. Urban and Regional Development and Decentralization	• Upgrade urban services • Limit car use in cities • Invest in ICT connectivity • Clarify and rebalance revenue and expenditure responsibilities of subnational authorities • Introduce subnational development fund		

Source: Centennial Group International (2013)

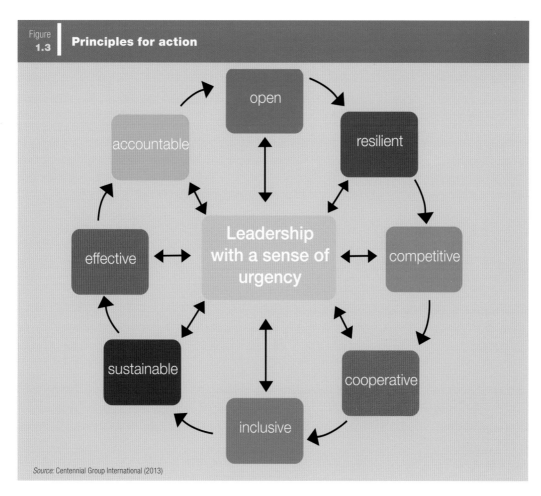

Figure 1.3 **Principles for action**

open

accountable

resilient

effective ⟷ **Leadership with a sense of urgency** ⟷ competitive

sustainable

cooperative

inclusive

Source: Centennial Group International (2013)

Only if domestic firms, government officials, and individuals face effective competition that stimulates performance, values results, and promotes on merit is the country likely to achieve competitiveness in the global marketplace.

4. *Cooperation*: Openness also brings with it responsibilities as a global and regional player, and competition needs to be matched by cooperation and partnerships, whether dealing with global climate change and food security, regional water issues or disaster preparedness, or a regional bank for seeds and other viable plant and animal tissues.

5. *Inclusiveness*: A cooperative spirit and sense of responsibility should extend not only to neighbors and the international community, but also toward all fellow citizens in the country. Inclusiveness plays a pervasive role in many of the seven priorities that we discussed in the preceding lines, both by contributing to an economic and political system that more effectively achieves the goals of the Vision 2050 and as an element of the quality of life.

6. *Sustainability*: This integral part of the vision underpins the long-term perspective of Kazakhstan 2050. It is embodied in the notion that 2050 is not merely seen as an endpoint, but as a threshold point by which Kazakhstan should have built a platform that can sustain a prosperous and stable society well into the second half of the 21st century. Beyond this, however, sustainability of natural, physical, human, and institutional assets and the services they provide for the people of Kazakhstan is a critical attribute of a successful strategy or initiative.

7. *Effectiveness*: Positing an ambitious vision and identifying key policies and programs that will contribute to achieving the vision are essential steps. But it is as important to ensure effective implementation of the policies and programs. Monitoring, evaluation, and adaptation are critical aspects of this process and clearly have to be strengthened throughout the policy making and implementation process.

8. *Accountability*: Finally, in order for the other principles to yield desired results it is essential that all economic and political organs and people—whether in the private or public sector, whether individuals or institutions—are held accountable. This extends to their use of resources, the legality of their actions, and the results they achieve.

Alternative Scenarios of Kazakhstan in 2050

We have developed four alternative scenarios using Centennial Group's model of the global economy. The purpose of our quantitative exercise is not to make predictions of what will happen 40 years into the future, but rather to ask "what if" questions and to highlight the long-term implications of broad trends and the country's economic strategies. The model we use is conceptually simple, based on the principle of convergence of low-productivity countries to the international high-productivity frontier (currently the US) depending on whether or not they are able to enjoy productivity gains (the distinction between "converger" and "non-converger" countries). Other key variables are labor force growth and capital stock growth (investment).

In past Centennial Group long-term outlook studies, such scenarios have provided a helpful anchor to focus the discussion with policy makers and attract public attention. However, the reader must be aware of the limitations of any long-term modeling exercise and not treat the scenarios as either predictions or projections. We discuss, as follows, results of two of the scenarios: the desired scenario—steady growth in the global economy with Kazakhstan in convergence—and a "business-as-usual" scenario under which the country does not converge (or falls into the middle-income trap).

Under the convergence scenario, by steadily closing the current productivity gap with the top-30 countries, Kazakhstan's economic growth rates could be sustained at between 4 to 5 percent for most the years of the coming decades. As a result, per capita incomes would reach over USD70,000 by 2050, compared with some USD13,000 in 2011(Figure 1.4). This would place Kazakhstan close to that of the United States. Its global rank would rise to 29th in terms of per capita income at market exchange rates. The country's GDP would be over USD1.5 trillion. Over 90 percent of GDP will be in non-oil sectors, successfully meeting the objective of building a diversified economy. In contrast, under a business-as-usual scenario Kazakhstan not only would not advance, but could even slip further behind from current rankings.

The difference in outcomes between the two scenarios is dramatic, both for the country and for individual citizens. Under the business-as-usual scenario, Kazakhstan's economic growth rate would steadily decline to 2 percent or less. Per capita income would be limited to around USD26,000 by 2050, or just double the 2011 level. GDP would also be only about one-third of that in the convergence scenario.

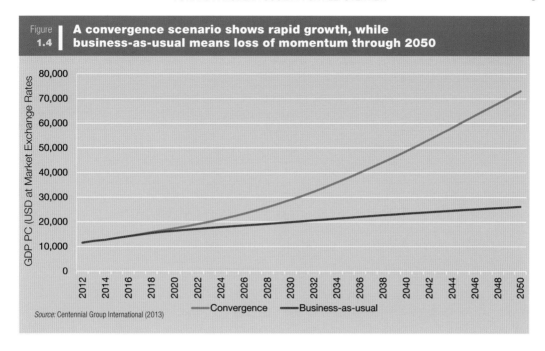

Figure 1.4 | A convergence scenario shows rapid growth, while business-as-usual means loss of momentum through 2050

Source: Centennial Group International (2013)

Convergence ——— Business-as-usual

Outline of the Book

Following this Overview, Chapter 2 provides a retrospective review of where Kazakhstan is coming from in terms of economic and social development, focusing on the years since independence and presenting a portrait of contemporary Kazakhstan. Chapter 3 considers the outlook for the long-term global environment in which Kazakhstan can expect to operate. Chapter 4 then develops our understanding of the vision of Kazakhstan for the 2050.

We then turn to the way forward and the strategy for achieving the vision. We present our analysis and recommendations for the seven key priority areas in which the vision will need to be implemented (see Figure 1.2). Chapters 5, 6, and 7 respectively address how Kazakhstan will manage its human, energy, and environmental resources, while Chapter 8 considers the spatial dimension with coverage of urban, regional, and decentralization issues. Chapter 9 builds on the preceding chapters in exploring how Kazakhstan can create a modern knowledge economy. Chapter 10 then considers how Kazakhstan should pursue international and regional integration as a way to ensure access to markets, finance, and ideas. Chapter 11 concludes the analysis of our seven priority areas by considering the all-important challenges of institutional development, which permeate and overlay all other priority concerns.

In pulling together the findings of this volume, Chapter 12 presents alternative scenarios of long-term growth of Kazakhstan, and Chapter 13 concludes by developing key crosscutting messages and exploring the eight principles for long-term policy formulation and implementation which we presented in the preceding lines.

A postscript summarized the key statements and discussions of Kazakhstan 2050 at the second Eurasia Emerging Markets Forum in Astana, September 10–11 2013.

1

Conclusion

To sum up, the seven priority action areas and eight principles for guiding the reforms are meant to serve as indicative pathways to achieve the ambitious vision of Kazakhstan 2050. Long-term economic scenarios show that Kazakhstan can indeed join the top 30 developed countries in terms of per capita income, but this is far from a foregone conclusion. In our view, these pathways will also help manage, though not eliminate, the two major risks the country faces in its march toward becoming a top-30 developed economy: the risk of suffering from the so-called "resource curse" and the risk of getting mired in the "middle-income trap".

While international conditions matter, Kazakhstan's own efforts will be key. First, management of extractive industries in a cautious and sustainable manner is crucial; second, in the non-resource sector, policies that achieve high productivity growth through private sector–led initiatives and high investment rates, focusing on technological deepening and innovation, are necessary for diversification. To become a top-30 developed country, rapid growth in Kazakhstan's non–natural resource-based economy will be the key; the notion that the non-oil sector will constitute nine-tenths of the economy by 2050 illustrates the magnitude of the task at hand.

Achieving the vision of Kazakhstan 2050 presents great challenges. The policy choices the country will have to make entail difficult economic and political trade-offs. In the end, the people of Kazakhstan have to decide for themselves what works for them and what does not.

What we have offered here are options for action based on objective analysis and international experience. From our perspective, the policy and programmatic choices matter, but the urgency with which they are tackled and the effectiveness and accountability with which they are implemented will be decisive. Implementation of these policies and programs will also determine whether Kazakhstan will be able to take advantage of its geographic location and harvest the best of the two continents to which the country belongs. Kazakhstan could both be a part of the fastest growing region in the world, as Asia drives to make the 21st century its own, and also create for its citizens the quality of life enjoyed by Europe.

Above all else, it is important to keep in mind throughout the ultimate goal of the whole effort: to offer all citizens of Kazakhstan on opportunity to participate in and enjoy the benefits of a successful modern economy.

Kazakhstan's Progress since Independence

Chapter 2

Richard Pomfret

Kazakhstan has a rich cultural and historical heritage, and since independence the country has made much progress in establishing itself as a sovereign nation state with a vibrant economy. This chapter reviews this heritage and draws a portrait of Kazakhstan's current opportunities and challenges as it aims to develop into one of the top 30 developed countries in the world by 2050. The chapter provides a summary of the key trends and turning points and offers a sketch of the economic and social platform on which Kazakhstan can build its future.

The Heritage

Before the 19th century, the geographic space of modern Kazakhstan was occupied primarily by Kazakh nomads. In the 1700s, some of these groups voluntarily sought Tsarist Russian suzerainty, and as Russian control tightened there was a gradual process of settlement by Slav farmers in the 19th century. The most favorable areas for settlement were the southeast of the country and the adjacent Chu Valley in northern Kyrgyzstan. After the Russian annexation of Central Asia and creation of a modern cotton economy there, Kazakhstan's districts adjacent to Uzbekistan also took up cotton growing.

With the transition to the Soviet Union came the introduction of central planning and the stronger government commitment to economic development and to provision of basic needs. The Soviet Union made major contributions to improving education, health, and housing, whose level had been low before 1917. Of all the republics, Kazakhstan was the one that resisted collectivization of agriculture most strenuously; the early 1930s saw massive slaughter of animals, rather than turning them over to collective ownership, and widespread famine with as much as 40 percent of the Kazakh population dying during the 1930s from starvation, epidemics, and executions. In this decade Kazakhstan also became famous as a destination for internal exile. After the outbreak of war in 1941 various ethnic minorities, including ethnic Germans from the west and Koreans from the east, were transported to Kazakhstan.

A further dramatic transformation of Soviet Kazakhstan was the Virgin Lands program introduced by Khrushchev in the 1950s in northern Kazakhstan. The program brought about 25 million hectares into cultivation (over 60 percent of current arable land). As a result, Kazakhstan became a major producer of wheat and barley. Variable climate led to volatile harvests, and the soils in some of the new lands (about 30 percent, according to the World Bank in 1992) were unsuited to long-term cultivation.

Immigration into Kazakhstan's three northern oblasts from the western Soviet Union had major demographic implications. The population of Kazakhstan grew from 7.5 million in 1954 to 10 million in 1960 and more than 12 million in 1965. The share of Kazakhs in the population, which was 57 percent in 1926, had fallen to 30 percent by 1959. Offsetting these demographic changes was the higher birth rate of Kazakhs relative to other ethnic groups. By the 1989 census the shares of Kazakhs and Russians in the republic's population were roughly equal, at just over two-fifths each, with a mix of other groups accounting for the other fifth. After the dissolution of the USSR and relaxing of exit restrictions there was an immediate and large emigration of people with German heritage taking advantage of citizenship rules in Germany and a more gradual emigration of people of Slavic background.

Although agriculture remained the largest sector of the economy by employment, there was also substantial expansion of mining during the Soviet era as many mineral deposits were explored and then exploited with the establishment of new "company towns." The most important single complex was the coal and iron production around Karaganda, but Kazakhstan was also a major producer of zinc, lead, uranium, and other minerals. In the post-1945 decades, Kazakhstan developed high-tech activity around the space center (cosmodrome) in Baikonur, from where Yuri Gagarin became the first man in space in 1961. Kazakhstan's low population density also made it a location for nuclear testing and research on chemical and biological weapons, which left a dangerous environmental legacy and would influence the independent country's strong stance against nuclear weapons and on environmental issues. Especially notable are the closing of the Semipalatinsk nuclear test site (also knows as "the Polygon") in 1991 and Kazakhstan's decision to give up its nuclear weapons after independence under the leadership of President Nazarbayev.

Some important infrastructure investments accompanied these developments. Kazakhstan is land-locked with limited river navigation and therefore has always been dependent on overland transport. In the Tsarist era, a regional rail network was rapidly constructed after the subjugation of Central Asia, consisting of two main lines with Tashkent as the hub; one line ran from the Caspian Sea to Tashkent, and the other headed northwest from Tashkent to western Russia. Rail connections to Kazakhstan were sparse. In the 1930s, construction of the Turksib line from Tashkent to Siberia provided a major rail lifeline through Kazakhstan. Furthermore, the mining centers were linked to the main lines, so that a reasonably efficient rail network connected the major cities.

Although the transport network was much improved by the 1980s compared with a century earlier, the dominant feature was that all railways and roads led to Moscow. It was only in the final years of the Soviet Union that the first rail line to China was built, crossing the border in eastern Kazakhstan, and there were no rail connections to the Soviet Union's southern neighbors until the Turkmenistan-Iran link was opened in 1997. The same inward-looking orientation applied to all economic flows, with trade being overwhelmingly intra-USSR, as were electricity and gas lines.

Toward the end of the Soviet period, the Kazakh Republic's energy resources became a focus of exploration and investment. Kazakhstan had potentially huge oil deposits around and under the Caspian Sea but did not have the expertise or capital to develop them. Foreign investment had been stifled for most of the Soviet era. As a harbinger of the future, negotiations were initiated in the final years of the Soviet Union for the largest joint venture deal in Soviet history with Chevron to develop the Tengiz oil field in western Kazakhstan.[1]

The Lean Years, 1991-98

When Kazakhstan became independent in December 1991, the new country faced three immediate major economic challenges: the transition from central planning, the dissolution of the Soviet Union, and hyperinflation and the breakdown of the ruble zone. The central planning system had been largely

---

1. The joint venture agreement was concluded after independence in 1993. Some small oil fields had been developed earlier, but Tengiz was striking for the scale of operations and acknowledgment of the need for the energy majors' technological input. See "Chevron Kazakhstan Fact Sheet, 2012" http://www.chevron.com /documents/pdf/kazakhstanfactsheet.pdf.

dismantled in the final years of the Soviet Union, but with Russia's January 1992 price liberalization other ruble-using countries such as Kazakhstan had no choice but to liberalize prices. Transition was inevitable, although the type of market-based economy was a policy choice.

The transition from central planning to a market-based economy in Eastern Europe and the former Soviet Union proved much more difficult and traumatic than anticipated, as all the economies experienced a deep transitional recession. For Kazakhstan this was exacerbated by the collapse of the Soviet economic space, leading to the breakdown of supply and demand links that was especially hard on "company towns" — referred to today as "mono-cities" — and on agriculture. As a final challenge, the structure of the ruble zone encouraged free-riding and led to hyperinflation and the eventual breakdown of the zone in November 1993.

Most of these problems were common to all fifteen Soviet successor states, but in Kazakhstan policy making in the 1990s was further affected by the priority of nation-building. In 1992 a widely held view was that many Soviet boundaries had been artificial and that some of the newly independent states would not survive. Kazakhstan, with its delicate ethnic balance and risk of secessionist movements in the Russian-dominated northern grain belt, was high on that list. President Nazarbayev responded with a skillful mix of political reassurances to non-Kazakhs while asserting the Kazakh heritage, most visibly by moving the capital in 1997 from Almaty in the southeast corner of the country to the more central town of Akmola, which was renamed Astana. And Kazakhstan successfully delimited its international boundaries with its neighbors.

Massive emigration did not help stability during the early and mid-1990s, as many of the emigrants were trained personnel. The population, which had been 16.4 million at independence, declined to fewer than 15 million in 2000 and had not regained the 1991 level in 2010 (Table 2.1). The population decline in the 1990s was exacerbated by a fall in the birth rate from more than 20 births per thousand population in the early 1990s to fewer than 15 by the end of the decade and an increase in the death rate from around 8 per thousand at independence to almost 11 in 1994 and 1996.

Aside from the demographic fallout of the breakup of the Soviet Union, which affected Kazakhstan's economy particularly negatively, the new country's economy was buffeted by the demise of central planning and severe disruption of long-standing trading relations among the former Soviet republics. This coincided with a cyclical downturn of international commodity prices that undermined Kazakhstan's hard currency earnings and complicated negotiations to develop the country's resources. In the early 1990s the Kazakhstani economy experienced a dramatic economic recession, with five consecutive years of negative growth, leaving the country with a cumulative loss of about 40 percent of its pre-independence GDP, similar to Russia.

Despite many obstacles, during the 1990s the foundations of a market-oriented economy were established by liberalization and privatization. Even more important for Kazakhstan's medium-term prosperity, Caspian energy exploration and exploitation moved forward after government negotiations with foreign energy companies to reach production sharing agreements for the exploitation of the potentially large oil and gas reserves. As a result, the Tengiz oil field was producing, and the massive offshore Kashagan oil field and the Karachaganak oil and gas field were discovered in time to benefit from soaring post-1999 oil prices.

By the end of the decade Kazakhstan had an effective macroeconomic policy framework that provided for a stable short-term outlook. Although buffeted by the 1998 Russian crisis, the economy responded strongly after devaluation of the tenge. At the same time, the government was the first in a former Soviet

2

republic to introduce far-reaching pension reform; assets in the privately funded program grew rapidly after 1999 and were equal to 12 percent of GDP in 2012, playing an important role in financial sector development.[2]

Most impressively of all, under the leadership of the President Nazarbayev the country adopted an ambitious long-term vision in 1997, at the trough of the transitional recession: the Kazakhstan 2030 Strategy (Box 2.1). In sum, despite a poor economic performance in 1991-99, the foundation was laid for future growth.

Table 2.1	Demographic trends, 1985-2012				
	Total population at the beginning of year (millions)	Annual rate of population change (percent)	Number of births per 1000 population	Number of deaths per 1000 population	Total number of net migration (thousands)
1985	15.7	n/a	25.1	8.0	n/a
1990	16.3	n/a	22.2	7.9	-92.6
1991	16.4	0.4	21.5	8.2	-57.7
1992	16.5	0.6	20.5	8.4	-156.3
1993	16.4	-0.2	19.3	9.5	-219.0
1994	16.3	-0.6	18.9	9.9	-406.7
1995	16.0	-2.3	17.5	10.7	-238.5
1996	15.7	-1.8	16.3	10.7	-175.5
1997	15.5	-1.2	15.2	10.4	-261.4
1998	15.2	-1.9	14.8	10.2	-203.0
1999	15.0	-1.5	14.6	9.9	-123.6
2000	14.9	-0.4	14.9	10.1	-108.3
2001	14.9	-0.2	14.9	10.0	-88.2
2002	14.9	-0.1	15.3	10.1	-62.0
2003	14.9	0.1	16.6	10.4	-8.3
2004	15.0	0.6	18.2	10.1	2.8
2005	15.1	0.8	18.4	10.4	22.7
2006	15.2	1.0	19.7	10.3	33.0
2007	15.4	1.2	20.8	10.2	11.0
2008	15.6	1.1	22.8	9.7	1.1
2009	16.0	2.6	22.0	8.0	7.5
2010	16.2	1.4	22.5	8.9	15.5
2011	16.7	2.9	22.5	8.7	5.1
2012	16.7	n/a	n/a	n/a	n/a

Source: Agency of Statistics of the Republic of Kazakhstan (2013).

---

2. However, poor investment decisions by the pension funds led to a major setback and they had to be nationalized in 2013.

> ### Box 2.1 | The Kazakhstan 2030 strategy
>
> The overarching strategic document for Kazakhstan's national development, "Kazakhstan 2030: Prosperity, Security and Improvement of Welfare of the Citizens of Kazakhstan," was adopted in 1997. It identified seven long-term national development priorities: (1) national security, (2) internal stability and social consolidation, (3) economic growth on the basis of an open market economy, (4) health, education and well-being of citizens, (5) energy resources, (6) infrastructure, transport and communications, and (7) professional government. The original Strategy 2030 document and all subsequent related documents repeat the theme of economics first, and then politics.
>
> The Strategy 2030 provides an overall vision, while implementation has been set out for shorter periods: 1998-2000 (preparatory stage), 2000-09, and 2010-19. The ten-year plans contain practical measures to achieve the long-term goals in light of current conditions, as well as play a monitoring function by providing interim targets. The 2000-09 strategic plan focused on reviving the economy after the transitional recession, addressing the most serious social issues and setting the foundations for long-term sustainable development. The national strategic plan for the second planning decade to 2020, drawn up in 2009 during the global crisis, focuses on enhancing Kazakhstan's competitiveness during the global economy's recovery. In the short term, strategic plans and sectoral programs are adjusted to priorities set out in the President's Annual Address, e.g., in 2011 these included the improvement of agricultural productivity, increased meat output, and high-quality water supply for the rural population.
>
> The 2010-19 Strategic Plan set five key priorities: preparation for post-crisis development, continued diversification of the economy, investments in the future (human capital and healthcare), improved public services, and continued stable interethnic and foreign relations. It identified several strategic goals to be met by 2020.
>
> *Source:* NAC of Nazarbayev University ("Place of Kazakhstan" 2012.)

The (Mostly) Boom Years, 1999-2011

After the lean years of the 1990s Kazakhstan experienced a sustained recovery in its economic performance during the first decade of the 2000s. Many aspects of this remarkable experience could be explored, but we focus here on selected key dimensions of Kazakhstan's economic recovery and then consider the government's economic macroeconomic management and its efforts at diversifying the economy and strengthen the country's human resource base. Many of these issues are treated in greater depth in subsequent chapters.

Recovery of economic growth

The decade beginning in 1999 saw a dramatic turnaround in Kazakhstan's economic fortunes (Figure 2.1). Between 2000 and 2007 the country grew at an average rate of more than 10 percent per annum, which made it one of the world's fastest growing economies and helped to boost its per capita income almost eight-fold between 2001 and 2011 (Figure 2.2). The turnaround was based on four elements: first, recovery from the transitional recession; second, good policy, such as the 1999 devaluation and continued economic reforms; third, rapid growth of the service sector and the construction industry; and, fourth, growth of the energy sector — oil output increased as world prices soared, while new pipelines reduced transport costs and the risk of having to rely on a monopoly transit supplier. The importance of the oil sector as a key driver of growth is shown in the overall trade accounts. Between 2000 and 2008

2

exports measured in current US dollars increased eight-fold, and, although export earnings dipped by 40 percent in 2009 in the wake of the global financial crisis, they recovered quickly in 2010 (Figure 2.3). Crude oil and other energy products accounted for around two-thirds of exports in 2010 (Figure 2.4). As a result of the oil export boom, the economy became significantly more open as trade turnover relative to GDP at purchasing power parity increased from 20 percent in 2000 to 46 percent in 2010. Finally, if one decomposes the growth performance of the economy into the oil and non-oil sectors, it is clear that in a number of years since 1999, the oil sector was a key driving force of the economy's growth performance (Figure 2.5).[3]

Another way to look at the post-independence growth performance of Kazakhstan is to decompose the sources of growth into the contributions of labor, capital, and total factor productivity (TFP). Figure 2.6 shows that, although labor and capital inputs declined in the early 1990s, it was the dramatic negative TFP changes that drove the recession of 1991-95. The negative TFP performance can be explained mainly by the disruptions in the economic system caused by the breakup of the Soviet Union. In contrast, both labor and capital contributions turned positive in the 2000s, but it was the dramatic reversal of TFP that drove the high economic growth rates of Kazakhstan during those boom years, reflecting the re-establishment of economic order and integration, a sound policy environment, and the beneficial impact of expanded oil production and exports at much higher world prices. During the financial and economic crisis of 2008-09 TFP growth dropped off dramatically but then turned positive again in 2010-11, albeit at levels below the exceptional highs of the early and mid-2000s.

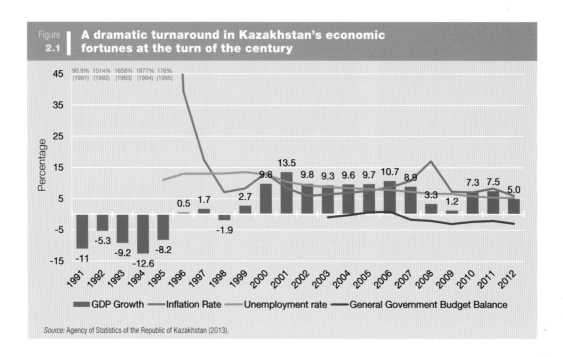

Figure 2.1 | A dramatic turnaround in Kazakhstan's economic fortunes at the turn of the century

Source: Agency of Statistics of the Republic of Kazakhstan (2013).

---

3. Figure 2.5 shows 3-year moving averages so as to help smooth out wide oscillations in oil price movements from year to year.

2

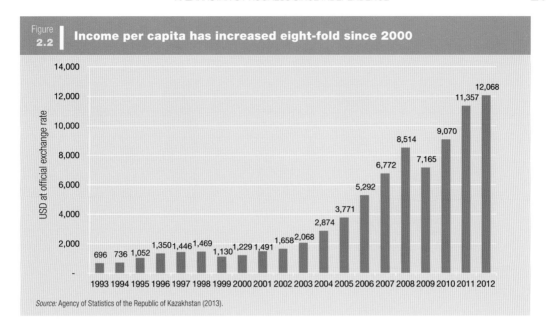

Figure 2.2 | **Income per capita has increased eight-fold since 2000**

Source: Agency of Statistics of the Republic of Kazakhstan (2013).

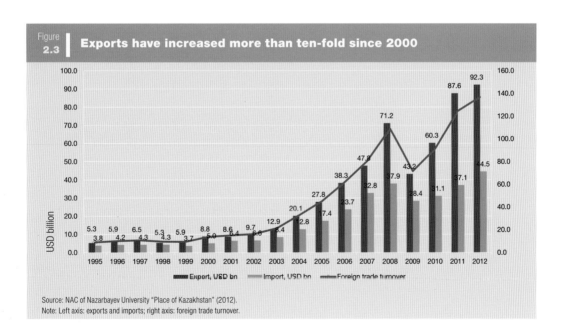

Figure 2.3 | **Exports have increased more than ten-fold since 2000**

Export, USD bn   Import, USD bn   Foreign trade turnover

Source: NAC of Nazarbayev University "Place of Kazakhstan" (2012).
Note: Left axis: exports and imports; right axis: foreign trade turnover.

2

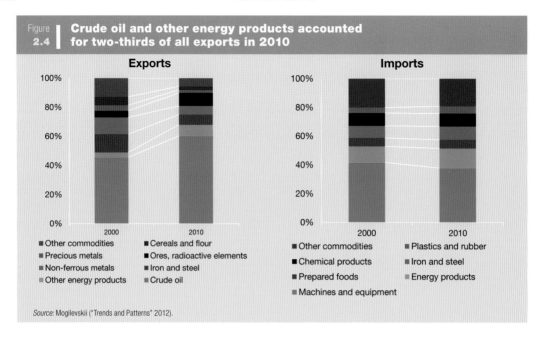

Figure 2.4 | **Crude oil and other energy products accounted for two-thirds of all exports in 2010**

Source: Mogilevskii ("Trends and Patterns" 2012).

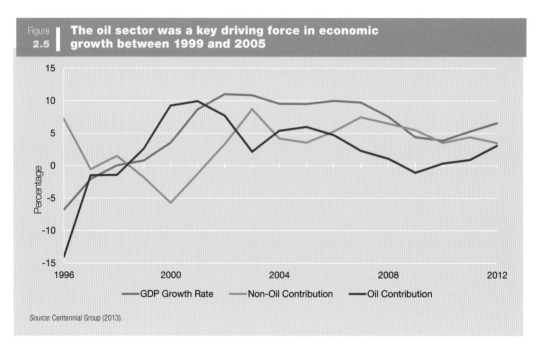

Figure 2.5 | **The oil sector was a key driving force in economic growth between 1999 and 2005**

Source: Centennial Group (2013).

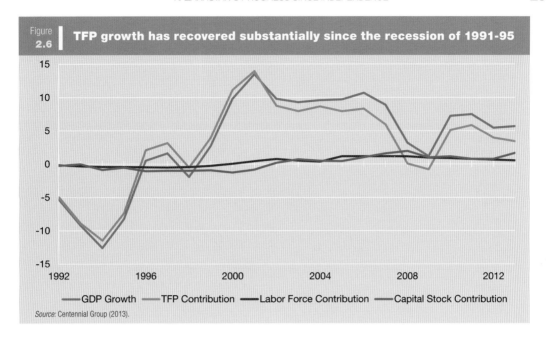

Figure 2.6 TFP growth has recovered substantially since the recession of 1991-95

GDP Growth ——— TFP Contribution ——— Labor Force Contribution ——— Capital Stock Contribution

Source: Centennial Group (2013).

The social impact

Resurgent GDP growth was accompanied by a revival of population growth (Table 2.1) and falling unemployment (Figure 2.1). Net emigration, which had still numbered over 100,000 in 2000, fell sharply, and after 2003 Kazakhstan became a country of net immigration, mainly consisting of returning Kazakhs and migrants from Central Asia attracted by relatively high wages for unskilled labor. The birth rate recovered from the low levels of the 1990s, and by 2007 was again more than 20 per thousand, setting off a baby boom period. In 2009 the death rate had fallen to the pre-independence level of eight per thousand. These demographic trends have important implications for the labor market in future decades, with fewer labor market entrants between 2015 and 2025 but a demographic bonus in the second quarter of the century before Kazakhstan faces the universal problems of an aging population. This is further discussed in Chapter 6.

The unemployment rate declined continuously from more than 12 percent in 1999 to about 6 percent in 2010 (Figure 2.1) and further to 5.3 percent in 2011. There was also a significant decline in poverty and an improvement in life expectancy after the dramatic deterioration in both welfare measures as a result of the transition recession after independence (Table 2.2 and Figure 2.7). However, poverty remains, and disparities between the regions are still significant. Especially striking are the stubbornly high poverty rates in South Kazakhstan and in Mangystau (Table 2.2).

Table 2.2 | Poverty levels have declined in all regions since 2007 but disparities remain

Share (%) of population with income below subsistence	2007	2008	2009	2010	2011	2012
Kazakhstan	12.7	12.1	8.2	6.5	5.5	3.8
Akmola	16.6	8.7	5.9	4.4	6.2	3.9
Aktobe	10.3	7.0	6.3	6.0	2.4	2.4
Almaty (province)	18.1	20.1	15.5	6.6	1.7	3.2
Atyrau	13.0	12.9	10.0	5.9	5.2	3.3
West Kazakhstan	10.3	10.2	8.2	6.7	4.8	4.1
Zhambyl	9.9	11.3	4.8	5.3	5.1	4.9
Karagandy	8.5	4.9	3.9	3.8	3.5	2.8
Kostanai	10.4	9.0	6.8	6.4	4.6	3.3
Kyzylorda	24.6	24.3	10.4	6.7	6.2	3.8
Mangystau	26.9	32.4	22.6	11.6	10.4	3.3
South Kazakhstan	14.3	13.0	11.7	11.5	10.4	7.9
Pavlodar	8.3	8.8	6.2	4.0	4.5	2.9
North Kazakhstan	16.0	11.0	7.3	5.4	9.6	5.7
East Kazakhstan	9.8	9.9	6.6	8.4	6.1	3.4
Astana	3.2	3.8	3.9	3.4	1.7	1.0
Almaty (city)	8.5	13.7	3.0	2.6	2.0	0.4

Source: Agency of Statistics of the Republic of Kazakhstan (2013).

Figure 2.7 | Life expectancy has improved since 2000

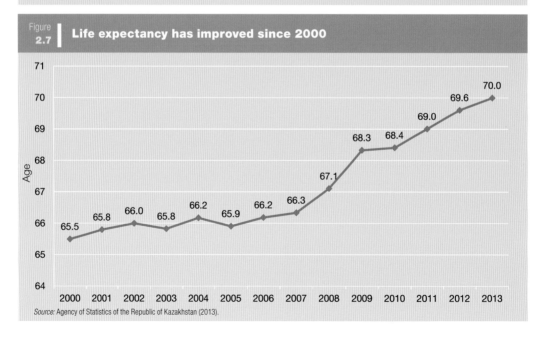

Source: Agency of Statistics of the Republic of Kazakhstan (2013).

One of the pervasive issues facing Kazakhstan's productive sector is the high degree of informality in the economy. According to World Bank data, Kazakhstan ranks among the bottom third of 150 comparator countries with a share of informal activities in GDP amounting to 38.4 percent (Figure 2.8). While this has declined from even higher levels in 1999 (43.8 percent), it remains a serious weakness for a county aspiring to join the rank of the most developed economies.[4] Particularly high levels of informal employment are observed in construction, food production, transportation, street food, commodity markets, and seasonal agricultural work.

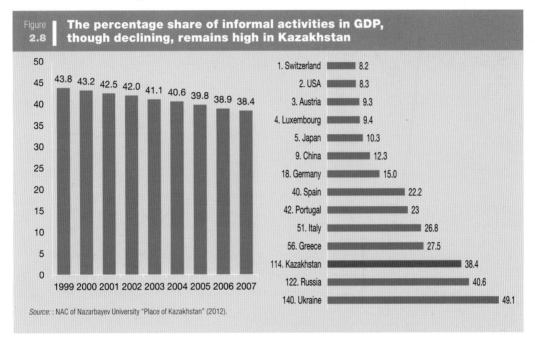

Figure 2.8 | **The percentage share of informal activities in GDP, though declining, remains high in Kazakhstan**

1999: 43.8, 2000: 43.2, 2001: 42.5, 2002: 42.0, 2003: 41.1, 2004: 40.6, 2005: 39.8, 2006: 38.9, 2007: 38.4

1. Switzerland 8.2
2. USA 8.3
3. Austria 9.3
4. Luxembourg 9.4
5. Japan 10.3
9. China 12.3
18. Germany 15.0
40. Spain 22.2
42. Portugal 23
51. Italy 26.8
56. Greece 27.5
114. Kazakhstan 38.4
122. Russia 40.6
140. Ukraine 49.1

Source: : NAC of Nazarbayev University "Place of Kazakhstan" (2012).

Inequality in Kazakhstan, as measured by the Gini coefficient, increased from a low 25.7 before independence in 1988 to a high of 41.1 in 2001 but then declined significantly during the boom years to 29.0, which is low by international standards (Table 2.3). However, recent research indicates that high-income earners are under-represented in the Statistical Agency's household surveys, resulting in a sampling bias toward low-income groups. The survey data may thus suggest a greater degree of income equality than actually exists and possibly less of an improvement than shown in Table 2.3. Nonetheless, since similar problems may affect other countries' Gini coefficient measurement, Kazakhstan's ability to contain inequality during periods of rapid growth appears to be a remarkable success story. For the future, however, it would be advisable to find ways to track income distribution more effectively so that policy makers are well informed on how widely and equally the benefits economic development are distributed across the country.

---

4. However, the Agency of Statistics of the Republic of Kazakhstan reports only a 19 percent share of unrecorded economic activity in GDP (which includes informal production and shadow/hidden activities). The difference is due to differences in the methodology of calculation. One confirmation of the high informality rates reported by the World Bank is the high proportion of self-employed (32.8 percent, or 1.2 million people) in the labor market of Kazakhstan.

Country	Year	Gini Coefficient	Country	Year	Gini Coefficient
Kazakhstan	1988	25.7	Brazil	2009	54.7
	1993	32.7	Mexico	2008	58.3
	1996	35.3	Argentina	2009	46.1
	2001	41.1	Georgia	2008	40.3
	2002	35.0	Russia	2009	40.1
	2003	33.9	Kyrgyz Republic	2009	36.2
	2004	32.3	Poland	2009	34.1
	2006	30.8	Azerbaijan	2008	33.7
	2007	30.9	Kazakhstan	2009	29.0
	2008	29.3	Ukraine	2009	26.4
	2009	29.0			

Table 2.3 | Measured inequality has been declining since 2001 and is low by international standards

Source: World Bank ("DataBank" 2013).

Looking at the gender dimension of equality, Kazakhstan does relatively well by international standards. According to the World Economic Forum's Gender Gap Index Kazakhstan ranks 31st among 135 countries (Hausmann et al. 2012). Equality among men and women in education and health is nearly or fully achieved (for tertiary education, women's enrollment is actually substantially above that of men). For economic opportunity, women still lag behind men and even more so for political representation (Figure 2.9). Over time, there has been some limited improvement in these two areas. The government recently introduced specific targets for women's representation in high-level government positions.

Figure 2.9 | Gender equality is high in education and health, but a gap remains for political empowerment and economic opportunity

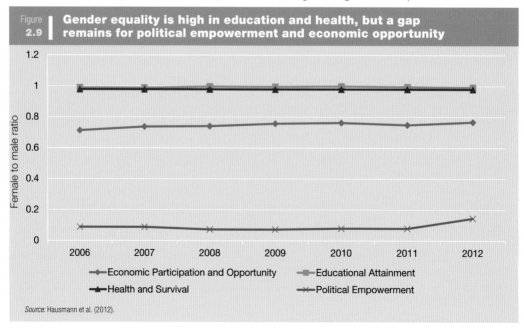

Source: Hausmann et al. (2012).

Effective macroeconomic management

Policy making during the 2000s was facilitated by energy revenues, which allowed the state budget to expand rapidly. But, as the "resource curse" literature makes clear, these resources could have been squandered. Fortunately, Kazakhstan generally managed its national resources wisely:

- Short-term macroeconomic policy has generally been good, despite a homegrown asset bubble and financial crisis in 2007 (Box 2.2), with a fairly stable exchange rate and inflation under control.
- The National Fund was established in order to save part of the oil revenues for future use; Fund resources were available for an emergency (e.g., during the 2007-9 financial crisis — Box 2.2) and for future generations. At the end of June 2013, the Fund contained USD 63.5 billion, according to the Kazakhstan National Bank website.
- There has been significant investment in infrastructure, including a pipeline from the Caspian oil fields to China, road improvements (notably upgrading a 2,700 kilometer highway across northern Kazakhstan from Khorgos on the Chinese border to Aktobe near the Russian border), a rail link to Turkmenistan and Iran, port upgrading on the Caspian, and improved air service through the twin hubs of Astana and Almaty.
- Long-term policy implementation has been characterized by an overarching vision (Kazakhstan 2030, see Box 2.1) and by flexibility (trial and response to successful or unsuccessful approaches).

Aiming for diversification

As the oil boom gathered momentum and energy sectors dominated production, the government became increasingly concerned about the need for economic diversification in the face of threatening Dutch disease, i.e., the shrinking of the non-oil traded goods sector. This argument is usually applied to manufacturing and services, but in Kazakhstan, agriculture, the sector with a larger share of employment than industries (Table 2.4), is also a priority for economic diversification beyond oil, gas, and minerals, as well as important for rural development.

Table 2.4	**The service sector dominates in Kazakhstan's economy**					
	Percentage of GDP			Percentage of Employment		
	1995	2005	2011	1995	2005	2011
Agriculture	12.9	6.8	5.5	n/a	32.4	26.6
Industry	31.4	40.1	42.1	n/a	18.0	19.0
Services	55.7	53.1	54.3	n/a	49.6	54.6

Source: : World Bank ("Databank" 2013).

At independence, the end of central planning and the dissolution of the Soviet Union hit agriculture hard, as supply chains were disrupted and subsidies dwindled, but at the same time many people retreated to agriculture when faced with loss of employment.[5] As a result, while agriculture's share of GDP dropped to 5.5 percent from 12.9 percent in 1995, agricultural employment increased from less than

---

5. The analysis of the agricultural sector is based on Pomfret (2013), which draws heavily on the 2013 OECD Review of Agricultural Policies: Kazakhstan.

2

Box
2.2 **The 2007 financial crisis and its aftermath**

The 2007 crisis arose because Kazakhstan's banks borrowed in international markets at shorter maturities than those on their loan portfolios to supplement the low levels of domestic deposits. The situation resembled underlying earlier crises, such as the 1997 Thai crisis when Bangkok, like Almaty and Astana in the mid-2000s, experienced a real estate boom. The banks lent to borrowers eager not to miss out in the property market, and the banks' creditors believed that Kazakhstan banks' liabilities were low-risk.

After the 1999 devaluation, the central bank reverted to a de facto exchange rate anchor. The exchange rate in February 2006 was KZT 130 per dollar, the same as at the end of May 1999, despite oil-boom pressures for currency appreciation. With the expectation that there was little exchange rate risk, banks could borrow in international markets at lower interest rates than they could charge borrowers at home. By 2006 Kazakhstan's banks were raising large amounts of capital abroad, where the cost of capital was less than the double-digit interest rates that they could charge borrowers at home. In the first half of 2007 medium- and long-term debt-creating capital inflows more than doubled, largely due to external borrowing by the banking sector. Kazakhstan's banks lent to higher risk borrowers who were willing to pay higher interest rates, while the foreigners lending to Kazakhstan's banks believed that they were lending to credit-worthy institutions.

Signs of stress in the financial sector emerged in 2007 when banks started to compete more actively in making deposits attractive. At the same time they substantially increased the interest rates on loans, which by the start of 2008 had reached about 20 percent, double the rates of the previous two years. In November 2007 the government provided support of around USD 4 billion, targeted at construction projects in danger of being abandoned half-finished, and the central bank raised the official refinancing rate, which had been unchanged at 9 percent since July 2006, to 11 percent. The full amount owed by Kazakhstan's banks to foreign creditors was unclear; according to the Financial Times, in October 2007 Kazakhstan's banks' international borrowings totaled USD 40 billion. As international credit access began to dry up in the first stages of financial stress in the US, international rating agencies began to downgrade the creditworthiness of Kazakhstan's banks in late 2007, and Standard and Poor's downgraded Kazakhstan's sovereign debt to BBB-.

When the real estate bubble burst in 2007, many borrowers were unable to repay their loans, and Kazakhstan faced a banking crisis. Kazakhstan's banks, and the government, still had cards to play. Some banks looked for a white knight to help resolve the liquidity crisis or to take an equity stake; the first substantial foreign investment in the banking sector was in November 2007 when the Italian bank UniCredit paid USD 2.1 billion for a 91.8 percent stake in ATF Bank, Kazakhstan's fifth largest bank.

The government reacted by drawing on the National Fund to bail out distressed banks and to finance a stimulus package. Four over-leveraged financial institutions, including the largest bank (BTA), had to restructure their debt and were de facto nationalized. The anti-crisis program launched in late 2008 pledged USD 10 billion, 9.5 percent of GDP, primarily channeled through the National Welfare Fund Samruk-Kazyna. The goal was to limit the decline in economic growth without stimulating inflation or increasing public debt. In 2009 Samruk-Kazyna reported that it had received 1,087.5 billion tenge from the National Fund, of which 486 billion was used to stabilize the financial sector, 360 billion for the real estate market, 120 billion for small and medium enterprise development, and 121.5 billion for implementation of innovative industrial and infrastructure projects (IMF 2012). Despite the efforts made to restore banking sector soundness since 2008, serious problems remain, with a large overhang of non-performing loans burdening some of Kazakhstan's banks (IMF 2012).

Source: Author.

20 percent of the workforce in 1990 to more than 30 percent in 2005, before dropping to 26.6 percent in 2011. This pattern is highly unusual by international standards and is shared only by the poorer and more rural Kyrgyz Republic and Tajikistan (OECD "Agricultural Policies" 2013).

Land reform was undertaken in several steps, with initial assertion of state ownership of land and granting of 99-year and then 49-year leases, followed only in 2003 by a law recognizing full private ownership of land; today there is still only a limited market in land.[6] Negative relative price movements, withdrawal of subsidies, and an uncertain land tenure system contributed to pervasive farm indebtedness by the late 1990s. At the same time the ubiquitous household plots provided a safety net for families whose formal incomes disappeared during the transition. Especially for meat, milk, and eggs, output came overwhelmingly from household plots by the turn of the century, and this remains true today.

Starting in 2001 with the aul (village) program and especially in 2002 with the billion dollar Agriculture and Food Program, the government adopted a more supportive position toward agriculture compared with a passive policy of the 1990s. Parastatal organizations were created or expanded to offer price support to farmers, and area and input subsidies increased rapidly. The value of farm output, which had been around 500 billion tenge in the early 2000s increased to 2,286 billion tenge in 2011.[7] The major component was wheat and other grains grown in the three northern oblasts, which accounted for over 45 percent of the national output. While the overall trend is obscured by the large variation in harvests in these regions, it is clear that agriculture responded to the policy shift. However, the extent to which these policies, and the parallel increase in the role of the public agency KazAgro, have promoted efficient use of inputs and appropriate output mix is debatable.[8]

Turning then to industry, in Kazakhstan the structure of industry is dominated by processing the outputs of the resource sectors — oil and gas, mining and metallurgy, and food and other agribusiness — and hence it is dependent on domestic supply and heavily influenced by world prices. As with agriculture, policy toward the manufacturing sector became more interventionist in the 2000s. Although tariff policy remained liberal, several protectionist non-tariff barriers were introduced, e.g., subsidies to farmers for the use of domestic fertilizers. The government also experimented with industrial policies, aimed at developing specific clusters of economic activity around perceived areas of competitive advantage.[9] Recent years, especially in the wake of the financial crisis of 2008, have seen increasing state involvement in the industrial sector, as in agriculture. The state-led concentration of economic power has been especially apparent in the growth of Samruk-Kazyna and its affiliates, raising the question of the appropriate balance between state-controlled and private firms. The People's IPO Program is a step toward privatizing some major Samruk-Kazyna affiliates between 2012 and 2015, but it is too early to judge its impact (see Chapter 11).

---

6. Rents on land leased from the state under the pre-2003 land reforms are so low that few tenants want to turn their lease-holding into private ownership.

7. According to data provide by the Agency of Statistics of the Republic of Kazakhstan.

8. The assessment is based on the 2006 report, Kazakhstan — Agricultural Policy Assessment, by the Joint Economic Research Program of the World Bank and the Government of Kazakhstan in collaboration with USAID and Food and Agriculture Organization (FAO), the 2009 World Bank report, Kazakhstan: Public Expenditure and Institutional Review for the Agricultural Sector, and the 2013 OECD Review of Agricultural Policies: Kazakhstan. One issue is the tendency of policy makers to see reform and modernization in terms of large capital-intensive farms, when the still large rural population indicates abundant labor, albeit workers unwilling to do back-breaking work like cotton-harvesting which increasingly relies on immigrant labor. Resorting to export controls in 2008 in order to protect food security also made little sense in efficiency terms.

9. The initial step, the 2003 industrialization program, was abandoned when the identified clusters failed to develop. The 2010 Development of Kazakhstan program supporting favored activities and establishing six special economic zones (SEZs) with specific industry focus (e.g., a textile cluster in South Kazakhstan) has been associated with successful establishment of an auto assembly plant, but otherwise has been criticized for being too fragmented (see Chapter 9).

Strengthening human capital

At independence Kazakhstan was, among Soviet republics, relatively well endowed with human capital. However, the situation in the 1990s was complicated by the large-scale emigration of non-Kazakhs, many of whom were well-qualified professionals, and by the transition from central planning. In the Soviet education system, primary education began relatively late (at 6-7 years old) and was preceded for many children by kindergarten education provided by their parents' enterprise. During the transition, state enterprises quickly closed down peripheral activities, including social services such as kindergarten, so that many children no longer had basic reading skills upon entering the school system. Better-off families paid for pre-schooling or provided home schooling, but poorer children were disadvantaged. At the other end of the education spectrum, in the post-Soviet era many universities and vocational schools were no longer offering useful education and training, and within high schools and universities competition for places in preferred subjects was often mediated by bribes to administrators. There were also reports of widespread corruption, as poorly paid teaching staff accepted bribes for grades, and of substantial exiting from teaching.[10]

As the economy recovered, spending on education increased after 2000. Especially significant were programs to address the shortcomings of the higher education sector. The Bolashak ("Future") Program launched in 1993 provided generous assistance for outstanding students to study overseas; numbers were small during the first decade, but with increased funding they soared from fewer than a 100 every year from 1995 to 2004 to a peak of 1796 in 2005. By 2012 the program had financed more than 8,000 students. Since independence some highly visible universities, such as KIMEP in Almaty and the Eurasian National University in Astana were developed, and in recent years the tertiary education system was reinforced by the well-funded Nazarbayev University, intended to become a world-class center of higher education and research in Astana. Chapter 5 explores these trends and policies in greater detail.

Kazakhstan's Standing in Cross-Country Comparisons

In concluding this chapter and setting the stage for the remainder of this volume, let us paint a portrait of Kazakhstan's current standing among other countries by drawing on various indicators of comparative performance, focusing first on how growth and progress with reforms compare with other transition countries in the former Soviet space, then considering Kazakhstan's ranking in various global country performance indexes, and finally drawing on a recent cross-country comparison of people's perception of their well-being.

Comparison of growth and reforms with other transition economies

Kazakhstan was, compared with other parts of the Russian Empire, relatively undeveloped in 1913. Although such numbers are highly approximate, Angus Maddison estimated present-day Kazakhstan's real per capita income in 1913 at purchasing power parity (in 2005 international dollars) to have been USD 925, which was the same as neighboring Kyrgyzstan and also the same as British India but lower than present-day Uzbekistan (Table 2.5). During the Soviet era Kazakhstan's real per capita income performance outshone that of all of these comparators and of independent countries such as Iran, Egypt, or Turkey, although the level of real per capita income was still lower than that of Turkey in 1988.

---

10. Exact numbers are hard to determine because in the early 1990s many teachers were paid only with a long time lag, and some stopped working temporarily. It may be presumed that some of the more energetic or with more appropriate skills (e.g., younger teachers with computing skills or English teachers) were among those permanently quitting teaching for better-paid work.

Table 2.5	**Kazakhstan's long-term economic performance is impressive relative to comparable countries**

Former CPEs	1913	1988	2008	Comparators	1913	1988	2008
Kazakhstan	925	7,219	10,469	India	925	1,159	2,781
Kyrgyz Rep.	925	2,395	2,043	Pakistan	925	1,569	2,317
Uzbekistan	1,376	2,004	2,455	Iran	1,376	5,440	10,398
Azerbaijan	1,669	6,075	8,024	Turkey	1,669	7,642	12,406
Russia	2,135	13,066	14,767	Egypt	1,241	3,047	5,216
Romania		8,896	11,793				
Bulgaria		8,323	12,005				
Poland		9,251	16,455				
Serbia		10,474	7,130				

Source: : Carlin, Schaffer, and Seabright (2012) – based on earlier estimates by Angus Maddison.
Note: All figures are at purchasing power parity measured in 2005 international dollars.
CPEs: Centrally Planned Economies

Kazakhstan's economic performance during the 1990s was average among the former Soviet republics and generally poorer than the performance of the Central and Eastern European transition economies. The energy boom raised Kazakhstan up to among the best of the former Soviet republics by growth in per capita incomes in the 2000s. Over the period 1988-2008 Kazakhstan outperformed poorer Eastern European transition economies, such as Bulgaria or Romania, but did not perform as well as more advanced Central European transition economies, such as Poland (Table 2.5).

Table 2.6	**EBRD transition indicators suggest mixed achievements with transition reforms**

	1998	2000	2005	2010	2011	2012
Large scale privatization	3.0	3.0	3.0	3.0	3.0	3.0
Small scale privatization	4.0	4.0	4.0	4.0	4.0	4.0
Governance/enterprise restructuring	2.0	2.0	2.0	2.0	2.0	2.0
Price liberalization	4.0	4.0	4.0	4.0	3.7	3.7
Trade and forex system	4.0	3.3	3.7	3.7	3.7	3.7
Competition policy	2.0	2.0	2.0	2.0	2.0	2.0

Source: : EBRD ("Transition Report" 2012).
Note: Indicators are measured on a scale from 1 (no reform) to 4 (developed market economy standards).

2

Following the dissolution of the Soviet Union, Kazakhstan was considered one of the more reformist successor states, as it followed Russia's 1992 price liberalization more fully than other Central Asian countries. The pace of economic reform in Kazakhstan slowed in the mid-1990s: by the EBRD transition indicators, Kazakhstan even fell behind Uzbekistan in 1996. However, with firmer macroeconomic control bringing inflation lower than 50 percent in 1997 and the 1999 devaluation putting the currency to a reasonable market-determined value, the process of creating a well-functioning market economy resumed.

The EBRD Transition Indicators suggest that progress with transition reforms was effectively over by 1998. Table 2.6 indicates that by 1998 Kazakhstan was a market-oriented economy with privatized small-scale enterprises and incomplete privatization of large enterprises, liberalized prices, and an open trade and foreign exchange regime, but at the same time with only limited progress in enterprise restructuring and competition policy. This characterization remained essentially the same a decade later, with some slight slippage on prices and the trade system, and no change to the indicators for competition policy or large-scale privatization.

According to the EBRD's 2012 Transition Report, a comparison of 36 countries in Europe, Central Asia and North Africa shows that the most thoroughgoing reforms have occurred in the Central European countries that are now EU members because of the pull exerted by accession to the European Union, followed by the southeastern European countries, Russia, Ukraine, Moldova, Armenia, and Georgia, all of which score above Kazakhstan, which in turn scores better than the Central Asian countries, Azerbaijan, Mongolia, and Belarus.

The EBRD indicators may understate Kazakhstan's transition insofar as banking and other financial sector reforms had created a vibrant banking system by 2007. A major challenge in 2013 is to determine whether that boom period's legacy can provide a launch pad for renewed financial development or whether the post-2007 state takeover of major financial institutions (Box 2.2) was a setback that will be difficult to reverse.[11] Similarly, Kazakhstan's pension system, which was innovative among transition economies when introduced in 1997, requires attention, but is potentially the basis for a sustainable approach to an aging population, while it has contributed through growing private asset holdings to broader financial sector development. Finally, the poor record on physical infrastructure is being reversed by the active rail, road, and pipeline construction described in the preceding lines (although a bigger challenge will be to improve the soft infrastructure that heightens trade costs), while communications via mobile phone, Internet, and aircraft, which are not well-covered in the EBRD indicators, are in reasonably good state in Kazakhstan.

Kazakhstan's standing in global comparisons

In this section we present a portrait of contemporary Kazakhstan, principally as seen through comparative country performance indicators. In the preceding section we showed the evolution of Kazakhstan's performance relative to other transition economies. However, in its quest to achieve top 30 status among developed countries, Kazakhstan will want to benchmark global performance indicators. We therefore summarize the evidence from relevant global performance indicators and explore in which areas Kazakhstan is ahead, even, or behind comparator countries in terms of its institutional and policy performance. Annex 1 at the end of the volume provides more in-depth background and information on country performance indexes.

---

11. The IMF (2012) flags the continuing overhang of non-performing assets in Kazakhstan's banking sector, and has highlighted concerns about the future of BTA, which was the largest bank in 2007 but is now struggling under the weight of perhaps four-fifths of its loans being non-performing.

Country performance indexes are subject to limitations that are briefly considered in Annex 1, but they provide a useful portrait of contemporary Kazakhstan. They show how far Kazakhstan has to go in reforming its policies and institutions if it wants to get closer to the international best practice "frontier" in a broad range of policy and institutional domains. Just as Kazakhstan wants to move up in the per capita income ranking from its current 70th position to join the top 30 in this ranking, so it will want to move up over the next few decades from its current position in the ranking of key country performance indexes to a position much closer to the top, whether for macroeconomic resilience, social indicators, economic integration, or institutional and governance performance. These improvements are important contributors to Kazakhstan reaching its goal of achieving top rankings in the per capita income league, but they also matter in their own right, since good governance and strong institutions, good social indicators, resilience to economic crises, and integration with the rest of the world contribute independently to the achievement of Kazakhstan's vision and thus contribute intrinsic value to the welfare of Kazakhstan's society.

Let us then turn to consider the main overall patterns and trends that emerge from 24 international country performance indexes collected by NAC of Nazarbayev University ("Kazakhstan Rankings" 2012). Overall the main results are as follows:

- Kazakhstan is currently positioned in the top 30 of countries covered in only three areas: macroeconomic policy, freedom of the labor market, and e-participation. For education, Kazakhstan is among the top 50 countries.
- Kazakhstan ranks poorly in governance and institutional performance. Its rankings are especially poor in corruption, voice and accountability, and press freedom. Moreover, trends in these areas are toward deterioration.
- Kazakhstan also ranks poorly in one of the three indexes covering the area of trade integration.
- In the other areas, Kazakhstan ranks either close to its current per capita ranking or somewhat worse.
- Relative to other countries in CIS (Commonwealth of Independent States), and especially in Central Asia, Kazakhstan does better in many of the global rankings. While this is relevant in demonstrating that Kazakhstan may have come further in its post-Soviet transition than other former Soviet republics, this only demonstrates that for the future Kazakhstan needs to look for relevant benchmarks elsewhere in the world.

These results point to the overall conclusion that, if Kazakhstan wants to achieve its vision of ranking among the top 30 performers in the world in 2050, it needs to improve significantly its performance in many areas of policy and institutional development, and especially so in the areas of governance and international trade integration.

People's perception of their well-being

An alternative approach to cross-country comparison is to ask people how they feel and what are the things with which they are satisfied and dissatisfied. The EBRD did this with the 2006 and 2010 Life in Transition surveys. In terms of happiness, Kazakhstanis generally finished slightly above middle of the pack. The problem, of course, is that respondents in different countries may have different benchmarks. Hence, when the sampled Tajikistanis report that they are the happiest people in transition, this may reflect their relief at no longer having a bloody civil war, rather than a meaningful comparison with people in other transition economies.

Nevertheless, we can draw some conclusions from Kazakhstan's respondents' statements about what they are more or less satisfied with life in Kazakhstan. With respect to public service delivery (Table 2.7), there is not a high level of public satisfaction. It is especially low with respect to civil courts (only in Mongolia, the Kyrgyz Republic, and Bulgaria are people less satisfied with their civil courts), but also with respect to the traffic police; despite a large improvement between 2006 and 2010, five-eighths of interviewees still reported having paid a bribe to traffic police in 2010. Improved healthcare, especially reduction of long wait times, is cited as the biggest priority among Kazakhstan's residents, and the relatively high percentage "satisfied" with public health services in Table 2.7 hides the fact that satisfaction in Kazakhstan ranked 23rd among the 28 transition countries surveyed. In sum, although the Life in Transition surveys paint a picture of improving citizen satisfaction in Kazakhstan, the country does not stack up well relative to other transition economies whose citizens are generally more satisfied with the maintenance of public service provision. At the same time, these surveys highlight the further progress that is needed to reduce corruption, which hampers perceived fair operation of courts and police.

Table 2.7	**Despite improvements, people's satisfaction with public service delivery (by %) remains low**						
	Public health	Traffic police	Official documents	Tertiary education	Unemployment benefits	Other social security benefits	Civil courts
2006	39	24	36	53	42	38	35
2010	54	40	50	62	43	50	27

Source: : EBRD ("Governance" 2012).

Conclusions

Kazakhstan is a young nation state with an important heritage. Economic conditions before 1991 were largely shaped by decisions taken elsewhere, mainly St. Petersburg and Moscow. Those decisions gave the new independent country a mixed legacy of good human capital and social conditions relative to its income level, extensive infrastructure (albeit not ideally suited to the post-1991 future) and a record of relatively rapid economic development and structural change within living memory. More immediately in 1992-93 the new country faced novel and huge economic challenges with the end of central planning, the dissolution of the Soviet Union, and hyperinflation, as well as political and social challenges arising from the country's complex ethnic structure and large-scale emigration.

From the perspective of 2013, the response to those challenges has been successful. Since the turn of the century Kazakhstan has benefited from massive oil revenues, but there are many examples of countries that have squandered resource wealth. In contrast, Kazakhstan has avoided a resource curse. Beyond mere survival, about which many observers were doubtful in 1992, Kazakhstan has been successful in increasing income levels and reducing poverty. For most of the population the quality of life is better than it was in the Soviet era and is continuing to improve. Substantial progress has been made toward turning Kazakhstan into a competitive economy as envisioned in the 2030 strategy.

There are lags in progress in some areas and there will be new challenges to face. Many of the challenges and debates of the past will carry over into the future.

Among the main challenges in the short to medium term is the need to protect the overall excellent macroeconomic fundamentals and to clean up the financial sector, especially the nationalized banks with large non-performing loan portfolios since the 2007-08 crisis. Macroeconomic policy has since 1996-97 been good in terms of managing the exchange rate and monetary policy to control inflation, and the central bank has established a good reputation, but strong macroeconomic performance remains to be firmly institutionalized. Similarly, creation and management of the National Fund has been a good response to the challenge of booming resource export revenues, but only time will tell if sound management is sufficiently institutionalized to weather stormy times and political pressures in the future.[12]

For the long term, as we will explore in the remainder of this report, the most important opportunities and challenges lie in the institutional and governance area and in building the human resource capacity of the country. Moreover, effective management of Kazakhstan's natural, environmental and human resource base and the creation a well-connected and increasingly urbanized knowledge-based society will have to be pursued in the quest to create a modern, sustainable economic and social platform for future generations in Kazakhstan. All of this has to be done in the context of an uncertain global and regional context, to which we turn next. The uncertainties that the country faces in the global and regional conditions put a great premium on continuing to build flexible and resilient institutions and policies for Kazakhstan.

---

12. As mentioned earlier (and in Box 2.2), the National Fund was tapped to finance bailouts and a stimulus program after the 2007 banking crisis. Subsequently an USD 8 billion annual limit on withdrawals was established to ensure prudent management of the Fund. However, the government has begun to increase its domestic (and to a lesser extent, external) debt, essentially borrowing against the Fund's assets; this had negative consequences, e.g., with respect to the financial health of pension funds encouraged to buy government bonds (Chapter 5).

THE GLOBAL
AND REGIONAL
OUTLOOK

The Global and Regional Outlook

Chapter
3

Shahid Yusuf

Kazakhstan's future trajectory is largely of its own making: how it uses its natural, capital, and human resources; how it saves and invests; how it governs itself; and how open it is to the rest of the world. But precisely that openness to the rest of the world, which is critical to Kazakhstan's long-term success, means that it is inevitably hitched to the fate of the geopolitical and regional economic trends, events, and lessons from experience.

Foretelling world, regional, or national events weeks, years, let alone decades ahead is a hazardous undertaking, as prophets of old learned the hard way. Even interpreting past lessons can be problematic.[1] Our techniques for looking into the future and applying the lessons of the past may have become more sophisticated, but our ability to forecast long-term economic, social, and political trends and events and to predict the impact of policy and institutional reforms remains at best limited. The financial crisis of 2007-8 and the long jobless recession that has followed in its wake has demonstrated once again that although forecasting may be unavoidable, accurate longer-term predictions are more the exception than the rule, and predicting turning points in economic activity has proven too much for model builders. In the mid-1980s, even the most knowledgeable observers did not perceive the hollowness of the Soviet economy or the coming demise of the USSR; it was impossible to conceive in the early 1970s, when a post-Cultural Revolution China was struggling back onto its feet, that its economy would become the second largest in the world just 40 years later; in the mid-1980s, Japan seemed to be on the cusp of global economic dominance only to plunge into two and possibly three lost decades a few years later;[2] and most recently, the Arab Spring is upending predictions regarding the future of the Middle East. Likewise, the New Economy of the 1990s and its successor, the computerized-digital world that has emerged since the turn of the century, were impossible to foresee in the 1970s, although many of the technologies responsible for the ICT revolution were being mainstreamed or were on the threshold of commercialization.[3]

Nonetheless, many, possibly most, decisions are influenced by expectations regarding the future. In particular, policy decisions by government agencies, business decisions by firms, and many household decisions hinge on future conditions and consequences and on lessons learned from the past. In

---

1. Note the furious debate among academics, pundits, and politicians about the impact of public debt on growth that is currently raging in the wake of an academic critique of a well-known analysis by C. Reinhardt and K. Rogoff on the topic. http://www.nytimes.com/2013/04/26/opinion/debt-growth-and-the-austerity-debate.html?nl=todaysheadlines&emc=edit_th_20130426

2. "Lost decades" only with reference to Japan's past record and that of other still flourishing East Asian Tiger economies. Averaged over the period 2000-2008, Japan's per capita GDP growth was almost level with that of the US, and the TFP growth at 1.5 percent per annum was a shade higher.

3. There is a famous remark attributed to Thomas Watson, the head of IBM in 1943, that he saw a market for no more than 4 or 5 computers. This has been since challenged and attributed instead to Howard Aiken at a somewhat later date. http://www.washingtonpost.com/wpsrv/style/longterm/books/chap1/historyofmoderncomputing.htm; http://www.freakonomics.com/2008/04/17/our-daily-bleg-did-ibm-really-see-a-world-market-for-about-five-computers/

3

exploring how Kazakhstan should move ahead in realizing its vision to join the top 30 developed nations of the world, we have to assess the likely global and regional context and the lessons from development elsewhere, based on which Kazakhstan can develop and deploy its considerable resources. We do so not in a deterministic manner, but try to highlight the potential tailwinds and headwinds that a country like Kazakhstan will face in the coming decades and what are the policy principles and priorities that emerge from international experience which might guide Kazakhstan as it looks ahead. Later in this volume (Chapter 12), we also explore some quantified future scenarios. These scenarios are not meant to predict the future, but are designed to help us frame the expectations for Kazakhstan based on alternative assumptions for key macroeconomic variables that help describe Kazakhstan's economy as it might develop in the future global context.

The chapter is divided into four sections. The first two sections consider respectively potential global and regional factors, or what today goes under the name of "known unknowns." The third section considers what development policy lessons of the past might tell us for the future. The last section draws the main conclusions relevant for the rest of this report.

The bottom line for this chapter is that, based on the immutability of resource depletion and on the assumption that the community of nations will change course slowly and insufficiently, countries need to prepare for uncertain, and possibly harder, times toward and beyond the middle of the 21st century. For Kazakhstan this calls for early action on its economic vision, exploiting the prevailing fair tailwinds over the next two decades or so, including the opportunities still latent in globalization, and taking advantages of technological catching up that all latecomers have. The essence of preparation lies in exploiting the time window of reasonably certain opportunity over the next two decades to build a prosperous, flexible, and resilient economy that is buttressed by institutions and a civil society that can take some hard knocks if and when they materialize and irrespective as to what they are and when exactly they occur.

Kazakhstan's Road to 2050 is Paved with Many Global Unknowns

The past four decades have been extraordinarily eventful for the global economy. Even with the knowledge and analytic capacity at our disposal in the 1970s, much of what happened during these years was impossible to predict. What is reassuring about this period is that the world avoided another catastrophic war and a major disease outbreak comparable to the influenza epidemic of 1918; localized famines were contained; and societies subject to droughts, floods, typhoons, heat waves, earthquakes, and tsunamis managed to absorb the costs without unraveling. Even countries wracked by destructive internal conflict such as Afghanistan, the Democratic Republic of the Congo, Liberia, and Rwanda or battered by a foreign invasion (Iraq) have not disintegrated, and their neighbors have more or less neutralized the spillovers.[4] Throughout this period, the world benefited from a steady stream of technological advances that have helped to raise the productivity of agriculture, manufacturing, and most services. Poverty has declined and the vast majority have benefited from increased longevity and improved quality of life.

We live in a more tightly networked world, and this interdependence is reflected in the mesh of globe-spanning institutions that monitor and regulate a multitude of activities. While the world's population has increased by almost 3 billion, food production has more than kept pace; for many people, dietary quality has risen. In short, when we look forward from the last quarter of the 20th century, the intervening years were gainful ones, and the world is a more prosperous place for many more people than it once was. However, the current prosperity was achieved at a price: it was based on the rapid consumption

---

4. However, the violent breakup of the former Yugoslavia and developments in the Horn of Africa argue for caution, while Afghanistan will be an important test case in the years ahead.

of non-renewable resources, including biodiversity. In addition, the quantum leap in consumption has stored huge problems for the future in the form of greenhouse gases, pollutants, and solid waste that are poisoning the biosphere.

Thus, when looking nearly four decades into the future, several unknowns — many of them troubling — may deflect what have been largely comforting trends over the past decades. We consider seven "apocalyptic horsemen" that potentially challenge an optimistic outlook[5] pertaining to the future of globalization, the advanced economies, technology, climate change, the availability of natural resources, the risk of war, and the threat from epidemics.

Could discontent with globalization triumph?

Questions have been raised as to the future of the ongoing globalization, with some observers predicting that it might soon falter and go into reverse much like how an earlier globalizing episode that commenced in the late 19th century was slowed by World War I and eventually undone by the Great Depression. The current round of globalization thus far appears robust, with trade growing at an average rate of 6 percent from 2000 to 2011 (Lamy 2012). Trade barriers have been gradually dismantled through a combination of multilateral agreements that have been superseded by regional and bilateral free trade agreements. Cross-border capital flows amounted to USD4.4 trillion in 2010 (Roxburgh et al. 2011); and foreign direct investment (FDI) reached USD1.24 trillion (UNCTAD 2011), further bolstering the salience of multinational corporations and their affiliates (MNCs) that collectively accounted for 58 percent of global GDP in 2007 (Alfaro and Chen 2012) and directly or indirectly control nearly 50 percent of global trade.

The economic liberalization that has undergirded these flows is responsible for the 3.5 percent average growth rate of the world economy since the beginning of the new century (Berry and Sirieux 2006). This is only slightly lower than the 3.8 percent rate achieved during 1970-1980 and is buoyed in large part by the phenomenal growth rates of Asia and a significant rebound in African and Latin American economies (Figure 3.1). Remarkably, the high growth rates have been achieved in spite of the financial crisis of 2007-8 and the ensuing Great Recession that has impaired the performance of leading advanced economies, pointing to the increasing economic weight and vibrancy of developing economies that accounted for 43 percent of global exports (Lamy 2012), with South-South exports amounting to 23 percent of the total in 2010. The intensifying globalization is also apparent from the large share of intermediate goods (60 percent) in trade and the rising import content of exports, averaging 40 percent worldwide (IMF 2008). The WTO now refers to goods as being "made in the world" rather than in any specific country because of the enormous spread of global (or, more accurately, regional) value chains and the fragmentation of value added for some commodities among countries.

Paralleling the flows of goods, services, and factors is the increasing interconnectedness among countries and cities made possible by ease of travel, as well as declining transport costs, great advances in communication technologies, and access to the Internet. Business and tourist travel has risen enormously, with expenditure on tourism exceeding USD1 trillion in 2011, as have information and technology flows, which are captured by a multitude of indicators such as international phone calls, licensing arrangements, numbers of international students, and cross-border research collaboration.[6]

---

5. Morris (2010) identifies five horsemen laying waste to and leveling civilizations in earlier eras: climate change, migration, famine, epidemic, and state failure. Looking ahead, he adds nuclear proliferation and population growth making a total of seven. More could emerge as mankind is an inviting — and welcoming — target.

6. Trade in services is expanding rapidly, with conventional tourism being augmented by medical and religious tourism and by the efforts of countries to attract foreign students to their schools and universities.

3

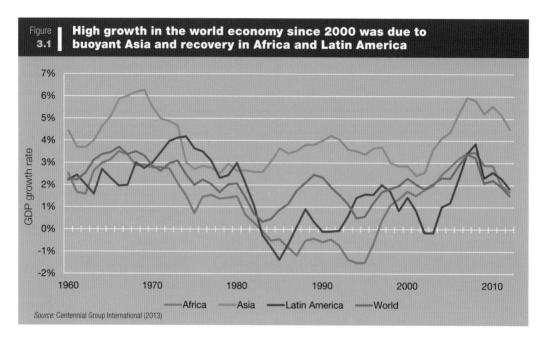

Figure 3.1 | **High growth in the world economy since 2000 was due to buoyant Asia and recovery in Africa and Latin America**

Africa — Asia — Latin America — World

Source: Centennial Group International (2013)

Alongside globalization, there has been a proliferation of transnational agencies and institutions with wide-ranging governance, regulatory, and research functions that complement, intersect, and at times, overshadow those of the state. These have added to and tightened the many-stranded ties binding countries to each other. They have, in addition, helped to bring together the world's decision-making elites and identified common issues for debate and resolution.

Is globalization likely to remain a growth-promoting force that expedites the management of global public goods, the resolution of shared problems, and the mediation of disputes among nations? After the experience of a century ago, it is impossible to be categorical. As Acemoglu and Yared (2010) indicate, a surge in nationalistic sentiments and militarism could result in a rollback of globalization, as could rising protectionist tendencies induced by prolonged slow growth and worsening inequality in leading economies that lead to economically dysfunctional but politically irresistible efforts to contain imports and to create domestic employment. Much depends upon the pace of recovery in the advanced countries and the success of efforts to correct structural problems. The minimizing of tensions associated with claims over land, continental shelves, or water (especially in Asia) would also diminish the probability of globalization going into reverse; as would the peaceful transition of several troubled Middle Eastern nations to political stability and rates of growth sufficient to productively absorb the youth bulge.

The effective tackling of globally systemic issues by international institutions — issues such as those associated with climate change, common pool resource depletion, poverty, international crime and terrorism, allocation of water resources, and financial interdependence — would increase the likelihood of strengthening global interdependence at least a couple of decades into the future, resulting in associated changes in governance that are mostly benign.[7]

---

7. According to the KOF Swiss Economic Institute Index of Globalization (2013), the financial crisis temporarily halted the march of globalization worldwide although there are signs of resumption in 2012. The small Northern European countries remain the most globalized, with Kazakhstan in 78th place. globalization.kof.ethz.ch

3

Retreat of the advanced economies?

Since the 1950s, the tempo of global economic activity and technological development has been set largely by a handful of advanced nations. These countries have also been the principal repositories of hard and soft power, although during the years when the Cold War raged, the West shared its monopoly of hard power with the Soviet Union. Since the onset of the Great Recession — a matter of five years — there has been a remarkable decline in the perceived economic weight of the West (including Japan), in its capacity to wield hard power with impunity, and in the sway of Western soft power (see Morris 2010). The nations that once bestrode the world now look weak, confused, vulnerable, and adrift. Not only has growth slowed in the United States, the EU, and Japan, the medium-term potential growth rates have been revised downwards as well. Worse, the emergence of a compelling vision that would inspire and propel a multitude of desirable national economic reforms is being rendered almost impossible by the spread of parochial and uncompromising political convictions, increasing inequality, and the rise of narrow, well-financed, and powerful interest groups. The clear superiority of the capitalist and democratic models of development and of income distribution is being widely questioned and rancorous disputes among different political forces and schools of economic thought have made it difficult to select among competing policy options, much less convince the public of their appropriateness.[8]

When emerging economies defied recessionary forces and rebounded in 2009-10, there was a brief moment when it seemed that the South had decoupled from the North and could push ahead irrespective of economic and financial conditions prevailing in Western countries. To a degree, such a decoupling has occurred thanks to the rise of Asian giants, but developments in 2011-12 and projections for 2013-14 suggest decoupling remains at best incomplete. The advanced economies still account for almost half of global GDP, their affluent middle classes (and the top 1 percent) are the consumers who count, their multinational corporations dominate virtually all key industries (Nolan 2012), their financial markets call the shots, and their innovation systems decisively influence productivity and growth.

In short, the developing world still needs Western locomotives to pull the global economy and this dependence is likely to persist for decades. With few exceptions, the developing world is not yet able to forge ahead on its own. The surge in African growth rates — to 5.3 percent per annum in the 2000s — was preceded by almost three decades of stagnation, and this surge is not buttressed by key fundamentals such as significantly higher domestic savings and private investment in productive capacity, improvements in quality of human capital, stronger market institutions, and diversified non-resource based exports. Similarly, Latin America also has a long history of stagnation, and its many structural, institutional, infrastructural, and human resource-related weaknesses are little changed from fifteen years ago. The growth acceleration experienced by a few countries, e.g., Peru, is wholly traceable to increased mineral exports and the higher prices commanded by these products (Edwards 2012). Turbulence in the Middle East imperils an already mixed economic performance, and parts of South and Central Asia confront grave uncertainties as one phase of the widely destabilizing conflict in Afghanistan draws to a close. Aside from China and some of its neighbors, the balance of this decade is unlikely to produce economic drivers that collectively could displace the Western locomotives.

Although the fiscal gaps, public and private indebtedness, systemic financial flaws, and burdensome medical and social insurance programs of leading advanced economies have attracted much attention, politics permitting, these in principle are amenable to solution within a matter of years. The more pressing

---

8. See for instance the exchange between Acemoglu, Robinson, and Verdier (2012) and Maliranta, Maattanen, and Vihriala (2012) on the relative innovativeness and efficiency of the US and Nordic models.

3

question relates to the growth prospects of Western countries and of the advanced East Asian econ-omies. In other words, what is the contribution these economies might make to global performance in what might be an even more integrated (and closely coupled) system?

All these countries will need to come to terms with the economic consequences of an aging and shrinking population, where dependency ratios will have doubled between 2000 and 2050 (Figure 3.2). These developments could dampen productivity, savings propensities, innovativeness, and demand for tradable goods and services. The aging trend could also saddle countries with rising healthcare costs, demanding possibly insupportable transfers from a smaller working population.[9] Declining populations in advanced nations will reduce the claims on the world's resources, but they could also set the stage for an economic implosion in the most severely affected countries, some already suffering from the onset of sclerosis such as in southern and southeastern Europe. It could also spread to other hitherto dynamic economies such as South Korea, Finland, and Switzerland.

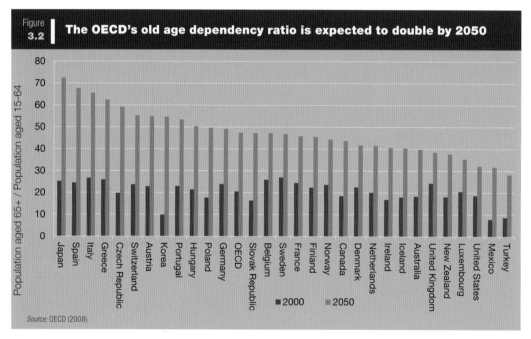

Figure 3.2 | **The OECD's old age dependency ratio is expected to double by 2050**

Source: OECD (2008).

Such a fate is by no means inevitable and there are a number of less painful intermediate scenarios, but renewing the dynamism of advanced countries depends ultimately on the evolution and effective harnessing of existing technologies that can contribute to sustainable growth and the appearance of new general purpose technologies that, after a period of assimilation, will contribute toward a steady increase in productivity in a more hostile physical environment. The productivity gains achieved between 1995 and 2006 were supported by innovations spawned by semiconductors, IT and the Internet. Other general purpose technologies stimulated investment and productivity growth in prior decades. Whether the high-income economies rise to the challenge, maintain their innovativeness, and are able to translate

---

9. Aging is also a challenge that will increasingly face the developing world, including China and Thailand. According to UN projections the share of the population in developing countries aged 60 and grow to over 20 percent by 2050, three times the rate in 1950; see http://www.un.org/esa/population/publications/worldaging19502050/pdf/81chapteriii.pdf

this via entrepreneurship into investment that employs a well educated but on average older workforce, will determine their weight in the global economy, their political influence, and the degree to which they drive development in other countries.

Technological innovation: savior or source of false hope?

The future of technological innovation is critical for the now advanced countries, but it also is critical for developing economies like Kazakhstan. Those observers who are technologically-inclined are among the most optimistic. They visualize a transformed, largely urbanized world, with big advances in urban design, land use, quality of structures, heating, ventilation, and air conditioning (HVAC), and transport; a vastly increased reliance on renewable energy; the advent of new materials courtesy of nanotechnology and the frugal use of resources with the help of recycling; the massive displacement of humans in most routine and many analytic tasks by robots, artificial intelligence, and digital technology; the emergence of a high-tech energy- and water-saving industrialized agricultural system with more food grown in factory-type conditions; the widespread use of IT, biotechnology, stem cell-based techniques, and implants to advance the quality of medical care and to extend life spans while lessening the incidence of chronic diseases and dementia; and geo-engineering to combat global warming. This is not by any means all that scientists have in store for us, but the aforementioned is a foretaste of the low carbon, automated world of the future that is more a vision of a hoped for scientific utopia than a world we will inhabit in 2050.[10]

But among the community of growth economists there is creeping doubt that productivity enhancing technological change will be as rapid in the future as it was in the past because low hanging fruit might have been largely plucked, leaving the trees denuded, at least temporarily. The doubters compare the quality and potential of long-run spillovers and linkage effects of recent innovations — associated with the Internet and social networking — unfavorably with the benefits derived from electricity and the internal combustion engine; they point to the diminishing number of influential innovations over the past three decades; they note the increased number of years it takes a scientist to arrive at the frontier of his chosen field (because of the quantum of knowledge to be mastered); they point to the increasing age of Nobel prize recipients; and they worry over the rising average age of the workforce and how it will affect the thirst for innovation, the supply of entrepreneurship, and the pace of new discoveries. The doubters foresee a slowing of innovation induced productivity growth in the advanced countries to a 1 to 1.5 percent per annum level, with steady state rates of growth approaching this or lower levels given the anticipated shrinking of populations.[11]

Doubting technology remains a minority position.[12] For the sake of developing nations and the future of the planet, it is of the utmost importance that the optimists are proven correct for three reasons. First, innovation is and will be the driver of growth and it is innovation that will ensure that growth is sustainable. Second, innovation will determine whether the productivity-constraining adjustment costs of going green (Howitt 2002) can be counterbalanced by productivity increases in other areas, especially in view of the likely stagnation or reduction in the rate of capital investment worldwide as graying reduces the volume of savings.[13] Third, only innovation that is, on balance, labor-intensive will create the number of well-paid

---

10. Brockman (2002) and Brockman (2009) assemble some of the speculations of leading scientists and thinkers.

11. See Huebner (2005); Cohen (2008); Cowen (2011) and Gordon (2012). For a more extensive discussion of global productivity trends see Chapter 9.

12. Acemoglu and Robinson are among those who believe that the future is likely to be rich in great innovations. They cite a number of papers that point to the innovation stimulating impact of incentives and of "inclusive institutions." http://whynationsfail.com/blog/2013/2/5/the-end-of-low-hanging-fruit.html

13. Household savings have plummeted in Japan and Korea and are now no higher than those in the United States, a savings laggard. Global rates of gross savings and investment were 19 percent of GDP in 2009 as opposed to 22 percent in 1995 (World Bank "Databank" 2013).

3

jobs that are needed to absorb the youth bulge in some countries and the retirement bulge in others and to keep income inequality from widening. Can advances in basic science and applied research deliver? It comes down to a matter of belief.

In any case, robust optimism regarding, for example, the myriad benefits from ICT/Internet-enabled smarter infrastructures must be tempered by an awareness that our increasing dependence on a seemingly all-encompassing cyberinfrastructure and potentially vulnerable server farms exposes us to cyberattacks that have the potential to cause severe disruption. This vulnerability has been brought home repeatedly by deadly attacks on financial institutions and other facilities and by the theft of valuable information from supposedly secure entities, both public and private. That government functioning can be partially disabled was revealed by the concerted denial of service attacks on Estonia in 2007;[14] moreover, the Stuxnet worm and other malware such as Flame and Gauss have demonstrated the capacity of experienced and well-equipped hackers to penetrate, monitor, and damage key infrastructure facilities, including those supplying power and water to cities and managing transport facilities. The first shots of cyberwarfare having been fired, one can anticipate more to come as the entry barriers are still relatively low. Hence, as the reliance on IT inexorably increases and more and more of the functioning of advanced and emerging societies becomes tied to digital technologies, reducing the vulnerability and enhancing the resilience of the IT infrastructure will be a continuing priority — a race between the creators of software and those seeking to mount "zero day attacks."[15]

Climate change: Force of drastic disruption?

Scientific progress, innovation, and optimal pricing of carbon will also, in part, determine how rapidly the rate of greenhouse gas emissions is slowed. Many other political and economic factors will decide the uptake of viable innovations, but first there must be innovation to draw upon — and pricing strategies to incentivize it. The tight grip of fossil fuels on virtually all activities; the enormous sunk cost of the infrastructure supporting their production, distribution, and utilization; the numerous interests arguing for continuing reliance on such fuels; and the volume of ongoing and planned investment in fossil fuel using long-lived power generating and other equipment, points to persisting dependence and rising emissions — unless there are technological breakthroughs that, in a matter of decades, revolutionize energy production and the efficiency with which it is used.[16]

If the breakthroughs do not materialize and the current fitful, dispersed, insufficient, and incremental efforts at greening remain the order of the day, the earth could warm by up to 4 degrees by mid-century, with potentially devastating consequences for some countries but with all countries paying a high and possibly escalating price.[17] The risk is that the earth's regenerative capacity is overextended, that it is in a state of overshoot that could beyond a tipping point result in runaway warming.[18] For landlocked Kazakhstan, the greatest risks will come from water shortages and desertification. Scantier (and more intense) rainfall and reduced flow of river water caused by the shrinking of Central Asia's hitherto abundant

---

14. http://blogs.law.harvard.edu/cyberwar43z/2012/12/21/estonia-ddos-attackrussian-nationalism/

15. https://en.wikipedia.org/wiki/Zero-day_attack

16. Jorgen Randers (2012) fears the worst, especially for the second half of the 21st century, and argues for a rapid shift away from fossil fuels to renewable energy use coordinated by global compact. He sees a rapid decline in population growth, plunging productivity because of social unrest, worsening poverty, and accelerating climate change.

17. See Cullen (2010). As yet there is little evidence of increasing heat tolerance in crops such as corn and soybeans; however, these crops show sharp reductions in productivity once temperatures rise above a threshold level, with the sensitivity being greatest during certain periods of the growing cycle.

18. See Meadows, Randers, and Meadows (2004); On the safe operating limits of the earth, see Rockstrom et al. (2009).

3

glaciers, forest cover, and lakes in catchment areas[19] will affect agricultural production, mineral extraction (coal requires washing), power generation using fossil fuel or water, and industrial output of energy and water intensive products, e.g., metals, electronics, petrochemicals, and foodstuffs (see Chapter 7).

Natural resources: will energy and water become binding constraints and food security threatened?

Looming uncertainty about energy supplies is a fourth factor that is focusing attention on the future. Since the industrial revolution, economic development has been inextricably tied to an elastic supply of cheap energy, based on readily available carbon fuels. Such fuels are far from being exhausted, but the richest and most accessible sources are being rapidly depleted. With population numbers rising and pointing toward a global total between 9 and 10 billion in 2050, incomes trending upwards as more countries join the race to develop, and energy intensive material and food consumption climbing in step, fossil-based energy will likely become more costly in the long term.[20] Some observers ascribe the slowing of growth in the advanced economies to higher energy prices; if current trends persist, growth reliant on existing technologies, modes of urbanization, consumption patterns, and lifestyles will become harder to sustain.[21] Of course, one of the benefits of increased energy scarcity and prices would be reduced carbon emissions and hence serve to address climate change, albeit likely only at a time when much damage will already have been done. As an energy surplus country for some decades to come, increasing energy scarcity and hence prices would be a helpful factor for Kazakhstan in terms of GDP growth, as long as the country can export energy. But, as in the past, energy prices are likely to be volatile, and periods of protracted declines and the attendant difficulties for energy exporting countries cannot be ruled out. At the same time Kazakhstan, too, will need to adjust its domestic prices so as to reflect world energy prices in order to realize greater energy efficiency in industry, transport, and urban design and to encourage greater reliance on alternative energy sources (see Chapter 6).

As with energy, global water supplies are getting increasingly scarce. Historically, Kazakhstan, along with its Central Asian neighbors has benefited from ample water resources supplied by the river systems of the region. However, as the death of the Aral Sea has demonstrated dramatically, as other river basins and lakes are similarly threatened, and as research on the impact of climate change demonstrates (Chapter 7) the region's usable water supply is at serious risk of depletion. This threatens not only the future of Kazakhstan's agriculture and requires its adaptation by relying on less water intensive crops, but also affects urban and industrial development, as the supply of water will be constrained and its costs may rise dramatically.

Climate change and water shortages will increase the salience of food security for most nations, Kazakhstan included, although given its land resources, it is likely to be both less vulnerable and in a position to become a significant supplier of food grain. According to the FAO, in 6 of the last 11 years, worldwide consumption of food has exceeded production and in 2012, global stocks of food grain were at their lowest level in almost 40 years. With populations and the demand for energy dense foods continuing to increase and global warming taking a toll on both cultivable acreage and yields, the FAO anticipates that prices will be 10-30 percent higher during the next 10 years and that production will grow more slowly — by 1.7 percent per annum versus 2 percent per annum in the preceding decade (OECD

---

19. http://www.chinafile.com/climate-change-not-grazing-destroying-tibetan-plateau

20. See some medium term forecasts by the IEA (for the 2020s) and views by James Hamilton. http://www.econbrowser.com/archives/2012/11/2012_world_ener.html; http://www.econbrowser.com/archives/2012/11/2012_world_ener.html

21. James Hamilton has carefully examined the relationship between economic activity and oil prices. See http://dss.ucsd.edu/~jhamilto/handbook_climate.pdf

and FAO 2012). In order to minimize the adverse impact of climate change on agricultural productivity and to profit from opportunities to supply countries that will be short of food grain, Kazakhstan must take steps to both strengthen infrastructure and extension services but also to engage in research on new biotechnologies and in particular GMOs (See Chapter 7).

Wars and violent conflict: can we keep the peace?

Steven Pinker (2011) has argued with an arsenal of statistics that the human race has become less violent and more peaceable.[22] It may be so. However, in Asia and Africa incipient arms races and domestic strife and tensions among countries are storing problems for the future especially in what is likely to be a multipolar world. The nuclear arms race may yet enter a new and more virulent phase, possibly in the Middle East and East Asia. Moreover, as Brzezinski (2013) has observed, "technologically sophisticated states can now gain the capacity to launch a non-lethal but paralyzing cyberattack on the socioeconomic system and the most important state institutions of a target country." Serious outbreaks of hostilities in existing hot spots could compound the damage from global warming and the exhaustion of the biosphere. Disputes over water and land fueled by climate change-induced migrations and the youth bulge could completely alter economic prospects and the course of technological change.

For Kazakhstan the biggest risks from armed conflict are — in some rough order of likelihood and potential impact on Kazakhstan — uncontrolled civil war and violence in Afghanistan spilling over into Central Asia; conflict in Central Asia over the waters in the Aral Sea basin; a major conflict in the Middle East; conflict on the nuclearized Indian subcontinent; conflict on the Korean Peninsula; regional conflicts in East Asia over disputed islands and marine resources, or over shared water resources (including rivers flowing through Kazakhstan).

A fundamental lesson of history is that a violent conflict is a serious threat to economic and social progress. Wars have always taken human lives and destroyed economic assets. Modern wars carry the risk of national, regional, and global annihilation. Even latent conflict causes economic damage through excessive spending on armies and armaments. So keeping the peace by searching for cooperative solutions to competing or conflicting interests must be an overriding goal for the world. More generally, such cooperation, mediated by local, national, regional, and international institutions, is critical for managing the many spillovers of human activity at all levels.

Global epidemics: the ultimate threat to mankind?

War- and climate-induced displacement of populations — including crowding in cities that are ill-prepared to supply water, sanitation, and waste management services; agricultural intensification; and further encroachment into forested areas — would be fertile soil for the spread of epidemics some caused by virulent zoonoses (e.g., diseases or infections that are naturally transmissible from vertebrate animals to humans; Quammen 2012). A world lacking effective global governance institutions and the will to craft and enforce enlightened rules[23] may ignore pressures that could have been avoided or at least minimized through precautionary action. Neglecting dangerous issues now could open the door for future global epidemics in the coming years to strip away the benefits of globalization and very likely lose decades of hard-won prosperity, as was the case with pandemics in centuries past (most notably the bubonic plague in Medieval times, and the wholesale extinction of native Americans in the wake of colonial conquests).

---

22. The skeletal remains of Stone Age humans suggest that 20-30 percent died violent deaths. In comparison, during the bloodstained 20th century, some 2-3 percent of the population fell victim to violence.

23. Kishore Mahbubani (2013) observes that where once the countries resembled "a flotilla of more than 100 separate boats"; globalization has brought us together to live "in 193 separate cabins on the same boat." It is our misfortune that this boat lacks a "captain or crew."

Recent scares of HIV/AIDS, the Ebola virus, SARS, and bird flu have threatened serious damage but have been contained to varying degrees. The pessimists among the experts are warning that the world may not able to repeat this feat for all future threats.

The Regional Dimension

Global trends and potentially disruptive events are some of the factors that will shape Kazakhstan's prospects. However, the impact of its immediate neighbors is likely to outweigh that of more distant countries. In this section we consider the potential developments in Eurasia, China, Russia, and other important neighbors. The implications for Kazakhstan's efforts to integrate globally and regionally are discussed in greater detail in Chapter 10.

Eurasia[24]

As noted in Chapter 1, Kazakhstan is located at the center of the most dynamic and increasingly important region of the world. Mostly as a result of Asia's rise, the share of Eurasia's GDP in the world economy stayed roughly constant at 62 percent between 1990 and 2010, but it could well rise to 75 percent by 2050 (Figure 3.3).

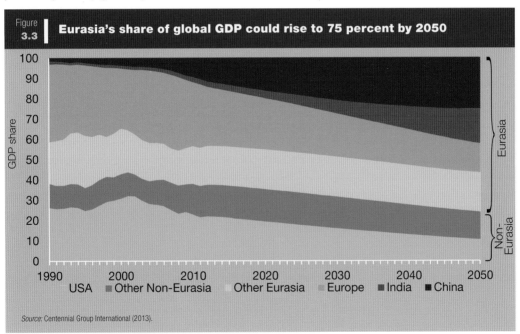

Figure 3.3 **Eurasia's share of global GDP could rise to 75 percent by 2050**

USA ■ Other Non-Eurasia　Other Eurasia ■ Europe ■ India ■ China

Source: Centennial Group International (2013).

As political barriers of the past (especially the Iron and Bamboo Curtains) have fallen and as cross-continental transport connections and electronic connectivity are dramatically on the rise, the Eurasian economic space has begun to catch up with globalization elsewhere in the world in terms of economic integration (Linn and Tiomkin 2006; Vinokurov and Libman 2012). This integration process, if it proceeds unimpeded, will support the growth of the major economies in the region, including Kazakhstan. On the

---

24. We include all of Europe and Asia in our definition of Eurasia.

other hand, if geopolitical, regional, or sub-regional political competition, or simply the inability to reach agreement on transcontinental transport infrastructure and transit facilitation impede the integration process, or if open conflict among Eurasian neighbors were to break out — in the worst case even with nuclear arms — this could slow down or even dramatically disrupt the Eurasian growth and integration process and hurt Kazakhstan's prospects. The exact impact of course depends on the nature of the obstacle and the location and severity of the conflict. Let us look then at the most important players among Kazakhstan's immediate neighbors: China, Russia, and Central Asia, including Afghanistan.

China

The country whose fortunes will impinge most on Kazakhstan over the long haul is likely to be China, followed by Russia, the other Central Asian states, and Afghanistan.[25] China's vertiginous economic performance has catapulted it into the limelight over a few decades and the expectation is that its GDP will exceed that of the US by 2018 if not earlier (Subramanian 2011). Already it is the world's largest consumer of key minerals — iron ore, coal, copper, etc. — and of concrete; moreover, with its automobile population increasing at double digit rates, China will soon also rank as the largest consumer of petroleum.[26] China leads the world in exports and its imports of raw materials and agricultural products are among the principal determinants of world prices. Thus, the pace and course of China's industrialization; the growth of its cities, car ownership, electricity consumption, water utilization especially by the agricultural sector, household consumption patterns (including of meat); and changing technology affecting the energy, water, and material intensity of China's GDP, will be key to the demand facing mineral exporters, and none more so than Kazakhstan.

The mainstream view, based on an extrapolation of recent growth rates with some adjustments, argues for continuing rapid growth tapering in the 2020s and beyond. The World Bank's range of projections for China through 2030 (Figure 3.4) shows an eventual decline in China's growth rates, but is on the more optimistic side than many others, who see a decline to a rate closer to 4-5 percent, much like South Korea, Taiwan (China), and others in the region, still very respectable by international comparisons. Indeed, recent economic developments in China are consistent with the lower end of the range of projections by the World Bank. Whatever the precise scenario, mainstream observers maintain that China still has close to 200 million workers to draw upon from the rural sector,[27] investment rates are high,[28] capital-labor ratios are a fraction of those in the United States,[29] the share of household consumption in GDP is under 40 percent,[30] there is considerable scope for productivity-driving technological catching-up in manufacturing and services, and increasing investment in R&D should result in growth-enhancing innovations.[31]

---

25. China's importance to Kazakhstan was demonstrated by the visit of President Nazarbayev to meet with China's newly appointed leadership on April 6, 2013. http://www.cacianalyst.org/publications/field-reports/item/12709-nazarbayev-visits-china-to-meet-its-new-leadership.html

26. It became the largest importer of petroleum in January 2013 with imports amounting to 6.3 million barrels per day. Much of the 2 million barrels per day increase in oil production since 2005 has been absorbed by demand from China. http://energy.aol.com/2013/03/11/china-surpasses-us-as-world-s-largest-oil-importer/

27. See symposium in the China Economic Review on whether China has passed the Lewis turning point: http://www.sciencedirect.com/science/journal/1043951X/22; and Das and N'Diaye (2013).

28. Lee, Syed, and Liu (2012) estimate that gross investment approached 50 percent of GDP in 2011 and probably exceeded that level in 2012.

29. According to Kuijs (2012) they were 14.3 percent of US levels in 2010.

30. Some commentators maintain that services consumption is understated and that household consumption as a share of GDP may have crossed the 50 percent mark.

31. R&D accounted for 1.83 percent of GDP in 2011 and is targeted to reach 2.2 percent in 2015.

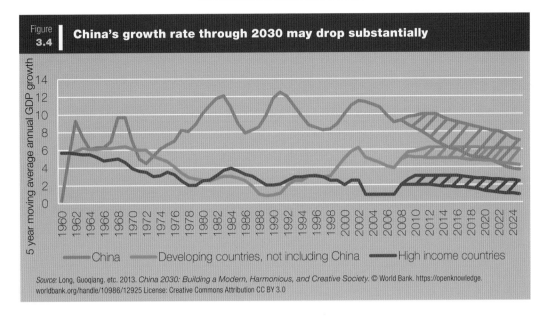

Figure 3.4 | China's growth rate through 2030 may drop substantially

Source: Long, Guoqiang. etc. 2013. *China 2030: Building a Modern, Harmonious, and Creative Society.* © World Bank. https://openknowledge. worldbank.org/handle/10986/12925 License: Creative Commons Attribution CC BY 3.0

Those questioning this sunny assessment of China's economic trajectory refer back to the experience of Russia and Japan, both of which invested heavily and ended up creating highly-lopsided economic systems that failed to deliver long run growth, the former by building an inefficient defense sector that absorbed between 22 and 27 percent of GDP in the early 1980s,[32] alongside increasingly ineffective central planning; the latter through overinvestment in an export-oriented manufacturing sector. China has not only invested far more of its GDP in manufacturing industries (using financial repression and a public sector-led industrial policy), but its export orientation has resulted in a more distorted and vulnerable economic system (Pettis 2013). The doubters point to the waste arising from the extraordinary building ahead of infrastructure demand with the help of financing through a poorly-regulated shadow banking network of off balance sheet vehicles, funds and investment banks;[33] the huge environmental costs of China's Big Push industrialization, its sprawling urbanization and its fertilizer-intensive agricultural production; the highly intensive (and in the longer run, unsustainable) use of energy and water to fuel development; the steeply increasing greenhouse gas emissions that since 2006 have made China the largest emitter of carbon;[34] worsening income inequality;[35] popular resentment of corruption and media control; and the continued reliance on a top-down, investment-led growth strategy.[36]

---

32. http://wais.stanford.edu/History/history_ussrandreagan.htm, other estimates range from 11 to 17 percent in the latter half of the 1980s. https://www.cia.gov/library/center-for-the-study-of-intelligence/kent-csi/vol14no2/html/v14i2a01p_0001.htm; http://www.globalsecurity.org/military/world/russia/mo-budget.htm
33. http://www.ft.com/intl/cms/s/0/7c76e8e0-80cf-11e2-9c5b-00144feabdc0.html#axzz2MJ7eiDmY; http://www.scmp.com/comment/insight-opinion/article/1138397/tackling-shadow-banking-china-needs-pick-small-target-first; http://www.bloomberg.com/news/2012-11-19/purple-palace-abandoned-shows-china-shadow-banking-risk.html
34. China's share of carbon emissions in 2011 was 28 percent of the global total. http://wattsupwiththat.com/2012/12/02/record-high-for-global-carbon-emissions-china-is-the-leader/
35. The Gini coefficient conservatively estimated crossed the 0.47 mark in 2012.
36. Several observers such as Francis Fukuyama, Acemoglu and Robinson, and Minxin Pei anticipate problems for China and a slowing of its economy because of dysfunctional politics and corruption.

For China believers, this is but a transitory and inevitable phase of China's extraordinarily rapid industrialization, one that is a prelude to a shift to a more sustainable growth path. An optimistic mainstream view is that China will come to grips with its many challenges and will move smoothly to a green growth path, to a stable pluralistic political regime, to displace exports with domestic consumption without sacrificing growth momentum, and to work constructively with other countries in steering the global economy in a sustainable direction. Pessimists, who recently appear to be gaining in credibility, visualize a sharper slowdown similar to Japan's, exacerbated by the shrinking ratio of the working age population (since 2012)[37] with unwelcome implications for employment, inequality, and political stability. A China having to cope with a slowing economy and possibly domestic unrest could turn into a more difficult neighbor for Kazakhstan than has been the case in the past.

Who is right, the optimists or the pessimists? In Zhou Enlai's words, "it is too early to say."[38] For Kazakhstan, the important conclusion is that either outcome is possible, especially in the medium-to-long term, and therefore it is essential for the country to be prepared to benefit from the upside of a dynamic, cooperative China, and to be resilient against the downside of a more troubled neighbor to the east.

Russia

Although China looms larger than others, Russia will undoubtedly exert a strong influence on the evolving economic and political calculus of the Central Asian region. Kazakhstan's ties — economic and political — with Russia are long-standing. Trade agreements, supply chains and the recently formed Customs Union (with Russia and Belarus) bind the country to Russia. The countries share common business practices and institutions. Russia remains an important destination of Kazakh exports, such as metal products and machinery.

But Russia's economic prominence as a trading partner and as a source of FDI and technology is diminishing for a number of reasons. Russia's growth rate that averaged 6.3 percent per annum between 2003 and 2008 has slowed since 2009 to under 4 percent range during 2010-13 and is projected to remain at that level in the near term.[39] The more serious concern looking to the future is that the Russian economy has so far failed to diversify, with oil and gas accounting for 70 percent of exports and for 50 percent of federal revenues. Moreover, Russian firms have had difficulties competing in global product markets, where they mostly are represented in the low-tech, low-value added product categories. An aging workforce, the erosion of technological capabilities built during the Cold War, a difficult business environment, and weakness in infrastructure represent important constraints.

In recent years Russia has tried to improve its international competitiveness, including an attempt to build a multi-nodal innovative ecosystem with Skolkovo, a new science city close to Moscow, as one of the first of several "points of light." This is modeled variously on Shenzhen and Silicon Valley and the jewel in the crown, which is a research university, has the active support of the Massachusetts Institute Technology and a generous budget.[40] Such technopoles have a long history (Castells and Hall 1994). They became popular starting in the late 1970s with the success of Silicon Valley, Route 128, and the Cambridge (UK) Cluster and became a focus of policy in France (Sophia Antipolis[41] and Saclay-Paris[42]),

---

37. The working age population included those in the 15-59 year age group. There numbers declined by 3.45 million. http://www.economist.com/news/china/21570750-first-two-articles-about-impact-chinas-one-child-policy-we-look-shrinking
38. http://www.ft.com/intl/cms/s/0/74916db6-938d-11e0-922e-00144feab49a.html#axzz2LI0V6WG5
39. Most recent data indicate a dramatic decline in Russia's GDP growth rate during the first quarter of 2013 to only 1.1 percent, attributed by one expert not to lack of demand, but to a serious decline in productivity growth (Aslund 2013).
40. http://www.economist.com/node/21558602
41. http://www.ft.com/intl/cms/s/0/86db17fa-5bd4-11e1-841c-00144feabdc0.html#axzz2LTIERlzw
42. http://regionomist.blogspot.com/2012/12/silicon-valley-la-francaise-paris-saclay.html

South Korea (Daejon), Japan (Tsukuba), Malaysia (Cyberjaya), and Singapore (One North). But the record is mixed: with the exception of the clusters in the two Cambridges and adjacent to Stanford, few have delivered on their promise of technology startup led virtuous spirals and repaid the sums invested by governments in infrastructure and venture financing.

It is uncertain whether Russia will be able to address the constraints it faces and to generate an economic renaissance, which extends well beyond Moscow and serves to instill a creative milieu in a number of Russia's leading cities. This upside cannot be ruled out and would be a great benefit to Kazakhstan, especially since Russia will remain a significant trading partner for Kazakhstan, not least because of the recent formation of the Customs Union between Russia, Kazakhstan, and Belarus. However, there is also a risk for Kazakhstan that Russia will not develop into a dynamic neighbor, and thus fail to become a source of rapidly growing demand, technological spillovers, and foreign direct investment.

Central Asia

For the foreseeable future, China and Russia will be the main factors for economic development and political stability in Kazakhstan's immediate neighborhood. However, Central Asia, and especially the developments in Afghanistan, is also potentially important for Kazakhstan's future development.

A strengthening of regional economic and trading linkages in Central Asia could be the making of a larger and more competitive market, promoting productivity gains and diversification. A regional trading area encompassing the Central Asian countries, possibly with Russia as a linchpin, collectively could become a powerful economic force. Between 2000 and 2012, the countries in the Caucasus and Central Asian Region grew at an average rate of 7.4 percent. The oil exporters plus the Kyrgyz Republic and Tajikistan had a combined population of 64.6 million in 2011 and if Armenia, Georgia, and Azerbaijan are included, the total rises to 81.5 million — about the size of the population of Germany. The addition of Russia raises it to 225 million, about 20 million less than the population of Indonesia, the fourth most populous country in the world. 40 years into the future, the total might be closer to 250-260 million with Russia's population having diminished and that of the Central Asian countries having increased. This could represent a sizable market with which to trade for Kazakhstan.

However, such a development is predicated on a prior settling of political and border disputes and a resolution of issues regarding the sharing of water resources; investment in transport and communication infrastructure connecting the principal urban and mineral producing centers, as well as strengthening links with European and Asian countries; and coordinated policy initiatives that increase investments in job creating productive activities, whether in manufacturing, mineral beneficiation, or services. Freer trade will be politically attractive and economically beneficial if in conjunction with complementary policies, it can deliver widely shared growth and employment opportunities (see Chapter 10).

Afghanistan

A much-discussed short-to-medium term concern that could also profoundly influence Kazakhstan's long-term prospects is the resolution of the conflict in Afghanistan once the international forces withdraw in 2014. A conflict-ridden Afghanistan could embroil its neighbors in increasingly bitter, costly, and politically-destabilizing disputes that would put development on hold and divert valuable resources into financing arms races. Alternatively, a burying of hatchets by the contending ethnic groups and an internationally-financed effort[43] to assist Afghans rebuild their war-torn country, could begin healing ethnic

---

43. This must factor in the absorptive capacity of the country but also take as a point of reference the sums spent in conducting a more than decade long and enormously destructive campaign without a strategy or an endgame.

fissures that imperil not only the future of Afghanistan but of the entire Central Asian region. An Afghanistan that is assisted in climbing back on its feet and integrated into the economy of the region could be a blessing for its people and an asset to its neighbors. Beyond Afghanistan, the unsettled outlook for Pakistan and Iran also present potentially troublesome long-term perspectives.

International Lessons for National Economic Policy

Aside from the direct impact of global and regional trends and events on Kazakhstan, there is also the more indirect effect of the lessons from the experience of other countries over the past decades in managing its own affairs as it looks toward 2050. Of particular relevance to Kazakhstan is the experience of selected comparator countries, either because they are large, sparsely populated, resource rich advanced countries (Australia and Canada), or because they are East Asian countries that have modernized rapidly and successfully (China, Japan, Singapore, and South Korea). Box 3.1 summarizes our findings.

Box 3.1 | Key success factors from selected comparator countries

Australia and Canada
- Good macro policy and prudent financial sector management to avoid the resource curse and create a good economic environment for private enterprise.
- Protectionist policies may (or may not) stimulate infant industries, but it is crucial to end such policies when infants either mature or fail.
- Industrial policy was pursued, especially in Australia, but "picking winners" has not been successful.
- Governments can promote resource exports by investment in transport, grain elevators, etc., and where such infrastructure is a private monopoly, the state can restrict abuses of monopoly power.
- Good institutions are key. Contestability matters: a loyal opposition provides an alternative to the government of the day, and an independent judiciary provides redress against abuse of government power.

China, Japan, Singapore, South Korea
- Effective national leadership with clear vision; focus on pragmatic, adaptive, evidence-based implementation; orderly leadership transition.
- Rapid global trade expansion offered market for export-driven strategy.
- High investment rate based on high national savings; FDI important for some, less for others; high investment in modern infrastructure.
- Human development, especially education, with stress on quality/deepening
- Effective institutions (meritocracy, accountability; effective public sector management; control of corruption; Japan's Ministry of International Trade and Industry, Singapore's Economic Development Board).
- A dynamic business sector (not state-owned enterprises).
- Development of modern innovation systems is expensive, takes time; big push may be infeasible/wasteful for small countries.
- Support for R&D (but degree varies – high in Japan, lower in South Korea).
- Specialization in strategically selected industries.
- Dirigisme worked, but there is no guarantee that it will work elsewhere.

Source: Background notes by Richard Pomfret and Shahid Yusuf.

Many of these lessons will be detailed in subsequent chapters, so the purpose here is merely to show where there are overarching agreements or uncertainties that will also concern policy makers in Kazakhstan. Much of the agreement is on the basic messages, most of the uncertainties are about how to implement them in practice.

- *Investing in human and physical capital:* There is little disagreement today that investing in human and physical capital is a major factor supporting long-term growth and inter-personal and inter-regional equity. It also is the key to achieve an inclusive and equitable social outcome. The key open questions relate to how much to invest, how to rank competing priorities, how to delineate roles of the public and private sector, and how to control the frequently high levels of corruption.
- *Effective management of mineral resource rents:* For resource-rich countries, macroeconomic management presents special challenges if they want to avoid the resource curse. Saving and prudently investing extraordinary resource rents, especially during upswings of commodity prices, is generally recognized as the way to manage.[44] There is less agreement on what is the optimal rate of exploiting known mineral reserves or how to achieve a diversified economic base.
- *Environmentally sustainable development:* More broadly, managing natural resource assets, including soil, water, air, and biodiversity, in a sustainable manner for future generations is widely accepted. However, the trade-off between growth today and a hospitable environment, including the control of climate change, remains a troublesome political and to some extent economic question. China's shift from a wholesale disregard of environmental concerns in the early phase of its growth spurt to a more balanced approach in the face of dire environmental threats represents one example of the difficulty of making the right choice at the right time.
- *Urban-industrial structure:* With the world becoming ever more predominantly urban, the role of effectively managed, smart, and green cities as centers of high-tech manufactures and services and as a response to the increasingly harmful impact of climate change is more and more recognized.[45] How and how quickly to bring about this change, how to assure sufficient labor absorption and what role market and state should play remains open to much debate.
- *Promotion of technological change:* Clearly, future growth will hinge on how fast the world can move the technological frontier outward and how fast those countries lagging behind, such as Kazakhstan, can catch up with the technology leaders. The open question again is the "how," and the "who" — the market and/or the state.
- *Integration into the world economy and cooperation with neighbors:* Openness to the rest of the world and effective collaboration with neighbors to minimize economic barriers and disruptive conflicts are important factors of long-term economic success. Whether and for how long to retain some protection for selected domestic industries, how to structure economic relations with the rest of the world — bilaterally, regionally or multilaterally – and how much, if any, of sovereign control to share with others through international agreements remains a matter of intense debate.
- *Effective institutions and governance:* There is little disagreement among development experts that effective institutions and good governance are critical for sustainable long-term growth and human welfare. What specifically this means, and how to achieve it, remains the subject of many

---

44. Frankel (2010), van der Ploeg (2011) and the contributors to the volumes edited by Lederman and Maloney (2007) and by Humphreys, Sachs, and Stiglitz (2007) offer tested suggestions to minimize the risk of exchange rate appreciation, smooth revenue volatility, and reduce rent seeking activities and the losses from corruption (e.g. through the distribution of revenues to the public or their transparent sequestration in sovereign wealth funds).

45. Edward Glaeser (2011) in his book Triumph of the City makes a convincing case for the role which cities can play in a innovation and environmentally friendly way.

debates: how to reform the civil service; how to combat corruption; how to assure the rule of law; how to create transparent, accountable public institutions; how much and how to decentralize central authority to subnational governments; and how best to empower individuals and civil society to participate effectively in public decision making? All these questions and more are widely debated around the globe.

Two additional, crosscutting lessons deserve mentioning:

- *Sound macroeconomic fundamentals:* Emerging market economies, which were resoundingly shaken by the East Asia economic crisis of 1997/8, have learned that conservative fiscal policy and management of debt, an ample supply of currency reserves, alertness to domestic asset bubbles, and openness to trade are essential for sustained economic growth and resilience to external shocks. They benefited from this resilience in their relatively painless adjustment to the global economic crisis of 2008/9.
- *Leadership:* Effective national leadership with clear vision is a major success factor, where effectiveness is closely linked to a focus on pragmatic, adaptive, evidence-based implementation.

It is now abundantly clear that none of the models of economic management on the shelf — East Asian, American, Nordic, German, Chinese, or Indian — offers a viable long-term strategy that helps to both diagnose the situation prevailing developing and developed countries and that defines a domain of action for sustainable growth.[46] Based on the earlier models and recent experience, the truth of the matter is that no one knows for sure, because each country's history, priorities and conditions matter; because technological change is transforming the characteristics of industrialization (and the nature of manufacturing processes themselves, e.g., 3D production); because after three decades of globalization the scope for export-led growth, whether by manufactures or by tradable services, is more limited for economies large and small; and because the era of rapid energy and resource intensive growth might not extend very far into the future without imperiling the life-supporting biosphere.

The Way Forward for Kazakhstan

A time traveler riding current trends into the future might discover that the world had learned a lesson from the crises and turmoil of the 2000s and the 2010s and had gravitated toward saner politics, better economic management, and stronger international institutions; had reined in population growth and terrorism; had hammered out policies for utilizing and supporting aging workforces; was focused on increasing "happiness" rather than mindlessly pursuing GDP growth; and most importantly, had come to terms with necessity of coordinated action to halt climate change. This would be the best of all possible worlds. With responsible and farsighted political leaders, who intelligently marshal the most well-grounded available scientific knowledge and persuade electorates to accept some not always palatable choices for the greater good of current and future generations, it is a world that could exist in 2050. Absent speedy action by the current generation, future generations might be disappointed. The clock is ticking, the window of opportunity is narrowing and the Cassandras are placing their bets.

And bet one must on the future, so it helps having some notion of what might be in store. In Table 3.1 we summarize some of the key external factors that might impinge on Kazakhstan's future from the earlier discussion, categorized by whether they are expected to exert a positive (tailwinds) or negative impact (headwinds), or both. The table also indicates the likely specific qualitative implications for Kazakhstan.

---

46. Rumelt (2011) provides a perceptive discussion of strategy from the standpoint of business.

The color of the circle indicates the balance of the likely impact on Kazakhstan: green for positive, yellow for mixed or uncertain, red for negative. Obviously, the table only can cover the most important of impacts and represent a broad qualitative judgment subject to great uncertainty.

Forewarned is forearmed. Kazakhstan has many strengths and can benefit from a number of favorable tailwinds, but it is also subject to quite a few global and regional headwinds, for which it must be prepared. One key conclusion from Table 3.1 is that over the next 15-20 years (short-to-medium term) the positive factors broadly outweigh the negative ones, while in the longer term the potential for negative trends and events, especially climate change, increase in likelihood. This argues for urgency in using the relatively favorable window in the next 15-20 years to develop the foundations of a modern, flexible, and resilient economy, which will be critical for meeting challenges in the long-term outlook through 2050 and beyond.

Based on this analysis of global and regional trends and potentially disruptive events, the remainder of this volume lays out the vision for Kazakhstan 2050 and then assesses what might be suitable pathways to achieve this vision. In the absence of any overarching models of development that it can or should follow, Kazakhstan will have to search for its very own model and solution, appropriate for its current state of development, and for the global and regional conditions it faces now and more uncertainly in the future. In doing so, it will want to draw on international experience for what worked elsewhere and what did not. It will need to continuously monitor and evaluate policies and programs that it has selected and modify and adapt them in light of the evidence, taking into consideration the changing global and regional conditions in which it is placed.

3

Table 3.1 **Global and regional tailwinds and headwinds for Kazakhstan: A summary**

● = positive impact   ○ = neutral or uncertain impact   ● = negative impact

Issue	Global/regional tailwinds	Global/regional headwinds	Implications for Kazakhstan	Likely net impact next 15-20 years	Likely net impact 20-40 years
Global					
Globalization	• Continued openness to trade and capital flows is likely, supporting further integration in short to medium term	• Increased regionalism, protectionism possible, esp. in outer years, with rising threats from climate change	• Mostly affected through impact on and in Eurasian economic space	●	○
Advanced country growth	• Stagnation, more likely in the longer term, reduces pressure on global natural resources and climate change	• Stagnation reduces global growth impetus; aging populations put pressure on global financial savings	• Stagnation will reduce commodity prices and reduce Kazakhstan's export potential, more likely in the long term	○	●
Technological innovation	• Continued innovation supports high productivity growth and helps mitigate/adapt to climate change	• Innovation and hence productivity growth slow; limits abatement of climate change impact; technology risks increase (e.g., cyberterror, etc.)	• Kazakhstan has opportunity to catch up and leap-frog; impact of slower global productivity growth more likely in long term as Kazakhstan approaches frontier	●	○
Climate change		• Potentially strong downside impact on global weather, sea level, economic growth, esp. closer to 2050	• Kazakhstan on balance will likely see negative direct impacts on water, weather, and agriculture, and negative indirect impact from worldwide economic impacts; esp. toward 2050	○	●

(contd...)

(Table 3.1 contd...)

Table 3.1	Global and regional tailwinds and headwinds for Kazakhstan: A summary				
Issue	**Global/ regional tailwinds**	**Global/regional headwinds**	**Implications for Kazakhstan**	**Likely net impact next 15-20 years**	**Likely net impact 20-40 years**
Natural resources		• In short- to medium-term limited impacts, but toward 2050 energy and water resource constraints could become serious	• Higher energy prices benefit Kazakhstan in short to medium term; price volatility a risk. Water scarcity a growing problem, esp. with climate change		
Wars and conflict	• Overall large-scale wars and conflicts have been on decline	• Significant, and possible growing risks, especially in Asia	• Significant risk from conflict in Afghanistan; less so Middle East; South Asia; Central Asia; Korean Peninsula, etc.		
Epidemics		• Significant and possibly growing risks, especially in Asia	• Outbreaks of SARS and bird flu have originated in Asia and recurrences could directly affect Kazakhstan		
Regional					
Eurasian Integration	• Eurasian economic integration will support regional growth	• Political obstacles and potential conflicts will limit inter-state cooperation and hence integration	• Kazakhstan as the hub of potential integration process, can benefit greatly if it proceeds unimpeded		
China	• Successful China continues as a major economic driver for world economy	• China slows down and could be a drag on world economy	• Impact on Kazakhstan of either scenario significant		

(contd...)

(Table 3.1 contd...)

Table 3.1	Global and regional tailwinds and headwinds for Kazakhstan: A summary				
Issue	Global/regional tailwinds	Global/regional headwinds	Implications for Kazakhstan	Likely net impact next 15-20 years	Likely net impact 20-40 years
Russia	• Continued open development of Customs Union a benefit to region	• Russia may not become a dynamic, modernizing economy; Customs Union maybe restrictive, not open	• Russia important partner, but limited impact on upside	○	○
Central Asia	• Central Asian cooperation and integration will support regional growth	• Political obstacles and potential conflicts among some countries pose risks for the region	• Kazakhstan will benefit directly from tailwinds and suffer from headwinds	○	○
Afghanistan	• A peaceful and stable Afghanistan would open up potential for regional energy, transport and trade development to and through South Asia	• A war-torn Afghanistan or one that became a haven for radical Islamist forces would seriously threaten Central Asia and wider regional/global peace	• Kazakhstan could be severely affected by the downside risk	●	●

Source: Author.

Kazakhstan's Vision 2050

Chapter
4

Aktoty Aitzhanova, Dennis de Tray, Shigeo Katsu, Johannes F. Linn, and Vladislav Yezhov

In this chapter we present the vision of Kazakhstan 2050 that has guided our work. Our task has been made a lot easier by the fact that the President of Kazakhstan, N.A. Nazarbayev, presented the vision for Kazakhstan 2050 in his speech to the nation on December 14, 2012. For the purposes of this report the core of the vision is reflected in this sentence in the speech: "By 2050 Kazakhstan must enter the top 30 club of most developed countries in the world." This is a highly ambitious, but broadly feasible goal in terms per capita income growth for Kazakhstan, as demonstrated by our scenarios developed in Chapter 12. It presumes that Kazakhstan takes the appropriate steps to ensure continued convergence in its productivity of national resource use toward the best practice worldwide.

However, the President's speech leaves no doubt that the vision of Kazakhstan in 2050 is not only concerned with economic growth as measured by per capita income, but also the well-being of the people of Kazakhstan. The vision foresees a country that provides for a well-educated and healthy citizenry, protected against unexpected shocks and supported by an efficient and pragmatic state apparatus that serves its citizens with accountability and according to the rule of law. It envisages a country in which entrepreneurship flourishes and diligence and determination are rewarded as the key ingredients to individual and national success and a future in which Kazakhstan's traditional values, culture, and patriotism are preserved, while openness, ease of communication, and peaceful relations with the rest of the world underpin the respect that Kazakhstan commands on the international stage. This includes prominently a focus on the quality of the country's economic and political institutions. They need to ensure good governance and a sense of equity and fairness, as Kazakhstan strives to become a wealthy, harmonious, integrated, and liberalized state that maintains the economic capacity and institutional agility to respond to inevitable but unpredictable change in the world and in Kazakhstan. Or in the President's own words:

> "I am strongly confident that Kazakhstani citizens of 2050 represent a society of educated, free people speaking three languages. They are citizens of the world. They travel. They are open to new knowledge. They are industrious. They are patriots of their country.
>
> "I am convinced that Kazakhstan of 2050 is a society of universal labor. It is a state with a strong economy, with everything devoted for a person. With a strong education, a great health care. With peace and serenity. With citizens who are free and equal, and the authority is fair. With supremacy of the Law.
>
> "We must work with dedication and inspiration, not losing sight of our primary objectives:
>
> - Further developing and strengthening statehood.
> - Transitioning to new principles of economic management.

4

- *Comprehensive support for entrepreneurship will be a leading force for the national economy.*
- *Forming the new social model.*
- *Creating modern and efficient education and health care systems.*
- *Increasing accountability, efficiency and functionality of the state apparatus.*
- *Setting adequate international and military policy that is responsive to the new challenges.*

"The only way to modernize our country and make it competitive is to progressively follow the path of political liberalization."

In January 2013 the NAC of Nazarbayev University conducted a focus group discussion with a small group of young Kazakhstanis on how they see the future of their country. Their vision is a powerful statement, fully consistent with that of the President, but it stresses the needs, goals, and interests of the individual, rather than the perspective of the state as a whole. The statement reads as follows:

"Our vision: We want Kazakhstan to be a country where it is good to be born, and that is attractive for living, for work and for retirement. At the center of our vision for 2050 are the people of Kazakhstan, their needs, goals, and interests. Kazakhstan in 2050 will provide well-being and safety for our children, our grandchildren, and ourselves; a clean and healthy environment, state-provided social protection; and availability of good education opportunities and healthcare. We want to have the opportunity to realize our dreams. We want long life expectancy.

"Our values: We want society built on friendship and trust not only among members of family and friends, but among our fellow citizens at large. We want a flexible society that is open to and can absorb well-educated immigrants. We want to be up to emerging global challenges and opportunities. We want to find the best synthesis of European and Asian traditions, cultures, and values incorporated in our lives. From Asian values we want to draw a strong commitment to society with a focus on a collective approach and on pursuing long-term interests with diligence. From European values we want to draw a sense of self-realization, creativity, individual initiative, and leadership. But we also want to keep our own values, such as flexibility, adaptability, and openness to new changes.

"Our strengths: We are a young country, open to the world, ready to learn, but also beginning to lead.

"The way forward: We need to decrease the dependence on natural resources. We want an innovative, competitive economy. We will look for possible opportunities provided for Kazakhstan by global climate change with its warmer climate and longer vegetative seasons, but we will prepare against the harm that climate models predict. We want democracy, protection of rights, freedom, and the rule of law. We believe that the development of information and communications technology that offers opportunities to establish a direct democracy with electronic elections, interactive decision making, and accountability of government to its citizens. We want to continue the traditions of our ancestors and protect our natural environment. We want to live in harmony with nature: be a part of nature, not its master."

4

We also benefited from the recently completed consultations led by United Nations Development Programme (UNDP) with many stakeholder groups in Kazakhstan about their vision for the future beyond 2015. The top concerns shared by the more than 2000 respondents involved were summarized in the UNDP report as follows:

> "Overall, the common development challenges most emphasized in the four consultation cities are: 1) environmental protection, 2) health, and 3) peace and security. Other areas noted strongly are: infrastructure, green economy, employment, good governance, local development, education, gender, culture, and issues related to the well-being and professionalism of young people.
>
> "Infrastructure, green economy, and health were strongly raised by government representatives, while NGOs and civil society were more concerned about the state of the environment, protecting vulnerable, and good governance. Issues related to health and education were voiced equally by various groups. Peace and security is seen as important for government and NGOs, to a lesser degree for vulnerable groups and local communities. Similarly, the latter two prioritize employment and local development. Interestingly, young people, family and cultural values were given considerable attention during discussions with a common view shared by various groups of participants."

We could have stopped here but decided to go one further step of "visioning." This step involves the difficult task of putting ourselves into the shoes of someone in the year 2050, living in Kazakhstan and looking at where the country and she or he is at that time and what was the pathway there. So we imagined first how two individuals might look back on their lives and their future in 2050. One story is told by a woman around 30 years old from Kyzylorda, who has a sharp sense of the environmental challenges faced by Kazakhstan. This retrospective is inserted after Chapter 7 on green growth. The second story is told by man from Karagandy who in 2050 in his early 50s and who has benefited from the development of a modern knowledge economy in Kazakhstan. This story therefore appears after Chapter 9. Finally, we imagined what the official historian of Kazakhstan's government might write in 2050 about the achievement of President Nazarbayev's vision of 2012. This statement lays out progress on the core elements of the vision that we will explore in detail in the remainder of the report. We have placed it as a bridge between Chapter 12 on scenarios and Chapter 13, which pulls together the main messages of the volume. These three visioned retrospectives demonstrate how it is hard to imagine life almost 40 years ahead, as we tend to extrapolate from what we have experienced, which is likely quite far off what will actually happen, but it is an interesting challenge, which has reinforced our sense that the key development priorities that emerge from the prospective vision statements with which we started this chapter are indeed the right ones.

In a nutshell, the vision we posit for Kazakhstan in this report is that the country intends to become one of the top 30 developed nations in the world, with:

- a strong human capital base of highly educated, healthy, and secure people, with good employment opportunities;
- an efficient, sustainable, and diversified energy resource base which contributes to the effective long-term development of the country;
- a prosperous country with clean air, water, and land, rich in biodiversity and using its natural resources sustainably in the face of growing threats from global climate change;

4

- a balanced and efficient urban and regional economy and decentralized governmental structure, which provides for the essential needs of Kazakhstan's people in an empowered and account- able manner;
- a diversified knowledge-based economy in which competitive entrepreneurs make effective and sustainable use of the country's natural resources;
- a country that is open to the rest of the world and a ready to work with its neighbors and to contribute to the solution of global challenges; and
- a strong, transparent, and inclusive economic and political institutional capacity that supports the effective management of the economy and the well-being of all people in Kazakhstan.

The next chapters in this volume explore each of these seven priority aspects of the Kazakhstan 2050 vision by looking at recent trends in Kazakhstan and around the globe, at how the broad vision needs to be refined in each of the seven areas, and at options for achieving the vision through appropriate action in the short, medium, and long term.

Throughout, we will reflect three overarching considerations: First, Kazakhstan needs to develop the resilience and flexibility to deal with and adapt to the many unexpected and unknowable events in the world, the region, and the country itself that will inevitably confront Kazakhstan in the coming decades. Second, urgency and a focus on implementation are key aspects of pursuing the vision, as Kazakhstan needs to take advantage of the window of likely relatively favorable external conditions for the next 15-20 years and of the fact that many of the changes needed will take time to implement and show results. Finally, the implementation of the vision is based on the presumption that, as the future historian con- cludes from the vantage point of 2050, it will help create a platform on which the country can continue to build a strong, prosperous future for the generations beyond 2050.

INCLUSIVE
HUMAN
DEVELOPMENT

Inclusive Human Development

Chapter
5

Michelle Riboud

Kazakhstan will be successful in its aspiration to join the ranks of the top 30 developed nations by 2050 only if it achieves high levels of human development, i.e., a highly educated, healthy population, with employment opportunities mediated by a flexible labor market and with a social safety net for those who fall behind. These four dimensions of a human development strategy — education, health, employment, and social protection — are essential for offering the Kazakhstani people a high degree of life satisfaction.[1]

It is well-established that human capital — education and health — affects economic growth through various channels. Besides its direct impact on productivity and indirect effects on health and fertility behavior, human capital will facilitate the transmission of knowledge and accelerate the rate at which Kazakhstan can take advantage of advances in knowledge, and notably, of technology transfers brought through foreign direct investment. It will also facilitate research and increase the innovative capacity of the economy as discussed in Chapter 9. More broadly, it will provide the flexibility and adaptability that Kazakhstan will need at each stage of the growth process.[2]

Nobel Prize laureate T.W. Schultz (1975) argues that growth is beset by constant changes in economic conditions to which businessmen, laborers, students, and housewives have to respond in modifying the allocation of their time and abilities. Decisions about participating in the labor market or not, quitting school or staying longer in school, choosing a particular field of study, working as self-employed or as a wage earner, transferring to a different job, migrating to another city, investing in a particular line of production, or altering investment in equipment are all taken on the basis of information about incentives (costs and expected returns) that are constantly changing in the process of a country's modernization. Those decisions cannot be anticipated or planned by central authorities. Responding to changes takes time and there is robust evidence that human capital enhances the ability to perceive, evaluate the consequences of changes, and determine whether and how to react.

High levels of human capital will come through a well-educated and healthy population but how they will translate into higher productivity and growth will depend on a labor market that rewards efforts and past investments and is flexible enough to facilitate the transition from low- to high-productivity jobs. As the objective is not only growth but also the well-being of the population, this will have to be accompanied by social protection mechanisms that provide for the elderly, disabled, and children and for those hit at times of economic crises.

This chapter is about Kazakhstan's path toward achieving high levels of human development and an institutional environment favorable to both productivity growth and protection for the most vulnerable. It comprises four sections that in turn deal with education, labor market, health, and social protection.

---

1. Educational opportunities for oneself and one's children, good health, employment, and protection from unexpected shocks are key elements identified by the growing literature on "happiness." See, for example, Graham (2011).
2. In this report we use the term "human development" and "human capital" interchangeably, although arguably the inclusion of employment and social protection dimensions go beyond the traditional definition of human capital dimensions in the economic literature.

Each section starts by examining recent trends and the conditions that Kazakhstan faces today, the vision for 2050, and a possible program of action for the next four decades that could make Vision 2050 a reality. The concluding section presents crosscutting recommendations and summarizes the detailed policy options proposed with a tentative time line.

Education

Trends and issues

Overall levels of education in Kazakhstan are relatively high, reflecting historically high levels of investment in education (World Bank 2004, 2012). There is a widespread network of public schools accessible to the majority of the population. Literacy rates are almost 100 percent for both men and women. Almost all youth make it through secondary or vocational and technical education, and higher education attracts a very high proportion (more than 50 percent) of secondary school graduates. Overall, more than 70 percent of the population aged 6-24 are attending an educational institution (general, vocational, or higher), and the average number of years of schooling of the population rose from 8.8 in 1995 to 10.4 in 2010, reaching a level similar to that in developed countries (World Bank "WDR" 2013).

Although at the time of independence the human capital endowment of the country was already relatively high,[3] the government gave priority to the development of the education sector and undertook a series of reforms supported by a gradual increase in public spending on education, which reached around 5 percent of GDP in 2012. Those reforms were motivated by the desire to have an educational policy that would be aligned with the cultural, social, and economic values of a newly independent state, by the awareness of the critical importance of high levels of human capital for economic development and global competitiveness, and by the desire to make Kazakhstan a player in the international community. The loss of some human capital with the emigration of qualified personnel of Slavic and German background after independence was an additional concern.

While Kazakhstan compares favorably with developed countries in terms of years of schooling, it does not fare equally well when a whole range of cognitive and non-cognitive skills are assessed (Table 5.1). In the 2009 PISA examinations (OECD "PISA" 2013), students' scores around 400 fell 100 points below the OECD average[4] and were below what could be expected given the country's level of GDP per capita. In a regional perspective, Kazakhstan stands below the Russian Federation and the average for Eastern European countries. Kazakhstan's ranking in the Global Competitiveness Index 2012-13 compared to the previous year worsened from 85 to 92 for the category "health and primary education," but improved from 65 to 58 for the category "higher education and training."[5] A number of enterprise surveys identified an inadequately educated labor force as a problematic factor for doing business, pointing to the lack of mastery of language, mathematics, and science as well as the lack of "higher order" skills (OECD "Private Sector" 2012; World Bank and EBRD 2013). Thus, the main issue faced by the education sector in Kazakhstan is not of access and quantity of education, but of quality. The challenge for the future is to ensure that each level of education provides the knowledge and skills that will permit Kazakhstan to pursue its growth and modernization process.

---

3. The economic depression during the first years of independence only affected temporarily secondary school enrollment rates (World Bank "Databank" 2013).

4. Math score is 405 (vs. 496 PISA average); science score is 400 (vs.501) and reading score is 390 (vs. 493).

5. According to the World Economic Forum (WEF) data, Kazakhstan's ranking with respect to the quality of its education system consistently had decreased over the period 2005-10 (National Center for the Education Quality Assessment 2011).

| Table 5.1 | Despite many years of schooling, Kazakhstan performs poorly on the PISA math test |

	Average years of schooling		2009 PISA Math test scores	
Countries	1995	2010	Math score	Rank
Singapore	7.4	9.1	562	2nd
Korea	10.6	11.8	546	4th
Finland	9.1	10.0	541	6th
Switzerland	9.6	9.9	534	8th
Japan	10.6	11.6	529	9th
Netherlands	10.5	11.0	526	11th
Belgium	9.9	10.5	515	14th
Germany	9.2	11.8	513	16th
Denmark	9.7	10.1	503	19th
PISA average	n/a	n/a	496	
Russian Fed.	10.2	11.5	468	38th
Kazakhstan	8.8	10.4	405	53rd

Source: World Bank ("WDR" 2013) and ("Education Quality" 2013).

The challenge that lies ahead to improve education quality in Kazakhstan is substantial, especially considering the large number of schools (about 7,465), teachers, and students (more than 4 million) that need to be reached (National Center for the Education Quality Assessment 2011). Fully aware of the quality issue, the government embarked on a series of reforms at all levels of education.

Preschool. Access to preschool used to be high during Soviet times. The motivation was to facilitate female labor force participation. Kindergarten services were usually provided by enterprises that employed the child's parents. With the closing of services offered by state-owned enterprises after independence, access fell drastically, affecting mostly children from poor families and rural areas. Reversing this trend has been one of the priorities of the State Program 2005-10. With the introduction and funding of the "Balapan" program, the coverage of children aged 3-6 has already more than doubled, increasing from 32 percent in 2007 to 71 percent in 2012 and the plan is to reach full coverage by 2020. The increased number of kindergartens or mini-centers is accompanied by a gradual increase in teachers' qualifications and improvements in curriculum and teaching materials, and private initiatives and public-private partnerships are being encouraged.

Primary, secondary, and tertiary education levels. At these levels, the objective has been to raise quality and reach world-class standards. Under the president's patronage a bold and innovative strategy was adopted with the development of a university (Nazarbayev University, NU) and a group of schools (Nazarbayev Intellectual Schools, NIS) serving as a driving force. These elite institutions, established with an international perspective, aspire to be the models for other institutions in the country and to have high impact on the whole network of educational institutions in the country (see Box 5.1).

5

| Box 5.1 | **Design and early implementation of education reform at the secondary and tertiary levels in Kazakhstan** |

NU is a research university created through partnerships with leading universities in the US, UK, and Singapore, and where English is the language of instruction. The NIS constitute a network of secondary schools focused on sciences and where the instruction is given in 3 languages, Kazakh, Russian and English. NIS have also established partnerships in the UK, US, Finland, Switzerland, and the Netherlands for curriculum and textbook development, teacher training, and evaluation. Both NU and NIS are well-resourced and autonomous institutions, and are not subject to the regulations and norms of the Ministry of Education. They seek to attain high standards of policy and good practice and to produce graduates comparable to those of the best institutions in the world. This is to be attained through innovation, experimentation, and adaptation of best practices to local circumstances (NU explicitly avoided the branch campus or franchise option). Admission is open to all communities from all parts of the country (NIS plans to be present in all provincial capitals and to admit children from Kazakh and Russian speaking households) but entrance processes are competitive and highly selective. NIS' teacher recruitment is equally competitive (about 1 selected out of 5 applicants) and open to foreign candidates. By focusing on science and mathematics, these schools intend to prepare students for a global world of rapid technological change.

The development of NU and NIS is happening at a fast pace and following a well-articulated pathway for scaling up. At NU, the Schools of Humanities and Social Sciences, Engineering, and Science and Technology opened in 2011; graduate schools of Business, Public Policy, and Education have started operation in 2013; and the Schools of Medicine and of Mining are scheduled for 2015. Research activities are growing with competitive funding subject to an international peer review process. The NU experience is being shared with other universities in Kazakhstan as they are to follow its model. Seven NIS are currently operational and the plan is to have 15 schools opened by 2013, and 21 by 2015. Along the way it will be important to monitor and evaluate progress and to adapt the programs in line with the evidence collected.

Source: Ruby (2012) and NU and NIS management.

In parallel, a number of other reforms have been introduced for the whole primary, secondary, and tertiary education system. One of the most significant is the participation of Kazakhstani students in all main international assessments (Trends in International Mathematics and Science Study, PISA, and Progress in Reading Literacy Study). This allows the country to compare the achievement of its students at both primary and secondary level with that of students in the best performing countries. Another is a deliberate move toward a trilingual society. While the teaching in the national language is encouraged and the number of schools using Kazakh as language of instruction is growing, there is also an intention to gradually introduce the teaching of English in primary schools along with Russian. A third important reform has been the introduction of a general exam taken by secondary school graduates, the Unified National Test (UNT), as basis for admission to tertiary education (formerly the responsibilities of higher education institutions). This national test was introduced in 2003-04 in an attempt to introduce a more uniform and transparent procedure, less amenable to corruption.

In higher education, the government adopted a new three-level structure based on the Bologna process. It authorized the establishment of private universities, created a National Accreditation Center in 2005 with its methodology based on best international practice, published new generation textbooks in 2012, and launched a scholarship program to study abroad ("Bolashak") in 1993. Particularly innovative was the introduction of tuition fees in public universities and the replacement in 1999 of a direct recurrent budget transfer by grants/vouchers that beneficiaries can use in public or private universities. These grants are awarded on a competitive basis, based on state orders for specific disciplines, to students who have passed the UNT (OECD and World Bank 2007).

Technical and Vocational Education and Training (TVET). The TVET system inherited from the Soviet period — which comprises both vocational schools (professional lyceums) and colleges[6] — was set up to support a command economy. Its rigid institutional structures, supply-driven orientation, and inefficient financing mechanisms made for a system unable to respond to the needs of a market economy (see World Bank 2010). Program contents and equipment were obsolete, and the curriculum overspecialized leading to narrow skills. After independence, private institutions entered the sector while the number of public institutions declined and limitations in public financing led even public institutions to admit fee-paying students.

Although the government was well aware of the need to make deep reforms in a system which attracts about one-third of graduates from secondary education and trains about 600,000 students every year, reforms lagged behind those introduced in the secondary and tertiary sectors, and a strategy with clear directions took time to develop. The 2007 Education Law provided a framework for restructuring TVET and for better integrating general and vocational education. With the planned transition to a 12-year cycle of compulsory schooling, general education is to be extended by one year, giving the opportunity to provide vocational students with more general and easily transferable skills.

The strategy that finally emerged[7] is similar to that applied to secondary and tertiary education. It builds on the experience of Asian countries, Canada, and Germany, and incorporates a well-designed scaling-up pathway. A set of eight new colleges managed under a holding organization, called "Kasipkor," will open in close cooperation with the industry and with support from international strategic partners. Once set up, these colleges will serve as models for all others and the approach will be rolled out gradually. The first college, about to open, is located in Atyrau. It will function in close partnership with Canada's South Alberta Institute of Technology and focus on skills required by the oil and gas industry. Others will follow in coming years, closely linked to the needs of industrial sectors identified as priority sectors such as machinery, energy, or consumer goods. In parallel, for the rest of the TVET sector, Kazakhstan has opted for the introduction of a dual system of vocational education and entered into partnerships with German entities to help adapt and use the dual system in 100 colleges. A new qualification framework was adopted in 2011, very similar to the European one, and employers' associations have been given the task to develop occupational standards. The development of educational standards and curriculum will follow.

The Vision 2050 for Education

The range of reform initiatives that have been launched over the past decade is impressive, but the task that lies ahead to make the vision become a reality is immense, considering the large number of schools, teachers, and students that need to be reached and "transformed." Box 5.2 summarizes a

---

6. Following nine years of general education, students can either pursue general education or shift to technical and vocational education (in professional lyceums). After 11 years of general secondary education, students can enter higher education institutions or colleges for a more advanced level of technical and vocational education.

7. See the State Program for TVET Development (Republic of Kazakhstan 2008) and the Industrial Development and Innovation Program (Republic of Kazakhstan "Industrial Development" 2010).

vision for a world-class educational system in Kazakhstan by 2050. The following pages discuss the challenges facing the country in the pursuit of this vision and a set of actions that could increase the chances of successful implementation.

Box 5.2 | **Vision 2050 for Education**

By 2050, Kazakhstan expects to have a strong and competitive human capital base, with students coming out of the education system with both high degrees of knowledge (comparable to those of the top 30 developed countries) and skills that are flexible enough to work in a diversified economy and adjust to a world of unpredictable changes. The vision is also to have Kazakhstan well-integrated in the world economy with a majority of students mastering English, Russian, and the national language.

Source: Author.

Program of Action

Preschool. As longitudinal studies of interventions in young children have shown (Heckman et al. 2012), preschool investment is likely to increase school readiness and performance (reducing the probability of repetition and dropout) and may also lead to better health, thus raising the efficiency of public expenditures in higher levels of education and in health. As mentioned here, in Kazakhstan implementation of the ongoing strategy for children aged 3-6 is already well-advanced and needs to be actively pursued. It is expected that, within a decade, all children will have access to preschool services and that a significant proportion of those services will be offered by the private sector or through public-private partnerships.

To promote even greater equality of opportunities among children of different socio-economic background, and in particular to address the disadvantages faced by children in rural areas[8] where the incidence of poverty is higher, the government should also consider introducing programs for children aged 0-3 targeted to families from disadvantaged backgrounds. Although there are no marked differences in access to school across income quintiles in Kazakhstan, there is some evidence that the poor spend less on education of their children than the more affluent households (World Bank 2004). It is also likely that poor households spend less time with their young children and provide a less stimulating learning environment. Differences in cognitive development between children coming from households with low and high socio-economic background have been documented consistently in developed and developing countries (Alderman 2011). Several studies have shown that early delays in cognitive development get worse as children get older and that some early stimulation inputs are especially critical in the first years of life, particularly the capacity to absorb language and differentiate between sounds (Naudeau et al. 2011). Whether high-quality primary schools can counteract earlier delays is still an open question, and more research is needed to answer it. However, it seems clear that intervening sooner rather than later in a child's life to remediate disadvantages is a cost-effective investment (Heckman and Pagés-Serra 2000).

Therefore, we recommend the following actions at the pre-primary level:
- fully implement the ongoing strategy for children aged 3-6 and
- introduce programs for early child development targeted at children aged 0-3 from disadvantaged backgrounds

---

8. In sparsely populated rural areas, many schools are small and multi-level or "ungraded," i.e., with a small number of children of different ages and grades attended by a single teacher. In 2010, 16 percent of students attended such schools and in 45 percent of those schools, the number of children enrolled per school did not exceed 10 (Republic of Kazakhstan 2011).

Primary education. Primary education (grades 1 to 5) in Kazakhstan is part of the 11 (soon to be 12) years of compulsory education and government programs, and statistics do not distinguish primary schools from others and only refer to general secondary schools which cover all 11 grades. Among the seven NIS that are currently operational (Box 5.1), only one starts at grade 1 while all others start at grade 7. This choice was made based on research which showed that cognitive intellectual capabilities benefited from intensive schooling as of grade 7. Moreover, the 2011 TIMSS results for Kazakhstan show that the gap between the achievement of Kazakhstani students and that of the best world performers increases with grade level (International Association for the Evaluation of Educational Achievement 2012).

This suggests that much of the effort to increase quality should concentrate on secondary and higher education, but also that a number of actions could usefully be taken regarding primary education:

- regularly analyze TIMSS data to monitor trends and better understand the causes of the gradual deterioration;
- assess to what extent there are significant quality differences (as measured by differences in learning achievements) between urban and rural schools; and
- compare the outcomes of the different experiments with the NIS schools to draw lessons about the relative effectiveness of a reform starting at grade 7 versus at grade 1.

Secondary and higher education. At the level of secondary and higher education, there are already a strategy and resources in place to make the 2050 vision become a reality. Success in reaching the desired outcome will, however, largely depend on two factors: the sustainability of leadership support for the approach and how implementation is phased in.

The development of NU will continue over several years: The first cohort of NU graduates will not enter the labor market before 2015 and for those who will enroll in the future medical school, the first graduates will only start their residency in 2019-20. Similarly, even though the opening of the NIS schools is on a fast track with 21 schools planned to be operational by 2015, it is quite possible that not all NIS schools will function by then at full capacity (all grades and all teachers)[9] with all new teaching materials fully developed, and the initial student cohorts which entered NIS in grade 7 will not complete secondary education before 2016. Continuous adjustments may also be required in the selection process for students and teachers and other aspects, such as diversifying the membership of the boards of trustees. As the strategy is to innovate, experiment, and adapt (Ruby 2012), it will take several years, perhaps a decade, before the system stabilizes.[10] During all these initial years and even beyond, sustained support, including human and financial resources, from the political leadership will be crucial to ensure success.

The biggest challenge, however, will be the scaling-up process, which involves roll-out of the approach to other universities and secondary schools. Although these other institutions may not expect to benefit from similar resources and to have the same international orientation, the ultimate aim of the reform is to ensure that the investments made in NU and the NIS generate benefits for the other institutions in the nation. NU and NIS are meant to be "models" that emulate replication and help raise the "quality" of education in the whole sector. The Graduate School of Education at NU is designed to provide Kazakhstan's future leaders of secondary and tertiary education with cutting-edge academic training.

---

9. The first NIS opened with only 5 international teachers although they aim to have 40 international teachers per school when fully operational (Ruby 2012). They also opened with only classes for grades 7, 8 and 9 but will progressively extend up to grade 12. Similarly, although work on curriculum is now completed, textbooks for all grades and all subjects need to be developed and will only be available gradually.

10. For example, NIS schools admit students from grade 7 except in one school which experiments starting at grade 1. In this latter school, more intense language training is being tried out (similar to what is done in Finland and Estonia). Another experiment will be the introduction of the International Baccalaureate (IB) in one school, in partnership with Switzerland. And there is the innovative potential of "MOOCs" (massive open online courses) which Kazakhstan's educational system, teachers, and students may benefit from.

5

In secondary education, the following types of action seem critical to ensure success:

- *Constantly test, evaluate, and adjust before scaling up.* Being able to demonstrate impact will be critical to induce others to change teaching practices. This demonstration can only occur if the transfer of good practice is done in such a way that one can compare those who change practices with those who do not and measure the outcome. Through the NIS Centers of Excellence, new training focused on pedagogical and teaching methods is imparted to teachers and school managers, and it is expected that, within five years, half of the teachers will have been trained and certified. It would be important to roll-out this training in a systematic way that would allow proper evaluation (with a control group) of the impact that the training has on teachers' attitudes in the classroom and children's learning achievements. The design of this evaluation has to start from the very beginning and requires statistical and econometric expertise.

- *Give time and carefully sequence each step to ensure success.* Changes are gradual, and actions need to be taken in appropriate sequencing. A number of years will be needed before a cohort of "new" teachers reach the classroom. In the meantime, changes are incremental. In schools, a new curriculum will be followed by the development of new books and teaching materials which will in turn influence teacher training. Currently, training provided at the Centers of Excellence focuses on pedagogy and teaching methods, but teachers will later have to become familiar with proposed changes in the curriculum. Similarly, the push for increased research activities at the university level is commendable, but funding needs to progress at a pace that matches the improvement in the quality of graduate programs and skills of graduate students.

- *Simplify and shift the focus of monitoring from inputs to outcomes.* There is a considerable amount of monitoring of regulations and control of standards exercised at the local and ministerial level, mostly related to inputs (size of classrooms, rehabilitation of buildings, hours of class by subject, program content, etc.). Leaving more flexibility to each school in the choice of inputs and focusing instead monitoring on measures of students achievement would provide a quality assurance system in line with the 2050 objectives. The NIS is currently working on the development and implementation of an evaluation system; it should gradually become part of the quality assurance system used by all other schools. In the meantime, or in parallel, some of the tests that students currently take at the end of grades 4, 9, and 11 (UNT) could serve as outcome indicators if their quality and reliability can be ensured. This is particularly important for the UNT, which is both a school exit test and a university entry exam. Similarly, a greater focus on outcomes could take place at the university level.[11]

- *Improve information flow and make it publicly available to facilitate individual choices.* Households would benefit from access to some of the information collected at the school or university level. In all cities where there are several schools, widespread and readily available information about the characteristics of schools (school scorecards indicating offerings, exit rates at exams, etc.) would help parents decide to which school send their children. Similarly, public information about entry requirements of universities, course offerings, graduation standards, pass rates, and career paths (time to get a job, stability of employment, salaries, etc.) of graduates of different fields would help

---

11. As autonomy is progressively granted to universities, one would expect that a greater diversity in course offerings and course content, examinations and graduation standards will emerge. The nature of the monitoring will have to change and rely mostly on an accreditation process. More information about pass rates and career paths of graduates once they enter the labor market (tracer studies) should be developed.

students make informed choices about fields of study and choice of university. A systematic collection, analysis, and dissemination of graduates' employment outcomes would also be of help to universities and policy makers in identifying fields of study and types of programs in demand.

- *Ensure that teacher incentives are aligned with the desired outcomes.* At the level of secondary education, the main channel through which the roll-out of the reform currently takes place is through training (seminars, online lessons, and methodological materials). The objective is to improve teachers' effectiveness. However, while it is widely recognized that raising teachers effectiveness in the classroom is a powerful means of raising quality of education (Glewwe and Kremer 2006), there is also a consensus from the international literature that many of standard teacher characteristics such as certification, degree held, training, and experience — which can reasonably be thought as encompassing "teacher quality" — are not good predictors of teachers' effectiveness and are not correlated with students' achievements (Slater, Davies, and Burgess 2009; Hanushek and Rivkin 2006). While training and exposure to new knowledge provides teachers with the capacity to do better, this capacity may only be utilized effectively when there is an incentive to do so.

  Kazakhstani teachers are obliged by law to take training every five years and will take the training offered by the Centers of Excellence but whether they will have the motivation and interest in being actively engaged in changing teaching practices and making children learn is uncertain. The lack of recognition and status of the teaching profession and the low salaries of Kazakhstani teachers relative to other professions are not conducive to greater efforts. The government is aware of this issue and has decided to offer salary increases linked to certification levels. Given worldwide research findings, this, too, is no guarantee for an impact on education quality. A more effective strategy would be to provide salary increases based on a combination of factors (certification being only one of them) as has been done in some other countries (Mexico, for example, see Box 5.3) and build a structure of pay that rewards outcomes. Alternative designs could be envisaged, adapted, and tested such as the Chilean model which fosters competition between schools (Box 5.3), or the Indian approach in which bonuses are given either to individual teachers or to all school teachers based on improvements in student achievements (Box 5.3). Whatever strategy is adopted, experimentation and evaluation are required before a large-scale implementation can be envisaged as results are very sensitive to design.

Rewarding outcomes (rather than training) would also be in line with the move toward per capita funding of schools that is to be introduced on a pilot basis in 2013 and scaled up in 2015. It envisages that funding could include grants for results and quality. Increased flexibility given to school managers and teachers in the choice of inputs and teaching methods has to be accompanied by rewards for greater efficiency and results.

In higher education, the roll-out of the reform will also be gradual with the NU sharing its experience with a first set of 18 universities, and some of them being gradually granted autonomy. Ensuring that this will be accompanied by a right set of incentives for changed behavior will be crucial. At this level also, low salaries and heavy teaching load provide minimal incentive for improving quality and should be revisited. In addition it will be critical the competition between universities leads to sector consolidation. There are currently 136 universities in Kazakhstan, and too many are of poor quality, badly governed, and even corrupt. While the accreditation process that was initiated may lead to some consolidation, greater autonomy will open the way for greater diversity. Given that universities get resources for their recurrent budget either from grants/vouchers or from fee-paying students, they will have to compete

5

to attract students. The recommendation made earlier that universities increasingly make public their offerings, course contents, graduation requirements, students' pass rates, and labor market outcomes could also play a role in increasing competition between universities. It would also contribute to reduce the role of the government in making decisions (state orders) on fields of study, leaving increasing room for individual and family decisions. Competitive funding for investment expenditures and for research based on soundness of proposals could also be introduced or, as in the case of research, extended. To promote even further competition, Kazakhstan could also consider the introduction of an assessment system of higher education quality as done in Brazil.

Box 5.3 | Incentive reforms for education in Mexico, Chile, and India

Incentive reforms linking teacher compensation to student performance were implemented in Mexico and Chile in the 1990s and in India in the 2000s. Although all countries share the common objective to raise the quality of basic education, they have followed different designs.

The Mexican program rewards individual teachers by granting permanent promotions (and higher compensation) to teachers based on a number of factors, including their education and professional experience, years of experience, and their students' performance. Each of these factors is evaluated using a point system. The total number of possible points is 100, out of which 20 correspond to the student performance component. Rewards are awarded when the number of points exceeds a national minimum cut-off point (70 points). The purpose of the reform was to establish incentives for teachers to improve both their qualifications and effectiveness in the classroom and to create opportunities for promotions without having to move into administrative positions. Participation into the program is voluntary but a majority of teachers have enrolled. The size of the bonus is substantial; its amount can range from 25 percent to up 200 percent of the base wage.

The Chilean program is a school-level performance-based pay program that awards a bonus to teachers in schools that outperform other schools on a national student exam. Schools are divided into homogeneous groups so that competition is between schools serving similar groups of students in similar settings. The bonus is awarded every two years. 90 percent of its amount is divided between the winning school teachers (the school director determines the use of the remaining 10 percent), and the size of the incentive varies between 5 and 7 percent of annual salaries.

In India, an experiment was conducted in 500 rural schools and a student population of 50,000 students in the state of Andhra Pradesh. Four different approaches to improving quality were tested: two incentive schemes (an individual teacher bonus and a group teacher bonus) and two input schemes (provision of an additional teacher and provision of a block grant to the school). The objective was to assess which approach would be most effective to improve quality. The experiment also had a comparison group of 100 schools that did not have any of the schemes. Evaluation showed that the incentive scheme was more effective than the input scheme.

Available evidence for these three country cases supports the view that incentives can work to improve quality. However, the analysis also showed that results are sensitive to design features and that adjustments can, at times, be necessary to make programs more effective.

Source: Vegas and Umansky (2005) for Mexico and Chile; Muralidharan and Sundararaman (2009, 2011) for India.

Technical and Vocational Education and Training (TVET). Transforming TVET into a system able to equip youth with employable skills is a major task. The TVET system comprises close to 900 schools and colleges attended by almost 600,000 students. The Kazakh authorities are well aware that success will depend on the existence of demand for the skills produced by the TVET system. For this reason, the government is taking a proactive approach by trying, through Kasipkor, to bring together three elements: a clearly identified source of demand for skills (through the partnership with a specific industrial sector), curricula aligned with the needs of this sector, and arrangements for implementing the corresponding programs (with support from strategic partners). Countries such as Korea and Singapore which have followed a similar approach have been successful, but their experience shows that it may take several decades until the experience gets mainstreamed and institutionalized (Tan and Nam 2011). In parallel to the development of new colleges under Kasipkor, a number of other measures have been introduced to modernize the TVET system. They include sending teachers for training in Singapore, introducing dual education in a group of enterprises, and developing new curricula following the redefinition of occupational standards.

While all these actions are valuable and should be continued, a number of additional actions should be considered:

- *Improve the collection and analysis of data on the labor market (firm and labor force surveys, tracer studies).* The monitoring of the labor market in Kazakhstan is clearly deficient. Knowing about existing vacancies by sectors and job categories is insufficient to organize an efficient training system. It is important to know what skills are in demand and get regular feedback from employers through periodic firm surveys. In other parts of the world, it has been shown that employers increasingly want a mix of job relevant competencies and personal qualities and place a high value on non-cognitive skills such as teamwork, flexibility, or ability to solve problems. Analysis of labor force surveys should be more systematic and detailed, and schools and colleges should undertake tracer studies to track employment outcomes of TVET graduates and better understand the career implications of the type of training they offer. Knowing whether trainees found a job after graduation is insufficient, what is needed is detailed information about the types of jobs found, length of job tenure, salary growth over the life cycle, etc. Relevant information is critical to improve the economic relevance of training programs and measure their cost-effectiveness.

- *Limit the degree of specialization and ensure sufficient general skills.* The very high number of fields and qualifications in Kazakhstan leads to workers having very narrow skills that can easily become obsolete in an economy that diversifies and changes rapidly. Workers have to prepare to change jobs and learn new skills over their working life. Increasing the compulsory number of years of general education from 9 to 10 before the start of vocational education by 2020 will help providing vocational students with more general and easily transferable skills. But training programs also have to respond to this need. They have to provide the mix of job relevant competencies and non-cognitive skills (such as teamwork, ability to solve problems, etc.) that employers increasingly want. The example of Germany described in Box 5.4 illustrates this point.

- *Provide greater autonomy to schools and colleges and demand stronger accountability.* Unless TVET management is given the authority to operate flexibly and redistribute resources according to identified needs, improvements will remain minimal. But this greater autonomy has to

5

be accompanied by strong accountability that requires capability to assess and measure performance. Thus a culture of monitoring and evaluation has to develop and feed into program
designs, and help implementation of these interrelated policies.

- *Introduce financing modalities that provide incentives to both training providers and employers.*
  Part of the financing — even for public colleges — now comes through fees. To the extent that
  students get access to accurate information about the labor market outcomes of specific training
  programs and are able to choose among schools and programs, this should create competition
  for resources among training providers and induce better program relevance and quality. But
  the rest of the financing should also reward linkages with employers and employability of graduates. In this sub-sector, also, monitoring should shift from inputs and norms toward outcomes.
  Incentives must also exist on the side of employers if a dual education system is to be promoted.
  Without the readiness of firms to provide training, the system is bound to fail.

It is worth noting that successful reforms of the TVET system as well as in higher education would
open the way for lifelong learning, that is, for greater opportunities for retraining workers whenever they
need to adjust to changing labor market conditions.

Box 5.4 | Broadening apprenticeship occupations to increase flexibility: The case of Germany

Germany has opted for a transition to broader apprenticeships that enable more mobility and flexibility
between pathways. The modernization of occupations is needed to increase internal flexibility (multitasking),
external flexibility, and facilitate further training to preserve employability over working life. In addition to developing more transferable skills (less vulnerable in the case of slowdowns of particular industries), this also ensures
that apprentices and future workers have a better understanding of their roles in work processes.

A good example can be found in the industrial metal trades that were revised twice because of fast changes
in technology and work organization. In 1987, 45 trades were combined to form 6 occupations with 16 different
specializations. In 2004, the distinction between occupations and specializations was abolished and training
was provided in five broad occupations. Instruction in joint core competences (such as teamwork) and occu-
pation-specific competencies is now provided throughout the entire training period.

Source: Evans (2012).

The Labor Market

Trends and issues

Over the past decade of fast growth, the labor market of Kazakhstan created some 2.3 million[12] new
jobs that have permitted a gradual reduction in the number of unemployed and provided income-earning
opportunities to an increasing labor force. Unemployment rates fell from 12.8 percent in 2000 to 5.2
percent in the third quarter of 2012 (Figure 5.1), reducing the number of unemployed from 900,000 to
about 470,000. The growth in the labor force is due to an increase in both labor force participation rates
and the working-age population. Labor force participation rates which fluctuated around 70 percent
in the early 2000s, have been slightly increasing in recent years to reach 72 percent in 2012, and the
working-age population rose following the overall population increase, which has been fairly rapid since
2002 (Agency of Statistics of the Republic of Kazakhstan).

---

12. Estimate given for the period 2000-2012 (Agency of Statistics of the Republic of Kazakhstan).

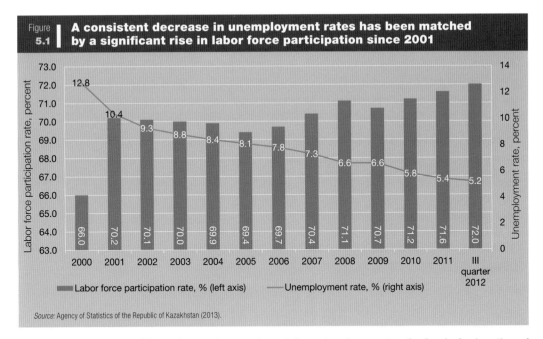

Figure 5.1 | **A consistent decrease in unemployment rates has been matched by a significant rise in labor force participation since 2001**

Labor force participation rate, % (left axis) — Unemployment rate, % (right axis)

Source: Agency of Statistics of the Republic of Kazakhstan (2013).

As could be expected from the previous review of the education sector, the level of education of the employed population is fairly high: 42 percent of workers have secondary education, 28 percent, vocational education and training, and the remaining 30 percent some tertiary education (Table 5.2). As the economy grows, the proportion of wage earners among the employed has been rising and now represents 68 percent of total employment, up from 57 percent in 2000. All newly created jobs have been in this category. The remaining 32 percent correspond to self-employment or informal employment. Most of the self-employment (two-thirds) is concentrated in rural areas and in the agricultural sector, and the rest corresponds mainly to non-manual jobs of short duration held in micro firms in urban areas (Rutkowsi 2011).

Despite these positive trends in job creation and reduction of the informal sector, the restructuring of the economy and the accompanying labor reallocation are still at an early stage. While the agricultural sector only contributes to 5.5 percent of GDP, it still employs 28 percent of the labor force (Table 5.2) and approximately half of those workers with only secondary education. Thus, there is still an important pool of low-income labor living in rural areas and working in the agriculture sector, and the transition out of agriculture and toward the other sectors of the economy is far from over. This labor pool, if appropriately redeployed to high productivity jobs, provides a demographic dividend that can support future growth. By the same token, continuous growth and job creation will be needed to absorb what is, in effect, surplus labor.

The share of labor employed in the public sector is decreasing slowly but is still quite high (a little over one-half) (see Table 5.3), indicating that the public sector continues to play an active and dominant role in the labor market. The public sector not only employs a sizable proportion of the labor force, especially in health and education services, but it also intends to play a proactive role monitoring and forecasting manpower requirements, as well as running programs aimed at boosting the employment of low income, self-employed, or unemployed citizens. In its Employment Program 2020, adopted in 2011, an array of interventions is envisaged, including job search assistance programs, training and retraining, wage and training subsidies, support for business development, and mobility support. In coming years, the challenge will be for the state to let the private sector be the main source of employment and only play a facilitating role.

| Table 5.2 | Composition of GDP and distribution of employment by sectors, distribution of labor force by level of education in each sector, 2011 |||||

	Percentage of employment	Total number of employed (thousands)	Tertiary education (percent)	TVET (percent)	Secondary education (percent)
Agriculture	26.5	2,196.1	10	17	73
Industry	11.6	960.3	26	39	35
w/o Mining	2.5	206.8	24	38	38
Construction	7.4	614.0	24	33	43
Trade	14.9	1,233.7	27	32	41
Transport	6.6	546.3	24	37	39
Information & communication	1.5	125.7	56	28	16
Other	31.6	2,625.5	52	29	19
Total	100.0	8,301.6	30	28	42

Sources: Agency of Statistics of the Republic of Kazakhstan (2013) and NAC of Nazarbayev University "Place of Kazakhstan" (2012).

| Table 5.3 | The public sector continues to play a significant but declining role in the labor market ||||

	2006	2007	2008	Change
Public	54.2%	52.4%	50.2%	-4.0%
Private	45.8%	47.6%	49.8%	4.0%
Total	100.0%	100.0%	100.0%	

Source: World Bank "Improving the Quality of Life" (2013).

The Vision 2050 for the Labor Market

How well the labor market functions is critical not only for growth but also for social sectors. No matter how well designed and effective reforms of the education and training sectors are in enhancing human capital, their ultimate success depends on the availability of jobs that can use the labor force's skills. Labor market developments also have critical implications for public finances, in particular for the design and financing of health insurance and pension schemes, as will be discussed later.

By 2050, the distribution of employment by sectors is likely to be quite different. Increases in agricultural productivity will not prevent the flow of labor out of this sector. In all developed countries, the share of employment in agriculture has fallen to below 5 to 6 percent. A similar pattern implies that Kazakhstan will need at least 1.8 million of new jobs created in sectors other than agriculture. Demographic trends will further increase the need for job creation. Depending on populations projections used,[13] one can anticipate that approximately 1.0 million to 1.7 million additional jobs[14] will be required by 2030 to absorb new labor market entrants and the number will further increase after 2030 when the new wave of baby boomers born in the 2000s hit the labor market.[15] To allow the creation of several million new jobs requires a flexible and adaptive labor market and supportive policies. Accordingly, Box 5.5 posits the vision for the labor market in Kazakhstan in 2050.

Box 5.5	**Vision 2050 for the Labor Market**

In 2050 Kazakhstan will have a labor market that values the human capital investments made in youth and adults and offers work opportunities that enhance the well-being of the active population. The dynamic private sector serves as the main engine of job creation and the public sector's role is principally to remove and mitigate the constraints that prevent the creation of employment.

In a global and national context when the nature and location of jobs in Kazakhstan changes and the work force has to adapt to new demands, the labor market will provide clear signals indicating what and where the high-productivity jobs are and be flexible enough to allow labor to move from low- to high-productivity jobs and adjust to new conditions.

Source: Author.

Program of Action

It is clear that the strength of the economy and its capacity to create work opportunities are the most important determinants of employment and of a dynamic labor market. This implies not only education policies leading to a highly skilled labor force, but also macroeconomic stability, and, as discussed in Chapter 11, an enabling business environment and institutional framework that foster private initiatives and facilitate adjustments. A well-functioning labor market is part of this critical institutional environment and a number of policies can play a key role.

---

13. UN population projections are more conservative than those of the Agency of Statistics of the Republic of Kazakhstan. The UN estimates that the population of Kazakhstan will rise to 18.8 million by 2030, while official projections foresee a population of 20.2 million by 2030.

14. Those numbers are estimated assuming that the labor force participation rate of the population remains approximately equal to what it is today (53.2 percent). Increases in participation rates of older workers that could result from an increase in retirement age would be offset by a likely decrease at ages 20-24 due to an increasing proportion of students in higher education.

15. Current projections by the UN for rural-urban population shifts imply a less drastic shift in population from rural areas to the cities. This could in part be due to the fact that rural off-farm employment will grow (as it has elsewhere), but it could also mean that urbanization will actually (have) to proceed more rapidly than projected by the UN, if Kazakhstan wants to join the ranks of the top 30 developed countries (see Chapter 8).

5

- *Reduce the costs of information for workers and employers.* In a world where the nature and location of jobs change rapidly, institutions and mechanisms that can facilitate access to information about new job opportunities reduce the length of periods of search and facilitate job mobility. On the demand side, mechanisms that can help employers detect the skills of potential employees reduce hiring costs and increase the speed at which vacancies are filled and the probability of a good match. Ease or low costs of job search or hiring promote employment through shorter unemployment spells and lesser job turnover.

  Employment centers could play this role in Kazakhstan. At the moment, this does not seem to be the case. The Ministry of Labor indicates that only 2 percent of employers report vacancies. This suggests that either information costs are high and/or that other information channels (possibly informal) are used by job seekers and employers. It would be worthwhile examining which institutional mechanism would work best and select the most effective. In this process, the government should only have a facilitating role, aimed at easing labor market adjustment.

  While improving information about labor demand and supply could facilitate job mobility, attempting to use this information to predict future manpower requirements is bound to fail and should be avoided. The longer the time horizon, the greater the details put in manpower demand forecasts, the less meaningful these forecasts become. As the experience of other countries has shown, forecasts based on past trends will never be able to anticipate and predict the sectoral and technological changes that will affect the nature and skill requirements of future jobs.

- *Maintain flexible contracting rules.* Labor market policies that regulate the employment relationship can have an impact on employment. Regulations that impose open-ended contracts with high costs of dismissal enhance job and income security. They foster stable employment relationships that are preconditions for trust and loyalty to the firm and thus, enhanced productivity. However, while protecting workers (those who have jobs) against layoffs, they may also reduce overall hiring in the economy, and the impact is likely to be greater for younger rather than older and more experienced workers. On the other hand, flexibility in the choice of work contracts and prospects of low severance payments allow employers to check whether the skills of the employee are a good match for the job and whether the level of the firm's economic activity is sustainable. They allow them to respond to short-term changes in the demand for their products. This flexibility provides greater efficiency and induces greater hiring.

  Although economists are still debating about the right level of employment protection, depending on the relative importance they give to flexibility or to social protection, available evidence from developed and middle-income countries (OECD 1999; Heckman 2008; Nickell and Layard 1999) indicates that a stricter employment protection legislation may protect the jobs of prime-age men at the cost of lowering employment for youth and women. There is also some evidence that stricter legislation is associated with lower job turnover and higher rate of self-employment. Many European countries that have a strict legislation currently face social problems linked to persistent long-term unemployment and high youth unemployment. In contrast, the United States — a country with limited interventions in the labor market — presents a record of long-term job creation (World Bank "Good Jobs" 2013).

The current disposition of the Kazakhstani labor code regarding job protection (hiring and firing regulations) does not appear very restrictive.[16] Given the need to ensure substantial job creation to absorb surplus labor and avoid long periods of unemployment, especially for young people entering the labor market, it seems advisable to favor flexibility and refrain from modifying and making the employment protection legislation more restrictive.

- *Allow flexible wage setting and ensure that human capital investments are valued by the labor market.* How wages are set, whether there is a minimum level or a cap, and to which extent wage differences reflect the investments in human capital made earlier are critical issues for a good functioning of the labor market. Many countries fix a minimum wage for unskilled and skilled labor. Kazakhstan is no exception. While a minimum wage regulation offers benefits to those who are covered, a number of studies have shown that it can have negative effects for those looking for jobs, in particular youth and migrants who are more likely to be at the low end of the wage spectrum. The magnitude of the impact depends on the level at which it has been fixed and the proportion of the labor force paid at this level. A general recommendation would thus be to make sure that the minimum wage is not set (or raised in the future) at a level that can deter formal employment of youth and less skilled workers.

  Wages are the main source of income of the population in Kazakhstan. Available statistics indicate that the average real wage has increased substantially over the last decade and that there are marked differences in average wages across occupations, economic sectors, and regions. However, no information permits assessing to what extent these wage differences are returns on past investments in education, training, and work experience or reflect other factors such as barriers to mobility. The Ministry of Labor acknowledges that it does not monitor how wages vary with education and work experience. It is thus impossible to assess how well the labor market rewards human capital investments. Moreover, there is no information showing whether wages are flexible enough to attract labor to occupations and sectors where there are skill shortages. It would however be critical to ensure that the labor market in Kazakhstan provides the signals and incentives that would guide students and workers in their choice of fields of study, careers and jobs. As discussed in the previous section, this would ensure that skills and knowledge acquired are appropriate to the economic circumstances of the country. Equally important are those signals for taking decision about migration to other cities or regions. Attempting to reduce wage inequalities through norms and regulations and imposing rigid pay determination processes would alter those signals and could prevent the labor market adjustments and job mobility that are needed. It could also create social tension if those who have invested time and effort in acquiring skills cannot get the benefits from these investments over their working life.

- *Test and evaluate employment programs before any scaling-up.* The Employment Program 2020 envisages the introduction of several interventions targeted to low-income and unemployed workers, including wage subsidies, training and retraining programs, self-employment assistance, and mobility support. International evidence on the impact and cost-effectiveness of these programs invites to some caution. Many of these programs have been implemented in developed and developing countries and show a very mixed record, according to evaluations from more than 300 interventions. (Betcherman, Olivas, and Dar 2004; Riboud 2012). The only type of intervention that seems to provide generally positive outcomes in countries with a large formal

---

16. There are, however, significant restrictions on employment of foreign nationals. This may put a break on modernization of the economy (see Chapter 10).

sector is counseling and job search assistance (it also happens to be the least costly). All other interventions work in some cases but not in others. The context in which programs are implemented matters: as could be expected, a growth environment is a factor of success. Results are also very sensitive to design features. Private sector participation, close monitoring and follow up, and a combination of complementary interventions (such as training with assistance for job placement) rather than isolated interventions increase the chances of success. When not well grounded in the realities of the labor market and/or badly administered, these programs are of little use and/or waste resources.

Given the uncertainty of positive outcomes, it is important to start with small-scale, carefully monitored and evaluated programs. It is prudent to maintain modest expectations about the employment effects of those programs. Even when these programs have been successful, international evidence shows that the impact remains modest. These programs may help (in particular at times of crisis) but not solve widespread employment issues. Growth and a business environment conducive to job creation remain the surest and most effective way to resolve employment issues, and the private sector needs to be the main engine. As pointed out in the 2013 World Bank World Development report, in today's rapidly changing times, the private sector is the source of almost 9 out of 10 jobs in the world (World Bank "Jobs" 2013).

Health

Trends and issues

After gaining independence in 1991, Kazakhstan was unable to maintain its large and inefficient health system inherited from Soviet times. The collapse of the health budget and the massive decline in living standards during the early years of the transition led to a worsening of health indicators. Life expectancy declined sharply from 68.8 years in 1990 to 64.6 in 1996, largely caused by an increase in mortality from cardiovascular diseases. The incidence of TB and other communicable diseases also increased throughout the 1990s. These factors led to a series of reforms of the health sector (Box 5.6).

While initial reforms were fragmented and volatile, a new phase of reforms providing more consistent policy directions started in 2004. The agenda set by the National Program for Health Care Reform and Development (2005-10) was ambitious, aiming at improving the quality and efficiency of health services. Goals were to shift toward primary and outpatient care, introduce international standards of health care services through new technologies and treatment methods, upgrade health facilities and equipment while downsizing the hospital sector, and train health specialists and managers. The State Guaranteed Benefit Package (SGBP), which covered emergency care and a set of outpatient and inpatient services, was expanded in 2005 to cover more groups of patients and diseases such as respiratory infections, hypertension, etc., and a drug benefit was also introduced for children, adolescents, and women of reproductive age. In 2010, funds pooling arrangements were modified so that, currently, there is a split of hospital and primary health care between national and oblast levels (around 67 percent for the republican budget and 33 percent for oblasts). The objective was to facilitate the implementation of the principle "money follows the patient" and to bring about more competition between providers.

Kazakhstan made progress on several fronts leading to a reversal of previously detrimental trends and some improvement in health indicators, according to the Agency of Statistics of the Republic of Kazakhstan: life expectancy started increasing again in 2000, the maternal mortality rate fell from 46.3 in 2007 to 17.4 in 2011, the infant mortality rate from 20.8 to 14.9 over the same period, and a 40 percent reduction in deaths from cardiovascular diseases was registered. Implementation of new clinical practice guidelines in pilot sites led to improvements in quality of care. However, not all key goals of the 2005-10 program were achieved, and the next stage of reforms was initiated in a new program "Salamatty Kazakhstan 2011-2015" and the strategic Development Plan 2020 (Republic of Kazakhstan "Salamatty" 2010).

Among the many issues that the "Salamatty Kazakhstan" program and its promoters will have to address, the main ones are the following:

Box 5.6 | Major health sector reform milestones

1991 – Private practices are permitted.

1996 – Mandatory Health Insurance Fund with payroll tax funding was created but then abolished in 1998 and replaced by a State Guaranteed Benefit Package provided for free and financed from budgetary resources.

1996 –2001 – Health financing and administration decentralized to the rayon level.

2004 – Adoption of the National Program for Health Care Reform 2005-10.

2009 – Adoption of the Concept on the Unified National Health Care System, based on free choice of provider and the development of competition and transparency in the health system and adoption of the Code on People's health and the Health Care System.

2010 – Adoption of the State Health Care Development Program for 2011-15 "Salamatty Kazakhstan."

- Adoption of new provider payment mechanisms (case-based hospital payment and capitation payment for primary health care centers.
- Introduction of evidence-based medicine as core of clinical practice, education, and research.
- Resources for hospital services under the State Guaranteed Package benefit are pooled back at the national level to allow implementation of free patient choice ("money follows the patient"). Financing primary health care centers remains the responsibility of local budgets (only bonuses paid by the republican budget).
- A number of state-owned health providers are granted autonomy due to a change in legal status.
- The principle of pay for performance (P4P) is adopted for health professionals.

Source: European Observatory on Health Systems and Policies (2012).

Health indicators are still substantially behind those of developed countries. Although health indicators have started improving, Kazakhstan still has a long way to go before the health status of the population is comparable to that of developed countries or even matches that of countries such as Turkey or the former Yugoslav republics, which have achieved steady progress (Table 5.4). Life expectancy at birth, equal to 70 in 2013, is one of the lowest in the whole European region and 12 years lower than the EU average (WHO Regional Office for Europe 2013). While life expectancy in most countries in Western Europe has increased by about 5 years over the last two decades, Kazakhstan has just recovered its 1990 level. The 10-year gap between men and women's life expectancy (64.34 vs. 74.34) is also much wider (the gap in the European region is 7.5 years), and there are substantial regional variations. Infant and maternal mortality rates and rates of TB are still high, and Kazakhstan faces a heavy burden of non-communicable diseases.[17] This low health status, which directly affects the population's well-being

---

17. However, there has been a distinct improvement in at least one important health indicator: According to UNICEF, as reported by NAC of Nazarbayev University, there has been a significant decline in under-5 child mortality between 1990 and 2012 (from 54.1 cases for 1,000 live births to 18.7).

MICHELLE RIBOUD

cannot be explained by lack of access to health services,[18] but rather by the low quality of those services and by lifestyle factors related to alcohol consumption, smoking, and diets high in fat. Environmental factors in industrial regions and poor sanitation and contaminated water in both urban and rural areas are additional public health concerns.

Table 5.4	Despite recent improvements, life expectancy in Kazakhstan remains low compared to Europe (measured in years)			
	Male		**Female**	
	1990	2009	1990	2009
Kazakhstan	64	64	73	74
High income countries (average)	72	77	79	83
Switzerland	74	80	81	84
Germany	72	77	79	83
France	73	78	81	85
Japan	76	80	82	86
Turkey	62	70	67	75
Croatia	69	73	76	80

Source: World Bank ("WDR" 2011).

Low efficiency of the health system. Although the 2005-2010 program put great emphasis on the restructuring of the health system with a shift toward primary health care and prevention, the current model is still based on outpatient care and hospital-based disease management and much of health financing is still directed at maintaining health care infrastructure. In 2008, inpatient care consumed 53.4 percent of public expenditures, whereas primary health care only received 16 percent (European Observatory on Health Systems and Policies 2012). Some reduction of the hospital network was achieved over the last decade while Kazakhstan started to modernize the infrastructure. Nevertheless, the ratio of hospital beds per person, level of unnecessary hospitalizations, and length of stay in hospitals are still much higher than in Western Europe.

There are indications that the quality of care is improving with the promotion of evidence-based medicine and the introduction of clinical guidelines, but there is still much scope for improving technical efficiency, in view of the poor performance indicators of inpatient care and narrowly specialized health facilities. Overall, inefficiencies are such that increased financial resources allocated to the sector have not translated into significant improvement in the quality of services. The attempt to shift the balance toward primary health care has not yet succeeded.

Financing of health care: Policy and practice are not fully aligned. After the failed attempt to introduce a mandatory health insurance in the late 1990s, the government introduced a State Guaranteed Benefit Package of services (SGBP) provided for free and financed out of general budget revenues. The package includes emergency care and inpatient and outpatient care and is subject to revision every two years.

---

18. Analysis of household budget surveys shows that about one in five people in Kazakhstan live within 10 minutes of a medical facility, and 85 percent live less than 30 minutes away. Regarding access to health facility, differences between rich and poor households are not significant (World Bank 2004).

User fees are allowed for services not included in the package, and those have to be covered by out-of-pocket payments, health insurance, or employers. An outpatient drug benefit has also been introduced. Children, adolescents, and women of reproductive age are entitled to pharmaceuticals free of charge.

Although, in theory, the range of medical services provided for free to the population is large (only non-essential services are excluded) and private participation in health care delivery is still limited to about 20 percent of services, private expenditures for health account for around 40 percent of total health expenditures.[19] The bulk of private expenditures are made for outpatient services (83 percent in 2007). Patients usually pay for pharmaceuticals, aids, and dentures from outpatient services and polyclinics. There are also indications that, at times, due to lack of funding, hospitals charge fees for goods and services that should normally be covered under the SGBP and that informal payments remain a frequent practice. The fact that patients admitted to hospitals can have the cost of pharmaceuticals covered while they have to pay in polyclinics creates an undesirable incentive for people to seek inpatient rather than outpatient care, in contradiction with the intended policy direction.

Almost all private expenditures are made out-of-pocket as private insurance is still minimal (about 1.2 percent of the population was covered by voluntary health insurance in 2009). Therefore, a significant financial burden for paying primary health care and outpatient falls on households, with a likely greater impact on poorer groups of the population who may face access barriers to health services.

Human resource issues affect the quality of health services. First, the quality of medical education and training of health managers needs much improvement. Second, the medical profession is not attractive financially, which has caused a decrease in the number of young professionals entering the sector. Third, there is an acute shortage of health personnel in rural areas, where living conditions are hard (almost four times fewer physicians per capita in rural areas than in cities). There is also an imbalance toward specialist services concentrated in urban areas, to the detriment of primary health care facilities. Fourth, medical center staffing is subject to regulations that prevent an optimal use of human resources. Nurses' and physicians' responsibilities are not clearly defined, with physicians often carrying out tasks that could be performed by nurses, and medical specializations are too narrowly defined leading to too many referrals. Finally, mobility is often constrained by lack or unaffordable housing.

Regional inequities. Regional differences in per capita allocations for health services (by oblast) were markedly reduced over the last decade. Between 2000 and 2008, the difference in health financing per capita between the richest and poorest oblast decreased from 4.2 to 2.1 times. However, inequities remain in utilization of health services and expenditures on drugs. Almaty and Astana host the most advanced clinical centers and spend significantly more per capita on drugs. The overall inpatient infra-structure is unequally spread and the shortage of rural health personnel — with almost four times more physicians in cities compared to rural areas — exacerbate problems in the provision of health services to the rural population. These differences translate in substantial variations in health outcomes (European Observatory on Health Systems and Policies 2012).

The Vision 2050 for Health

Despite its many laudable efforts in health sector reform, Kazakhstan has a long way to go before it can match the health outcomes of the most developed nations and achieve the vision for the health sector reflected in Box 5.7. Making this goal a reality will require long and sustained efforts with a focus

---

19. The information in this and the next two paragraphs is based on European Observatory on Health Systems and Policies (2012) and interviews with Ministry of Health staff in Astana.

on effective implementation of initiatives. Bringing health outcomes to the level observed in developed countries will likely take several decades, if one considers that it took 20 years for countries making steady progress to achieve a five-year gain in life expectancy. This calls for urgency in implementation as well as patience in regard to outcomes.

Box 5.7 | Vision 2050 for Health

By 2050 Kazakhstan will have built a new model of health care that ensures availability of health services to the whole population and brings health outcomes close to those observed in most developed countries. This model relies on greater emphasis on prevention and primary health care, highly qualified health professionals, and the full use of up-to-date knowledge and modern technology. Kazakhstan will have a modern health management and an efficient provider payment system. Incentives will be in place for responsible patient behavior and high quality standards of health services. The cost-sharing of health expenditures with the population will be compatible with budgetary resources and aligned with social objectives.

Source: Author.

Program of Action

The policy directions specified in the recently approved "Salamatty Kazakhstan" Program and other related documents are consistent with the aforementioned vision. The challenge will be to achieve a full implementation of announced or ongoing reforms and to make sure to bring the incentive framework in line with policy directions. Action will be required in seven principal areas.

- *Promote patient responsibility and prevention.* There is some evidence that the high incidence of diseases of the circulatory system in Kazakhstan (which can be related to lifestyle factors) plays a predominant role[20] in explaining the low life expectancy. Accidents are also a major cause of deaths. As shown by the experience of Western Europe, education, information campaigns, continuity of medical attention with a primary care doctor, and appropriate incentives (taxes on tobacco and alcohol for example) can change lifestyle behaviors and disease management and reduce the risk of cardiovascular mortality and accidents due to alcohol consumption, smoking, diets high in fat, and lack of physical exercise. In Kazakhstan budget allocations dedicated to preventive and public health care have been small (about 2 percent of total current expenditures) in recent years and would need to grow.

- *Ensure that incentives created by provider payment mechanisms are aligned with policy directions and accompanied by a less rigid budget planning process and greater autonomy in the use of resources.* Payment mechanisms for health services, hospitals, and outpatient providers have been modified several times over the last decade and are still evolving in search of the most appropriate setup. They are meant to create incentives for greater efficiency and better quality of services. However, expected efficiency gains may not materialize if budget processes continue to encourage capacity increases and if rigid rules prevent providers from cost-effectively reallocating resources. Changes in budget planning rules and granting greater autonomy have to go in parallel with the introduction of the new incentive framework.

---

20. According to WHO, the leading cause of death in 46 percent of cases is cardiovascular disease (Ministry of Health, Republic of Kazakhstan, and Oxford Policy Management 2010 and 2011).

- *Introduce gradual and careful application of pay for performance principles.* P4P offers rewards for providing high-quality care and promotes better outcomes. Many performance incentive schemes have been implemented over the past few decades, most extensively in the UK and US. France also has a national program, Spain and Italy have local-level or small-scale programs, and an increasing number of developing countries are using this approach in pilot projects. Evaluations, although limited, have shown positive outcomes (WHO 2010). The decision taken by the government of Kazakhstan to introduce P4P in primary health care in addition to the capitation payment system fits with the policy objective of improving outcomes. If successful, it could facilitate the desired shift toward primary health care. So far, preparatory work has been done and initial implementation has started.

  To ensure success, implementation needs to be gradual, cautious, and well-coordinated with other actions, as international experience suggests (see Box 5.8). Performance measures should be designed to motivate providers to produce more services in priority areas such as maternal and children's health. They should also be designed to induce transparent and honest reporting of actual performance and not seen as a system imposing sanctions for not achieving targets.[21] It is highly recommended to precede full-scale implementation with well-evaluated pilots. The roll-out may take several years and require numerous adjustments. Moreover, introduction of P4P needs to be well-coordinated with the implementation of other reforms, in particular the development of quality audit processes with international standards and of information systems. Communication campaigns would also be useful to ensure that methods of remunerations and associated incentives are well understood by health personnel.

- *Pursue and complete implementation of some other key reforms.* These include (1) the revision and improvement of the content of clinical practice linked to evidence-based medicine and rational drug use, (2) the phased transition of health facilities to the legal status of state economic enterprises which gives them greater autonomy in managing resources, (3) the introduction of accreditation and internal audit processes for health providers which should become the main tool for managing quality of services, and (4) the free patient choice for primary health care providers and hospital care. Greater autonomy and quality audits are critical for achieving and monitoring quality improvements and are necessary complements of the introduction of pay for performance schemes. The exercise of free choice will promote competition between service providers.

- *Ensure efficient and sustainable health care financing by:*
  - *Improving efficiency first and only then increasing public spending.* Total health expenditures, both public and private, have grown rapidly in absolute terms, in recent years, largely driven by high GDP growth rates. In percentage of GDP, total spending amounted to 4.5 percent of GDP in 2009 and public spending to 2.7 percent (WHO 2010).[22] Overall, Kazakhstan spends little on health as proportion of GDP relative to what is observed in low and middle-income countries or in the European region (on average 8.5 percent). This lower level of expenditures seems partly due to a lower utilization of inpatient and

---

21. Care should be taken to develop informed, feasible, yet challenging performance measures, well aligned with priorities and not to create perverse incentives. As many countries have done, it would be good to initially use simple indicators of structure and process that are easy to measure with existing information systems and easy to attribute. More complex indicators of outcomes/results and quality could be used at a later stage of development of the system once adjustments to the information and administrative system have been introduced and medical compliance has been achieved.

22. According to NAC of Nazarbayev University, health related spending from the budget amounted to 4 percent of GDP in 2012.

outpatient services (WHO). The government has indicated its intention to further increase public spending on health as a percentage of GDP. In the short run, however, the priority should be on implementing the ongoing reforms and bringing greater efficiency in the health system. Increasing spending without addressing inefficiencies is not likely to bring better outcomes.

Box 5.8 | Pay for performance: Lessons from international experience

P4P ties compensation to the achievement of specified goals in patient care and prevention. It is usually combined with base salary or fee-for-service payments. Amounts vary (in the UK for example, 18 to 25 percent), but international experience suggests that a 7 to 13 percent range may be adequate at the time of introduction. A choice can be made between group and individual rewards. Non-financial incentives such as opportunities for continuing medical education and training, career opportunities, and availability of clinical protocols can be used jointly with financial incentives.

Implementation of P4P is complex and requires that a number of conditions be met. Besides the development of a regulatory framework and appropriate funding, it requires the selection of performance measures, operational methods, and the capacity to evaluate, revise, and refine. It can thus only be implemented in areas where there is sufficient evidence base to measure results and requires that physicians have trust in the reliability of data and the transparency and fairness of the process. What many countries have done is to initially use simple indicators of structure and process that are easy to measure with existing information systems and easy to attribute. More complex indicators of outcomes/results and quality can be used at a later stage of development of the system once adjustments to the information and administrative system have been introduced and medical compliance has been achieved.

Although there is still limited evidence, evaluation of P4P in developed countries suggests that these schemes have improved physician and/or hospital performance against a set of measures that vary but include quality indicators, such as adherence to best practices. In developing countries, P4P has often been introduced as a pilot project and improved performance has been reported in several areas of care, including the number of antenatal visits and child immunization coverage. A correct implementation of the scheme appears key for positive results.

Source: WHO (2010); Ministry of Health, Republic of Kazakhstan, and Oxford Policy Management (2010 and 2011).

○   *Introducing an explicit co-payment policy.* One of the key objectives of the health reform program is the financial protection of the population in health care. To this end, the government has consistently increased spending for the SGBP and the drug benefit over recent years. At the same time, it has expressed concerns about the moral hazard cost of excessive health care utilization and stressed the importance of "shared responsibility." Introducing co-payments is being considered. Cost-sharing of health expenditures in practice already exist since private expenditures amount to around 40 percent of expenditures. Some co-payments are implicit corresponding to payments for services that should have been free; others to services or goods not covered under the SGBP. Introducing an explicit policy about co-payments consistent with the emphasis on primary health care could be preferable to maintaining the status-quo. To ensure incentives for effective utilization one could consider introducing co-payment rates that would vary depending on the type of care and for example, apply low or no co-payment on preventive care visits or basic pharmaceuticals. These modifications in the distribution of the burden could be done without changing the overall share of private expenditures.

- *Controlling the growth in public spending to levels that are fiscally sustainable in the long term.* The share of health expenditures covered by out-of-pocket payments is high in Kazakhstan (around 40 percent) relative to what is observed in high-income countries (where the average is 25 percent). However, attempting to reduce significantly the overall share of expenditures supported by households to increase financial protection of the population may not be advisable. The long-run sustainability of public funding is at stake. In Organization for Economic Co-operation and Development (OECD) countries, health expenditures have increased faster than GDP for 40 years and are projected to reach 15 to 20 percent of GDP in most countries. It is highly uncertain that these countries will be able to maintain the private sector's share of direct payments at its current level. In Kazakhstan, as in other parts of the world, the pressure for increased public spending will be strong even without an attempt to change the cost-sharing proportion and in no country would public finance be able to pay for total health expenditures. Rather than trying to reduce the overall share of private contributions, it could be preferable to move gradually toward prepayments and risk-pooling arrangements as discussed below and only design special protection programs for those who cannot contribute.

- *Developing voluntary private insurance plans.* Currently, while private sources contribute to about 40 percent of current health expenditures, only 3 percent of private spending comes from pre-paid risk pools, managed by private insurance companies. Even if the contribution of voluntary private health insurance is not likely to cover all private expenditures,[23] facilitating the development of insurance plans would increase the share of pre-paid resources and decrease the share of out-of-pocket expenditures, reducing the risk of fluctuations in the utilization of health services.

- *In the medium term, the government could consider moving toward health financing based on pre-payment and pooling.* The objective would be to reduce the dependence on out-of-pocket payments and increase the proportion of the population covered by formal insurance. In the short run, however, it might be preferable to maintain the practice of a benefit package (suitably adjusted) financed out of general budget revenues and wait for such a move until a large fraction of the population working in agriculture or in the informal sector has transited to the formal sector to avoid fragmentation and inequality. In countries such as Mexico which initiated this move when there was still a large informal sector, inequalities and inefficiencies were exacerbated with workers in the formal sector better covered than others, and with the coexistence of different types of pooled funds covering different population groups with different levels of benefits (Levy 2008; WHO 2010).

- *Improving the quality of medical education and motivating health workers.* Health workers are at the core of the health system. Inadequate training and compensation undermine efficiency. Improving the quality of medical education requires the use of up to date instruction manuals and the establishment of close links with hospitals for clinical practice. The profession also needs to

---

23. Private insurance covers only about 10 to 15 percent of total health expenditures in high-income countries (WHO 2012).

5

become financially appealing to attract young and talented young professionals into medicine and address the shortage of health personnel in rural areas. The introduction of pay for performance may be a motivating factor if well explained and understood but it may also be necessary to increase basic salary levels and offer greater prospects for career advancement.

Social Protection

Trends and Issues

High and sustained growth during the last decade has resulted in substantial poverty reduction. The share of the population living with an income below the poverty line (or subsistence minimum)[24] fell from 46.7 percent in 2001 to 4 percent in 2012 (Figure 5.2). Concurrently, as mentioned before, the unemployment rate fell from 13 percent to 5.2 percent. The incidence of poverty as indicated by household budget surveys is higher in rural areas than in urban areas, and in particular, among unemployed or self-employed in agriculture (Table 5.5). As in other countries, important determinants of poverty are low levels of education, employment status of the household head (lack of job), number of children, and household size. The "oblast" of residence also matters as growth has been stronger in resource-rich Western regions and large cities (See Chapters 2 and 8).

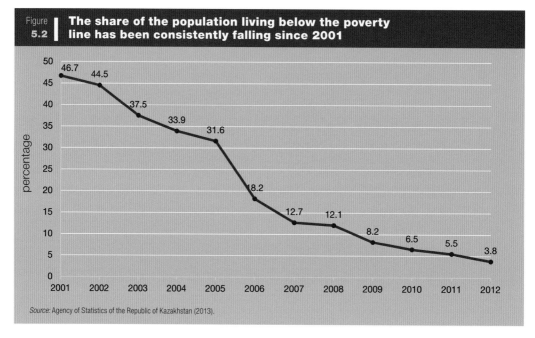

| Figure 5.2 | The share of the population living below the poverty line has been consistently falling since 2001 |

Source: Agency of Statistics of the Republic of Kazakhstan (2013).

Between 1998 and 2002 Kazakhstan embarked on a series of major reforms of the social protection system. Up until 1998, the pension system was pay-as-you-go (PAYG), publicly managed, with a defined benefit linked to pre-retirement salary. The 1998 reform introduced a fully-funded, defined contribution pillar and a gradual phasing out of the PAYG component. The pension system was further adjusted in

---

24. The subsistence minimum or poverty line is established by costing out a food consumption basket and inflating this basket to account for non-food consumption.

2005 with the introduction of a flat-base pension component. Social assistance programs were also reformed. Numerous benefits and subsidies with categorical eligibility were monetized and consolidated in 1999-2000 and means-tested assistance was introduced in 2002.

Table 5.5	**Poverty headcount rates vary greatly depending on status of employment and settlement type**			
	Poverty headcount (percent)	Distribution of population (percent)	Poverty headcount (percent)	Distribution of population (percent)
	Rural		Urban	
Employee	19.2	57.1	10.3	63.4
Self-employed	25.0	20.5	14.4	14.5
Unemployed	34.6	1.1	17.8	1.4
Retired	21.4	17.5	13.9	16.9
Out of Labor Force	26.0	3.8	22.8	3.7
TOTAL	21.2	100.0	12.1	100.0

Note: Poverty headcount rate determined by household head's status of employment and settlement type.
Source: Household Budget Survey 2008 (World Bank "Safety Net" 2011); World Bank staff calculations.

As a result, the current social protection system in Kazakhstan comprises three components: the pension system, three means-tested programs (the Targeted Social Assistance program or TSA, housing benefits, and allowances for dependent children under 18 introduced in 2006) and two categorical programs (Social Allowances and Special Allowances). The Social Allowances program provides disability and survivor allowances, as well as old-age allowances for those who reached retirement age and are either ineligible for pension payments or whose entitlement is below the guaranteed minimum. The special allowances are monetized benefits and subsidies formerly known as "privileges" which are paid to specific categories of the population such as veterans, victims of Chernobyl, or families with many children. In addition, the unemployed may get financial support during a period of one to four months after losing their job if their former employer has contributed to the State Fund of Mandatory Social Insurance. At the end of this period, they may become eligible for the TSA.

While consolidated government expenditures on social protection represented 10 percent of GDP in 1997, the share fell to 6.6 percent in 2002. The drop was due to both diminished government liabilities toward pensioners following the introduction of the reform and the move away from untargeted benefits toward means-tested benefits. Later on, spending on social protection continued to decline as poverty rates and the number of beneficiaries fell. Between 2007 and 2011, the number of beneficiaries from the targeted social assistance program fell by close to 40 percent. Spending on social protection represented 4.3 percent of GDP in 2011.

A large fraction of households receive social transfers. Although income earned is the most prevalent and most important source of income, pensions come second and represent about 21 percent of total household incomes (Table 5.6). Close to 40 percent of households received a pension, and around 30 percent received some form of social assistance in 2002. Recent data suggest that these proportions have remained fairly stable over time. Table 5.6 also shows that pensions and social transfers represent an important share of the income of the poorest households (belonging to the bottom expenditure quintile) and that a large fraction of them benefit from them.

Table 5.6 | Pensions and social transfers represent an important source of income for the poorest households

Source of Income	Percent of households income by source		Share of total household income by source	
	Bottom quintile	Total	Bottom quintile	Total
Income earned	99.3	99.2	63.2	65.0
Pensions	30.6	39.1	14.5	21.2
Rental income	0.7	1.8	0.1	0.3
Social transfers	50.3	31.7	15.8	7.2
Private transfers	52.2	49.8	5.7	5.7
Other income	6.1	5.9	0.7	0.6
Total			100.0	100.0

Source: Kazakhstan Household Budget Survey 2002 (World Bank 2004).

The coverage rates of social assistance programs decline with wealth, and the lowest two quintiles receive 60 percent of all social assistance transfers. The TSA has a good targeting performance, comparable to that of best programs worldwide (Table 5.7), with more than 70 percent of the benefits accruing to the lowest quintile. In contrast, other means-tested program, the housing allowance program, is not well targeted.

Table 5.7 | Some social assistance programs, particularly the TSA, are well-targeted, while others are not, such as the housing assistance program

	Distribution of income benefits* by income quintile					
	Total	Q1	Q2	Q3	Q4	Q5
All social assistance	100.0	39.6	19.5	15.6	11.8	13.5
TSA	100.0	72.4	13.8	7.0	1.0	5.8
Housing assistance	100.0	24.4	17.2	18.3	15.7	24.4
Social allowances	100.0	38.8	19.9	15.6	13.1	12.6
Special allowances	100.0	39.9	20.0	16.1	11.0	12.9
One-time transfers	100.0	21.8	22.7	12.7	17.7	25.1

* defined as the amount of benefits received by individuals in a quintile. It takes into account the value of benefits as well as the coverage.
Source: Household Budget Survey 2008 (World Bank "Safety Net" 2011)

Overall, available evidence suggests that the social protection system has been effective in reducing poverty. It was estimated that, in the absence of social protection programs, poverty would have increased from 15 to 30 percent in 2002 (World Bank 2004). A similar calculation made in 2008 also indicates that the poverty headcount rate would have been 19 percent higher in the absence of social protection programs (Rutkowski 2011). The government also demonstrated its capacity to provide a temporary safety net at times of crisis. When the economy declined in 2008, a large-scale public works program was implemented where unemployment risks were highest.

The elderly have benefited from adequate protection. Their living standards seem quite comparable to those of the working population. Currently, almost all elderly receive the base pension and the defined benefit pension (since they worked part of their life under the PAYG system). The latter is only gradually declining for new retiree cohorts. An analysis of income and pension data (World Bank "Pension" 2012) shows that the average pension from the two combined benefits provides around 50 percent of the annual wage income of formal workers and that, taking into account all sources of income, the elderly receive around 83 percent of the income of working-age population. This finding is consistent with data in Table 5.5, which show fairly similar poverty rates among retired and the working-age population.

Looking ahead, the main concern is the adequacy of future pensions and the impact it would have on the living standards of the elderly. As the PAYG is gradually phased out, future pensioners will increasingly rely on just two pension components: the base pension and the defined contribution benefit. While currently, the replacement rate is at about 45 percent, projections of current trends indicate that replacement rates could progressively decline and drop to the 10 to 12 percent range by 2040 (World Bank "Pension" 2012). Two factors, not anticipated at the time of the reform would contribute to it. First, the contribution periods of the insured population has been shorter than expected: only 60 percent of the working-age population contributes to the pension funds and, on average, for only 8 months per year. The second and most important factor is that rates of return on investments of pension savings have been close to zero until 2006 and turned negative since then.

Given the importance of pensions as a source of income for a large proportion of households, the risk of rising poverty for the elderly looms large. This also leaves the government facing substantial liabilities. The law on pension guarantees that the value of pension assets at time of retirement be at least equal to the real value of past contributions. These guarantees will continue to be triggered if positive investment returns cannot be achieved. It is also conceivable that there would be social pressure for even greater intervention as this guarantee might not be sufficient to avoid a sharp drop in the living standards of the elderly. In addition, the government would still have to attend the needs of those who have not contributed (the remaining 40 percent of the working-age population) with the base pension or the social old-age allowance.

Fully aware of these pending issues, the government has decided to increase the level of the base pension (Ministry of Labor and Social Protection of the Population of the Republic of Kazakhstan 2013). It was set at 50 percent of the subsistence minimum in January 2012 and will be raised to 60 percent by 2015. Subsequently, it is expected that it will continue to increase gradually until it reaches the level of the subsistence minimum (which is also aligned with the minimum wage). In addition, the president ordered in January 2013 that pension savings of all 11 private pension funds (which amount to about 10 percent of GDP) be transferred into a state-owned fund managed by the National Bank. In 2013, two laws were approved: These new laws establish: (1) a single state pension savings fund which integrate all former pension funds, (2) starting in 2018, a gradual increase over 10 years of women's retirement age from 58 to match men's retirement age (63), and (3) a 5 percent contribution of employers to the pension fund in case of work under dangerous and hazardous conditions.

A second future issue is related to the targeted social assistance program that is the last resort program for the poor at times of crises or loss of employment. The program works on demand, and the majority of recipients have received the TSA for more than one year and 40 percent for three years. In principle, beneficiaries can receive benefits indefinitely. This raises an issue of possible long-term dependency on social assistance, which concerns the government. This risk does not appear very high under current circumstances. It could, however, increase if the program was made more generous and the eligibility threshold higher.

The Vision 2050 for Social Protection

An affordable, effective social safety net is a core human development pillar of a successful developed economy. So the vision for Kazakhstan 2050 includes this as an important element. Box 5.9 provides a specific Vision 2050 for social protection.

Box 5.9 | Vision 2050 for Social Protection

The Vision 2050 for social protection is for a society which aims at reducing poverty and at providing social protection for the elderly, children, and disabled and safety nets in times of crisis or individual hardship. Programs will be fiscally sustainable, targeted to provide support only to those who need it, designed to avoid dependency, and help people transition from reliance on social transfers to employability.

Source: Author.

Policy Decisions To Be Taken and a Program of Preparatory Steps

The area of social protection raises a number of important, complex questions about trade-offs across different policy and political goals that need to be carefully assessed by the government.

Pension system

Ensuring the sustainability of the pension system and its ability to provide protection to the elderly is a critical issue. Maintaining the pension system under current conditions was clearly not a viable option in the medium term. Nevertheless, the recent decision to put all private funds under central bank authority and the recent draft laws still leave a number of important policy decisions to be made.

In re-examining options and what should be the long-term pension strategy, a number of questions need to be addressed and examined:

- *What level of financing of pensions can Kazakhstan sustain out of general budget revenues, and in particular, what level of the base pension?* This needs to be ascertained through a careful fiscal analysis. In the short and medium term, public financing is unavoidable as cohorts of retirees still have to be partly supported under the PAYG defined benefit system. Public financing is also required if the state guarantees for the defined contribution component are triggered. The decision to introduce and raise the level of the flat base pension added a public liability which has long-term fiscal implications, especially if the level of the base pension is going to reach and stay equal to the subsistence minimum and therefore, be indexed on inflation. Currently, the subsistence minimum is at around 19 percent of the average wage. Finally, the expected population increase resulting from the increase in life expectancy and the rise in fertility rates since the early 2000s will also have cost implications. Without an in-depth fiscal analysis, we do not feel it is possible for us to assess whether the proposed level of the base pension is sustainable and we would recommend conducting such analysis before taking a final decision.
- *Should years of contribution, and therefore retirement age, be increased?* This is always an unpopular and very difficult political decision, but it seems unavoidable to raise the retirement age. As health indicators improve and life expectancy gradually catches up with levels in developed

5

countries, retirement age will have to follow a similar path. In the short run, the recent decision to raise the retirement age of women, through a gradual increase of half a year during ten years starting 2018, is a step in this direction. Women in Kazakhstan retire much earlier than men (58 instead of 63) and have longer life expectancy (20.5 years at time of retirement versus 12.5 years for men). Ten years from now, life expectancy in Kazakhstan may well have increased by two or three years for both men and women and financing requirements for pensions are likely to increase accordingly.

- *What coverage should be given to self-employed and informal workers who still represent 40 percent of the working-age population?* Labor market developments are critical to address this question. Hopefully, with growth and the opening of new job opportunities, many self-employed and informal workers will gradually join the ranks of formal and insured workers. An attractive social insurance system would also be a conducive factor. In the short run, however, the majority of them do not contribute. Those self-employed who contribute (about one-third) do so on the basis of the minimum wage, not their actual income, and farmers and unpaid family workers do not contribute. Yet, they are eligible for a base pension or a social old-age allowance financed out of general revenues.[25] This coverage issue of informal workers could even become more serious if there were not enough job opportunities for the larger youth cohorts that are expected to enter the labor market after 2020.

- *How to address the poor performance of the defined contribution funded pillar?* This issue requires immediate attention. The aforementioned draft laws currently under discussion establish a single pension fund under the central bank, but leaves decisions pending regarding the fund's operation guidelines and investment rules. Those will be decided by a council under the President of Kazakhstan, following the model of the National Fund (see Chapter 6). It is clear that changes in investment rules and a restructuring of the sector are required. The poor performance of the pension funds resulted from lack of profitable investment opportunities in a small domestic market and a portfolio structure overexposed to domestic fixed income instruments that yield negative real returns. Domestic and international portfolio diversification is needed as well as the removal of obligations to invest in government bonds that yield negative real returns. Such diversification strategy has been followed in countries with funded pillars, and in most of them real rates of return have been satisfactory (World Bank "Pension" 2012). Real rates of return in Latin America have averaged 8 percent until 2007 and even after the impact of the 2008 crisis still averaged 6.4 percent. In Eastern Europe, returns have averaged 3.9 percent and have remained positive after the crisis. In Kazakhstan changes in investment rules should be accompanied by a restructuring of the funds to bring broader international expertise and higher efficiency and achieve lower administration fees.

- *What guarantees does Kazakhstan want to provide to the elderly?* Kazakhstan's implicit promise to provide adequate pensions to the elderly needs greater clarity. Is the focus on a minimum pension or an income replacement level? There is some trade-off between those objectives, and pension systems across the world give a different weight to each, depending on the priority they give to poverty alleviation versus income replacement. Under the earlier reform, the government opted for providing a flat-base pension for all and a guarantee related to the value of pension

---

25. In his study of the social protection system in Mexico, Santiago Levy (2008) demonstrates that the design of the system in Mexico is such as to give strong incentives both to firms and to workers to stay in the informal sector (since only formal sector firms contribute, but informal sector workers also benefit). It would be desirable to study whether a similar link exists between social protection system and informality in Kazakhstan, and how best to avoid creating one in any future social protection reform.

5

assets (to be at least equal to the real value of pension contributions to the funded pillar). There was no guaranteed replacement rate. If a decision were to be taken to also guarantee that the replacement rate of future pensioners be at a high level, for example, similar to that of current pensioners, this could lead to huge implicit debts in the future and would be inconsistent with the 1998 decision to introduce a defined contribution component. It would practically amount to a return to a defined benefit system. A preferable option would be to restructure the pension man-agement structure to ensure positive returns on pension savings without specific guarantee on the level of the replacement rate. This would still leave some flexibility, depending on the outcome of a fiscal analysis and political choices, for raising or lowering the base pension, and reducing or increasing the contributions to the funded pillar as some countries of Eastern Europe have done.

Safety net

With regard to the safety net, the challenge is to maintain adequate protection while not creating disincentives to work. Currently, the eligibility threshold for the TSA program is set at 40 percent of the subsistence minimum, and the number of program beneficiaries has fallen from year to year in line with the decrease in the incidence of poverty. As now only around 1 percent of the population benefit from the TSA, an increase in the eligibility threshold is under consideration to cover more people (Rutkowski 2011). Two facts, however, invite some caution before such a decision. First, the TSA is not the only program that favors the poor. The majority of TSA households receive more than one form of assistance (World Bank "Pension" 2012). As shown in Table 5.8, 39 percent of benefits from social assistance programs other than the TSA go the bottom quintile and close to 60 percent to the bottom 40 percent. It would thus seem necessary to consider the total package of benefits to determine whether the coverage and generosity of the safety net are adequate. Second, the subsistence minimum is also the minimum wage, which around 16 percent of the labor force is paid. As the eligibility threshold gets closer to the minimum wage, the risk of disincentives to work increases.

Our recommendation is to only let the eligibility threshold increase automatically through upward adjustments in the minimum subsistence (maintaining the same proportion) and to improve the targeting of the other two means-tested programs (housing assistance and allowances for dependent children), perhaps by applying the same procedures than for the TSA since these have proved to be effective. Linking the means-tested programs with the employment programs discussed in the previous section through the design of mutual obligations or co-responsibilities[26] would also reduce the risk of dependency and facilitate the return to work. Beneficiaries of social assistance programs could lose their benefits (or see them reduced) if they do not make use of opportunities to increase their employability and do not show willingness to adapt to changing labor market conditions.

Conclusion and Recommendations

Kazakhstan has undoubtedly been an impressive reformer in the human development area and has not shied away from embarking on structural reforms that many developed countries would hesitate to undertake. Even if there are still areas where policy choices need to be firmed up, policy directions are all geared to make the Vision 2050 become a reality. Objectives appear achievable, but there is

---

26. See World Bank (2013) for a more detailed discussion of how to address the issue of work dependency through the design of 'social contracts' and activation programs.

still a long way to go before reaching 2050. Along the way, a lot has to be done over several decades as was discussed in this chapter. The following priorities appear most important for action across all human development:

- *Sustain support from the political leadership for the strategies that have been outlined.* It is only through incremental changes that Kazakhstan will come closer to its objectives. Many of the desired transformations will take years, even decades. Changes in priorities and policy directions could delay or even derail the process.

- *Ensure that incentives are in place and in line with the desired objectives.* More resources allocated to human development may be necessary, but there is robust international evidence that adding resources without a supportive institutional structure will not lead to highly functioning education, health, and social protection systems and a flexible labor market. The performance of each sub-sector is affected by the incentives that actors face, and the Kazakhstani authorities constantly need to make sure that rules and regulations as well as financing mechanisms do not produce incentives that work against policy goals.

- *Match incentives with responsibility and autonomy.* Those three elements cannot be introduced as isolated policies. Improved incentives can only be effective if students, teachers, doctors, nurses, hospital managers, and so forth have some leeway for independent choices and decisions. Many aspects of the reforms and strategies discussed in this chapter complement each other, and implementation requires careful coordination and sequencing.

- *Improve the capacity to measure outcomes, monitor, and evaluate programs.* This is consistent with the increased emphasis on performance and results. Making teachers and doctors accountable for greater performance implies being able to measure this performance. Constant efforts will be required to improve the quality and reliability of tests that measure students learning achievements and of indicators of quality of health care. Similarly, ensuring that education and training programs provide the skills needed for economic growth or that social policies provide effective protection to the most vulnerable implies being able to monitor labor market outcomes and evaluate the impact of programs.

- *Systematically scale up (only) what has been demonstrated to work, based on solid evidence.* In the area of human development policies and programs Kazakhstan has some excellent examples of systematically pursuing scaling-up pathways for specific programs, such as the concept of Nazarbayev University as an incubator of country-wide university reform. Given the massive task that Kazakhstan faces in upgrading its human development programs, only a systematic application of a scaling-up principle, which includes a careful monitoring, evaluation and adaptation of the results and lessons, will allow the country to reach the ambitious goals set for the year 2050.

In this chapter we made a number of specific recommendations[27] and stressed the importance of appropriate sequencing. Table 5.8 collects these recommendations and presents their suggested sequence in the short, medium and long term. In pursuing these reforms one must recognize a number of important challenges and trade-offs: (1) implementation of reform takes time, persistence, resources, and urgency, (2) long-established habits and expectations among education and health workers, students, patients, and social protection recipients need to be changed with appropriate incentives, accountability, and autonomy, (3) links with the macroeconomic and institutional environment and business climate are critical for effective employment policies, and (4) international experience and lessons are helpful, but provide no blueprints for application in Kazakhstan.

---

27. Most of these recommendations are consistent with those made in Rutkowski (2011).

5

Table 5.8	Human development: Time frame for implementation of recommended actions		
Area	**Short term**	**Medium term**	**Long term**
EDUCATION			
Pre-School	• Achieve full-coverage of preschool age (ages 3-6)	• Implement program for children aged 0-3 from disadvantaged background	• Evaluate impact and revise if necessary
Primary & Secondary	• Monitor and analyze TIMSS and PISA test results and use results to inform decision making • Roll out teacher training and other reforms in a way that allows impact evaluation (with control group) • Develop a quality assurance system focused on outcomes; improve quality and validity of tests (UNT in particular); ensure fairness & transparency • Design an incentive system that links compensation to outcomes (recognition, promotions, salary increases); implement on a small scale, evaluate & adjust Simplify monitoring of inputs (standards & norms) leaving more flexibility to each school (but demanding accountability)	• Monitor trends in students achieve-ment'; use results to inform decision making • Proceed gradually with scaling up: at each stage, experiment, evaluate and adjust • Assessment/exams aligned with learning goals	• Idem • Monitor impact of reform
Tertiary	• To emulate replication of the NU model, ensure that right set of incentives (career paths, salaries) induces changed behavior. Apply to a limited number of universities. Test and evaluate. • Accompany incentives with auton-omy and accountability. Simplify control mechanisms Continue with accreditation process • Improve the quality and valid-ity of UNT; ensure fairness and transparency • Collect, analyze and disseminate information about university require-ments, offerings, pass rates and graduates' employment outcomes	• Expand implementation of reforms to an increasing number of universities. Evaluate impact • On-going • On-going • Promote competition between uni-versities for funding (recurrent and investment expenditures) • Match pace of increased funding for research with improvements in quality of graduate programs. • Consider possible introduction of a quality assurance monitoring system for universities	• Continue implementation • On-going • On-going

(contd...)

(Table 5.8 contd...)

Table 5.8	Human development: Time frame for implementation of recommended actions		
Area	**Short term**	**Medium term**	**Long term**
TVET	• Undertake regular and detailed analysis of labor market and enterprise surveys • Limit the degree of specialization and ensure sufficient general skills in TVET programs • Provide greater autonomy to schools and colleges (while demanding greater accountability) • Introduce financing modalities that facilitate competition between providers and encourage linkages with employers • Track employment and wage outcomes of TVET graduates. Evaluate returns and cost effectiveness of training programs	• Regular undertaking and analysis of labor force and enterprise surveys • Apply gradually to an increasing number of colleges/schools • Disseminate information about effectiveness of programs and schools/colleges	• Regular undertaking and analysis of labor force and enterprise surveys • Adjust program contents as needed
LABOR MARKET			
	• Conduct detailed analysis of labor market); move away from manpower planning • Maintain flexible contracting rules (hiring and firing regulations); avoid imposing rigid pay determination processes & regulations that would alter market signals; ensure that minimum wage level does not deter employment of low skilled and youth • Test, evaluate employment programs before any scaling up	• Regular monitoring of labor market trends and dissemination of information • Idem • Set up mechanisms to reduce costs of search and ease job matching; Adjust design & scope of employment programs based on evaluation	• Idem • Idem

(contd...)

(Table 5.8 contd...)

5

Table 5.8	Human development: Time frame for implementation of recommended actions		
Area	Short term	Medium term	Long term
	HEALTH		
	• Use education channels, information campaigns, medical attention & incentives (taxes) to promote prevention & patient responsibility. Increase budget allocation to prevention • Gradually change budget planning rules and grant autonomy in parallel with introduction of provider payment mechanisms • Pursue use of accreditation and introduction of internal audit processes • Introduce a co-payment policy consistent with emphasis on primary health care • Pilot introduction of pay for performance (P4P) principles: ensure coordination with complementary actions; evaluate before large-scale implementation • Motivate health workers with adequate compensation and training; address rural shortages; ensure trust in P4P process	• Continue with information campaigns, medical attention & incentives to change lifestyle behavior • Pursue phased transition of health facilities to legal status of state economic enterprises to allow granting of autonomy • Evaluate and improve tools for measuring quality of services • Facilitate the development of voluntary private insurance plans • Gradually extend application of P4P principles: adjust as measurement capacity improves; ensure trust of health workers in reliability of indicators and transparency/fairness of P4P process	• Idem • Evaluate possibility to move toward health financing based on pre-payment and pooling • Continue evaluating and adjusting measurement and reward mechanisms
	SOCIAL PROTECTION		
Safety Net	• Monitor poverty levels, causes and characteristics and effectiveness of social assistance programs • Improve targeting of housing program and child allowances • Maintain well-targeted programs closely linked to employment programs	• Idem • Idem	• Idem • Idem
Pensions	• Undertake a fiscal analysis to determine financing level compatible with budget resources; set a ceiling to base pension; define coverage of self-employed and informal workers and fix the level of state guarantees • Restructure administration of private pension savings (maintaining defined contribution pillar) and change investment rules to allow for portfolio diversification • Increase the retirement age for women	• Ensure that level of base pension and other guarantees are compatible with budget resources • Increase retirement age of both men and women	• Adjust retirement age in line with increases in life expectancy.

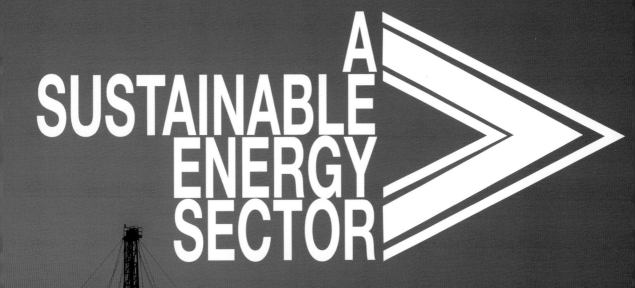

A SUSTAINABLE ENERGY SECTOR

A Sustainable Energy Sector

Chapter
6

Hossein Razavi

Kazakhstan's oil and gas resources have played an instrumental role in fueling the country's impressive economic growth in recent years and the strategic use of this important asset will be critical for the country as it aims to join the top 30 developed countries. The government has done very well in attracting foreign investment into the oil and gas sector and in expanding oil exports and export revenues that have been instrumental in supporting the country's economic growth. It also has accumulated a substantial portion of export revenues in the National Fund that was created in 2000 and serves as an instrument to save financial resources for the future generation and to play a stabilization role against the volatility of international oil prices. Thus the government utilized very effectively the resources of the National Fund in minimizing the impact of the 2008-09 international financial crises on the Kazakhstan's economy.

Going forward, Kazakhstan will need to preserve its long-term oil export potential. This will require: (1) diversification of domestic energy consumption, (2) improving energy efficiency, and (3) sustainability of the oil supply capacity through reserve expansion and/or reserve conservation. If prudently managed, Kazakhstan's oil (and other mineral) resources can support, rather than impede, the rapid transformation of the economy of Kazakhstan by efficiently converting natural capital into highly productive physical and human capital. This will, however, require that Kazakhstan follow the examples of countries like Botswana, Chile, and Norway to avoid the pitfalls of the "resource curse," which has so often stood in the way of successful development of resource-rich developing countries.

In this chapter we will review the current situation in the management of energy resources in order to identify its advantages and disadvantages and present a Vision 2050 for future development of energy resources considering the global trends and best practices. We will then analyze the prospects as well as policy and institutional requirements for the development of green energy (renewable energy and energy efficiency) and finally present recommendations for policies and institutional reforms for consideration in the short, medium, and long term. Aside from energy, Kazakhstan also has substantial reserves, production, and export capacity in non-energy minerals. Box 6.1 summarizes some of the key aspects of the mining sector.

Current Situation in the Energy Sector

Kazakhstan has abundant energy resources, including oil, gas, coal, hydropower, renewable energy, and uranium. Some of these sources of primary energy have been exploited rather well for domestic and/or export purposes. Development of these resources is also intertwined with the energy requirements of the power sector. Table 6.1 contains information on the basic trends in energy production, consumption, and trade.

6

Box 6.1 | The non-energy minerals sector in Kazakhstan

In addition to oil, gas, and coal, Kazakhstan has a variety of other minerals. Kazakhstan's mining industry accounts for approximately 7 percent of the country's GDP. The country's share of global reserves is 18 percent for uranium, 30 percent for chromite, 10 percent for copper, 12 percent for lead, and 13 percent for zinc. In terms of its production capacity, Kazakhstan holds the first place in the world in uranium, third in chromite, seventh in zinc, and eighth in lead. The output of ferrous metals was partly used in the domestic market to support the machinery industry. However, an estimated 80 percent of the output was exported to various destinations, mainly India, China, Japan, Germany, and Australia.

Kazakhstan's uranium resource base is estimated at 900,000 tons, giving the country the second rank in the world after Australia. Kazakhstan's uranium production has grown dramatically (by about ten-fold) in the last 10 years. In the early 2000s, Kazakhstan produced about 2,000 to 3,000 tons of uranium annually, far less than the outputs of the other large producers, Australia and Canada. However, since 2006 the growth in output accelerated reaching 21,000 tons in 2012. This is larger than the combined outputs of Australia and Canada. Going forward, the country's strategic interest is to increase its participation in the downstream value chain. The national uranium company – Kazatomprom – has developed partnerships with leading international firms, such as Areva and Cameco, to transfer and develop Kazakhstan's technological base. The ultimate goal for Kazatomprom is to participate in all elements of the nuclear fuel cycle, either by investing in Kazakhstan or internationally. Kazatomprom's present plans address most areas of the value chain. It is working with Toshiba to construct a processing plant, with RusAtom to build an enrichment plant, with Areva to construct fuel assemblies, with Japanese and Chinese companies to produce pellets, and with Russian companies to build a small scale reactor. There is also a plan (not yet approved) to build a nuclear plant by 2020.

Kazakhstan's chromium reserves are the second largest in the world behind South Africa's. Chromite production reached 3.8 million tons in 2010, ranking Kazakhstan the third after South Africa and India. Although chromite mining has been dominated by the Kazakhstani company ENRC, there has been a strong push by the Russian mining conglomerate Mechel to enter the market through its acquisition of London-based Oriel Resources. Copper mining also offers strong prospects. With some 40 million tons in proven reserves, Kazakhstan is within the top four copper rich nations of the world. However, its profile in the international market was raised in 2010 when it became one of the top 10 producers of copper. Kazakhstan's copper production is dominated by the domestic firm Kazakhmys. However, there is now an interest by some leading international firms such as Rio Tinto to enter the country's market. Kazakhstan is ranked first in terms of zinc and lead reserves. Both zinc and lead production are dominated by major domestic firms Kazzinc and Yuzhpolimetall. Kazzinc is particularly active in employing advanced technologies into the mining sector.

Source: Author.

Oil sector

The oil sector has played a major role in the energy sector and the economy. Until the early 1990s the country's oil production was barely sufficient to meet Kazakhstan's domestic requirements. However, presently domestic consumption accounts for only 13 percent of total production. This dramatic change is due to the rapid expansion of oil production capacity from about 400,000 barrels/day in early 1990s to 1.8 million barrels per day (mb/d) in 2012. Kazakhstan's proven oil reserves are estimated at 30 billion barrels. The bulk of the country's reserves lies in three western Kazakhstan fields: Karachaganak, Tengiz, and Kashagan, with the first two currently producing about half of Kazakhstan's total oil output. Tengiz is located onshore northwestern Kazakhstan and is the world's deepest operating field at 12,000 feet. It is the largest producing oil field in Kazakhstan, with an output of approximately 520,000 bbl/d in 2011. Karachaganak, also onshore northwestern Kazakhstan close to the Russian border, produced 244,000 bbl/d of condensate in 2011, accounting for about 15 percent of total production. Uzen oil field, located in southwestern Kazakhstan in the Mangystau region, produced about 100,000 bbl/d in 2011. The

Table 6.1	Kazakhstan's energy production, consumption, and trade					

	1992	1995	2000	2005	2010
Petroleum					
Production (mb/d)	0.57	0.45	0.77	1.40	1.82
Consumption (mb/d)	0.40	0.27	0.19	0.23	0.21
Net Exports (mb/d)	0.17	0.18	0.58	1.17	1.61
CO_2 Emissions (mln tons)	62.5	40.4	29.4	33.0	34.5
Natural gas					
Production, total (bln cubic meters)	7.3	5.3	8.2	13.5	17.6
Consumption (bln cubic meters)	13.1	10.5	6.8	9.3	8.2
Net Exports (bln cubic meters)	-5.8	-5.2	1.4	4.2	9.4
CO_2 Emissions (consumption and flaring) (mln tons)	39.4	21.3	27.3	26.5	16.8
Coal					
Production (mln short tons)	139.5	93.1	85.4	96.1	122.3
Consumption (mln short tons)	100.1	72.4	49.2	71.4	86.7
Net Exports (mln short tons)	39.4	20.7	36.6	25.2	33.4
CO_2 Emissions (mln tons)	159.0	77.5	76.0	110.0	133.1
Electricity					
Capacity (MW)	18,862	19117	16,306	18,763	18,735
Generation (GWh)	78,557	63,176	48,621	64,168	78,089
Consumption (GWh)	82,879	58,533	44,469	57,092	72,613
Imports (GWh)	28,620	8,000	3,100	3,518	2,914
Exports (GWh)	15,447	2,500	85	3,648	1,757
Distribution losses (GWh)	8,851	10,143	7,167	6,946	6,633
Carbon intensity					
(tons of CO_2 per thousand 2005 USD)					
Kazakhstan	6.2	4.5	3.8	3.0	2.4
US	0.6	0.6	0.5	0.5	0.4
China	3.7	3.1	2.0	2.4	2.2

Source: EIA (2012); ADB (2009); ADB ("Infrastructure Roadmap" 2012); author's analysis.

Mangystau oil field, in the same region, produced 117,000 bbl/d in the same year.

Growth is expected primarily at Kashagan and Tengiz fields. The Kashagan field, believed to be the largest known oil field outside the Middle East and the fifth largest in the world in terms of reserves, is located off the northern shore of the Caspian Sea near the city of Atyrau. Development of the Kashagan field poses technical difficulties: very high-pressure gas, high sulfur content, and environmental problems. Nevertheless, the first phase development is expected to start production in the second half of 2013 with about 100,000 b/d and to reach 450,000 b/d by the end of Phase 1 development (2020). At the same time, there are significant uncertainties over the prospects and timing of the larger second phase that could bring overall production from the field to the 1.5 mb/d mark.

Kazakhstan has been successful in attracting foreign investment into the oil sector. As a result, after a period of stagnation during the first half of the 1990s, oil output started to grow in the late 1990s and has more than doubled over the last 10 years (Figure 6.1). Kazakhstan's liquid oil production was about 1.8 million barrels per day (mb/d) in 2011, of which about 1.6 mb/d was exported to world markets by pipelines to the Black Sea via Russia, by barge and pipeline to the Mediterranean via Azerbaijan and Turkey, by barge and rail to Batumi, Georgia on the Black Sea, and by pipeline to China.

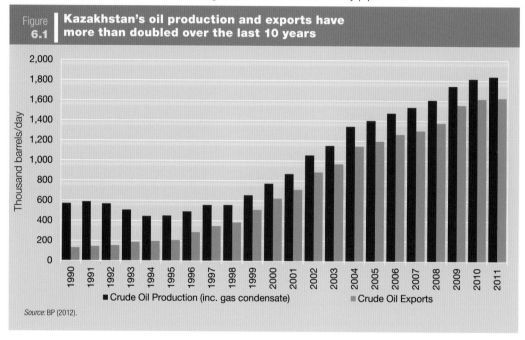

Figure 6.1 Kazakhstan's oil production and exports have more than doubled over the last 10 years

Source: BP (2012).

The rapid increase in oil production in the second half of 1990s became questionable on the account of sufficiency of oil reserves. However, the sharp increase in new discoveries resulted in a five-fold jump in oil reserves estimates, providing clear support for the expansion of oil output (Figure 6.2).

Management of oil revenues

The government was quick to recognize the need for a comprehensive approach to the management of oil revenues. In 2000, it established the Kazakhstan National Fund, which was designed in line with that of the internationally known best practice, i.e., the Norwegian Fund. Kazakhstan's National Fund is not a legal entity but a fund owned by the Ministry of Finance. The guidelines for the operation of the fund

6

are set by a Management Council,[1] while the day-to-day operation is managed by the National Bank of Kazakhstan. Within the National Bank, its Treasury Department manages the fund's portfolio. The overall investment strategy is evaluated and modified once per year.

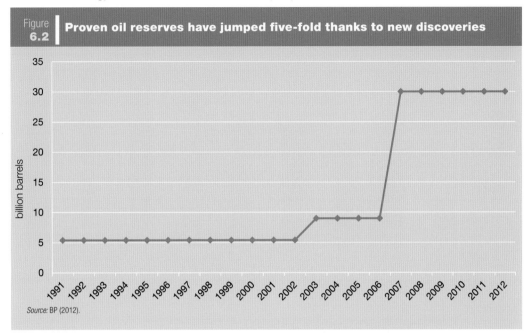

Figure 6.2 Proven oil reserves have jumped five-fold thanks to new discoveries

Source: BP (2012).

The National Fund has two main functions: to provide economic stability and to accumulate savings for future generations. There are two distinct portfolios serving each of these functions: a dollar-denominated stability fund and a dollar-denominated savings fund. The portfolio of the stability fund preserves a high degree of liquidity, with the six-month US T-bill as the benchmark. The portfolio of the savings fund aims at long-term return. It was initially intended to invest 40 percent in global equities and 60 percent in global fixed income. The strategy became much more conservative by 2008 when the portfolio shifted to 20 percent equity and 80 percent fixed income assets. This new strategy paid off during the financial crises when the National Fund lost only 2.5 percent while most other sovereign funds lost large amounts.

The assets of the National Fund have grown steadily from about USD 1.2 billion in 2001 to USD 8 billion in 2005 and to USD 41.6 billion in 2010. Aside from an initial budget transfer to establish the Fund, the inflow into the Fund consists of direct taxes and other oil sector receipts, revenues from privatization, sales of land, and investment income. The inflow has varied as a function of overall economic activity and the world price of oil. Figure 6.3 shows the growth in the value of the National Fund.

---

1. The Council members, appointed by the President of Kazakhstan, are the President, the Prime Minister, the Head of the Presidential Administration, the Chairman of the Senate, the Chairman of the Majilis (the lower house of the national parliament), the Chairman of the National Bank, a Deputy Prime Minister, the Ministers of Finance and Economy, and the Chairman of the Accounting Committee for the Control of the Execution of the National Budget.

6

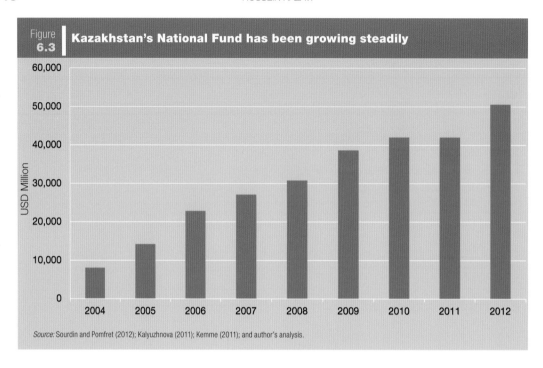

Figure 6.3 **Kazakhstan's National Fund has been growing steadily**

Source: Sourdin and Pomfret (2012); Kalyuzhnova (2011); Kemme (2011); and author's analysis.

Gas sector

Gas reserves are estimated at 85 trillion cubic feet (less than 1 percent of global reserves and less than 8 percent of Turkmenistan's gas reserves). Most of Kazakhstan's natural gas reserves are located in the west of the country, with about 80 percent of total natural gas reserves located in four fields: Karachaganak, Tengiz, Imashevskoye, and Kashagan. Natural gas production is almost entirely associated gas, which makes its availability dependent on the amount and location of oil production. Therefore natural gas production capacity has increased in conjunction with the rapid expansion of oil. At the same time, gas use in power and industry has grown in the recent years. Gas consumption in these sectors is expected to accelerate with the projected availability. Kazakhstan produced 19.3 bcm of natural gas in 2011 (BP 2012) and plans to increase the gas output to 60-80 bcm a year by 2015. Kazakhstan has become a net gas exporter since 2003. The main gas export goes to the Orenburg processing plant in Russia. Export to Russia goes through the Central Asia and the Bukhara-Uralsk pipelines.

Coal

Coal is the largest source of energy in Kazakhstan. The country's coal reserves are estimated at 34.5 billion tons (about 4 percent of global and 20 percent of Russia's reserves). Kazakhstan's coal reserves are mostly of anthracitic and bituminous form. Major coal fields are Bogatyr and Severny. Coal production amounted to 125 million tons in 2011, of which about 70 percent was used domestically in the power, industrial, and household sectors, and about 30 percent was exported to neighboring countries.

A program of transition of coal industry operations to international standards was completed in 2011. The program involved implementation of some 133 national standards that meet ISO requirements. As a result, all coal mining operations are considered compliant with international requirements; this allows the industry to expand the geographical scope of its exports. The flexibility in export may enable Kazakhstan to increase its coal production. However, until the transformation to a green economy is substantially achieved, it is expected that coal will continue to constitute the major share of domestic energy supply, particularly in the power sector.

Power sector

The government of Kazakhstan has recognized that the availability of sustainable power and heat service is essential for economic and social prosperity and human development as well as for attracting private sector investments in the country. The government has therefore a clear policy of securing reliable supply of power through a competitive electricity market. To this end Kazakhstan adopted a new electricity law in 2004 that was aimed at creating a fully competitive electricity market. The subsequent reform of the power sector resulted in the creation of 69 power plants of different forms of ownership. The aggregate capacity of these plants was 19,798 MW in 2012, of which 15,765 MW is considered as available capacity. The fuel mix of power generation in 2012 comprised 74 percent coal, 11 percent natural gas, about 4 percent fuel oil, 10 percent hydropower, and less than 1 percent other renewables.

Electricity demand dropped from 105 TWh in 1990 to about 54 TWh in 1994 but then gradually recovered to reach 88 TWh in 2011. Electricity generation that stood at 87 TWh in 1990 has now recovered to almost the same level, indicating the need for expansion of the domestic generating capacity. It is important to note that Kazakhstan's electricity system is interconnected and operates in parallel with power systems of Russia and Central Asian countries (except for Turkmenistan) and that Kazakhstan has consistently received power from Kyrgyzstan while transmitting some amounts to Russia and Uzbekistan.

The power sector faces significant challenges. Most power plants are old and inefficient and private owners do not have a clear financial incentive to upgrade the facilities. The power transmission and distribution systems are also in need of rapid reinforcement to lower the electricity losses (currently estimated at more than 20 percent). The Draft Concept Decree of Electricity Industry (prepared in 2012) envisages that electricity demand will reach about 145 TWh by 2030, requiring a generation amount of 150 TWh. The Draft Decree foresees an investment requirement of 9.5 trillion KZT (5.5 trillion KZT for generation, 1.4 trillion KZT for transmission, and 2.5 trillion KZT for the distribution network) to deal with the outstanding and projected needs for the reinforcement of power supply facilities. It is further noted that the ambitious target that the government has adopted for development of renewable energy would add significantly to the amount of investment needs.

Development of the power sector is intertwined with that of the heat supply system. Forty of the 69 power plants are combined heat and power units. Rehabilitation of these units should be considered in the short-to-medium term. The efficiency of the centralized heating systems will need to improve significantly through the repair and replacement of heating networks (see Chapter 8).

Renewable energy (RE)

Development of renewable energy resources is one of the priority areas in Kazakhstan's electric power industry and the energy sector as a whole. An important incentive for using RE sources is the fact that Kazakhstan committed itself to reducing its CO_2 emissions by 15 percent by 2020 and by 25 percent by 2050 against the 1992 level. This goal will be difficult to achieve just by reducing the energy intensity of the economy. Thus, the role of RE in reducing greenhouse gas emissions becomes essential. The government is also aware of other benefits of RE development such as transfer of technology, employment creation, etc.

The country's RE potential is substantial. Hydroelectricity accounted for about 10 percent of total generation in 2011. The overall hydro (including small sites) potential is estimated at about 22,000 MW, of which only 10 percent is presently developed. The potential for solar energy is very large with an estimated level of 1,300 kWh to 1,800 kWh of electricity per square meter. Bioenergy can be produced from agricultural residue, particularly considering the fact that Kazakhstan produces annually some 10 to 17 million tons of wheat. Biogas can be also produced from the wastes of agricultural livestock and poultry. However, Kazakhstan's most substantial and promising source of RE is wind power.

The overall potential of wind energy is estimated at more than 900 TWh/year compared with the country's present annual consumption of about 90 TWh. Table 6.2 contains the regional distribution of wind resources. It indicates that areas adjacent to the Caspian Sea, Almaty, Zhambyl, Mangystau and Atyrau in the south, Akmola in the north, and Karagandy in central Kazakhstan have high potentials for wind power development. Table 6.2 indicates the distribution of wind resources.

Table 6.2	Many regions in Kazakhstan have high potential for wind power development		
Region	**Wind speed (m/s)**	**Potential wind capacity (MW)**	**Potential wind energy (GWh)**
Akmola	15.5	108,500	285,100
Karagandy	0.3	2,100	5,500
Almaty	5.3	37,100	9,7500
Zhambyl	1.2	8,400	22,100
Southern Kazakhstan	3.2	22,400	58,900
Northern Kazakhstan	15.2	106,400	279,600
Eastern Kazakhstan	1.2	8,400	22,100
Mangystau	4.8	33,600	88,300
Kyzylorda	3.8	26,600	69,900
Total		**35,3500**	**929,000**

Source: Wind Energy (2013).

The government has recognized the abundant wind power potential and has launched joint programs with UNDP to develop a wind atlas for the country. The Atlas contains the general map of Kazakhstan and eight detailed sites that were investigated in 2006-07. In conjunction with the UNDP effort, the government has prepared a draft program for development of 300 MW wind power capacity by 2015 and 2000 MW capacity by 2024. The investment requirement for the 2000 MW is estimated at USD 2.5 billion.

Organization and regulation of the energy sector

In March 2010, the Ministry of Energy and Mineral Resources was replaced by the Ministry of Oil and Gas, with responsibility for the petroleum industry, and the Ministry for Industry and New Technologies, with responsibility for electricity and mining sectors. The reorganization on the oil and gas side aimed at giving the state sole responsibility for sector regulation, with the national oil and gas company, Kaz-MunaiGas (KMG), dealing primarily with the commercial side of the business. KMG, which was created in 2002 to represent the state's interests in developing Kazakhstan's natural resources, has a number of subsidiaries, including KMG Exploration and Productions (upstream operations), KazMunaiTengiz (offshore oil and gas operations), KazTransOil (oil pipeline operations), and KazTransGas (gas pipeline operations). KMG holds significant equity interest in the main oil and gas fields, including 15 percent in Kashagan, 20 percent in Tengiz, and at least 50 percent in most of the offshore blocks.

Kazakhstan has seen a significant increase in foreign investment in the oil sector. There are a number of international oil companies (most notably Chevron, ExxonMobil, Shell, Total, ConocoPhillips, Eni, CNPC, PetroChina, LUKoil) that are involved in the country's major projects. Kazakhstan's Law on Subsoil Use governs the transfer of rights relating to subsoil use. It was amended in 2005 to give the state the authority to exercise preemption rights on any oil assets put up for sale in the country. The law was amended again in 2007 to allow the state to make retroactive changes to any existing oil contracts or even break the contracts if they are deemed a threat to the country's security. A further amendment in 2010 established strict local content requirements for oil and gas contracts and formally abolished the production-sharing agreements. As a result, joint ventures have now become the most common type of investment. Rather than awarding exploration licenses through an open bidding process, the government now offers the exploration blocks to KMG, which in turn negotiates with potential partners. Based on this new procedure, KMG signed in 2010 exploration agreements with Total and Statoil for two offshore Caspian blocks. State-to-state deals with national oil companies, particularly Russian and Chinese, are also practiced.

The Ministry of Industry and New Technologies is responsible for policy and strategic management of the power sector. The Law on the Power Industry, which was enacted in July 2004 (and amended in December 2012), is aimed at creating a competitive energy market, promoting investment in the modernization of the power industry, and developing renewable energy. This and the Law on Natural Monopolies (which was also amended in December 2004 and in December 2012) determine the role of the government as well as the role of the regulator — the Agency for Regulation of Natural Monopolies (ANMR). Accordingly, the government regulation in the field of electric energy would include technical regulation (reliability, safety, grid code, licensing of market participants, etc.) and economic regulation (tariffs, de-monopolization, and privatization of the market.) Following the de-monopolization objective, the power sector was functionally divided into production, transmission, distribution, and marketing while many of the emerging companies were privatized. Presently about 85 percent of electric power generation is managed by private sector. There are also 18 regional distribution companies. The transmission system is owned and operated by the state-owned company Kazakhstan Electricity Grid Operating Company. The entire power system including all plants and networks represent Kazakhstan Unified Energy System that is united by a common mode of operation and a centralized dispatch. Kazakhstan United Energy System is divided into three sectors: Northern (Akmola, Aktobe, Kostanay, Pavlodar, Karaganda, Northern and Eastern Kazakhstan); Southern (Almaty, Zhambyl, Kyzylorda, Southern Kazakhstan); and Western (Atyrau, Western Kazakhstan, Mangystau).

One of the objectives of the Law on the Power Industry was to modernize the power supply facilities. This objective has not been achieved due to the lack of financial incentives for private owners. A major barrier in this regard is the low price of electricity that is set based on a "cost plus" principle that does not take into account the replacement costs necessary for modernizing the Soviet-era infrastructure. To remedy the situation, a new system of "limit tariffs"[2] was established by the government in 2009 to be maintained for a period of at least seven years (from 2009 until 2015). This system takes account of investment required for reconstruction and upgrade.

The government has prepared follow-up laws and amendments to deal with any shortcomings of the original laws. An important law was passed in 2009 to enable the development of renewable energies. The Law provides the following incentives for renewable energy development: (1) the grid operation companies shall purchase all power and/or heat from renewable energy installations, (2) power and/or heat off-take agreements should cover a period of at least the payback period of the installation as determined in the project's feasibility study, (3) the power off-take price shall be set by the energy producer at its own discretion but will not exceed the value in the feasibility study, (4) the energy producer can enter into delivery agreements with consumers, and energy distribution companies should make their grid available free of charge, and (5) the construction of infrastructure to connect a renewable energy project to the grid should be included in the project development costs.

A further important draft law on energy savings was prepared in 2009. Subsequently various amendments were prepared to improve the effectiveness of the law. The final law on Energy Saving and Increase of Energy Efficiency was signed by the President in January 2012.

A Vision for the Energy Sector

Natural resources and especially the energy sector would play an essential role in enabling Kazakhstan achieve its 2050 vision. Therefore the vision of the energy sector should state the enabling role that the sector can play in the country's development. The President's speech of December 2012 articulates the main ingredients of this vision by requiring the country to manage natural resources and transfer them into sustainable economic growth that would deliver maximum efficiency; develop alternative energy sources, e.g., solar and wind power so that by 2050 these sources would account for at least a half of the country's total energy consumption; make an accelerated transition toward low carbon economy; form partnerships for transfer of technologies; and become the regional magnet for investment.

Based on these requirements and the current conditions of the energy sector, we propose the vision statement for the energy sector shown in Box 6.2.

> **Box 6.2 | Vision 2050 for the Energy Sector**
>
> The energy sector should be developed in a coherent, sustainable, and environment-friendly manner to meet domestic energy needs, support the growth of a diversified national economy, improve the standard of living of the nation's citizens, and enable Kazakhstan to meet international standards expected of an industrial country.
>
> *Source:* Author.

The strategic framework for achieving this vision comprises three main pillars: (1) development of renewable energy, (2) improving energy efficiency, and (3) sustainability of energy resource utilization. The remainder of this chapter is devoted to the review of the strategic aspects of these pillars.

---

2. Within the frameworks of this system, all power plants were classified into 13 price groups considering the type of plant, type of fuel, and distance from fuel source. Each price category has a limit tariff ranging from 3.63 to 7.9 KZT/kWh. Each producer can charge a price up to the ceiling in its category but has the option of applying for an individual tariff if the set tariff is insufficient to meet the investment obligations of the producer.

Setting a Target for Energy Efficiency

Kazakhstan has substantial room for improving its level of energy efficiency. The energy intensity of the country's economy in 2010 was 0.68 tons of oil equivalent (toe) per 1000 dollars of GDP, which is six times the ratio for Western Europe (0.11), almost quadruple that of the US (0.16), and comparable only with Russia (0.69) (Figure 6.4). The main reasons for inefficiency of energy consumption are the use of outdated technologies (particularly in the industry and the power sector) and lack of strong incentives for energy conservation. The thermal efficiency of coal use in the power sector is estimated at less than 20 percent compared with the international average of 34 percent (ADB 2009). Energy audits of selected public buildings (schools, kindergartens, hospitals) indicate that the potential for energy saving in these buildings is as high as 40 to 50 percent (MVV Decon 2010). The industrial sector, which accounts for about 40 percent of total energy consumption and 70 percent of electricity use, is considered to have the highest potential energy savings. The energy audits of four large industrial enterprises (JSC "Aksu Ferroalloy Plant," JSC "Petropavlovsk Heavy Engineering Plant," JSC "Kazzinc," and JSC "Khimpharm") indicate a potential of 15 to 40 percent energy saving potential in the industrial sector.

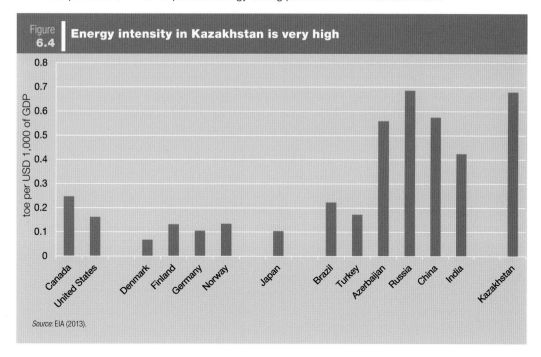

Figure 6.4 **Energy intensity in Kazakhstan is very high**

Source: EIA (2013).

The potential for energy savings is well-recognized by the government. A draft law on energy savings was prepared in 2009. Subsequently, various amendments were prepared to improve the effectiveness of the law. The final law on Energy Saving and Increase of Energy Efficiency was signed by the President in January 2012. At the same time, the Ministry of Industry and New Technologies prepared a comprehensive energy saving plan that consists of 47 measures, including 25 inter-sectoral measures, 5 pilot projects, and 24 measures in the spheres of industry, electricity, heat generation, and housing and utility services. The comprehensive plan will cover all national companies, government agencies, administrations of oblasts and of the cities of Almaty and Astana, and housing and utility service entities. Once implemented, the comprehensive plan will provide for GDP energy intensity reduction of 2.5 percent per annum, with the annual savings amounting to 16 billion kWh of electricity, 11 kilocalories of heat power, 7 million tons of coal, and about KZT 200 billion. The implementation of the plan would require the adoption of 22 identified subordinate regulatory acts that would establish the requirements of energy efficiency for buildings, vehicles, electric motors, energy saving accreditation, energy audits, and energy efficiency expertise, as well as the creation of the State Energy Register (SER). The SER is expected to serve as the main mechanism for measuring and monitoring the achievement of the goals of the comprehensive plan. It will monitor energy use of some 28,000 energy consuming entities including government agencies, major industrial enterprises, and other large consumers.

Implementation of the aforementioned plan will lead to the establishment of a modernized industry. Therefore, the benefits of the plan go beyond energy efficiency and into transfer of advanced technologies and competitiveness of the economy. The design of the plan has been based on substantial analytical work. The overarching law and the system of regulation and administration seem well thought through. However, the next challenge is to enable various components of the plan to secure sustainable and transparent financing, and Kazakhstan is not unique in addressing this challenge. Below we describe how various other countries deal with the same set of issues.

Global perspective in energy efficiency

Energy efficiency (EE) improvement has received significant attention in all OECD countries and a number of developing economies. Globally, energy intensity has declined at the rate of 1.0 percent per annum during 1980 to 2010. Energy efficiency is now on the top of energy policies in almost all countries around the world. The latest estimates (IEA 2012) indicate that worldwide energy intensity is expected to decline at the rate of 1.8 percent per annum during 2010 to 2035. Efficiency improvement will result in a reduction of 70 percent in the projected global energy demand in 2035, compared with the business-as-usual (BAU) scenario. China, the US, the EU, and Japan account for more than half of the energy savings. It is also estimated that energy efficiency improvement would require an additional investment of USD 3.8 trillion during the years from 2010 to 2035. The payback period for most of these investments is rather short (two to eight years), but there are significant implementation barriers that would make the EE programs challenging.

Implementation barriers have been extensively analyzed through various studies (see Singh, Limaye, Henderson, and Shi 2010; World Bank Development of Clean Energy" 2013). The major barriers to the implementation of energy efficiency projects are classified in the following categories:

- low (subsidized) energy prices
- lack of formal institutional framework for developing and implementing energy efficiency strategies, policies, and programs
- emphasis on increasing energy supplies rather than on reducing energy consumption
- lack of confidence in the energy efficiency improvement projects to deliver substantial savings
- lack of "champions" for promoting energy efficiency initiatives
- limited knowledge and comprehension of energy efficiency by consumers
- financing barriers

These barriers are being addressed in the energy policies of most countries through various instruments, including energy efficiency laws, mandatory energy audits, energy intensity reduction targets, codes and standards for buildings, appliances, and vehicles, information and awareness campaigns, and training and certification. Kazakhstan has also addressed the barriers through incorporation in the energy efficiency deliberations and law mentioned earlier.

However, for most countries including Kazakhstan, the financing barriers have proved to be complex, challenging, and persistent. The first important issue in financing is whether energy prices are sufficiently high to create an incentive for EE. But even in countries where prices are sufficiently high, the mobilization of finance for EE projects faces further constraints due to small project size, project development costs, lenders' risk perception, and collateralization mentality of commercial lenders.

A number of financing mechanisms have been designed and implemented to facilitate and enhance financing of EE projects. The two most important mechanisms are: energy efficiency funds and energy service companies (ESCOs).

Energy efficiency funds. This category refers to special purpose funds established by governments, regulators, utilities, and/or donor agencies (such as the World Bank, EBRD, and ADB) for financing energy efficiency projects. An illustration of the structure of energy efficiency funds is provided in Figure 6.5. Examples of these funds can be found in the United States, Korea, Thailand, China, Brazil, and Norway.

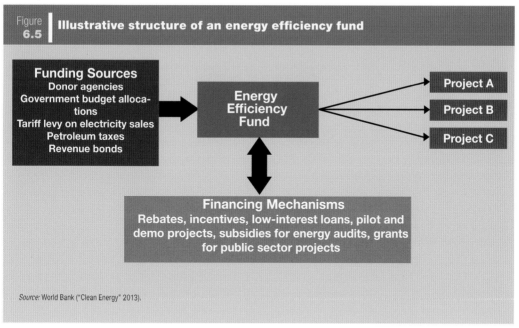

Figure 6.5 **Illustrative structure of an energy efficiency fund**

Source: World Bank ("Clean Energy" 2013).

ESCOs. ESCOs are private entities that:
- offer a range of EE services (design, engineering, construction, commissioning, etc.);
- finance (or facilitate financing of) EE activities. The main principle is that the energy savings will pay for the cost of efficiency improvement. In certain cases ESCO is the financier. It agrees to pay for the capital cost and recover it by keeping part of the savings. In other cases ESCO works with financiers to provide the link and comfort;
- provide sustainability: ESCOs typically provide performance guarantees, based on the level of energy and/or energy cost savings, for the entire project (as opposed to individual equipment guarantees offered by equipment manufacturers or suppliers); and
- take risk. Most of the technical, financial, construction, and performance risks are often borne by the ESCO.

The ESCO model and the performance contracting concept have been successfully applied in the United States, Canada, Western Europe, and China, but the experiences in other countries have been limited. An important barrier is that, at inception, an ESCO company has a limited track record in implementation of EE projects and not much credibility with energy consumers. Another barrier is that at the early stage, ESCOs normally have a small capital base and face difficulty in accessing project funding from commercial financial institutions. Therefore, currently the ESCO model along with performance contracting is feasible where there is a mature banking sector and a viable energy services delivery infrastructure. In countries where these conditions are not met, governments have used a modified version of ESCO in the form of a "public ESCO" that refers to publicly-owned, or partially public-owned, ESCOs. Often this is done when the local ESCO industry is nascent and some public effort is deemed necessary to create the industry.

The concept of a "Super ESCO" has recently evolved as one of the mechanisms for overcoming some of the limitations and barriers hindering the large-scale implementation of energy efficiency projects. The Super ESCO is a special case of a public ESCO. It is established by the government to: (1) function as an ESCO for the public sector market (hospitals, schools, municipalities, government buildings, and other public facilities), (2) support capacity development and project development activities of existing private sector ESCOs, and (3) help in creating new ESCOs. The government capitalizes the Super ESCO with sufficient funds to undertake public sector projects and to leverage commercial financing. A primary function of the Super ESCO is to facilitate access to project financing by developing relationships with local or international financial institutions. With their size and credibility as a public institution, Super ESCOs have the capability to support the growth of a nation's private domestic ESCO business and can have the capacity to provide financing for EE projects (see Limaye and Limaye 2011). Figure 6.6 illustrates the structure of a Super ESCO. While the concept of Super ESCO is still new, a number of countries, e.g., Belgium, China and India, have already implemented the model while many other developing countries are in the process of establishing such a fund (World Bank "Development of Clean Energy" 2013).

Proposed energy efficiency strategy for Kazakhstan

As discussed earlier in this section, Kazakhstan has prepared a comprehensive energy efficiency plan after a long process of analysis and deliberation. The plan is expected to reduce the country's energy intensity by 2.5 percent per annum during 2012 to 2020. We propose two supplements to this plan: an extension of a more ambitious target for energy intensity to 2050 and a financing mechanism that would facilitate the implementation of energy efficiency programs.

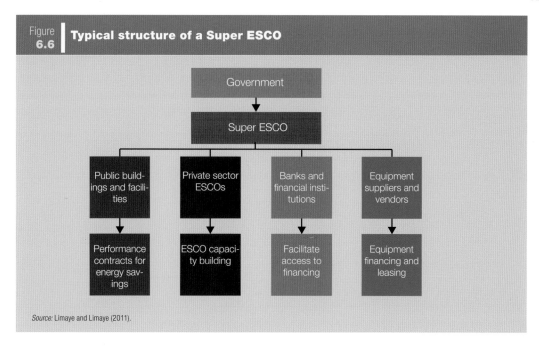

Figure 6.6 | **Typical structure of a Super ESCO**

Source: Limaye and Limaye (2011).

The recommended 2050 target. The present plans indicate that Kazakhstan's energy intensity will decline at the rate of 2.5 percent per annum during 2012-20. The same rate is expected to continue over the next three decades under a business-as-usual scenario. However, a more ambitious target should be adopted if Kazakhstan is to approach the efficiency of comparable advanced countries. Some analysts (see Ziesing 2008) have advocated energy efficiency of Western Europe as a long-term target for Kazakhstan. We believe it is unrealistic and perhaps unreasonable to assume that Kazakhstan can achieve the same level of energy efficiency as Western Europe. In our view, the efficiency trends of the United States and China are more relevant to Kazakhstan because these countries also rely heavily on coal and have comparable geographical and climate conditions. China's central government sets an ambitious target for reducing energy intensity per unit of GDP every five years and enforces it. The projection of China's energy intensity indicates a continuous decline and an eventual convergence to that of the US. We recommend that Kazakhstan also set as a target long-term convergence to the US energy intensity, which can also be interpreted as using the target energy intensity of China as a benchmark.

Figure 6.7 depicts the energy intensity of the United States and China, which are expected to converge rather rapidly. Kazakhstan's energy intensity under the current, BAU scenario is projected to decline from 0.51 in 2020 to 0.24 in 2050. Although this would be an impressive achievement, the energy intensity in 2050 will remain 42 percent above that of China. In order to close this gap, Kazakhstan's energy intensity should decline at a target rate of 3.5 percent per annum during 2020 to 2050.

The recommended financing mechanism. As described earlier, international experience shows that mobilizing finance presents a severe barrier to the implementation of the EE projects. The experience also indicates that in most countries, a combination of financing instruments is used to fit various projects. The financing framework normally entails some public support at the initial stage but aims at long-term sustainably and increasing participation of private sector and commercial financing. Energy efficiency

6

funds are normally used as a method of providing public support, while ESCOs are utilized to rely on private sector finance based on monetizing the achievable savings of energy. As described in these lines, the Super ESCO model is used to indicate public support for a transitional phase, while the mechanism would over time convert to a vehicle that mobilizes commercial finance and relies fully on private sector for project implementation. Considering the international experience and the present conditions and objectives of Kazakhstan, the Super ESCO model seems to be the most suitable financing mechanism for energy efficiency projects.

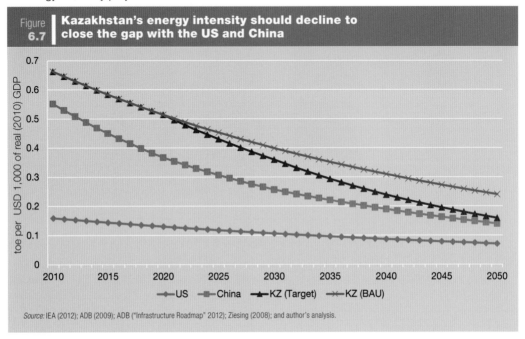

Figure 6.7 | Kazakhstan's energy intensity should decline to close the gap with the US and China

Source: IEA (2012); ADB (2009); ADB ("Infrastructure Roadmap" 2012); Ziesing (2008); and author's analysis.

The Super ESCO should be structured as an independent legal entity initially funded by the government. Its responsibilities should include identification, financing, and implementation of projects, generally using the performance contracting approach. Its immediate priority will be to target energy efficiency projects in the public sector. The efficiency potential in the public sector is generally substantial, but the implementation of energy saving programs is complicated by numerous factors, including a lack of commercial orientation of public agencies, limited incentives to lower energy costs, complex and strict budgeting and procurement procedures, and limited access to budgetary or commercial project financing. The Super ESCO will sign memoranda of understanding with public agencies for conducting the basic ESCO functions including audits, project design, engineering, equipment procurement, financing, construction management, etc. A Super ESCO can also play a major role in the private sector. It has the capacity to develop and implement projects in the private sector. However, it is more desirable to build the capacity of the local private sector ESCOs and create a competitive private market for ESCO services. Therefore an appropriate role for the Super ESCO may be to engage private ESCOs as contractors for parts of the implementation (such as installation, commissioning, and performance monitoring), thereby helping to build their capacity. The Super ESCO may also be in a position to arrange financing for small private

ESCOs to help them implement projects and build their capacity and credentials. Finally, the Super ESCO should assume the responsibility of providing training and capacity building to the private ESCOs, thereby contributing to the development of the energy services delivery infrastructure.

Governance and management of the Super ESCO should be carefully devised to enable a transparent and flexible operation and to ensure that it transitions to a private sector entity in the medium term. The transition to private sector should be embedded in the plan so that one avoids the risk of bureaucratic capture. It is preferable to establish the Super ESCO as an independent corporation that would operate under an appointed board. Its initial shareholding will be 100 percent by the government, but after conducting some initial projects and gaining experience, the Super ESCO may invite domestic or international private sector partners to make equity investments to increase its capital base. At that stage, the ownership and board composition may be suitably altered to reflect a private-sector-led commercial operation.

The government of Kazakhstan has decided to establish an energy efficiency entity (MVV Decon 2010). The terms of reference of this entity and the Super ESCO should be designed together to ensure consistency, synergy, and effectiveness. It is anticipated that the initial set up of Super ESCO would involve some complexity in designing the rules, procedures, etc. However, once established, the Super ESCO will operate as a commercial enterprise and will not impose much complexity on the government.

The size of Super ESCO. The international experience indicates that a well-structured energy efficiency program can close the country's energy efficiency gap by 1.5 percent per annum (Limaye and Limaye 2011). Kazakhstan's energy efficiency gap is estimated at about 35 to 40 percent of total energy consumption (MVV Decon 2010). The potential benefit of reducing this gap at 1.5 percent p.a. would amount to an energy saving of USD 150 million to USD 200 million/year. The international experience also indicates that the benefit-cost ratio of a well-designed energy efficiency program can range from 1.5 to 2.0. Therefore, a rough estimate for Kazakhstan's energy efficiency budget requirement would be in the order of USD 100 million to USD 120 million/year. The size of the Super ESCO should be devised to meet the budget requirements for about five years (World Bank "Development of Clean Energy" 2013) after which the government support should be withdrawn in order to enable the facility to transition to a private sector entity.

Achieving the Renewable Energy Target

The government has in recent years emphasized the need for developing renewable energy (RE). For the medium term, the government has set a target to meet 3 percent of its electricity generation (about 2.5 TWh) from RE by 2020. For the long term, the recent (December 14, 2012) President's speech mentions a goal that Kazakhstan should by 2050 meet 50 percent of its energy requirements from alternative energy resources. This is a very ambitious target that should be studied in the context of the emerging global trends, the country's RE potentials, and the implementation challenges in Kazakhstan.

Global perspective

Development of renewable energy has attracted substantial attention in the last decade mostly in conjunction with the concerns about climate change. Globally renewable energy (RE) comprised 20 percent of electricity generation in 2010. A significant share (16 percent) corresponds to hydropower, which is a traditional source of electricity generation. However, most of the debate and analysis of RE development focus on "new RE" that comprises wind, solar, bioenergy, geothermal, etc. It is this category of RE that is subject to substantial attention, promotion, and investment. In the 2000s, investment in the new RE first experienced significant growth after the signature of the Kyoto Protocol, then a slowdown during the period of financial crisis, and a rebound afterwards. The EU has served as the champion of RE development. Denmark and Germany are considered the pioneers in the development of wind and solar technologies, respectively. United States deployment of RE has been encouraged at the federal and state level, with an explicit policy for RE development reflected in the Clean Energy Standard Act of 2012. This act sets the first nation-wide targets for clean electricity (defined as electricity produced from renewables, nuclear power, and gas-fired generation). In practice, however, China is the country that has made the most sizable progress in deployment of RE. Its 2005 Renewable Energy Law formed the RE framework. In 2009 the government adopted a target to increase the share of non-fossil energy (nuclear and renewables) in the power sector to 15 percent by 2020. The target contains explicit components of 200 GW for wind and 50 GW for solar capacity by 2020.

Globally, there are two noticeable prevailing trends in RE deployment. First, China leads the world in terms of investment expenditure (Figure 6.8). Second, wind dominates all RE sources due to the fact that cost of wind electricity development has now declined to the levels that are low enough to compete with traditional sources of electricity generation (Figure 6.9).

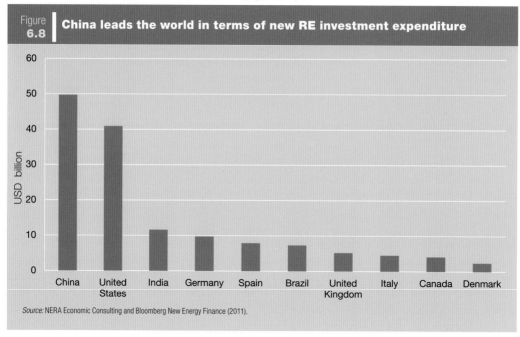

Figure 6.8 China leads the world in terms of new RE investment expenditure

Source: NERA Economic Consulting and Bloomberg New Energy Finance (2011).

Investments in RE development are expected to accelerate during the next three decades. IEA estimates that investment in renewables (including hydropower) would amount to USD 6.4 trillion during the years from 2012 to 2035. The power sector would account for 94 percent of the total with wind (USD 2.1 trillion), hydro (USD 1.5 trillion), solar photovoltaic (USD 1.3 trillion), and the remainder in biofuels. It is fully understood and generally accepted that RE development would need to be subsidized. The global subsidy to RE projects was about USD 80 billion in 2010. The annual subsidy is projected to grow and reach about USD 240 billion in 2035. Although the subsidy is vital for the growth of RE, the general expectation is that these subsidies would decline over the long-run as the costs of newly deployed technologies decline.

6

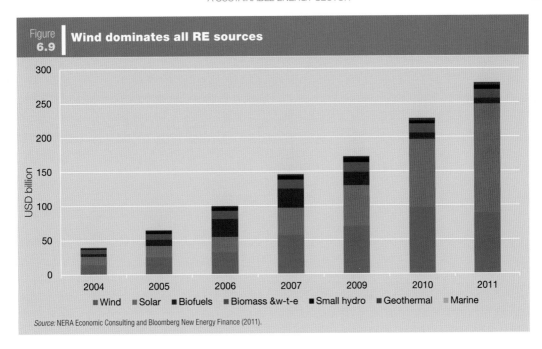

Figure 6.9 **Wind dominates all RE sources**

USD billion

Wind ■ Solar ■ Biofuels ■ Biomass &w-t-e ■ Small hydro ■ Geothermal ■ Marine

Source: NERA Economic Consulting and Bloomberg New Energy Finance (2011).

Kazakhstan's RE development strategy[3]

Kazakhstan has a strong resource base of renewable energy. The government's medium-term plan rightly emphasizes the development of wind resources. The plan contains some small projects in solar and bioenergy and 300 MW of wind power to be developed by 2017. The plan also indicates development of 2000 MW wind power plants by 2024.

The medium-term plan is rather ambitious but is in line with the global practice. Table 6.3 shows the projected growth of RE for the world and a select number of countries. The share of RE in the global electricity generation was 20 percent in 2010. Bioenergy accounted for 2 percent, wind for another 2 percent, and the remaining 16 percent was based on conventional hydropower. The new RE had a small share in all individual countries except for the EU, which had approximately 10 percent contribution from bioenergy, wind, and solar power. However, the projections for growth of new RE indicate substantial growth, with wind playing the dominant role. The main driving force for the growth of wind power is its corresponding investment cost that has declined substantially in the last three decades. The investment cost of solar power is still very high but is forecast to decline in the next 20 years.

Wind power technology is an energy technology that has been successfully improved and widely spread around the world. The cost of wind power depends on site characteristics, but the average cost has declined from more than 20 cents per kilowatt-hour (kWh) in the early 1990s to 6–7 cents per kWh today. There are clear prospects for further cost reductions with larger-scale wind turbine production and advances in technology. R&D efforts are focusing on building larger wind turbines, reducing the material weight of turbine blades, and designing more intelligent rotors to improve reliability. There are also initiatives to improve the availability of wind power through storage facilities or through combinations with other energy resources, such as hybrid systems that use wind and gas or wind and solar.

---

3. Chapter 7 considers the issue of renewable energy further from the green growth perspective.

6

Table 6.3	Targets for the share of renewable energy in total electricity generation

	2010						2030						2050
	Hydro	Bio	Wind	Solar	Other	Total	Hydro	Bio	Wind	Solar	Other	Total	Total
World	16	2	2	0	0	20	15	4	7	3	1	30	44
US	6	2	2	0	0	10	6	5	8	3	1	23	38
Japan	7	2	0	0	0	9	9	4	6	6	2	27	41
EU	11	4	5	1	0	21	11	7	18	6	3	45	55
China	17	0	1	0	0	18	14	3	8	3	0	28	43
Kazakhstan	12	0	0	0	0	12	10	1	9	2	0	22	50

Source: IEA (2012) and author's analysis.

Wind power is also a good example of a case in which technology development has been accompanied with other economic benefits, e.g., employment and market niche. Advances in wind power technology were initiated in Denmark, when the country decided to develop a comparative advantage in this industry. Since then it has spread to many other industrial countries like Germany, Spain, and the United States. Very impressive progress has also taken place in China, India, and Korea. Local firms in these countries have progressed in a span of less than 10 years from no wind turbine manufacturing to the state-of-the-art wind systems. In 2009 China overtook the United States in having the largest wind power capacity. Its success is due to a very ambitious strategy that aims at specific targets, clear incentives, and exceptionally effective method of technology transfer.

Clarifying the RE target. Kazakhstan's program of developing 2,000 MW of wind power capacity by 2024 can be achieved, provided that a proper financing scheme is put in place to facilitate resource mobilization. Afterwards, the wind power capacity development should be further accelerated to enable a 9 percent contribution to total electricity generation by 2030. The total power generating capacity is expected to reach about 35,000 MW by 2030. Wind power would need to reach about 6,000 MW to account for 9 percent of electricity generation.[4] Extending the trends to 2050 we assess that the power generating capacity would need to reach approximately 50,000 MW, of which wind power should amount 20,000 MW in order to maintain the 16 percent share of its contribution to total electricity generation. The share of hydroelectricity is expected to decline somewhat while solar and bioenergy may account for a maximum of 4 to 5 percent of electricity production. Thus, the share of RE in total electricity generation is not likely to exceed 30 percent even if all the promotional facilities are put in place. Therefore, Kazakhstan's target of 50 percent should perhaps be interpreted in a broader sense.

As mentioned earlier, both China and United States have broadened their targets to indicate "clean energy" rather than referring strictly to RE. Kazakhstan could clarify its 2050 target to indicate 50 percent clean energy from RE and gas-based generation in line with the United States definition. This definition

---

4. Electricity generation from a wind turbine varies constantly depending on the wind speed. On average wind farms have a capacity factor of 20 to 40 percent compared with 60 to 80 percent for a thermal plant. A further disadvantage of wind (and solar) energy is that they should be accompanied with proper back up capacity that is often in the form of additional gas turbines.

6

would still encompass a very radical and ambitious shift out of coal-based generation so that the share of coal would drop from 72 percent in 2010 to 48 percent in 2050 (Table 6.4). This share could be dropped even further if the nuclear option is included in the long-term development plan.

Table 6.4	The impact of energy efficiency and renewable energy on energy and electricity supply for Kazakhstan					
	2000	**2010**	**BAU scenario**		**Target scenario**	
			2030	**2050**	**2030**	**2050**
Primary Energy Supply (MTOE)	42.2	68.0	102.3	128.9	84.0	86.8
Electricity Generation (TWh)	51.4	83.7	145.7	200.3	119.8	135.1
Coal (%)	70.3	72.2	69.0	64.0	59.0	48.0
Oil (%)	4.5	4.0	3.0	2.0	3.0	2.0
Natural Gas (%)	10.7	12.7	14.0	17.0	16.0	20.0
Hydropower (%)	14.5	10.6	9.0	7.0	10.0	10.0
Renewables (%)	0.0	0.5	5.0	10.0	12.0	20.0

Source: IEA (2012); ADB (2009); (ADB "Infrastructure Roadmap" 2012); Ziesing (2008); and author's analysis.

Establishing a financing scheme. Achieving the RE targets for 2030 and 2050 would need a proper legal and regulatory framework, vast technical preparation, an attractive business environment, and access to finance. Kazakhstan has done well in developing legal and regulatory requirements. The Renewable Energy Law contains the required provisions to enable RE developers to sell the generated power to the grid. EBRD has continued to support the government in setting a feed-in-tariff to encourage RE investment, and also on the structure of power purchase agreements and technical requirements for the connection of RE plants to the transmission grid. Considering the ongoing assistance from EBRD and UNDP and others, it seems that the regulation and institutional development activities are on the right track to enable RE development. However, the major bottleneck to implementation of the RE projects appears to be financial viability and access to finance. As mentioned before, the global experience indicates that RE development would need substantial subsidy. Kazakhstan's RE Law seems to assume that the subsidy can be provided by the purchasing utility and absorbed into the cost of supply of electricity. This assumption is unrealistic. The subsidy requirement for RE development is very large and not affordable by the purchaser of power. Like many other countries, Kazakhstan would need to establish a transparent mechanism for channeling government subsidy to support RE investments. This is normally done through establishment of a renewable energy fund with a clear organizational and governance arrangement. EBRD prepared in 2012 a project to establish financing instrument — Kazakhstan Renewable Energy Financing Facility (KazREFF). This facility should be considered as a pilot and evaluated as soon as operational. Thereafter, consideration should be given to establishing a much larger fund with a capacity to support multi-billion dollar investments in RE development.

Reducing technical and financial risks. Renewable energy is a new business with substantial uncertainty in its profitability. The technology, construction, and operation of RE plants have a short track record. The resource base is subject to significant variation depending on time and location. These uncertainties add to the project risk that in turn would result in a higher premium in the required electricity tariff. The government can reduce some of these risks by carrying out upstream work. The international experience indicates that money spent on project preparation and upstream development is money well spent as it contributes to a reduction in the technical and business risks. Spending an initial amount of money on project preparation pays off in terms of reduced delivered cost of supply as well as more rapid and competitive reception by the private sector. The government should prepare a clear plan for: the preparation of feasibility studies for wind and solar projects and measurement of wind and solar resources. Wind speeds (at various heights) and solar direct normal insolation should be measured in potential project locations. Actual measurements for a period of at least 12 months are necessary in carrying out the feasibility studies for wind and solar projects.

Sustainability of Oil Resource Utilization

Global perspective

World oil demand is projected by IEA to grow from 87 mb/d in 2011 to 110 mb/d in 2035. The incremental demand is largely due to the growth in consumption in non-OECD countries. The increase in oil supply comes mostly from non-OPEC countries in the form of unconventional supplies such as tight oil, natural gas liquids, shale gas, etc. Although there is substantial potential for expanding supply of unconventional oil, the cost of supply will remain high. As a result, the price of oil will also remain high under various demand-supply scenarios. Figure 6.10 shows the IEA projected oil price scenarios. Under the current policy (a BAU scenario) the oil price would increase to USD 150/bl in real (2011) terms. This projection takes account of current plans for efficiency improvement in the OECD and non-OECD countries. There are, however, two other scenarios under which efficiency gains accelerate due to introduction of new technologies (referred to as New Policy Scenario) and efficiency gains beyond the new technologies in order to meet the climate change benchmarks (referred to as the 450 Scenario). Even under the lowest demand scenario the price of oil will remain above USD 100/bl. In summary, the global perspective indicates that Kazakhstan is likely to be able to export its oil at attractive prices under any demand-supply scenario.[5]

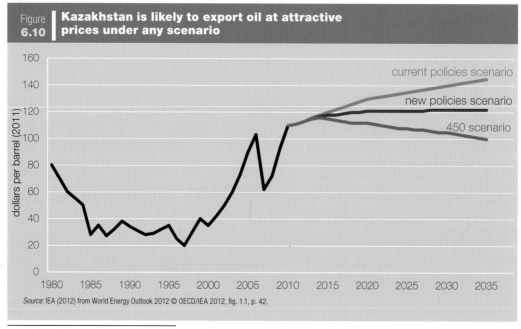

Figure 6.10 | Kazakhstan is likely to export oil at attractive prices under any scenario

Source: IEA (2012) from World Energy Outlook 2012 © OECD/IEA 2012, fig. 1.1, p. 42.

---

5. It is also possible that unforeseen supply shocks affect oil prices (e.g., rapid expansion of shale-based production). Below we consider a case of an unexpected drop in oil prices.

With the historic increase in oil prices in recent decades, the international community and individual countries have put an increasing emphasis on the proper management of government oil revenues. Empirical evidence (Bhattacharyya and Collier 2011; Gupta, Kangur, Papageorgiou, and Wane 2011) shows that the governments of oil exporting countries failed to optimize the use of export revenues in the first oil boom of the 1970s. They channeled most oil export revenues into their domestic economies, resulting in appreciation of their real exchange rates, rapid expansion of imports of goods and services, weakening the non-oil sector, inefficient (and often corrupt) management of the public sector, etc. The collapse of international oil prices in mid-1980s brought to the forefront the need to establish mechanisms and arrangements to protect the economies of oil exporting countries from the impacts of oil price fluctuations. The debate also clarified the distinction between the need for some stabilization tool and inter-generational arrangement. Subsequently most oil exporting countries launched an effort to establish some type of sovereign wealth fund that would help them address the problem of volatility in public spending, control the appreciation of the real exchange rate (in order to reduce the likelihood of Dutch disease), and save financial resources for the future generation. Box 6.2 summarizes the international experience with sovereign oil funds.

Kazakhstan's oil production strategy

Kazakhstan's oil production has tripled since 2000. Accordingly oil exports have increased from 600,000 b/d to 1.6 mb/d while a major part of government's oil revenue has been saved in the National Fund. Both oil production and exports are likely to expand particularly in the next few years as the Kashagan field comes online. The field's recoverable reserves are estimated at 11 billion barrels of oil. The current timetable indicates a start-up in 2013 with the output gradually increasing to 400,000 bl/day by 2020. The oil output of this field is expected to increase to 1.5 mb/d in the second phase (after 2020) for which plans are not clear yet. It is understood that development of Kashagan and other future projects require significant expansion of Kazakhstan's export capacity, and several projects are under consideration for construction of new pipeline systems or expansion of existing transport systems.[6] The overall projection for the liquid oil production indicates a sustained increase to a peak of 3.8 mb/d by 2035. Figure 6.11 shows the IEA forecast for Kazakhstan's oil production.

This projection by IEA indicates the confidence that there is continued interest by foreign investors in Kazakhstan's oil sector. However, the impact of the projected oil production on the remaining reserves sounds a policy alarm. Although it is widely believed that proven oil reserves can be upgraded over time with new discoveries, it is worthwhile to note that many other oil producing countries, e.g., Mexico, Malaysia, and Indonesia, did not experience the discoveries that they were anticipating. A particularly relevant case is Norway (Figure 6.12), which increased its oil production rapidly based on the logic of anticipating more discoveries and monetizing the oil reserves while the price was high. It ended up selling a major part of its oil at USD 20/bl. It exercised firm discipline, saving money in its oil fund. Although Norway is known for promoting the most advanced oil exploration and development technologies and for maintaining a transparent national fund, one could see that, in retrospect, the country would have been better off if it had taken a more conservative path toward resource depletion.

6. Kazakhstan is promoting the Kazakhstan Caspian Transportation System, which includes the construction of an 830-kilometer, 600,000 bbl/d capacity onshore pipeline from Eskene in western Kazakhstan to Kuryk on the Caspian near Aktau, where a new 760,000-bbl/d oil terminal is to be built. Other options include expanded transportation capacity to China. In August 2012, CNPC officials reported that the company is considering building a second crude oil pipeline to source volumes from the Caspian Sea region. There are also proposals for construction of the Trans-Caspian oil pipeline and the Kazakhstan-Turkmenistan-Iran pipeline. These new pipeline systems are mostly needed within a medium- to long-term framework if and when oil production exceeds 2 mb/d.

Box
6.3 **International experience with sovereign oil funds**

Although the first sovereign oil fund, now called the Kuwait Investment Authority, was founded in 1953, most other oil-related funds were established in the 1990s and 2000s. Presently, the largest oil-related sovereign funds include those of the United Arab Emirates — with USD 620 billion in financial assets, Norway — with USD 400 billion, Saudi Arabia — with USD 300 billion, and Kuwait — with about USD 250 billion. The reviews of these as well as many other smaller funds (Qatar, Libya, Brunei, Malaysia, Iran, and Azerbaijan) point out the importance of governance and transparency in the long-term stability and purposefulness of the sovereign oil funds. These issues have been discussed widely at international forums, particularly those organized by the IMF that in 2008 led to formation of the International Working Group of Sovereign Wealth Funds. The Working Group comprises 26 IMF member countries with sovereign wealth funds; it prepared and adopted in 2009 a set of generally accepted principles and practices referred to as the Santiago Principles. These generally accepted principles and practices draw upon the international best practices to provide guidelines for institutional structure, governance, and investment operations of the sovereign wealth funds in order to serve the objectives of the funds and remain consistent with a sound macroeconomic policy framework. The Working Group also decided in April 2009 to establish an International Forum of Sovereign Wealth Funds. The Forum is a voluntary group of Sovereign Wealth Funds that will meet to continue discussion and understanding of the Santiago Principles. The members of the International Working Group include some relevant industrial and developing countries among which many oil producing countries (United States, Norway, Russia, Azerbaijan, Iran, Kuwait, Libya, Qatar, and United Arab Emirates) are active participants. Kazakhstan is neither a member nor an observer of the International Working Group or the International Forum.

There have been some systematic attempts (see Truman 2010) to measure the effectiveness and the transparency of the governance of the sovereign wealth funds. The most frequently referenced system is the scorecard developed by Truman (2008). This scorecard uses 33 criteria that are grouped into indicators that evaluate the structure, governance, transparency, accountability, and behavior of the funds. Truman uses this scorecard to evaluate the sovereign wealth funds of 37 countries. The scores range from 11 to 97. The highest score is for Norway's sovereign fund at 97. The lowest scores (of less than 20) go to the sovereign funds of the United Arab Emirates and Qatar. Kazakhstan's National Fund is ranked somewhere in the middle with a score of 65, while Azerbaijan's State Oil Fund is scored 76. Aside from Truman's scorecard, reference is also made (Kemme 2011) to the Linaburg-Maduell index which focuses on the transparency of the governance of the sovereign wealth funds. The Linaburg-Maduell Index score ranges from 1 to 10. The Norway Fund and the US-Alaska Fund are scored at 10. Azerbaijan's Fund is also scored at 10, Russia at 5, Abu Dhabi at 3, Saudi Arabia at 2, Iran and Venezuela at 1. Kazakhstan is scored at 6.

Source: Author.

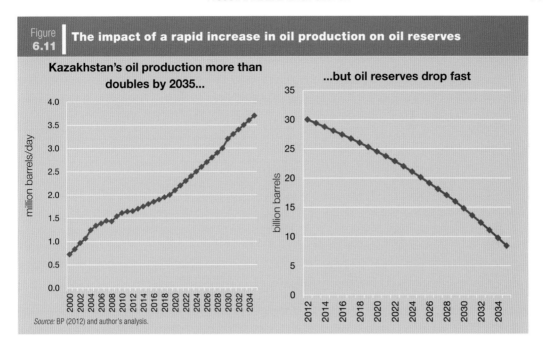

Figure 6.11 | **The impact of a rapid increase in oil production on oil reserves**

Kazakhstan's oil production more than doubles by 2035...

...but oil reserves drop fast

Source: BP (2012) and author's analysis.

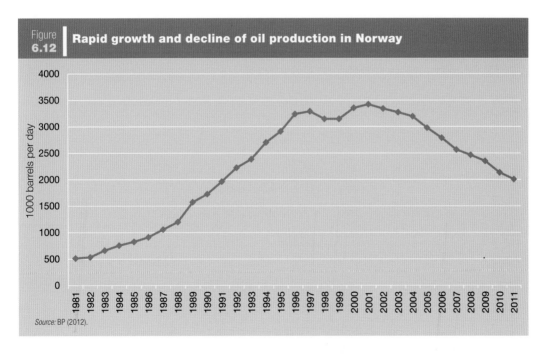

Figure 6.12 | **Rapid growth and decline of oil production in Norway**

Source: BP (2012).

6

Kazakhstan would need to manage the pace of oil depletion. One priority is to ensure that the business environment is conducive to upstream exploration activities that may result in upgrading the oil reserves. However, it is also important to consider scenarios that would slow down oil depletion. The oil production decision should be viewed in the broader context of managing the nation's assets. The value of the associated assets at any point in time would consist of the value of the stock of accumulated capital (mostly physical and social infrastructure), the accumulated financial assets, and the value of the remaining oil reserves in the ground. Policy makers are often tempted to allocate much of oil export revenues to investment in infrastructure hoping to accelerate and sustain economic growth. Empirical research (Gupta et al. 2011) indicates that the productivity of the accumulated capital stock often falls short of what policy makers envision at the time of allocating funds to infrastructure investments.[7] This implies that policy makers should give more weight to accumulating financial assets if these assets have a safer return. Research (Razavi 1983) also shows that in the event that there is substantial uncertainty in the rate of return on financial assets, the policy maker should take a conservative approach toward the extraction of oil resources. It is pointed out that the combination of uncertainty in the policy environment and the irreversibility of oil depletion imply that one should avoid an aggressive oil extraction strategy.

Considering this framework Kazakhstan may want to slow down the expansion of oil extraction until and unless it discovers more oil reserves. Within the 2013-50 time frame one can compare two alternative scenarios. The first scenario is based on the current projections that oil production would reach 3.8 mbd by 2035 after which it has to drop quickly to a level of about 500,000 b/d that would be needed for domestic consumption. The second scenario is based on the assumption that Kazakhstan would cap its oil production at two mb/d in order to ensure a sustainable output through 2050. Figure 6.13 depicts two scenarios for future oil production.

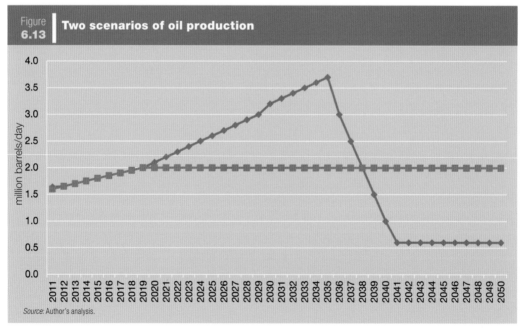

Figure 6.13 | **Two scenarios of oil production**

Source: Author's analysis.

7. The reasons for these shortfalls are likely to be manifold, but key challenges are generally effective project identification and design, sound cost-benefit analysis, competitive and transparent procurement, and disciplined project implementation. Kazakhstan would be well-advised to improve its capacity and deployment in these regards, but until such time as it has reached developed country standards, ensuring high returns in infrastructure investments, it would do well to err on the side of caution in managing its physical and financial energy reserves.

6

The cap of 2 mb/d is a threshold above which the level of oil production would not remain sustainable to 2050. However, this cap can well be adjusted upward as more oil reserves are discovered. It is also pointed out that capping oil production at to two mb/d is not likely to require limiting the expansion of the fields that are under development.[8] Nevertheless, to the extent that this possibility may arise, the two mb/d should be treated flexibly to accommodate short-term deviations from the target.

Management of the National Fund

Kazakhstan's National Fund has been used strategically. The resources from the National Fund were utilized in 2009 to limit the impact of the global financial crisis on the domestic economy. A bailout package of about USD 10 billion was formulated to recapitalize banks, real estate and construction firms (see Chapter 2). Although the bailout package was evidently successful, this type of transactions is considered a "one-time" event. Indeed the Presidential Decree (No. 962, dated April 2, 2010) – that is also referred to as the "New Concept" — provides much more specific guidelines for withdrawal from the National Fund. The Decree clearly points out that the Fund should play a smaller role in the functioning of the economy now that the financial crisis has been resolved. It emphasizes that while the National Fund has two roles — stability and savings — the stability role is reserved for one-time events like the financial crisis, and the Fund is not to become an ongoing source of funding.

Kazakhstan's new guidelines for the National Fund set two explicit targets: Transfer to the budget is limited to USD 8 billion/year, and the level of the National Fund should be increased to at least 30 percent of GDP (or about USD 90 billion) by 2020. These are indeed admirable targets that would prevent inefficient use of the Fund's resources. However, there are a number of questions that need to be examined to provide policy guidance.

First, it is useful to ascertain the impact of the two scenarios of oil production on the accumulation of National Fund assets. The impact of these alternative scenarios on the accumulated National Fund is presented in Figure 6.14. Under the first scenario, the National Fund grows faster in the years prior to 2035 and then starts to decline afterwards. Under the second scenario the National Fund grows continuously. Under both scenarios the government transfers an annual amount of USD 8 billion (in real 2012 dollars) to the development budget. It is well understood that the scenario of oil production should be selected based on a wide range of considerations. However, maintaining the oil production at the level of 2 mb/d seems to be a conservative strategy that would not impose much difficulty on the government budget and saving policy.

Second, it is useful to examine whether the government should provide any flexibility in the limit of USD 8 billion per year transfer to the budget. The question has become more pronounced recently as proposals have been made for additional transfers to fund high priority undertakings. The international experience indicates that allowing flexibility in the fiscal rule often results in a continuous drawdown.[9] At the same time a constant USD 8 billion ceiling may prove to be too rigid to take advantage of exceptional opportunities when they arise. Even under the scenario of capped oil production the accumulation of assets in the National Fund is likely to reach about 40 to 45 percent of GDP by 2020, exceeding

---

8. Under current contracts, a major expansion is foreseen in the Kashagan field with about 100,000 b/d in 2013-14 and 450,000 b/d by 2020. This expansion would partly replace declining outputs in other fields and partly add to total production that is likely to stay around 2 mb/d.
9. Norway is considered as a best practice in maintaining a firm fiscal rule. The rule is based on the justification that the principal assets of the national fund should be kept for future generations while the financial return on these assets can be transferred to the budget. Applying this rule to Kazakhstan's National Fund would limit the annual transfer to a small (USD 2 to USD 3 billion) amount. However, the rule may become applicable after 2020 when National Fund reaches a more substantial scale.

substantially the 30 percent target set by the government. The difference gives an indication of the magnitude of additional transfers that the government may allow. It translates into a margin of about USD 5 to USD 6 million per year that could be considered for funding exceptional high priority undertakings.

Third, it is necessary to provide a sense of the resilience of the National Fund under a possible downturn cycle of international oil prices. We examined a hypothetical scenario in which the price of oil drops by 40 percent in 2015 and stays at this low level for 3 years after which it would return gradually to its previous trend. Under this scenario, the accumulated assets in the National Fund will reach about 25 percent of GDP by 2020, while allowing for the regular transfer to the budget of USD 8 billion/year, plus an exceptional transfer of USD 5 billion/year to stabilize the economy.

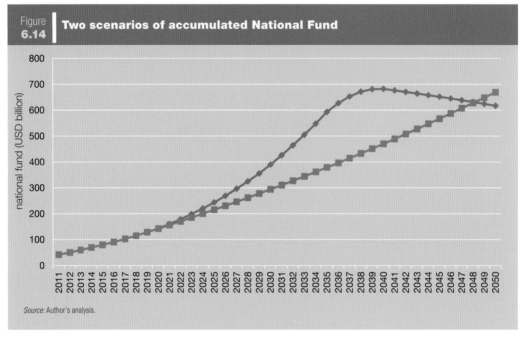

Figure 6.14 Two scenarios of accumulated National Fund

national fund (USD billion)

Source: Author's analysis.

Fourth, it is important to point out that government borrowings should not be planned based on the assets of National Fund. Linking such borrowing to the National Fund jeopardizes the main purposes (avoiding the potential resource curse and saving for the future generations) of the fund.

Finally, it is perhaps useful to mention that our review of management of National Fund indicates that the Fund's portfolio is invested in a professional and transparent manner. The withdrawal will be also considered well-disciplined under the new guidelines. However, we recommend that Kazakhstan accepts the membership in the International Working Group of Sovereign Wealth Funds in order to make known the National Fund as an international best practice. Kazakhstan would also be well-advised to complete the requirements of the Extractive Industries Transparency Initiative (EITI) to achieve full membership[10] since this reflects widely accepted international standards of transparency in this important sector.

---

10. Kazakhstan produces EITI reports that disclose revenues from production of oil, gas, and minerals. It also completed EITI validation process in 2010 with a follow-up in 2011. The EITI required further remedial actions by August 2013 to ensure full compliance.

Conclusions and Recommendations

The recommendations of this chapter relate to the achievement of four targets:

- First, to pursue the vision of green energy, Kazakhstan would need to reduce its energy intensity at the rate of 2.5 to 3.5 percent p.a. in the next four decades. This target will lead to improving Kazakhstan's energy efficiency to the level of China, which will converge to the energy efficiency of the US.

- Second, to achieve the target of 50 percent renewable energy by 2050, Kazakhstan would need to develop some 20,000 MW of wind power in addition to smaller amounts of hydro, solar, and bioenergy. Still, the share of renewable energy in electricity generation is not likely to exceed 30 percent. It is therefore suggested that Kazakhstan's target of 50 percent should be perhaps interpreted in a broader sense to indicate 50 percent clean energy (including RE and gas-based generation).

- Third, Kazakhstan's new guidelines for the National Fund set two explicit targets: Transfer to the budget is limited to USD 8 billion/year, and the level of the National Fund should be increased to 30 percent of GDP by 2020. These are indeed admirable targets that would prevent inefficient use of the Fund's resources. The government's stream of export revenues indicates that these targets are achievable.

- Fourth, current projections of oil production indicate that oil output will reach 3.8 mb/d by 2035. This magnitude of expansion is likely to cause a rapid exhaustion of oil reserves. It is recommended that Kazakhstan caps its oil production at 2 mb/d in order to ensure a sustainable output through 2050. This cap may well be adjusted upwards if new oil reserves are discovered. However, assuming current price projections even under the cap of 2 mb/d the National Fund will increase substantially exceeding 30 percent of GDP by 2020 while allowing transfer of an annual amount of USD 8 billion (in real 2012 dollars) to the development budget.

Achieving these targets would require a set of well-designed, complementary, and consistent strategies for improving energy efficiency, promoting renewable energy, and managing oil revenues.

Energy efficiency

The energy efficiency strategy should:

1. *Establish a long-term target for reducing the country's energy intensity*. Kazakhstan has prepared a comprehensive energy efficiency plan that is expected to reduce its energy intensity by 2.5 percent per annum during 2012 to 2020. This target should be extended to 2050 at a more ambitious rate of 3.5 percent for 2020 to 2050. As indicated in the country's energy efficiency plan, the achievement of the targets for energy efficiency and renewable energy would require continuous adjustment of energy prices to reflect full cost recovery.

2. *Strengthen the institutional set up to enable all stakeholders to work together to implement this ambitious energy efficiency plan*. A high-level decision-making body with political clout is needed to bring all parties together and provide strategic directions to the energy efficiency agenda. Since the same body is missing in the case of renewable energy, we recommend that a Clean Energy Committee be formed to provide strategic directions to the energy efficiency and renewable energy programs. In addition, there is a need for a specialized entity that would function as the country's hub for promoting energy efficiency. It should have the overall strategic responsibility for implementation of energy audits and surveys, enforcing energy efficiency standards and labeling programs, promoting R&D and dissemination of advanced energy technologies, facilitating market

6

penetration and commercialization of high-efficiency equipment, and mobilizing financial support for energy efficiency projects. The recently established Center for Energy Efficiency and Clean Production is mandated with some of these responsibilities. Its mandate should be expanded and clarified to an executive body with authority to carry out a comprehensive EE agenda.

3. *Establish a Super ESCO.* To attract public and private capital to the energy efficiency market, specific financing strategies and mechanisms are needed for the various sectors and stages of energy efficiency development. Considering the international experience and the present conditions and objectives of Kazakhstan, the Super ESCO model seems to be the most suitable financing mechanism for EE projects. The term Super ESCO is used to indicate public support for a transitional phase while the mechanism would over time convert to a vehicle that mobilizes commercial finance and relies fully on the private sector for project implementation. The Super ESCO should be structured as an independent legal entity (a corporation) that is initially funded by the government. Its immediate priority should be to target energy efficiency projects in the public sector. The Super ESCO will sign memoranda of understanding with public agencies for conducting the basic ESCO functions including audits, project design, engineering, equipment procurement, financing, construction management, etc. The Super ESCO will engage private ESCOs as contractors for parts of the implementation (such as installation, commissioning and performance monitoring), thereby helping to build their capacity. The terms of reference of the Super ESCO and the Center for Energy Efficiency should be designed together to ensure consistency, synergy and effectiveness as well as provide for a built-in transition timetable of the Super ESCO to a private entity.

Renewable energy

The renewable energy development strategy should:

1. *Clarify Kazakhstan's vision of 50 percent RE by 2050 and establish targets for each type of RE.* Based on our proposed clarification of the 50 percent target, Kazakhstan should develop by 2050 about 20,000 MW of wind power capacity and 5,000 MW of solar and bioenergy.

2. *Strengthen the present institutional arrangement.* The proposed Clean Energy Committee would provide strategic directions including the targets and incentive framework for the development of renewable energy. In addition the government should consider the establishment of a specialized agency as a vehicle for research and development, technical capacity building, and preparation and implementation of renewable energy projects. It would be perhaps a stretch for the Center for Energy Efficiency and Clean Production to play the required role in the renewable energy area but should be considered as an option.

3. *Establish a financing scheme.* Achieving the RE targets for 2020, 2030, and 2050 would need a proper legal and regulatory framework, vast technical preparation, an attractive business environment, and access to finance. Considering the past and ongoing preparatory work, it seems that the development of legal and regulatory framework is on the right track. However, the major bottleneck to implementation of the RE projects appear to be financial viability and access to finance. Kazakhstan would need to establish a renewable energy fund with a clear organizational and governance arrangement.

4. *Reduce the technical risks*. Renewable energy is a new business with substantial uncertainty in its profitability. The uncertainty adds to the project risk that in turn would result in a higher premium in the required feed-in tariff. The government can reduce some of the risk by carrying out upstream work such as preparation of feasibility studies for renewable energy projects and assessment of wind and solar resources in various locations.

Energy sustainability:

The energy sustainability strategy should:

1. *Ensure that the business environment is conducive to upstream exploration activities that may result in upgrading of oil reserves.* Kazakhstan has a good track record in attracting and managing the interests of foreign investors in the petroleum sector. The incentives should be directed to encouraging new exploration activities and discovery of additional reserves.
2. *Manage the pace of oil depletion.* The government should consider an alternative scenario of oil production that slows down resource depletion. Particularly, the combination of uncertainty in return on financial assets and the irreversibility of oil depletion imply that one should avoid an aggressive oil extraction strategy. The strategy should limit oil production capacity to around 2 mb/d until and unless substantial additional oil reserves are discovered.
3. *To make known the operation of the National Fund as an international best practice.* It is pointed out that the National Fund's portfolio is invested in a professional and transparent manner. However, we recommend that Kazakhstan accepts the membership of the International Working Group of Sovereign Wealth Funds in order to make known the National Fund as an international best practice, while also completing the requirements of the EITI to achieve full membership.

Challenges and time table for implementation

The aforementioned recommendations are expected to face a number of challenges including: (1) ambitious targets for energy intensity and alternative energy, (2) political resistance to a cap on oil production, (3) pressure against a firm fiscal rule for transfers out of the National Fund, (4) the need to manage any subsidies for energy efficiency and renewable energy carefully and (5) the need to prevent bureaucratic and political interests from preventing transition from a Super ESCO to private ESCOs.

The time frame for and sequencing of implementation of these recommendations is as envisaged in Table 6.5.

6

Table 6.5 | **Time frame for implementation of recommended actions**

Short term	Medium term	Long term
• Establish a high level Clean Energy Committee		
Energy Efficiency		
• Design the Super ESCO's terms of reference in conjunction with the terms of reference of the Center for EE and Clean Production • Design the governance and management structure of the Super ESCO • Establish and capitalize the Super ESCO • Select a group of pilot projects from public buildings, commercial buildings, and industrial plants • Carry out energy audits and implement the pilot projects	• Evaluate the results of the pilot program • Establish medium-term targets for reducing energy intensity • Formulate and implement large-scale programs in each category • Evaluate the performance of the Center for EE and Clean Production • Evaluate the performance of the Super ESCO • Promote private ESCOs by contacting out the implementation activities of Super ESCO	• Withdraw government funding of the Super ESCO • Revise the governance structure of Super ESCO to function on a commercial basis • Establish 2050 targets for improving energy intensity • Review private sector incentives for EE improvement • Establish cross-subsidy arrangements that may be needed to promote EE projects
Renewable Energy		
• Establish RE targets for 2030 and 2050 • Establish an RE agency or expand appropriately the scope and authorities of the Center for EE and Clean Production • Prepare a clear plan for measurement of wind and solar resources with immediate installation in identified locations • Carry out feasibility studies for identified wind and solar projects • Implement the identified RE projects using KazREFF and other facilities • Establish a comprehensive solar and wind resource monitoring program for Kazakhstan	• Review and revise RE targets for 2030 and 2050 • Review the performance of KazREFF • Review and adjust the feed-in tariffs based on the international experience • Establish a large RE Fund that would support feed-in tariffs and other types of subsidies • Carry out feasibility studies for the identified RE projects Implement the identified RE projects • Design grid models and develop new technologies to enable rapid and safe integration of renewable energy into the country's network	• Review the performance of the RE Fund • Review and adjust feed-in tariffs based on the international experience • Review and adjust the 2030 and 2050 targets Evaluate the feasibility of withdrawing government subsidies from the development of RE projects • Evaluate the possibility of converting the RE Fund into a public-private partnership (PPP) corporation • Implement the identified RE projects

(contd...)

(Table 6.5 contd...)

Table 6.5	Time frame for implementation of recommended actions		
Short term	**Medium term**	**Long term**
Sustainability of Oil Resources		
• Set a clear ceiling for petroleum production based on the current proven oil reserves • Review the incentive system for upstream petroleum development to ensure strong encouragement for exploration activities and discovery of additional reserves • Accepts the membership of the International Working Group of Sovereign Wealth Funds • Complete the requirements of EITI for full membership	• Evaluate the upstream activities and their contributions to production and proved reserves • Evaluate the reserve/production ratio and the possible need to adjust the ceiling for oil production • Evaluate the accumulation and the governance of the National Fund • Examine the need to adjust the policy regarding withdrawals from the National Fund	

6

A GREEN GROWTH PATH >

A Green Growth Path

Chapter
7

William Y. Brown

We now turn to a broader set of questions about the use and protection of Kazakhstan's natural resources in the interest of a successful, sustainable, "low carbon" growth path, often referred to as representing "green growth." Kazakhstan carries a heavy legacy of environmental damage from Soviet times (Chapter 2) and the next four decades may bring increasingly severe global and regional challenges which will also affect Kazakhstan's potential for economic growth and social welfare, especially as it approaches the middle of the 21st century (Chapter 3). Chapter 6 laid out a promising strategy for one important area of Kazakhstan's natural resource endowment and use, the energy sector, but there are many other dimensions to green growth that we will consider in this chapter.

We first explore what we mean by "green growth," take stock of the current ecological situation in Kazakhstan and the implications of climate change for the country, and then consider the vision of green growth for Kazakhstan 2050. The subsequent sections address specific questions of how to achieve a green growth vision: first, the crosscutting question of what role pricing and regulatory policy can play in environmentally-sound carbon emission management, followed by specific green growth policy initiatives that Kazakhstan may wish to pursue in the coming decades in the areas of alternative energy, industrial waste management, agriculture, and biodiversity. We also briefly survey the role that cities, education and research, and governance play in supporting green growth, all areas covered in other chapters in greater depth. A concluding section summarizes the implications and recommendations.

The Concept of Green Growth

Green growth has been advanced recently as a central objective in development by a multitude of national and international organizations. It was the principal theme of the Rio+20 summit in June 2012, and it was addressed in advance of that meeting by a flurry of reports, articles, and institutional comments (UN "World Economic and Social Survey 2011" 2011; UNEP 2011; OECD "Toward Green Growth" 2011; OECD "Tools" 2011; FAO 2012). The concept warrants evaluation by Kazakhstan in formulating its vision for 2050. There is no accepted definition for the term, but it generally refers to growth of an oconomy that provides for progress on both conventional economic measures such as GDP per capita and on environmental protection. Green growth commentary also generally emphasizes the role of the private sector in providing goods and services whose production and use are environmentally preferable. This chapter interprets green growth consistent with these perspectives. Other treatments go further, and weave into the concept a full plate of objectives for societal well-being.[1] Those additional objectives are important to government planning, but conflating them with green growth begs the question of why they are given a green label rather than simply considered desirable or good.

Several international organizations and private institutions have developed models that generate "scenarios" for the economic and social consequences of investing in green growth. The United Nations Environment Programme (UNEP) used the "Threshold 21 World Model" developed by the Millennium Institute, and estimated that GDP per capita and other measures of global well-being will be significantly increased by investing incrementally 1 or, better, 2 percent of GDP in green growth (UNEP 2011). Figure 7.1 shows UNEP's estimates for the effects of 2 percent GDP investment compared with "business-as-usual" for 2015, 2030, and 2050. The UN Economic and Social Council drew from different models, and concluded that investing 3 percent of GDP is preferable (UN "World Economic and Social Survey 2011" 2011). While models of this type are not conclusive, they broadly confirm that many high-return investments can improve the environment, including investments in drinking water treatment and supply, wastewater management, irrigation, heating, cooling, and transportation vehicles and corridors. Given such scope of opportunities, even a 3 percent GDP investment target may be sub-optimal.

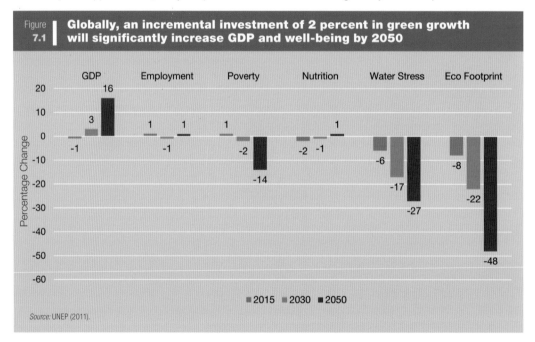

Figure 7.1 | Globally, an incremental investment of 2 percent in green growth will significantly increase GDP and well-being by 2050

Source: UNEP (2011).

The jury is still out on the profitability of private sector investments in green growth, which will vary from case to case, and on the reliability of modeled scenarios for the benefits of green growth investments. The Republic of Kazakhstan is well-advised to be cautious about assuming that commercial markets for environmentally-preferable technologies and practices will form in scale because of short-term government financial incentives. However, a middle road for green growth is supported by experience.

---

1. This was done in the final declaration for the Rio+20 summit (UN Conference on Sustainable Development 2012). Paragraph 58 "affirms" that "green economy policies" should address 16 different items including, for example, to be consistent with international law; respect national sovereignty; involve all relevant stakeholders; enhance the welfare of minorities, women, children, youth, persons with disabilities, and others; promote social inclusion; and contribute to poverty eradication.

Sensible governmental policies for environmental protection, such as those established in many developed nations, will be beneficial to Kazakhstan. These policies typically aim to prevent unacceptable risks to human health and the environment and to promote sustainable use of renewable natural resources. Quantitative cost-benefit assessments of such regulations are done in many developed nations. In the United States, which summarizes results of these studies annually, overall benefits of environmental protection exceed costs significantly. If this path is accepted as green growth, then Kazakhstan will benefit from taking it. Identifying steps for progress on that road begins with a look at the environmental resources at stake — air, water, land, and biodiversity — and how they are faring in Kazakhstan.

Environmental Resources of Kazakhstan[2]

Clean air

Air pollution is monitored by sampling ambient pollutant concentrations and concentrations in discharges[3] and then managing discharges to meet air quality objectives. Pollutants regulated in national regimes commonly include particulate matter less than 10 micrometers (PM_{10}) or 2.5 micrometers ($PM_{2.5}$) in diameter ($PM_{2.5}$ is more dangerous to health), carbon monoxide, sulfur dioxide, ground-level ozone, nitrogen oxides, and lead. The specific limits for these pollutants are set with reference to differing protocols that can be complex. In addition, a large number of hazardous air pollutants, including metals such as mercury and carcinogenic hydrocarbons such as benzene, have been identified and are regulated at the emission source. The risks posed to human health at different concentrations have been assessed for these pollutants, and the established limits are based on risk.

Kazakhstan's size and low population density would appear to suggest that much of the country will have only limited anthropogenic air pollution, including in particular large areas of steppe to the north, desert to the southwest, and high mountains to the east. However, reports indicate many problems in areas of industry and higher population density where pollution is measured. The national state-run Kazhydromet is the main environmental monitoring institution in the country. It operates a network of fixed and mobile measuring stations and laboratories that analyze air, water, and soil for pollution. Kazhydromet is thinly funded, but it is charged with monitoring hundreds of pollutants, some of which have maximum allowable concentrations established under the Kazakhstan Environmental Code. The maximum allowable concentrations reportedly have no consistent foundation in benefit or cost, and where actually measured they are often exceeded several-fold with no realistic, immediate prospects for compliance. Some maximum allowable concentrations are set at levels below those that available technology can detect. Despite the long list of items legally mandated for monitoring, some of the most harmful pollutants in Kazakhstan are not consistently covered.[4] The four pollutants that are in fact regularly monitored in most Kazakhstani cities are total suspended particles, nitrogen dioxide, sulfur dioxide, and carbon monoxide.

---

2. The 2008 Environmental Performance Review of the United Nations Economic Council of Europe (UNECE 2008) provides extensive information on these resources in Kazakhstan and policies concerning them. Unless otherwise noted, specific facts presented in this section on Kazakhstan's environmental resources and management are provided in that review.

3. Carbon dioxide has global impacts and is addressed in the discussion of climate change. This section addresses air pollutants generated in the country that have significant local impact.

4. These include ground-level ozone, small particulate matter, many heavy metals, volatile organic compounds, and persistent organic pollutants. Pollution from high levels of particulate matter $PM_{2.5}$ is a particular concern worldwide. In China, for example, it is a continuing source of protest and unrest.

7

Available data give an overall picture on air pollution in the country, but they do not generally allow identification of activities that violate standards. The primary sources of air pollution are oil and gas production, mining for coal and metals, and emissions from other industries, including metallurgy and chemicals. The high sulfur content in Kazakhstan's oil and gas leads to release of sulfur oxides in production, and sulfur oxides are also released by power plants burning the low-quality coal used for domestic electricity consumption, which are often located near coal mines. Acid precipitation from atmospheric sulfur dioxide is a problem within Kazakhstan and across its borders downwind. Both underground and surface coal mines are "gassy" with methane, and coal mine methane is a significant environmental and safety issue.[5] Operating mines are typically ventilated, but methane recovery for energy use is limited, and the methane that accumulates in abandoned mines presents risk of explosion. Metals and metallurgy operations emit high levels of pollutants including sulfur dioxide, carbon monoxide, nitrogen oxides, hydrocarbons, heavy metals, and particulates including silicon dioxide. Plants are frequently located in cities near where people live and work. Vehicular emission pollution is also an increasing problem in Kazakhstan's cities.

The data available on the Internet from the Agency of Statistics of the Republic of Kazakhstan (2013) are very general and not very useful,[6] but technical reports drawing from the Agency's data indicate serious local air pollution and the need for action. Vitaliy and Karatayev (2011), for example, observe that air pollution in Kazakhstan is a "significant environmental problem," with maximum allowable concentrations often significantly exceeded and the highest levels of pollutants registered in Ridder, Ust-Kamenogorsk, Almaty, Zyryanovsk, Aktau, Atyrau, Shymkent, Taraz, Petropavlovsk, and Temirtau. The report investigates air pollution in the Rudnyi Altay Industrial Area of eastern Kazakhstan in detail, and concludes that it is correlated with the occurrence of malignant tumors there. A recent World Bank team also concluded that air pollution is a significant health problem in Kazakhstan, in its case focusing on harm from particulates (World Bank "Modern Companies" 2012).

Clean and ample water

Kazakhstan has abundant water in some areas and is water-stressed in others, with significant pollution in surface and groundwater near cities and facilities for mining and fossil fuel production. About 44 percent of Kazakhstan's surface water flows into the country from neighboring Kyrgyzstan, Uzbekistan, China, and Russia. Transboundary rivers include the Ural, which is shared with Russia and flows into the Caspian from the north; the Irtysh, which flows from China to Russia through Kazakhstan; the Syr Darya, that rises in the Tian Shan mountains of Kyrgyzstan, and flows through fertile agricultural areas of Uzbekistan before entering Kazakhstan and moving to the Aral Sea; and the Ili River, which flows into Kazakhstan from China and feeds Lake Balkhash. Up to 90 percent of river flow is in the spring, and that feature in conjunction with long cold winters and short hot summers guides patterns of water use. Pipes must be laid deep to avoid freezing in winter, crops are generally limited to one growing season, and high evaporation requires and also challenges irrigation. Demand for water to produce hydroelectricity peaks in the winter, although supply is restricted by freezing, and demand for irrigation water peaks in the summer. As is widely known, the Aral Sea dried up because of diversion of water for irrigation, although it is now partially restored in its northern portion. Less well known is the fact that Lake Balkhash is shrinking because of water overdraft from the lake and diversion of water from the rivers that feed it, especially the Ili river from China (see also Chapter 10).

---

5. Methane emissions also contribute to global warming as a greenhouse gas. Methane has a much shorter life in the atmosphere than CO_2, but it has a much greater warming effect when present.
6. The Agency of Statistics of the Republic of Kazakhstan has more detailed information collected by Kazhydromet, and should present it online.

Kazakhstan's water future is heavily dependent on cooperation with its neighbors and efficient coordination with internal constituencies. China will play a growing role in water availability through its upstream position on the Black Irtysh and the Ili Rivers. Negotiations are ongoing with China on these two rivers, but China is actively increasing irrigated acreage (Agency of Statistics of the Republic of Kazakhstan 2013). Discussions are also ongoing with Russia on allocation of water from the Ural Basin, but a coordinated approach has been elusive. The Ural currently has an annual water deficit of 4.7 km³ and suffers from degraded floodplain vegetation, reduced fish stocks and other biodiversity, and high level of industrial pollution, including hexavalent chromium from its Ilek River tributary (Agency of Statistics of the Republic of Kazakhstan 2013). Kyrgyzstan also draws from the Ili upstream, and both Uzbekistan and Kyrgyzstan use the Syr Darya upstream of Kazakhstan for hydroelectric power and agriculture.

Kazakhstan's surface waters carry significant pollution. This includes metals and hydrocarbons generated by mining, oil and gas, and other industrial facilities; effluent from inadequately treated sewage in urban areas; and runoff from past land contamination such as radioactive substances from the Semipalatinsk nuclear site. Mercury pollution is high in a large area of the Nura River basin, which includes Lake Tengiz and Karagandy, Kazakhstan's fourth largest city. About 56 percent of Kazakhstan's drinking water supply is from groundwater, and some 100 aquifer segments are considered unsuitable for drinking water supply because of contamination (UNECE 2008).

As is the case for air pollution, water use monitoring and protection in Kazakhstan is complicated by the involvement of a multiplicity of national and local authorities, limited staff capacity, and insufficient and poorly located observation stations. The lead national agency has been the Committee for Water Resources, which has been part of the Agriculture Ministry, but was transferred to the Ministry of Environmental Protection on January 16, 2013 by Governmental Decree 466. The Water Resources Committee works with River Basin Organizations established for each of the eight river basins. Other agencies have additional water monitoring programs, but they do not coordinate with each other, and the data are not complementary. While important steps have been taken on both fronts, reportedly to include a new, leading role for the Environment Ministry, internal coordination remains weak.

Clean land

Kazakhstan's vast territory includes substantial non-degraded areas, such as designated natural reserves and likely other areas whose status is not monitored but which are remote from settlements. However the country's climate makes land prone to desertification when disturbed, and about two-thirds of its land area — some 180 million hectares — reportedly has been degraded to some degree because of Soviet era agricultural and water management practices. This is most significant in wheat growing areas in the north, and in southern cotton and rice growing areas. About half of the country's territory is considered at risk of desertification.

Development of Kazakhstan's extensive fossil fuel and mineral reserves presents environmental challenges. Producing and transporting these fossil fuels and other minerals degrades land significantly and causes air and water pollution. Releases from the country's high sulfur ("sour") oil deposits are hazardous to ecosystems and human health. The sulfur is separated and used as an ingredient in other industries, but its supply exceeds demand, and so it must also be managed and stored as waste. Sulfur waste is currently placed in blocks on pads in the open air, and is accumulating in the millions of tons. Waste heaps near mines for non-fuel ores exceed 25 billion tons, and contaminate soil and water. Current uranium mining methods do not produce tailings, but old, radioactive tailing deposits are found at various sites in the country, including a site eight kilometers from the Caspian Sea near Aktau. Nearly 500 Soviet nuclear weapons tests at the Semipalatinsk site in the northeast have left a legacy of massive surface radioactivity.

Biodiversity

Kazakhstan's major natural ecological systems are desert, steppe, mountain, forest, and the Caspian Sea, with the remaining area committed to agriculture and intensive human uses (Convention on Biological Diversity "Kazakhstan" 2013; UNECE 2008; Ministry of Agriculture of Kazakhstan Republic 2007). Desert and steppe amount to about 60 percent of the land area, but mountains provide the greatest biodiversity. Kazakhstan species reported on the website of the Convention on Biological Diversity include 6,000 vascular plants, 5,000 mushrooms, 485 lichens, 2,000 algae, 178 mammals, 489 birds, 12 amphibians, and 104 fish. Obviously, there are also many other species, including insects and other invertebrates.

Kazakhstan has established a network of protected areas covering about 208,000 km^2, or about 7.6 percent of the country (Table 7.1).[7] The kinds of protected areas and the protection they are intended to provide vary. The best represented ecosystems are in the mountains; the steppes are less well represented; and few of the desert and semi-desert areas are protected. The country has promulgated laws and plans to protect endangered wild hoofed animals, sturgeon, and forests, and it is an active party to a range of international agreements for biodiversity conservation. The Agriculture Ministry has been responsible for implementing these laws, but government staff have indicated that the responsibility will be transferred to the Environment Ministry.

Table 7.1	Protected areas cover more than 200,000 km^2 of Kazakhstan	
Category		**Area (km^2)**
Reservations		12,035.7
National Parks		16,531.3
Protection Regimes		56,213.1
Natural Sanctuaries		64.8
Botanical Gardens		4.2
Areas of Outstanding Natural Beauty		113,505.0
Wildlife Reserves		9,401.3
Total		207,755.4

Source: Ministry of Agriculture of Kazakhstan Republic (2007).

With the exception of vertebrate animals, little is known about the status and trends of Kazakhstan's biodiversity outside of protected areas. Furthermore, most reserves do not prescribe complete protection, and monitoring and enforcement of conservation requirements are underfunded and not considered very effective. Many species are endangered, mostly due to habitat destruction and hunting. These species

---

7. The text of Ministry of Agriculture of Kazakhstan Republic (2007) states that total reserves amount to 15 million hectares or 5.4 percent. The percentage used here divides the 208,000 km^2 presented in Table 7.1 by the total national territory of 2,725,000 km^2.

include some 125 vertebrates, 85 insects, 96 other invertebrates, and 287 higher plants. The situation is thought to be critical for many species. Even rare, hoofed animals, which are afforded the most protection, continue to decline from poaching.

The Specter of Climate Change

Green growth requires action to address the full spectrum of local environmental challenges to air, water, land, and biodiversity in Kazakhstan. However, it also requires action on another, overarching, challenge: climate change.

A torrent of research and modeling before and after adoption of the UN Framework Convention on Climate Change in 1992 and the Kyoto Protocol in 1997 has demonstrated that the concentration of atmospheric carbon dioxide is increasing because of human activity, mostly from fossil fuel emissions, and that such activity is causing the Earth's surface temperature to rise. The most definitive, widely participatory and closely-reviewed assessment of this issue has been done by the Intergovernmental Panel on Climate Change (IPCC). The IPCC's latest fourth assessment was completed in 2007 (Core Writing Team, Pachauri, and Reisinger 2007), and its upcoming fifth assessment is expected in 2014. Other international work keeps coming, including a November 2012 World Bank report (Potsdam Institute for Climate Impact Research and Climate Analytics 2012). National governments and institutions are also addressing the issue, and a particularly useful, recent, detailed, technical, peer-reviewed, consensus report was issued in 2011 by the US National Research Council (NRC 2011).

The scientifically non-controversial facts presented in these reports are as follows: gaseous carbon dioxide (CO_2) is a "heat-trapping" molecule (a greenhouse gas), which absorbs and re-emits solar radiation. Its presence with other greenhouse gases warms the Earth's surface, and makes life as we know it possible. Without CO_2 we would be in a deep freeze. However, the concentration of CO_2 in the Earth's lower atmosphere has risen from about 280 parts per million (ppm) before the industrial revolution to 400 ppm in May 2013 — the highest level in at least 800,000 years (Earth Systems Research Laboratory 2013).[8] The concentration is rising about 2 ppm each year, and is expected to continue rising in the next decades. This increase in CO_2 is largely anthropogenic, and very likely accounts for most of Earth's warming over the past 50 years.

The parties to the United Nations Framework Convention on Climate Change and Kyoto Protocol have taken the position that global temperature increase since industrialization began should be limited to 2°C and, if possible, to 1.5°C.[9] Neither number has definitive support as a tipping point, and each is best appreciated as a political line drawn in sand. Unfortunately, the sand has shifted, and there is little question that global temperature will increase by more than 2°C by 2100, possibly as much as 4°C with potentially dramatic global impacts (Box 7.1).

Observations on the effects of climate change for Eastern Europe and Central Asia place Kazakhstan in a mixed or intermediate category among potential winners and losers. One study, reported in Fay, Block, and Ebinger (2010), projects an agricultural yield increase between 11 and 28 percent by 2080, although then notes that these numbers are probably an overstatement. Fay, Block, and Ebinger (2010) also ranks Kazakhstan low among the Eastern European and Central Asian countries in likely experience of greatest climate extremes by 2100.

---

8. Measured at a height of 3,400 meters on Hawaii.
9. Asserted in the Copenhagen Accord of COP 15, Cancun Agreements of COP 16, Durban Platform of COP 17, and COP 18 Doha Statement on Advancing the Durban Platform.

Box
7.1   **Expert views on the global impact of climate change**

In his foreword to Potsdam Institute for Climate Impact Research and Climate Analytics' *Turn Down the Heat* (2012), the Bank's President Jim Yong Kim states that the report "spells out what the world would be like if it warmed by 4°C, which is what scientists are nearly unanimously predicting by the end of the century, without serious policy changes." This may overstate the degree of certainty warranted, but four degrees is in the ballpark. NRC (2011) provides a particularly useful way to look at this, and is generally concordant with the World Bank report. The NRC report concludes that Earth's surface temperature rises in a more or less linear fashion by about 1.75°C for each trillion tons of carbon added to the atmosphere, and it notes that about 0.5 trillion tons of carbon have been added to the atmosphere since 1800, resulting in the current, global temperature increase of about 0.8°C. Extrapolation to 2100 using US Energy Information Administration estimates for business-as-usual future global carbon emissions, multiplied by the NRC temperature increase/emissions ratio, projects a temperature increase of between 3 and 4°C by 2100 (tons are metric tons) (EIA 2013). Core Writing Team, Pachauri, and Reisinger (2007), NRC (2011), Potsdam Institute for Climate Impact Research and Climate Analytics (2012), and many other reports predict that the global effects of climate change will be ecologically and economically adverse, and dramatically so at higher temperature levels. Rising temperature will increase average global precipitation. Both temperature and, especially, precipitation will vary geographically and with greater extremes. Summers will be longer and hotter with less cooling at night. High latitudes will become wetter, and the subtropics drier. Periods of both drought and heavy rains will increase in frequency, as will the frequency and intensity of hurricanes. The oceans will become more acidic from increased dissolved CO_2. Corals, mollusks, and other invertebrates with calcareous exoskeletons will be especially impacted. Much permafrost and perhaps deep sea "clathrates" — reservoirs of frozen molecular complexes holding methane — will melt, and may release substantial methane and accelerate warming.

Much ice considered permanent during human history will melt from glaciers, the Arctic Sea, and perhaps Greenland. Sea levels will continue to rise, estimated at 0.5 to 1 meter globally by 2100, with regional variation. In the millennia ahead, if emissions are not curtailed, sea levels may increase by 1 to 4 meters because of thermal expansion of seawater and glacier and ice cap loss. Sea level will rise even more — an estimated additional 4 to 7.5 meters — if the Greenland ice sheet melts, and much more if the Antarctic sheet shrinks significantly. Rising sea levels may submerge low-lying cities and settlements, especially in Asia.

These changes will be costly for the global economy and welfare. For a limited temperature rise, within 2°C, higher latitudes may see an overall increase in agricultural productivity from longer growing seasons and greater crop growth at night. Winter heating costs at high latitudes should drop with warming. The negative impacts from climate change are much greater, however, especially if mean global temperature rises above 2°C, as nearly every close observer now expects. NRC 2011 estimates some specific effects per degree Celsius of global warming: 5 to 10 percent change in precipitation in a number of regions: 3 to 10 percent increase in heavy rainfall; 5 to 10 percent change in stream flow in many river basins worldwide; 15 percent decrease in the extent of annually averaged sea ice; and 25 percent decrease in the extent of September Arctic sea ice. The report estimates that global agricultural productivity will decrease by 5 to 15 percent for each degree Celsius increase in temperature, with some crops impacted much more than others. In general, "C3" plants such as rice and wheat respond to increased CO_2 levels with faster growth, whereas "C4" plants such as corn, sorghum, and millet do not.

Source: Author.

Reports specific to Kazakhstan are more troubling (UNDP "National Human Development Report" 2008; Esserkepova 2009). The average temperature in Kazakhstan has risen by 1.5°C since 1936 — about twice the global temperature increase since the industrial revolution. The most rapid warming has occurred in winter temperatures, but summers have warmed as well. There is no clear observed trend in total rainfall, but desert, semi-desert, and adjacent areas have become more arid, and glaciers have shrunk. Average national temperature and precipitation are expected to increase in the future. Scenarios based on five principal climate models forecast additional rise in average national temperature by 1.4°C as of 2030, 2.7°C as of 2050, and 4.6°C as of 2085 — substantially more than the expected global increase (UNDP "National Human Development Report" 2008). Average national precipitation is expected to increase from the current level by 2 percent (2030), 4 percent (2050), and 5 percent (2085), but will vary with location and time of year. Water resources are expected to increase in mountain areas but diminish in the plains, and most increased precipitation will be in winter, with little or no increase, and perhaps a decrease, in the summer. The currently "humid" zone of northern Kazakhstan may shift further north, and lead to more drought and adverse impact on grain production. Effects on hoofed animal productivity will be mixed, but will be negative overall. Coastal flooding is a possible concern only for the Caspian Sea, whose level has varied dramatically in history. The Caspian might be expected to rise to higher levels in the next decades because of expected increased volume in the Volga River, which provides 70 to 80 percent of the Caspian's surface flow. However, climate models instead project a 6 meter decrease by 2100 because of increased surface evaporation (Fay, Block, and Ebinger 2010).

As the reports by the World Bank, the UN and OECD vigorously advance, it is possible to change policies and practices to mitigate climate change, and this chapter addresses steps to that end in the context of green growth. However, the widespread implementation of new policies, better alternatives, or breakthrough technologies is not a good bet for the next several decades — perhaps not for the remainder of this century — and Kazakhstan should not count on them. It also should be noted that Kazakhstan cannot significantly affect the impacts of climate change by reducing its own greenhouse gas emissions. The nation has very high per capita energy use and carbon emissions, but its emissions amount only to 0.6 percent of the global total (see Chapter 6; EIA 2013). Nevertheless, Kazakhstan has taken steps consistent with its responsibility among nations to help protect the global commons from carbon emissions. It is a party to the United Nations Framework Convention on Climate Change and the Kyoto Protocol, and it is implementing a pilot initiative for carbon cap-and-trade. The government also is aware that failure to reduce carbon emissions may have negative consequences in international commerce and financial assistance, and it has ambitions, not yet bearing fruit, to earn carbon credits by reducing emissions. The best way to address carbon mitigation is in the context of energy production and efficiency, and environmental quality generally. Kazakhstan can pursue avenues of green growth that respond to the nation's local environmental needs, mitigate emissions, adapt to changing climate, and also defuse potential public unrest of the kind that air pollution is causing in China. A combination of regulatory and non-regulatory initiatives is needed, and establishing a sound program for the former is a good first order of business.

A Vision for Green Growth

Against this background and the general vision for Kazakhstan 2050 presented in Chapter 4 we propose a vision statement for green growth in Kazakhstan through the middle of the 21st century (Box 7.2). The subsequent sections will explore how Kazakhstan can aim to achieve this vision through prompt and sustained action in a number of key areas.

> Box
> 7.2 | **Vision 2050 for Green Growth**
>
> In 2050, the people of Kazakhstan will enjoy not only a country whose prosperity places it among the top 30
> developed countries of the world, but also a country with clean water and land, rich in biodiversity, and using
> its resources sustainably. Increasing summer droughts from climate change will not have undermined human
> well-being. Moreover, Kazakhstan will be seen to be a responsible global citizen of the world, by contributing
> its share to the protection of the global environment. The nation's citizens will understand and support the
> government and private initiatives that led to these results.
>
> *Source:* Author.

Pricing and Regulation for Green Growth

Environmental quality in "commons" can be degraded by pollution or overuse of shared resources — such as atmosphere, fish in the sea, groundwater, and non-renewable energy resources — when costs are not borne by those causing them. This is the underlying principle for most environmental laws of developed nations. These laws have addressed national environmental concerns through rules and regulations with reasonable levels of success, except for climate change. Such rules can work by changing prices (with taxes or subsidies) to ensure producers and consumers face the true costs of their actions, or by setting standards of behavior through regulation. Perhaps the most significant general criticism of mainstream developed nation environmental laws is that they were for the most part established through political processes which did not consider costs and benefits of standards imposed with any rigor, and for the most part they do not include mechanisms specifically promoting economic efficiency, such as emission taxes or trading mechanisms. However, environmental laws and regulations have reduced and cleaned up much pollution, prevented degradation of many sensitive ecosystems, and are widely publicly accepted. Furthermore, they increasingly incorporate cost-benefit review and mechanisms for efficiency.

In this section, we first address a prime example of green pricing and regulation, namely the pricing and regulation of carbon content. Other environmental areas also raise pricing and regulatory issues, especially the pricing of water for residential, industrial, and agricultural use, and the pricing of pollutants (where the "polluter pays" principle is most widely recommended by experts). However, a detailed exposition of these issues is beyond the scope of this chapter. In any case, in many areas of environmental policy, regulatory intervention will be necessary. We next consider the regulatory process, addressing how environmental regulation can best be implemented to assure the regulatory benefits outweigh its costs.

Green pricing and regulation: The case of the carbon price — Tax, cap-and-trade or mandates?

Kazakhstan's economy is fossil fuel-intensive, with high energy use per capita and per GDP in comparison with the OECD, and roughly the same profile as Russia (see Chapter 6). From an environmental perspective, improving the efficiency of fossil fuel energy consumption and production is a key priority, and carbon pricing is an attractive vehicle for that objective.

An important step for Kazakhstan in managing carbon prices is eliminating subsidies for fossil fuels and implement a carbon tax. That will provide an incentive to reduce fossil fuel consumption and to increase alternative energy and industrial technologies generating less carbon and other pollution. The various subsidies in place for fossil fuels could be replaced with support through other spending vehicles to achieve the social and economic objectives for which the subsidies are intended.

Carbon taxes are efficient and effective instruments for reducing carbon emissions. This view was recently convincingly argued in de Mooji, Keen, and Parry (2012), whose main lessons are listed in Box 7.3. Carbon taxes or prices are best set "upstream" on all fossil fuels in proportion to their carbon content, at the point where they first enter the economy (e.g., coal mines, petroleum refineries, fuel importers), with refunds for any carbon capture technologies installed at industrial facilities. This upstream, fuel content-based pricing, in combination with removal of fossil fuel subsidies, sends a price signal for reduced emissions and low-carbon innovation to all users. Downstream pricing is less comprehensive, harder to monitor, and more vulnerable to arbitrary manipulation.[10]

Box 7.3 | IMF lessons on climate fiscal policy

- Comprehensive carbon pricing policies can effectively reduce emissions and at least cost.
- Design details for carbon pricing are important.
- Studies suggest that a reasonable startling level for emission prices in large emitting countries would be about USD 20 per ton of CO_2 or more by 2020.
- National payments for forest carbon sequestration are promising if carbon can be measured.
- Small-emitting developing economies should focus first on energy pricing reforms that are in their own interest.
- International aviation and maritime charges are a promising source of climate finance, although there are other options.

Source: de Mooji, Keen, and Parry (2012).

An alternative to a carbon taxes is the cap-and-trade system, which limits emissions by regulation, but allows trading of unused permits. However, cap-and-trade systems are undermined if free emission allowances are granted, they require provisions to limit price volatility, and they are "not appropriate for countries lacking institutions to support credit trading" (de Mooji, Keen, and Parry 2012). Indeed, some policy experts are less reserved than de Mooji, Keen, and Parry (2012) about the advantages of a carbon tax over cap-and-trade systems. For example, the Carbon Tax Center argues that the carbon tax results in more predictable of energy prices, and is more transparent, easier to implement, less subject to arbitrary and corrupt treatment, and applicable to many sectors. Moreover, carbon taxes can be made to be revenue neutral by lowering other taxes on business or people (Carbon Tax Center 2013). This does not mean that carbon taxes are simple to implement. Careful planning and transparent implementation are needed, as the experience in countries using this scheme has shown. (Flannery, Beale, and Hueston 2012; de Mooji, Keen, and Parry 2012) But with the lessons learned it appears that carbon taxes can be more readily implemented than cap-and-trade measures.

Regulation and mandates are less effective than carbon taxes or cap-and-trade, although they can be reasonable alternatives if carbon pricing is not initially politically possible. One potentially effective instrument is "feebates" (de Mooji, Keen, and Parry 2012). A feebate provides a fee or rebate for items such as new vehicles or power generators based on whether they produce more or less carbon emissions than a set "pivot point" level. Alternatively, some countries mandate energy efficiency standards by national

---

10. However, in the absence of an upstream carbon tax, downstream taxation of energy use can be appropriate. For example, taxing gasoline at substantial rates (as done in Europe) provides incentives for reduced automobile use and for using more energy efficient cars. The revenues from this tax can be earmarked for funding road infrastructure and subsidizing public transport (see Chapter 8).

laws, such as the CAFE for motor vehicles in the United States and similar standards in the EU and New Zealand, whose effect is to increase gas mileage (UN "World Economic and Social Survey" 2011). Yet another approach is to provide guidance and incentives to domestic producers and users of energy using end-use products, especially machinery and appliances, as under the Japanese "Top Runner" program (Agency for Natural Resources and Energy 2010; Kimura 2010). The concept is to identify the most energy efficient commercial offering for a specific product (e.g., refrigerators), and establish that level of efficiency as the target for all manufacturers of the product. Mandates for achieving specific percentage minimums for renewable energy — such as wind, solar, or hydroelectric energy — are the least effective approach to emission reduction.

Kazakhstan has developed a one-year cap-and-trade program whose implementation was originally planned for 2013 but has been deferred to 2014. However, it did not auction allowances, and the program does not include provisions to limit price volatility. Furthermore, well-understood problems with corruption argue against more complicated cap-and-trade systems. The cumulative worldwide experience in our view supports a reconsideration of the current program with a view toward a possible replacement by a carbon tax.

At what level should Kazakhstan set its carbon tax? Studies cited in de Mooji, Keen, and Parry (2012) suggest that a reasonable starting level for emission prices in large emitting countries would be about USD 20 per ton of CO_2 by 2020. Furthermore, a carbon tax at the USD 20 per ton level would provide substantial new revenues — globally in the neighborhood of USD 250 billion annually from developed countries, which could be combined with USD 40 to USD 60 billion from subsidy reform. We suggest that Kazakhstan move forward with planning for an initial carbon tax at the USD 20 per ton of CO_2 level, but assess before implementation whether differences between it and the large emitting countries reviewed by the IMF indicate that a different level or phase in strategy would be appropriate. The revenue from carbon taxes and subsidy reform would be available for any social or economic policies, including at least initial support for people and enterprises currently dependent on cheap fossil fuels. Alternatively, carbon taxes can be kept revenue neutral by lowering other taxes in the economy. As de Mooji, Keen, and Parry (2012) notes, distributional concerns about scaling back fossil fuel subsidies or adding tax are "better addressed through more targeted policies (e.g., safety nets, investments in primary education), rather than holding down energy prices (which benefits everyone, and often the rich more than the poor)."[11]

Regulatory policy

Kazakhstan has promulgated multiple, detailed requirements concerning the environment, including codes on water, land, forests, and the environment generally. Even the Constitution of the Republic of Kazakhstan includes provisions addressing the environment and natural resources in Articles 6.3, 31, 38, and 61. These requirements are very specific in process and technology, and include elements of policies in wide use internationally. However, they are generally seen as overly prescriptive, punitive in application, and as providing enforcing official discretion that can easily be turned to graft (see Chapters 2 and 11). Also, the requirements promulgated are frequently ineffective in their objective to protecting the environment. Kazakhstan needs a more effective regulatory program that will achieve objectives for clean air, water, and land, and for conservation of water and natural ecosystems.

---

11. Several authors have noted that carbon taxes are a good way to raise revenue in general (Morris 2013; McKibbin et al. 2012).

The question for Kazakhstan is therefore how it should regulate specific activities that significantly impact the environment within the country. The OECD provided excellent guidance for coherent, transparent, participatory, fair and effective regulatory policy practice in the Recommendation of the Council on Regulatory Policy and Governance, adopted March 22, 2012 (OECD "Recommendation" 2012), which also applies to the case of environmental regulation. Implementing the OECD regulatory policies would help condense, clarify, and improve the purposes and operations of regulations now in place. The OECD policies would make environmental regulations more welcoming to investors who are prepared to comply with the law, and will thus help advance green growth.

One particularly important policy in the OECD recommendation (Principle 5) is to regulate only when the benefit of regulation is greater than the cost, and to maximize net benefit. A level of pollution is not acceptable if regulating it to a lower level will provide greater net benefits. The United States has applied this policy, through initial work begun during President Ronald Reagan's administration and by executive order of President Clinton. Most of the significant US regulations addressed have been environmental, and most of them concern air pollution. The White House reports to Congress annually on benefits and costs of major regulations issued, and overall the benefits have significantly exceeded costs, with the greatest impact from environmental regulation (Office of Management and Budget 2012). Determining net benefit requires effort, but it will justify regulatory actions taken and prove their value.

After thorough review of the international experience, the government should consider issuing a decree requiring that all existing and new laws be reviewed and, as needed, revised to meet principles drawn from the OECD recommendation, including in particular the net benefit principle and the requirement of Principle 9 that regulations be effective in accomplishing their objectives, which is not the case now.[12]

Beyond pricing and regulation

Sound pricing and regulatory policy is necessary, but it is only part of the passage to green growth. Indeed, most commentary on green growth does not address pricing and regulatory policy. Instead, it is premised on the belief that investment in a range of environmentally preferable alternatives to the status quo will also provide economic benefits such as increased GDP for a nation or corporate profits. That perspective is popular because everyone appears to win: government, business, and the environment. This chapter has emphasized the need for a sound regulatory foundation to protect the environment, because market externalities for pollution exist in Kazakhstan as they do elsewhere, and because Kazakhstan's approach to environmental regulation has been ineffective. No one wins under the current system, except the polluters.

There are, however, many opportunities for green growth beyond pricing and regulation in Kazakhstan. Opportunities exist in areas such as diversification of energy sources; industrial waste management; agriculture; biodiversity; and, finally, green cities, green education and research, and green governance. Sensible steps forward on these fronts can improve the environment, address climate change, and benefit the people of Kazakhstan overall. These are the topics are covered in the remainder of this chapter.

Alternative Sources of Energy

Kazakhstan produces most domestically consumed electricity by burning dirty coal, which not only generates high carbon emissions, but is a significant source of air and water pollution harmful to human health and the environment. Increased use of natural gas in lieu of coal would be a big step forward for

---

12. These principles are consistent with President Nazarbayev's December 2012 instruction to ban permits and licenses that have "no direct influence on the security of Kazakhstan."

Kazakhstan's environment, and will contribute significantly to achieving President Nazarbayev's target of 50 percent alternative energy for the power sector by 2050.[13] The country can draw from its enormous conventional gas reserves for supply, estimated to be some 2 trillion m^3, and it may find additional non-conventional "tight" gas accessible through "fracking" technology. Kazakhstan is also, sensibly, interested in whether to produce "syngas" through gasification of underground or surface coal. Coal gasification has a nearly two century history from when first used for city lights. Interest in underground coal gasification has resurged recently with new projects, including those in China, India, South Africa, and Australia (World Coal Association 2013). Underground coal gasification is especially suited for coal veins that are lower grade or difficult to mine, and recent improvements in drilling technology make it more attractive. Underground coal gasification is potentially an important untapped energy source for Kazakhstan, although the technology's long history of pilots without large-scale success suggests smaller scale efforts and review before more is considered. Natural gas, conventional or fracked, is currently cheaper.

Whether gas is "natural" or manufactured, newer combined cycle gas turbines are more efficient and environmentally less damaging than the old coal plants now used in Kazakhstan, especially once the health and other environmental benefits secured by not digging up and burning coal are considered. So long as human health and longevity is valued in Kazakhstan at levels endorsed by more developed nations, there is little doubt that reducing coal burning pollution will produce net benefit. One option is to require existing plants to retrofit with good air pollution control technology, and for new plants to come with it. However, fixing up the old coal-fired plants that predominate in Kazakhstan would be expensive and would not significantly reduce carbon emissions. A better option may be to rebuild or replace them to burn natural gas.

Beyond gas, there are renewable, non-fossil sources of energy, which have the virtue of not running out in the future or potentially becoming exorbitantly expensive to produce when supplies dwindle. Kazakhstan has considerable potential for wind, hydroelectric, solar, and even biofuel energy (NERA Economic Consulting and Bloomberg New Energy Finance 2011). The government should explore investments in these areas, with careful assessment of the costs and benefits, sustainability, and eventual commercial viability of particular projects before any public funds are invested. Global experience shows that these renewable energy resources are valuable assets, but they are not likely to scale-up to significant replacement of fossil fuels by 2030, or even by 2050 (Brown 2012). Experience also shows that it is easy to expend huge resources with limited benefit in this area, so Kazakhstan will want to proceed with caution.[14]

Despite perennial, perhaps never-ending controversy, nuclear energy has an important place in the global energy future, and it is entitled to contend for the green label. Environmentalists are understandably ambivalent about nuclear energy as an alternative to fossil fuel energy. Reactor accidents are a risk, and waste disposal an issue, but newer reactors present less risk than older designs, and existing nuclear power plants are significantly less dangerous to human health than burning coal per unit of energy delivered (IEA 2002). Nuclear waste disposal concerns could be addressed substantially by consolidating material in large national or regional disposal sites at geologically appropriate locations with the best provisions for environmental safety and material security. Kazakhstan has no nuclear power plants currently, and developing plants could augment natural gas and renewable energy to achieve President Nazarbayev's goal of 50 percent alternative energy by 2050. The government has decided to move forward with one plant, most likely to be sited in Aktau, but it will take more to bring scale.

13. The Environment Ministry has indicated that "alternative energy" includes both natural gas and nuclear power. See also Chapter 6.
14. See Chapter 6 for a discussion of renewable energy targets.

Green Management of Industrial Waste

Like any other country, Kazakhstan has significant challenges in safely disposing of its industrial and residential waste. The latter issue is addressed in Chapter 8 as part of the need to provide for effective urban services, but this leaves the important problem of industrial wastes. In his December 14, 2012 address, President Nazarbayev instructed that "all extracting enterprises must introduce only ecologically harmless production techniques." This is a powerful vision. Mining and metallurgy dominate environmental concerns for extractive enterprises, in combination with fossil fuel production, and impacts on air, water, and land can be extreme in the vicinity of facilities, some in densely populated areas. Accomplishing this vision will require process improvement, effective regulation of ongoing waste generation, and remediation of past contamination, which is serious in view of the environmental legacy of the Soviet Union.

In conjunction with pollution control and cleanup, Kazakhstan may wish to explore the option of developing a capacity for industrial waste management that goes beyond purely national needs, but also allows for treatment for imported waste. The market for global waste management services is large. Proprietary information and differing statistical methods make precise estimates difficult, but one public estimate from August 2012 predicts that the global market for waste management and remediation services will grow about 4.7 percent annually over the next five years and will reach approximately USD 263.4 billion in 2017 (PRWeb 2012). Another study from 2011 put the European industrial waste management market at USD 75 billion annually, with demand for recycling and recovery services driving growth (Frost and Sullivan 2011).

The option for Kazakhstan to offer nuclear waste management services internationally is sensitive and controversial, but the case can be made. Some 50 nations have high-level nuclear waste, most as spent fuel from reactors.[15] Across the board, these countries are struggling to find places for permanent storage. Most spent nuclear reactor fuel is now "temporarily" stored at the power plants where it was used. National governments, including the United States, France, and Germany, are engaged in public debates, so far unresolved, about where to store waste within their boundaries. Finland has started digging a site for its waste at Onkalo. But overall, the problem is in search of a solution, and there is significant international interest in identifying sites to which nuclear waste can be exported and safely kept.

There are various international initiatives (including the Association for Regional and International Underground Storage and the International Federation for Nuclear Energy Cooperation), which are exploring modalities for international cooperation on nuclear waste disposal. A particularly interesting aspect of the International Federation for Nuclear Energy Cooperation's work for Kazakhstan concerns interest in "fuel leasing." Currently, when a utility buys uranium from a mining company in another country, the importing country is usually responsible for used fuel. However various proposals have been made for fuel leasing, where the supplier takes back used fuel for reprocessing or disposal.[16] Kazakhstan could consider fuel leasing and take back of the uranium it supplies. The country has a big stake in uranium, with 15 percent of global reserves and current world leadership in production. Providing for spent fuel return would strengthen its competitive position with buyers that have limited, poor disposal options. Furthermore, the waste management services provided would generate significant foreign revenue.

---

15. See the World Nuclear Association Website for further information.
16. Russia is the main proponent of used fuel take back. It requires take back of uranium that it supplies to Iran, it takes back used reactor fuel from some other states that it supplies, and it processes other nuclear wastes from France and Britain for reuse. Russia considered allowing importation of spent reactor fuel that it did not supply, but has not followed through on it.

To carry out an initiative of this kind, Kazakhstan would need to develop facilities for nuclear waste processing and disposal, which most economically would be combined with facilities for managing other industrial waste. A spent fuel take back policy will be simpler to implement if Kazakhstan produces nuclear fuel ready for reactor use and not just pellets, as it reportedly plans, although spent fuel take back could be arranged through new contracts or through established joint ventures between Kazatomprom and enterprises in Russia, Japan, China, and other countries.

Kazakhstan might wish to explore entering the industrial and nuclear waster market as part of its industrial diversification strategy, but more importantly it may be the only way for it to effectively deal with its national industrial waste challenges. Long-term sustainability of sophisticated industrial waste treatment requires private sector engagement and thus commercial viability. That can likely only be warranted if the waste management capacity operates at a scale significantly above what is required for national disposal needs.

Moving forward with industrial and nuclear waste management services on a big scale is a big decision, and will require careful technical and commercial assessment. Since waste would have to be transported to land-locked Kazakhstan through third-country territory, Kazakhstan would also need to engage in diplomatic exchanges with its neighbors to ensure their willingness to let the potentially hazardous materials cross through their territories. If the government is interested in pursuing the matter, it would be important to understand the market and the government's role before proceeding. A good, cost-effective way to do that would be to invite competing proposals from private enterprises, and to ask those proposing what they would expect from the government other than authorization to do business. Such a process would provide due diligence, and would help determine what waste streams and technologies make the most sense.

Even if justified on its merits, proposals for large-scale waste treatment will inevitably provoke controversy. The government would be well advised to approach the matter in a very transparent way with a careful public outreach and consultation process.

Green Agriculture

Agriculture contributes to natural resource depletion or contributes to its preservation, depending on how it is managed. In turn, agriculture's contribution to the economy and to the welfare of the rural population is vitally dependent on the environment. We first look at general issues of whether and how agriculture contributes to green growth and then consider one specific option for furthering this contribution in the coming decades to the use of genetically modified crops.

Agriculture and the environment

Agriculture constituted 5.5 percent of Kazakhstan's GDP in 2011, but employed 28.3 percent of the workforce (Chapter 2). 61 percent of the country's area (76.5 million hectares) is classified as permanent pasture, and 32 percent (24 million hectares) is classified as "arable" (systematically cultivated for production of row crops) (Foreign Agricultural Service 2010; Ministry of Agriculture of Kazakhstan Republic 2007).[17] About two-thirds of the arable land (18 million hectares) is cultivated for grain. Some 5 million hectares of arable lands are currently idle (unplanted for several years), but only 2 million idle hectares are considered suitable for crop production. The land is mostly flat, lending itself to large-scale farming, but the soils are highly variable. Wheat fields in the north are not irrigated because of high salinity in groundwater, and they are considered to be in a zone of "risky" agriculture, with droughts occurring in

17. See also Pomfret ("Kazakhstan's Agriculture" 2013) for an historical review of Kazakhstan's agriculture since independence.

two out of five years. Drought reduces production quantity significantly, but enhances quality, measured in protein content. Compared with most other wheat growing nations, productivity in tons per hectare is low, which may be attributable to the environment, management, or both. As noted previously, past water diversion to grow cotton drained much of the Aral Sea, and future reduction in available water may occur in southern Kazakhstan from upstream, transboundary diversion and from increased summer droughts caused by climate change.

Wheat, barley, oats, and oilseeds are sometimes conventionally tilled as they were during the Soviet era. Low or no-tillage practice has been used in some fields, keeping soil moisture higher. This environmentally favorable practice is sometimes referred to as "conservation agriculture," whose basic components are permanent soil cover, minimal soil disturbance, and crop rotation. No-till practice requires adding chemicals for weed control (assuming GMOs are not used), and also requires expensive, new machinery, but it demands less fuel. The government subsidizes purchase of herbicides and fuel, and provides an extra subsidy for no-till rotation to encourage it.

Climate change poses a daunting threat to Kazakhstan's agricultural future, particularly to the rain-fed spring wheat production that is its most important agricultural export. Even accounting for increased photosynthesis from higher CO_2 concentration, a steep drop in spring wheat productivity is forecast by climate models, to between 25 and 60 percent of current production by 2085 in Kostanai, Akmola, and Pavlodar oblasts, and to between 70 to 90 percent of current production by 2085 in North Kazakhstan (Esserkepova 2009).

In his December 2012 speech, President Nazarbayev called for a substantial increase in agriculture's share of Kazakhstan's GDP by 2050 by drawing on the country's "vast 'green' territories capable of producing eco-friendly foodstuffs." This is an ambitious goal, not least in light of the expected adverse effects of climate change. In any event, efforts to increase production can and should be made.

One good, fundamental step is to eliminate subsidies, let the market set prices, and support social objectives through other funding vehicles. President Nazarbayev's instruction to "resolve…the supply of irrigation water…by 2040" is also a positive move. The existing irrigation infrastructure in southern Kazakhstan is in bad shape, and upgrading it will improve productivity there. Although northern spring wheat does not appear to be a candidate for irrigation, there are opportunities for increased production of various crops in the south, such as winter wheat, maize, soybean, and cotton.

Kazakhstan's support for conservation agriculture of spring wheat, and no-till rotation particularly, is another plus for productivity and the environment, except for likely increased herbicide use, and the government's plans to improve transportation from field to buyer will address a key bottleneck, most acute in the form of bad rural roads, which President Nazarbayev has instructed to be fixed. Less certain in value, but potentially more dramatic in result, is to investigate markets for crops that will require little or no irrigation, and that can grow in the large areas not currently considered arable. Biofuel crops are a case in point, but the search should extend to potential new crops of all kinds, whether or not currently grown in Kazakhstan, including GMOs.

Biotechnology and GMOs

Advancing agriculture in Kazakhstan will also require avoiding mistakes, and the Republic should avoid the mistake of rejecting its greatest opportunity for agricultural innovation, in the form of genetically modified organisms (GMOs). Box 7.4 lists just a few strands of GMOs that have been developed. GMOs of some kind are now used throughout the world. As of 2012, GMO crops were planted in 170.3 million hectares in 28 nations, and their production has grown steadily (Figure 7.2) (James 2012).

7

> **Box**
> **7.4** | **The growing list of GMOs**
>
> Dry spells can inhibit plant growth, and a range of GMO crops including wheat, peas, and corn are being engineered for continuing, faster growth with less water, leaving more water in the ground. Flood-tolerant GMO rice varieties have been developed that can survive underwater where others die. Tomatoes have been engineered to resist frost and grow in salty, inhospitable soils. "Golden rice" has been engineered to produce iron and beta-carotene for Vitamin A, improving developing nation diets where vitamins are scarce. A vaccine for hepatitis B has been engineered into bananas. Tomatoes and other vegetables have been modified to stay fresh longer on the shelf. Algae has been modified to produce ethanol. Bacteria have been modified to digest cancer-causing hazardous waste. GMO salmon grow faster in aquaculture. GMO "BT" corn and other crops produce a pesticide that would otherwise be less discriminately sprayed. "Roundup Ready" crops and other plants, including lawn grasses, resist harm from herbicides sprayed on them to eliminate weeds. GMO goats have milk with a drug that prevents blood-clotting in humans, and GMO bacteria make insulin. Jellyfish genes are being put into other species to make them glow — a key marker for research.
>
> Source: Brown "Conserving Biological Diversity" (2011).

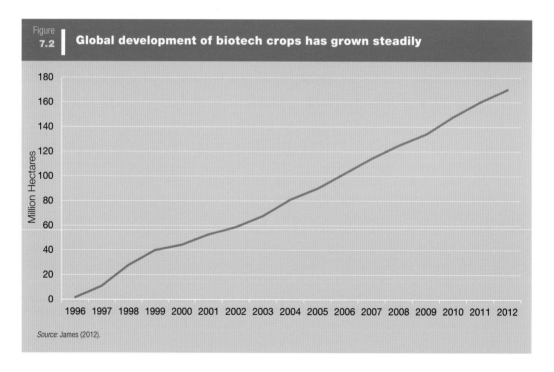

Figure 7.2 | **Global development of biotech crops has grown steadily**

Source: James (2012).

Kazakhstan should invest in research and development for GMOs, and it should facilitate production of GMO crops as markets indicate. Controversial or not, the genetic plasticity of life is a powerful, environmentally responsive, and responsible tool for economic growth and social welfare. We are entering a period where the management of biology by changing DNA will match the great advances in information technology. The importance of GMOs for agriculture has widespread support from the global scientific community, including an early report by seven national academies from the developed and developing world (NRC 2000). The report unequivocally supports the value of GMOs and the need to advance that value, while noting that regulation is needed to assure that the benefits are not compromised by unaddressed issues concerning the environment and human health. More recent studies are also supportive. For example, NRC (2010) finds that "genetic-engineering technology has produced substantial net environmental and economic benefits compared with non-GE crops in conventional agriculture." A 2009 OECD report on the "Bioeconomy to 2030" states that "[B]iotechnology . . . can increase the supply and environmental sustainability of food, feed and fibre production, improve water quality, provide renewable energy, improve the health of animals and people, and help maintain biodiversity by detecting invasive species" (OECD 2009).

GMOs do pose risks, and they need sound regulation. Concerns have been expressed about the possible escape and uncontrolled spread of transgenic organisms, about growing insect and weed resistance, about fair access to the new technology and, perhaps most passionately, about food safety. However these risks are manageable and, as NRC (2000) concluded, they do not countermand the huge potential that GMOs offer for good. Where national laws are lacking, they should be introduced and implemented (Brown "Conserving Biological Diversity" 2011).

Kazakhstan's Environment Ministry is interested in facilitating "organic" agriculture, without GMOs and with little or no use of chemical pesticides. As noted here, GMOs are a way to avoid the environmental impacts of spraying chemical pesticides and herbicide. Kazakhstan's large area could support growing both GMO and non-GMO crops, and the smart path is to explore both markets, and to let the cost of production and the demand guide investment and any government involvement. Indeed, estimates of economic impacts for potential GMO crops in Russia and the Ukraine indicate a significant advance in value over conventional crops (Brookes and Blume 2012). Table 7.2 presents estimated effects on yield and productivity if GMOs crops currently in production elsewhere are used in Russia.

Table 7.2	The economic impact of potential GMO plant development in Russia is significant		
Crop	**GMO trait**	**Change yield**	**Profitability**
Maize	Herbicide Tolerance	0 to +5	0 to +9
	Insect Resistance	10	+11 to +16
Oilseed Rape	Herbicide Tolerance (Glyphosate)	+3 to +12	+13 to +14
	Herbicide Tolerance (Glufosinate)	+10 to +12	+5 to +8
Soybeans	Herbicide Tolerance	+5 to +15	+14 to +29
Sugar Beets	Herbicide Tolerance	+3 to +15	+16 to +26

Source: Brookes and Blume (2012).

In the face of climate change, drought-resistant wheat is of particular interest for Kazakhstan. In 2009, wheat growers associations in Australia, Canada, and the United States agreed to coordinate in advancing GMO wheat, and field trials with many strains have been conducted with government support in Australia and China, among other locations (Canadian, American, and Australian Wheat Organizations 2013; Office of the Gene Technology Regulator 2012; International Service for the Acquisition of Agri-biotech Applications 2011). The trials have been accompanied by controversy, including destruction of a plot in Australia by Greenpeace (Gough 2011), but publicly reported results from early trials in Australia demonstrated 20 percent more productivity than conventional wheat under drought conditions (GMO Safety 2008). Figure 7.3 presents estimates run for Kazakhstan from a model used to estimate the added value of GMO wheat in Argentina, modified to reflect circumstances in Kazakhstan.[18]

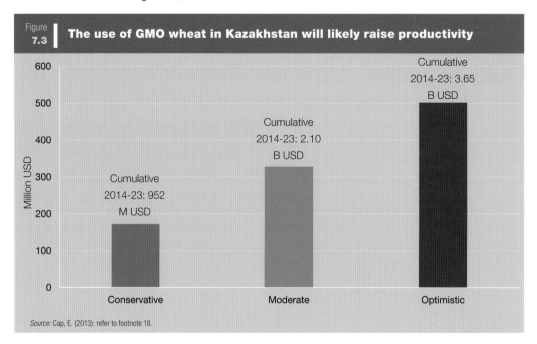

Figure 7.3 | The use of GMO wheat in Kazakhstan will likely raise productivity

Source: Cap, E. (2013): refer to footnote 18.

GMOs could jump-start discovery, generate revenue for Kazakhstan, and facilitate development of intellectual capital within the country over the longer term. Kazakhstan might consider taking equity stakes in biotech ventures abroad that are developing GMOs for market, with priority for those in which it might eventually take a controlling interest. There are many companies engaged in such work, some associated with universities or with university faculty members. Many of these companies are big and well established, but many in turn are seeking capital. The United States is a leader in this arena, with hotbeds for companies in several cities, particularly Cambridge, Massachusetts, relating to Harvard

18. Personal communication from Eugenio Cap, Director of the Institute of Economics and Sociology, with the National Institute of Agricultural Technology (INTA), Buenos Aires, Argentina (cap.eugenio@inta.gob.ar). Dr. Cap developed the mathematical simulation SIGMA model and ran it for this report. For this particular case, a 28% reduction in drought-losses using GMO wheat in Kazakhstan is assumed, based on productivity data from international field trials and an average of two droughts every five years reported for Kazakhstan. The three scenarios presented in Figure 7.3 were built, using combinations of both adoption parameters and wheat world prices (1) Conservative: Adoption half-time: 4, 5, and 6 years (for high, medium and low tech farmers, respectively), adoption ceilings of 60%, 70%, and 90% of total planted area (H, M and L tech), world wheat price USD 150 per ton; (2) Moderate: Adoption half-time 3, 4, and 5 years, adoption ceilings of 70%, 80%, and 100%, world wheat price USD 250 per ton; (3) Optimistic: Adoption half-time 2, 3, and 4 years, adoption ceilings of 80%, 90%, and 100%, world wheat price USD 350 per ton. Dr Cap notes that these results should be regarded with caution because of uncertainty in the validity for Kazakhstan of the values chosen for the adoption parameters, but that the three combined scenarios probably encompass a reasonable expectation.

and M.I.T., and La Jolla, California, through universities there and the J. Craig Venter Institute. Europe is highly engaged also, and the OECD estimates that biotechnology could contribute up to approximately 2.7 percent of GDP in the OECD by 2030 with business-as-usual, and more in the non-OECD "due to the greater importance to GDP of primary and industrial production compared to OECD countries." (OECD 2009) A strong niche for Kazakhstan in this industry would be to take stakes in biotech ventures whose products complement the country's resources and needs, including GMOs for agriculture (e.g., drought-resistant wheat), but also energy (e.g., biofuels), and environment (e.g., bacteria modified to metabolize and breakdown hazardous waste). These products could be tested and deployed as useful within the country, but would also have international markets which through sale of patented products could be a significant new, non-depleting revenue stream for Kazakhstan.

Russia is an important competitor to Kazakhstan in international markets for agricultural products. Unlike China and India, Russia is not currently growing GMO crops, but its position is changing (Vassilieva 2012). On April 24, 2012, the Russian government adopted "The Comprehensive Program for Development of Biotechnology in the Russian Federation through 2020." The document "acknowledges that Russia is lagging behind both developed and developing countries in the development and use of biotechnology (including agricultural biotechnology) and sets targets to create a biotech-oriented economy by 2020, including 200 billion rubles (USD 6.7 billion) for development of agricultural biotechnology." The document observes that Russia does not use genetic engineering for plant crops which are "wider and wider used in the world," and that without GMOs Russian agricultural production will remain "high cost and will not be able to compete with foreign countries ." Russia is positioning itself to fix this problem, and Kazakhstan needs to do the same or risk being left behind.

Green Biodiversity

Kazakhstan has a great variety of biodiversity resources that it needs to preserve for future use in natural habitats and in specially created storage facilities. We take these initiatives in turn.

Natural habitat preservation

Kazakhstan reports natural reserves covering 208,000 km^2, amounting to 7.6 percent of the nation's territory, as noted here. These reserves vary widely in the degree of protection intended to be conferred, and they are subject to extensive poaching and other illegal extraction. At its 2010 meeting in Nagoya, Japan, the Conference of the Parties to the Convention of Biological Diversity adopted a target that: "by 2020, at least 17 percent of terrestrial and inland water areas, and 10 percent of coastal and marine areas, especially areas of particular importance for biodiversity and ecosystem services, are conserved" (Convention on Biological Diversity 2013). Kazakhstan should consider embracing these targets, and attaining these percentages by 2020, with natural reserves designated for at least 10 percent of the Caspian Sea under Kazakhstan's jurisdiction. Outstanding areas of desert and more steppe should be included along with other categories. However, an even more important and more difficult issue than the size of area covered is to actually provide the "conservation" protection which reserve designation is intended to convey. Many nations have established "paper" parks with little or no real protection against extraction of resources or settlement. Kazakhstan can strive to do better.

Over the past two decades natural resource managers have increasingly recognized that areas afforded complete protection not only protect resources within them but also provide breeding grounds for fish and wildlife which move beyond the borders of protection and are available for harvest. This has been a central finding and supportive argument for the vast marine protected areas established recently by the United States, United Kingdom, and others. The same concept can be applied for the natural reserves of Kazakhstan. Some designated reserves should be set aside from all extractive use or development. In these, only carefully managed research and accommodations for ecotourism should be allowed, providing financial support for conservation, and advancing public appreciation. The role of government in ecotourism should not be to establish government enterprises, but to set environmental standards and to facilitate competition and investment by the private sector.[19]

There is no general practice or generally accepted standard for the percentage of national area that should be given full protection, and the amount appropriate will differ as a nation's biodiversity differs. However, as a starting premise, Kazakhstan might consider providing such protection to 10 percent of the lands and waters under its jurisdiction. Other designated reserves might allow limited extractive use and development so long as consistent with conservation of biological diversity. Providing for conservation within reserves where some extraction is allowed requires mapping and management of key ecological features.[20] The central management objective is to approximate an undisturbed state and to prevent unsustainable uses. The same conservation standards can be applied in a more flexible way to development activities not in natural reserves through a policy of "no-net-loss" of biodiversity. That policy was adopted widely for wetland development, and first extended to biodiversity generally in 1990 by a major multinational corporation. More recently, it has been advocated by the International Union for the Conservation of Nature.[21] The concept of "no-net-loss" allows developers to compensate for harm caused to biodiversity by countervailing investments, such as protecting adjacent areas, or funding biodiversity protection at other locations. Ease of implementation varies with sector: no-net-loss is more easily accomplished by enterprises whose geographic footprint is relatively small in light of revenues produced (e.g., manufacturing, oil and gas, and even mining) than for those premised on lower financial yield per unit area developed (e.g., agriculture). Kazakhstan should consider at a minimum requiring land developers to assess the impact of proposed projects on biodiversity, and to offer measures that, to the extent compatible with the purpose of the project, will provide for no-net-loss of biodiversity.

Preservation in storage

Biodiversity in the wild (or "in-situ") is the top priority for conservation efforts, but many species will become extinct overtime because of human activity, and the species of Kazakhstan and Central Asia are no exception. Consequently it is also important to provide for ex-situ conservation in the form of frozen seeds, viable animal cells, and also frozen dead cells whose DNA can be sequenced. One recent publication proposes an initiative for this purpose which it refers to as "DNA Net Earth" (Brown 2013). The concept builds on the work of many institutions, including the Smithsonian Institution in the US, Kew Gardens in the UK, and the Svalbard Seed Bank in Norway. Kazakhstan reports accessions of more than 75,000 plant specimens in various facilities as of 2007, but it also reports that temperature and other conditions are variable, and do not assure long-term preservation.

---

19. *The New York Times* recently reported (January 13, 2013) that Mongolia has set a goal of one million annual overseas tourists by 2015 — roughly double the number who visited in 2011. New hotel chains are opening in anticipation of the increase, Mongolian Airlines is adding international routes, and tour operators are offering camping trips with rides by horse to the steppe grassland and other remote areas. Other nations have found big markets for ecotourism, often in combination with culture (Brown "Cultural Heritage and Development" 2011).

20. These include: (a) kind, abundance, and distribution of indicator species and ecosystem types, including age structure of harvested species such as trees or fish, and vulnerable and invasive species if present; (b) habitat coverage showing any fragmentation and corridors that impede or facilitate movement or spread; and (c) sources and levels of any harmful pollutants. See (Brown "Conserving Biological Diversity" 2011) for discussion.

21. See, for example, UN Global Compact and International Union for the Conservation of Nature (2012). The company adopting the policy was Waste Management, Inc. (1990).

DNA Net Earth proposes establishing a global network of facilities, relying mostly on existing institutions, to preserve DNA for every known species and for new species as they are described. It is intended to be a safety net for biodiversity, provide genetic libraries for research and commerce, be used to recover species that are endangered, and offer the potential to selectively restore species that have gone extinct. Only a small fraction of the 1.9 million known species are currently maintained as living organisms in cultivation or captivity or maintained frozen as viable seeds or cells. Just a fraction more species have DNA in dead cells that is kept in long-term frozen storage. Three specific steps are suggested in the DNA Net Earth proposal: developing a website to track progress on preservation whose key information is managed directly by contributing facilities; establishing new incentives and mandates for contributing specimens, including grant, publication, and permit requirements; and engaging the public in collection. Kazakhstan could play a leading role in this effort for the species of Central Asia.

A facility for frozen storage in Astana could be managed by the Agriculture Ministry in coordination with agricultural universities in Astana and Almaty, and could be used by researchers worldwide. Liquid nitrogen is the cooling medium of choice, and a facility handling specimens from Central Asia, acquired over time, would be modest in cost and space required. Seeds are especially compact and readily stored. A logical, initial priority for collection and research would be species of known or potential value in agriculture and species that are endangered. Kazakhstan also could play a significant role in the global development of DNA Net Earth, for example playing a leading role in developing the website contemplated, or being the first nation to establish incentives and mandates for contributing specimens through grant, publication, or permit requirements. The "Green Bridge" initiative designed to serve as a regional forum for green development initiatives would be a good vehicle for regional and international cooperation on this issue.

Other Green Initiatives

There are many other areas in which green growth can and needs to be pursued. Many of these are treated in other chapters of this study. We only briefly touch on three here, because of their particular relevance and importance for green growth: green cities, green education, and green governance.

Green cities and infrastructure

Cities are potentially a key driver of green development, provided high-density land use, transportation, building standards, urban services and provision of green spaces are geared to reduce the negative ecological footprint of the urban population (Glaeser 2011). Roughly half of the population of Kazakhstan is clustered in Almaty, Astana, and a small number of other cities. The country's population and its share living in cities will continue to increase. These growing cities should be "green" and function well in the event that climate change is unmitigated. Chapter 8 discusses Kazakhstan's urbanization trends and policies in detail. Much of what is recommended there will contribute to making the country's cities develop in a more efficient and greener way for the rising number of urban citizens. Four priorities in particular represent a green city perspective: (a) high-density development that minimizes harm from sprawl and improves resource use efficiency, (b) conservation of green spaces, (c) "smart" transportation, and (d) improved infrastructure.

Kazakhstan is developing the concept of the "Green4 Project" based on four satellite cities around Almaty, and EXPO 2017 in Astana is expected to give a "powerful impetus" for a green path in Kazakhstan. Although the details are yet to be developed for either of these, Almaty and Astana could be useful showcases for advances on the four green urban priorities referenced in this section. A key consideration, however, is to make sure the steps taken and facility investments made address the most fundamental issues, and have the potential to scale up. For example, new municipal recycling programs and separation facilities probably make sense, but they should be developed in conjunction, and in balanced proportion, with programs for collecting and transporting the waste that is not recycled, and for managing that waste through incineration or sanitary disposal. There will be waste residues, and Almaty needs one or more state-of-the-art, lined landfills just as much as it needs recycling services. Wastewater infrastructure presents a similar point. It would be relatively easy to build a new wastewater treatment plant in Almaty or Astana with the most sophisticated, and expensive treatment technologies. However, it might not be feasible to scale-up such a plant to cover fully the needs of these cities or other cities in Kazakhstan. Furthermore, fixing leaking sewage pipelines and expanding the capacity of existing wastewater treatment facilities to avoid combined storm water and sewage overflow, may be a higher, albeit less visible, priority.

Green education and research

Green growth depends on innovative thinking and discovery. That will require a significant, continuing investment in science and technology, including formal and informal education at all levels, and research and development by academic and private enterprises. Special depth should be established for the topics central to green growth in Kazakhstan discussed in this chapter, including environmental quality, renewable energy and waste management.[22] Research and development on GMOs, combined with investment in biotech companies, is also a path forward, as noted in these lines. The relationships developed with researchers in these international companies would facilitate development of intellectual capital within Kazakhstan, without being dependent on such internal capability at the outset. Nazarbayev University could play a key role in arranging and managing such an initiative. The analysis and recommendations in Chapter 5 have a direct bearing on assuring an effective development of a quality educational system that can support green growth.

Green governance

Two governance issues stand out for green growth in addition to those addressed elsewhere in this report. First, the Environment Ministry needs a strong hand. It should be strengthened in its role of setting environmental standards concerning pollution of air, water, and land, and protection of ecosystems from destructive land-use and resource extraction. Personal communications from Kazakhstan officials in February 2013 indicate that lead responsibility is being transferred to the Environment Ministry for renewable energy, water, and wildlife, which is good. But the Ministry also will need to carry out its lead coordinating role in working with other ministries such, as Oil and Agriculture, to assure that their plans and activities are consistent with green growth. That does not mean that the Environment Ministry should direct the other ministries on such matters, but it should be empowered to convene their representatives, discuss issues and concerns, and either work things out or report to the Prime Minister or the President for resolution of differences.

A second governance need for green growth in Kazakhstan is for the nation to work with immediate and more distant neighbors. The "Green Bridge" initiative by Kazakhstan is an important vehicle for that, whose concept is to serve as a venue for coordination and innovation on environmental issues within Central Asia, and in Europe and in the Asia-Pacific region generally. An exact work plan for the Green Bridge initiative is yet to be formulated, and it may be a work in progress indefinitely. However, the Green

---

22. Special consideration should be given to use of MOOCs, which are growing rapidly and include science and technology.

7

Bridge initiative can help to keep Kazakhstan connected to those beyond its borders on an important and enduring topic. Kazakhstan is also well-advised to stay on track, and enhance work on the full range of regional and international environmental activities that currently concern it. Some initiatives are specific, such as cooperation on water withdrawals from rivers shared with China, Russia, Uzbekistan, and Kyrgyzstan; establishing a regional DNA bank; and cooperation on regional waste management. Others are more general and long-term, such as participating in international climate initiatives; international benchmarking efforts relevant to green growth; and research and development on GMOs. Both specific and more general international cooperation is critical.

Conclusions and Recommendations

Green growth is a good direction for Kazakhstan, and should address local environmental needs and climate change together. Four overarching fundamentals stand out:

- The government should continue to completion the many good initiatives it has launched on this front, such as infrastructure improvements and increased use of renewable energy. President Nazarbayev's December 2012 instructions address several needs for green growth, and priority should be given to effective implementation of those goals.
- The government should explore a carbon tax and mandate agency review of all existing and new regulations with the goal of assuring that all regulations maximize net benefit to the people of Kazakhstan.
- The government should identify innovations that may encounter initial resistance, but that are well-suited to the country's natural and social strengths and are fundamentally a good thing to do for the environment and economy of Kazakhstan. One outstanding example for this is the application and adaptation of GMOs for agriculture and other sectors. Ways to break from the pack are rarely obvious or risk-free, but they are the way to excel.
- The government should search for opportunities that will bring international enterprise and intellectual assets to Kazakhstan without requiring, at least near-term, that those business and human assets be located within the nation. Two examples of such opportunities are taking equity in biotech firms whose labs and administrators are elsewhere, and engaging students and others in massive, open, online courses prepared abroad. Such initiatives can enrich Kazakhstan's home-based business and intellectual capital, and at the same time avoid the potential failure of independent domestic initiatives not yet ready to perform or to compete successfully internationally (see also Chapter 9).

In the remainder for this chapter we summarize the principal specific recommendations for green growth with specific proposed actions and their timing.

Carbon taxation

Explore and eventually move to adoption of a carbon tax in lieu of continuing Kazakhstan's 2014 cap-and-trade pilot effort. Such a tax will be more efficient, will provide an incentive to reduce fossil fuel consumption and carbon emissions, and will promote alternative energy and industrial technologies generating less non-carbon pollution.

Proposed actions
- Short term: Explore, design, and promulgate a carbon tax with staged implementation requirements and any adjustments needed to maintain or improve existing social policies.
- Medium and long term: Review administration of the carbon tax and revise it as experience indicates.

7

Regulatory review

The government of Kazakhstan should issue a decree incorporating the 2012 OECD recommendation on regulatory policy. That decree would mandate review of all national laws and regulations to ensure that regulations are issued only when unregulated markets will not accomplish the same objectives and when regulations will provide net benefit. The review will also aim for regulations to be flexible, efficient, timely, competitive, transparent, and effective.

Proposed actions
- Short term: Prepare and issue the regulatory review decree.
- Medium-to-long term: Prepare and issue annual reports estimating net benefits of new regulations

Benchmarked environmental regulations

Kazakhstan needs an effective regulatory program achieving performance objectives for clean air, water, and land, and for conservation of water and natural ecosystems. The program should be benchmarked against proven objectives and practices in developed economies, and it generally should be similar to them in design and effect unless cost and benefit analyses indicate otherwise. The environmental parameters currently monitored should be reviewed and upgraded, and information on monitored items and the program generally should be posted and updated regularly on a publicly accessible website.

Proposed actions
- Short term:
    - Develop tentative criteria and protocols defining requirements for clean air, water, and land, and for conservation of water and natural ecosystems. Draw from practices of other nations that have been effective in protecting these resources, including approaches taken in Australia, Canada, and the United States, and include review of current criteria and practices in Kazakhstan.
    - Estimate the benefits and costs of implementing these requirements.
- Short to medium term: Promulgate in tranches revised requirements for the resources covered, and post the requirements and statistics monitored on a publicly accessible website.
- Medium-to-long term: Review and as warranted revise requirements at least once every five years to improve their effectiveness in achieving environmental objectives and their administrative efficiency.

Alternative energy[23]

Kazakhstan should reduce coal consumption for domestic energy, and it should increase domestic consumption of natural gas. Pollution controls at coal-fired power plants should be evaluated, and the plants should be brought to acceptable standards, closed, or converted to natural gas. Kazakhstan should also establish new hydro, wind, and solar power generating facilities, but should assess the full costs and benefits before major investment, including the costs of upgrading and expanding existing electrical grids or establishing new grids. Kazakhstan should also consider one or more pilot projects for coal gasification.

Proposed actions
- Short term:
    - Develop a plan for developing an integrated mix of energy sources as described here, incorporating cost-benefit analysis.

---

23. See also recommendations in Chapter 6 on alternative and renewable energy.

  ° Complete review of all existing coal-fired power plants, and either confirm that adequate pollutions controls are in place or decide on conversion to natural gas, pollution upgrades, or closure.
- Medium to long term: Achieve scheduled targets and at least 50 percent alternative energy for electricity production by 2050, and achieve a lower but ambitious percentage for total energy consumption.

Biodiversity preservation

Kazakhstan should expand and strengthen its network of natural area reserves, including significant areas of complete protection, and it should facilitate ecotourism in key places. A policy of "no-net-loss" of biodiversity should be implemented outside designated reserves. Kazakhstan should establish and manage a repository for seeds and other DNA carriers of Central Asian plant and animal species.

Proposed actions
- Short term: Develop and begin implementing a biodiversity plan: to place at least 17 percent of Kazakhstan's land and inland waters in natural areas reserves, place at least 10 percent of Kazakhstan's share of the Caspian Sea in such reserves, provide complete protection from extractive uses in natural area reserves for at least 10 percent of the territory of Kazakhstan, provide for "no-net-loss" of biodiversity in development of lands and waters not within natural area reserves, facilitate ecotourism, and establish and manage a repository for seeds and other DNA carriers of the plant and animal species of Central Asia.
- Medium-to-long term: Implement, monitor and report at least once every five years on implementation of the biodiversity plan, and amend the plan as warranted to improve it.

Industrial waste recycling

Kazakhstan should assess the costs, benefits, and public-private process of providing state-of-the-art waste recycling, treatment, and disposal services for domestic (and possibly foreign) industrial and nuclear waste generators. This could include radioactive waste cleanup and storage of spent fuels from nuclear power plants. The initiative would also include a complementary investment in research, development, and education for waste management and reduction, and establishment of consulting services to help companies reduce waste and manage what they generate effectively. If the assessment is positive, Kazakhstan should move forward with the initiative.

Proposed actions
- Short term:
  ° Issue an international RFP to solicit competitive proposals for industrial and nuclear waste services as described here. The RFP should flexibly allow service providers to demonstrate that they will excel in environmental protection, security, cost, and reputation.
  ° Complete a cost-benefit analysis of the waste management initiative, taking into account information from the RFP process.
  ° Decide whether to go ahead with a major initiative on waste management, and select or permit one or more service providers to go forward with plans.
- Short-to-medium term: Review government programs and funding for research and development in waste management, and announce plans for enhancement if the subject is made a major initiative. Nazarbayev University could play a key role.

- Long term: Monitor activities and adjust government support and management on a continuing basis.

Green agriculture

Kazakhstan produces a range of crops and livestock, but wheat is Kazakhstan's current predominate agricultural export product, and managing it right is key. The wheat is not irrigated, and the effects of climate change are expected to be adverse. Increased no-till practice is desirable, particularly in the face of climate change, as is the improvement in roads and in irrigation called for by President Nazarbayev. Kazakhstan has so far stepped back from GMOs, which offer great value for agriculture in Kazakhstan. The government should take a positive stance on them, and should invest in their research and development.

Proposed actions

- Short term:
    - Continue plans for improving agriculture, including improving rural roads and removing other "bottlenecks" in Kazakhstan for transport of agricultural products to buyers; restoring sound irrigation infrastructure in the south; and expanding use of no-till agriculture to maximize preservation of soil moisture.
    - Revisit the potential use of GMOs in agriculture and other sectors, and establish a fundamental government position in support of such technology.
    - Fund a continuous research and development initiative for GMOs. This may or may not be supported through the Ministry of Agriculture, but in any event should involve the agricultural universities, to provide the academic excellence and independence needed for innovation and education. Include in this initiative a project on genetic modification of wheat for improved drought resistance and a project to identify biofuel crops that can grow without irrigation in the desert of Kazakhstan.
    - Establish a steering committee including representatives of appropriate government agencies and Nazarbayev University to explore potential equity investments in biotech firms abroad, and request it to report initial findings and recommendations.
- Medium to long term: Implement, monitor and adapt as appropriate.

Green cities

Four major green city priorities stand out in Kazakhstan and include promotion of high density urban living, urban green spaces, smart urban transportation, and modernized urban infrastructure. Implement the actions recommended in Chapter 8.

Science and R&D

A significant, continuing investment in science and technology is required for innovation and green growth, including formal and informal education at all levels, and research and development by academic and private enterprises. Talent from abroad is needed to help catalyze such change, and Kazakhstan should pay what is takes to secure that talent, and do what it takes to keep it.

Proposed actions
- Short-to-long term: Request Nazarbayev University or another university in Kazakhstan to annually evaluate and make recommendations on needs and funding requirements in science and technology for green growth, including formal and informal education at all levels, and research and development by academic and private enterprises.
- Short term: Commission Nazarbayev University to provide two reports by January 2016: one report reviewing needs and making recommendations on attracting and retaining a world-class faculty in areas relevant to green growth, and the other report assessing the potential of MOOCs in Kazakhstan and making recommendations on how to increase participation in MOOCs and how to enhance their value to securing employment and promotions.

Green governance

The role of the Environment Ministry in green growth should be strengthened. Its role in directly setting environmental standards should be maintained and strengthened, and transfers of responsibility for renewable energy, water, and wildlife should be completed. But the Environment Ministry also should have a lead coordinating role in working with other ministries such as oil and agriculture to assure that their plans and activities are consistent with environmental protection. Resolution of any differences would be the purview of the top authorities.

Proposed actions
- Short term: Review and revise as needed existing policies for interagency review of environmental issues, to assure that the Minister of the Environment has clear authority to convene representatives of other agencies, seek consensus on issues, and report to the top authorities if differences cannot be resolved.
- Short-to-long term: Periodically review the role of the Environment Ministry in all new regulations affecting the environment, and provide clear authority as needed for it to assure that environmental performance objectives are achieved.

Green Bridge

Kazakhstan should continue active involvement in the work of regional and international organizations and regimes, implement the Green Bridge initiative, and seek agreement on shared use of trans-boundary water.

Proposed actions
- Short-to-long term: Continue participating in regional and international organizations and regimes, and explore membership in appropriate additional entities as opportunities arise.
- Short to medium term:
  ○ Support the Green Bridge initiative broadly as a vehicle for exchange and cooperation on the environment and economy within Central Asia and throughout Europe and the Asia Pacific.
  ○ Establish an initial small secretariat for the Green Bridge initiative in Astana and incorporate it as a non-profit organization in one or more nations to facilitate funding.

○ Facilitate adoption of a strategic plan for the Green Bridge initiative identifying major, measurable objectives. Include consideration of contributions to the concept of DNA Net Earth, such as a regional seed bank; efforts at cooperative resolution of transboundary water issues affecting nations of Central Asia and their neighbors; cooperation on GMOs; and international solutions and coordination on industrial and nuclear waste management.

Table 7.3 pulls together the recommendations in tabular format for ease of reference. They are offered as options for consideration by the government of Kazakhstan and for action as it may consider appropriate. We note that there are challenges and trade-offs concerning these recommendations. For example, the long, gradual time frame for impacts from climate change may not seem urgent to the broader public or the political elite, and implementation of a carbon tax will present administrative and political issues. The recommendations on GMOs and industrial waste management, while strongly supported by the merits, will encounter opposition from those whose are predisposed against them. Especially the issue of industrial waste management for nuclear waste is fraught with sensitivities. Furthermore, the recommendation to strengthen the Environment Ministry and overall government coordination on the environment will likely be resisted by agencies with differing, entrenched agendas and constituencies — a feature not limited to Kazakhstan.

Table 7.3	**Short-, medium-, and long-term options for green growth**		
	Short term	**Medium term**	**Long term**
Carbon taxation	• Explore, design and promulgate a carbon tax with staged implementation requirements and any adjustments needed to maintain or improve existing social policies	• Review administration of the carbon tax and revise it as experience indicates	
Regulatory review	• Prepare and issue the Presidential regulatory review decree	• Prepare and issue annual reports estimating net benefits of new regulations	
Benchmarked environmental regulations	• Develop tentative criteria and protocols defining requirements for clean air, water, and land, and for conservation of water and natural ecosystems; estimate the benefits and costs of implementing these requirements		
	• Promulgate in tranches revised requirements for the resources covered, and post the requirements and statistics monitored on a publicly accessible website		
		• Review and as warranted revise requirements at least once every five years	
Alternative energy	• Develop a plan for developing an integrated mix of energy sources, incorporating cost and benefit analysis • Complete review of all existing coal-fired power plants, and either confirm that adequate pollutions controls are in place or decide on conversion to natural gas, pollution upgrades, or closure	• Achieve scheduled targets and at least 50 percent alternative energy for electricity consumption by 2050, and achieve that or a lower but ambitious percentage for total energy consumption	
Biodiversity preservation	• Develop and begin implementing a biodiversity plan with specific targets	• Review and as warranted revise biodiversity plan once every five years	

(contd...)

(Table 7.3 contd...)

7

Table
7.3 **Short-, medium-, and long-term options for green growth**

	Short term	Medium term	Long term
Industrial waste recycling	• Explore feasibility of industrial waste management program (including nuclear)	• Monitor activities and adjust government support and management on a continuing basis	
	• Review government programs and funding for research and development in waste management, and announce plans for enhancement if the subject is made a major initiative		
Green agriculture	• Improve agricultural services and rural infrastructure	• Implement, monitor, and adapt as appropriate	
	• Explore possible development and use of GMOs		
	• Explore potential equity investment in foreign biotech firms		
Green cities	• Promote of high density urban living; of urban green spaces; of smart urban transportation; of modernized urban infrastructure		
Science and R&D	• Nazarbayev University (or another university) to assess regularly scientific research and R&D needs for green growth		
	• Nazarbayev University (or another university) to study how to attract world class faculty and whether and how to implement MOOC teaching		
Green governance	• Explore how to upgrade coordination function of the Ministry of Environment		
	• Periodically review the role of the Ministry of Environment in all new regulations for effective engagement		
Green Bridge	• Participate in relevant regional and international organizations		
	• Develop and implement "Green Bridge" concept with establishment of secretariat in Almaty and initiatives in selected areas (seed bank, cooperation on GMOs, trans-boundary water issues, etc.)		

Kazakhstan in 2050 — Lyazzat Bertassova Remembers

Lyazzat Bertassova was born some 30 years ago in the Kyzylorda oblast, then still one of the poorer regions. After graduating from the Agrarian University in Almaty she returned to her family business, a combination of small-holder farming and services activities, such as a small flourishing restaurant and a mechanical equipment repair service. She reflects on her life:

I don't know where to start. I am the oldest child of a traditional farming family; I have three younger siblings, a brother who helps me with our family business and two sisters, one doing her MBA or something similar in Tashkent next door in Uzbekistan and one who is studying in Almaty's design school and dreams about revolutionizing Kazakhstan's fashion. My father inherited a small farm from his parents in the old days but had a bad tractor accident when he was in his 40s and is unfortunately not able to do much work, but he is a commanding presence and a magnet in our little restaurant because he is always in a good mood in spite of his physical setbacks. So my mother has been the backbone of our family; she had to learn to run a business on the fly. She always told me incredible stories of how she struggled with the local *akimat* people to protect our little business and how difficult it was to get any financing from banks for modest firms like ours. After my father had to stop working she and my father's parents had to go through bureaucratic hassles to obtain his disability pension.

You see, this all happened when I was still a schoolgirl, and so I don't remember too well. I only remember my mother working hard from early morning to late at night. Farming income was so little, and the weather became more and more unpredictable, so mother decided to open the restaurant where she could serve meals relying on the modest production of meat and poultry from our farm. Because of growing oil prospecting in this oblast and of its growing importance as a transit corridor, the restaurant helped balance the dwindling income from the farm. I don't want to brag, but my mother was one of the few who still knew how to prepare a proper *bisbarmakh*, and she had an assistant cook from Uzbekistan who cooked the best *plof*, so our place was very popular with locals and travelers alike. It was good for my father as he had a place where he felt really useful.

Some 10 years ago (I was a student then) I told my mother that we should take advantage of all the transit traffic and set up a little repair shop. I also offered to find some smart young repairmen, probably from across the border. I was scared if we would find people who could take on this job — it all looked so complicated. But actually I found out that replacing spare parts and so on is the easy part — almost all spare parts can be printed, and anything more complicated can be put together by our little robots, but what has been difficult is to find young workers who can speak and engage customers properly. I wonder what they teach in school these days, and I am not that far removed from study myself!

So it was natural that I returned home after my studies. I miss Almaty with its beautiful mountains — I was told that they used to have a snow cap almost all year round, but that seems like a fantasy to me — and its beautiful boulevards — I was told that once the downtown city streets were clogged with many cars, but they managed to get rid of them and have everybody use these convoys of electric wheelers that somehow never collide and are always respectful of the people who walk around or ride on bicycles.

I miss the clean air, scented by the lush trees all year round. And of course the food and the culture, everything at your fingertips and everything made just for you using virtual materials, this is something I want to introduce here as well.

But duty called — five years ago mother had to scale back her pace. The constant exposure to air pollution, especially during bad winter air in the early part of her life, gave her chronic asthma, so I had to increasingly take over. One would think that with the state of medicine and the ability to regrow lungs and so on it should be easy to regrow mother's organs, but we discovered that that seems to be the easy part; it is more difficult to find specialists willing to oversee the robots doing their surgery. It seems that going to medical school takes too long for most people, so there is a serious shortage. Mother is now on the waiting list, but we are also thinking of trying our luck with medical treatment right next door in Uzbekistan since we now have open borders. The good news is that the cause of my mother's health issue — which is so typical for many of her generation — is now a thing of the past; all our coal-based heaters have been replaced: We have electricity from a combination of solar, wind, and natural gas. We have taken advantage of an energy credit that the central government introduced about the time I was born but that never reached us until 10 years ago (it is phased out now because somebody declared victory) and have installed our own wind and solar power plant. Now we sell to the public grid.

My grandparents used to tell me, wistfully, how easy it was to travel to visit their friends in neighboring countries; apparently the borders didn't mean anything. My parents then told me that times had changed and that they hardly remember what Tashkent or Samarkand looked like — it was such a hassle to get the permits, and in any case traveling there was such a hassle. Unbelievable, but now it's so easy. No more border controls — we can dial up specialized travelators that take us wherever we want to go in a matter of minutes. And yes, we repair them too and started to think of operating them as well.

So everything should be fine, no? We have good clinics and hospitals — well, short of staff, but well equipped — a good government that we are proud of, a good community where we trust each other, even the people from other *jus* (a quaint sound, this word, but history books tell us that there was a lot of rivalry still during my grandparents time). We now have clean air. I can get or order everything that I had in Almaty. And our children — I forgot to mention that I serve as the godmother to many of the children here — I love the way they are educated in school, with access to the latest technology as if they were in the big cities, but at the same time with these wonderful teachers' careful attention. So I for one am not worried about their values when they grow up, and I know whatever happens to me, my large family will support me.

So what am I worrying about? Yes, I do worry about our beloved river, the Syr Darya; we see the water levels going down in general, but then torrential rains create terrible flash floods followed by long droughts. I learned in school that, almost 50 years ago, our northern part of the Aral Sea was once saved through bold action, but now we worry about it drying up once more. And we worry that the water shortage is leading to real conflict in this region this time. So yes, I hope that our government takes the lead and find a solution for our quarreling neighbors.

Source: Visioned by Shigeo Katsu.

URBANIZATION, REGIONAL DEVELOPMENT, AND DECENTRALIZATION

Urbanization, Regional Development, and Decentralization

Chapter 8

Johannes F. Linn

Efficient, safe, vibrant cities, an integrated regional space, and effective urban and regional management with citizen participation are essential ingredients for a country's competitiveness and for the quality of life of its citizens. For a large country that is landlocked and sparsely populated, such as Kazakhstan, spatial connectivity of its rural and urban population is a particular challenge. And for Kazakhstan to reach and sustain its goal of becoming a top 30 developed knowledge economy, the development of an efficiently managed, attractive and competitive structure of large and medium-sized cities is especially important (see Chapter 9).

This chapter provides a brief overview of the trends in urbanization, regional development, and decentralization in Kazakhstan in recent decades, and reviews key government programs in these areas. The chapter then presents a vision of what Kazakhstan may wish to look like in terms of its territorial development by 2050, and what are the main pathways that it could pursue to achieve this vision.

Urban, Regional, and Decentralization Trends in Kazakhstan

Urbanization: A steady, but moderate trend

By international standards, Kazakhstan is moderately urbanized and will likely remain so until 2050, with more than one-third of the population projected by the United Nations then to be still living in rural areas. As shown in Table 8.1, the country's urban population share increased from 44.5 percent in 1960 to 57.1 percent in 1990, but then declined somewhat to 54.4 percent by 2010, due to the differential impact of migration, fertility rates, and reclassification of settlements from urban to rural.[1] By the year 2050, according to the UN, Kazakhstan will have an urban population of 13.7 million, or 64.4 percent of the total. This will be below the world average (UN "Urbanization" 2012), and Kazakhstan, along with much of Asia and Africa, will occupy a middle tier of urbanized countries in a highly urbanized world. Moreover, Kazakhstan's urban areas cover a relatively very low share of total land area and of arable land, a trend that will continue through 2050, and the average density of Kazakhstan's large cities by international standards falls in the medium range (Angel 2012).

Kazakhstan's largest city, Almaty, had a population of 1.45 million in 2012. Almaty, although large, is no mega-city (defined as a city with a population of 10 million or more). In 2011, the world had 23 mega-cities, and it is projected to have 37 by 2025 (UN "Urbanization" 2012). Almaty will not be among them. Nor will it be among the 59 cities in the world expected to have populations between 5 and 10 million, but instead it will be one of 573 cities between 1 and 5 million. Furthermore, the primacy of Almaty (i.e., its share of Kazakhstan's total population) is moderate at 15.9 percent in 2012, and less than would be expected by international standards, according to which it would have to be about twice the size (Angel

---

1. For a commentary on the impact of reclassification, see Makhmutova (2012).

8

2012; Coulibaly et al. 2012). The low degree of primacy is also reflected in the fact that Kazakhstan does not conform to what is known as Zipf's Law of city size distribution, since Kazakhstan's medium-sized cities (defined as cities with populations between 100,000 and 1 million) are consistently larger than expected relative to the size of Almaty.[2] This pattern is explained in part by the territorial planning of Soviet times, but also more recently by the emergence of Astana, whose rapid growth has surely limited the growth of Almaty. City population projections indicate that this pattern of lower-than-expected primacy is likely to persist for the next few decades (Figure 8.1).

Table 8.1	Kazakhstan's urban population share is relatively moderate and likely to remain so in 2050					
Population	Total	Urban	Rural	Share (%)	Urban	Rural
1960	9,995,997	4,445,751	5,550,246	100	44.5%	55.5%
1970	13,109,992	6,585,935	6,524,056	100	50.2%	49.8%
1980	14,898,332	8,066,255	6,832,077	100	54.1%	45.9%
1990	16,297,981	9,300,779	6,997,202	100	57.1%	42.9%
2000	14,901,641	8,397,566	6,504,075	100	56.4%	43.7%
2010	16,204,617	8,806,952	7,397,665	100	54.4%	45.7%
2020	17,680,023	9,451,122	8,228,902	100	53.5%	46.5%
2030	18,872,994	10,545,067	8,327,927	100	55.9%	44.1%
2040	20,047,661	12,059,198	7,988,463	100	60.2%	39.9%
2050	21,210,040	13,650,054	7,559,986	100	64.4%	35.6%

Source: Compiled by NAC of Nazarbayev University based on World Bank (1960–1990), Agency of Statistics of the Republic of Kazakhstan (2000–2010), UN World Population Prospects (2020–50).

City infrastructure and management: major challenges

The definition of cities in Kazakhstan spans a wide range of settlement sizes. In addition to Almaty, defined as a large city (with 1 million inhabitants or more), Kazakhstan has 20 medium-size cities (100,000 to 999,999 inhabitants) and 65 small cities (less than 100,000).[3] The nature of the challenges and opportunities across this wide array of cities differs. Our focus here is mostly on the issues faced by the large and medium-sized cities, which had about 80 percent of the total urban population in 2012.

The urban infrastructure and management that Kazakhstan inherited at independence was, in many ways, a favorable asset for the country, as in the rest of the former Soviet Union (Coulibaly et al. 2012). The cities of Kazakhstan offered good access to public transit, water and sanitation, and recycling. District heating was almost universally available, as were public education and health services. Soviet

---

2. Zipf's Law states that the distribution of cities conforms to a power function: $r \times P^q = K$, where r is the rank order of a particular city, P is its population, K is the population of the largest city, and the exponent q is a number equal to or close to 1. If q=1, then following this equation the population of the second largest city should be half the size of the largest city, the third largest city should a third of the size of the largest city, and so on down the city ranks. This "law" is based on an observed regularity of city size distributions in the world. Angel (2012) estimated that the equation is statistically significant not only at a country level, but also at a global level, when he fitted it to the populations of 3,646 cities worldwide, with the estimated exponent q = 1.053 at the 95 percent confidence level.

3. According to Kazakhstan's legal definition, the country's 87 cities are categorized according to levels of significance: Two cities have "national significance" (Almaty and Astana), 40 cities have "regional significance," and 45 cities have "district significance." All city demographic data in this section are based on Agency of Statistics of the Republic of Kazakhstan, provided by the NAC of Nazarbayev University.

cities even had some favorable "green" characteristics, such as recycling and combined heat and power plants. Moreover, private car ownership was low, and hence transport-related pollution and congestion were limited. However, central planning also left Kazakh cities with liabilities, such as provision of urban services linked to firms that no longer maintained these services after central planning was abandoned; "mono-cities" that depended on a single firm for much of its employment, income and local revenues; and so forth. Moreover, with the transition toward a market economy and institutions, the management of all urban services had to be fundamentally restructured, the housing stock privatized, and new municipal funding sources developed.

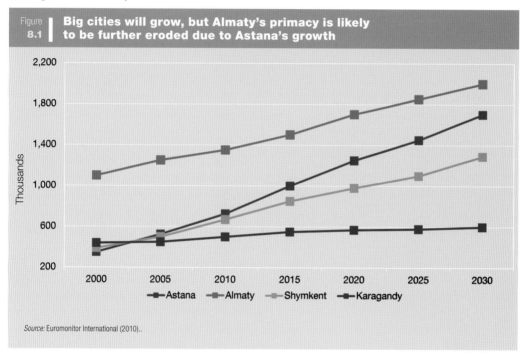

Figure 8.1 | **Big cities will grow, but Almaty's primacy is likely to be further eroded due to Astana's growth**

Source: Euromonitor International (2010)..

While many of the urban infrastructure assets remain in place, the cities of Kazakhstan face serious challenges in managing what the Asian Development Bank refers to as "the country's aging and dilapidated municipal infrastructure" (ADB "Sector Assessment" 2012):

- *Water and sanitation infrastructure* is rapidly deteriorating due to lack of maintenance and inadequate funding. The Asian Development Bank (ADB) estimates that 86 percent of the population has access to drinking water and 81 percent to sanitation, but the quality of the water is variable and the sanitation services frequently involve discharge without effective treatment (ADB "Sector Assessment" 2012). Moreover, three-quarters of the infrastructure needs replacement, there is a high rate of water that is unaccounted for, and water tariffs do not cover operational, let alone capital, costs (ADB "Sector Assessment" 2012; OECD "Ten Years" 2011; World Bank "Targeting" 2012). According to the EBRD Transition Indicators 2012 (EBRD "Transition Report" 2012), the gap between Kazakhstan's water and waste water sector market structure and institutions and those of advanced industrial countries remains large.

- *Urban solid waste disposal* needs are growing rapidly but collection is limited to 40 to 60 percent collection of waste generated, and what is collected is disposed of mostly in untreated landfills with significant risks to ground water supplies and the environment (ADB "Sector Assessment" 2012).

- *Centralized district heating* is widely relied on by the inhabitants of Kazakhstan's cities to keep warm in the grueling winters. The existing systems suffer from poor maintenance of the distribution network, high losses of heat in the distribution network and residential structures, lack of metering among end users, and limited cost recovery due to low tariffs (ADB "Sector Assessment" 2012; ADB "Infrastructure Road Map" 2012).

- *Affordable housing* is also a serious problem in the cities of Kazakhstan. The vast majority of urban housing is now in private hands, with only about 3 percent publicly owned (UNDP 2010). However, very little (only 3 percent) of the housing stock is rental property, which makes for a very inflexible housing supply that impedes mobility (World Bank "Targeting" 2012). Poor maintenance of the existing housing stock is prevalent, in part due to the lack of effective homeowner associations (World Bank "Targeting" 2012), and, on the suburban fringes, unplanned, illegal residential development is not uncommon (UNDP 2010). Overall, a significant shortage of cheap housing is reported in the large cities, especially in Almaty and Astana (Laruelle and Peyrouse 2013).

- *Urban transport and transit* is dominated by the private automobile, as motor vehicle ownership has rapidly increased from about 100 per 1,000 of population in 2003 to about 220 in 2010 (World Bank "DataBank" 2013). While this remains far short of the ownership levels in advanced industrial countries, such as Germany and Poland (570 and 540 motor vehicles per 1,000 people in 2010), the modal split in transit for the three largest cities of Kazakhstan shows that there is an overwhelming reliance on the use of cars for urban transport, comparable to that in the US (Dopazo et al. 2012). This causes significant problems of congestion, pollution, and traffic accidents[4] in Almaty and increasingly also in other cities of Kazakhstan. With a great potential for continued rapid growth of automobile use, there is also the potential for resulting severe additional problems. Low gasoline prices and an absence of effective management of traffic and parking compound the urban transit problem (ADB "Sector Assessment" 2012), and public transport companies suffer from financial losses due to low tariffs and resulting poor service (ADB "Sector Assessment" 2012; ADB "Infrastructure Road Map" 2012; World Bank "Targeting" 2012).

- *Exposure to natural disasters, especially earthquakes*, is very significant in the south of Kazakhstan (Linn 2011; Thurmond 2011). Southern Kazakhstan is part of a vast belt of high seismic risk that extends throughout Central Asia and the Caucasus. Severe earthquakes devastated Almaty between 1887 and 1911. And as recently as January 28, 2013 an earthquake of 6.6 magnitude was reported to have taken place within 250 km of Almaty.[5] Kazakhstan is better prepared to respond to natural disasters than its Central Asian neighbors, but its disaster preparedness and response capacity remains weak in the face of major threats (Gurenko and Dumitru 2009; UNDP and ECHO 2011).

---

4. The mortality rate from traffic accidents is three times higher in the Former Soviet Union (FSU) than in Western Europe, and Kazakhstan has the highest mortality rate in the FSU (Coulibaly et al. 2012). According to World Health Organization data, Kazakhstan rates 38th highest among 178 countries in terms of the incidence of road traffic deaths. http://www.photius.com/rankings/road_traffic_deaths_country_rankings_2009.html

5. http://www.rferl.org/content/earthquake-kazakhstan/24886635.html

- *Social disparities* are significant across cities. Per capita incomes, poverty rates, and unemployment rates differ substantially across cities of different size, with incomes lower and poverty rates higher in the smaller urban areas. Urban service quality is also lower in the smaller cities (Ferré, Ferreira, and Lanjouw 2010; Makhmutova 2012). However, poverty rates have come down everywhere, and unemployment rates are nearly equalized throughout the country (UNDP "Decentralization" 2008).

- *Urban management capacity* is generally weak. According to the ADB, there is a "lack of planning and development coordination between the central government and the regional and city *akimats* (mayors); slow institutional, policy, regulatory, and tariff reforms to support municipal development; weak institutional capacity and experience to develop municipal projects suitable for PPP delivery; and a lack of ability to attract and involve institutional investors and various forms of private sector participation" (ADB "Sector Assessment" 2012, p. 1). Moreover, according to the World Bank, "urban land markets are active, but land-use planning and approval is cumbersome and non-transparent" (World Bank "Targeting" 2012, p. 10).

These challenges will get more severe as cities continue to expand. Demands on stretched transport networks and ecosystems will become severe unless concerted action is taken to improve the quantity and quality of urban service provision and limit the rapidly growing use of automobiles.

Regional development: Disparities and connectivity[6]

Kazakhstan is a large country (ninth largest in the world, equal in size to all of Western Europe; World Bank "Country Partnership" 2012) with a low average population density, except in the south. Unless urbanization proceeds more quickly than currently projected, Kazakhstan in 2050 will still have between 30 percent and 40 percent of its population living in rural areas, likely more than seven million people (Table 2.1 here). This presents Kazakhstan with the challenge of how to assure a reasonable economic and social balance across regions and across the rural-urban divide in terms of opportunities for economic and human development. Kazakhstan's future political stability will likely depend on how effectively it addresses this challenge. Moreover, economic growth requires a high degree of connectivity of business and people across the vast geographic space of Kazakhstan and with the rest of the world.

Looking, first, at regional economic and social development, while overall social conditions have improved throughout the country during the 2000s, regional and urban-rural differences within Kazakhstan remain significant. Following USAID (2006) one may categorize regions by oil-extracting "oblasts" (provinces), non-oil industrial oblasts, agricultural oblasts, and municipal districts (Almaty, Astana). About 60 percent of the country's GDP is produced in the two largest cities (municipal districts) and in oil-extracting oblasts. While per capita income grew in all oblasts in recent years, there remain substantial divergences in GRP (gross regional product) per capita across oblasts: In 2011 GRP per capita in oil-rich Atyrau (USD 43,700) was more than 10 times that in agricultural Zhambyl (USD 4,100). There is no evidence of regional income convergence (Frey and Wieslhuber 2011). Poverty dropped in all oblasts, but there remain significant differentials in poverty rates (see Chapter 2). Surprisingly, however, some of the oil producing oblasts have poverty rates significantly above the national average.

The differentials in per capita income and poverty rates are matched by differences in access to public services (housing with water supply, sanitation, central heating, gas, and hot water supply) across oblasts and across the urban-rural divide. Rural housing is by far the least well-supplied with public

---

6. Unless otherwise stated all figures in this section are based on NAC of Nazarbayev University analysis, drawing on data provided by the Agency of Statistics of the Republic of Kazakhstan.

services (except for gas). Across oblasts, Kyzylorda, West Kazakhstan, and North Kazakhstan are least well-supplied in urban and rural areas, while the cities of Almaty and Astana generally have access rates far above the national average. The same holds broadly true for access to health services across oblasts as measured by the availability of medical staff per population.

A second key issue for Kazakhstan, with its large land area and low density, is the extent to which its population in different locations is connected to each other, markets, and government service providers. The road and rail network, as well as air traffic and Internet connectivity, are key in this regard.

The road transport sector in Kazakhstan faces significant problems, which are well-summarized in the following quotes from a recent ADB report:

- "Much of the road network is in poor condition: about 60 percent of republican roads require major rehabilitation and proper maintenance. Moreover, the feeder road network serving the rural population is not fully developed, and is characterized by poor conditions and a low service level, especially during winter. These result in a high cost of transporting goods: the transport cost component is about 10 percent of the cargo value, which is far above the average of about 4 percent in developed economies" (ADB "Sector Assessment" 2012, p. 1).
- "Technical and operational characteristics of roads are below international standards, with traffic exceeding allowable loads. The average driving speed along the Europe, Caucasus, Asia transport corridor is less than 20 km per hour." (ADB "Sector Assessment" 2012, p. 1)
- "The road sector has long-standing operational and institutional bottlenecks: (i) the network is incomplete, and some sections are in bad condition; (ii) truck overloading is frequent, cutting into the economic life of road assets; (iii) revenues from transit are low, affecting cost recovery and reinvestment capabilities; (iv) inefficient cross-border procedures increase the burden on trade and raise the cost of doing business; (v) weak road sector planning affects sound investment sequencing; and (vi) project management shortcomings create inefficiencies. Although road accidents have been falling by 7 percent per year, speeding and inadequate road design and operations still cause many accidents and high fatality rates" (ADB "Sector Assessment" 2012, p. 2).

Railway traffic is also of great significance for Kazakhstan internally and for connecting it with neighbors and with international markets (see Chapter 10). After the collapse of the Soviet Union, railway use collapsed throughout the FSU, but it recovered most quickly in Kazakhstan, growing substantially beyond its pre-independence level (Coulibaly et al. 2012). However, the operation of the railway system confronts significant challenges. There is a shortage of wagons, a majority of the passenger cars that are in service require repair, two-thirds of locomotives are beyond their design lifespan, and the ownership of freight wagons is fragmented, with many small owners unable to provide adequate maintenance (Laruelle and Peyrouse 2013).

With regards to air traffic services, the system was highly developed in the Soviet Union, where in 1990 it accounted for about 35 percent of all intercity travel (Coulibaly et al. 2012). However, Moscow and Saint Petersburg (Russia), and to a lesser extent Tashkent (Uzbekistan), were the main hubs of national and international air traffic; following the breakup of the Soviet Union, the fragmentation of the aircraft fleet across the new countries and the rise in energy costs and lack of central subsidies led to a significant reduction in air traffic. Over time, as in other FSU countries, air traffic recovered in Kazakhstan, and the government invested in new infrastructure capacity and supported the development of a private national flagship airline (Air Astana). However, Kazakhstan's airline connectivity remains relatively low by international standards (Coulibaly et al. 2012). According to an index of air connectivity developed

8

by the World Bank, Kazakhstan rates 128th out of 209 countries and territories in 2007 (compared to Russia at 47th, and Uzbekistan at 120th). Moreover, according to the WTO Aviation Liberalization Index Kazakhstan was among the least liberalized countries in 2008 (Piermartini and Rousova 2008). Moreover, total turn-around costs at Almaty airport were high by international standards, more than three times the cost at Frankfurt, according to World Bank data (Coulibaly et al. 2012).

Considering finally Internet connectivity, the use of the Internet has dramatically risen in recent years in Kazakhstan, from 15 users per 100 persons in 2008 to 50 users per 100 persons in 2011, not far short of developed country rates. Internet use varies across oblasts, but in general the level of use is close to the national average even in the poorer and remote oblasts (with the exception of Zhambyl and Kyzylorda oblasts, where the user rate is only somewhat above half the national level). While this is an encouraging development, Kazakhstan's overall conditions for ICT development — reflecting prevailing ICT infrastructure and ecosystem variables in the country — fall short of advanced country levels and access to broadband Internet remains low (Figure 8.2).[7] Since broadband access is critical for modern IT development and connectivity and the development of a modern knowledge economy, this remains an important area where Kazakhstan needs to catch up. Finally, according to the World Economic Forum's Network Readiness Index 2013, Kazakhstan is ranked 67th in the world out of 138 countries, with strong marks on government usage (rank 31), good individual readiness (rank 53), but weak standing on market development (rank 97) and the policy and regulatory environment (rank 100).[8]

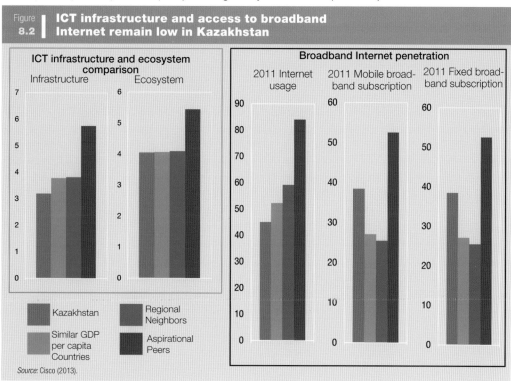

Figure 8.2 | **ICT infrastructure and access to broadband Internet remain low in Kazakhstan**

Source: Cisco (2013).

---

7. Figure 8.2 is based on research carried out by Cisco and applies a framework in which key factors representing the state of ICT development are divided into a category representing ICT infrastructure and a category representing the general conditions in the country that influence the ability of users to apply ICT.

8. http://www.weforum.org/issues/global-information-technology/the-great-transformation/network-readiness-index

8

Decentralization: Placing responsibility and resources where they belong?[9]

After the collapse of the Soviet Union and the demise of its central planning system, the new republics experienced a haphazard, complex, and non-transparent process of partial decentralization (Dabla-Norris 2006; UNDP "Decentralization" 2008). Kazakhstan was no exception. Since independence the country went through six stages of reform that determined the current functions and responsibilities of the four levels of government[10] (NAC of Nazarbayev University "Policy Brief" 2012).

As a result of various reform initiatives and experiments the intergovernmental structure in Kazakhstan shows a significant deconcentration of administrative functions to subnational levels of government. In 2011 subnational finances accounted for 39 percent of total state expenditures (republican and subnational). Subnational spending on education and housing are the largest two expenditure items, and each is more than twice the republican-level expenditure. The third largest item is health spending, which is approximately at the same level as republican spending. Transport and communication also loom large, but here national-level spending exceeds its subnational counterpart. The share of subnational spending in total state spending has stayed approximately constant in recent years, although the shares of subnational spending on education and health have declined.

Three issues arise with the current system of territorial administration in Kazakhstan. First, there are significant overlaps in the distribution of administrative functions across the four levels of government. While successive reforms have attempted to provide for greater clarity in the division of responsibility, this has not in practice resolved the many areas of uncertainty (NAC of Nazarbayev University "Policy Brief" 2012).[11] The current distribution of expenditure responsibility shows with a striking frequency more than one level of government responsible for a given function (Table 8.2).

Second, control over local decisions remains centralized at the national level as part of a unitary, presidential political and administrative system, in which the cascading appointments of the executive leadership from the President on down to the local level results in a "dominant vertical." According to a recent UNDP classification Kazakhstan ranks among the less decentralized among four groups of transition countries (UNDP "Decentralization" 2008). The government has taken some measures of decentralization that potentially give greater accountability of local administrations to the local electorate, such as the introduction of elected oblast and rayon level representative bodies (*maslikhats*), and more recently the introduction of elections of rural *akims*, which were announced in December 2012 and which are to be held in 2013.

Third, the current administrative capacities of subnational administrative bodies are weak, especially with regards to effective land-use planning, operation and maintenance of infrastructure, and the planning and implementation of public-private partnerships (Bhuiyan 2010, ADB "Sector Assessment" 2012; World Bank "Country Partnership" 2012).

The prevailing patterns of deconcentration combined with centralization of control also can be observed on the revenue side. The revenue structure of subnational governments (oblasts and rayons) is dominated by two sources of funding: tax revenues and grants from the central government. Starting from a

---

9. Unless otherwise stated all figures in this section are based on NAC of Nazarbayev University analysis, drawing on data provided by the Kazakhstan Ministry of Finance and the Agency of Statistics of the Republic of Kazakhstan.

10. The four levels are: republican or national level, oblast level, district level, and local level. The local level consists of "aul (rural) okrug," regions of a town and village settlements. Note that only the first three levels have their own governmental and budgetary structures. At the local level there is a mayor (akim), who until 2013 has been is appointed by the district level akim, but will be elected as of 2013 for rural jurisdictions.

11. According to NAC of Nazarbayev University ("Policy Brief" 2012), the government is committed to carry out so-called "functional reviews," which are to assess and help clarify, among other things, the distribution of functions among different levels of government in specific areas of government responsibility (e.g., education, health, etc.). It is too early to tell whether these reviews have a significant impact in streamlining the division of functions among levels of government.

small share of 12 percent in 2001, grants have steadily grown in importance and now account for more than 60 percent of subnational revenue (Figure 8.3), with the territory's own revenues covering less than 40 percent of total subnational expenditure needs. While in principle local executive bodies may receive budget loans (according to budget code Article 177) we have not come across any information that indicates that local governments actually borrow. But the extent to which subnational (province and local) bodies borrow, and under what conditions deserves further in-depth analysis, which to our knowledge so far has not be carried out.

| Table 8.2 | Significant overlaps exist in the expenditure powers of the different levels of government | | |

Expenditure powers by public administration spheres	Distribution among budgets		
	Republican Budget	Oblast Budget	Local Budget
General state services	+	+	+
Defense	+	+	+
Public order and safety	+	+	+
Legal, judicial, penal enforcement activities	+	-	-
Education	+	+	+
Health care	+	+	-
Social assistance and security	+	+	+
Housing and utility service	+	+	+
Culture, sport	+	+	+
Tourism and information space	+	+	-
Agriculture, land relations	+	+	+
Water, forest, fishing industries, specially protected natural areas, environmental and wildlife protection	+	-	-
Industry and sub-surface management	+	-	-
Architecture, city planning and construction activities	+	+	+
Transport and communications	+	+	+
Energy saving and energy efficiency	+	+	+
Economic activity regulation	+	+	+
Miscellaneous	+	+	+

Source: Ministry of Finance of the Republic of Kazakhstan (2011).

Subnational government's own revenues are based principally on revenues from the individual income tax (38 percent), the social tax levied on salaries (30 percent), and the property tax (12 percent). The remaining 20 percent is accounted for by excise duties, other minor taxes and fees, and revenues from natural and other resource usage. While this revenue structure is in principle quite appropriate, all tax

8

rates and bases are set by the national authorities, leaving no freedom for subnational governments or their electorates to set their own revenue policies. The income tax rate of 10 percent is very low by international standards, and property taxes, while not exceptionally low by developing country standards, also generally do not represent an elastic revenue source (World Bank "Targeting" 2012).

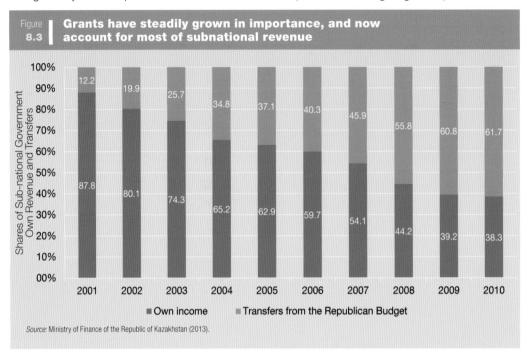

Figure 8.3 Grants have steadily grown in importance, and now account for most of subnational revenue

Source: Ministry of Finance of the Republic of Kazakhstan (2013).

With regards to grants, Kazakhstan employs two sets of transfers from central to subnational authorities: general transfers and targeted development transfers. The allocation of both transfer types is determined by the budget law as follows (see NAC of Nazarbayev University "General Transfers" 2013 for further information):

- *General transfers* use a complex allocation system that is principally designed to provide general revenue support to subnational governments aimed at broadly equalizing per capita revenues across jurisdictions. This objective is only partially achieved, as the post-transfer revenues tend to be higher in the oil-rich oblasts and in Almaty (World Bank "Targeting" 2012), even though the general transfer system actually requires Mangystau Oblast and the two largest cities (Almaty and Astana) to transfer some of their own revenues to the other oblasts. One of the strengths of the grant allocation process is that transfers are fixed for a three-year period, which assures a reliable flow of resources for subnational entities (NAC of Nazarbayev University "Policy Brief" 2012).

- *Targeted transfers* are designed to finance specific investment programs in a wide array of provincial and local development functions, such as housing and communal services, including water supply, heating, gas, and electricity distribution. They are the principal source of subnational investment and, at USD 4.2 billion, a substantial resource. The allocation and program selection process and criteria are specified in detail in the legal and budgetary provisions, but according to a recent review by the World Bank, they are "complex," "cumbersome," and "opaque." In effect, grants may be awarded not according to the criteria, but "on the basis of the stamina and or persistence of their sponsors" (World Bank "Targeting" 2012, p. 5). About 50 percent of the targeted transfers has gone in recent years to Astana and Almaty, with exceptionally high per capita allocations to Astana for the construction of the new capital city. Overall, the allocation of targeted grants reinforces, rather than alleviates, the disparities in subnational revenue distribution.

Thus, while a sequence of reforms of the intergovernmental system in Kazakhstan over the last two decades has resulted in a governmental structure that is relatively de-concentrated, the public sector remains highly centralized in terms of a "dominant vertical," where decisions flow from the top (the national authorities) to the bottom (local communities), rather than the reverse.

Government Programs and Initiatives: Responding to Opportunities and Challenges

The Government of Kazakhstan since independence has been well aware of the opportunities and challenges represented by the country's vast territory at the center of the huge Eurasian landmass, the unevenly distributed population, and the legacy of Soviet-built urban and regional infrastructure. Accordingly, the authorities pursued many programs and initiatives that were designed to provide overall strategic direction and address specific areas in urbanization, regional development and decentralization. In this section, we briefly review some of the more important initiatives, but this by no means is intended to present a comprehensive summary of all programs that have been pursued.

Astana

The single most significant decision in spatial planning was to move the nation's capital city in 1997 to Akmola, renamed Astana, in the center-north of the country, which provided for a rebalancing of the demographic, economic and political center of gravity away from the hitherto dominant southern fringe of the country centered in and around Almaty. The process of planning and implementation of the Astana project is an outstanding example in long-range scaling up: having defined a goal for the year 2030 — a modern capital city of 1 million people, representing the best of Kazakhstan in terms of infrastructure, efficiency, style, and quality of life — the authorities developed a well-articulated pathway toward achieving that goal. Based on an overall master plan developed by the renowned architect Kisho Kurokawa, who was selected in an international competition, three subsidiary plans (a land-use plan, a transportation plan, and a town regulation plan) have provided comprehensive guidance for the development of the city over the last 15 years (Berlyne 2013). Implementation has been carefully monitored, including at the highest level of government, and plans were adapted to incorporate lessons and new opportunities, such as the setting up of Nazarbayev University and attracting Expo 2017 to Astana.[12]

As Astana moves forward toward 2030 and beyond to 2050, a number of important issues need to be addressed, including: (1) how to convert what is currently a relatively dispersed and low-density design into a compact, "green," and "smart" city that allows for effective mass transit, low congestion and pollution, and a high degree of IT connectivity; (2) an effective integration of Astana into the national and international transport and IT grids; and (3) a financing and management process that reduces the call on national resources to sustain the continued expansion of the city and to assure maintenance of the rapidly constructed infrastructure and buildings — already, some of the construction shows significant wear and tear, and serious shortfalls in essential maintenance.

---

12. http://kazakhworld.com/2012/11/28/astana-expo-2017/

The Territorial Development Strategy and other regional development initiatives

In 2006, the government approved a Territorial Development Strategy of Kazakhstan. The strategy focused on the development of three major country-wide transportation axes or corridors (north, east, and south) with two "leading cities" (Almaty and Astana) playing the role of national and international hubs and a set of medium-sized "key cities" as national and regional hubs within Kazakhstan (Junussova 2012). The national transport corridors envisaged under this strategy are broadly consistent with the regional transport corridors developed for Central Asia under the auspices for the Central Asia Regional Cooperation Program (CAREC), in which Kazakhstan is a member (CAREC 2010). Makhmutova (2012) critiqued the government's approach to regional planning for paying too little attention to smaller cities and towns; moreover, Junussova (2012) noted that most sub-regional development strategies, which the government developed based on the national Territorial Development Strategy, paid insufficient attention to external linkages.

Complementary to the Territorial Development Strategy the government also developed a Transport Infrastructure Development Program 2010-14, which covered sector investments as well as institutional and policy reforms (ADB "Sector Assessment" 2012). The government also has been implementing a railway modernization program in recent years (Laruelle and Peyrouse 2013).

Currently, OECD is engaged with the government in an assessment of oblast-specific industrial development and investment opportunities (OECD "Regional Competitiveness" 2012). Starting in 2012 with pilot assessments in three oblasts, the program is designed to identify priority sectors of investment and develop supporting investment promotion activities. Once experience has been gathered with implementation of these activities in the pilot oblasts, the program is to be rolled out in all oblasts in 2015.

Urban development programs

Improvements of urban infrastructure have been pursued at national and city levels. The Akbulak Water Program 2011-20 aims to improve access to safe urban water and sanitation, while a regional program of modernization of housing and utilities for 2011-2020 is designed to raise housing and district heating utility standards (ADB "Sector Assessment" 2012). The program "Affordable Housing — 2020" was approved in June 2012 to support the construction of 69.05 million m^2 of housing in Kazakhstan between 2012 and 2020 (OECD "Regional Competitiveness" 2012). Master plans have been prepared, or are under preparation, for a number of cities, including Almaty and Astana. For Astana, a five-year sustainable transport program is under implementation.

To deal with the problem of cities dependent on single, declining industries left over from Soviet days, the government in 2012 approved the "Mono-Cities Program" (Republic of Kazakhstan 2012). It identified 27 mono-cities with a total population of 1.5 million people. Having differentiated mono-cities according to their development potential (high, medium, or low), those with medium and high potential receive support for diversified business development (including anchor investments by Samruk-Kazyna, grants for modernizing existing firm capacity or exploration of mineral deposits, investments in infrastructure, and support for small and medium enterprise development). People in low-potential mono-cities are supported in their search for employment elsewhere. Since only two such cities were identified, the government appears to have considerable optimism about its ability to support the diversification of a large majority of mono-cities.

8

Infrastructure Road Map for Kazakhstan 2040

ADB commissioned the preparation of an infrastructure road map for Kazakhstan through 2040, which was prepared by a Spanish consulting firm. In its report published in July 2012, the team of consultants laid out a long-term infrastructure development vision and road map for the energy sector, transportation, and urban services. The road map provides for about 100 detailed recommendations in each of the three areas for the short term (0-5 years), medium term (5-15 years) and long term (15-30 years) (ADB "Infrastructure Road Map" 2012).

Recent decentralization initiatives

Two recent developments have the potential to contribute significantly to decentralization in Kazakhstan. First, in December 2012 the President announced that the *akims* (mayors) of rural villages are to be elected, rather than appointed. Second, 4,500 civil servants are to be transferred from national government departments and agencies to local administrations in 2013. Both initiatives will require significant effort for effective implementation.

Creation of the Ministry for Regional Development[13]

In January 2013, the President of Kazakhstan announced the establishment of the new Ministry of Regional Development with a far-reaching mandate regarding regional and urban development in Kazakhstan. The new ministry oversees various departments and committees (agencies), including the Committee for Regional Development and the Department for Regional Policy, and the agencies for construction, land management, enterprise development, coordination of local authorities, city planning, and housing and utilities. With this broad range of responsibilities, the new ministry has virtually all the levers for developing and implementing comprehensive urban and regional policies, except for the allocation of revenue authority and budgetary transfers to subnational governments. This should facilitate the coordination and integration of hitherto fragmented governmental policies and programs in regard to urban and regional development.

A Vision of Kazakhstan 2050

In recent years the authorities have initiated many programs designed to address the country's issues of urbanization, regional development and decentralization. However, looking toward the future, Kazakhstan faces major challenges for how it will create a well-integrated system of modern cities, a balanced regional economic and social structure, and an effectively decentralized system of intergovernmental relations. Let us then consider what vision for 2050 might guide the country in responding to these challenges, consistent with the overall vision presented in Chapter 4.

In his speech on December 14, 2012 President Nazarbayev[14] focused on a number of issues of direct relevance to the topic of this chapter, including the need for balanced regional development, creating access for small towns and low density areas, enhanced coordination in the government's regional development activities, and decentralization of some control to local governors and electorates, while

---

13. This section is based on an interview with a senior official in the Ministry for Regional Development.
http://fininfo.kz/iris/news/449210;jsessionid=1B340068EA8D873562E0A09DD9146508
14. The speech is available at
http://www.bksoc.org.uk/documents/KZ%20president%20address%202012.pdf

8

maintaining the "vertical of power." The last point reflects the tension that the Kazakh authorities face, at least in the short term, in supporting decentralization while wishing to retain key elements of central control.

We therefore suggest in Box 8.1 the vision for Kazakhstan 2050 in the three areas under consideration here. The question then is how to achieve this ambitious vision. The next section presents some options and suggestions for initiatives that Kazakhstan may wish to pursue in its quest for a modern society in regard to urbanization, regional development and decentralization.

Box 8.1 | Vision 2050 for Urbanization, Regional Development, and Decentralization

- Efficiently urbanized: a balanced urban structure; strong urban administrative capacity throughout with effective service provision in public/private partnerships; two world-class metropolitan areas and high-quality mid-sized cities ("competitive," "smart," "green," "safe," and "fun" cities); and effective control of crime and preparedness for natural disasters.
- Highly integrated regionally: major population centers are linked through efficient transport, logistics, and communications systems, with smaller towns and cities and rural/agricultural communities linked to major transport and communications hubs and corridors through high-quality secondary and tertiary networks; this also provides essential behind-the-border support for international integration; in this vein, national and supra-national regional integration strategies are effectively linked; access to economic and social services is balanced across regions.
- Effectively decentralized: While retaining its unitary governmental structure, Kazakhstan will have an efficient, equitable, and decentralized intergovernmental system, with local executives accountable to local voters; clear expenditure and effective revenue assignments; national transfer systems that provide appropriate incentives; well-developed municipal bond markets supervised by the Central Bank; and strong administrative capacities at the subnational level.

Source: Author.

How to Achieve the Vision

In pursuit of the above vision, Kazakhstan may wish to consider three overlapping aspects of policy and programmatic engagement. The first area is city planning and implementation: the way cities use their limited space, how they connect business and people across that space, and how they finance the investments needed to assure their effective functioning. The second area is territorial planning and implementation: shaping the way people are connected across the vast geographic and economic space of Kazakhstan. The third area is decentralization: to what extent and how local government and individuals are empowered to make decisions about spatial planning, both across regions and within regions and cities. We look at each of these areas and assess what might be ways for the authorities of Kazakhstan to shape urbanization, regional development, and decentralization trends in the coming years so as to help achieve the vision of Kazakhstan 2050.

City planning and implementation

We focus here on city-level planning and implementation rather than on the issue of control of urbanization and city size distribution, since the latter issues in our view are not relevant goals of policy-making in the case of Kazakhstan, but rather the by-product of other decisions, in particular the effectiveness of city planning, territorial planning, and decentralization decisions. We do not believe that in the case of

Kazakhstan looking ahead it is necessary or appropriate either to force or restrict the speed of urbaniza-tion, or to plan for accelerating or holding back the growth of any particular city or city size category. As noted here, however, it is possible that the modernization strategy that Kazakhstan is poised to pursue will result in a more rapid pace of urbanization than that projected by the United Nations. In this case, the need to plan for an effective absorption of this additional urban population growth will have to be reflected in future urban planning exercises based on careful monitoring of trends.

The key features of city planning and implementation are represented in Figure 8.4, where the yellow boxes represent goals of modern city planning consistent with the vision Kazakhstan 2050, and the blue boxes represent instruments for achieving the vision. At the core of the goals for city planning is the creation of a *competitive city*: one that can compete in the national, regional, and global marketplace by attracting innovative and productive business and labor. This is complemented by the creation of a *smart city*: one that provides and uses the tools of modern information and communication technology for business, government and people. The goal of a creating a *green city* is related to city that uses natural resources, such as energy, water, and air, efficiently and sustainably and limits emissions and pollution. The goal of a *safe city* relates to ensuring that people and businesses are prepared for and as far as possible protected from natural disasters and crime. Finally, the city should be a *fun city* to live in: one that allows people to enjoy culture, sports, green spaces, and the city's heritage. Each of these goals, as shown in Figure 8.4 by the yellow boxes and arrows, is related to the other goals in multiple ways, such that achievement of one goal supports the achievement of the others.

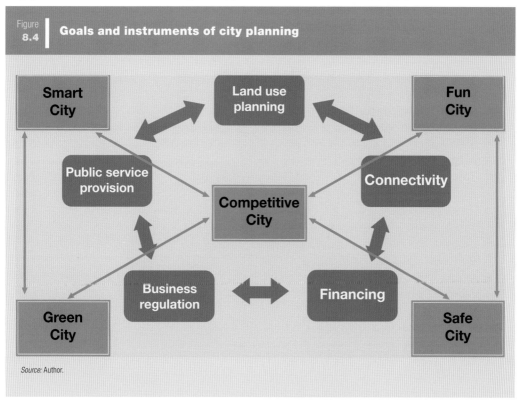

Figure 8.4 | **Goals and instruments of city planning**

Source: Author.

8

In the remainder of this section we will focus on key instruments for achieving the compound goal of a modern city, which are represented in Figure 8.3 by the blue boxes: land-use planning, connectivity, public service provision, business regulation, and financing. As for goals, the use of the five sets of instruments is, as we shall see, interconnected, and need to be planned and implemented in a mutually supportive manner.

Land-use planning

The first instrument in the urban planning and implementation tool kit is land-use planning. Usually the planning process is embedded in the preparation of city master plans and the land-use plans are implemented through infrastructure investments (roads, water and sanitation, schools, universities, hospitals, and so forth) and by application of land use regulations. These include the permission of land development at the periphery, restrictions on density of development (e.g., floor-area ratio regulations, set-back requirements, etc.), and building permits consistent with land use restrictions, building safety, and so forth.

A key consideration for land-use planning in the future must be the maintenance of a compact city development. The potential differences are huge. Compare Atlanta (US) and Barcelona (Spain), cities roughly of equal population size in 1990 but with Atlanta occupying more than 10 times the area of Barcelona. The resulting increase in infrastructure requirements, commuting distances, ecological footprint, and so forth for low-density development along the lines of Atlanta compared to the higher-density development of Barcelona is dramatic (Suzuki, Cervero, and Iuchi 2012).

Six requirements of effective land-use planning are relevant for Kazakhstan:

- Effective and early land-use planning as cities grow is particularly important as the physical structure of a city, once established, is long-lasting and difficult to change (Angel 2012).
- A key ingredient of effective land-use planning is the existence of effective cadastral mapping and clear property rights.
- Sufficient allocations have to be made for public land use (especially roads, schools, green space, etc.) and these spaces have to be protected from encroachment. According to Angel (2012), about 5 percent of urban land should be set aside for transport rights of way, and another 5 percent for public use and open space.
- Care needs to be taken not to impose excessively restrictive floor-area ratio restrictions on urban residential and business construction. This has been a common mistake in cities around the world and has led to highly inefficient urban land use patterns (e.g., in Mumbai, India) (Bertaud 2010).
- The regulatory framework for the implementation of land-use plans and its actual application has to be kept simple, transparent, and free from corruption.
- A close link between land-use planning and urban infrastructure planning needs to be fostered, especially as regards the development of transport and transit, and of water and sanitation trunk lines.

Recommendations: In the next few years, Kazakhstan should take stock of its land-use planning and implementation approaches and its institutional capacities in all large and medium-sized cities to assure that they effectively respond to the aforementioned requirements. Appropriate changes then should be implemented and the modernized system of land-use planning applied consistently in the coming decades.

8

Intra-city connectivity: Efficient transport and transit planning and implementation

Intra-city connectivity involves two key elements: efficient transport/transit and Internet connectivity. We discuss here transport/transit only and leave the discussion of Internet connectivity to the next section dealing with territorial planning and implementation, since the issue of IT access has to be tackled primarily at a national level. However, this should not be taken as an invitation to neglect IT connectivity at the city level. Increasingly, electronic interchange (especially live video connections) will serve as a key way of communication not only for long distance, but also for every day exchanges over short distances, in connection with home-based work, for business or personal meetings, or for online shopping. This has the potential of significantly enhancing the efficiency and productivity of urban life, as well as cutting down on the need for transport and transit. At the same time, electronic connectivity cannot replace face-to-face interaction, and hence, as cities grow, the need for transport services will also continue growing.

In considering transport and transit planning, a key factor is the growth of the principal mode of transport used by commuters during rush hour times: walking and cycling, automobiles, or public transport. Automobiles require by far the greatest amount of urban space for transit and for parking. In addition of course, the energy and ecological footprint of cars is much greater than of alternative forms of transit. A key priority for urban transport planning therefore has to be the control of the growth of automobile use. The wide differences in the share of cars used for transport in cities in different parts of the world is clearly correlated with the different policies employed with regard to urban transit modes (Suzuki, Cervero, and Iuchi 2012).

Kazakhstan still has a relatively low level of car ownership in comparison with today's developed countries. However, judging from the recent rapid growth in automobile ownership in the country and in the rest of the world and its close correlation with increasing prosperity of the population, one can predict that Kazakhstan will have a high rate of car ownership in the future, comparable to developed countries. Kazakhstan has four sets of instruments to control the use of automobiles in its cities: limit the growth in car ownership, limit the use of cars for urban transit, offer preferential treatment for alternative modes of transit, or utilize land-use planning and infrastructure investments to help make transport more efficient and facilitate transit other than by car.

Control of car ownership: Short of outright control over the number of cars individuals or business can own, which would be highly restrictive and difficult to enforce, taxation of automobiles, either at the time of purchase or through an annual license fee, provides a disincentive to car ownership, as well as revenue for the construction of urban transport infrastructure and for subsidies to public transit. There are dramatic differences in the purchase price across cities worldwide: the price of buying a car in Shanghai is more than four times that in London (Economist.com 2013). The scope for taxation of automobile as an asset is therefore significant.

Limit the use of cars in cities: Ideally, however, one would focus on limiting the use of cars rather than of car ownership, since it is the use of cars, rather than their ownership per se, that imposes high social costs (high investment requirements, congestion, pollution, accidents, etc.) not fully reflected in the costs the user has to bear. Car use could be constrained by regulating the use of cars in cities at certain times or in areas of high congestion (Suzuki, Cervero, and Iuchi 2012). Some cities have done so by permitting only cars with odd or even license plate numbers on alternate days during periods of high pollution (e.g., in Beijing). Singapore and London have restricted the use of cars in the central city districts by charging high fees. Many European cities have permanently designated pedestrian-only areas in the central cities. Many countries, especially in Europe, tax gasoline at high rates, which raises the cost to the user of, and hence discourages, automobile use. There are considerable differences in the cost of

8

automobile use (in addition to differences in the of car purchase) across selected cities in the world, again indicating considerable latitude in the potential for taxing automobile use (Suzuki, Cervero, and Iuchi 2012). One important cost of car use relates to the price of gasoline. Gasoline prices in Kazakhstan are among the lowest in the FSU, and much lower than in Western Europe (represented by Spain), although they are somewhat higher than in the US (Coulibaly et al. 2012). So the scope for raising gasoline prices in Kazakhstan appears substantial.

Preferential treatment for alternative transit modes, particularly public transit: Another way of accounting for the high social costs of car use is to subsidize the use of public transit or give it preferential treatment in the use of available road space. When subsidizing public transit, it is critical that these subsidies be explicitly budgeted, so they do not impair necessary spending on operations and maintenance. Alternative cross-subsidies among users can be considered, with the fiscal resources required for the cross subsidy raised by taxing car use or car ownership as suggested here.

Preferential use of road space or provision of separate rights of way is of particular relevance for two forms of public transit: Bus Rapid Transit (BRT) and Light Rail systems. Both modes are especially suitable for large and medium-sized cities, where they can form the backbone of a planned urban transit system. For cities above 1 million people, subways can also serve as an appropriate transit mode, but they need to be combined with other public transit forms if they are to provide a serious alternative to the use of cars. A number of cities have used one or the other of these two transit systems with considerable success, including Bogota, Curitiba, and Seoul (Suzuki, Cervero, and Iuchi 2012). Kazakhstan is already planning a light rail system for Astana and has recently expanded the subway in Almaty.

Land-use planning and transport infrastructure investment: As noted in the preceding lines, land-use planning needs to make adequate provision for public rights of way, if congestion is to be kept to acceptable levels. Bangkok shows the dramatic impact of inadequate planning for trunk road space (Angel 2012). Moreover, road and urban rail investments are a critical way to influence the shape of a city and its density, since commercial and residential land development tends to take place along such major lines of transit. Effective maintenance of the road and rail assets is essential to keep transport costs down for private users and to limit the replacement costs for the public or private owners of the infrastructure. Finally, transport modes other than automobiles can be supported by allowing or encouraging higher densities, by setting aside space for and investing in walk ways, pedestrian zones and in bicycle paths, and by offering pedestrian-friendly interfaces between public transport and pedestrian walking areas (residential and commercial). Of course, climate is a significant factor: where the weather is characterized by extreme cold and/or heat, as in many parts of Kazakhstan, the potential for creating a "walkable city" or "cyclable city" will by necessity be limited.[15]

Constraints and opportunities: Worldwide experience shows that the control of automobile ownership and use in cities is difficult for two interrelated reasons. First, with high income elasticity and a low price elasticity of the demand for automobiles, which reflect the universal intensity of people's preferences for owning and using private cars, price mechanisms are relatively ineffective in controlling the use of automobiles in cities. Second, given this strong preference it is also difficult politically to introduce and enforce strict limits — price or non-price — on the ownership and use of private cars. This means that Kazakhstan's leadership will have to be particularly forward-looking, courageous, and persuasive in assuring public understanding and support for appropriate policies in this area. On the other hand,

---

15. Note that Montreal (Canada) has dealt with this challenge by constructing extensive underground pedestrian walkways in its city center; however, this option is expensive and may not be viable everywhere, given geological constrains (e.g., high ground water levels in Astana).

technological advances may help in future by creating more effective electronic traffic management tools, driverless cars, car-sharing systems, reduced commuting needs, and so forth. But the challenge of effectively managing urban connectivity will likely remain significant, nonetheless.

Recommendations: Effective intra-urban connectivity is critical for Kazakhstan to develop competitive, smart, green, safe, and fun cities in the coming decades. Accordingly, we recommend that Kazakhstan should:

- provide for BRT and light rail transit in large and medium-sized cities, and further extension of the Almaty subway system, with budget subsidies helping to offset the continued cost advantage of cars;[16]
- apply land-use planning and investment to encourage high density development, and allow for dedicated rights of way for pedestrians, bicycles, and public transit;
- assure effective operation and maintenance of urban transport and transit assets through improvements in management and funding;
- limit the use of cars in urban transportation by a suitable combination of taxes and fees on the use of cars in cities, combined with area and time-based restrictions on the use of cars in city centers; and
- cover the cost of urban transport and transit infrastructure investments and subsidies by taxes on automobile ownership and use.

Urban communal services, housing, and public safety

As mentioned here, Kazakhstan has a significant backlog in urban communal services, and with the continued growth in the urban population through 2050 it will need continued investments, improved operations and management, and better financing. This section reviews the initiatives required for this sector in the coming decades to help meet the vision for Kazakhstan 2050.[17] It also briefly considers how to help meet urban housing needs and provide for public safety, especially in regard to natural disaster preparedness.

Municipal water supply and sanitation. ADB ("Sector Assessment" 2012) presents a program of action that aims to increase access to water and sanitation services in urban areas to 100 percent by 2015 and then maintain universal service coverage through 2040 (and beyond), taking into account expected growth in the urban population. The initial phase of this program is consistent with government's Akbulak program for the period 2011-2020. Total investment cost of rehabilitation and new construction of production, treatment, distribution and collection is about USD 5 billion through 2040. In addition to these investments, the program envisages 100 percent meter coverage (up from 76 percent currently), measures to reduce water losses, and a monitoring system for the water and sanitation sector implemented by an independent regulatory body. In addition, for long-term sustainability, water tariffs need to be raised to cost-covering levels, through use of appropriate lifeline tariffs which protects the low income consumers from undue burdens. Finally, private sector participation in the sector is already significant and is to be further encouraged under the Akbulak program.

---

16. According to ADB ("Sector Assessment" 2012) a combination of investments in improved public transportations and measures to discourage the use of cars the modal share of cars in Almaty could be reduced from 70 percent now to 37 percent by 2040, and in the case of Astana from 70 to 52 percent. The investment costs are estimates at USD 804 million for Almaty, and USD 548 million for Astana (in constant 2010 US dollars).

17. We draw on the analysis and findings of ADB ("Sector Assessment" 2012), which lays out a plan a action for the urban communal services sector in Kazakhstan through 2040.

8

Urban solid waste management.[18] ADB ("Sector Assessment" 2012) recommends that by 2040 all urban solid waste is to be collected, with two-thirds sorted for recycling, composting or incineration, and the remaining one-third disposed in sanitary landfills. This requires investment in dual collection capacity, incineration and composting plants, construction of sanitary landfills, and closure of open dumps. ADB estimates the cumulative investment costs at USD 4.0-4.5 billion and annual operating costs at USD 303-363 million per annum (in constant 2010 US dollars). In addition, ADB ("Sector Assessment" 2012) recommends "gradual involvement of private operators in the solid waste sector and the introduction, initially as a pilot, of Extended Producer Responsibility, in which manufacturers are made financially responsible for the management of the product end-of-life, [which] will ensure that the private sector invests in the collection and treatment of waste streams included in the Extended Producer Responsibility schemes (e.g. vehicles, packaging, electronic and electric equipment)" (p. 58). Effective regulatory, enforcement, financing and public education mechanisms will have to be developed to ensure compliance with collection requirements by commercial and residential users. In view of the significant externalities involved, some subsidy by the public sector from general tax revenues, especially for residential and small business waste, will likely be required.

Municipal district heating. ADB ("Sector Assessment" 2012) notes the urgent need to upgrade the municipal district heating system in Kazakhstan and proposed a comprehensive program for the upgrade. An estimated 78 percent of distributed heat could be saved through the introduction of heat and hot water meters in homes and offices, improving the heat distribution system to increase efficiency and reduce losses. In addition, the program envisages the progressive conversion of current low-efficiency heat-only boilers to high-efficiency and low-polluting boiler technology, relying on clean coal or gas-fired equipment. In this sector, too, over time heating tariffs need to be raised to cost covering levels (see also Chapter 6).

Urban housing. Provision of housing is generally best left to the private sector. However, the public sector can assist in a number of ways to ensure that the housing supply meets the needs of the widest possible spectrum of the urban population. Five elements of public policy are important, based on international experience:

- Urban land-use planning and regulation must ensure that adequate land is available in accessible locations for residential development, and that density regulations do not restrict choices for building high-density settlements where this is economically the most appropriate (especially in or near the city center).
- Credit markets still need to be more developed to provide mortgage finance for a wide range of households, especially among the poorer population. Developed countries have in place various schemes to support mortgage credit for low-income households. Kazakhstan may want to review the worldwide experience and adapt it to its own institutional, financial, and cultural requirements.
- Adequate rental housing is an important feature of a well-developed housing market. Worldwide experience demonstrates that, rather than public construction and ownership of rental housing, it is better to support private construction, ownership, and management of rental housing, either through suitable land-use regulation or by requiring developers to construct a minimum share of rental housing along with owner-occupied housing. Subsidies should be used sparingly, if at all (Coulibaly et al. 2012).

---

18. For a proposed approach to deal with industrial waste, see Chapter 7.

- In Kazakhstan, as in other FSU countries, homeowner associations are not well-developed and widely supported by apartment-owning households. It will be essential to develop mechanisms to support the development and acceptance of such associations through public information campaigns, regulations, and limited financial support.

Public safety: Disaster preparedness and crime prevention. As noted earlier, many of Kazakhstan's population centers, especially in the southeast of the country, are at risk of major earthquakes and other natural disasters (floods, landslides, and so forth). Two types of intervention can help reduce the damage caused by such disasters, as discussed at length for Central Asia in Linn (2011):

- *Disaster-proofing*: Buildings and public infrastructure can be constructed to minimize the damage from earthquakes and human settlements can be kept out of flood-prone areas. Appropriate regulation and land-use planning goes some way toward addressing these issues, but are often not sufficient, due to lack of enforcement. In addition, encouraging the setting up of disaster insurance — possibly as a private-public partnership — has a good track record in developing self-regulation of building standards by the insurance industry and in providing financial resources to rebuild after a disaster struck.[19] In addition, the Kazakhstani authorities, especially at the local level, should develop programs to disaster-proof existing public buildings, especially schools and hospitals.

- *Disaster preparedness and response:* Severe disasters will cause damage, even if buildings and infrastructure are built to highest standards, as the experience with earthquakes in Japan has demonstrated. Therefore, it is critical that national and subnational authorities are prepared for responding quickly and effectively to disasters when they occur. Kazakhstan has some capacity in this regard, but it could be strengthened. Since the worst natural disasters are likely to strike border regions of the southeast of the country, it will be important to engage with the neighboring countries, especially the Kyrgyz Republic and Uzbekistan, in developing a joint preparedness and response capacity. The Central Asia Center for Disaster Response and Risk Reduction, which was established provisionally in Almaty with support from Kazakhstan, the Kyrgyz Republic, and Tajikistan, is an excellent start toward a coordinated regional approach to disaster preparedness and response, but needs to be fully developed and if possible extended to bring Uzbekistan also to the table.

Violent crime in cities is a major issue in many countries, including the United States, Mexico, Jamaica, Brazil, Kenya, and South Africa, just to name a few. For Latin America, there is a whole literature on the issue of urban crime (Heinemann and Verner 2006). A recent long-term prospects study for Mexico devoted a whole chapter to the high level and surging crime rate in that country (Loser and Kohli 2012). In contrast, violent crime in the cities of Kazakhstan appears to be less on the front pages of the international news and development research. However, UN statistics indicate that the homicide rate in Kazakhstan is in the middle-to-high range by international standards (UNODC 2011), and recent press reports for Central Asia have pointed toward a rise in crime rate in the country (Kosolapova 2012). This, combined with the reports of high level of corruption, drug trafficking, occasional violence, latent Islamic extremism, and so forth can quickly generate impressions of a lack of safety for people living in Kazakhstan's cities. As Kazakhstan progresses further on the path toward a modern, affluent society, keeping

---

19. Mexico and Turkey have developed such insurance schemes with World Bank support, and efforts are underway to introduce them in the Balkans region. There are hurricane insurance programs in the Caribbean Islands.

a watchful eye on crime and developing a comprehensive, effective, and yet humane approach that is consonant with Kazakhstan's own culture and history as an inclusive society will be an important element in assuring Kazakhstan's cities are attractive places to live and do business.

Recommendations: Effective provision of urban communal services is a hallmark of a modern society. Countries whose cities do not meet advanced standards of water and sanitation, waste disposal, heating, housing, disaster preparedness and security will have problems attracting the industries and services that will make the country into a modern knowledge economy. Kazakhstan has an opportunity to take the following basic steps to ensure effective urban service provision:

- The authorities should review the detailed recommendations in ADB ("Sector Assessment" 2012) for the upgrading of urban communal services, adapt them as appropriate to include tariff reforms and increased engagement by the private sector, and then implement them in a phased manner, which would aim for completing urban communal infrastructure rehabilitation and closing gaps by 2025 and ensuring that the high level of quality services is maintained as the urban population continues growing.
- Kazakhstan needs to address the shortage of affordable housing with appropriate land-use planning, support for the development of broadly accessible mortgage finance, incentives for rental housing development, and strengthening of homeowner associations.
- Kazakhstan needs to strengthen its disaster proofing, preparedness, and response capacity, in close engagement with its Central Asian neighbors, and it needs to be alert to rising urban crime.

Business regulation

Many business regulations in Kazakhstan, while usually mandated at the national level, are implemented by the oblast and rayon administrations. This includes the whole panoply of regulatory practices commonly monitored by such surveys as the World Bank's *Doing Business* survey (World Bank "Doing Business" 2012) or the EBRD-World Bank *Business Environment and Enterprise Performance Survey* (BEEPS),[20] including land-use regulations, building safety and fire inspections, business licenses, and so on. Improvements in the way these regulations are managed at the city level will be critical in ensuring a business environment that is supportive of entrepreneurship, new investment, innovation, and employment creation. This requires the development of single window licensing, repetitive inspections, control over corrupt practices, and business complaint mechanisms. While official intentions in improving the business environment are well-established in Kazakhstan, implementation would benefit from effective monitoring of results at the oblast or rayon level. This could be effected by implementing the *Doing Business (DB)* index and BEEPS approaches at the subnational level as has been done for selected countries in the case of the DB (World Bank "Doing Business" 2012),[21] and for Russia (Plekhanov and Isakova 2011) and Kazakhstan (Berglof 2013) in the case of the BEEPS. Figure 8.5 shows that there are some notable differences in the perception of business obstacles in different oblasts in Kazakhstan.

Recommendations: Implement the DB and BEEPS surveys at city level for the ten largest cities. Based on the results, assess the reasons for differences across cities and implement measures to promote better implementation, especially of those regulations for which there are major weakness encountered in specific locations.

---

20. The BEEPS is a survey of business executives' opinions (some 500 executives were surveyed in Kazakhstan) of the actual obstacles encounters in doing business; Doing Business in contrast is an expert assessment of the statutory length of time and cost required for dealing with various regulations. They measure therefore different aspects of the regulatory system and ideally should be implemented side-by-side.
21. Note that the specific observations for DB are current collected solely in Almaty. For countries where subnational DB indicators have been collected, the results differ considerably across jurisdictions (World Bank "Doing Business" 2012).

Figure 8.5	Notable differences exist in business climate perception by oblast

Region	Skills	Business inspections	Access to finance	Electricity	Corruption	Crime	Transport	Tax administration	Access to land	Business licensing	Courts	Informal sector	Customs & trade	Compulsory certificates
Kazakhstan														
Akmola*														
Aktobe														
Almaty														
Almaty City														
Astana City														
Atyrau*														
East														
Karaganda														
Kostanai														
Pavlodar*														
South														
West														

Source: Berglof (2013).
Note: The different shades of blue indicate different intensity of perception of an obstacle to doing business (the darker, the more severe).
* denotes oblasts with fewer than 25 observations.

Financing[22]

In principle, user fees should cover the operations and maintenance costs of urban services, including a provision to fund the capital costs replacement. This rule is justified for efficiency reasons (to avoid wasteful consumption) and for financial viability (to assure the sustainable financing of the service). Externalities (e.g., environmental costs or benefits) or distributional reasons (e.g., helping poor consumers) can justify deviating from the full cost recovery principle. Additionally, political reality often gets in the way of a rational service pricing policy, especially when users have not been accustomed to pay for communal services, as was the case in the Soviet Union. So it comes as no surprise that in Kazakhstan currently cost recovery from users and beneficiaries for urban services is low relative to costs. From a long-term perspective, it will be important that beneficiary charges increasingly cover the costs (both the financial costs, and any additional social costs from environmental damage or congestion) of communal services, with few exceptions. And where subsidies are needed, it is important that these are explicitly budgeted and paid for from general tax revenues, so as to avoid the risk of underfunding the service and thus the sustainability of quality service provision.

---

22. For a detailed discussion of the principles and practice of urban service financing see Bahl and Linn (1992) and Bahl, Linn, and Wetzel (2013).

8

User fees or beneficiary charges can be based on the amount of services consumed in the form of service tariffs, which usually requires metering of service for the end user. This is possible for water and sanitation, public transport, district heating, and, in principle, solid waste disposal. Such tariffs are a good way to cover recurrent costs — and are widely used around the world — but are generally less well-suited to cover capital costs, especially where large and lumpy investments have to be made in production, distribution, or collection facilities.

Capital costs can, however, be covered in other ways. One way is to recover the investment costs from the owners of the properties in the service area, on the grounds that they benefit from the invest-ment in the form of windfall gains as a result of increases in the value of the property with access to the improved service. Such "value capture" financing[23] is especially well-suited for infrastructure investments in water and sanitation, urban road and rail infrastructure (including subways), and parks and recreation areas. It has been used in many industrial and developing countries, including the US, Germany, Japan, Colombia, Hong Kong, and South Korea. A special form of value capture takes place in so-called "land readjustment" schemes (e.g., in Korea) or "town planning" schemes (e.g., in Ahmedabad, India), where rural land at the edge of a city is subdivided and serviced by the municipal government and the costs are recouped by the sale of a fraction of the developed land, while the remainder and main portion of the land is returned to the original owner (Suzuki, Cervero, and Iuchi 2012). While value capture financ-ing methods can be technically and administratively demanding — they require a clear legal base, good land-use planning, and an effective cadastral system — the main obstacle tends to be political. Property owners who are not used to the idea that windfall gains should be taxed away to cover development costs, and who have influence over policy makers to avoid this from happening, will often win the day, with the result that costs are passed on to the general taxpayer or other users. Moreover, most land value capture mechanisms require that land is privately owned, land rights are clearly established and well documented in cadastral records, and land values are regularly assessed. These conditions would have to be gradually built up in the case of Kazakhstan.

Another way to cover capital costs is to borrow the money from the capital markets (or from inter-national financial institutions, such as the World Bank or ADB) and fold the debt service cost into the user tariff. This option is often not available to subnational authorities due to constraints put on such borrowing by the national government, as in the case of Kazakhstan.[24] However, over the long term, it is appropriate for Kazakhstan to explore how to develop this capital financing tool, which is commonly used in developed countries to fund communal services in urban areas. This option is further discussed below, in the section on decentralization.

In Kazakhstan capital investments (and, to some extent, even recurrent costs) are currently funded by grants from the national budget, and thus in effect by the national taxpayer. In a country that has large resource rents, as is the case for Kazakhstan's oil resources, it is appropriate to consider this option as a way to share the natural resource benefits with the broader citizenship. However, two issues arise. First, since benefits from urban communal service investments tend to be capitalized in land values, and since the (de facto, if not de jure) ownership of land is skewed toward the more wealthy and influ-ential, the benefits will reinforce income inequality in the country. Second, since natural resources are exhaustible and therefore the rents they generate are also exhaustible, there will come a time when this mode of financing is no longer readily available. The risk then is that beneficiaries of urban services will

---

23. There are many terms for this form of financing, including "betterment taxes," "special assessments," "valorization," etc.
24. Local executive bodies are in principle entitled to receive loans from the national budget (Budget Code Article 177), but we were not able to confirm that such loans were actually provided or, if so, in what amounts and under what conditions. This deserves more investigation as the government considers its strategy for subnational government finance.

8

have come to see high subsidies as an entitlement that will be difficult politically to take away. For these reasons, systems of effective, if partial, cost recovery for urban services should be a core element of the approach to funding urban services. Third, allowing cost recovery is a key element of a successful strategy to involve the private sector more directly in the provision of urban services.

Recommendations: Kazakhstan needs to increase the cost recovery for urban services, aiming ultimately for full recurrent and capital cost recovery, unless clear externalities or distributive grounds justify subsidies, in which case these should be explicitly and transparently budgeted. Specific recommendations include the following:

- Recurrent costs are generally best covered by service fees or user charges and should be gradually raised to at least that level.
- In the long run, lumpy capital costs can be financed either by value capture from property value increases associated with investments in urban services, or from loans, with loan service charges recouped from service tariffs. Kazakhstan should gradually develop the subnational capacity to engage in value capture and to borrow for capital investments.
- As the capacity to fund urban service investments from beneficiary charges increases, Kazakhstan should gradually reduce the funding from national grants.

Territorial planning and implementation

Two aspects of territorial planning and implementation, i.e., the policies toward the distribution of economic activity across the country, deserve special attention. First, there is the issue of connectivity between businesses and people (transport and telecommunications). Second, there are policies toward distribution of governmental services and financial transfers across regional jurisdictions which affect the way people benefit differentially from governmental activity, depending on where they live. We take each of these aspects in turn.

Connectivity

Connectivity of economic actors across a country's geographic space is always important for economic and social development, but it is especially important in a huge, sparsely populated country like Kazakhstan. If businesses and households face high costs of transport and communication, or if they have no or limited access to markets, information, and public services, then they are hampered in their ability to create productive, competitive enterprises and to obtain key inputs for production, investment, or consumption. Governments may wish to locate certain industries in particular locations, due to political, social, or economic considerations, but if these enterprises, whether private or public, do not have ready access to input and output markets, information, and clients, then the regional economic development efforts of the government will soon be thwarted. Thus, developing the transport and communications infrastructure must be a central element of any territorial development initiative. For Kazakhstan this means that it needs to assure effective access to roads and/or railways, air transport, and information technology (IT) throughout its territory. Let us start by considering transport.

Transport. For roads and rail, the best way to consider connectivity is to start with transport corridors that are, or could be, connecting major border crossing, and principal domestic hubs, usually major cities. Building on the corridor approach of the Territorial Development Strategy 2006-15 described here and the CAREC corridors, ADB ("Sector Assessment" 2012) recommends the implementation of the Territorial Development Strategy through 2015 to be followed by further investments and improvements that would pursue the following objectives:

- investment in roads that would "have over 5,567 km of high quality roads link all provincial capitals and border crossing points in all parts of Kazakhstan;" (p. 38)
- investment in railways to upgrade and modernize the system of 9,950 km track with rails speed of 100 km/hr, the international standard; also, exploration of the option of investing in a high speed rail network, consisting not only of a north-south line from Astana to Almaty, for which construction started in 2013, but also an east-west line from Urumqi through Almaty to Tashkent and Samarkand;
- investment in the creation of "a network of state-of-the-art logistics and intermodal centers to help establish Kazakhstan as a regional logistics hub;" (p. 29);
- substantial improvements in border crossing procedures, customs harmonization agreements implemented between Kazakhstan and its neighbors, and possible extension of the customs free border crossing of the Customs Union with Russia and Belarus;
- introduction and funding of a traffic safety program (monitoring, enforcement, education, etc.);
- effective collection of transport user charges based on costs and establishment of a National Transportation Fund for earmarked sector revenues and expenditures; and
- development of a sound legal and regulatory framework for private-public partnerships in the sector.

Total cost of the program for the period 2011-40 would fall in the range of USD 55-125 billion, depending on the specific components included. As a result of the proposed program there would be substantial reduction in travel time requirements (by 35 to 43 percent for road transport, and by 65 to 71 percent for rail), while shipment costs would drop by an estimated 24 percent.

In addition to the road and rail corridors and logistics improvements at the principal cities envisaged by ADB, other considerations deserve to be reflected in the government's approach to transport policy. First, the secondary and tertiary road network around the primary highway corridors should be also consistently developed so that people living along and between the corridors can benefit through improved access. In other words, the goal would be to move from transport corridors to economic development corridors. Second, air transport also needs further development. Key steps will be to reduce restrictions on competition among airlines and operators and to reduce turn-around costs at Kazakhstan's major airports, which are high by international standards (see the preceding lines).[25]

IT connectivity. IT connectivity, and in particular the spread of broadband access, according to World Bank estimates (cited in Cisco 2013), has a direct impact on growth in developing countries, such that a 10 percentage point expansion in broadband usage is associated with a 1.4 percentage point increase in GDP growth. Since Kazakhstan is only in the middle of the pack of countries in the development of its IT connectivity (see the preceding lines), and well behind advanced industrial countries, it will have to develop a strategy in the coming years for rapid catch-up and, ultimately, universal access to broadband and whatever successor IT communications technology may emerge. Such a strategy would focus both on supply-side issues of broadband availability, and on demand-side issues, designed to foster the

---

25. Kazakhstan would be well-advised eventually to pursue an open sky policy, which gives Kazakhstan the benefits of competition among international and domestic airlines. However, at present the government has decided to build up a competitive domestic airline industry, ruling out this option for now.

use of broadband networks.[26] In developing such a strategy, Kazakhstan should consider alternative technological choices and systems approaches, with a view to ensure that the approach chosen is "future-proof" and scalable in the specific context of the large geographic space and generally low density of the country. The examples of Australia, Canada, and Mexico, countries that have pursued different approaches, can serve as reference points.

Regional economic and social balance

Most governments around the globe are concerned about the distribution of economic activity and of social welfare of people across the regions of their country. The rationale may be supporting national economic growth by supporting lagging regions to catch up with the leading regions, or assuring equal access to economic opportunity for all citizens, or in terms of assuring the political cohesion of the country and avoiding social unrest and or inter-regional conflict.

In the case of Kazakhstan all three motivations have been at work, and Vision Kazakhstan 2050 includes a pursuit of balanced regional development, where lagging regions have a chance to participate in national growth and prosperity and, over time, regional disparities are reduced. Judging by international experience, Kazakhstan at its current stage of development may face an easier time in pursuing this goal than in the past, since research has observed that in early stages of economic development regional disparities tend to increase, while the opposite is true in later stages of development as countries move through middle income status and approach high income levels (Henderson 2002).

However, the natural process of convergence may not be fast and certain enough for Kazakhstan's policy. Moreover, Kazakhstan faces the special challenge and opportunity created by its oil and mineral wealth, which is not evenly distributed across regions. Those regions that have oil and mineral wealth have higher per capita GDP. How to share this wealth with other regions is a major issue that clearly needs to be addressed. Many of the government's recent and current regional initiatives (such as the mono-cities program, the OECD-supported program for regional investment promotion, and others that we reviewed here) reflect the government's intentions to work toward narrowing the gaps in regions' economic and social status. However, the Territorial Development Strategy also reflects a goal to support especially the development of the country's leading cities as a way to advance the modernization of the country and its international competitiveness (Mahkmutova 2012; Junussova 2012).

The tension between the objectives of supporting regional convergence principally in the interest of equalizing opportunities and supporting political stability and cohesion on the one hand, and fostering growth in the leading regions, and especially in the largest cities, as a way to incubate a modern economy (and perhaps to meet the needs and expectations of the political and economic elite) on the other, is not surprising. Indeed, it pervades much of the history of economic and political thought on regional development policies (World Bank 2008). Two aspects will help Kazakhstan resolve this tension: the fact that its policy makers have a long time perspective, and the fact that it has relatively ample resources due to its oil wealth. By prioritizing for each of the two objectives what are the most effective ways of meeting them and by appropriately phasing initiatives over time it should be possible to achieve both: rapid modernization in the center, and effective development in the periphery.

---

26. Cisco (2013, p. 4) includes the following items under supply-side policies: competition and investment; spectrum allocation and assignment; reducing infrastructure deployment costs; core network expansion; and inclusive broadband availability. Under demand-side policies fall the following items: affordability of devices and access; government leadership to utilize and promote broadband; ICT skills development; facilitation of online and local content, applications, new technologies and services; and consumer protection and empowerment.

Recommendations: In developing and pursuing a strategy for long-term territorial development Kazakhstan may therefore wish to consider the following key elements:

- First and foremost, develop effective connectivity across the country through investments in modern, high-speed and low-cost transport, and IT communications systems;
- Assure that the advanced regions, and especially the cities, are managed for competitive, smart, green, fun, and safe growth, financed in the long run mostly by their own resources, rather than drawing on national grants;
- Assure access to quality education, health, and communal services in the lagging regions, with financial support from the central budget so as to assure that people, and especially young people, have access to minimal quality of life and long-term opportunities wherever they live (see Chapter 5);
- Support the modernization of agriculture by investing in rural connectivity (roads and IT), by rehabilitating agricultural infrastructure (especially irrigation) and by support for the development of value chains;
- Support industrial development in lagging regions and cities (including mono-cities) only where there are clear opportunities for private enterprise to develop productive activities without sustained public subsidies; and
- Streamline and coordinate government initiatives for regional development, monitor and evaluate results, keep bureaucratic processes simple, and adapt the approach based on lessons learned.

Decentralization: Responding to people's preferences

There are conflicting arguments for and against more decentralization to be found in the literature, and the actual practice varies widely across advanced and developing countries (Bahl and Linn 1992; Bahl, Linn, and Wetzel 2013). Many experts argue that the principle of subsidiarity — i.e., pushing the authority for decision making to the lowest possible level of government that is closest to the people — is best in reflecting individual and collective preferences in governmental decisions and hence most efficient from an economic perspective. Moreover, it meets the expectations of those who argue that greater democratization has to start from the base, by empowering people at the local level. The argument against decentralization is made by those who consider that the spillovers across jurisdictional boundaries are significant and who believe subnational government does not have the institutional capacity to manage governmental responsibilities effectively. However, there is little doubt that, as countries develop economically and institutionally, the need and scope for more decentralization increases (Dabla-Norris 2006; UNDP "Decentralization" 2008). Indeed, over the last two decades the developing world has seen a general trend toward decentralization, along with increased democratization (Bahl, Linn, and Wetzel 2013).

As one moves from general principles to the specifics of allocation of expenditure responsibility and revenue authority across jurisdictional levels, there is even less agreement on general rules that could be universally applied and there is little guidance from the experience around the world, since actual practice differs widely (Bahl, Linn, and Wetzel 2013). There is a presumption that national government should not only retain the obvious national security, diplomacy, rule of law, macroeconomic policy and trade integration functions, but also should have policy and supervisory functions for the financial sector, education, health, food security, and agriculture, and for national transportation networks, energy and environmental policy. Local governments typically are allocated responsibilities for communal services (water and sanitation, solid waste disposal, local transport, district heating, housing land-use regulation, urban planning, firefighting, and local policing). There is less clarity about the potential role of intermediate-level governments (provincial, state or "oblast" governments). Especially in unitary coun-tries, like Kazakhstan, these intermediary-level authorities are often quite weak and have overlapping responsibilities with national governments and/or local governments. The overlaps tend to be especially significant in the areas of education and health, where provincial level authorities usually have at least some responsibilities. They also often and quite appropriately have important functions in dealing with rural administration and service provision, and for regional infrastructure (especially provincial roads, irrigation networks, etc.). However, despite these broad guidelines, the simple truth remains that there is no blueprint that Kazakhstan could follow in designing its intergovernmental fiscal system when it comes to allocating expenditure responsibility.[27]

The same is true for the allocation of revenue authority. General practice around the globe points to national governments retaining for themselves those sources of revenues that are most productive and could generate the greatest distortions if administered separately and with different terms by subna-tional authorities. Accordingly, income taxes, wage taxes, value-added taxes, general taxes on wealth and inheritance and trade-related taxes, along with natural resource taxation are usually reserved for national governments. Local governments are generally left with taxes on real estate, local business taxes, and user charges (Bahl, Linn, and Wetzel 2013). Once again, provincial-level governments, espe-cially in unitary governmental structures, have very mixed revenue allocations, with the most common one being sales/value-added taxes. Kazakhstan is unusual in that subnational governments benefit from income and wage taxes. However, this creates anomalous requirements of channeling surplus resources from the three better-off oblasts to the poorer ones, which sets up predictable tensions among oblast governments.

The vision of Kazakhstan 2050 envisages a more decentralized governmental system. The fact that Kazakhstan already has a relatively deconcentrated system of government, in which subnational agen-cies administer a relatively large share of public expenditure responsibilities, in principle facilitates a move toward actual decentralization, i.e., where subnational authorities also assume control over the resources they administer and where they are accountable to their local constituent populations. In practice, however, international experience shows that effective decentralization is difficult to implement, needs to be carefully phased so that local capacities match local responsibilities, and can easily conflict with political priorities of the central government. In the case of Kazakhstan, the tension between the intention to decentralize and the expectation that the power of "the vertical" — i.e., central control — be maintained is evident from the President's speech, as noted earlier. The best way to resolve the tension is to pursue a gradual and phased approach, which in any case is advisable in view of the need to build up local government capacity.

Given the current state of de-concentrated but centralized government, the following are areas in which we believe Kazakhstan can proceed in pursuing its long-term goal of creating a more decentral-ized state.

Place more reliance on subnational elected offices

The recent decision to introduce elections of rural *akims* could be followed up with a decision to have all *akims* elected, even in the big cities. At the same time, it would be advisable over time to strengthen the role of local representative bodies (*maslikhats*), which are already elected, to assume greater respon-sibility of oversight of the activities of the *akim* and his local administration.

---

27. As noted earlier in this paragraph, there is especially little guidance in the literature on the role and functions of the provincial-level authorities. For Kazakhstan, this means more research needs to be done on how the oblast-level authorities best fit into a decentralized inter-governmental administrative and fiscal system.

8

Clarify expenditure responsibilities

The government is already carrying out functional reviews of all national ministries. As part of this process, a systematic analysis should be carried out of the extent of overlap of functions between the central and subnational (oblast and rayon) governmental bodies, with a view to assign clear and non-duplicative function to each level of government. The broad principles laid out here can serve as guidelines, but in the end Kazakhstan needs to find a solution that fits its own historical precedents and current needs.

Have more staff reporting directly to the local executive

As noted here, there are currently plans to transfer 4,500 central government employees to join the subnational administrations. As part of the government's functional reviews of its ministerial structures, a systematic inventory of staff should be made which can be transferred to subnational government along with a decentralization of functions.

Give subnational authorities greater authority over subnational revenues

This involves two possible types of action. One option is to give subnational governments the right to set their own tax rates for existing taxes. The other option is to give subnational governments the right to access new revenue sources. Here particularly good candidates for city governments are the instruments of value capture.[28] It appears that this instrument has so far not been used in Kazakhstan, so its introduction should be phased in, starting with a pilot and careful legal, regulatory and administrative institution building and only moving to full implementation once experience has been gained and capacity created.

Structure intergovernmental grants in a way that is simple, predictable, and rewards good subnational performance

Over the long haul intergovernmental grants should be restricted to support those areas where local action has clearly significant spillover effects beyond local boundaries or where vital national interests are at stake, such as assuring an appropriate regional balance. Among the functions with strong spillover effects are education, health and disaster preparedness. In addition, support for poor, rural oblasts is a valid national objective. On the other hand, the large cities should in the long term become largely self-sufficient financially, without having to rely on transfers for their infrastructure investments, let alone operations. To the extent grants are provided, they should be structured according to simple rules that are transparently applied. Some countries, e.g., Russia, have structured grants so that they reward subnational governments for the achievement of well-articulated goals (Zinnes 2009). In the case of Kazakhstan, this could also be explored. For example, subnational authorities could be rewarded for demonstrated improvements in the local business climate.

Introduce loan finance for subnational government

Many developed countries permit subnational authorities to borrow for capital investments, subject to stringent controls usually exercised by the Central Bank. In recent years, this practice has also spread to some emerging economies (e.g., Colombia, India, Korea). In principle, loan finance — which broadly matches the benefit stream of investments with the cost stream — is an efficient and sound way to finance lumpy local infrastructure investments, especially in cities. Of particular interest is the Colombian FINDETER example. Kharas and Linn (2013, p. 408) report that, according to a World Bank evaluation, this involved creation of "(a) a successfully functioning intermediary Municipal Development Fund (see

---

28. See Smolka (2013) for a summary of the experience with and lessons from land value capture in Latin America.

below); (b) the development of local credit rating institutions; (c) improved municipal credit worthiness; (d) improved fiscal performance of the municipal sector based on improved cadastral services and local revenue collection; and (e) improved municipal services."

However, a number of important preconditions need to be met, before loan financing for subnational government can play a significant role in Kazakhstan:

- Subnational governments must have developed the capacity to prepare sound investment projects and to finance the loan repayments reliably — in other words, they have to be creditworthy.
- An independent subnational credit rating mechanism will be important to help develop the subnational credit market.
- National regulations for municipal credit markets have to be put in place, usually by the Central Bank, or the bank supervisory agency. Such regulations would need to include limitations on subnational public agencies in taking on foreign currency debt and the question of how subnational bankruptcies will be handled.

Develop private sector participation in subnational infrastructure programs

Kazakhstan has some valuable experience with private sector participation (PSP) in the urban infrastructure sector, in particular in the municipal water sector (OECD "Ten Years" 2011). Under the Akbulak Program (2011-20) for water sector development, a systematic expansion of PPP is envisaged (ADB "Sector Assessment" 2012). However, according to OECD (2011) the track record of PSP initiatives in Kazakhstan to date is mixed. This confirms the worldwide experience with efforts to increase private participation in urban infrastructure provision (OECD "Ten Years" 2011; Kharas and Linn 2013). The conditions for a successful implementation of PSP and PPP are many, including:

- Subnational authorities have to have the capacity to prepare and negotiate appropriate contracts with potential private partners.
- The national legislation for PPP, and in particular the law on concessions, needs to be supportive of effective PPP initiatives.
- The national and subnational policies on tariff setting have to allow the private concessionaire or owner to set rates at a financially sound level.

Currently, these conditions are generally not met in Kazakhstan: Subnational governments have only limited capacity to engage with private partners, the regulatory framework, and in particular the concessions law, needs to be suitably revised, and tariff setting policies in practice remain a constraining factor. Therefore, ADB ("Sector Assessment" 2012) appropriately recommends a cautious and phased approach to PSP and PPP development in the urban infrastructure services sector, building the capacity, the legal, regulatory and policy infrastructure, and introducing pilots especially in sectors where PSP/PPP approaches have hitherto not been used, including in the municipal solid waste sector.

Build the subnational capacity for an effective decentralized governmental structure

The lack of capacity to deliver on larger responsibilities is generally seen as a key constraint to effective decentralization, and such concerns are not unfounded, whether in Kazakhstan or elsewhere. Thus, a systematic process of capacity building is required. This will take time and must involve various elements of institutional building support, including assuring that the cadre of subnational civil servants is well trained and qualified for the jobs they are expected to handle. Many urban administrative jobs are highly specialized and wide-ranging, including city planning, infrastructure engineering, traffic management, business regulation, cadastre design and management, not to mention budget and project management,

8

structuring of contracts with private partners — the list goes on. Therefore, the provision of skill-specific training and technical support is critical, but is not enough. The same skills are in high demand in the private sector, and only with appropriate subnational civil service pay, working conditions, and merit-based career prospects will the qualified people be attracted to serve in the subnational government structures. A carefully designed plan and sustained implementation for subnational capacity building are therefore necessary ingredient of Kazakhstan's progress toward more decentralized government.

Provide national support for building an effective decentralized government structure

The recent creation of the Ministry of Regional Development is potentially a significant step forward in Kazakhstan's effort to develop an effective national institutional and policy making structure in support of decentralization. It will provide for an effective focus on urban, regional, and decentralization issues at the ministerial level, and aid coordination of planning and implementation across the many governmental agencies currently engaged in this area. It will now be important that the ministry develops a clear agenda of short-, medium-, and long-term action for its mandated tasks. The options explored in this paper can serve as an input into this process. One of the aspects that will be important is ensuring that the ministry principally focuses on strategy, planning, policy formulation, and monitoring and evaluation of implementation, rather than getting into the nitty-gritty of day-to-day implementation, which should be left to implementing agencies under the ministry's supervision and increasingly to local authorities.

One of the options that the government and the ministry may wish to explore is to create a *subnational development fund*, which provides a combination of services to subnational governments in helping them develop the capacity to take on decentralized functions. These services would include the following:

- provision of grant and loan finance for subnational development projects and programs;
- technical assistance to subnational government units in project preparation and supervision;
- training for subnational government staff; and
- advisory support for institutional capacity building efforts of individual subnational government entities.

Examples of such funds can be found in various countries and have been supported by the World Bank in recent decades (Annez, Huet, and Peterson 2008).[29] A good case in point is the Colombian FINDE-TER, mentioned here. The experience with such funds is not universally positive, but when appropriately structured and seen as an instrument facilitating a difficult transition rather than an institutional set up that will be sustained indefinitely, subnational development funds can play a useful role. This dynamic and transitional role is well reflected in ADB (2008). It shows the evolving role that a subnational development fund can play in a three stage process: In stage 1, the fund serves as a conduit for funding and capacity building; in stage 2 it assists in making the subnational entities into creditworthy institutions that can begin to access the financial market; and in stage 3 the fund turns itself into a private entity which competes with other financial institutions in mobilizing infrastructure finance.[30] If Kazakhstan opts to develop and implement a subnational development fund, then its financial resource transfers to subnational governments should replace the current transfer system, which in any case suffers from excessive complexity and, hence, opacity.

---

29. Such funds go under different names, including "Urban Investment Funds," "Municipal Development Funds," "Regional Development Funds," etc. The World Bank proposed the exploration of a Regional Development Fund for Kazakhstan and cites examples from Canada, Colombia, European Union, Poland, and United States (World Bank n.d.).

30. The argument for a transitional public sector role in municipal development funds is very similar to the argument made in Chapter 6 for a transitional public sector role in Super ESCOs, which would help develop financing for energy efficiency initiatives.

Recommendations: Decentralization is a difficult and politically sensitive process, in which one needs to balance the national government's legitimate concerns for vertical control with the need to push responsibility and authority to the lowest efficient level of government. It needs to be undertaken with caution, but also with a clear vision and determination. The aforementioned exposition on nine areas of potential engagement provides some guidance for key actions that Kazakhstan may wish to explore in pursuing a course toward decentralization:

- expand the electoral processes for subnational government and strengthening the role of elected local government bodies;
- use the government's functional reviews for determination of an appropriate delineation of expenditure responsibilities of governments at different levels of government and for determining which civil servant contingents can be shifted from national to subnational service;
- provide subnational governments with more authority to raise revenues, including urban land value capture instruments;
- adjust existing grant systems to meet the tests of simplicity and predictability, to provide funding for functions where spillovers dominate and to jurisdictions that do not have a sufficient own resource base to meet essential social needs, and to provide incentives for effective subnational management;
- develop over the long term the potential for subnational government to borrow and strengthen the capacity to initiate and manage private-public partnerships; and
- support capacity building of subnational authorities, possibly with the support of a newly to be established subnational development fund, under the guidance and supervision of the Ministry of Regional Development.

Conclusions: Main Findings and Summary of Recommendations

Urbanization, regional development, and decentralization are three important components of a successful Kazakhstan 2050 vision and strategy. They provide key mechanisms for achieving energy efficiency, green growth, and a modern, knowledge-based economy. An effective institutional transition and human development strategy are critical factors for a successful urbanization, regional development, and decentralization process. This chapter summarizes the main conclusions and recommendations for these three policy areas. It is important to recognize that the issues and actions across these three areas are inextricably linked with each other. While we consider them separately, they form a continuum of issues on a critical spectrum of government policy and engagement. Figure 8.3, at the end of the chapter, summarizes the recommendations.

Urbanization. The speed of urbanization and the degree of urban primacy in Kazakhstan are moderate, and Kazakhstan will likely maintain a relatively large share of its population living in rural areas by 2050. Urban services infrastructure and management are generally weak. Urban transport challenges will become more pressing as the ownership and use of private cars will likely rise dramatically. For the future, effective urban planning and management will be critical.

The vision for 2050 is for a balanced urban structure; strong urban administrative capacity throughout with effective service provision in public/private partnerships; two world-class metropolitan areas and high-quality mid-size cities ("competitive," "smart," "green," "safe," and "fun" cities); effective control of crime and preparedness for natural disasters.

8

Regional development. Kazakhstan is a large country with low population density and with significant regional diversity and disparities. Accordingly, two key factors, connectivity and balance, matter greatly for an effective long-term development strategy for sustained growth, inclusive human development, and political stability.

Connectivity requires support for spatial integration and access through effective transport corridor development linked to international transit corridors (especially those promoted by CAREC), as well as the development of the secondary and tertiary transport network to link the smaller towns and rural hinterland to the larger hubs. The measures to be taken not only cover the "hard" infrastructure investment and maintenance, but also the "soft" aspects, including effective institutional development, transport and transit facilitation, and development of the logistics infrastructure. Connectivity also requires that Kazakhstan move quickly from the middle of the pack to top position in the ranks of countries that have effective and wide coverage of broadband technology, supported by policy that pursues both supply side and demand side dimensions.

As far as regional balance is concerned Kazakhstan has to address the tension between a policy that focuses on the development of the large cities as the primary engines of modernization and a policy that assures that there is a convergence in economic opportunities and human welfare across the regions of the country in terms of business investment, access to employment, social and infrastructure services, credit, etc. By approaching this from a longer-term perspective, with a balance and phased approach, and using available energy resources judiciously to meet priority needs both at the center and the periphery, to resolve this tension.

The vision for 2050 is then a Kazakhstan that is highly integrated regionally: major population centers are linked through efficient transport, logistics, and communications systems, with smaller towns and cities and rural/agricultural communities linked to major transport and communications hubs and corridors through high-quality secondary and tertiary networks; national and supra-national regional integration strategies are effectively linked; and access to economic and social services is balanced across regions in the interest of a converging economic trend across regions.

Decentralization. By international standards, Kazakhstan has a de-concentrated administration, but with centralized control by the national authorities and little bottom up accountability at the subnational level. Decentralization, which would bring benefits in terms of an effective delivery of public services, a flexible response to differentiated local needs and increasing the empowerment of local communities is a difficult and long-term process, which requires making trade-offs between central and local control. International experience shows that there are two key conditions for effective decentralization. First, decentralization of expenditure control has to go hand-in-hand with decentralization of revenue authority. Second, effective decentralization requires the building of subnational government capacity and modalities for citizen engagement.

The vision for 2050 is therefore an effectively decentralized Kazakhstan: i.e., while retaining its unitary governmental structure, Kazakhstan will have an efficient, equitable, and decentralized intergovernmental system, where the local executive is accountable to local voters, with clear expenditure and effective revenue assignments, national transfer systems that provide appropriate incentives, well-developed municipal bond markets supervised by the Central Bank, and strong administrative capacities at the subnational levels.

8

In considering these goals and recommendations, a number of challenges and trade-offs will have to be borne in mind: (a) the fact that urban structure and infrastructure, once put in place, is of long duration and requires that the correct policy and investment decisions be taken as early as possible; (b) there will be special interest and popular opposition to some of the recommendations, especially where they limit the use of cars and restrict land use for those who previously had unfettered ability to appropriate the benefits of urban land development; (c) the financing needs of urban development are large, local capacity is limited and the scope for corruption is substantial; (d) there are opportunities, but also limits, for involving the private sector; (e) there are tensions between maintaining a "strong vertical" and "decentralization"; (f) there is a tendency to overdesign bureaucratic systems, such as the current transfer system; and finally, (g) public agencies, such as the subnational development fund are difficult to transform into commercial and ultimately private entities due to bureaucratic interests that wish to maintain the public agency.

8

Table 8.3	**Recommendations for urbanization, regional development, and decentralization**

Recommendation area	Short term	Medium term	Long term
Urbanization			
1. Land-use planning	• Inventory land-use planning practices	• Introduce modern land-use planning	• Maintain land-use planning
2. Connectivity	• Public transit: BRT/LRT/Metro depending on city size • Limit car use (taxation, congestion control/pricing, etc. funds urban transport investment and public transit) • Improved management/funding of public transport • Land use planning and infrastructure investment for high density • Universal access to high speed Internet (phased national plan)		
3. Urban commu-nal services	• Implement/accelerate current programs and review ADB program • National disaster preparedness	• Fill infrastructure gaps in line with ADB program suitably amended • Regional disaster preparedness	• Assure modern service quality is maintained • Maintain preparedness
4. Business regulations	• City-level DB and BEEPS surveys	• Support cities in improving business regulations	• Maintain effec-tive business regulations
5. Financing	• Develop plan for urban financing	• Recurrent costs cov-ered by user charges	• Capital costs funded by value capture, loans, grants
Regional Development			
1. Regional transport	• Review/adapt ADB LT transport plan	• Implement/monitor/adapt plan	
2. ICT connectivity	• Develop ICT connec-tivity strategy	• Implement/monitor/adapt strategy	
3. City man-agement (see also urbanization)	• Develop strategy for self-financed large cities	• Implement/monitor/adapt	
4. Support for lag-ging regions/towns	• Develop minimum package of HD and comm. services; funded (partially) by grants	• Implement/monitor/adapt package • Support industrial dev. only if sustainable without subsidies	

(contd...)

(Table 8.3 contd...)

8

| Table 8.3 | Recommendations for urbanization, regional development, and decentralization |

Recommendation area	Short term	Medium term	Long term
5. Agricultural modernization	• Rural connectivity, ag. infrastructure, value chains	• Implement/monitor/adapt	
6. Coordination and M&E	• Improve coordination/M&E	• Implement	
Decentralization			
1. Expand subnational electoral process and control	• Implement elections for all mayors; Strengthen role of maslikhats (sub-national representative bodies); Support development of civil society at subnational level		
2. Local authority	• Use functional reviews of ministries to assess distribution of func-tions and staff; explore options for defined roles for oblast governments	• Implement/monitor/adapt	• Ditto
3. Subnational rev-enue authority	• Explore options for increased local reve-nue authorities, esp. value capture	• Implement/monitor/adapt	• Ditto
4. Intergovern-mental grants	• Review/redesign grants according to international best practice	• Implement/monitor/adapt	• Ditto
5. Subnational borrowing	• Review international best practice	• Design/plan and begin implement.	• Complete implementation
6. Subnational capacity building	• Develop approach to capacity building, incl. subnational develop-ment fund	• Implement under guidance of Min-istry of Regional Development	• Ditto

Source: Author.

KNOWLEDGE-
BASED
ECONOMIC
GROWTH

Knowledge-Based Economic Growth

Shahid Yusuf

Mineral resource-rich countries that manage their affairs prudently can count on secure medium-run prospects barring unforeseen and prolonged slumps in global economic activity. However, if a country wants to grow rapidly on a sustained long-term basis, its growth will have to be driven by productivity gains in the sectors other than resource extraction, unless one predicts continued increase in minerals reserves and/or prices. Moreover, there are risks that the natural resources will eventually be depleted or their economic worth reduced by technological advances. Hence, the forward-looking resource-rich nations plan ahead and lay the foundations of an economy that can sustain and build upon the temporary prosperity bestowed by mineral wealth.

Kazakhstan shares this vision and is intent on pursuing a transformation that will make it an affluent knowledge economy with a diversified industrial, service, and export base by the middle of the century and thus enter the ranks of the top 30 developed countries by 2050. The currently advanced economies owe their relative affluence to the fruits of industrialization and a deepening services sector, the steady upgrading of technology in all activities, and incremental innovation that has contributed to rising productivity. Kazakhstan's intention is to emulate a variant of this strategy adapted to its own circumstances and responsive to the evolving global environment and the imperatives of greening.

The purpose of this chapter is to synthesize the relevant international experience for Kazakhstan on the making of a knowledge-based economy and to inform this with views on trends that could expedite or impede the process through the middle of the century. As will become apparent from our discussion, in essence this means making progress with all the elements of the development priorities covered in this study: a highly developed human resource base, efficient and sustainable use of natural resources, a balanced, effective, and decentralized process of urban and regional development, an economy that is integrated with the rest of the world, and modern institutions. However, additional elements of policy also need to be addressed as one considers how to turn Kazakhstan into a diversified, highly productive economy, and a strategic approach toward diversification and productivity growth will be essential if Kazakhstan is to reach its goal of joining the top 30 developed countries.

Tho chapter is divided into five parts. The first synthesizes factors that have contributed to growth in countries that have already made a similar journey and the emerging trends that will impinge on those starting out in the second decade of the 21st century. The second presents lessons for Kazakhstan based on international experience. The third section examines Kazakhstan's current capabilities and its readiness to engage in transformation. The fourth section presents the vision for Kazakhstan's development of a modern knowledge economy and spells out a menu of strategic policy options. A final section presents some summary guideposts and potential actions for the short, medium, and long term.

9

Growth: How and How Much?

Looking back over a half-century of GDP growth in industrialized East Asia and the leading European economies, the evidence suggests that rapid growth during much of the latter half of the 20th century was facilitated by macroeconomic and political stability and spearheaded by capital. Countries such as Japan and Korea that invested more in industry and infrastructure grew faster (Jorgenson and Vu 2011). For Korea and Taiwan (province of China) — joined in the 1980s by the southeast Asian "tiger" economies and by China — rapid growth extended into the 1990s, driven principally by capital. However, this rich and telling experience also highlights four additional factors that would allow countries such as Kazakhstan to achieve a high long-term growth rate, albeit gradually declining as the country approaches the productivity level of the most advanced countries, as suggested in the high-performance scenarios developed in Chapter 12. The four factors are: investment allocation, productivity gains, technological progress, and a domestically-nurtured innovation system that buttresses technological advances and productivity.

The experience of the 20th century: four pillars of economic growth

First, more investment was advantageous up to a point, but excess led to misallocation and a distorted industrial structure that forced costly adjustments in later years. The 20th century experience suggests that an investment rate of 35 percent is at the upper end of the desirable range and an investment rate closer to 30 might be more easily absorbed by economies in the earlier stages of industrialization. High rates can strain the absorptive capacity of even those economies with the financial and other market and public institutions to intermediate the efficient allocation of capital and the human capital to utilize it productively. Germany did not much exceed a rate of 25 percent of GDP during its years of rapid growth in the 1960s. The Northeast Asian economies and Singapore approached rates closer to 40 percent of GDP. These initially did yield higher growth rates, but they were also responsible for hypertrophied industrialization excessively dependent on exports and for the building ahead of demand of gilt-edged infrastructure projects, not all of which delivered adequate returns. The intense focus on investment and broad-based industrialization of the leading East Asian economies, by inviting misallocation and squeezing consumption, was welfare-subtracting. This tendency was exacerbated by the substitution of (relatively) cheap capital for labor, resulting in widening income disparities in Korea, Japan, Singapore, and China, as well as in Europe and the US. Moreover, the industrial systems bequeathed by the investment-led Big Push, while seemingly advantageous in an era when trade was being liberalized and opportunities in Germany, Japan, and Korea appeared limitless, is less well-suited for a time when the rate of globalization has decreased.[1] A world subject to large trade imbalances is a far less welcoming place for economies whose health continues to be closely tied to the export of manufactures.

China is the most recent and most conspicuous entrant into the league of industrialized nations wedded to trade. In fact, the Chinese case further underscores the risks and the huge welfare costs of excessive investment in industrial diversification and in infrastructure.[2] Double digit growth, aside from setting global records, has also saddled China with a vast industrial system that will need to be streamlined and geographically concentrated in multiple nodes, its ownership and governance reformed, its orientation shifted more toward domestic markets, and its intensity of noxious emissions greatly

---

1. The huge increase in China's trade surplus after 2001 was made possible by its entry into the WTO and the elimination of many of the barriers confronting China's exporters (Taylor 2013).
2. Estimates of the cost of resource misallocation as a consequence of China's investment compulsion range from 4 percent of GDP to 10 percent and more.

reduced in the interests of China[3] and of the planetary biosphere. China — and earlier cases of Japan and Korea — draw attention to another drawback of a long-running, investment-based strategy noted by Acemoglu, Aghion, and Zilibotti (2002). They observe that an investment-biased approach that entrenches large capital-intensive producers (e.g., Korean chaebol and the lead firms in Japanese keiretsu) frequently producing standardized goods can give rise to a "rent-shield" effect; that is, cash rents earned by insiders protect them against competition from more efficient new entrants. For this reason, an economy can remain focused too long on investment and delay the switch to a strategy that exploits innovation opportunities. One outcome of such delay is that the economy becomes stuck in a "non-convergence trap" and technology gaps cannot be closed.

A second factor affecting long-term performance, now validated by extensive research, is that increasing productivity will pace growth in mature advanced economies.[4] Undoubtedly gains in total factor productivity (TFP) are not independent of capital investment because technological advances embodied in plant, equipment, and associated production practices account for some of the improvements in productivity, but with services enlarging their share of GDP and intangibles[5] identified as an increasingly important source of productivity growth, new investment is likely to contribute a diminishing share of growth relative to TFP in the future. This is apparent from the stable increase in Japanese TFP over the past two decades even though investment as a share of GDP has declined. A related characteristic of productivity gains is that they have tended to be high during earlier stages of development when economies are catching up and approaching the technological frontier, when labor is transferring from lower- to higher-productivity occupations (most notably from agriculture to industry, and later to more productive manufacturing activities), and when competition leads to the intra-sectoral convergence of individual firms. For example, in both Japan and Korea, TFP rose at rates in excess of 2.5 percent before slowing and stabilizing in Japan at 1.5 percent. In Korea, which lags Japan in terms of development (and per capita GDP), the rate still exceeds 2 percent, but in all likelihood, Korea too will experience a slowing of productivity growth.

Over a period spanning two decades (starting in 1989) data from 122 countries shows that TFP has risen by an average of 0.96 percent per annum. In the G7, the average was 0.37 percent per annum; it was 2.75 percent in developing Asia and 0.16 in Latin America (Jorgenson and Vu 2011). This pattern of change in TFP has occurred in the face of rising expenditures on R&D[6] and also of the increasing educational qualifications of the workforce in the advanced countries. In other words, more and better-educated workers and the faster accumulation of knowledge capital may partially compensate for a decline in TFP from other sources but does not push TFP to a higher trend rate.

If the admittedly limited experience of a few leading advanced countries is a guide to long-term steady-state rates of increase in TFP, it would appear that a third determinant of economic performance is significant scientific advances spawning major innovations that ripple through the system impinging on and modifying a vast number of activities, including many low- and middle-tech manufacturing activities

---

3. The cost of pollution to China is enormous and rising. It is estimated that the losses amount to between 4 and 6 percent of GDP, and the life expectancy of the 500 million Chinese living North of the Huai river has been reduced by almost 5.5 years. China's carbon emissions have now edged well ahead of those released by the United States (World Bank "Cost of Pollution in China" 2007; Ekstrom 2012).

4. Comin and Hobijn (2006, 2011) emphasize the contribution of technology to growth. The role and importance of productivity is highlighted by the annual productivity briefs of the Conference Board (2013). On the history of TFP, see Hulten (2001).

5. Managerial skills and learning embedded in the organizational practices of a firm have a large role. Corrado, Hulten, and Sichel (2006) estimate the large contribution of intangibles to growth in the United States. The low levels of management skills in Central Asian economies, including Kazakhstan, have been described by Bloom, Schweiger, and Van Reenen (2011) and van Ark and Hulten (2007).

6. This raises questions as to the productivity of R&D and the risk of diminishing returns as spending increases, the quality of inputs diminishes, and evaluation is not rigorously enforced.

9

and services.[7] The internal combustion engine, the semiconductor, the Internet, and myriad digital technologies are all examples of innovations based on a multitude of scientific discoveries that have diffused through the economy, stimulating investment and productivity. Between the mid-1990s and 2000, almost two-thirds of the productivity gains in the United States were directly linked with investment in ICT (and a third between 2000 and 2006), while European and Asian countries have registered more modest gains because their services sectors are less competitive (Jorgenson, Ho, and Stiroh 2008). Absent such technological events, incremental innovation can maintain the momentum of TFP for some time (including in sectors such as agriculture, logistics, and food processing), but with the tempo diminishing as the quality of collateral innovations gradually sinks, a process of decay begins, which some fear is already becoming apparent (Cowen 2011; Gordon 2012; Huebner 2005). Countries in a catching-up mode can maintain higher rates of TFP growth by raising capital intensity and moving closer to the technological frontier, but this is temporary. Once the frontier is close, and marginal innovations become the drivers, growth must inevitably slow — until the next round of technological change sweeps through.[8]

A fourth factor that is interlaced with the other three but deserves independent treatment is the creation of an indigenous innovation system that initially accelerates technological absorption, contributes to incremental innovation, and eventually can be a source of more radical leaps in technology. The successful industrializers' post-World War II experience shows that prowess at technological catching-up and innovativeness underpinning gains in productivity, rested on three pillars of what has become known as the "triple helix": the manufacturing, technological, and organizational capabilities of firms and their ability to compete in the global marketplace, government support for R&D, and research universities. The strands of this "triple helix" are described in more detail below.

The knowledge-suffused innovation system ("triple helix")

In building an innovation system, each advanced country gradually established the institutional foundations of a highly competitive manufacturing sector dominated by large private firms supported by a network of smaller specialized suppliers. Manufacturing capability and globally-oriented firms, which invested in R&D and saw their future competitiveness as inseparable from technological excellence, are central to the development story of the United States, Japan, Germany, Korea, and others. In Western countries and Japan, world-class firms took shape over the course of several decades. Korean chaebol — some of which germinated in the 1920s and 1930s under Japanese colonialism — were quicker off the mark (e.g., Daewoo), as were Taiwanese firms, and a number of Chinese companies are enlarging their global market shares at amazing speed (Kohli 1994). Firms that can hold their own on the global stage constitute the first strand of the triple helix.

The importance of technology and the advantages of rapid innovation came into focus during the Second World War and left a lasting imprint on corporate and government thinking. Prior to the war, much government spending on research in the United States was funneled into agriculture. From the 1950s onwards, industrial technologies of military relevance came to the forefront.[9] The war years had indicated convincingly to policy makers that resources devoted to research, combined with the mobilizing of scientific talent, could speedily lead to practical results of (eventual) commercial significance. As

---

7. See Jovanovic and Rousseau (2005) on general purpose technologies.

8. This is consistent with the approach embodied in the model we have used in Chapter 12 to develop long-term scenarios for economic growth of the world and Kazakhstan.

9. Mowery (2011) discusses the government's role and the contribution of research for military; insights from research in other sectors can be found in Henderson and Newell (2011). How Germany built its research system starting in the 19th century is the topic of a paper by Lenoir (1998).

a result, the second strand of the triple helix became the special attention henceforth assigned to the government's research and technology policies, which directly and indirectly influenced industrial development. These came to be viewed as a means of promoting advancement in specific areas of strategic interest including defense, space, energy, telecommunications, and healthcare, but also as a means of building the scientific (intangible) capital that could nourish innovation throughout the economy.

The involvement of university-based scientists in the war effort (e.g., in the Manhattan Project and the development of radar) drew attention to research universities' potential to be producers of key scientific findings and of upstream applied research. Research universities emerged as the third strand[10] of what from the early 1990s came to be widely known as the "innovation system,"[11] the intellectual centerpiece of a modern knowledge economy and the primary source of long-term productivity dividends.

From these beginnings, the analysis of innovation, whether viewed in the context of a system or independently, has blossomed and become a fixture in the economic growth and business literature. What makes a knowledge economy the holy grail of development for countries looking deeper into the 21st century — Kazakhstan being one of several — is the belief that only by transitioning to such an economy can a country fully harness the creative powers of innovation. The currently certified "knowledge economies" countries such as Finland, Singapore, and the US spare no effort to maintain, if not further embellish, this much prized status to the extent that budgetary realities permit. Others, such as China, now the nerve center of global manufacturing, are eager to gain entry to the club of highly innovative countries. Even China, which could coast along for a few decades more on the strength of its manufacturing capabilities,[12] realizes that only by dint of innovation can it remain a diversified, highly productive and internationally competitive economy that steadily enhances the welfare of its people.

Innovation indexes and country growth performance

In response to the demand for recipes to create an innovative knowledge economy, it has become fashionable to compute innovation indexes to rank countries based on indicators capturing aspects of "knowledgeableness" or "innovativeness."[13] However, in addition to establishing a pecking order among nations, the indexes also conveniently identify the ingredients that in principle should enable a country to ascend the ladder and join those at the top. By sparking contests or races among countries with their eyes fixed on reaching the uppermost rungs, the indexers have ensured that terms such as "innovation" and "knowledge" are burned into the minds of policy makers so that when budgets are carved up, the drivers of the knowledge economy receive their due. The game of policy making by reference to indexes has also made it appear deceptively easy to become an innovative economy if sufficient resources can be mobilized. Once inducted into the club of high performers, there is the expectation that growth underwritten by productivity gains is then largely assured.

In practice, a glance at the innovative frontrunners' GDP growth data suggests that there is more to rapid growth than a high innovation index ranking. Switzerland for example is widely perceived to be one of the most innovative of economies, yet its growth between 1980 and 2012 averaged 0.42 percent and the maximum rate ever was 1.90 in 1989 (Fontes 2013). Finland, another innovative wunderkind, averaged a growth rate of 3.5 percent per annum during its boom years from the mid 1990s through the 2007.

---

10. The triumvirate that is the business community, the government, and the research university are elements of the so-called triple helix at the heart of the innovation system (Leydesdorff and Zawdie 2010).

11. The term was apparently coined by Chris Freeman (1982; Lundvall 2007).

12. China's capital to labor ratio in 2011 was a fraction—14 percent—of the United States, leaving plenty of room for catching-up (Kuijs 2012).

13. The indexers include the WEF, INSEAD, European Business School, ITIF, and others. See Archibugi, Denni, and Filippetti (2009).

9

Of the three countries with the highest patent counts — one popular indicator of innovativeness — Japan and Germany have struggled to make productivity respond to accumulating patent statistics between 1990 and 2010. The third country, the United States, did better between 1995 and 2005, but only marginally when measured by productivity.[14]

One can pin the blame for Germany's stagnant growth performance in the last two decades on the headwinds generated by the unification of its western and eastern halves following the dismantling of the Berlin Wall;[15] Japan's lackluster productivity growth can be ascribed to repeated mishandling of macro-economic policies and the reluctance to grasp the nettle of banking reform in the 1990s; the inability of the Unites States to become the productivity leader of the elite club can be blamed on the vagaries of its science and technology policy, its infrastructure failings, and the weaknesses of its schooling system. Nonetheless, the experience of these advanced knowledge economies suggests that while moving up the rankings ladder of the knowledge indexes can be an important factor in achieving higher productivity, it is no guarantee for sustained high growth, especially once countries approach the productivity frontier (DeLong 2013).

Is Singapore the innovator to follow?

Then there is Singapore, also one of the top-ranked innovative economies. It has with adroitness unusual among the nations of the world managed to minimize self-inflicted policy injuries. It also has pursued the objective of knowledge-based innovativeness with a single-mindedness borne of the realization that its prosperity rests on the quality and the creativity of its workforce. Singapore has spared no effort and resources to build a triple helix innovation system that assiduously translates into practice all the lessons harvested from two decades of global experience with innovations systems. Starting with a finely tuned schooling system emphasizing science, technology, engineering, and mathematics (STEM), Singapore has invested in a highly ranked research university, partnered with leading western business schools to provide students with managerial and entrepreneurial training, established institutions to impart world-class vocational training, and, by bidding for diverse talent from across the world, staffed a state-of-the-art research infrastructure to hunt for commercial innovations in fields considered to have the greatest promise: microelectronics, biotechnology, stem cells, optoelectronics, and new materials.[16] Singapore has put forth every effort to make itself into a business friendly and livable metropolis and a conference hub for the southeast Asian region. It is justifiably proud of its financial, legal, and infrastructural services sectors, and startup firms benefit from access to public and private venture capital. Singaporean domestic capabilities are powerfully reinforced by the presence of numerous multinational firms that have located regional headquarters and production facilities in the city. They are further buttressed by the presence of more than 100,000 highly trained foreigners who have made Singapore their temporary home. Despite these efforts, Singapore's TFP grows not much faster than that of the United States or Japan.[17] Its researchers (many of whom are foreign nationals resident in Singapore)

---

14. On productivity comparisons, see Asian Productivity Organization (2004).

15. In 2007, Hans Werner Sinn described Germany as Europe's laggard and published a book asking "Can Germany be saved?" http://ideas. repec.org/p/ces/ceswps/_1708.html; http://www.voxeu.org/article/can-germany-be-saved; five years later, in the wake of the most serious recession in decades, Germany was touted as Europe's strongest and most competitive economy.

16. http://www.research.a-star.edu.sg/

17. Depending upon the methodology used, Singapore's TFP grew at between 0.94 percent per annum and 1.6 percent per annum between 1991 and 2001. http://app-stg.mti.gov.sg/data/article/21/doc/NWS_2002Q3_TFP.pdf; http://www.eastasiaforum.org/2012/12/26/singapore-in-2012-balancing-growth-with-domestic-imperatives/

are establishing a credible track record by winning patents and publishing in refereed journals, but an innovative powerhouse Singapore is not. It is not a hive of high-tech startup activity, and unlike the case of Switzerland, Finland and Sweden, no Singaporean firm has emerged, or looks like it will emerge, as a global giant.

Was it worth the trouble and expense for Singapore to build the elaborate innovation system and to strive to become a knowledge economy? The answer is arguably yes. Can the system in place, with some improvement and immigration, deliver productivity-led growth well into the future — even as the core population ages? That is debatable once investment spending slows, as it has begun to. Should other small countries pursue variants of Singapore's "model" and set about constructing their own innovation systems because these constitute the best — or the only — insurance against future economic stagnation and shocks and against deteriorating environmental conditions? The answer is a qualified "yes." For middle-income countries such as Kazakhstan, as for advanced countries, there is no turning back from the road to the knowledge economy if they want to try and safeguard their longer-term economic prospects once non-renewable resources are exhausted or rendered uneconomic and climate change results in a more hostile environment. However, what sort of innovation system is assembled, how elaborate and specialized it is, and what is expected of this system, will vary from country to country and will be profoundly influenced by the evolving characteristics of the global "knowledge environment" and the modes of research.

The Messages for Kazakhstan Looking Toward 2050

For Kazakhstan, as it faces the daunting task of quickly moving up the productivity ladder, the specific relevant findings from growth economics and the research on innovation systems can be summarized as follows.

General lessons for Kazakhstan

During the stage when Kazakhstan is urbanizing and building its production base of mining, energy extraction, manufacturing, and services as well as its communications and research infrastructure, capital is likely to be the leading source of growth. Thus, from the standpoint of growth, investment at 30-35 percent of GDP, if efficiently allocated, could deliver rates of growth that result in a doubling of the national product in ten years or less. As noted earlier, and in Chapter 3, the window of opportunity for rapid catching up is arguably in the region of 15-20 years. A big push, as demonstrated by China or Singapore, could impart growth momentum that would be highly advantageous for the leaner, climatically challenged middle decades of the century and beyond.

Kazakhstan's interior location (absence of a coastline) could handicap growth because of infrastructure deficiencies and weak services trade policies (Gallup and Sachs 1999; Sachs and Warner 1997).[18] However, its proximity to China and proposed infrastructure investments might offset its "peripherality" through neighborhood effects, if China continues to grow into a powerful economic center (Easterly and Levine 1997; Behar 2008). Positive spillovers from China's growth could put additional wind into Kazakhstan's sails; a slow-growing and turbulent China would be a brake on Kazakhstan's growth. Likewise, conditions prevailing in Kazakhstan's other neighbors could buoy or dampen growth (see Chapter 3).

---

18. http://www.voxeu.org/article/landlocked-or-policy-locked; http://wber.oxfordjournals.org/content/15/3/451.short

Cross-country research, though frequently challenged, also urges countries in which several ethnic communities coexist to exercise due political caution in conducting their affairs because ethnic fractionalization is correlated with internal strife and slow or uneven growth (Easterly and Levine 1997; Alesina and La Ferrara 2004; Campos, Kuzeyev, and Saleh 2009; Posner 2004). Central Asia, with its potentially deep ethnic divisions, is susceptible to the ethnic pitfall, and countries in the region must tread warily if they are to realize their growth objectives. The literature on resource-rich countries cited in Chapter 3 underscores another correlation between mineral bounties and slow growth because exchange rate appreciation encourages the diversion of resources into the non-tradable sectors, and a combination of rent-seeking activities, a dominant state, and socio-political pathologies drain economic dynamism.

East Asian economies that started down the road to industrialization in the 1960s had the advantage of relatively egalitarian income and wealth distributions. These served to mute social tensions and were widely viewed as a source of national cohesion around growth objectives that involved initial sacrifices for all. Sustaining such a distribution contributed to social stability during the years of rapid growth and was part and parcel of the successful efforts at containing rent-seeking activities. Closer to the present, each of these economies now faces creeping income inequality, a retreat that throws doubt over the future of the social contracts in these nations and the strains it might impose on the political economy of development. It may be that worldwide we are witnessing an increased tolerance for inequality, but even if that is the case, the risk is that it will be paralleled by a weakening of commitment to and belief in a vision of future shared prosperity, political estrangement — or disengagement — and a reduced willingness to make present sacrifices for future gains. Kazakhstan, with its relatively equitable income distribution (see Chapter 2), has a chance to avoid the broader trends of rising inequality and thus the disruptive social and political stresses that high and rising inequality is like to bring about.[19]

Last but not least, as noted here, every currently innovative knowledge economy has arrived at this juncture after long and successful apprenticeship as a manufacturer progressing from low- to medium- and higher-tech activities over the course of decades, with the East Asian countries moving at a faster clip than the Europeans. Research offers no guidance on whether Kazakhstan and other mineral rich countries must also develop a competitive medium-tech manufacturing base now that the contribution of manufacturing to GDP is much reduced as a consequence of productivity gains. And there are few clues as to which specific industries could serve as stepping-stones to an innovative economy. We do know that some industries tend to have many input-output and employment linkages and spillovers,[20] are research-intensive, prolific patenters, generators of sizable quasi-rents, and buoyant exporters with good prospects in global markets. But for late-starting, small economies, leapfrogging into such industries is far from easy because of entry barriers arising from high startup costs, the importance of achieving scale economies, and the need for a lengthy period of learning and accumulation of tacit knowledge to achieve a high level of innovativeness. For these countries, currently low- and medium-tech activities might offer better options. It is apparent from countries' experience with textiles, food processing, and agriculture that there is much room for technological innovation and productivity gain remaining in these areas. For example, the innovativeness and economic performance of the Nordic countries and Germany derives not just from their high-tech telecommunication and pharmaceutical industries but more so from white goods, paper, escalators, marine diesels, technical textiles, dairy products, and many

---

19. However, as noted in Chapter 2, there may be biases in the survey data on which the income distribution figures for Kazakhstan are based. Collection of more accurate income distribution data is a high priority.

20. The ideas and diagrams produced by Di Tella (2011) identify candidate industries based on their location in a product space, but they give no guidance on how a country even if it can establish such industries with the help of its mineral wealth, can render them competitive and use them to vault into the league of innovative economies.

other not especially glamorous items that contribute vitally to the working of the modern economy and quality of life. Vinod Khosla, one of America's most astute venture capitalists, believes that the biggest payoffs are likely to come from innovations in air-conditioning, glass, and cement that are intrinsic to the infrastructure of society.[21]

The view that long-run growth is subject to endogenous factors — that is, those that determine technological change[22] — has increased the salience of human capital because ideas will, for the foreseeable future, emanate from the minds of (mostly) highly trained people,[23] and the technologies that arise from these ideas and research findings will also be developed by engineers and technicians and brought to the market by savvy entrepreneurs. In other words, human capital is the linchpin. Andrei Shleifer (2012) echoes the mainstream opinion with his claim, after examining the role of institutions and other variables, that "[I]f there is a fundamental cause of growth, the best candidate is human capital." The quality of human capital and its ability to generate and utilize technologies is the key to growth. The importance of quality emerges from the research conducted by Eric Hanushek and his colleagues.[24] Whether this (improved) human capital creates and develops productivity-enhancing technologies is a function of the design and operation of innovation systems and the environment — local and global — within which they operate. According to Vandenbussche et al. (2006), the closer a country is to the technological frontier, the greater the contribution of technical and skilled workers to closing the gap and pushing the frontier outward.

The accumulation of human capital in cities appears to partly underlie the productivity benefits accruing from agglomeration economies and the capacity of large cities to diversify, to move up the value chain, and to recover quickly from adverse shocks.[25] Urbanization economies arising from industrial diversity also reflect the abundance and diversity of human capital and of "thick" labor markets in cities and the opportunities some cities provide for rich interaction. Many fruitful ideas, and the products or services that they give birth to, evolve from the intermingling of knowledge from multiple disciplines. Thus, the returns from investment in human capital are enhanced by urban locations that attract and bring together talented people drawn from many different parts of the knowledge spectrum. The enormous interest aroused by Richard Florida's book (2012) on the creative class and its urban roots has brought to light the close and mutually reinforcing relationship between human capital, creativity, and the conducive urban environment, physical as well as social. That cities served as the crucible for innovation — places where ideas germinated, entrepreneurs brought the ideas to the marketplace,[26] and industrial clusters with traded and untraded interdependencies formed — was previously on the fringes of economic thinking, but the notion that the city feeds the innovative process is relatively new and now widely acknowledged.[27]

---

21. http://www.ncbi.nlm.nih.gov/pubmed/21265326

22. According to Howitt, "Endogenous growth is long-run economic growth at a rate determined by forces that are internal to the economic system, particularly those forces governing the opportunities and incentives to create technological knowledge." http://www.econ.brown.edu/fac/Peter_Howitt/publication/endogenous.pdf

23. This was not necessarily true in the past. Individuals quite innocent of scientific qualifications albeit with at least basic education conceived many path-breaking inventions. Interestingly, it appears that many of the signal advances of the 18th and 19th centuries were by a small number of highly prolific inventors. See Meisenzahl and Mokyr (2011).

24. http://hanushek.stanford.edu/ ; http://ideas.repec.org/p/stl/stledp/2009-19.html

25. Boston, with its seven major universities and its storehouse of human capital, is one example of a city that has extracted maximum mileage from the production of diverse and high quality human capital. See http://ideas.repec.org/p/fth/harver/2025.html ; http://ideas.repec.org/p/nbr/nberwo/6271.html ; http://ideas.repec.org/p/nbr/nberwo/10166.html

26. http://relooney.fatcow.com/OREP-Solow_2.pdf

27. http://www.creativeclass.com/rfcgdb/articles/WSJ%20The%20Joys%20of%20Urban%20Tech.pf; http://www.creativeclass.com/rfcgdb/articles/WSJ%20For%20Creative%20Cities,%20the%20Sky%20Has%20Its%20Limit.pdf ;

9

The heightened interest in the city goes hand in hand with the realization that subnational innovation systems are the building blocks of national systems. Work by Keller, Adams, and others[28] shows that research on the frontiers of a field tends to diffuse slowly because it is largely tacit and arises from the working, face-to-face interaction, familiarity and trust of groups of researchers in an urban location. Hence, local "attractors" (housing, schools, services, security), incentives, institutions (universities, tech extension providers), environmental reinforcers (as in San Francisco), angel investors, venture capitalists, developers and local banks are at the root of innovation, and the success of a national innovation system derives from the aggregated performance of a few local innovation systems.

Excellence in schooling

For Kazakhstan and resource-rich, middle-income countries such as Russia, Saudi Arabia, South Africa, Argentina, and Chile in broadly similar circumstances and with similar objectives, the road to an innovative economy that will deliver long-run growth via productivity gains in a sequence of manufacturing and service based activities depends upon raising the quality of human capital and extracting maximum mileage from a suitably tailored innovation system. What is the guidance from research on these two determinants?

Raising education quality for a modern knowledge economy is a much debated and exhaustively researched topic. Surveys of the vast literature single out the following four points, with the caliber of teachers being the most consequential (these are discussed in detail in Chapter 5). They are:

- teacher quality, motivation, and drive for results linked to (periodically refreshed) qualifications, incentives, autonomy, and social status. The top performers among the participants in the PISA and TIMSS tests (e.g., Singapore, Finland) drew their teaching staff from among the best college graduates;[29]
- curricula, books, school physical facilities, and computers/IT access/ Individually, none of these is highly significant, but collectively they matter, with the effectiveness of computers and IT for science and math education depending upon the competence of teachers and how effectively they integrate IT into the pedagogical process;
- family circumstances and cultural environment that attaches significance to learning and to high scholastic achievement (as in the Republic of Korea or Finland);[30] and
- preschool education and/or affordable day care offering some learning inputs (as in Finland)[31]

Few countries, the United States included, have had much success in translating these findings into universal practice because of the cost of good pre-schooling, the difficulty of attracting the best graduates into the teaching profession, and the inability to tailor incentives to consistently obtain student quality outcomes, and because influencing the culture of learning and assuring that children grow up in nurturing, intact families is beyond the capabilities of governments and communities. Neither Koreans nor Singaporeans are entirely happy with their high-pressure environments, even if they lead to outstanding

---

28. http://www.nber.org/papers/w16683.pdf ;http://ideas.repec.org/p/nbr/nberwo/7509.html; http://ideas.repec.org/p/rpi/rpiwpe/0612.html; http://ideas.repec.org/a/tpr/qjecon/v108y1993i3p577-98.html

29. http://ideas.repec.org/p/ags/umciwp/120033.html; http://www.teacherqualitytoolbox.eu/news/4/mckinsey_report_how_the_world_s_best_performing_school_systems_come_out_on_top; www.oecd.org/pisa/46623978.pdf

30. http://www.oecd.org/pisa/pisaproducts/46581035.pdf

31. http://www.newamerica.net/blog/early-ed-watch/2008/how-finland-educates-youngest-children-9029

9

science and math scores. And Singapore has struggled to balance rote learning with analytic reasoning skills and creativity.[32] Nonetheless, it is of critical importance for Kazakhstan's future that the country mimics these leaders' focus on human capital development.

Good schools that graduate students literate in science and mathematics and adequately equipped with analytic, communication, and soft skills are the foundation of an innovation system for the decades ahead. In many, if not most, industrializing countries, schooling deficiencies pose a major challenge and could take years, if not decades, to correct. Transplanting wholesale a Singaporean, Finnish, or Korean model can be ruled out because these models are culture-bound, path dependent, and creatures of local politics and institutions (not to mention flawed) that others cannot and should not replicate. However, improving education quality is a must, and China is demonstrating that focused and well-financed efforts can produce results in a decade.[33]

A 21st century innovation system

A creative innovation system that can support a growing diversified economy rests on the nation's learning economy. For Kazakhstan, the quality of its schools and universities must be a priority as these comprise the bedrock of a knowledge economy (see Chapter 5). However, an innovation system appropriate for the next several decades must also create and mesh a number of other key elements. Research to date points to the following elements of a knowledge economy strategy, although, as we will indicate below, technological change and trends in globalization could drastically rewrite the rules of the game.

Firms as innovators and anchors. As noted earlier, in the past manufacturing capability and competitiveness in medium and high tech industries was a sine qua non of an innovative economy. West European countries and the industrialized East Asian economies that developed productive innovation systems and are now classified as "knowledge economies" sourced between a quarter and a third of their GDPs from the manufacturing sectors and in every case demonstrated the capability to absorb advanced technologies and to produce complex components and capital goods. Manufacturing capability was not established by the building of turnkey petrochemical plants or showpiece steel mills or tariff-sheltered auto assembly plants, but by domestic design, technology assimilation, integration, and production skills. These then served to initiate incremental innovation and local R&D. In many instances foreign firms played a substantial role in the manufacturing sector and in imparting manufacturing capabilities, but homegrown firms always or eventually had a dominant part.[34] The most successful model combined a number of giant multinational corporations with a global market for their products. These firms based their competitiveness on management skills and long-term global strategies, incremental innovation backed by own R&D, by absorbing learning into their organization and work practices so as to steadily enhance productivity, and by successfully building a supply chain that facilitated the diffusion of learning.[35]

The objective of much formal R&D is product and process innovation. Firms — generally private ones — do most of the applied research and development and employ the vast majority of researchers Thus, research-oriented innovative firms are the rootstock of an innovation system and drive diversification. One sees this not only in the European countries but also in East Asian economies such as Korea and Taiwan (China); other East Asian economies that have not incubated innovative firms have struggled to create viable innovation systems and diversify their economies and worry about middle-income

32. http://www.bbc.co.uk/news/business-17891211
33. http://www.nytimes.com/2010/12/30/world/asia/30shanghai.html?pagewanted=all; http://www.bbc.co.uk/news/business-17585201
34. This is not so in the cases of Singapore and Ireland, although in Singapore Keppel Corp is an important manufacturer of oil rigs, and Ireland has major food processing firms and firms producing construction materials. http://www.kepcorp.com/en/
35. http://ideas.repec.org/p/nbr/nberwo/18017.html; http://ideas.repec.org/p/nbr/nberwo/15712.html

9

traps — Malaysia, Thailand, and the Philippines are in this category. From the experience of leading clusters, it is also apparent that one or a few anchor firms can determine the fortunes of a local innovation system. In Silicon Valley, Lockheed and Fairchild served as the anchors and their spin-offs and affiliates ("Fairchildren") helped initiate the virtuous spiral; in Cambridge, UK, it was Acorn, Cambridge Consultants (CCL), and later Advanced RISC Machine (formerly Acorn RISC Machine) that launched Silicon Fen;[36] TSMC was the force behind the fabless-chip-designer boom in Hsinchu Park (near Taipei); and firms such as Siemens, Vestas, Ericsson, and Nokia have performed similar functions in their respective countries. Anchoring, however, is most fruitful when it occurs in an urban locale offering locational advantages, connectivity, services, and livability. Thus for example, Medicon Valley, which straddles the Copenhagen metro area and extends across the Oresund strait to Malmo, has thrived because of anchor firms such as Novo Nordisk, Astra Zeneca, and Carlsberg Brewery but also because the urban environment is among the most attractive in the world.

The role of research universities. Although firms enjoy pride of place, the research university is a second anchor and will in the years to come very likely enjoy equal billing with firms in the engine room of the innovative economy for two reasons:[37]

First, the direction of much technological development, e.g., in bioengineering or nanotechnology, is becoming more knowledge-intensive, more closely linked to advances in basic science, and arguably the products being developed rely more on cross-disciplinary expertise. Research universities are uniquely placed to harness all three — the larger ones having both breadth and depth; the smaller ones through specialization and networking.

Second, large vertically integrated corporations once maintained research establishments employing thousands of scientists,[38] where they conducted basic and curiosity-oriented research alongside the bread-and-butter applied research and developmental work. Most now find it too costly to do so; the focus of R&D has narrowed to mainly applied R&D, and the outsourcing of research is becoming a commonplace. As a consequence, institutions with the scope and resources of Bell Labs[39] exist, if at all, in a much shrunken form. As the ambit of corporate research has narrowed while the importance of ideas and basic science has risen, universities have stepped into the breach (attracted by the financial opportunities as well and governments anxious to lighten budgetary responsibilities), and university-industry linkages have gained in number and significance.

The great research universities in the advanced countries established traditions for excellence and for scientific productivity over centuries.[40] Only a handful of these have garnered multi-stranded and mutually advantageous linkages with the business sector. Making universities fulfill a commercial role alongside their more central functions has proven difficult. Incentivizing university researchers — whose primary objectives can be teaching or publication in refereed journals — has been an uphill task, and only a trickle of research makes it into the commercial realm, and most of this is from a handful of the leading research universities. This may change as more universities develop the capability of both doing a lot of high-quality upstream research and translating this into innovations, but it has been slow going with universities still accounting for a minority of patents and a small minority of innovations in all advanced economies.

---

36. http://en.wikipedia.org/wiki/Cambridge_Consultants; http://en.wikipedia.org/wiki/ARM_architecture
37. The seminal role of Stanford University in the Silicon Valley context, of the Massachusetts Institute of Technology and Harvard in the context of Route 123, and of the University of Copenhagen in Medicon Valley has long been recognized. However, universities were secondary to the anchor firms and other corporate players clustered in technology parks and science cities. This is changing as universities gain importance.
38. Only Google and Microsoft now maintain research campuses on such a scale.
39. http://www.nytimes.com/2012/02/26/opinion/sunday/innovation-and-the-bell-labs-miracle.html?pagewanted=all&_r=0
40. On the making of world-class universities, see Etzkowitz (2002); Kaiser (2010); Altbach and Salmi (2012).

Industrializing countries pursuing ambitious plans of creating research universities of their own and making them serve the needs of industry have thus far registered few successes. China, Singapore,[41] Korea, Taiwan (China), Hong Kong (China), and most recently, Saudi Arabia and Qatar, have all invested substantially in establishing the physical infrastructure of a research university — an expensive proposition — have with varying degrees of success staffed these institutions with instructors and researchers with adequate qualifications and have begun to train a student body that will serve as the innovators of tomorrow.[42] However, all this is work in progress: These institutions might well serve as anchors, but whether they do will depend upon three factors:

- How the university evolves in the face of rising costs, encroaching digital technologies,[43] and the impact of the commercialization of university research on the pursuit of ideas for their own sake. The university of the future is likely to be a different animal, and no one knows quite what it might be yet.
- It is an open question as to whether or not the most talented will be drawn to the often only moderately rewarding activity of university research, with uncertain career paths. It is equally uncertain as to how universities might go about developing the entrepreneurial skills and spirit that would translate ideas into innovations. Both China and Singapore are experimenting and waiting for results.
- A world-class research university is more likely to flourish in some urban centers than others, to attract a sufficiently diverse and high-caliber staff and student body, and to serve as an anchor of a business cluster. Large metropolitan regions that are tightly interconnected nodes in the global network of cities offer a more open, diverse, economically variegated environment with many more job opportunities and sources of financing, plus the cachet that comes from living in a big city with brand recognition. From the standpoint of innovation, the nodal city is more likely to be plugged into the global innovation system, which serves as a conduit for information and enables researchers to participate in vital national and trans-national networks.

Governments as energizers and catalysts. Ever since the Second World War, governments have been drawn into making policies that affect research, technological development, training of the workforce, and industrial strategy. Top-down, highly dirigiste approaches — as practiced by the USSR and China prior to the 1980s — have proven counterproductive. However, all governments, irrespective of ideological inhibitions, have found it desirable to engage in technology and industrial policy — in the United States it is camouflaged as defense policy — in the interest of promoting innovation and long-term growth. Intervention has paid the largest dividends in four areas:

- Successful countries have created a high-powered government body backed by the top leadership, which in consultation with key government departments and the business community, proposes broad strategic guidelines for technology/industrial development, defines (market compatible) incentive policies, and has sufficient fiscal clout to pursue their coordinated (with other stakeholders) implementation. Perfection is a rarity. However, the Economic Development Board in Singapore,[44] the Economic Planning Board in Korea, Finnish Funding Agency for Technology

41. For a more detailed discussion of the Singaporean research system, see Yusuf and Nabeshima (2006). http://www.sup.org/book.cgi?id=9923; http://sciencecareers.sciencemag.org/career_magazine/previous_issues/articles/2009_03_06/science.opms.r0900067; http://www.nature.com/nature/journal/v468/n7325/full/468731a.html; The recent ups and downs are explored in http://www.nature.com/nature/journal/v468/n7325/full/468731a.html
42. On the experience of HKUST, which effectively tapped the diaspora, see Salmi (2012).
43. The growth and prospects of online courses (MOOCs) are examined by Waldrop (2013).
44. The workings of the Economic Development Board and the factors contributing to its effectiveness are explored in Yusuf and Nabeshima (2012) and in Heart Work 2 http://www.stpressbooks.com.sg/Heart-Work-2.html.

and Innovation/Sitra/Academy of Sciences in Finland, IDA in Ireland, and the Office of the Chief Scientist and the Ministerial Committee for Science and Technology in Israel[45] have all contributed significantly to the technological advancement and industrialization of their respective economies.[46]

- With private companies finding that basic research is no longer a core competence and unlikely to enhance shareholder value, much basic research — essential for innovation — must now be financed by the state and largely conducted by public universities and public research institutes (although this varies among countries).[47] The state has the responsibility for scanning the scientific horizon in collaboration with the research and business communities, assigning priorities, distributing budgetary resources among competing claimants and importantly, evaluating results periodically to ensure that the objectives were well justified, the project design and management was effective, and the returns measured up to expectations. However, the bulk of R&D spending continues to be financed by the private sector — almost 70 percent in the U.S., 72 percent in Germany, 82 percent in Japan, and 75 percent in Korea and in China (in 2009) (Veugelers 2013).

- Few private companies are willing to engage in costly blue skies research with an uncertain and distant pay-off as in the case of many green technologies, the Internet, and shale gas extraction. A state agency such as DARPA, suitably staffed, empowered, and held accountable to the legislature must then shoulder the task of canvassing proposals, commissioning research, vetting results and, if promising, finding ways of commercializing the resulting innovations. In many instances, for example with green technologies, government subsidies and/or procurement (semiconductor chips) have enabled promising technologies to acquire traction. Setting product standards, certification requirements, and regulations governing performance, also stimulates innovation and higher-quality production (with the help of metrological and testing facilities).

- Training a high tech workforce is an expensive business, and the cost of acquiring advanced science and engineering degrees (and the associated risks of not finding jobs or receiving research grants) can be an inhibiting factor (Romer 2001). Thus in addition to other enabling policies, it falls upon the state to not only underwrite some or much of the basic research conducted but also to partially cover the costs of training the workforce that is responsible for advancing science and giving birth to innovations.

The aforementioned elements constitute some of the relevant findings and lessons for Kazakhstan as it charts its way forward toward an innovative knowledge economy with the potential to diversify and grow. Before examining Kazakhstan's current capabilities and how these might be augmented, it is useful to note how innovation systems might be affected by changes in the global knowledge economy.

Globalization of knowledge: What does the future hold? The increasing cross-border traffic in ideas and technologies together with the communications revolution has helped to globalize the innovation system. Companies and institutions of research and learning are beginning to embrace "open innovation," realizing that with partnerships and collaboration more good ideas can be born and harvested. Because of deepening knowledge pools and the complexity of technologies being brought to light, the

---

45. On state innovation policies in Israel, Taiwan, and Ireland, see Breznitz (2011) and http://ec.europa.eu/invest-in-research/pdf/download_en/psi_countryprofile_israel.pdf
46. Yusuf and Nabeshima (2012): http://publications.worldbank.org/index.php?main_page=product_info&products_id=24201; See also Darius Ornston (2012) How Small States Make Big Leaps, Cornell University Press.
47. Data on R&D by academic institutions and its financing can be found in http://www.nsf.gov/statistics/seind12/c5/c5h.htm; universities account for 36 percent of basic and applied research in the US and 14 percent of total R&D in 2009.

lone inventor/innovator is becoming a rarity, and much research is conducted by teams, especially international teams. Individuals and institutions are specializing and joining forces to conduct research because it is too difficult and costly for a single person or all but the largest universities to internalize the breadth of the knowledge that needs to be assembled to conduct cutting edge research. The globalized innovation system is also strengthening the advantage of nodal innovative cities/metro regions, and these in time could become even more dominant by exploiting economies of agglomeration, scale, and scope. In other words, the globalization of innovation could enhance the comparative advantage of key local innovation systems with an early start, an established ecology, a high degree of connectedness, and a solid reputation. Were this to happen, secondary cities (in the innovation ranking) and more remote locations would lose out and have difficulty retaining their best talent. Start-up activity would also become more concentrated.

Should there be a retreat from globalization that resulted in a balkanization of research, this could allow some countries to pursue independent technology development strategies, provided they have the necessary resources, but innovation would suffer globally and is unlikely to thrive locally especially in smaller countries. Moreover, a retreat from the globalization of research would undoubtedly parallel a step back — or several steps back — from the globalization of trade and capital, which would be bad for growth in other respects as well. In fact, the progress of innovation, the building of knowledge economies, the diversification of smaller economies, and the resolution of threats to planetary well-being are all predicated on the continuing and benign character of globalization. The first half of the 20th century — from the outbreak of World War I through the 1940s — are a stark reminder of what can happen were globalization to stall or backpedal because of an upsurge of populism and political and trade tensions.

With this backdrop derived from a half century of cross-national research, let us look at Kazakhstan.

Kazakhstan in the Innovation Scales

An overview of Kazakhstan's performance since 2000 presents a mixed picture. Growth of GDP has averaged a respectable 7 percent per annum (2004-12), which is comparable to that of the East Asian economies. This was supported by rising investment from 23 percent in 2000 to a peak of almost 32 percent of GDP in 2005 and by high commodity prices (Chapter 2). However, since then, investment has declined to 22 percent of GDP in 2012 almost entirely because of sharply slowing of private investment, the share of which fell from almost 28 percent in 2005 to 14.3 percent in 2011. FDI provided a partial offset, rising from USD 1.2 billion in 2000 to USD 12.4 billion in 2012. Data on the distribution of investment shows that the primary sector was by far the largest recipient, followed by transport and logistics, real estate, manufacturing, and utilities. Between 2003 and 2010, replacement and renewal of capital equipment from 1999 through 2006 contributed to gains in TFP. However, since 2006, TFP across all sectors has plunged and become a drag on growth. The projected rates of growth through 2015 are in the 5.8-6.0 per annum range (World Bank 2012), which assumes some recovery in investment and a reversal in the rate of change in TFP bolstered by improvements in the growth performance of manufacturing and agriculture that have contributed little to aggregate growth during the past 15 years.

As of 2011, the mining sector accounted for 18 percent of GDP and processing/manufacturing for 12 percent. Services were responsible for 57 percent of GDP, and agriculture trailed with just a 5.5 percent share — less than that of the construction sector (7 percent). The export picture is one of increasing concentration on mineral — mainly petroleum — exports. In 2000, minerals accounted for 67 percent of exports; by 2010, their share had climbed to 81 percent with petroleum exports responsible for 60 percent of earnings. The number of firms engaged in cross-border trade has declined since 2005, and

SHAHID YUSUF

only 5 percent of firms are exporters. Manufactured exports, mainly to Russia, Japan, and Iran are predominantly metal and chemical products. The share of labor-intensive exports was a minuscule 0.6 percent in 2010 and that of high-tech goods was 4.4 percent. In the interim period, the export share of capital-intensive products halved to 13 percent from 27.6 percent. In terms of sophistication, Kazakhstan's exports ranked low, and there has been no change since 2000 (Table 9.1).

Table 9.1 | Kazakhstan's exports rank low in terms of sophistication

2000	Share in exports %	Share in imports %	Index of revealed comparative advantage	Exports, USD mln.	Imports, USD mln.
Material-intensive goods	67.3	21.7	0.8	5,707	1,051
Capital-intensive goods	27.6	23.6	0.2	2,341	1,144
Labor-intensive goods	1.7	13.0	-0.4	140	633
High-tech goods (easily imitated)	1.4	12.3	-0.7	122	591
High-tech goods (not easily imitated)	0.2	29.5	-1.5	169	1,430

2010	Share in exports %	Share in imports %	Index of revealed comparative advantage	Exports, USD mln.	Imports, USD mln.
Material-intensive goods	81.4	19.5	1.0	45,876	4,762
Capital-intensive goods	13.1	15.5	-0.1	7,369	3,717
Labor-intensive goods	0.6	17.1	0.5	316	4,110
High-tech goods (easily imitated)	4.4	12.4	-0.5	2,462	2,970
High-tech goods (not easily imitated)	0.6	35.5	-1.6	336	8,504

Source: UN (2010).
Note: Data compiled by NAC of Nazarbayev University.

As noted in Chapter 2, there has been a significant improvement in Kazakhstan's global competitiveness ranking and business environment between 2011-12 and 2012-13, from 72th to 51th for competitiveness[48] and from 56th to 49th for business climate (Schwab 2012).[49] However, obtaining construction permits, trading across borders, and obtaining credit and electricity remain problematic;

---

48. A 2006 study by Michael Porter gave Kazakhstan low marks for competitiveness on most scores; http://www.isc.hbs.edu/pdf/Kazakhstan_Competitiveness_2005.01.26.pdf
49. http://www.doingbusiness.org/data/exploreeconomies/kazakhstan/

the legal and regulatory environment is non-transparent, subject to change, and weakly enforced by the court system; and acquiring visas is time-consuming (see Chapter 2; issues relating to governance and corruption are dealt with in Chapter 11). At the same time, Kazakhstan's ranking on the Logistics Performance Index, important for such a sprawling country, is a low 86th in 2012.[50] Recent indications are that foreign investors perceive deterioration in the investment climate in Kazakhstan (see Chapters 2 and 11).

Kazakhstan's manufacturing sector is small and at an early stage of development. According to data compiled by NAC of Nazarbayev University the food and beverages industry is the largest with a 3.8 percent share of GDP followed by the engineering industry with a 2.1 percent share.[51] Other sectors of note are: construction materials (1 percent); chemicals (0.6 percent); rubber and plastics (0.5 percent); and metal products (0.5 percent). All three of the top-ranked subsectors have seen their shares in GDP decline since 2007 by 12 percent, 0.3 percent and 1.0 percent respectively. Chemical and rubber have maintained their shares, while metals have experienced a small slippage. On balance, manufacturing, which could be focus of diversification and innovation, is in retreat.

Kazakhstan's innovativeness is ranked by two reports, one issued by the European Business School (Innovation for Development Report 2010-11)[52] and a second by INSEAD (Global Innovation Index 2012).[53] In the first, Kazakhstan is in 54th place among 130 countries, flanked by Croatia and Romania. Surprisingly it is two rungs above the Russian Federation. The INSEAD index ranks Kazakhstan much lower — in the 83rd spot among 141 countries — flanked here by Swaziland and Paraguay. The Russian Federation is ranked 51st. In addition, the World Bank's Knowledge Readiness Index ranked Kazakhstan 73rd with a score of 5.2 (the average score for Europe and Central Asia was 6.45; Russia ranked 60th).

Other data on patents and scientific publications reinforce the impression of a country close to the starting gate. But if the WEF Technological Readiness rankings are accurate, Kazakhstan is sliding backwards, with its ranking deteriorating from 75th in 2008-09 to 87th in 2011-12.[54] Kazakhstanis have received on average a single patent each year from the US Patent and Trademark Office since 2000 and less than one from the EPO between 2000 and 2011. Patent applications per one million people were only 93 in 2010 as compared to 196 in Russia and 2,591 in Korea (UNECE 2012). Spending on R&D is low: between 0.21 percent and 0.23 percent during 2007-09 and falling to 0.16 percent of GDP in 2010. In PPP terms it amounted to USD 23 per capita as compared to USD 165 in Russia.[55] Innovation intensity is also low, with "innovative products" accounting for 1.2 percent of products sold in 2010 (mainly overseas). Most of the research outlay is on applied research and technical services with natural and agricultural sciences receiving 30 percent and 9.4 percent respectively. Few firms pursue innovation, as demand for innovation is weak — and these tend to be private ones. Food processing and machinery businesses tend to be more innovative, but again the number of firms engaged in innovation is small and the impact on productivity is negligible. Unlike in Singapore, FDI has not boosted R&D or innovation, in large part because FDI is mostly in the resource-based sector and firms active in this sector tend to

---

50. World Bank (2012) http://siteresources.worldbank.org/TRADE/Resources/239070-1336654966193/LPI_2012_rankings.pdf; Just 1 percent of the container traffic between Europe and Asia passes through Kazakhstan.

51. However, almost half of the value added in the engineering and machinery sector comes from the repair and maintenance of vehicles and equipment.

52. http://www.innovationfordevelopmentreport.org/

53. http://knowledge.insead.edu/innovation/global-innovation-index-2012-481

54. Chapter 5 discusses the weaknesses of the education system.

55. The number of workers engaged in R&D has declined from 50,000 in 1990 to 17,000 in 2010, in part because of the emigration of two million people during the 1990s, many of them among the most skilled, draining the country's stocks of human and research capital (see Chapter 2). Chemistry, mathematics, engineering, materials science, and mathematics have attracted the largest number of publications.

9

be conservative and to spend less on R&D ("Innovations in Energy" 2013).[56] A report issued by the UN Economic Commission for Europe specifies the structure of the innovation system, further evaluates its current limited potential, describes the many initiatives underway to improve governance, provides supporting services and use special economic zones (SEZs) to incubate clusters, and offers a number of specific recommendations.[57]

Becoming an Innovative and Diversified Economy: The Road to 2050

The overarching vision for Kazakhstan 2050 is to join the top 30 developed economies. We believe this is only possible if Kazakhstan turns itself into a modern knowledge economy as succinctly stated in Box 9.1.

Box 9.1 | **Vision 2050 for a Modern Knowledge Economy**

The vision for Kazakhstan is to create by 2050 a private sector driven, diversified and resilient economy with competitive knowledge-based manufacturing, agriculture, and service sectors, supporting a top 30 ranked performance.

Source: Author.

The flurry of initiatives by the Kazakhstani authorities to diversify economic and in particular industrial activities, to increase R&D spending to 1 percent of GDP by 2015, and to make the country an innovative hot spot are impressive indeed. The State Program for Accelerated Innovative Development (SPAIID 2010-14) that emerged from the Development Strategy 2020 — and is backed by the Law on State Support to Industrial Innovative Activity (2012) — is ambitious. Time-bound sectoral targets for rapid ("forced") industrial and export diversification and industrial growth averaging 8 percent per annum are detailed in the Innovative Industrial Development Strategy for 2003-15 and in the State Program for Forced Industrial Innovative Development 2010-14. The latter program lays out a number of targets: raising GDP by 50 percent over the course of five years; increasing the share of processing industry to 12.5 percent; raising non-oil exports to 40 percent of the total; and increasing labor productivity by 150 percent. However, the government budgeted what is by international standards a relatively modest USD 1.3 billion for this industrial effort. These programs also introduced requirements to increase local content and for foreign firms to hire mostly nationals. Such regulations undermine competition and efficiency and constrain the transfer of skills from abroad.

The Ministries of Industry and New Technologies and of Education and Science have been empowered to put the strategy into effect and it is expected that a cross-ministerial Council on Technology Policy chaired by the Prime Minister will oversee their activities. Additional support for innovation as well as oversight will come from the National Innovation Fund. Increased budgetary outlay and tax incentives are being introduced to enlarge the private share of R&D spending, which was less than 19 percent of the total in 2010. New offices and institutions have been created. Nine SEZs[58] have been set up to develop manufacturing industries (e.g., in Aktau and Atyrau), tourism (e.g., in Burabai), and R&D

---

56. MNCs are unlikely to locate much innovative activity in a country unless it has a large pool of scientific talent and is demonstrating progress in innovative activity e.g., Israel and Switzerland.
57. http://www.unece.org/fileadmin/DAM/ceci/publications/icp5.pdf
58. Companies operating in the zones are exempted from taxes and customs dues.

9

intensive businesses (e.g., in Alatau/Almaty and Astana New City). Moreover, incubators were established following the phasing in of a Technology Business Incubation Program in 2010, with innovation funds put in place and bilateral agreements signed. The government also made efforts to advance regional integration and took steps to improve the business climate and harness foreign expertise to conduct foresight analysis and identify promising areas of research. In addition, the government has proposed policy priorities and instruments in a Business Roadmap 2020 (diversification, social effectiveness, favorable industrial environment, assistance for small and medium enterprises, and encouragement of entrepreneurship via a special fund known as DAMU) and identified priority sectors — energy, chemicals, machinery, pharmaceuticals, construction materials, agribusiness, ICT, biotechnology, nuclear power, and engineering industries.

It is clear that Kazakhstan's policy makers have closely observed the recent and not so recent strategies of their successful Asian neighbors and, in planning ahead, have cast their policy net widely, adopting a top-down approach that to varying degrees was the norm in East Asia and is currently being implemented at great speed by China. The range of policies initiated in a short space of time and the scope of the economic diversification planned is breathtaking for a country with a population of less than 17 million, albeit one with mineral wealth sufficient to bankroll many expensive projects — as Saudi Arabia, Malaysia, and the UAE have demonstrated. However, this raises the question whether a top-down strategy with multiple stretch ("forced") objectives is an efficacious way forward for a country only recently emerged from "transition," with a limited pool of human and business related intangible capital (depleted by emigration), and with a number of thorny outstanding governance issues to settle. Undoubtedly, government leadership, commitment, strategic guidance, and financial underwriting of projects and activities that the private sector would shun, are critical at this juncture. But a broad top-down industrial diversification strategy orchestrated by the state and entrusted to state owned enterprises[59] (which world-wide experience shows are generally among the least innovative) can quickly turn into a costly growth subtracting debacle — something that China might soon discover with its hugely expanded renewable energy and transport sectors.

It is now becoming clear that the manufacturing sector will not produce more than about 15 percent of GDP at its peak and will not employ much more than a tenth of the workforce in mid-sized economies, especially resource rich ones. Moreover, unless the manufacturing sector is serially innovative, it is unlikely to generate the productivity gains and the quasi-rents that can significantly contribute to material affluence and an investable surplus. The production of commodity-based manufactures, e.g., petrochemical feedstock (ethylene, benzene/toluene), fertilizer, basic medical ingredients low in the pharmaceutical value chain, synthetic textiles, construction materials, standard machine tools, plastics etc. as Saudi Arabia has done, only minimally promotes growth and employment. As Saudi Arabia has also discovered, this kind of industrial widening does next-to-nothing for TFP growth (it has been negative in Saudi Arabia since 2004). Even under the best of circumstances, manufacturing will not be the growth driver it was for the East Asian tigers and for China. An industrial sector biased toward heavy chemical- and resource-based activities that is inappropriate for Kazakhstan and unsuited for the evolving international environment would squander resources and arguably put the economy on a sub-optimal development path.

---

59. Some 30 state-owned enterprises are to serve as the standard bearers of the industrial and export diversification program.

There is no dearth of studies on what an aspiring industrializer should consider when looking out over the next two to three decades — including such frontier areas as nano- and biotech based products, medical devices and prosthetics,[60] new materials, green manufactures, smart textiles, robots, sensors, filters, and catalysts. Among the popularizers of a so-called Third Industrial Revolution, Jeremy Rifkin (2011) has touted the potential of renewable energy: green buildings that would generate a surplus of energy, the potential inherent in a switch to a hydrogen economy, the benefits to be derived from an Internet enabled smart grid, electric or fuel cell based vehicles, and 3-D manufacturing. The list is long and not especially illuminating for government planning purposes. A transition to a green economy can be advantageous because it gives Kazakhstan an early start. However, most technologies are still in a gestation stage and dependent on subsidies, and Kazakhstan for now is unlikely to derive much advantage from the industrial spillovers of green technologies (because of size and limited technological and manufacturing capabilities). Similarly, the findings of Hausmann-Hidalgo product space analysis (suggesting that some of the top items are iron reservoirs, chocolate preparations, structures and parts of iron and steel, paper board, PVC, glazes, parts of machines, cocks, valves, accessories, etc.) also are of little value.

In our view supply push alone — through investment in higher education and R&D, infrastructure, and manufacturing facilities — will not bring about the viable, long-term, growth-promoting diversification that Kazakhstan is seeking. It must be matched, and in fact pulled, by the demand for innovation. The government and universities can serve as essential handmaidens of the innovation process and satisfy the necessary conditions for a virtuous spiral. It is demand-pull that must lead, and demand comes from the entry and growth of firms relying on innovation to pass the market test and achieve profitability. In the absence of entrepreneurial firms to transform ideas into marketable innovations, the return on investment in R&D is small, and there will be few employment opportunities for graduates.

Therefore, Kazakhstan's growth, economic development, and future innovativeness during the next three decades will depend mainly on three drivers: entrepreneurial dynamism of its firms (including state-owned enterprises [SOEs] that are likely to remain important players like in China and Vietnam), how these are enabled by the local innovation systems in one or two of the leading cities, and government policies that enhance the quality of the human capital, create an environment hospitable to new ideas and innovation, and furnish it with services — including and in particular, ICT services - and institutions. We already discussed the role of education in general in Chapter 5, and specifically for the knowledge economy earlier in this chapter. Let us then in the remainder of this section explore the role of firms and cities and which priority sectors Kazakhstan may want to focus on.

Firms

All the success stories from East Asia revolve around the emergence and rise of internationally competitive firms, e.g., Japan's auto and electronics firms, Korea's manufacturers of transport equipment, consumer electronics, and white goods, Taiwan's silicon fabs and chip designers and contract manufacturers (TSMC, Hon Hai Precision), Israel's software and defense electronics firms (Checkpoint, VocalTech),[61] agribusinesses in Malaysia and Thailand (e.g. Sime Darby and Charoen Pokphand), and China's producers of telecommunications equipment, wind turbines, white goods, computers, and trans-

60. The medical devices cluster in Warsaw, Indiana headed by firms such as Zimmer Corp., Depuy, Symmetry Inc., and Medtronic Inc. is an example of successful development in a small city largely as a result of the initial founding of Zimmer Inc. in 1927, a firm that produced aluminum splints, the evolution of this firm as a world leader, the emergence of other firms also producing medical devices, and the support provided by Purdue University.
61. http://www.ft.com/intl/cms/s/0/166799a0-fdda-11e1-9901-00144feabdc0.html#axzz2PQbey2i7

port equipment. There are other interesting examples of relevance for Kazakhstan, such as Fonterra from New Zealand,[62] the world's leading producer of dairy products (30 percent); JBS of Brazil, one of the world's largest producer of meat products and the largest player in the beef market;[63] Stora Enso and PM of Finland, leading producers of pulp and paper; and Cemex of Mexico, one of the two foremost producers of cement and construction materials (the other is Lafarge). Most firms that have proven to be game changers for their countries have been homegrown and privately owned; however, Singapore's Keppel Corp[64] is state-owned, as are several of the rising Chinese stars. In Singapore as well as in China, foreign MNCs have played important roles, transferring technology, and helping the countries diversify and climb the value chain. In Brazil, the big four agribusinesses, Cargill, ADM, Bunge, and Louis Dreyfus, work alongside local corporations.

The story of Europe's "hidden champions" (e.g. TetraPak, Winterhalter GMbH, Alfred Karcher GMbH), well-narrated in Simon (2009),[65] brings out the contribution to innovation, job creation, productivity, exports, and growth of mid-sized companies (one of the top three in the world in their business lines with revenues below €3 billion). By setting ambitious targets, specializing in carefully selected market segments, keeping core competencies and all essential production activities in-house, and through intensive applied research and incremental innovation informed by continuous feedback from clients, these generally closely-held firms have forged a place for themselves in the domain of global manufacturing.

Cities[66]

Large and medium-innovative cities are the focus of most R&D, innovation, corporate headquarters, prototyping plants, and startup activity. There are few such cities in even the largest countries,[67] and inevitably there will be few potentially innovative/smart cities in Kazakhstan. Almaty stands out from the rest, by virtue of location, climate, size (population is 1.47 million, the country's largest, and its share of GDP at 17.8 percent, overshadows that of the next largest, Astana, at 8.4 percent), ethnic diversity, and long history as the political, commercial and cultural center of the country. Competition from other cities would be desirable to spur innovation; however, the effectiveness of multi-level initiatives to develop the innovation system of Almaty could determine whether and how rapidly Kazakhstan moves toward its longer-term objectives. Dispersing resources (human, organizational, and material) over a number of specialized (science or smart) cities and many SEZs, as Saudi Arabia is doing, may detract from the success of any one city, and particularly, the lead candidate.

Smart cities are well-furnished with housing and social services, and increasingly they are focused on technologies and institutions that contribute to resilience in the face of economic and other shocks and adapt in response to emerging opportunities. All put great store in the quality of their ICT infrastructure, and in this regard, Kazakhstan has much ground to cover. Internet costs are high, and only a third of the adult population has access, with broadband users comprising little more than a tenth of the population. Fully mobilizing the "intelligence" of its smart cities will be critical to realizing the vision of a knowledge

---

62. http://en.wikipedia.org/wiki/Fonterra
63. http://en.wikipedia.org/wiki/JBS_S.A.
64. Keppel Corp. has thrived because of its access to state provided patient capital, managerial autonomy, and the quality of its management, product quality and innovativeness, and the steady demand for rigs.
65. http://www2.simon-kucher.com/hiddenchampions/
66. Chapter 8 explores the urban structure and policies in Kazakhstan in general. The focus here is on the role of cities in a modern knowledge economy.
67. http://www.businessinsider.com/the-20-most-innovative-cities-in-the-us-2013-2?op=1

9

economy within a 15-year window. There is intelligence inherent in local cross-disciplinary,[68] knowledge networks and in this regard, research universities such as Nazarbayev University in Astana and Al-Farabi Kazakhstan National University in Almaty can play a vital role in encouraging university-industry linkages and entrepreneurial activity. There is the collective intelligence that derives from the mature and coordinated functioning of the many agencies and institutions that the government has created during the past decade and that need to prove their worth in the urban setting. There is the intelligence that accrues from the progressive deepening of industrial activities grounded in domestic comparative advantage and their many associated, value-adding services, a thickening process that occurred in Stavanger (Norway) in the 1980s and 1990s. And then there is the intelligence that is the outgrowth of ICT-supported learning networks now augmented by "big data" that through global connectivity enable a smart city rich in human capital to draw upon the stores of knowledge accumulating in key urban nodes across the world.

The challenge for Kazakhstan during the next decade or two is to make one or perhaps two of its cities into knowledge hubs of Central Asia. As with economic diversification, a selective and measured application of policies commensurate with the administrative capabilities of the public sector has a higher likelihood of producing results. A localized industrial-cum-innovation strategy coordinated by a high level body that is focused on one or two urban centers might be the optimal way forward. It would be easier to design, implement, finance, manage, tinker with, and evaluate. A fast-growing and innovative city would be a beacon for the rest of the country.

Leading sectors for long run growth

High-tech industries or services exert a compelling fascination on policy makers because they are associated with the prosperity of advanced countries, but for many countries, the long run comparative advantage and the lucrative quasi-rents may be elsewhere. In Kazakhstan's case the comparative advantage — in addition to mineral extraction — would appear to lie in the mining engineering industry (as in the case of South Africa and Australia) as well as nuclear fuel fabrication and waste processing in light of the country's large reserves of uranium, and in agriculture, food processing, and agricultural equipment (as in the United States, Brazil, and Argentina). A notable element of the growth process in industrializing East Asian economies and leading western economies is that rising agricultural productivity contributed to growth, facilitated the transfer of workers to rural or urban industries, and generated surpluses that could be plowed into other productive activities. Kazakhstan has yet to exploit the full potential of its agricultural sector to augment its growth rate and, as indicated in Chapters 2, 3, and 7 to lay the groundwork for future food security and exports of food grains. The country's huge land mass offers considerable scope for expanding and raising the quality/productivity of grain, meat, and dairy products. If the food processing industry is included, agriculture's share of GDP is 9 percent with agro-processing diversified relatively evenly across grain milling, dairy products, dressed meat, confectionery, and animal fats.

The case for focusing on the food sector and its value chain is compelling.[69] The rising global population and higher incomes, in conjunction with climate change, will steadily increase the demand for grain, meat, dairy products, and fats (Brown 2012; Cline 2007; Evenson et al. 2004). In order to meet the demand, the climate challenge, and, very likely, shrinking supplies of water, food producers and processors will

---

68. The absence of cross-disciplinary research, a legacy of past compartmentalization of research in specialized research institutes, is a weakness to be remedied by merging some institutes with either universities or firms and using research universities as axes of cultural and knowledge-based activities in cities. A major university can contribute enormously to the intellectual and cultural life of a city through suitable location and the cultivation of linkages, not just with businesses, but also with other educational and social entities.

69. Almaty's chocolate producer Rakhat could, for example, become the nucleus of a regional and eventually global confectionery business through ambitious goals, good management, and targeted marketing and innovation.

have to seek answers in the most advanced forms of genetic engineering and tissue culture (see Chapter 7). They will need to develop many new technologies, including: (1) disease- and drought-resistant and nutrient-rich strains and compatible chemicals and pesticides; (2) efficient, energy-frugal land preparation, seeding, fertilizing, harvesting, and zero tillage production practices with the help of better machinery and the use of GPS, sensor technologies, and drones that map the condition of the soil and its moisture content; (3) techniques that economize on water use and pollution; (4) minimal spoilage and losses in storage, handling, and transport; (5) new methods of processing and packaging, ways of improving the utilization of the cold chain, and techniques for maximizing the shelf life of products; and (6) the use of hydroponics and aeroponics for growing high value products close to cities to further reduce energy and water use.

The potential in the food sector for apparently "high-tech" development that is labor-using and fits perfectly with Kazakhstan's comparative advantage is very large. And there are valuable lessons to be derived from the experiences of both advanced and middle-income countries on how to do good research, enhance productivity, diversify products and services, and create linked manufacturing and services subsectors. Countries such as the United States, Brazil,[70] Argentina, China, and Israel can be a source of important policy insights. Argentina for example, has successfully developed state-of-the-art seeders; and Brazil (because of the Brazilian Agricultural Research Corporation, or EMBRAPA) is the leader on research in land reclamation and on soybeans, citrus, and coffee; Israel is a key player in irrigation systems, and, along with the Netherlands and Singapore, is active in advancing technologies related to water filtration, greenhouses and hydroponics; China has created a world-class wind-power industry;[71] and the US is the preeminent researcher and user of GM technologies, aside from having the most sophisticated agro-food value chain.

Mining engineering and the manufacturing of mining equipment would be much harder for Kazakhstan to develop and to sustain, as Chile and South Africa are finding. Nonetheless, it is an option worth considering, especially the possibility of attracting firms that are currently scaling back their operations in South Africa or acquiring firms with relevant technological expertise in Canada, the US, Australia, and Latin America that could be transplanted in whole or part to Kazakhstan and would be able to contribute to the deepening of the resource-based sector. For that to work, Kazakhstan would have to move quickly to augment its managerial and entrepreneurial capital and infrastructure — hard and soft — the former initially via a variant of the Bolashak program that enables 30 and 40 year olds (who actually engage in start-up activity) with technical skills and firm-level experience to learn about start-up activity and the management of high-tech firms through stints in Silicon Valley, Cambridge, Munich, or Sophia Antipolis. As the Norwegian and Abu Dhabi sovereign wealth funds have demonstrated, a well-crafted long-term strategy tuned to the country's development objectives can serve as the basis for a selective acquisition of foreign firms that can contribute to industrial diversification, increased domestic value added, and technological advancement of the mineral extraction and beneficiation sector. Such an approach has its risks, but with advance preparation, with a scouting of the possibilities in targeted sectors and on a scale commensurate with the managerial capabilities of the National Investment Corporation this is an option for Kazakhstan to explore.

---

70. See on Brazil: http://www.fao.org/docs/eims/upload/305935/Brief%2033.pdf; http://www.economist.com/node/16886442; http://www.agricultureandfoodsecurity.com/content/pdf/2048-7010-1-4.pdf; Sabel offers some interesting information and references on innovation broadly and in Argentina: http://www.iadb.org/res/laresnetwork/files/pr325proposal.pdf

71. The policies that contributed to the growth of wind power in China and in the US are detailed in Lewis (2012) and Aggarwal and Evenett (2012).

9

Conclusion: Strategic Guidelines and Actions for the Short, Medium, and Long Term

Comparative advantage in complex multi-stranded activities with long run potential does not materialize overnight. However, several East Asian economies have shown that a focused strategy, implemented with vigor, that has the backing of major stakeholders and the public and that is adequately financed can achieve results in a decade or less and drive development for decades. Kazakhstan has the resources; now it needs to fine-tune its development strategy so as to fully exploit the 15-20 year window of greatest opportunity. It is difficult to neatly compartmentalize actions into short, medium and long term as all need to be pursued over the foreseeable future. But many of the specific actions underlying the strategic thrust presented in this chapter are detailed in other chapters of this report that deal with improvements in the institutional and business climate, green growth, human development, and urban and regional development. The following eight strategic guidelines for the modern knowledge economy deserve priority consideration.

Avoid policy overload. An excess of priorities and policy initiatives that greatly exceed the absorptive and implementation capacities of the national and subnational bureaucracies can be highly counterproductive. An illusion of vigorous developmental activity belies the confusion, lack of coordination and eventually disillusionment and cynicism that results from trying to do too much in haste. Korean, Taiwanese, and Singaporean experience suggests that few objectives, pursued with well-chosen and competently executed policies, delivered the goods. Perhaps the policy makers of the 1970s and 1980s were fortunate in that they were not overburdened with good advice and lessons from other countries and were required to innovate — "cross the river by feeling the stones" — and their policy innovations are now the stuff of legend.

Catalyze industrialization. The state can initiate an industrializing spiral by improving the business climate, easing infrastructure constraints and strengthening the institutional (legal, regulatory) scaffolding of markets. But it can also go further in a situation where a jump-start appears warranted — like in Kazakhstan — by selectively acquiring foreign firms with desirable technologies and relocating some of their production to Kazakhstan. A carefully planned program of acquisitions financed through the National Fund could help to create the nucleus of a cluster that is suitable for Kazakhstan and would attract private local and foreign investment.

Outsource industrial policy. Although much is made of the role of the East Asian state in the pursuit of industrial policy, the state only provided fairly broad guidelines and in fact outsourced most of the details of industrial policy and its implementation to firms. Undoubtedly the state eased access to credit, provided incentives, and invested in infrastructure, but the drivers of industrial deepening, diversification, and export-led growth in Korea, Taiwan, and China were and are the entrepreneurial managers of firms. Success was not the outcome of micromanagement by "enlightened bureaucrats," although sound incentives certainly helped. It did not arise from huge leaps in the conduciveness of the business environment (which still leaves much to be desired in China for example, while the gains made by Saudi Arabia have yet to show results). Visionary, ambitious, globally focused entrepreneurs made Huawei, Haier, Wanxiang, Samsung, LG, TSMC, and Quanta into leading players and the engines of growth. SOEs can be successful, but only if managed purely on commercial terms along private sector lines. This has proven difficult in practice, with only a handful of success stories, and therefore we believe principal reliance on private business initiative is critical. For Kazakhstan the challenge ahead is to strike a balance between identifying and grooming future "winners" and working to create a more competitive enabling environment conducive to the entry and exit of firms. An element of strategic selectivity, including in the acquisition of foreign firms, must be combined with a commitment to minimizing the risk of bureaucratic capture by rent-seeking special interests and of an open ended support for "losers."

Develop light regulatory touch and supportive institutions. The rise of Indian software companies such as Infosys, Wipro, TCS, HCL, Satyam, and others was assisted by relative freedom from regulation of the IT sector, public investment in high level skills and research, FDI, and liberalizing reforms starting in the 1990s that prioritized IT development. Local authorities also played a role in assisting the sector to grow, as did spillovers from defense industries located in Bangalore.[72]

Provide state-of-the-art and secure ICT infrastructure and incentives for greening. The development of software businesses, smart urban technologies, and innovation in Seoul, Singapore, Copenhagen, and Helsinki have all benefited from investment in and easy and cheap access to broadband Internet and advanced telecommunications infrastructure. Such infrastructure has also contributed to the level of connectedness, to productivity and to the greening of urban transport and energy utilization. For Kazakhstan, this would be an easy win and one that could be achieved within a few years. However, a focus on "hardened" ICT in the face of increasing security risks from aggressive hacking and related threats will become ever more important.

Develop a vibrant community of high-quality research universities. Research universities with effective links to the private sector will be a critical component of the modern knowledge economy in Kazakhstan. The early success of Nazarbayev University and the roll-out of its model to other universities in Kazakhstan will be a key ingredient of a successful innovation system for the country.

Provide cities with administrative and fiscal autonomy and the incentive to develop. What is so striking about the Chinese (and South Indian) experience is how subnational governments have taken the lead in spurring industrial activities, encouraging start-ups, attracting FDI, and tirelessly marketing the economic virtues of their cities. Chinese mayors (and some Indian chief ministers), motivated by clear incentives, have spared no effort in mobilizing public and private entrepreneurial energies to build their urban economies and have been spurred by the intense competition from other cities.

Create an open and attractive urban environment for knowledge workers. The growth of creative industries will be vital to the economic health and innovativeness of leading cities. An open, cosmopolitan environment that encourages the circulation of international knowledge workers is one factor that nurtures creative activities. Steady progress in strengthening IP rights and making it easier for firms to enter and to access credit are others. These require not just institutional reforms but also change in culture and outlook. This is a medium-term project. From the experience of Singapore and Japan, we know that culture changes slowly, but change it must, if a society, or a city, wants to be an active participant in the global innovation system.

In the preceding sections we indicated a number of possible specific actions that would support the creation of a modern knowledge economy. Table 9.2 brings them together with a suggested sequencing for the short, medium and long term. As indicated at the outset, the other priority areas addressed in this report also serve to underpin the development of the knowledge economy. So many, if not all, of the actions recommended in the preceding sections are relevant but not repeated here.

As in other areas, there are challenges and trade-offs that need to be faced squarely in the design and implementation of policies for the building of a modern knowledge economy. There is a clear tension between an approach of "picking winners" versus an approach of creating a favorable business environment. Moreover, in practicing strategic selectivity there is always a risk of favoring special interests. And

---

72. This is not the whole story, of course. The Indian diaspora played its part also, as did the nimbleness and initiative of the leading Indian firms.

what are intended to be "temporary" state engagements, subsidies, and protection can be very difficult to reverse once firmly entrenched. Throughout, maintaining competition, transparency, and a strict results orientation for all interventions by the state in support of particular sets of activities will be critical.

Table 9.2 | Actions for creating a modern knowledge economy

Areas	Short term	Medium term	Long term
Government leadership and support	• Government to provide long-term vision and credible commitment to development with selectivity of priority areas	• Interagency coordination; implementation, evaluation and adaptation of policies	
	• Leadership on science and technology by sponsoring blue skies research and support for research universities; forging of university-industry linkages; funding of R&D, SEZs and initial procurement and time-limited subsidization of new technologies		
Development of firms (see also Chapter 11)	• Intensify improvement in business environment, including flexibility of attracting foreign expertise; attract or buy into international firms to establish subsidiaries as a way of jump- • starting local development in selected sectors, with focused marketing campaign aimed at a few overseas cities where firms located and persuading targeted firms to locate subsidiaries in Kazakhstan with promise of incentives and supporting infrastructure, skills and enabling institutional environment		
		• Maintain world class business environment; ensure sunset of special government support for specific firms, foreign or domestic; evaluate progress and adapt policies as needed	
Development of research universities (see also Chapter 5)	• Build up research capacities to world class standards of Nazarbayev University; modernize TVET; establish linkages with private firms; provide competitive funding for innovative research		
		• Scale up NU model to other universities; implement, evaluate, and adapt	
Development of smart, green, fun, and safe cities (see also Chapter 8)	• For a few large cities, invest in secure broadband connectivity; ensure efficient city and international transport services and effective communal services; give local authorities leeway and incentives to attract firms	• Scale up these policies to all large and medium-size cities	

Source: Agency of Statistics of the Republic of Kazakhstan (2013)

Kazakhstan in 2050 — Seryk Baikanov Remembers

Seryk Baikanov was born in the first years of independence. Now in his 50s, he is the owner/manager of one of the successful Kazakhstani environmental engineering firms that he founded in his early 30s. He reflects on Kazakhstan's trajectory:

I vaguely remember the tough conditions in the country when I was born, but my parents often mentioned that as tough as it was — they had lost their jobs in the foundry in Karagandy when the company collapsed — they made sure my siblings and I had enough to eat and enough warm clothes to get us through the harsh winters; they never lost hope and were convinced that we children would have a better future. Things indeed started to improve when I went to secondary school — this must have been in the first decade of this century — schoolbooks were regularly available and teachers started to be able to concentrate on teaching us rather than worrying about their pay. At home we again had running water and stable electricity (my parents told us that that was how it used to be before independence). I studied hard; I vowed that I would get into Nazarbayev University so that I would receive the best higher education in the country. There I studied mechanical engineering; I must say that I myself, all my study mates, and my uncles who were engineers were quite baffled by the teaching and curriculum, but we had access to tools considered very advanced then such as CAD and 3D printers.

I was fortunate to be able to continue to study engineering at Massachusetts Institute of Technology to get my graduate degrees and to be exposed to an environment of entrepreneurship and risk-taking. With some friends I created my first company in the US, providing engineering services for the design of water conservation tools and advanced soil measurement equipment. But about 25 years ago, I felt I had to come back here because of my parents, as I had vowed to look after them in their old age. I was quite surprised and impressed by the Kazakhstan that I found upon my return: the general standard of education and health care was already much better, so I could put my children into the local public school without trepidation. And my kids were impressed that their new friends spoke pretty good English. Learning Kazakh for them was made easier because the country had shifted to the Latin alphabet.

Childhood friends that I visited in their villages all had small but neat houses in good sanitary conditions and had access to communication equipment that was not too out of date. Indeed what impressed me were the efforts to put the whole country onto what they used to call the "Internet highway." So I came back at the right time. Attitudes toward small professional businesses had changed; people started to feel that striking out on one's own was OK, the government helped me with a little bit of start-up support that I paid back in eight years, and I was able to get good talented young people to join my new firm. They preferred to join a start-up rather than pursuing a career as managers in a big company, and I had lots of business because the country started to be serious about "greening." I also found that people were more relaxed, the press was able to report what happened — actually, that's how the coal sector scandal about price-fixing and throttling entry of cleaner energy sources blew up.

But of course not everything was as good as it is today: Bureaucratic red-tape persisted, but at least one didn't have to pay on the side anymore, so registering a small new business, although easier than before, was still a bit cumbersome. Traffic was awful, with too many gas guzzlers that used the highways as parking lots; the coal lobby was still strong, and it took some major air pollution scandals and scolding from our international partners to finally break through with concrete investments to shift to cleaner energy. What startled me was how much climate change was already felt 25 years ago. I witnessed more volatile cycles of torrential rains and drought; winters had changed — I missed the crisp, biting cold air of winter of my youth.

The last two decades went by in blur because I was building my practice in environmental engineering — it's still small, but we have highly trained staff that I can source from my alma mater here as well as the best universities anywhere. We have modern equipment, some of which I designed and patented myself to help in water and soil conservation. As I said, business has been booming, and I have also set up an energy conservation consultancy. We have expanded to the neighbors, with some of our best clients in Pakistan, Thailand, and Western China. Our economy has been steady, and we have weaned ourselves away from depending on oil and gas, sort of like Norway has been able to. There are quite a number of people like me, who have been able to set up small technology oriented firms. We have been able to grow together and create a veritable *Mittelstand*, this old word for the German system of mid-sized companies. We now work very well with our government. It has gotten out of our — the business sector's — way and has focused on building the good infrastructure that you see here, really fun cities, and really cleaned up the air, water, and soil. What has helped is that our revered founding president's stretch goal for citizen and government, namely for Kazakhstan to become part of the 30 most developed countries, was taken seriously by all his successors, who followed each other in a stable and open process. I have traveled to pretty much all of the developed countries east, south, and west and think we have gotten there.

Recently my wife and I talked about when I should think of handing my businesses over to my children because she is also thinking of retiring from her practice as obstetrician, but she smilingly complains that young couple today feel so bullish about the future that she has long waiting lists and she doesn't want to disappoint her fans — after all she has been looking after two generations of the same families who are now good friends. But what am I to do? It's way too early for me to hang up my tools; maybe I should just create another company.

Source: Visioned by Shigeo Katsu.

KAZAKHSTAN'S
ROLE IN THE
REGION AND IN
THE WORLD

Kazakhstan's Role in the Region and in the World

Chapter
10

Richard Pomfret

Openness to and integration with the rest of the world has been one of the hallmarks of the successful emerging market economies over the last three decades. For Kazakhstan, openness will be just as important, if not more so, in the coming four decades as the country aims to propel itself into the top 30 developed economies. Kazakhstan needs market access for its energy and agricultural exports and will benefit from cooperation with its neighbors on key green growth challenges. Kazakhstan's students and skilled professionals need access to the best worldwide knowledge, its cities will need to be connected to the global network of smart cities, and its remote rural border areas will benefit from easy trade across borders. The development of a knowledge economy will depend on being able to access and adapt the best technological solutions in the world.

Kazakhstan in 2050, as a mid-sized country by population with one of the world's most competitive economies, will seek to balance policies that work in its national economic interests with its responsibilities as a global citizen. It will want to be prepared for unexpected economic and political shocks that may well strike from outside its borders: having a resilient, flexible, and adaptive economy and institutions will be critical.

At the same time, as noted in Chapter 3, geography matters, and regional relations will be especially important, both with the large neighboring powers of Russia and China and with the poorer neighbors to the south. Although the focus in this chapter is on economic aspects of regionalism and globalization, these cannot be separated from international policies on security, the environment, and other cross-border issues.

Kazakhstan's location presents opportunities as well as challenges. As a landlocked nation, Kazakhstan must interact with at least some of its neighbors for transit purposes. In this vein, it is fortunate to be surrounded by three of the BRICS, the large economies powering global economic growth in the 21st century.[1] On security matters, it will be difficult to avoid being affected by the competition between the superpowers, and geopolitically (as in international sporting events) Kazakhstan may find itself pulled between a European and an Asian orientation. Culturally, as a majority Islamic nation with a secular tradition from the Soviet era, Kazakhstan may find itself exposed to competing visions of an Islamic state like Turkey or Iran, while striving to maintain traditions of tolerance and multiculturalism. Finally, although relations with Kazakhstan's Central Asian neighbors to the south have not flourished in recent years, the region is defined by two great rivers flowing into the Aral Sea, the Amu Darya and the Syr Darya, as

---

1. BRICS are Brazil, Russia, India, China, and South Africa. Empirical studies in which the country is the unit of analysis find that landlocked status is a curse because there are many poor landlocked countries in Africa, and to a lesser extent South America and Asia. However, when the data are weighted by trade flows, landlocked status turns out to be a boon because the results are dominated by European landlocked countries such as Switzerland, Austria, the Czech Republic, and Slovakia who benefit from their location (compare Raballand 2003 with Sourdin and Pomfret 2010). Neighbors matter.

10

well as many elements of culture, language, and history. As a mid-sized and prosperous regional actor, Kazakhstan will be expected to provide leadership in a fragile and fractured region, much as Australia now does in the South Pacific or South Africa in southern Africa.

Kazakhstan's approach of multivector diplomacy — aimed at balancing relations with its neighbors, as well as with other external powers, with varying emphasis from issue to issue[2] — has served the country well in its first two decades and provides a sound foundation for future policy. Kazakhstan also has some useful niches as a mid-sized power, most notably unique anti-nuclear proliferation credentials that allow it to act as a bridge between, say, Iran and the UN Quartet. With regards to regional cooperation, President Nazarbayev played an important role in December 1991, ensuring that the dissolution of the USSR was not immediately followed by regional disintegration, and has remained a strong supporter of the CIS. The paradox of the 1990s, however, was that, despite many regional cooperation and integration agreements among CIS members designed to maintain the unified economic space, there was minimal implementation. Kazakhstan's international economic policies were *de facto* multilateral rather than regional, although, despite lodging an application in 1996, Kazakhstan (unlike the Kyrgyz Republic) did not join the WTO. The overall pattern in economic relations up to the mid-2000s was diversification of economic partners and regional disintegration.

The most striking recent initiative in regional cooperation is the customs union of Kazakhstan with Armenia, Russia, and Belarus. Options for expansion include upgrading this union to a common economic space and perhaps widening it with the accession of the Kyrgyz Republic and Tajikistan. The customs union highlights several possible alternatives for Kazakhstan's future. What are the implications for economic sovereignty, and does the customs union signify a shift to a more northern, rather than eastern focus? Alternatively, if the custom union's trade barriers are low (open regionalism rather than exclusive regionalism), will it facilitate Kazakhstan's role as a Eurasian land bridge? If so, Kazakhstan could link China (and eventually the Indian sub-continent) to Europe via Russia and could also provide a north-south corridor from Siberia to Central and South Asia. This would be entirely consistent with continued multivector diplomacy. At the same time, Kazakhstan can scarcely ignore its Central Asian neighbors, given the need for cooperation to address regional problems of water scarcity and potential instability. Accession of the Kyrgyz Republic and Tajikistan to the customs union would facilitate cooperation with Kazakhstan within the common economic space, but would it cement divisions between those three countries and Uzbekistan? These are just some of the examples of the complex questions of regional integration and cooperation with which Kazakhstan's diplomacy must grapple.

This chapter starts by describing the evolution of Kazakhstan's international economic diplomacy since independence, stressing its role in promoting regional integration (albeit with limited success up to 2005). The second section describes changes in actual international economic relations since independence and analyzes future challenges and prospects. The third section breaks down Kazakhstan's external relations by country. The fourth section analyzes the reasons behind the customs union and its likely consequences. The last two sections lay out a vision for regional and global integration for Kazakhstan in 2050 and explore various possible scenarios for regional and global integration in the context of achieving the Kazakhstan 2050 goals. While the domestic reform priority will be to achieve the vision of creating and maintaining a competitive economy and polity, in the face of changing global conditions

---

2. On security matters the major organization is the Russian-led Collective Security Treaty Organization. On environmental issues, a major source of conflict is water, especially the desiccation of the Aral Sea, but also rivers flowing from China into Kazakhstan.

10

the government will need to remain flexible. The most successful economies in the last third of the 20th century were those able to prosper both in the boom periods pre-1973 or pre-2007 and also in the less flourishing global conditions that followed these booms.

Kazakhstan's International Economic Diplomacy, 1991-2005

In December 1991, as the Soviet Union collapsed, the CIS was initially conceived, with Kazakhstan's support, as a framework within which to maintain economic ties among the Soviet successor states.[3] In both the political and economic spheres, however, the replacement of the Soviet Union by sovereign nations created conflicts that the CIS framework was unable to contain. The CIS made no progress in introducing special treatment for trade among members, although some members' trade and tax policies continue to favor CIS partners and intra-CIS visa-free travel remains the norm.

In 1992, Kazakhstan joined the United Nations, the International Monetary Fund and the World Bank. Kazakhstan participates actively in the main UN agencies and is also a member of organizations outside the UN system, such as the International Organization for Migration and the World Customs Organization. In 1992, at the UN General Assembly session, President Nazarbayev initiated the Conference on Interaction and Confidence-Building Measures in Asia as a counterpart to the Organization for Security and Cooperation in Europe, of which Kazakhstan is also a member.[4]

Also, following independence, Kazakhstan supported the creation of and joined numerous regional organizations and regional trading arrangements (RTAs). The principal regional bodies are listed in Table 10.1 with their respective membership. While in general these organizations and agreements have had little impact, a few of them, including the SCO and CAREC (and potentially the more recently created customs union between Belarus, Kazakhstan, and Russia), have developed political and economic significance in providing a platform for mutual trust building and regional cooperation. In addition, there were various bilateral trade agreements, which are, however, hard to track.[5] These often overlapping agreements, to the extent that they envisage preferential treatment of regional or bilateral trade, exhibit a spaghetti bowl effect (UNDP and CIS 2005) and were generally ineffective.

In sum, despite the many proposals and varied institutional initiatives, the period from the early 1990s to 2004-05 was one of regional disintegration (Linn 2004). Attempts to revive regional cooperation (UNDP and CIS 2005; ADB 2006) and a more active role for CAREC after 2005 brought only limited achievements. Even in areas of pressing need for regional cooperation (such as the Aral Sea), little happened.

President Nazarbayev was visible during this period as an important figure in many international forums (e.g., in CIS formation in 1991 and 1992 or at the 2005 SCO summit), but Kazakhstan's role in regional diplomacy was generally low key. Senior officials participated in meetings of the various organizations, but while Kazakhstan was never the cause of breakdown, nor was it particularly proactive between 1992 and 2005. A similar assessment applies to Kazakhstan's relationship with multilateral organizations (UN, IMF, World Bank, World Customs Organization, OSCE). This was most obvious with respect to the World

---

3. The Baltic countries did not join the CIS and Turkmenistan and Ukraine have never ratified the treaty, although they participate in meetings. Georgia withdrew in 2008.

4. The Conference on Interaction and Confidence-Building Measures in Asia Secretariat is located in Almaty. Kazakhstan is also a member of the European Bank for Reconstruction and Development, the Asian Development Bank, and the Islamic Development Bank.

5. Kazakhstan signed bilateral trade agreements with Moldova in 1995, Azerbaijan in 1997, and Georgia in 1999. Lists of such agreements (e.g., Tumbarello 2005, Table 1) are both too long, because some agreements have not been implemented, and probably too short, because some agreements may have been omitted.

Trade Organization (WTO); Kazakhstan applied for membership in 1996, and initially prospects of a rapid accession, similar to that of neighboring Kyrgyzstan, which joined the WTO in 1998, seemed good, but negotiations stalled and have still not been completed.

Table 10.1	Kazakhstan is a member of numerous regional organizations*							
	CIS	EurAsEc	UES	CACO	SPECA	ECO	SCO	CAREC
Kazakhstan	x	x	x	x	x	x	x	x
Azerbaijan	x					x		x
China							x	x
Kyrgyz Rep	x	x		x	x	x	x	x
Mongolia								x
Tajikistan	x	x		x	x	x	x	x
Turkmeni-stan	x**				x	x		
Uzbekistan	x	x		x	x	x	x	x
Russia	x	x	x	x			x	
Iran						x		
Pakistan						x		x
Turkey						x		
Afghanistan						x		x
Armenia	x							
Belarus	x	x	x					
Georgia	x							
Moldova	x							
Ukraine	x*		x					

Source: updated from Pomfret (2009).
Notes: CIS = Commonwealth of Independent States; EurAsEc = Eurasian Economic Community; UES = United Economic Space; CACO = Central Asian Cooperation Organization; SPECA = Special Programme for the Economies of Central Asia; ECO = Economic Cooperation Organization; SCO= Shanghai Cooperation Organization; CAREC = Central Asia Regional Economic Cooperation Program
UES became moribund in 2004. Uzbekistan joined EurAsEc in 2005, and CACO became redundant. Afghanistan joined CAREC in 2005 and Pakistan and Turkmenistan in 2010. Uzbekistan suspended its EurAsEc membership in 2008.
*For up-to-date details of the various schemes, see Laruelle and Peyrouse (2012) and Libman and Vinokurov (2012).
** Turkmenistan and Ukraine are unofficial CIS members, and Georgia withdrew from the CIS in 2008.

Changes in the Direction of Trade, Capital, and Labor Flows

After independence, Kazakhstan saw large changes in the direction of trade, capital, and labor flows. These changes had little connection to the economic diplomacy described in the previous section and much more to do with the transition from central planning, opening to the global economy, and the post-1999 energy boom.

In the late Soviet era, Kazakhstan, like the other Soviet economies, had an open economy, but its trade and other economic relations were overwhelmingly with other Soviet republics, plus a small amount of trade with Eastern Europe. Virtually no trade occurred with the rest of the world. As described in Chapter 2, the entire infrastructure was oriented toward intra-USSR trade and transport until the very end of the Soviet era, when the first rail link to China was built. Similarly with capital movements, the only significant extra-USSR investment agreement involved Chevron in Tengiz, which was only signed in 1990.

With independence, dramatic changes in trade and financial flows occurred. Historical economic and personal ties, including established infrastructure links and the shared Russian language, encouraged the continuation of established economic relations. Against these forces for constancy, however, there were powerful pressures to become more involved in the global economy.

On the export side, Kazakhstan's natural resources are in universal demand and, allowing for logistic and transport issues, reap the highest returns when sold on the global market. For oil and many minerals, the final consumer's identity may not be known, and for that reason the direction of trade statistics are often not particularly useful (e.g., if oil sales are to an offshore company and booked as exports to the British Virgin Islands). For grains, export values depend upon the harvest in Kazakhstan and world prices (i.e., harvests in other regions). On the import side, there was pressure to access goods and services that had been unavailable in the Soviet era, both intermediate inputs and consumer goods. An immediate phenomenon in the early and mid-1990s was the proliferation of shuttle traders who operated on a small scale, bringing consumer goods in person from Turkey, China, the Gulf states, and elsewhere.

The 1990s thus witnessed a major reorientation of Kazakhstan's trade away from the CIS. By the end of the decade, intra-CIS trade was well below half of total trade. Data are poor from the early years, and much trade was unrecorded over the decade, but the size of the change is apparent in estimates such as those of Islamov (2001), who calculated that, in 1992, 88 percent of Kazakhstan's exports and 94 percent of imports were intra-CIS trade, but in 1999 the CIS shares had dropped to 26 percent and 43 percent. Although trade was substantially reoriented in the 1990s, Russia remained the single largest partner.

As trade channels became more formalized in the 21st century, Russia remained the major supplier of imports. However, China has become at least as important a trading partner, both as a market for Kazakhstan's exports of hydrocarbons, minerals, and metals, and also as a source of imports. Imports from China have grown rapidly since the turn of the century and are not always recorded. Figure 10.1, reporting trade flows in the first half of 2012, highlights the dominant role of Russia and China as trade partners, while other large flows on the export side of the trade ledger (e.g., Italy, the Netherlands, and France) are related to investment flows and tend to be volatile.

Foreign investment in Kazakhstan during the 1990s was substantial, mainly in oil and gas (at least three-fifths of the total, with "business services" being the next largest category) and primarily by the major multinationals (Table 10.2). In the early 2000s, there was a policy reaction against western multinationals, reflected in the increasing involvement of KazMunaiGas in energy projects at the cost of foreign companies and in a shift toward favoring Russian and Chinese investors. Libman and Ushkalova (2009) ascribe this in part to dissatisfaction with the practices of multinationals, but it also reflected the recovery of the Russian economy and a more general warming of relations with China. A major turning point was the debate over development of the Kashagan offshore megafield in which Agip/ENI was the lead operator. After delays in 2007, both Prime Ministers Berlusconi and Prodi flew to Astana to renegotiate with President Nazarbayev. In February 2008, the government stopped any negotiations with respect to production sharing agreements. The government's desire to renegotiate (or insert KazMunaiGas into) production sharing agreements made before oil prices soared after 1999 is understandable, as is the difficulty (or problem of asymmetric information) in assigning responsibility for delays in large complex project such as Kashagan, but the salient responses by the government followed no apparent or predictable rule.

UNCTAD estimated the stock of foreign capital in Kazakhstan to be USD 93.6 billion in 2011, up from USD 10.1 billion in 2000, and Kazakhstan's outward stock of FDI in 2011 was USD 19.9 billion, up from a mere USD 16 million in 2000. The size of these stocks and of the flows reported in Table 10.3

are second only to Russia's in the CIS and far ahead of any other CIS country (UNCTAD 2012).[6] There are many anecdotal reports of FDI from China, especially near Kazakhstan's eastern border, and from Russia, especially since the customs union came into effect, and other CIS countries, but little reliable aggregate data.[7]

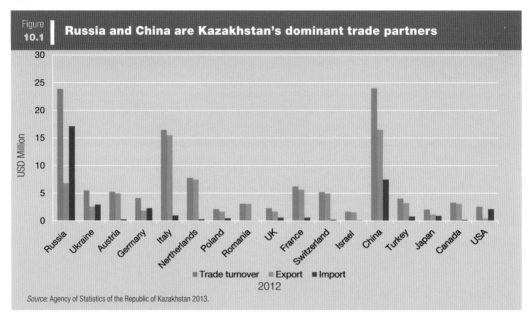

Figure 10.1 | Russia and China are Kazakhstan's dominant trade partners

■ Trade turnover ■ Export ■ Import
2012

Source: Agency of Statistics of the Republic of Kazakhstan 2013.

Table 10.2 | FDI in Kazakhstan was substantial during the 1990s,* mainly in petroleum

Sector/industry	FDI (million USD)	Percentage of total FDI
Agriculture, hunting, forestry, and fishing	11.7	0.1
Petroleum	8,699.1	59.4
Mining and quarrying	408.7	2.8
Food, beverages and tobacco	434.8	3.0
Metal and metal products	492	3.4
Other secondary	402.2	2.7
Business activities	2,507.5	17.1
Other tertiary	1,324.9	9.1
Unspecified	362.0	2.5
Total	14,642.9	100.0

Source: UNCTAD World Investment Directory Country Profile: Kazakhstan (2008). * 1993-2002

---

6. In 2011 Turkmenistan had the third-largest inward stock with USD 16.6 billion and Ukraine the third-largest outward stock with USD 8.2 billion.

7. Alexander Libman claims that Russian companies relocated to Kazakhstan "to take advantage of lower taxes and a better regulatory environment," but he adds that "there is almost no reliable data on cross-border investments in the post-Soviet space" (Kassenova, Libman, and Smith 2013).

Table 10.3	Kazakhstan's inward and outward FDI flows are high					
	2006	**2007**	**2008**	**2009**	**2010**	**2011**
Inward FDI flows	6,278	11,119	14,322	13,243	10,768	12,910
Outward FDI flows	-385	3,153	1,204	3,159	7,837	4,530

Note: Flows are measured in millions of US dollars.
Source: UNCTAD World Investment Review (2012).

The foreign investment climate in Kazakhstan is difficult to assess. According to the World Bank's Doing Business 2013 report Kazakhstan ranked 10th out of 185 countries in protecting investors, but this is heavily weighted toward protection of domestic minority shareholders (World Bank "Doing Business" 2013). More generally, indexes of the business climate in Kazakhstan paint a mediocre picture and one that appears to have deteriorated in recent years. (see Chapters 2 and 11). The view of foreign investors is less positive and appears to have more to do with implementation than legislation. Thus, revising oil and gas production sharing agreements, while understandable on a case-by-case basis, creates an impression that contracts are not secure and that the national treatment principle for foreign investors is not observed. The impression of discrimination against foreign investors is reinforced by reports that major companies such as Kazakhmys or Eurasian Natural Resources Corporation, although listed on the London Stock Exchange, appear to fall short of international standards of behavior toward foreign minority shareholders.[8]

Between 2005 and 2007, practically all of Kazakhstan's largest banks had foreign operations, following their clients into Russia, Ukraine, and Georgia in particular.[9] BTA and Kazkommertsbank were the two largest private banks in the CIS; BTA had four subsidiaries in Russia and owned banks in Belarus, Ukraine, Georgia, Armenia, and Tajikistan, while Kazkommertsbank, through its subsidiary Moskommertsbank, became the third-largest mortgage lender in Russia by 2007 (Libman and Vinokurov 2012). Halyk Bank, Alliance Bank, ATF Bank, and Bank Centercredit all had subsidiaries in Russia. More slowly, Russian banks have entered the Kazakh market. Alfabank in Almaty and VTB operate on a modest scale, but Sberbank aims to become one of the biggest banks in Kazakhstan. The Russia company VimpelCom, through its Beeline affiliate, offers mobile and online services and high-speed wireless and broadband access in Kazakhstan.

Kazakhstan continues to rely on Russia for elements of its power supply, reflecting the pre-independence networks, which were integrated across republican borders. Despite completion of the north-south power line in 2008, Kazakhstan's domestic grid is not fully integrated. As a result Kazakhstan imports electric power from Russia to western Kazakhstan, while northern Kazakhstan exports electricity to Russia. Russian and Kazakhstani investment in hydroelectricity projects in Kyrgyz Republic and Tajikistan could increase the pressure to improve transit from Tajikistan to Russia and would improve supplies to southeastern Kazakhstan, but these projects are subject to significant funding and political constraints

---

8. Both Kazakhmys and ENRC have a very small free float, i.e., the percentage of shares openly traded (18 percent in ENRC's case, which is below the 25 percent limit being introduced by the UK's financial regulators). For reports of irregularities in Kazakhmys and ENRC see Financial Times (London), March 27, 2013 and The Guardian (London), February 14, 2013. Strict requirements of local hiring by foreign firms also are seen as limiting foreign investors' appetite for engagement in Kazakhstan.
9. There had been an earlier movement of Kazakhstani banks into the Kyrgyz Republic after the 1998 Russian crisis.

10

that may impede their implementation in the coming years. However, for the long term, it will be in Kazakhstan's interest to see an integration of the Central Asian and Russian power grid and significant expansion of hydropower capacity in its southern neighbors.

Emigration was massive until the early 2000s, constituting a substantial brain drain in the early post-independence years, as the emigrants contained a disproportionate number of the country's well-educated and skilled people (see Chapter 2). The exodus slowed substantially with the Russian crisis in 1998, but even in 2000 annual net emigration was still over 100,000. It only began to drop substantially with the oil boom. In the 21st century there has been a small continuing immigration of returning Kazakhs, as well as significant flows of temporary immigrants from Central Asia attracted by the booming construction industry and seasonal agricultural work, such as cotton harvesting. Estimates go as high as one and a half million unskilled immigrants, four-fifths from Uzbekistan and the remainder from elsewhere in Central Asia and the Caucasus, although poorly monitored visa-free borders make quantification difficult. The ADB estimated that outflow of remittances exceeded USD 3 billion in 2006 (NAC of Nazarbayev University "Determinants" 2013); this probably increased at the height of the construction boom and fell after 2007, but remittance outflows are difficult to measure, and more recent estimates are unavailable.

Transport links have been reoriented. Roads are being upgraded, some with CAREC funding as part of international corridors, e.g., a northern east-west route from China to Russia and a southern route between Shymkent and the Uzbekistani border. A second rail link to China was opened in 2009, and a railroad through Turkmenistan to Iran was completed in 2013. Air connections have been improved, with Astana and Almaty as emerging hubs, although air connectivity is still relatively low by international standards (see Chapter 8).

One consequence is that Kazakhstan is replacing Uzbekistan as the crucial link in major north-south and east-west routes traversing Central Asia. The north-south rail link between Kazakhstan, Turkmenistan, and Iran will become the fastest land route from Russia to southwest Asia. The customs union between Russia, Kazakhstan, and Belarus was accompanied by a September 2010 agreement between the national railroads of Russia and Kazakhstan to simplify customs requirements for transit goods, clearly aimed at reviving the rail transit trade from China to the EU (and bypassing the southern route via Tashkent and Baku favored by the Transport Corridor Europe-Caucasus-Asia). Since 2011, a Eurasian Landbridge service has been available on existing rail lines that is cheaper than air and faster than sea; a container from Chongqing to Duisburg costs USD 10,000 compared to USD 30,000 by air and takes 21 days by rail compared to 42 days by road and sea (Roberts et al. 2012).[10] The Landbridge route will determine which Central Asian country provides transit services, but countries on the line will also benefit from reduction of their own trade costs; countries not on the line are likely to be marginalized.[11]

---

10. A driving force has been the shift of major manufacturing operations from China's high-wage east coast to inland cities such as Chongqing or Chengdu, and the municipal authorities' active pressure to cut transport costs by avoiding the multi-modal route via, say, Shanghai and Rotterdam to Central European destinations. The Landbridge service is used by Hewlett-Packard, Acer, Foxconn, and other companies who produce in western China and sell in Europe, and by German car producers to send components to their factories in China.

11. China also has plans to link its high-speed rail network to that of the EU, but there will likely be room for only one project, and with current national attitudes that is likely to be an all-Kazakhstan route through Central Asia, avoiding Uzbekistan. China's plans are ambitious but not infeasible. The first high-speed trains in China were introduced in April 2007, and by June 2011 China had 9,676 kilometers of high-speed rail in service, the largest national network in the world. The plan is to increase the domestic network to 18,000 kilometers by 2015 and to create international links to the south and west. With current technology high-speed rail primarily serves passenger traffic, but parts of the Chinese network (e.g., Chongqing-Lanzhou) are designated for mixed freight/passenger service with speeds of 200 kmph (compared to 300-350 kmph on the major passenger routes). For background information on the Chinese plans see, for example, Xinhua's English language website, including "Backgrounder: Chinese high-speed rail development" posted December 26, 2012 at http://news.xinhuanet.com/english/china/2012-12/26/c_132065182.htm.

10

To take full benefit, Kazakhstan must pay attention to the soft infrastructure of trade; its low rankings on the Doing Business trade component or the Logistics Performance Index are cause for concern, and recurring anecdotal reports of problems with customs, border guards, visa services, and other agencies involved with trade reinforce the impression of a difficult and inhospitable partner.

During the 1990s oil exports were constrained by Russia's Transneft pipeline monopoly, but rising oil prices and increasing output were the catalyst for completion of a private pipeline through Russia to the Black Sea in 2001, for construction of the Baku-Ceyhan pipeline from 2003 to 2005, and for construction of a pipeline from western Kazakhstan to China since 2007. The oil boom was also the stimulus for upgrading the Caspian ports, especially Aktau, in order to ship oil across the Caspian Sea to pipelines going west from Azerbaijan. The gas pipeline from Turkmenistan to China built in 2009 passes through Kazakhstan and offers opportunities to export Kazakhstan's gas to China.

In sum, Kazakhstan's external economic relations have changed dramatically over the two decades since independence, from a predominance of intra-CIS linkages to a more diversified global orientation. The hard infrastructure associated with trade has changed correspondingly, with transport and pipeline links much diversified from the exclusively northbound orientation of the Soviet era. This provides the basis for a global economic outlook, while having especially strong links with its large geographical neighbors and natural trading partners.

Kazakhstan's External Economic Relations by Country

Chapter 3 addressed the economic outlook for Kazakhstan's neighbors and major trading partners. This section examines Kazakhstan's external economic relations on a country-by-country basis.

At independence the dominant external partner was Russia, with whom Kazakhstan shares a border that is 7,000 kilometers long and is relatively free from natural obstacles. Although Russia's relative influence declined during the 1990s and early 2000s, it has been dramatically revived with establishment of the Customs Union, which will be analyzed in the next section. However, the biggest change has been the growth in economic relations with China, which were minimal in the late Soviet era. Since independence, Kazakhstan has also developed good ties with the United States, albeit less intensive in economic terms than with the two big neighbors. This has created a triangle of large powers, Russia-China-US, seeking close relations with Kazakhstan. Kazakhstan also has significant economic ties with the European Union, Japan, Turkey, South Korea, and Iran. Last but not least, relations with southern neighbors need to be reviewed to answer the question of whether Kazakhstan is part of Central Asia or is distancing itself from its relatively poorer neighbors.

Russia

Immediately after independence Kazakhstan's priority was nation-building, and, although President Nazarbayev was a strong supporter of the CIS, Kazakhstan was keen to establish its sovereignty and avoid subservient status to Moscow. Russia's diminishing influence was highlighted by the changing trade patterns described in the previous section and by Russia's economic and political weakness, culminating in the Russian crisis of 1998.

With Vladimir Putin's ascension to the presidency in 1999, Russia became more assertive in its "near abroad," and the energy boom reduced the resource constraints that had hamstrung Boris Yeltsin. EurAsEc was established in 2001 and the Collective Security Treaty Organization in 2002.[12] The color

---

12. Kazakhstan has also had bilateral military ties with Russia since the early 1990s, allowing Russia use of several firing ranges and of missile launch centers in western Kazakhstan, as well as the Baikonur Cosmodrome, in return for cash rents and military equipment.

10

revolutions in Georgia in 2003, Ukraine in 2004, and Kyrgyzstan in 2005 further strengthened solidarity between Russia, Uzbekistan, Tajikistan, and Kazakhstan. Nevertheless, when Russia recognized the independence of South Ossetia and Abkhazia, Kazakhstan and its Central Asian neighbors refused to follow. One recent study characterized the Kazakhstani position this way: "the Kazakh elites are increasingly autonomous in relation to Russia, and although Nursultan Nazarbayev remains a major supporter of the Kremlin's strategies for regional integration, Kazakhstan is seeking to attain geopolitical autonomy and an equal status with Russia" (Laruelle and Peyrouse 2013). Whether this balancing act can be maintained within the Customs Union is the subject of the next section.

China

In the decades before independence, direct connection with China was restricted, and official relations went through Moscow.[13] Although China quickly established good relations with independent Kazakhstan (Prime Minister Li Peng visited Kazakhstan in 1994 and President Jiang Zemin in 1996), the main concerns during this period were delimitation of the ill-defined borders and demilitarization of border areas.[14] These were the main agenda items of the Shanghai Five Forum[15] established by China, Russia, Kazakhstan, Tajikistan, and Kyrgyzstan in 1996. Trade increased from a low base. According to Chinese customs data, Kazakhstan's exports to China reached USD 958 million in 2000 and imports were USD 599 million; Kazakhstan customs figures are smaller, USD 670 million in exports and USD 154 million in imports, reflecting the substantial amount of unrecorded trade across the porous border.

Economic links between China and Kazakhstan have continued to expand, largely driven by strong economic complementarities. China's imports are overwhelmingly raw materials: coal, iron, steel, and increasingly energy in the 21st century. The construction of an oil pipeline from western Kazakhstan to the Chinese pipeline network has been built in installments since 2007, while Kazakhstan can also potentially use the Turkmenistan-China pipeline built in 2009. Kazakhstan's imports from China are primarily consumer goods. Small traders evade customs duties when importing many of these goods, and the trade is often unreported; some of the imports are routed through the massive Dordoi bazaar outside Bishkek, others are traded in free economic zones at the border. Chinese companies and individuals have invested in Kazakhstan, primarily in mining and energy and, on a smaller scale, in support of manufactured imports.

China's primary motivation appears to be to promote regional stability in order to restrain separatist pressures in Xinjiang and to protect its economic interests. China is also concerned about ensuring access to energy supplies that do not have to pass through chokepoints like the Strait of Malacca, although there are alternatives to Central Asian oil and gas. Finally, China is interested in developing alternative overland routes to Europe, including internationalization of China's high-speed rail network.

---

13. All border crossings between Kazakhstan and China closed after the Sino-Soviet split in the early 1960s, and only Khorgos reopened when relations improved in the early 1980s. The first rail link opened in 1990. Border crossings at Bakhty and Jimunai, plus some informal crossings and river ports of entry, were opened in 1990-91.

14. China and Kazakhstan signed a border demarcation treaty in 1994, but the last disputes were not settled until 1999. Disputes over Chinese withdrawal of water from the Ili and Irtish rivers remain unresolved despite 2001 and 2011 agreements.

15. This Forum later was converted into the SCO.

The Chinese government has maintained a low profile, preferring to work through the SCO.[16] The SCO is accorded high status by Kazakhstan and other members, whose heads of state attend the annual summits. During Kazakhstan's 2011 SCO presidency, the country hosted over a hundred meetings. The SCO is useful to the smaller members, including Kazakhstan, as a forum for counterbalancing Russian and Chinese influence. In May 2012, new premises of the SCO Secretariat, double the size of the old Secretariat building and in a more prestigious central location in Beijing, were formally opened in a ceremony attended by foreign ministers of all six members, the Secretary-General of the SCO, and the Executive Director of the Regional Anti-Terrorist Structure, an important agency of the SCO. After the SCO's early emphasis on borders and then on counter-terrorism, drugs, and migration, China advocated shifting the focus to trade and economic matters such as financial cooperation and banking. China has labeled projects in Central Asia and provision of financial assistance to poorer Central Asian countries during the 2009 economic crisis as SCO economic activities, but these initiatives have been bilateral in every respect.

Also relevant to relations with China, Kazakhstan has participated in CAREC, which brings together the Central Asian countries and regions of China. Following the adoption of an approach to transport and trade facilitation centered on developing several major corridors, loans from multilateral institutions have been identified with CAREC Corridors passing through Kazakhstan from China to Russia and from China to Uzbekistan. However, these projects are essentially bilateral loans taken by Kazakhstan to improve the country's transport network and to establish a central role in China-EU road transport.[17] More generally, these activities under the aegis of regional initiatives are consistent with Kazakhstan's multivector diplomacy.

A curious element in the foreign expert literature is the wide disagreement about the relative influence of Russia and China in Central Asia. Stephen Blank (2011) argues that Russia's position is so weak and overextended by poor policy and poor economic conditions that it will inevitably continue to lose ground, to China in particular, and the outcome will be a "New Chinese Order" in the region. The International Crisis Group (ICG 2013), in stark contrast, sees Central Asia as a problem for China because Chinese analysts do not understand the region and China does not have the military capacity to combat any influences on the volatile Xinjiang region; hence, China works with Russia in the SCO. For Kazakhstan, such conflicting analysis suggests a fertile ground for multivector diplomacy as it can interact with both large neighbors rather than facing a monolithic hegemon.

---

16. The current membership of SCO currently consists of China, Kazakhstan, the Kyrgyz Republic, Russia, Tajikistan, Turkmenistan, and Uzbekistan. Mongolia received observer status at the 2004 SCO summit, Pakistan, India, and Iran at the 2005 summit, and Afghanistan at the 2012 summit. In 2008 the position of Dialogue Partner was created for states sharing the goals and principles of the SCO and wishing to establish relations of equal mutually-beneficial partnership with the SCO; Sri Lanka was granted Dialogue Partner status at the 2009 summit and Belarus was also accepted as a Dialogue Partner at the 2009 SCO Summit, but its application for observer status was rejected on the grounds that it was a purely European country. Turkey was granted Dialogue Partner status at the 2012 SCO summit, and Turkish Prime Minister Recep Tayyip Erdogan has publicly raised the possibility of abandoning Turkey's EU candidacy in return for full membership in the SCO "Turkey Looks Forward, Talks SCO," *Eurasia Daily Monitor* 10 (27), February 13, 2013. Available at http://www.jamestown.org/single/?no_cache=1&tx_ttnews%5Btt_news%5D=40454.

17. A large World Bank loan for road construction and improvement in northern Kazakhstan was the result of bilateral negotiations between Kazakhstan and the World Bank, and the project was for upgrading the national road network as well as being part of a China-Russia link, yet it is listed on the CAREC website as a CAREC corridor project. CAREC's structure with six multilateral partners ensures that almost all multilateral assistance to Kazakhstan in areas such as transport or energy can be listed as CAREC projects.

10

The United States

The third major power in Kazakhstan's multivector diplomacy, the US, has much less direct influence. After Kazakhstan's independence, the US moved quickly to establish an embassy and provide oversight of the decommissioning of Kazakhstan's nuclear weapons. Kazakhstan has also received US funding for the dismantling of infrastructure for production of bacteriological and chemical weapons. Since Kazakhstan's independence, much of the US strategic aim in Central Asia appeared to be limiting the influence of Russia and Iran, but those regional powers had a relatively low profile in the 1990s. Moreover, the US leaned to Uzbekistan as its main contact in the region. After the start of military operations in Afghanistan in 2001, the US focus on Central Asia increased, but its main bases for its operations in Afghanistan were located in Uzbekistan and Kyrgyzstan. The US has also been concerned about the militarization of the Caspian Sea and Russian naval superiority, although, again, Kazakhstan is not its main partner; Azerbaijan is. In the meantime, the US provides financial, technical, and training aid to Kazakhstan, which has been keen to retain interoperability status with NATO. Moreover, the US continues to recognize Kazakhstan's anti-nuclear credentials, with one-on-one Obama-Nazarbayev meetings associated with nuclear proliferation events (e.g., in Washington in April 2010 and Seoul in March 2012).

Overall, the US economic footprint in Kazakhstan has been small, apart from the role of Chevron, ExxonMobil, and ConocoPhillips in the Tengiz and Kashagan oil fields and in some areas of agricultural equipment; in aggregate, the US accounts for about 3 percent of Kazakhstan's foreign trade. The 2009 establishment Northern Distribution Network (the supply route from Western Europe to Afghanistan) and the 2011 New Silk Road initiative were intended to increase economic interaction, but the fundamentals are not strong. Moreover, after a surge of transport of non-lethal equipment in 2014, the Northern Distribution Network will become redundant as US forces withdraw from Afghanistan. The US is far away and without obvious special complementarities, apart from as a political counterweight to Kazakhstan's two biggest neighbors.

Other partners

Kazakhstan has also managed to keep middle-sized partners among its foreign policy vectors. President Nazarbayev is a frequent traveler, e.g., meeting UK Prime Minister Cameron in August 2012, Turkish President Gul and Prime Minister Erdogan in October 2012, French Prime Minister Hollande in November 2012, and King Juan Carlos and Prime Minister Rajoy of Spain in February 2013. At home, President Nazarbayev hosted Organization for Security and Cooperation in Europe meetings in 2010, multilateral negotiations with Iran in March 2013, and a conference of the Istanbul Process[18] in April 2012. The economic basis for some of these relations is slim but enough to keep them on the radar, e.g., announcements that Kazakhstan will form joint ventures with Peugeot-Citroën and with EADS' Eurocopter, and that Talgo will provide rolling stock for the high-speed rail link between Astana and Almaty. More than 3,000 joint ventures have Turkish partners, mainly in construction, and Kazakhstan also shares strong cultural ties with Turkey. At the institutional level, Kazakhstan has had formal relations with the EU since 1999 through a Partnership and Cooperation Agreement, which is expected to be superseded by a new agreement in 2013 or 2014.[19]

---

18. This is a regional initiative to plan for stable post-2014 development in Afghanistan after the departure of NATO troops. See http://kazworld.info/?p=29349.

19. Relations with the EU are distinguished by inclusion of a human rights dialogue, which is unique among all Kazakhstan's agreements with foreign partners.

Within Central Asia, cooperation has been weaker than anticipated. Water issues are dominant in relations, especially with Kyrgyzstan and Tajikistan. With Uzbekistan, economic connections remain important, especially labor and remittance flows, even though formal diplomatic relations have not always been easy. The direct rail line to Turkmenistan will strengthen bilateral links with both Turkmenistan and with neighboring Iran. A major issue with the Caspian littoral countries is delimitation of the Caspian Sea, which remains fundamentally unresolved despite agreement on national and economic zones (i.e., a 25-mile limit) and on some biodiversity issues and sturgeon conservation. Since 2001, Kazakhstan has provided some aid to Afghanistan and Mongolia, and with the establishment of Kazakhstan's Agency for International Development, further assistance is likely to focus on Kyrgyzstan and Tajikistan. Through its membership in the Eurasian Development Bank, where it is the second largest shareholder after Russia, Kazakhstan has also provided crisis-related financing to its smaller Central Asian neighbors. Although oil and gas exports are constrained by pipelines and other transport options, Kazakhstan has shown flexibility in its grain exports, seeking out new markets in Georgia, Iran, Afghanistan, and the Gulf region, as well as using established export routes through Russia and selling to its Central Asian neighbors.[20]

Elsewhere in Asia, Kazakhstan cultivates relations with Korea, Japan, Malaysia, India, Gulf states, and Israel (Laruelle and Peyrouse 2013). Partly due to the large Korean community in Kazakhstan, Korea is the most important of these, with regular direct air services, major infrastructure projects (e.g., the USD 4.5 billion Balkhash power plant in which Korea Electric Power Corp and Samsung will hold a 65 percent stake, Samruk will hold 25 percent, and Kazakhmys will have 10 percent), investment in oil and gas, car assembly plants, and other joint ventures. Relations with Japan and India have lagged in recent years, but both of these major economies are showing renewed interest in Kazakhstan, and Kazakhstan is responding positively to these countries as potential customers and as counterweights to the neighboring great powers.[21] In Southeast Asia, Kazakhstan has special links with Vietnam, Indonesia and Malaysia via joint OIC membership, and with Thailand as a popular tourist destination.

Finally, Kazakhstan is establishing a global presence through embassies and consulates on other continents, including Brazil and Cuba in Latin America, Egypt and South Africa in Africa, and Australia. As a leader in the Central Asian Nuclear Weapon Free Zone, Kazakhstan has woven special links with New Zealand, the major advocate of a nuclear-free Pacific. From an economic perspective, however, a trade agreement with New Zealand would be of marginal importance.

The Customs Union with Russia and Belarus

The customs union with Russia and Belarus is by far the most significant regional integration move by Kazakhstan since independence. The agreement was signed in November 2009, and a common external tariff and customs code established in 2010. In July 2011, customs controls at the members' common borders were abolished. The customs union's significance is reflected in the statement by Libman and Vinokurov (2012, p. 49) that it is "the only truly functioning integration institution in the FSU."[22]

---

20. In 2008, however, during a shortfall in domestic production and a spike in world wheat prices, Kazakhstan halted exports, with some damage to its liberal trade image and hardship to neighbors dependent on grain imports from Kazakhstan.

21. One indicator of the revival of links with Japan, which were stronger in the 1990s, is the start of renewed negotiations on direct flights to Japan. India has had little direct presence in the past, but is increasingly concerned about energy security (taking over ConocoPhillips' Kazakhstan operations), and is viewed by Kazakhstan as a force for stabilizing the AfPak region, which is a necessary condition for opening up pipeline and overland transport links to South Asia.

22. A harbinger of the change was the creation of the Eurasian Development Bank in 2006 (mentioned in the text here), as a joint initiative by Kazakhstan and Russia. The Bank's membership also includes Armenia, Belarus, the Kyrgyz Republic, and Tajikistan. The Bank finances projects that promote integration, provides technical assistance to members, and funds the Center for Integration Studies, which conducts research on integration. The EADB also hosted a regional crisis fund in 2009 to help poorer members weather the global economic crisis.

10

In economic theory it is clear that a customs union is a second-best arrangement, which may or may not improve over the preceding tariff-ridden situation, but which is inferior to non-discriminatory trade liberalization (see Box 10.1). The empirical evidence of customs unions and free trade areas is that they have been harmful when they have erected a wall around a protected market, but beneficial if they have low external protection and focus on integrating the internal market by trade-facilitating measures. The argument that a customs union is necessary for a small economy to achieve economies of scale is false, because, with open trade policies, the world is the market. The scale economy argument is belied by the success of the relatively small first generation new industrializing economies (Hong Kong, Singapore, Taiwan, and South Korea), and by the dismal performance of the most populous counties as long as they sheltered their producers from global competition (rapid growth in China, India and Brazil dates from major opening up of their economies in 1978-79, 1991, and 1995, respectively).

How does the customs union work out in practice for Kazakhstan? The common external tariff as negotiated under the union was weighted toward the Russian tariff. Whereas Russia was able to keep 82 percent of its customs tariffs unchanged, lower 14 percent, and increase 4 percent of its tariffs, the corresponding shares for Kazakhstan were 45 percent, 10 percent, and 45 percent (Libman and Vinokurov 2012). Raising the external tariff while allowing duty-free imports from Russia was a recipe for trade diversion (see Box 10.1), and a simple but plausible model by IMF economist Patrizia Tumbarello (2005) estimated substantial welfare loss for Kazakhstan. Moreover, non-tariff barriers, such as newly designed sanitary and phytosanitary (SPS) rules, will make it harder for the Kyrgyz Republic to export its farm products to Kazakhstan (Djamankulov 2011) and tighter controls on the customs union's external borders will discourage informal, or previously poorly monitored, imports into Kazakhstan from the Kyrgyz Republic and China (Mogilevskii "Trends and Patterns" 2012).[23]

Why did Kazakhstan take this step when ex ante studies suggested that the customs union would yield negative returns to Kazakhstan? Libman and Vinokurov (2012) emphasize the reassertion of Russian power and economic strength as important long-run trends in making a Russian-centered RTA attractive, and the financial crisis of 2007-08 as the short-term stimulus for a defensive partnership. Laruelle and Peyrouse (2012) find that the empirical literature indicates potential short-run benefits for Kazakhstan but a longer-term negative impact as foreign investment, technology, and knowledge transfer flows decline. The EBRD study (Isakova, Koczan, and Plekhanov 2013) is more agnostic, forecasting small, negative short-term effects on Kazakhstan but uncertain long-term effects, perhaps suggesting that forming the customs union was a political, rather than economic, decision.

One debate that had occurred in the mid-2000s was whether it was better to prioritize multilateral tariff liberalization or RTA formation, with the general conclusion that the former would be better because it would more likely lead to more open regionalism with low external trade barriers. The customs union took the regionalism-first path but effectively came to the same destination. In 2012, Russia joined the WTO, and its commitments included substantial tariff reductions, to an average tariff of 8 percent by 2020; elimination of some non-tariff barriers to trade; and written clarification of other non-tariff measures that

---

23. Silitski (2010) argues that the main reason for Russia promoting the customs union was to control imports from the EU and China, which were evading tariffs, taxes, and other restrictions by routing via Belarus and Kazakhstan respectively. Laruelle and Peyrouse (2012) highlight the drastic effect of the customs union on Kyrgyzstan's role as a platform for re-exporting Chinese goods and report estimates that the number of Kyrgyz wholesale traders fell by 70 to 80 percent in 2010-11. Apart from the physical difficulties of controlling Kazakhstan's long border, there are reports of competition between border guards and customs officers and of corrupt practices.

| Box 10.1 | **Regionalism and multilateralism in the global economy: Lessons for the customs union** |

10

The foundation document for current international trade law, the 1947 GATT, took a negative stance toward preferential trading arrangements. The splitting of the global economy into exclusive trade blocs was viewed as one of the contributors to economic depression and war in Europe in the 1930s. GATT Article 1 required unconditional MFN treatment, i.e., every signatory must treat all other signatories as well as the most-favored trading partner. Trade policy in the high-income countries during the 1950s consisted of reduction of tariffs and removal of quantitative restrictions, which were generally multilateralized via MFN treatment.

However, six Western European countries pursued economic integration as a path to future peace, creating the European Economic Community in 1957 with the plan of completing a customs union by 1968. Seven other European countries formed the European Free Trade Association in competition, and many groupings in the Western Hemisphere and in Africa created customs unions and free trade areas. The EEC customs union was successful and formed the basis for the EU, but all of the other RTAs stagnated or collapsed. The fundamental reason, highlighted by Jacob Viner (1950), is that discriminatory trading arrangements lead to trade creation and trade diversion; the former, where new trade displaces inefficient producers or satisfies increased demand, is welfare-augmenting, while trade diversion, where preferred trade displaces more efficient non-preferred producers, is welfare-reducing, so that the net welfare effects are ambiguous. While the EEC customs union in manufactured goods was trade-creating, the principal impact of the Central American Common Market, the East African Community, and many others was trade-diverting. The larger European Free Trade Association countries eventually joined the more dynamic EU.

During the 1960s and 1970s, the major trading nations, led by the US, held multilateral trade negotiations and agreed to substantial tariff reductions (in the 1964-67 Kennedy Round) and to the removal of many non-tariff barriers (in the 1973-79 Tokyo Round). However, this was followed by a major retreat from the non-discrimination principle. The US signed RTAs with the Caribbean Basin countries, Israel, and Canada during the 1980s, and then formed the North American Free Trade Area (NAFTA) in the early 1990s. The EEC created the Single Market, expanded to twelve members, and changed its name to the European Union. Australia and New Zealand signed the Closer Economic Relations agreement in 1983.

With another change in broad direction, the Uruguay Round of tariff negotiations, which had stagnated in the 1980s, was brought to a successful conclusion in 1994, tying up loose ends from previous rounds, bringing agriculture, textiles, and clothing into GATT, and signing a first agreement on trade in services (GATS). Reflecting the enhanced significance of multilateralism, the GATT Secretariat was replaced by the World Trade Organization (WTO) with beefed up responsibilities and a more serious dispute resolution mechanism.

In the 21st century, a new wave of regionalism is occurring. It has centered in Asia, where the two previous waves had largely been absent. Starting in 2000, Asian countries went on a spree of signing trade agreements, both within and beyond the region, and on a bilateral or plurilateral basis. These were primarily "new age" or WTO+ agreements targeting specific practices at or behind the border that hindered trade. In many cases they were to facilitate operation of supply chains based on greater fragmentation of the production process.[24]

In sum, since 1947 the world trading system has seen three waves of RTAs amid a general trend of multilateralism and strengthening of world trade law. The waves differ, and apart from the unsuccessful schemes of the 1960s, do not involve classic free trade areas or customs unions discriminating in favor of members whose internal market is protected by high external trade barriers; this type of exclusive RTA failed because it diverted rather than created trade. The successful RTAs (EU, Closer Economic Relations, NAFTA) have been those with low external trade barriers, which have worked on reducing trade costs to promote greater economic integration without losing the benefits of operating in the liberal global economy. The "new age" RTAs of the third wave involve successful open economies (Singapore has signed the most trade agreements since 2000) pushing to reduce trade costs so that they can reap still further benefits from specialization and trade.

Source: Author

---

24. More historical and theoretical details on are in Pomfret (1997). East Asian regionalism is covered in Pomfret (2011). Baldwin (2011) sets out the development benefits of participating in supply chains.

10

affect trade.[25] All of these policies would be implemented de facto as changes in the customs union's common external commercial policy. Therefore, once the 2020 external trade policies are in place, the customs union is likely to be much less harmful to Kazakhstan than suggested by estimates made before Russia's WTO accession. Nevertheless, the long-term net benefits remain uncertain.

In January 2012 the creation of a Common Economic Space (CES) began. The aims of the CES include creation of a common market in goods, services, labor, and capital; coordination of monetary, financial, and tax policies; development of unified transport, energy and information systems; and unification of systems of state support for innovation and priority sectoral development. In July 2012, the Eurasian Economic Commission, a supranational executive body comprised of deputy prime ministers, was established.

How far will creation of a common economic space go? Both widening and deepening are on the horizon. Kyrgyzstan and Tajikistan, both already members of EurAsEc, are the most likely new members of the CES along with Armenia. A steering committee for integrating the Kyrgyz Republic into the CES already meets (although reconciling Kyrgyz WTO commitments with the external tariff of the customs union is a major obstacle). Ukraine is a more distant, and more challenging, future member. These potential new members are all in the WTO and, assuming that Kazakhstan finalizes its own WTO accession, could reinforce steps toward an open rather than an exclusionary regionalism. There is greater uncertainty about how far integration will go. In the European Union there have been continuous pressures for deeper integration, although the process over the 60 years since the Coal and Steel Treaty has been uneven and slow. Successful completion of the customs union led to pressure to complete the single market and have a common currency, common banking rules, and supranational fiscal oversight. Unlike the EU, Russia holds a majority voting position within the customs union and is thus likely to be the driving force (as in the case of Russia's unilateral WTO negotiations affecting the customs union's external policies), albeit with other members having a seat at the negotiating table. In any case, the considerable difficulties which the European integration process has faced argues for caution in projecting a similar pathway for Kazakhstan and its neighbors.

The Vision 2050 for Kazakhstan in the Region and the World

The CIS was meant to replace the Soviet Union, but it had little practical impact (see Chapter 2). Kazakhstan's political efforts in the 1990s were primarily focused on nation-building and domestic economic policy. Many agreements were signed, but in practice Kazakhstan's economic relations were on a bilateral and multilateral basis rather than a preferential or regional basis. The period 1990-2005 was one of regional disintegration rather than integration. Kazakhstan's international economic relations changed substantially in the 1990s; market forces largely drove the process, and it resulted in wider global connections and reduced relative importance of pre-independence regional links. In recent years Kazakhstan adopted a more layered approach, with a trend toward hierarchical regional engagement with the northern-oriented customs union at the top, China brought in through the SCO, and Central Asia, largely relegated to receiving assistance through Kazakhstan's Agency for International Development, at the bottom. At the same time Kazakhstan is broadening its diplomatic reach with more active participation in some international organizations and representation on all continents. The lead role it

---

25. WTO accession commitments go beyond tariffs and NTBs. The Final Report on Russia's accession is 758 pages long, excluding the specific commitments on goods and services, which are in annexes, and it includes, inter alia, rules for the treatment of foreign investors; constraints on trade-distorting (amber box); agriculture subsidies; and rules on intellectual property, public procurement, and foreign trade regime transparency. Shepotylo and Tarr (2012) calculated that in 2020 after the transition period Russia's weighted average bound tariff will be 8.2 percent and the applied tariff 7.6 percent.

aspired to in connection with its Organization for Security and Cooperation in Europe presidency, its active engagement with the OECD, and its multiple initiatives in hosting in Astana major events of global or regional significance attest to that active pursuit of a stronger regional and international profile.

For the future, much depends on how the rest of the world, and especially Kazakhstan's immediate neighbors, will develop in terms of their economic trajectory, their domestic political stability, and their relations with Kazakhstan, with each other, and with the rest of the world. However, Kazakhstan can play an active role in helping to bring about an outcome that is supportive of its own national aspirations, and in any case it can and must prepare itself for any potential eventualities. The vision we suggest for Kazakhstan's regional and global engagement is summarized in Box 10.2.

Box 10.2 | Vision 2050 for Kazakhstan's Regional and Global Engagement

Kazakhstan will have constructive, peaceful relations with all of its Eurasian neighbors. It will play a lead role in regional organizations that provide for effective cooperation on security, on economic integration (esp. transport and transit) and on the management of the regional public goods (especially shared water and energy resources).

Kazakhstan will do its best to keep regional economic structures open to the rest of the world and will participate as a respected global citizen in international institutions, focusing especially on those which are effective in addressing important global challenges that also involve a clear national interest. This will inevitably involve selectivity based on significance for Kazakhstan and ability of Kazakhstan to play a positive role.

Kazakhstan will be prepared for unanticipated external economic and political shocks by developing a resilient, flexible, and adaptive economic and institutional capacity.

Source: Author

Future Scenarios and Possible Actions

Future scenarios for Kazakhstan's regional and global engagement and options for appropriate action can be traced across different time horizons. Table 10.4 at the end of the chapter summarizes possible actions under different assumptions regarding future international and regional scenarios for Kazakhstan.

In the short term

In the short term, there is much that is positive about Kazakhstan's current approach, and the process of multivector diplomacy remains valid. The two major economic issues requiring short-term action are WTO accession and creation of the Common Economic Space.

Earlier WTO accession could have been useful but was less important in the 1990s when Kazakhstan faced more urgent priorities of nation-building and none of Kazakhstan's neighbors were WTO members. The Kyrgyz Republic (1998), China (2001), and Russia (2013) are all members now, so trade across most of Kazakhstan's borders can now be carried out by a common set of international rules. WTO rules are a good basis for world trade law, which is why almost all of the world's economies are WTO members. The main exceptions (Iran, Uzbekistan, Azerbaijan) are not models that Kazakhstan should follow if it wants to be a top-30 economy. All successful economies are engaged in the global economy and recognize and (largely) abide by WTO rules. The WTO has a dispute settlement mechanism that protects traders against WTO-incompatible measures, even when applied by the largest trading nations.[26]

---

26. In one of the earliest dispute settlement mechanism cases, Venezuela successfully complained about US fuel policies that effectively discriminated against oil imports from Venezuela, and the policies were changed. The EU lost a high-profile banana case, brought by small South and Central American countries. For Kazakhstan, a specific area where the dispute settlement mechanism could be used is in combating anti-dumping measures imposed on iron and steel exports.

A second short-term issue arises in the rapid implementation of the customs union and its extension to a CES: the extent to which the CES evolves into an open or an exclusionary economic arrangement. Kazakhstan should use its influence to ensure that deepening or widening the CES is in the context of remaining open to the global economy. An exclusionary grouping will pose challenges for economic sovereignty and also for Kazakhstan's multivector diplomacy. The CES will provide Kazakhstan with access to a larger internal market, but, for an open economy, the market is the world. If all CES members are WTO members committed to liberal trade policies, then the arrangement should follow the more open regionalism of ASEAN, the EU, or the Closer Economic Relations rather than the failed Latin American or African model of protecting the internal market. None of the high-performing emerging economies of the past half-century used an RTA as their main route to prosperity (Box 10.1).

In addition, action on regional cooperation regarding transport and trade facilitation, energy and water issues, security, and other matters is important in the short-, medium-, and long-term. As a landlocked country, Kazakhstan needs transit access and efficient air services, with an early move to an "open sky" policy. Currently, its neighbors include two large dynamic economies, and Kazakhstan should seek to improve transport links to Russia and China and also act as a Eurasian land bridge. Taking full advantage of such links will require improved soft infrastructure (trade facilitation) as well as investment in hard infrastructure. Water and environmental issues are important and require bilateral cooperation with Russia over the Ural River and with China over the Ili and Irtysh rivers. The water and energy issues in the Aral Sea Basin need urgent regional cooperation with Afghanistan, the Kyrgyz Republic, Tajikistan, Turkmenistan, and Uzbekistan (Box 10.3). These are ongoing issues that will not disappear even in the longer term.

Finally, Kazakhstan should continue on the path to greater global involvement. Not only big powers matter. Australia and Korea have been drivers of G20 and Singapore of 3G. Kazakhstan will and should continue to promote alternative forums, such as G-Global, and play an active role in existing organizations, such as chairing OSCE and OIC, and hosting the Istanbul Process in April 2013, the ADB 2014 annual meetings, and EXPO 2017. Middle powers can also identify niches via reputation, which Kazakhstan has done with respect to nuclear proliferation.

In the medium term

Medium-term scenarios are more difficult to predict, especially given the potential for instability across much of Kazakhstan's neighborhood, let alone the global economy. Some factors may be beyond Kazakhstan's control. The current regional balance may become unstable if China continues to grow and Russia does not. Kazakhstan has, at best, partial control over what happens in its neighborhood. Will the SCO expand to incorporate Afghanistan, Turkmenistan, Pakistan, India, Iran, and Turkey to become a major Eurasian organization, but with greater emphasis on the south and east, rather than the customs union? What if Russia, with its majority voting power within the CES, decides to take it in a more exclusive and less desirable direction? Finally, Kazakhstan has little say over whether its southern neighbors prosper or become failed states. As the largest Central Asian economy, must Kazakhstan play a leadership role in addressing Central Asian problems such as the Aral Sea or terrorism?

Although there is no escaping geography and the primacy of relations with Russia, China, and Central Asia, choices of how Kazakhstan interacts with these partners, and with the rest of the world, can be made. Within the customs union, Kazakhstan can use its influence to ensure that the union is open rather than exclusive, and focuses on integration through reduced obstacles to the movement of goods, services, labor, and capital rather than on creation of a trading bloc protected by high barriers to external trade. The SCO can be a vehicle for engaging with China through institutionalized meetings of leaders

Box 10.3 | Need for cooperation and leadership on Central Asia regional water and hydro-energy issues

Central Asia has significant water resources that can be used for agricultural and energy production. During Soviet times, engineers constructed huge reservoirs in the water-rich upstream republics (the Kyrgyz Republic and Tajikistan) and major irrigation schemes in the water-poor downstream republics (Kazakhstan, Turkmenistan, and Uzbekistan). This permitted the conversion of large tracts of desert into vast cotton fields. The intensive use of water from the Amu Darya and Syr Darya rivers led to the drying up of the Aral Sea in a matter of decades, causing a major ecological disaster of historic proportions. At the same time, a regional power grid was established, which allowed the region-wide distribution of hydroelectricity generated in the system. A core feature of this system was to store water upstream in the winter so it could be released for irrigation use in the summer. Upstream republics were rewarded for restricting the release of water – and hence power generation when they needed it most – during the winter months by the provision of free gas, coal, and oil fuel from the downstream republics.

After the breakup of the Soviet Union the coordination and barter mechanisms that had kept the system operating were interrupted. Downstream countries discontinued the provision of free fuel supply in the winter, which forced the upstream countries to release water for hydropower generation instead, thus reducing the amount of water available to downstream countries for irrigation in the summer. This resulted in great waste and underdevelopment of water and energy resources and created the potential for conflict among the countries about the allocation and use of water among them. An already complicated situation is further aggravated by the fact that the region faces potential short-term crises of water, energy, and food security due to recurring regional drought. Moreover, the potential impact of global warming on the region adds another layer of uncertainty and potentially serious risk, since it may threaten the survival of Central Asia's extensive glacier system and hence its supply of water for irrigation and hydro energy. Pervasive shortages of water and electric power would seriously undermine the economic development of the region and could give rise to interstate conflict. So far, this conflict potential has been contained by ad hoc negotiations and agreements, but no longer-term solutions have yet been found.

Central Asian countries, regional organizations, and international financial institutions have made efforts to develop more effective and cooperative approaches to the management of water and energy resources. This includes the Aral Sea Basin Program supported by international donors; the regional water sharing agreements among key countries in the region; the regional energy strategy being developed under the auspices of CAREC; the efforts of the international community under UNDP leadership to assess the current threats to regional prosperity and stability from a possible crisis of water, energy and food security; and the World Bank's efforts to mediate in the latent conflict between Tajikistan and Uzbekistan over the construction of the Rogun dam.

There are great benefits from concerted improvements in regional water and energy resource use in Central Asia. There are also great political, technical, and financial obstacles. Ultimately governments have to work with each other, with private investors and with users to ensure effective solutions. This presumes a readiness to cooperate and compromise by the governments in the region, but this will require the building up of trust and will take time. As it has recently started to do, Kazakhstan can take a lead in terms setting an example of water and energy conservation measures, in working on bi- or trilateral, if not region-wide, resolution of potential conflicts over water resource use, and in proactively encouraging the regional and international institutions to play a strong role in intermediating conflicts and guaranteeing possible agreements, drawing on the experience with other regional water basin agreements and management solutions elsewhere in the world.

To facilitate the development of selected large scale hydropower generation investments and transmission projects Kazakhstan, as a key downstream country, could encourage the other Central Asian leaders to join project-specific consortia with the support of international financial institutions and other partners. With appropriate safeguards for the downstream countries guaranteed by multilateral or bilateral actors, it may be possible to satisfy the requirements of downstream countries through shared responsibility for the successful implementation of the projects.

Sources: UNDP (2005), Linn ("Links" 2008), and Linn ("Crisis" 2008).

and senior officials. Broader regional forums can play a similar role, and some (e.g., CAREC for regional transport and trade facilitation) may be useful vehicles for developing, financing, and executing regional investment and cooperation strategies. Participation in these regional cooperation efforts must be selective and judged on a case-by-case basis in terms of likely results; no government can engage with all of the countries of the world to an equal extent. Within Central Asia, Kazakhstan's superior economic performance brings responsibilities to lead; the most difficult issues require region-wide cooperation, which may not be forthcoming under current political conditions. Nevertheless, Kazakhstan needs to search for imaginative ways to lead where possible and quickly respond to opportunities that may arise in moving the regional cooperation agenda forward for Central Asia.

The complexity of these options should not distract from the general principles, which are apparent from global best practice: to think globally, contribute to creating a good neighborhood, and remain flexible. Some factors will be beyond Kazakhstan's control, but flexible responses are possible.

Top 30 economies are all open to the global economy and engage with multilateral institutions. They abide by international rules and norms and participate in the institutions that set these rules and norms. Kazakhstan is already engaging in the UN, IMF/World Bank, World Customs Organization, World Intellectual Property Organization, OSCE, International Olympic Committee, etc., but it will benefit from joining the WTO and collaborating increasingly with, and eventually joining, the OECD. An important consideration is Kazakhstan's human capacity to participate in global institutions, which involves selectivity as to where to put the most effort. Looking at the intersection between national contribution by a regional and global organization and international impact and visibility for Kazakhstan could be the key criteria for this choice. CAREC and the Rome-based international agriculture and food security organizations (FAO, UN World Food Programme, and International Fund for Agricultural Development) could be good candidates (Box 10.4).

Also as part of thinking globally, upgrading of trade and trade facilitation is an ongoing process, with some more high profile projects like the Eurasian Landbridge or adopting open skies arrangements, but with many less glamorous but important aspects such as road improvements or customs simplification. As mentioned in the preceding, deepening and widening the CES should be about creating a more competitive, economically-integrated region, and not about sharing a larger protected market; this is likely to be an ongoing issue, as many changes will involve losers as well as winners, although trade facilitation has the potential to be win-win.

Cooperation among Kazakhstan and its Central Asian neighbors and Afghanistan has been disappointing over the last two decades. As by far the richest economy in the neighborhood, Kazakhstan can expect to play a lead role in addressing issues such as water and energy, and, perhaps security, while the poorest neighbors may require assistance in emergencies in order to help them avoid becoming failed states. Again, this might involve selectivity and flexibility in identifying windows of opportunity for addressing the more intractable issues.

In the long term

Creating a scenario for 2050 is fraught with uncertainty. Apart from predictable but uncertain events, there may be entirely unforeseen shocks (see Chapter 3). Nevertheless, lessons can be drawn from successful emerging economies. The best strategy for achieving Kazakhstan 2050 goals will depend on changing global and regional situations. While it is unclear what ultimately will be the main defining conditions, among the main candidates surely count energy markets, Russia's economic fortunes, East Asia's increasing weight in the global economy, developments in Central Asia, Afghanistan, and South

Asia, and the overarching process of Eurasian integration. The primary lesson from the most agile most successful East Asian economies is that it is crucial to remain open to the global economy and for economic agents to be free to respond to external changes rather than be sheltered from them.

Box 10.4 | Two examples of regional and international organizations in which Kazakhstan may wish to play a stronger role

CAREC has been repeatedly referred to in this chapter. It is a unique entity in Central Asia, in that it brings together not only ten key countries, but also six international financial institutions. With a limited, but clear focus, especially on transport investment and trade/transit facilitation, it meets a key interest of Kazakhstan in its efforts to connect with its neighbors and through them with the rest of the world. CAREC has developed an excellent regional transport sector strategy and by combining national transport investments with the financial clout of the international financial institutions has begun to implement the strategy. Core features of the strategy and its implementation are long-term perspective, a clear link between individual projects and the development of priority corridors, and the measurement of cost and time reductions in transit along the corridors region-wide. CAREC's organization would benefit from reinforcement and stronger engagement at the highest level by its member countries, including the introduction of bi- or tri-annual summit meetings. Kazakhstan could assume a lead role in working with the other partner countries and international financial institutions in assuring that CAREC's plans are effectively implemented and that there are stronger links between CAREC, SCO, and the CES (Linn 2012).

The three major international organizations dealing with global agriculture and food security issues are based in Rome: the FAO, the International Fund for Agricultural Development, and the World Food Programme. Kazakhstan is not a member of the World Food Programme, and so far as played a low-key role in FAO and International Fund for Agricultural Development. As a major agricultural producer and exporter, Kazakhstan should have a considerable interest in assuring that there is an effective international institutional framework in place to help address global and regional agricultural policy, regulatory, investment, and information needs. Moreover, since Kazakhstan still faces considerable challenges in managing the transition from an agricultural sector that employs large numbers of people to one that is in line with developed country standards of very limited agricultural employment it could significantly benefit from the global expertise and knowledge embodied in these institutions. With significant food security issues among its neighbors in Central Asia, Kazakhstan has a great interest in assuring that the international bodies dealing with this issue, and especially the World Food Programme, pays sufficient attention to the needs of Central Asia. Therefore, it seems a natural fit for Kazakhstan to play a much more active role in the Rome-based international agriculture and food security organizations.

Source: Author.

10

Table 10.4	Short-, medium-, and long-term options, 2013-2050

Short term

- Join WTO
- Ensure CU/CES is open to the global economy
- Maintain multivector diplomacy

Medium term

Scenario	Options/Actions
Russia positive • Economic prosperity and political stability	• Strengthen regional integration (CES), while remaining open to the world economy • Cooperate on Eurasian land-bridge
Russia negative • Social unrest, populist/ nationalist government	• Avoid pressures for an exclusive RTA • Diversify economic relations
China positive • Continued economic growth, political stability	• Strengthen relations, pursue economic opportunities, resolve cross-border environmental issues • Cooperate on Eurasian landbridge
China negative • Growth slowdown, unrest and conflict	• Be ready to redirect trade and investment flows
Central Asia positive • Improved relations with Uzbekistan • Increased living standards in Kyrgyz Rep & Tajikistan • Opening up of Turkmenistan	• Engage with neighbors, facilitate 3Ts (trade, transport, transit), assist poor neighbors, cooperate and collaborate on water/energy, disasters, etc • Take on leadership role in key regional organizations (e.g., CAREC, International Fund for Saving the Aral Sea)
Central Asia negative • Succession crises, social breakdown, interstate conflict	• Help to mitigate harmful consequences, engage where possible
Global positive • Liberal trade and investment system, no major long-lasting crises	• Benefit from economic opportunities as signaled by world prices • Recognize global rules and norms, and be a good global citizen • Reinforce presence in key international organizations (e.g., Rome-based institutions)
Global negative • Economic depression, conflict between major powers	• Benefit from economic opportunities as signaled by world prices • Recognize global rules and norms, and be a good global citizen • Resist temptations to turn inwards

Long term

- Scenarios are hard to predict, so flexibility is critical
- Create a strong and competitive economy that can respond to global opportunities
- Do not respond to adverse external changes by closing off global relations

Sources: Author and Centennial Group International 2013

INSTITUTIONS
FOR A
MODERN
SOCIETY

Institutions for a Modern Society

Chapter
11

John Nellis

Institutions are at the core of successful long-term development. The effective and sustainable development of Kazakhstan's human resources and natural resources, of a balanced, decentralized, and thriving urban and regional economy, of a modern knowledge society, and of successful integration into the global economy and constructive relations with its neighbors are embedded in and require the development of mature and effective institutions. And good institutions affect people's welfare directly. The rule of law, absence of bureaucratic hurdles, corruption, and arbitrary treatment, ease of doing business, and ability to participate in local and national political life and civil society are now accepted as essential aspects of a human life endowed with dignity, fairness, and a sense of empowerment. To a large extent, it is the quality of institutional performance that will determine whether or not Kazakhstan will, by 2050, exhibit a sufficiency of the eight characteristics required to achieve the report's vision: openness, resiliency, competitiveness, cooperation, inclusiveness, sustainability, effectiveness, and accountability (see Chapters 1 and 13).

To date, Kazakhstan's institutional framework has helped to make it an open, market-oriented, and thriving economy well ahead of its Central Asian neighbors (Cohen 2008). Nonetheless, for Kazakhstan to continue to progress and to join the top 30 developed countries by 2050 this framework requires further adaptation. Since progress on the institutional front is such an important underpinning for the design and effective implementation of good policy in other spheres of the Kazakhstan's economic and social development, and since institutional development is inherently a long-term process, early and persistent action in this area is of great urgency in providing the foundation for lasting success.

In this chapter, we examine key aspects of the institutional basis of Kazakhstan. We examine the country's current economic, legal and judicial, regulatory and public management, and governance frameworks. We analyze their present performance and call attention to trends, accomplishments, and challenges, as judged by domestic actors, both official and non-official, external analysts, and the findings of the inquiries conducted for this report. We then suggest steps the government might take to improve the institutional framework and help Kazakhstan achieve the goal of becoming a stable, peaceful, prosperous, and agile state, accountable to its citizens by 2050.

As we delve into the details of Kazakhstan's institutional development, we need to be modest in the expectations we raise regarding analytical rigor and definitiveness of conclusions, since the professional literature on institutional development remains one of many open debates and few definitive agreements beyond the view that institutions matter (see Box 11.1).

Drawing on some of the literature (e.g., Acemoglu and Robinson 2012) we have adopted what we regard as a useful organizing device in addressing the institutional dimensions of Kazakhstan's development prospects: We consider economic and political institutions separately. Economic institutions are those that shape and guide the way in which actors in a society carry out their productive activities.

11

Political institutions are those that mediate the political interactions between and among citizens and authorities. The dividing line between these two spheres, as we shall see, is by no means watertight; in fact there is considerable overlap and interaction among them. However, in the professional literature on institutions, as well as in Kazakhstan's public discourse, these two spheres are commonly treated as separable. In fact, the notion that Kazakhstan has been following a strategy of "economy first, then politics" was central to the first two decades of Kazakhstan's approach to development.[1] A main contention of this chapter is that this approach overall has worked as intended until now, but that the time has come to start the shift to a parallel process and address more fully the "politics" part of the equation. Steady progress toward more "liberal constitutionalism" (i.e., a contestable and accountable political system, based on the rule of law) will position Kazakhstan not simply to enter the "top 30 club" but to stay in it. This study fully concurs with the President's statement that "[t]he only way to modernize our country and make it competitive is to progressively follow the path of political liberalization" (Nazarbayev 2012).

Box 11.1 | The nature and function of institutions

In the past quarter-century, many scholars and analysts of growth and socio-economic development have come to assign great importance to the nature, number, quality, and manner of functioning of a society's political and economic institutions. These are now seen as major factors shaping economic performance and human welfare.[2] However, the study of institutions is still in flux. Analysts do not agree on precisely what institutions are, how they come into being, and how they function and influence outcomes. A good part of the problem stems from the large span of social activity that institutions are thought to affect. Institutions are perceived as systems of "shared beliefs, internalized norms, rules and organizations that motivate, enable and guide individuals to adopt regular behaviors that reduce uncertainties and risks in social action" (Shirley 2008, summarizing Greif 2006). They can be formal and codified, as in decreed rules, laws, and constitutions; and they can also be "informal constraints (norms of behavior, conventions), and self-imposed codes of conduct, and their enforcement characteristics" (Shirley 2008, p. 17, summarizing North 1990). They are the social "rules of the game," the "core social factors that influence…human behavior" (Davis 2009, p. 3).

Attempts to narrow the unsatisfying breadth of these scholarly definitions do not get very far: Acemoglu and Robinson (2012, p. 74-65) see "inclusive economic institutions" (i.e., the "right" ones) as "those that allow and encourage participation by the great mass of people in economic activities that make best use of their talents and skills." The inclusive economic institutions "must feature secure private property, an unbiased system of law, and a provision of public services that provides a level playing field in which people can exchange and contract…[They] permit the entry of new businesses and allow people to choose their careers."

Source: Author

---

1. Commonly associated with Singapore's approach to development, this phrase has been used frequently by President Nazarbayev in recent years. See his interview on Euronews, January 14, 2010 (http://www.euronews.com/2010/01/15/nazarbayev-economy-first-then-politics/) and his speech to the nation on December 14, 2012 (http://www.kazakhembus.com/document/address-by-the-president-of-the-republic-of-kazakhstan-strategy-kazakhstan-2050)

2. One study concludes: "In countries whose economic performance has lagged…it is now standard to search for institutional causes and solutions" (Davis 2009). A second observes a "broad consensus…that political systems influence performance…that democracies tend to have 'better' business environments…and that better business environments tend to be associated with stronger economic growth" (Commander and Nikoloski 2010). A third, econometric study argues that the "quality of institutions 'trumps' everything else…in determining income levels around the world" including geography and a country's trade regime (Rodrik, Subramanian, and Trebbi 2002). A fourth, elaborate historical analysis posits a matrix of political and economic institutions, either set of which can be classed as "inclusive" or "extractive," and concludes: "Nations fail economically because of extractive institutions." (Acemoglu and Robinson 2012)

Box 11.1	**The nature and function of institutions (continued)**

This helps, but two important questions remain: First, passage or issuance of a decree or a law endorsing or codifying some desired behavior does not necessarily bring an institution into being. All too frequently, policies are not implemented and laws not enforced or obeyed. The core of a social institution is the creation of a "mind set," when the desired or required behavior becomes internalized and routinized in a critical mass of actors in a society. Thus, a policy or law is not automatically an institution. But it may become one over time, as the behavior elicited by the policy or required by the law takes root and becomes embedded in society. This crucial process of institutional formation, of how they pass from legal or policy concept to ingrained behavior and social norms, is not well understood. It is also why institutional development tends to take so long. Institutions must become embedded in a country's culture before they are fully effective; thus, one of the great challenges that Kazakhstan faces in achieving its 2050 goals is to accelerate the process of embedding new institutions in the Kazakhstan culture, as that process has in other countries often taken decades, if not generations.

The second unanswered question is: Just how can states go about creating and sustaining the right sort of institutions? Leading students of the issue believe that institutions cannot be engineered by decree of even the most enlightened political leaders nor parachuted into a state by means of technical assistance or foreign aid. Institutional specialists think that societal "outcomes are determined by interlocking networks of economic and political institutions that are numerous, subtle and complex" (Shirley 2008, p. 118-19). Acemoglu and Robinson put it more starkly: It is not "the ignorance of politicians" that hinders growth and development, "but the incentives and constraints they face from the political and economic institutions in their societies." These institutions cannot be switched on and off; they have developed and evolved over many years from deep within the local society.[3] Thus, analysts see institutional alteration and development arising from forces within a society, as evolving over the long-term out of numerous small group interactions that change the norms and accepted patterns governing how citizens interact. This perspective unfortunately produces minimal policy guidance. But it does suggest two lessons: The first is that if Kazakhstan wants world-class institutions by 2050, it needs to start delivering on that goal aggressively now; the second is that since institutional development take so long, staying the course – that is, consistency – is fundamental to success. Of course there must be an ability to make midterm corrections in the long-term process of institution-building, but changing the rules frequently will rapidly undermined institutional credibility, and credibility is essential that if institutions are to bring about the behavioral changes that they are designed to induce.

Source: Author.

However, we think that the academic approach summarized in Box 11.1, while correct in stressing the long-term nature of institutional development, goes too far in downplaying the role of political leaders and individual change agents in a state. It is clear to us that a number of successful institutional

---

3. In fact, many governments, from the Egypt of Mehmet Ali through Meiji Japan, Ottoman Turkey and numerous others, have tried to import "modernizing" institutions. Many contemporary post-colonial and post-Soviet states have attempted to alter their economic institutional frameworks, either on their own or with outside. The outcomes have sometimes been at least partially positive (e.g., Meiji Japan) but have often fallen flat. Many of the imported policies have not taken root and endured to become institutions, or the institutions that resulted produced outcomes quite different from those anticipated by their instigators.

11

transformations — in Singapore, the Republic of Korea, China, Brazil, Chile, Botswana, Estonia,[4] and elsewhere — are at least partly attributable to the actions of far-sighted governments and leaders. To us it is clear that Kazakhstan's social stability, economic growth and poverty reduction achievements to date, which are clearly superior to the performance of regional comparator countries and a number of non-Asian resource-rich states as well, is not a matter of physical endowments or good political fortune alone. Part of this good performance stems from the policies chosen and implemented by the country's leadership, working with and through the social institutions that have evolved in Kazakhstan over time.

In sum, we conclude that institutions, and the culture and history that form them, matter and that inclusive political institutions are vital to societal health and enduring prosperity. How and how quickly institutions develop depends on many factors, but we believe that leadership is an important one and that it helps to expose a forward-looking leadership to assessments of the country's current institutional framework, good historical and contemporary policy practice, and examples of how a leadership can assist and guide the development of an appropriate, productive institutional set up. This is what the rest of this chapter attempts.

Kazakhstan's Present Institutional Situation

Kazakhstan was, until 1991, a Soviet Socialist Republic of the USSR. As such, its political and economic institutions were mainly those imposed and tolerated by the Soviet state. Kazakhstan's pre-independence policy and political autonomy was thus minimal. Kazakhstan now finds itself in a cohort of countries, the so-called "transition economies," which have all started off from a common institutional framework built on the predominance of the state and the one-party system. As indicated in Chapter 2, the transition to a market-oriented system is a complex and difficult endeavor that naturally takes time. At independence, the administrative institutions Kazakhstan inherited were designed to implement directives from a central planning-oriented system, not to construct and function in a free-market setting. Moreover, as also noted in Chapter 2, between 1989 and 2002, large numbers of Russian, Ukrainian, and ethnic German residents migrated out of Kazakhstan, many of them taking with them crucial expertise needed to run the institutions of the state and the nascent private sector.

Despite many obstacles, Kazakhstan has made remarkable progress in terms of economic growth, poverty reduction, and building the framework of a modern, market-oriented state. Credit must be given to government's successful efforts to open the energy and mineral sectors to Western investors who brought in the managerial and technical expertise needed to exploit the resources, to governmental efforts to build comparatively competent public management systems in general, and economic and financial management institutions in particular, and to government's efforts to share – more equitably than many resource-rich states – the newfound wealth among the population at large. Some observers have pointed to the positive influence of the country's rich and still vibrant traditional culture in general and of the "jus" (i.e., family clans) in particular. These "informal social institutions" are seen to have an indirect

---

4. The institutional accomplishments of Singapore, the Republic of Korea, and China are discussed in detail below. But successes have not been limited to Asia. In Latin America, both Brazil and Chile made transitions from military-autocratic to democratic political systems, while at the same time undergoing economic transformations that unleashed their domestic private sectors, served and promoted by increasingly competent public bureaucracies. In Africa, Botswana — landlocked, small, and resource-rich — has defied geographical shortcomings and maintained a, if not the best, growth record in Sub-Saharan Africa, mainly because of sound, prudent economic policies and an accountable leadership.

but nonetheless significant effect on political decision making and resource allocation (see Collins 2006).[5] But so far no in-depth analysis exists that probes the extent of these informal institutions in economic and political matters.

Let us then assess the institutional underpinnings of Kazakhstan's economic performance before we turn to consider the country's political institutional framework.

Kazakhstan's current economic institutional framework

Overview of selected indicators of economic institutional performance. While the quality of institutions may be difficult to assess precisely, we now have many tools to evaluate their general efficacy; that is, we can now draw on a number of international indexes ranking the comparative economic policy and institutional performance of states. Despite their limitations, noted in Chapter 2, these indexes are revealing and useful. They show that, particularly in economic terms, Kazakhstan generally scores well compared to its peer group of countries of similar per capita income when the focus is on economic institutions.

For example, Kazakhstan was ranked in 50st place, out of 148 countries assessed, in the World Economic Forum's *Global Competitiveness Index* (GCI) 2013-2014, placing it just behind 49th place Italy, and ahead of Mexico (55) and Brazil (56). The GCI ranking is important to the government: Being consistently classed in the top 50 states on this index is an announced short-term objective, and, as noted, gaining a ranking in the top 30 positions is one partial measure of attaining the stated principal goal for 2050 (Nazarbayev, 2012 p. 27). On the World Bank's *Doing Business 2013* index, Kazakhstan ranks a respectable 49th (185 countries surveyed), placing it between Mexico and Tunisia (World Bank "Doing Business" 2013). Again, the government watches closely its ranking on this index and takes pride in both top 50 placement and any noted improvements. According to the latest version of the *International Property Rights Index*, Kazakhstan's legal and political environment and safeguards for physical property rights are superior to those of Russia.[6] The Heritage Foundation's 2013 *Index of Economic Freedom* ranks Kazakhstan at 68th place (177 countries surveyed). This score places the country in the third (of 5) or "Moderately Free" category, while most other CIS states, including Russia, are placed in the fourth, "Mostly Unfree" category. Note that Kazakhstan is in the same Economic Freedom category as several OECD countries including Mexico, Belgium, Portugal, France, and Spain. Finally, Kazakhstan scores a respectable 6.25 (out of 10) on the "Market Economy" dimension of the Bertelsmann Foundation's *Transformation Index 2012 (BTI)*, obtaining placing it 48th among the 128 countries reviewed.

Another gauge of the institutionalization of sound economic institutions is that the government of Kazakhstan has to date maintained prudent macroeconomic and fiscal policies, even when there was domestic pressure in the opposite direction. As noted in Chapter 2, various indexes rate Kazakhstan's macroeconomic management among the top 30, and BTI states approvingly that the government has so far "largely evaded succumbing to populist policy changes" (Bertelsmann Foundation "Kazakhstan" 2012). One particular source of institutional strength has been the performance of the National Bank, Kazakhstan's central bank. The ability to maintain a policy in the face of political pressure is an indication of institutionalization. The challenge is now to cement this institutionalization and, as importantly, to improve further the institutional framework so that Kazakhstan will join the top 30 performers not only in a few selected areas but across a range of key areas of economic institutional performance. This is the topic we turn to next.

---

5. As noted in Chapter 1, this volume does not delve into the cultural foundations of Kazakhstan's modernization process. This is not to minimize the importance of this dimension, especially for a comprehensive understanding of how Kazakhstan can develop an institutional system best suited to its own conditions.
6. But Kazakhstan's much lower ranking with regard to intellectual property rights leads both countries to be ranked, overall, quite similarly.

Key areas for strengthening economic institutions. The available evaluations of Kazakhstan's current economic institutional framework point to areas where progress is needed if the country is to deepen, broaden and maintain its achievements. The most important areas for improvement include the following:

- *The Kazakhstani workforce, in both the public and the private sectors, needs improved skills for a diversified economy.* This is of direct relevance to institutional development since building and sustaining strong institutions require highly qualified and motivated people. The lack of an adequately skilled workforce is seen a major problem by senior government officials and investors both domestic and foreign.[7] Investors face increasingly severe local hiring requirements, but find it difficult to obtain nationals with the necessary skills. Respondents to the latest GCI survey of business people in Kazakhstan listed an "inadequately educated workforce" as the "most problematic factor for doing business" in the country (Schwab 2012). Kazakhstani respondents in the last available *Business Environment and Enterprise Performance Survey* (World Bank and EBRD 2009) rank "skills and education of workers" as their number one problem, out of a list of 14 issues, ahead of taxation, corruption, and access to financing.

- *Full implementation for early results of the many programs launched to modernize the civil service is essential.* Regarding administrative reform, studies show that progress has been less than planned in a number of areas, including decentralization, the introduction of "results-based management systems," the transfer of activities from the state to the private sector, the introduction of standards and regulations for all state services, the delineation of responsibilities between political appointees working with the executive and the professional civil service, and several other areas. (NAC of Nazarbayev University "Administrative Reform" 2012). The NAC of Nazarbayev University review stresses that the effort to implement, monitor and evaluate programs and initiatives "needs improvement." The problem is that current actions do not focus on outcomes. Follow-up actions "are not regularly taken. Therefore, the monitoring and evaluation do not bring results to be included in the next stage of planning" (NAC of Nazarbayev University "Kazakhstan's Development Strategies" 2013, p. 9). Senior ministerial officials interviewed acknowledged a tendency to respond to the latest directives from on high, to the detriment of monitoring and evaluation efforts of existing programs. The last available BTI views the entire administrative reform program as "largely academic" (Bertelsmann "Kazakhstan" 2012).

- *More generally, the discrepancy between the many broad and ambitious reform initiatives, especially those regarding rule of law, governance, and public management, and their partial or lagging implementation needs to be addressed.* Investors, for example, complain that implementation (of rules and regulations affecting them) is "uneven, irregular, and non-transparent." They note, and officials interviewed in Astana agree, that rules regarding hiring have become much more cumbersome and "onerous" in the last few years (OECD "Kazakhstan" 2012).

- *There are persistent concerns about corruption.* There is much evidence that corruption negatively affects businesses, both domestic and foreign-owned. For example, 23 percent of respondents in a 2012 OECD survey of 260 business leaders in Kazakhstan ranked "bribery and the unfairness of government" as the "top barrier that limits the development of your business." When asked to give "the most important government services in the eyes of businesses," 28 percent responded, "fighting corruption" (OECD "Kazakhstan" 2012). Corruption is listed as the second most problematic factor for doing business in Kazakhstan by the 2012 GCI. In the 2009 BEEPS survey, managers listed corruption as their third most vexing issue, behind tax rates and difficulty

---

7. Many government officials interviewed in Astana raised this issue.

in finding good workers (World Bank and EBRD 2009).[8] Business respondents indicated that the frequency and magnitude of corruption was significantly higher in Kazakhstan than the averages reported for Eastern Europe and Central Asia as a whole. A 2012 review by the Extractive Industries Transparency Initiative notes that in 2009 substantial transfers from extractive firms to government, estimated at US $939 million, "were not disclosed" (EITI 2012).[9] Every index and every commentator agrees: "Corruption remains a serious challenge in Kazakhstan" (OECD "Kazakhstan" 2012), despite numerous and well-publicized government statements of intent and initiatives to combat it.

- *Legal/judicial reforms*: Observers perceive "major shortcomings" in various aspects of the legal/judicial framework affecting business operations and "ensuring effective corporate governance." Weaknesses are cited in both insolvency and concessions laws. Concerns are expressed about both the competence and especially the independence of the courts (ADB 2011, p. 4).

- *The soundness of the banking system* is regarded as a problem. As noted in Chapter 2 the global financial crisis revealed that a number of banks in Kazakhstan were overleveraged and heavily exposed to weak real estate loans. As with many governments the world over, GOK has been reluctant to force the banks to write-down these debts and sell them at market value. An IMF review concluded that the program adopted by Government "is insufficient to resolve problem loans," and, in any case, was being implemented very slowly (IMF 2012).

These concerns indicate where institutional reform priorities must be focused; we return to these themes below when identifying areas for action. But first let us address a concern about the direction of change in economic institutional management that we have observed.

The role of the state: Reemergence of a state-led economy? After two decades of considerable prudence and market-oriented reforms, it appears now that there has been intensifying involvement of the state in a wide variety of economic affairs. While the seeds of this process may have been planted some time back, the global economic crisis of 2008 added greatly to the statist pressures in Kazakhstan. While appropriate under the crisis conditions, the government rescue of a number of troubled banks opened the door to protectionist demands from other sectors and interests. The state-owned National Welfare Fund Samruk-Kazyna added a substantial portion of the equity in distressed banks to its already massive holdings. It is estimated that Samruk-Kazyna presently controls a very large share of the economy through its partial or complete ownership of a reported 561 companies, institutions, and legal entities having an estimated total value of $83.3 billion, a sum equal to about 45 percent of Kazakhstan's 2011 GDP. Firms wholly or partly owned – often between 45 percent and 51 percent — include the national oil and gas company, the national railways corporation, the national telecommunications firm, the state airline, the national uranium firm, the postal services, the development bank, the electricity grid and most

---

8. BEEPS is a joint product of the EBRD and the World Bank. The last survey in Kazakhstan was in 2008-2009. 544 "business owners and managers" were interviewed. Thirteen of the survey questions directly related to corruption; e.g., "are you expected to give gifts to public officials" to obtain contracts, licenses, tax relief, permits, utility connections, etc. In every case the percentage of firms responding positively was significantly higher than the average positive responses in the rest of the region as a whole. Moreover, "the value of the gift expected to secure a government contract" was three and a half times higher in Kazakhstan than the regional average. Forty-four percent of Kazakhstani firms identified "corruption as a major constraint" versus 39 percent in the region as a whole. It is available online at: http://www.enterprise-surveys.org/Data/ExploreEconomies/2009/kazakhstan

9. Non-disclosure of transfers by no means proves the presence of corrupt dealings, but non-disclosed sums of this magnitude are cause for concern and a seeming violation of the reporting procedures agreed to when Kazakhstan entered into the EITI.

11

other major companies (OECD "Kazakhstan" 2012; Peyrouse 2012).[10] Samruk-Kazyna is governed by a thirteen-member board, chaired by the Prime Minister. When major decisions are made, they are often portrayed as directives of the Head of State. For example, a February 2013 news brief announced that the President "instructed Samruk-Kazyna to withdraw from the capitals (sic) of BTA Bank, Alliance Bank and Temirbank," three of the four institutions taken over during the crisis (TengriNews 2013). Samruk-Kazyna's size and reach, and its governance structure, indicate the extent to which the Kazakhstani state is a primordial economic actor.

Recently released data indicate that the financial and operational performance of many of Kazakhstan's state-owned enterprises are unsatisfactory. In May 2013, the Kazakhstan Auditing Committee announced that of 300 SOEs surveyed, more than 40 percent were unprofitable in calendar 2012; total losses that year were USD 22.6 million, and the largest 40 SOEs accounted for close to half of these losses (Voloshin 2013).

The 2008 crisis spurred demands in some business circles for increased state assistance and direction, in financial and policy terms. "Lobbying for industrial policies, tariffs and other trade protection continues" (Bertelsmann Foundation "Kazakhstan" 2012). Sentiment appears to be growing for restrictions on foreign investors and for the setting up of "national industrial champions" supported by the state (Cohen 2008). The government's recent policy of "forced industrialization" (see chapter 9) suggests a penchant for large public investments in industry and retaining a strategic state stake in most important sectors and firms.

The 2012 OECD Investment Review (OECD "Kazakhstan" 2012) noted the breadth of both investment and national security legislation specifying limits on foreign, and in some cases any private sector participation, in a wide range of sectors, including telecommunications, mass media, banking, transport, real estate, forestry, and agriculture. The review stressed that the many recent changes to the investment-relevant legal framework have tended to erode the incentives and guarantees previously accorded to investors. For example, new or modified legislation has weakened the strong "stability clauses" in most contracts concluded in the 1990s that gave foreign investors legal protection against ex-post amendments. Investors have also complained that new legislation is less clear concerning access to, and the "binding nature of international arbitration judgments" (OECD "Kazakhstan" 2012).

Investors have also expressed growing concern about government efforts to ensure that the percentage of Kazakhstanis employed in foreign-owned firms quickly reaches stipulated levels. It is perfectly rational for the government to wish to ensure that the number of foreign managers and workers is minimized and that the percentage of Kazakhstanis employed in these firms, at all levels, increases as soon as possible. However, in pursuing this goal the government risks adopting unreasonably short-term or even counterproductive policies, resulting in firms either putting unskilled people in positions for which they are not yet qualified or inflating employment numbers to unjustified levels merely to obtain the proper ratio. Neither outcome is desirable. A more systematic, longer-term plan for the training and placement of national workers and managers is needed.

Another possible indicator of increasing economic nationalism is that in 2010, in response to a widespread perception that the original contracts had been excessively generous to the investors, 21 oil and gas contracts with foreign firms were renegotiated "due to alleged violations of terms." One foreign

---

10. As of May 2013, a new holding company, "Baierek," was organized as part of Samruk-Kazyna. Under the umbrella of this new structure are now grouped ten entities whose function is oriented toward development and diversification of the economy, and attracting investment and support for development clusters. Among the ten agencies are the National Agency for Technological Development, Kazakhstan Development Bank, Entrepreneurship Development Fund (DAMU). With one exception (the Kazkahstan Mortgage Company), Baierek owns100 percent of these enterprises.

observer thought that the increasing number of fines imposed on energy and minerals investors for environmental and regulatory violations was more a form of extracting resources from the vulnerable than a rigorous application of the rules (Cohen 2008); others see this as an overstatement. The Ministry of Finance reports that while receipts from business fines did rise in 2009 and 2010, they declined considerably in 2011 (the last year for which data are available).

Overall, and in contrast to overall positive perceptions of the country's economic conditions, there is a concern that the country is becoming more, not less, difficult for investors to deal with. The EBRD notes: "State interference in business processes needs to be reduced" (EBRD "Transition Report" 2012). The Asian Development Bank reported in 2011 that "there had been significant deterioration in investor perception" (ADB 2011). Kazakhstan is presently ranked as the 12th most restrictive state (out of 51 surveyed) on the OECD's "FDI Regulatory Restrictiveness Index," with a score of 0.091, well below (worse) than the OECD average of 0.137 (OECD "Kazakhstan" 2012).

We note that the crisis of 2007/8 and its fallout justified a more intense engagement by the state in the economy on a temporary basis. However, the key will be to reverse the trend quickly and effectively as economic and financial conditions normalize, lest the pressures for continued and even increased state engagement in commercial activities take on a life or their own and become embedded for the long term in Kazakhstan's institutions. This undoubtedly would take the country away from its Vision 2050. We shall return below to the measures needed to retain and deepen what has overall been a strong economic institutional performance and to the critical issue of the role of the state in economic matters.

Kazakhstan's current political institutional framework

An assessment of Kazakhstan's governance and political institutions is more difficult than for economic institutions since perceptions about priorities and outcomes differ widely depending on the vantage point taken.

The position of the government, strongly supported by a number of external analysts (for example, Cohen 2008 and especially Socor 2012) is that the continuation of growth and the maintenance of stability require strong and steady leadership. Kazakhstan exists in a difficult political location, and faces numerous economic and social challenges that argue against the introduction of the entire panoply of western democratic overnight. Ethnic and religious differences in the population, to date quite muted, could spark negative, destabilizing consequences. Indeed, the experience with the political transition in the Kyrgyz Republic, Georgia, and Ukraine is seen as a clear argument in favor of a gradual political transition.[11] At the same time, Kazakhstan's leadership insists that as the economic position solidifies and as the population grows in political maturity and sophistication a faster, but still evolutionary, pace of political reform will be introduced so that in the longer run Kazakhstan will possess a governance system closely resembling most advanced western industrial societies. As noted earlier the often-repeated statement sums up the past approach: "Economy first, then politics" (Nazarbayev 2012, p. 8).

It is thus perhaps not surprising that Kazakhstan's ranking in international comparisons of governance and political system indicators is not as good as in the economic institutional sphere. Figure 11.1 shows the assessments for Kazakhstan of the Worldwide Governance Indicators (WGI) project concerning six governance factors, at three different points in time since 2000. The graph suggests relatively high ranking for political stability, government effectiveness, and regulatory quality, but low rankings for accountability, control of corruption, and rule of law. Regarding changes over time, the indicators show improvements

---

11. See President Nazarbayev's interview on Euronews, January 15, 2010 (http://www.euronews.com/2010/01/15/nazarbayev-economy-first-then-politics/).

11

over the last decade in government effectiveness, regulatory quality, and rule of law, declines in voice and accountability and political stability, and a recent decline in control of corruption, following earlier improvements. How do these perceptions of Kazakhstan compare with those for the Russian Federation, and for comparator countries, such as Korea and the Kyrgyz Republic?

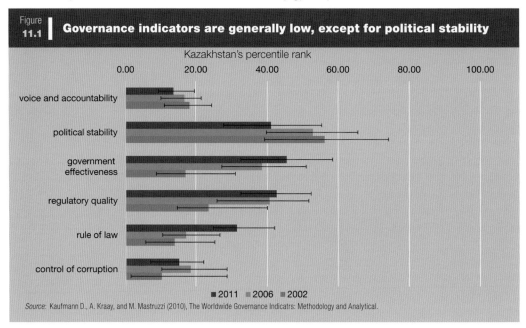

Figure 11.1 | Governance indicators are generally low, except for political stability

Kazakhstan's percentile rank

■ 2011 ■ 2006 ■ 2002

Source: Kaufmann D., A. Kraay, and M. Mastruzzi (2010), The Worldwide Governance Indicatrs: Methodology and Analytical.

The composite comparisons in Figure 11.2 reveal that, as of 2011, governance in Kazakhstan is perceived as appreciably better than in the Kyrgyz Republic and the Russian Federation (not to mention Afghanistan) but far below that of the Republic of Korea. Note that Kazakhstan's relatively high placement on the element of Political Stability and Absence of Violence is the factor that accounts for most of its superior ranking, compared to Russia and the Kyrgyz Republic. Indeed, Kazakhstan's ranking on this dimension is closer to that of the Republic of Korea's rather than those of its neighbors.

Beyond these broad governance indicators, Kazakhstan's political institutions have been criticized by a few internal critics and, more widely, in international circles, particularly in Europe and the US. Critics claim that the country's political framework, following an initial period of openness, shifted toward a system lacking "autonomous and sustainable political institutions" (Freedom House 2011). These observers assess the government's numerous democratization initiatives as declarations that mask a reluctance to promote pluralistic politics and full accountability to the public.[12] They further argue that, particularly in the years since 2007, there has been a reduction in the contestability of the political marketplace, first, by strengthening the already dominant executive; second, by adding to the powers of the economic and technocratic elites; and third, by increasing the barriers to organization, action, and

12. The government has periodically issued policy statements identifying democracy as a prime goal and outlining a general approach to democratization. See in particular the 2006 statement forming the "State Commission for the Development of Democratic Reforms," which was to launch measures aimed at enhancing the powers of parliament, devolving authority to regional governors, and increasing the powers and competencies of civil society organizations. See in particular Section 5, "Further Strengthening of the Statehood and the Development of the Kazakhstan Democracy," in President Nazarbayev's December 2012 policy speech.

media access on the part of opposition political parties and civil society organizations. [13] Both Freedom House and a UN-sponsored report (Makhmutova and Akhmetova 2011) observe that, despite governmental pronouncements on the need to stimulate and finance grassroots organizations, present political arrangements actually hinder or stifle civil society formation in Kazakhstan; they severely "constrain the development of an autonomous space where genuinely independent and self-organized associations and non-state actors can emerge" (Freedom House 2011).[14]

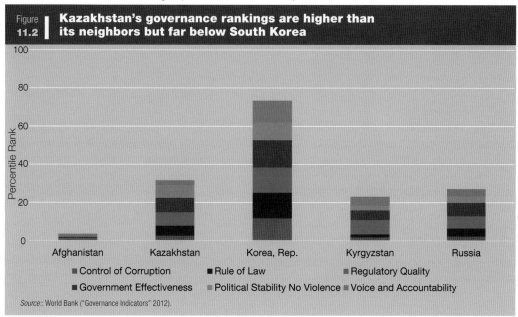

| Figure 11.2 | **Kazakhstan's governance rankings are higher than its neighbors but far below South Korea** |

Legend:
- Control of Corruption
- Rule of Law
- Regulatory Quality
- Government Effectiveness
- Political Stability No Violence
- Voice and Accountability

Source: World Bank ("Governance Indicators" 2012).

Reflecting the difficulties of the legacy issues, the transition economies in the region, Kazakhstan included, have consistently received low rankings on all seven of Freedom House's dimensions of what constitutes democracy: electoral process, civil society, independent media, governance (at both the national and subnational levels), judicial framework, and corruption. Kazakhstan's 2012 overall rating of 5.5 (placing it in the "Not Free" category) is the same rating as that of Russia, superior to that of neighboring Turkmenistan and Uzbekistan (rated at 7) and China (rated at 6.5), but well below that of Mongolia, the only country in the region classed as "Free" (rated at 2) (Freedom House 2012). Media observers rank Kazakhstan deficient in terms of press and Internet freedom. The Reporters without Borders' 2012 Index of Press Freedom ranks Kazakhstan in 154th place (out of 179 surveyed), a fall from its 2009 and 2007 rankings (142nd and 131st, respectively).[15] The latest Bertelsmann Transformation Index concludes that

---

13. Besides Freedom House, other analysts noted the limitations of Kazakhstan's current political system, such as Bertelsmann Foundation and the European Forum for Democracy and Solidarity, which noted in September 2012 that in Kazakhstan "elections are still not being held in accordance to (sic) democratic standards, the media is not free" and "all power is concentrated in the hands of the executive."

14. The government has sponsored and financed a large number of "non-governmental organizations," but some, including the OECD, question their independence. They are viewed as largely "affiliated with the ruling party," and dominated by government officials or political representatives (OECD "Anti-Corruption" 2011).

15. Russia is ranked 142nd; the Kyrgyz Republic was 108th, and the Republic of Korea 44th.

there has been a recent "decline in civil liberties and media freedom" (Bertelsmann "Kazakhstan" 2012, p. 2). In all these areas Kazakhstan can and will need to move forward in order to attain the quality of life for all citizens envisaged in the vision of Kazakhstan 2050.

Overall assessment

How should one then assess Kazakhstan's present overall economic and political institutional makeup? Many emerging economies now economically developed *and* classified as functioning democracies have passed through prolonged periods of autocratic rule and severe restrictions on political competition — e.g., Brazil, South Korea, Indonesia, and Chile. Furthermore, states can launch and sustain for some time economic growth and poverty reduction in the absence of competitive, pluralistic politics. China is the key example. Finally, unsettled post-revolutionary political events in neighboring Kyrgyz Republic and several Arab Spring countries such as Tunisia and Egypt confirm that the path to pluralistic politics is neither straight nor easy to follow and that the initial stages of democratic governance may impose both social tensions and economic costs on a country. Even assuming the validity of Acemoglu and Robinson's core thesis — that inclusive political institutions are prerequisites for long-run prosperity — the fact remains that no one can say how long countries can persist on the autocratic path before doing serious harm to their chances for an "inclusive" future or until the prospects of making the shift by evolutionary, not revolutionary, methods decline to zero. And, as noted here, we have but very general ideas on just how a state shifts from an extractive to an inclusive framework.

For Kazakhstan today few would challenge the notion that the country's *economic* institutional framework is relatively strong, especially in the macroeconomic domain, as good or better than those of its regional comparators, and as good as that of a number of other, non-regional states in roughly similar circumstances. However, Kazakhstan's *governance/political* institutions are widely perceived as relatively much weaker and overall are still a long distance away from the long-term goals articulated by the government.

This creates tensions in at least two ways. Most important, there is a wide, and perhaps growing, gap between what the government states as its objective (increased accountability and pluralistic politics) and the measures implemented (not just proposed) to achieve the goal. The citizenry may not be greatly incensed about this gap at present, but their indifference may not last indefinitely. Second, while Kazakhstan's political/governance systems are viewed as better than those of its near neighbors, this is not the comparison that matters. In order to safeguard for the longer-term the many accomplishments to date and in order to achieve and maintain the status of being ranked in the top 30 club of most developed states in the world by 2050, Kazakhstan will want to address challenges in its governance/political institutional framework sooner rather than later.

This may be a particularly opportune time for moving forward with political reforms, since a recent study shows a high ranking on the indicator of generalized trust within Kazakhstan. The EBRD "Life in Transition" survey revealed that, in Kazakhstan in 2010, about 55 percent of those interviewed had a high or complete trust in others. This figure was higher than that recorded in the country in 2006, much higher (in both years) than the average figure recorded in the transition region as a whole and indeed significantly higher than the average figure recorded in Western Europe in 2010 (40 percent). Respondents' trust in the presidency, the parliament, and the government in general was also "very high," though down from 2006.

(The courts, police and NGOs received much lower trust levels, EBRD "Transition Report" 2012, p. 81.)[16] This implies that, at the moment, the government has "social capital" to draw upon. These widely-shared, market-supporting beliefs appear to provide a good foundation on which to build Kazakhstan's needed institutional reforms.[17] Recent decisions, such as in the 2011 adoption of a transparent competitive grant system based on international peer review for science research, are examples of institutional reform that will have lasting impact in the years to come. The institutionalization of the concept of meritocracy in senior civil service appointments (called "Corpus A") and upcoming local mayoral elections are promising steps of such reforms. Throughout, it will be important that a transparent process is used to inform and engage a public used to the traditional ways of the transition state.

A Vision of the Institutional Basis of a Prosperous, Agile, and Accountable State

Our analysis given here laid out the institutional areas needing maintenance and strengthening in order to achieve, by 2050, Kazakhstan's strategic vision. In terms of the specific institutional dimensions of this vision, Box 11.2 presents key aspects of the institutional framework underpinning the overall vision of Kazakhstan laid out in Chapter 4.

Box 11.2 | **Vision 2050 for Institutions**

In 2050 Kazakhstan possesses economic and political/governance institutions that are the foundation of its expanding and durable prosperity. This has meant not just adopting and adapting the best institutional structures from around the world but also creating or reinforcing the culture and incentives needed to make those structures deliver. The country has laws and regulations that are developed with open and diverse public input, demonstrably achieve the policies they espouse, reward private initiative, and operate in the public interest. The judicial system and judges are speedy, fair, transparent, and impartial. The civil service is competent, accountable, and honest. A free, independent, and vibrant media and press connect Kazakhstan with the world and help its citizens shape their future with reliable information and diverse opinions.

In 2050 Kazakhstan also possesses a mature and accountable democracy with effective representation of citizens' interests, appropriate checks and balances for the parties and individuals in power, and sensible delegation of responsibilities to each level of government. It has a decentralized system of governance and delivery capacities at the level of oblast and rayon governments, with local accountability of elected local officials, coupled with open and fair national elections. Corruption is now kept at bay by a disciplined public sector and by the vigilance of active civil society and the openness, transparency, and oversight that characterizes processes and procedures at all levels of government.

Source: Author

In the remainder of this chapter we offer options for achieving this vision, providing the society of Kazakhstan, by 2050, with the institutions that will consolidate the gains previously achieved, address perceived gaps in policy and behavior that hinder full achievement of the vision, and deal with new challenges that the study predicts will occur.

---

16. For comparison, a 2008 survey found 78 percent of interviewed Swedes, 71 percent of Canadians, and 58 percent of Americans agreed with the statement, "Most people in society are trustworthy." Interesting to note, the highest degree of trust – 79 percent – was recorded in China (Wike and Holzwart 2008). Note, however, that a 2011 survey carried out as part of a report on civil society in Kazakhstan found quite "low levels of trust among members of the society" (Makhmutova and Akhemtova 2011). These findings do not necessarily contradict the EBRD findings here; they simply confirm that differently worded questions among different survey populations, even in the same society in the same time period, can and do produce differing results.

17. Buiter and Rahbari (2011) state: "social capital – trust between unrelated individuals and/or between the citizen and the state – is a determinant of the quality of a country's economic and political institutions." Social trust "facilitates collective action and impersonal exchange."

11

Reform of Institutions Affecting Economic Development and Business

As regards the further development of economic institutions we recommend action in four specific areas.

First, the government will want to safeguard and reinforce the policies that have produced Kazakhstan's remarkable growth and its comparatively equitable distribution of the fruits of that growth. We recommend that state leaders sustain their commitment to encouraging investment and private business by maintaining their sober and prudential macroeconomic, monetary, financial, and fiscal policies, by redoubling efforts to minimize administrative and legal barriers to entry into the country's markets, by persisting with actions to boost competition and ensure level legal and regulatory playing fields for foreign and domestically-owned businesses, by eliminating exemptions to procurement, trade and regulatory regimes, and, in general, ramping up actions to maintain "stability and predictability in both the rules and their implementation" (OECD "Kazakhstan" 2012).

Kazakhstan's leaders should not consider their successful economic policies set in stone. Just because a positive policy has been formulated, put in practice, and become more or less institutionalized does not mean it will or even should persist indefinitely. First, setbacks can and often do occur. Interests that would benefit from a weakening or revision of a policy or an approach are always at work; they must be contained. Second, the macro- or market environment in place when the policy was devised will change overtime, requiring revisions or even wholesale alterations. Monitoring, evaluation, enforcement, and amendment processes must all be in place to provide the requisite agility. That is, state administrators and leaders need the information to understand the workings of, the authority and ability to defend, and the flexibility to revise their economic policies and institutional framework. No matter how good its planning and forecasting efforts, Kazakhstan, like all countries, must prepare for inevitable surprises. In addition to creating a meritocratic senior corps, Kazakhstan will need to continue to strengthen its public administrative policy, supervisory and regulatory systems and speed up the concrete implementation of its many proposed reforms. For an idea of how this might be done, see Box 11.3, which summarized what Singapore has done to develop a strong, disciplined, and motivated civil service.

Second, the state leadership may wish to focus explicitly on limiting the growing pressures for a dominant role of the state and roll back recent increases in state engagement in the commercial sphere associated with its response to the 2007/8 financial crisis. Many extractive sector contracts concluded in the 1990s were generous to the private partners and, in retrospect, perhaps overly so. The more secure and prosperous Kazakhstan of today may well expect more equitable terms. But the country still needs the managerial and technical know-how of the private sector, domestic and international, if it is to achieve its essential objective of diversifying the economy away from its dependence on oil, gas, and minerals. The OECD's concluding recommendation concerning investment in Kazakhstan could well serve as Kazakhstan's general rule regarding the role of the state: "While safeguarding essential national security interests, Kazakhstan's policy should be designed to ensure the smallest possible impact on investment flows and be guided by the principles of non-discrimination, proportionality, transparency, and accountability...." (OECD "Kazakhstan" 2012).

Concrete measures to achieve this goal include the following:

- *Conclude its protracted negotiations and enter the WTO*.[18] WTO membership may require the relaxation or modification of a number of current policies regarded, by the OECD and other observers, as hindering private activity and tilting toward state intrusion (for example, regard-

---

18. Kazakhstan first applied for entry into the WTO in 1996. Negotiations have taken place since, with frequent announcements by both parties of imminent and successful conclusion (for example in 2005). A joint statement of the GOK negotiators and WTO officials in 12/2012 noted "positive momentum in Kazakhstan's accession process" and expressed the "hope that Kazakhstan would reach the finishing line in 2013." See also Chapter 10.

| Box 11.3 | **Civil service reform in Singapore** |

The civil service of Singapore is regarded as "one of the most efficient and least corrupt in the world" (Tay 1999). Operating on the principles of "discipline, efficiency, rationality, and capacity," it has become the government's "major institutional vehicle to deliver development" by preparing national development plans, coordinating their implementation, and efficiently delivering services to the people (Saxena and Bagai 2010). How was Singapore able to build and sustain this vital public institution? What can Kazakhstan learn from the Singapore experience?

Since independence in 1965, Singapore has followed a multi-pronged strategy to improve its civil service. First, government leaders established and then maintained a strict policy of no tolerance for corruption of any sort of any public official and of any political leader. Second, meritocracy prevails. Recruitment is based only on qualifications and competence, established by examination and strict assessment of experience. Pay increases are also based on careful objective evaluation of performance. For example, for promotion, a non-political agency assesses whether the candidate possesses the requisite skills, attitudes, and "potential" for advancement. Third, there is a constant stress on leadership by example, transmitting "strong values and principles of good governance socially rather than formally throughout the organization" (Saxena and Bagai 2010). Leadership comes from the very top; all government ministers and senior managers subscribe to, and publicly practice, an ethos of competent and clean governance. Fourth, Singapore maintains a generous but flexible pay system for public servants. Base salaries are kept similar to those prevailing in the private sector and substantial bonuses are paid for exemplary work.

Singapore's leaders have emphasized attitudinal change as much or more than policy, procedure, and techniques. Singapore's civil service has computerized its operations, adopted best-practice structures and procedures, and sought performance-enhancing innovations and enhancements aimed at improving organizational effectiveness and service delivery. But the ultimate key to success has been the emphasis on instilling in all civil servants a shared meritocratic ethos based on integrity and a commitment to national development goals and to serving the public. This mindset is created and sustained by a system of rigorous initial training and frequent re-training, exemplary leadership demonstrating commitment to the ethos, and prestige and financial incentives to adhere to the ethos.

Is this success replicable elsewhere? Singapore is small in size and population, with a tradition of hard work and entrepreneurial effort. The state is politically unified. This allows the unchallenged ruling party to focus attention on administration rather than politics (but this also leads to criticism that Singapore is not a fully functioning democracy). Singapore's economic success has provided the resources needed for its approach; its civil service is one of the highest paid in the world. The country's early leaders played a crucial role: Lee Kwan Yew, Keng Swee, and Rajaratnam believed deeply in the central role of an efficient, competent, and respected civil service and provided the political force necessary to launch and sustain it.

For Kazakhstan to emulate Singapore in this regard it will have to deepen its existing efforts to improve both incentives and surveillance of the public administrative system. It must continue its current programs to improve civil servant selection, pay, grading, and training, decrease the number of senior administrative positions appointed outside the formal civil service ranks, and better establish the independence and objectivity of the personnel management system. However, the harder and most important tasks are the non-technical ones: Kazakhstan needs to alter the attitudes and behavior of those who set the standards for accepted practice and its public servants.

Visible and sustained commitment to the Singaporean "principles of good governance" listed in the preceding lines must first come from the leadership. Then it must be transmitted and ingrained in the administrative class. How? In Singapore, the government set up a Political Study Centre, which conducted courses for senior civil servants to change their attitudes and increase their awareness of the local contextual constraints to development" (Saxena and Bagai 2010). This training has now been folded into the operations of Singapore's Civil Service College, a "learning institute" made up of three training departments, five centers of expertise, and five corporate services units.

Source: Saxena and Bagi (2010) and Tay (1999).

11

ing "local content" requirements, unclear investment policies, restrictions on foreigners owning agricultural land and forests, restrictions on foreign banks opening and operating branch offices, limitations on competition in the telecommunications and a number of other sectors, etc.) It will also require an extensive building of administrative capacity to implement the agreement. This effort is well worth it: WTO membership will signal investors of the state's renewed commitment to openness, global market integration, and market orientation.

- *Implement the People's Initial Public Offering program*. A very promising initiative is the recently launched People's Initial Public Offering (People's IPO) program (see Box 11.4). This program will sell off between 5 percent and 20 percent of equity in a number of firms. This will result in a relatively modest change in the firms' capital structure. Management figures, board members, and state control will probably not change. Will partial privatization make any difference? It certainly can. Studies in India have shown that "partial privatization has a positive impact on profitability, productivity, and investment" of firms, even when the state retains majority control (Gupta 2005). Why? First, as in India, to be listed on the Kazakhstan Stock Exchange large firms such as those in the People's IPO program must meet strict accounting, audit, credit agency, and profitability standards for a period of three years or more prior to the offering. These listing requirements increase and make public the amount of information on firm activity. Transparency is improved. Second, even in small stock markets with limited activity, the quotation of the price of a tradable stock spurs managers to focus on performance issues affecting the stock price. Neither firm managers nor government supervisors want the bad publicity associated with a dramatic decline in the share price. Principals are given a handy indicator of their agents' performance. More broadly, Di Tella (2011) and others note an association between widespread private ownership of property and increased pro-market and anti-corruption pressures. The People's IPO program is a positive step in many respects.

- *In addition, promote more extensive and transparent privatization measures*. If Kazakhstan is to bring the economic weight of the state more into line with norms prevailing in the advanced industrialized OECD countries, it should speedily implement the Presidential instruction to Samruk-Kazyna to divest the equity it holds in three of the four large bailed-out banks, with foreign banks allowed to bid, consider private-public partnerships for the expansion and improvement of Kazakhstan's infrastructure, and use a competitive tendering process, not private trade sales, with competitively selected, established, and reputable international financial advisers to manage the details of each and every substantive transaction (subject, of course, to supervision by state authorities) (Goldberg and Nellis 2007). As indicated here, Kazakhstan needs to place the assets presently under-managed in SOEs in more competent and productive hands. As Kazakhstan moves to divest the remaining larger firms in Samruk-Kazyna's portfolio, it can learn from the extensive and well-studied privatization experiences, good and bad, of other formerly Soviet or formerly socialist states in East, Central, and Southern Europe. Transparency in procedures and decisions at every step in the process has the dual advantage of maximizing the chances of finding good owners for the firms and persuading the public that the general interest has been safeguarded.

Third, Kazakhstan needs to ramp up the struggle against corruption. All available independent evidence, from Transparency International, the Bertelsmann Transformation Index, Freedom House, the WGI, the CGI, the Asian Development Bank, and others, indicate an increase over time in the public's

| Box 11.4 | People's Initial Public Offerings, 2012-15 |

The People's IPO program, which would allow citizens of Kazakhstan to become co-owners of the nation's largest companies, was presented by the President Nazarbayev in February 2011 at the 13th Congress of Nur Otan Party. In July 2011, the Board of Directors of Samruk-Kazyna National Welfare Fund approved the placement of subsidiaries and affiliated companies' shares in the stock market, and in September the Government of Kazakhstan approved the Program. A list of Samruk-Kazyna companies, whose shares will be offered for sale in stages from 2012 and 2015, was drawn up. The businesses included in the People's IPO are companies with no significant dependence on world prices for raw materials, e.g., oil and gas pipelines, electricity, airline, power plants, shipping, and railways.

Stage	Companies	Stage	Companies
2012	KazTransOil	2013	Kazmortransflot (maritime shipping)
2013	Kazakhstan Electricity Grid Operating Company	2014	Temir Zholy (railroad)
2013	Air Astana	2014	Kaztemirtrans (rail cargo)
2013	KazTransGas	2015	Kazatomprom
2013	SamrukEnergo (power generating)	2015	Kazmunaigas

Minority stakes will be offered for sale, and the state will retain control over the enterprises. People's IPO shareholders can only be Kazakhstani citizens. In order to avoid the concentration of securities in the hands of a small group of individuals, the program involves restrictions on the maximum number of shares to be purchased by any individual. The securities can be purchased by the pension funds of the country. The shareholders will be able to participate in the management of the national companies, in particular, to vote at general meetings of shareholders, and are entitled to dividends.

Preparation of candidate companies for People's IPOs consists of three main phases. Preliminary preparation includes audit of financial statements, diagnosis and improvement of corporate governance and risk management, internal control and audit systems. Preparing for the public offering involves a comprehensive review (due diligence), final determination of underwriting and cost of services, legal support (preparation of the prospectus and other related legal documents), business valuation, and marketing. Finally, the offering of shares requires investor education, development of information and investment memorandum, PR support, the collection of applications (published preliminary prospectus, conducting road shows, demand analysis, pricing), and events in the secondary market after the offering (stock keeping in an active market). A secondary goal is to boost the Kazakhstan Stock Exchange.

In the first People's IPO, KazTransOil, citizens and pension funds were offered for purchase 38,463,559 shares at a price of KZT 725 per share. In November and December 2012, 34,687 applications were received for a total of KZT 59,409 million, i.e., the demand was more than double the supply, demonstrating a high level of interest in investing in the shares among the population (retail investors bought 79.1 percent of the offered shares) and Kazakhstan's pension funds. There was also a significant increase in brokerage accounts opened by citizens of Kazakhstan; more than 52,000 accounts have been opened, which is several times the number before the People's IPO program.

Source: Richard Promfret, based on information provided by NAC of Nazarbayev University ("Government's Participation" 2012).

11

and observers' perceptions[19] of the incidence and intensity of corruption. Experience has shown that the problem with corruption is perhaps not that it directly and negatively effects economic growth.[20] Its most negative effects lie rather in the extent to which pervasive corruption erodes trust in government and increases the level of cynicism in society. Kazakhstan's booming extractive sectors may mute this impact of corruption, but available survey data suggest that the prevailing high level of public trust in core government institutions — important for future institutional progress — may be at risk of erosion.

Worldwide, corruption has proven resistant to quick solutions. This has led many to conclude that corruption is a condition rooted in "the mentality" of a society, thus requiring years of effort to resolve. However, Box 11.5 reports on the experience in Georgia, which shows that this need not always be the case. Georgia's unusual combination of a public reaching the boiling point at the same time that a fiercely anti-corruption government was coming into power may not be easily replicated. One must also note that over time the implementation of the anti-corruption program has drawn criticism from both internal and external (e.g., Transparency International) observers as riding roughshod over legal due-process measures. One of the reasons the reformist government lost the late 2012 elections was public concern over high-handed actions of the executive in the name of anti-corruption. The reforms were not reversed, but the new government seems less likely to pursue the issue with equivalent vigor. Whether the process will be sustained is unclear. Nonetheless, the story gives hope to all those who seek to end quickly the scourge of corruption.

Kazakhstan already possesses a number of anti-corruption initiatives and programs. High-ranking officials, including the President, have repeatedly pronounced on the necessity to attack and eliminate this problem. The issue is not the written or announced policy; it is the lagging implementation resulting in a gap between policy and practice that needs urgently to be addressed. What precise and practical corruption reduction methods can one recommend for Kazakhstan?

- *Change the rules of the game, monitor, create incentives.* Rule-changing involves, as in Georgia, reduction of the activities offered or controlled by the state, thus reducing the need for contacts – and the opportunities for corrupt dealings — between officials and citizens. Another mechanism is decentralization of government programs down to levels where local communities can more easily watch over processes and results. Once rules have changed, monitoring of results is critical. The difficult part is to establish independent and dedicated monitors, willing and able to fight against the established way of conducting business, with the high-level backing that allows them to run the risk of offending the powerful. Moreover, recent research concludes that all these measures "have the potential to reduce corruption" but "monitoring is ineffective without a simultaneous incentives program or when the incentive is not large enough." (Hanna et al. 2011, p. 1) Incentives help, such as higher pay and/or bonuses for state agents who produce results in terms of reduced corruption.
- *Introduce asset declaration by public officials.* Di Tella (2011) examined the efficacy of many anti-corruption measures worldwide and concluded that among the best is that of "insisting that politicians sign a statement of their wealth (prior to entering politics)," and then monitoring

---

19. Almost no person using public position or contacts for purposes of illegal enrichment admits his or her crime. Thus, efforts to measure the scope and breadth of corruption must rely on a second-best metric: the subjective assessments of citizens and businesspeople affected.
20. Earlier studies (e.g., Mauro 1995) argued that corruption did constrain growth but the enduring and high growth rates of states perceived as highly corrupt weakened that contention. Recent anti-corruption arguments acknowledge the need to nuance the previous assertions (Cockcroft 2012).

Box 11.5 | Georgia's successful anti-corruption campaign

As recently as 2003, the Republic of Georgia was in a state of "pervasive corruption, ever-present crime and dysfunctional public services" (World Bank "Fighting Corruption" 2012, 1). In that year, Georgia ranked near the very bottom of Transparency International's Corruption Perception Index, in 124th (out of 133) place, alongside Tajikistan and Angola, and well behind every other transition state.

In short order this situation changed dramatically. By 2010, Georgia earned Transparency International's ranking as the most relatively improved country of all examined in that year, and by 2012 its ranking was a respectable 51st (out of 174), a 13 place improvement over its 2011 placement. (Kazakhstan, in contrast, was ranked 133rd by Transparency International in 2012, a 13-place decline from the previous year.) By 2010, the percentage of Georgians reporting illegal payments – to obtain licenses, permits, entry to and graduation from the university, electricity or water connections, social security payments, or in response to demands from the traffic police or other officials – declined to levels reported in the core five countries of the EU. Average reported levels of such payments in the rest of the former Soviet Union states were almost 10 times higher than in Georgia. In 2010, only 2 percent of surveyed Georgians reported paying a bribe in the previous year (World Bank "Fighting Corruption" 2012). (Note the 2011 EBRD finding that 62 percent of interviewed Kazakhstanis reported bribing the police alone in the previous year.) How was Georgia's rapid transformation accomplished?

A World Bank team reviewed Georgia's anti-corruption campaign and found the core factors contributing to its success. First and foremost was the active and sustained leadership from the highest political level, i.e., the President, his Prime Minister, and several members of the inner cabinet. They empowered and defended a small team of aggressive and dedicated reformers, mostly drawn from outside government circles. The program established early credibility by launching "a frontal assault" on many blatantly corrupt officials who were charged and convicted of criminal offenses. Thousands of the widely detested traffic police were dismissed overnight and replaced with new, young personnel. In fact, there was an overall reduction in public security employees, from 63,000 in 2003 to 27,000 in 2011. Licenses and permits were annulled in many areas, and entire agencies and departments were simply abolished. Tax collection and utility bill collections rose greatly. Privatization and decentralization were pushed for many formerly central government activities and some became e-government measures (e.g., getting a passport). Indeed, a hallmark of the reform, according to the former Georgian Minister of Economy, was a belief that "limiting the interface between the citizen and the state was essential to reduce the opportunities for corruption" (World Bank "Fighting Corruption" 2012).

These tactics met with success, in large part due to the intense and widespread disgust among the Georgian public with the previously prevailing situation, combined with the near revolutionary change of government in 2004 bringing determined anti-corruption figures into high office. This group used outside assistance, from the Open Society Foundation, the UNDP, and others, and made very effective use of an anti-corruption public media campaign to reveal enrichment of past politicians, announce reform objectives, and publicize arrests and other measures.

Source: World Bank "Fighting Corruption" 2012.

11

their consumption and level of wealth while they are in office. A program of asset declarations by public officials has been in place in Kazakhstan since 1996, but it not clear how closely it has been monitored or enforced.

- *Implement key recommendations of the OECD anti-corruption report.* The priority recommendations of the 2011 OECD anti-corruption report on Kazakhstan were: establish "as soon as possible a law on access to public information," make public past internally-conducted surveys of citizens' perceptions of the incidence and importance of corruption, restructure the existing public consultative councils on corruption which at present are dominated by government representatives or officials, "ruling party representatives," and NGOs affiliated with the ruling party, strengthen the independence of the judiciary ("a major problem"), criminalize corruption, reduce the number of political appointees to administrative posts (who thus avoid competitive selection procedures), increase training on ethics and proper behavior for civil servants, and reform the system of internal audit of government agencies and programs (OECD "Anti-Corruption" 2011).

Fourth, Kazakhstan would progress to the next stages of its jurisprudence reform program. Legal observers give the country considerable credit for the progress that has been made since independence, when judicial and court systems were viewed as severely deficient with "weak and ineffective courts... and poorly trained and underpaid" judges. Allegations of corruption were frequent (Baker and McKenzie 2009). Both foreign and domestic users currently report greatly improved levels of satisfaction with the system. A UNDP-financed survey, in 2012, of 6,000 Kazakhstani citizens revealed that more than 80 percent of respondents were content with the overall competence and fairness of court proceedings (UNDP in Kazakhstan 2012). However, the remaining problems are significant. First, the process of legal resolution is very slow, which causes hardship for the citizenry and greatly increases transaction costs for businesses. Second, as noted here, the rules concerning the resolution of business disputes through arbitration remain confused and unclear, another large problem for investors both foreign and domestic. Third, the independence of many judges from the political process continues to be questioned.

To address the remaining issues, Kazakhstan might consider some international good practice, for example, the successful Philippine and Indonesian approaches to speeding up court cases, Nepal's experiences in strengthening judicial independence, integrity, and accountability, and the experience of a number of other Asian countries in judicial training efforts.[21]

Reform of Institutions Affecting Governance and Political Institutions

In many respects the distinction between economic and governance/political institutions is artificial: Corruption corrodes both economic and political capacity, as do weaknesses in public administration, ineffective regulation, and judicial proceedings, and large and enduring gaps between policy pronouncements and actual practices. Thus, most of the reasoning and the recommendations presented in the previous economic section apply equally to governance and political issues. Moreover, external observers must be doubly careful when intruding on matters relating to a country's internal political system – especially since the timing and magnitude of governance changes are often as important as the changes themselves. Therefore, the suggestions offered in this sub-section are of necessity more general and tentative. However, this does not mean they are of less importance — on the contrary.

---

21. These and many other practical suggestions drawn from real-world judicial reform experience are presented and discussed in Armytage (2009).

The encouraging news is that, as noted here, numerous countries have successfully accomplished the transition from pre- or partially democratic status to fully functioning pluralism. To illustrate: Brazil, Chile, Indonesia, the Republic of Korea, and Turkey each have had an autocratic past, and all have managed to combine formidable economic progress with deep, sustained, institutionalized democratization measures. Box 11.6 summarizes the experience with democratization in two Asian countries: the Republic of Korea and Indonesia. The principal lessons to be drawn from these highly compressed and simplified histories are these:

- Don't wait too long. Inaction on the political institutional front increases the chances that the nature and pace of the reform that will eventually, inevitably arise will be decided for you, not by you.
- There is no blueprint, no set best method, for how the democratization process will or should unfold. In each country the specific transition path is different, responding to the specific conditions of the economy and society. That will undoubtedly hold true for Kazakhstan — as and when it chooses to move its transition forward.

Based on the lessons from other countries and the current political institutional opportunities and challenges that we observe in Kazakhstan, we recommend that the government consider a broad and sustained concretization of the many governance and democratization initiatives previously launched. In general, we believe that the time has come to begin the shift from an approach of "economy first, then politics," to implementation of the two processes in parallel. We do not and cannot go into great detail on what form these further initiatives should take, or in what precise sequence they should be implemented. It is up to the Kazakhstani people and leadership to determine the exact dates and details of the specific actions needed to implement these principles. We can only give our considered opinion that for Kazakhstan to attain and maintain a position among the leading nations of the world it must do more than solidify and diversify its economic achievements: It must also put in place a system of "liberal constitutionalism" that is open, contestable, accountable, and with the appropriate checks and balances. The general areas for action that we offer for consideration are as follows:

- *Loosen restrictions on media and Internet activity.* Such measures provide the people of Kazakhstan with the information needed to function as responsible citizens and to place them in a position to effectively exercise their political "voice." As Kazakhstan moves to deepen its decentralization program, greatly expand the number of elected regional and local officials, and strengthen parliament (actions described in the President's December 2012 strategy statement, Section 5), the populace will need access to a variety of independent information sources and better channels of expressing their approval or disapproval of government or bureaucratic initiatives. This will enhance their capacity to choose the proper candidates and policies, and it will greatly add to their capacity to hold those elected officials accountable to their commitments and the public interest.
- *Loosen restrictions on the formation and operation of independent civil society organizations and legitimate political organizations.* The institutional literature (for example, Shirley 2008 and Acemoglu and Robinson 2012) stresses heavily the importance of independent, civil society institutions in building sustainable and just prosperity, good governance, and accountability to the public. Buiter and Rahbari (2011) note that the variety and "depth" of a country's independent civil society network is very important; it is a "determinant of economic efficiency and political stability."

11

Box
11.6   Paths to democracy in Asia

In the last 40 years, a large number of countries have transformed themselves from seemingly stable autocracies to functioning, if not always flourishing, democracies. Instances of the process can be found in Africa, the Middle East, Latin America (Argentina, Brazil, Chile), East and Central Europe (the many states emerging from Soviet dominance), and Asia. We focus on two Asian cases of particular relevance to Kazakhstan: Indonesia and the Republic of Korea (South Korea). In both there were long-standing, strong centralized governments, headed by powerful and paternalistic leaders. Both systems were characterized by stable macroeconomic performance and good growth rates – as well as intolerance of formal opposition, or indeed of any political organization outside the state structure. In both countries the leaders were popular for an extended period during their tenure, in good part due to the substantial development benefits brought to the citizenry during their rule.

Despite the good economic growth records (as well as the strong US support for both regimes during their autocratic periods), both societies – starting in South Korea in the 1970s and Indonesia in the 1990s – began to face increasing public pressures to open the political process and make leaders more accountable.

South Korea's transition process was long and very difficult: Student-led protests against the regime, violently suppressed by the military in 1980, were constant, and many of the protestors' initial demands were quite radical. The persistent internal protests finally combined with international pressures to convince parts of the elite that a democratic opening was the best way to maintain the country's stability. South Korea's first free and fair elections were held in late 1987. Since that time, a cautious, evolutionary process of political liberalization has produced contestability for political office, increases in the impartial rule of law, and an expansion of protected human and legal rights. All this has been paralleled by continuing high growth rates and a more than doubling of GDP per capita. A state that 25 years ago was classed as thoroughly autocratic has now "joined the ranks of industrialized liberal democracies" (Chaibong 2008).

Indonesia's transition to democracy was less lengthy and somewhat less fraught. A vibrant set of civil society organizations had been partially tolerated by the autocratic regime. The media were fairly free to express dissenting opinions. Several members of the elite, including the daughter of Sukarno, the founding father of the nation, established themselves as a shadow democratic opposition. Students took the lead in anti-autocracy protests, but many from the religious community joined them as well. Once again, as protests mounted, foreign supporters of the regime began to counsel accommodation, fearing that a hard-line crack-down against dissent would open the door to more revolutionary forces. In May of 1998 a set of massive, and this time violent, riots (costing at least 500 lives), led a group of senior insiders, including half his personally appointed cabinet, to advise the President to resign. He did so, and the democratic transition began.

Since 1998, Indonesia has conducted free and fair elections, reformed the court system, including the Supreme Court, transferred substantial budget powers to district governments, held elections for district officials, and had several peaceful transitions of leadership.

Serious cleavages and political issues remain. One cannot state unequivocally that democracy will never again be threatened in these two systems. But it is clear that both countries have made tremendous progress.

Source: Bush (2011) and Chaibong (2008)

Countries lacking such networks are "less resilient in the face of unexpected developments." Government can assist this process by empowering communities, devolving some service activities to non-governmental organizations, and promoting more volunteering and philanthropy.[22]

- *Decentralize political decision making and empower subnational governments with clear accountability and transparency to their electorates.* As noted in Chapter 8, while the degree of decentralization varies across developed countries, they all have a greater degree of empowerment of subnational authorities, electorates, and communities than is currently the case. The recently announced election of rural mayor is a step in the right direction.

- *Continue nation-building toward shared prosperity and consolidate the gains by inter alia incorporating also agreed processes of political leadership transition.* As noted in Box 11.6 successful modernizing states have managed leadership succession in various effective ways, while failure to do so has been shown to result in serious risks of instability and potential economic losses (Mueser and Giersch 2012).

Conclusion: Sequencing Reform, Sustaining the Optimal Institutional Setting, and Meeting the Challenges of Implementing the Reforms

The previous section is filled with a plethora of suggestions. The real question, of course, is how this all is to happen. Who is going to issue the instructions, and precisely how and why will the actions proposed be implemented and take effect? These are the most vexing questions in institutional development. While persuaded of the power and importance of leaders and policy makers, we recall the many students of institutions who stress the evolutionary nature of their development and the difficulty of "engineering" them into existence. Moreover, it should be noted that Kazakhstan, unlike a number of post-socialist states in Central and Southeastern Europe, does not enjoy the prospect of early accession to the European Union, the factor that served as a very strong incentive to institutional change in countries from Estonia to Croatia. What course of action can be proposed in Kazakhstan?

Timing of measures is part of the answer. So we propose that the government may wish to consider the following sequencing of the suggested reforms. Table 11.1 at the end of the chapter summarizes the key actions.

In the shorter term:

- Concerning *civil service reform*, the government would implement the ongoing civil service report; it would also examine the utility of a training program along the lines of the Political Studies Center in Singapore. We believe that a major lesson from Singapore is that the foundation of good governance is instilling in government staff at all levels an ethos and attitude of fair, impartial, and competent government. But this does not arise overnight; it will take time to shift the mentality of administrators away from their inherited mind-set, and toward a more open, trusting, service delivery approach. As the changing of ingrained mentalities is so obviously a long-term process, the time to start is now.

- The same logic applies to a loosening of the political reins and providing new impetus to the process of building liberal constitutionalism. Given the reasoning in the Chapter 2, i.e., that Kazakhstan can look forward to a decade and a half or so of ample resources and economic ease, possibly followed by an increasingly constrained position – and given that almost all successful transitions from paternalist to pluralist political systems have taken place in times of

---

22. This is the three-part strategy to promote civil society adopted by Great Britain. See Her Majesty's Government (2010).

relative economic prosperity, the suggestion is that the focus now change from stating eventual targets to that of concrete action. One way to lead into this process is by an immediate *ramping up anti-corruption efforts*; this should provide popular support for further governance initiatives.

- On the economic front, the essential shorter term concerns have already been listed; i.e., *WTO membership, expanding the privatization program, safeguarding the sound policies already well-established, and containing the pressures for economic populism and state intrusion*. All presently require attention.

In the medium term:

- The Government of Kazakhstan has ambitious programs in progress for regional development, including increasing the responsibilities and authority of local and regional level officials. Devolution of central powers is a time-tested method of engaging and empowering the citizenry of a nation and boosting political pluralism. Establishing the policy, legislative, regulatory, and electoral procedures for this *decentralization process* is underway, but it will take 5 to 10 years to complete. The next stage will be to match the devolved political and administrative functions with a *local capacity to finance these functions*. This is always a delicate matter: One must at the same time expand local generation or retention of resources while protecting the poorer districts and regions whose local tax base is weak (usually handled through some form of continued central funding). To institutionalize the decentralization process will require, in the medium term, a fleshed-out *program of subnational public finance* (see Chapter 8).

- The government would complete the *privatization process*. The level of public ownership and involvement in industrial or infrastructure enterprises should be reduced to that prevailing today in the most industrialized countries of the OECD. This means that the "valuation of the SOE sector relative to GDP" in Kazakhstan should decline from its present figure of above 60 percent to 20 to 30 percent. Note that this range is the high end of OECD countries; it is found in "countries that have recently made a transition toward more market-based economies: the Czech Republic, Finland, Israel, Poland, and Norway. The average for all reporting countries is around 15% of GDP" (OECD "Working Party" 2011).

- The *governance/political initiatives* suggested in this chapter would be substantially consolidated. Perceptions of the incidence and intensity of corruption should decline beyond "best in CIS" levels, and start to approximate EU averages.

In the longer term:

- The most important long-run institutional need for Kazakhstan is to apply the competent, agile, and resilient set of state structures built in the earlier period to deal with the more difficult, and possibly much more difficult, economic and environmental, and hence social and political conditions the country might face by the mid-21st century. Difficulties will arise out of climate change and shifts in the supply of and demand for Kazakhstan's energy and mineral resources. All possible mitigations to these risks — including continued economic diversification away from extractive industries, successfully adapting the skills in the public and private sectors, finding additional, non-energy ways for Kazakhstan to link up with the massive markets of Russia, China, and India, and managing the expectations of a populace accustomed to the largesse of oil wealth – require much enhanced institutional capacity in both the economic and the governance/political areas.

11

Monitor, evaluate, and adapt at all stages:

- Throughout the implementation process it will be critical to monitor and evaluate progress and adapt the measures and approaches as needed. For this, it will be useful to track progress in absolute and relative terms by reference to one or more of the institutional development indexes mentioned in the text here.

The bottom line is that early, visible, and significant action is essential in order to assure credibility and widespread trust in the government's commitment to institutional change. A clue to rapid and successful institutional transformation is found in the Georgian experience with anti-corruption activities (Box 11.4). The most visible feature of this success was the fearless and firm actions of a committed leadership group willing to attack entrenched vested interests and behaviors. But the reform group would not have succeeded without overwhelming support from a citizenry whose reaction to corruption had passed from resigned disgust to active outrage. That is, the Georgian leadership accurately judged that a social moment had arrived, in which previously unthinkable actions would garner widespread and enthusiastic popular support. The reformers then had the courage and the capacity to act.

At the same time we recognize that institutional change is a process and takes time, persistence, and a committed leadership. The point is that political leaders are actors embedded in their society; they have to tailor their institutional approaches to suit prevailing norms and beliefs. Throughout history, successful political leaders have been those able to judge public sentiment and pick the right moment to deviate from past practice. The capacity to assess what "society" needs and wants and to judge when and how to go about the process of translating those needs and wants into action or legislation are the characteristics of the successful leader. An advisor to Russian Empress Catherine the Great once congratulated her on "the blind obedience" of her subjects to her many decrees and laws. Catherine replied that what the advisor mistook for blind obedience was really the intense efforts she made to be sure of issuing only those laws that she knew the people would accept and obey.

Numerous challenges face the implementation of the broad reform strategy presented. We feel safe in claiming that if our proposed reforms are adopted and institutionalized, the broad mass of the Kazakhstani people of 2050 will be better off. But costs as well as benefits will be imposed; there will be groups and individuals who will lose out in the process of reform and resist the changes. At the same time, rising public expectations for change may outrun the readiness and implementation capacity of government. Managing the reform path means building and maintaining a pro-reform coalition, while satisfying the rising expectations of an increasingly articulate and empowered electorate. This will be a delicate and difficult task. The overarching challenge is how to maintain the admirable stability — in both the economic and social senses — that has propelled Kazakhstan's good achievements to date while introducing, over the next three to four decades, the increased citizen voice, political participation, and accountability required to firmly set the country in the top 30 club of developed states.

The clear and repeated conclusion of this entire chapter is that the process of institutional development is essentially homegrown. In the final analysis, institutional development in Kazakhstan is up to the people of Kazakhstan.

Table 11.1 | Institutional reforms: Actions in the short, medium, and long term

Area	Short term	Medium term	Long term
Economic institutions	• Join the WTO • Expand privatization • Adopt OECD recommendations on anti-corruption and investment promotion Maintain and implement sound economic reforms • Resist pressures for statist policies • Implement civil service reform	• Develop and implement system of local public finance • Further advance privatization process (SOEs no more than 20-30% of economy) • Advance anti-corruption agenda beyond best-of-CIS and close to EU levels	• Achieve and maintain top 30 ranked economic institutions, resilient and flexible
Political institutions	• Increase media and Internet freedom • Loosen restrictions on CSOs and political organizations • Ensure transparent local elections	• Decentralize decision making and accountability • Introduce agreed processes of leadership transition	• Achieve and maintain resilient and flexible top 30 ranked political and governance institutions
Implementation	• Select suitable cross-country indexes and monitor/evaluate progress both in absolute and relative terms • Adapt programs in light of evidence		

Source: Author

SCENARIOS FOR THE FUTURE >

Scenarios for the Future

Chapter 12

Harpaul Alberto Kohli and Johannes F. Linn

Throughout the preceding chapters the focus was on a broad vision of Kazakhstan's future, encompassing the manifold dimensions of human and natural resource endowments, of urban and regional development, of a modern knowledge-based economy, of a nation linked to the rest of the world and its neighbors, and institutional capacity. We finally turn to the question of whether it is reasonable to expect the country to transform itself in the next four decades from the current middle-income economy to a top 30 developed economy, measured in the simple metric used by economists to categorize the wealth of countries — namely per capita income. Alternatively, there is the possibility of Kazakhstan getting stuck in what is sometimes referred to as a "middle-income trap," an outcome that has widely characterized the performance of many middle-income developing countries in recent decades, especially in Latin America and the Middle East.[1] And of course, there are many intermediate outcomes that could be envisaged.

In order to give some rigor to the development of alternative scenarios we have applied a quantitative framework to trace out possible paths of future economic development of Kazakhstan. The purpose of our quantification exercise is not to make predictions of what will happen forty years into the future, but rather to ask "what if" questions and to highlight the long-term implications of broad trends. In past Centennial Group long-term outlook studies the scenarios have been a helpful anchor to focus the discussion. However, we must be aware of the limitations of any long-term modeling exercise.

The model we use is conceptually simple, based on the principle of convergence of low-productivity countries to the international high-productivity frontier (currently the US), depending on whether or not they are able to enjoy productivity gains (hence the distinction between "converger" and "non-converger" countries in the model application). Other key variables are labor force growth and capital stock growth (investment). Detailed explanations of the model have been published in a journal article (Kohli et al. 2012).

Despite its conceptual simplicity, the model is highly data intensive (as it covers 187 countries) and it is sophisticated in some of its computational aspects. The model is particularly useful for multi-country (global or regional) scenario analysis, since it is sufficiently aggregated to be relatively simple but disaggregated by country to allow the development of meaningful alternative global or regional scenarios.

In its standard version the model does not disaggregate structural components of the economy (sectors, regions, urban/rural) and is therefore less useful for building country-specific scenarios, although it can in principle be adapted by applying suitable sub-models for specific issues and has thus been adapted for the agriculture sector. For the case of Kazakhstan, we have developed a special adaptation of the model by breaking out the oil sector from the rest of the economy and treating it in effect as an exogenous component, driven by expected oil production and world prices for oil.[2]

---

1. See Kharas and Kohli (2011) for a full analysis of the middle income trap concept and experience.
2. See Annex 2 at the end of this volume for a description of the model structure and assumptions.

12

We use two sets of assumptions for the oil sector consistent with our analysis in Chapter 6: One assumes production grows rapidly until 2038 but then drops off dramatically as known reserves are being exhausted; the other assumes that oil production is capped at two million bbl/d and continues at that rate until 2050. Oil prices are assumed to rise gradually at an annual rate of 0.5 percent.

In addition we explore alternative assumptions for two dimensions of performance of the non-oil sector in Kazakhstan:

- One dimension is *Kazakhstan's TFP growth* in the non-oil sector, for which we consider two different options: For the "Kazakhstan high" and "Kazakhstan medium" cases we assume that Kazakhstan's TFP will grow continuously, approaching the US TFP level in the long term (i.e., Kazakhstan is a "converger"), while for the "Kazakhstan low" we assume that TFP growth will decline to the US TFP growth rate over a 10-15 year period and then stay there (i.e., Kazakhstan is a "non-converger").
- The other dimension is *Kazakhstan's investment-to-GDP rate* in the non-oil sector: For the "Kazakhstan high" case we assume the investment rate will rise from 30 percent in 2013 to 35 percent by 2018 and stay at that level until 2046, after which it will decline to 32 percent by 2050. This is an investment rate performance broadly commensurate with that of the East Asian "tigers."[3] For the medium and low cases we assume that the investment rate drops to 25 percent by 2019 and stays at that level throughout. This is above the average level of the non-oil investment rate for the last decade, which was about 20 percent.

With these alternative sets of assumptions we explore four different scenarios. These can briefly be described as follows:

- *Scenario 1:* Kazakhstan high performance ("converger" and high investment rate), capped oil production
- *Scenario 2:* Kazakhstan medium ("converger" and low investment rate), capped oil production
- *Scenario 3:* Kazakhstan low ("non-converger" and low investment), capped oil production (this scenario is also referred to as "business-as-usual")
- *Scenario 4:* Like Scenario 1, but uncapped oil production

Let us first consider the results for the global economy and for key sub-regions. Global GDP at market prices will expand 4.3 times, and 3.8 times in 2010 PPP constant dollar terms, while GDP per capita will expand 2.9 fold. Asia's share of global GDP will increase dramatically from 37 to 56 percent, while the European share will drop from 26 to 15 percent and that of North America will drop from 21 to 12 percent.

Let us then look at Kazakhstan's three big neighbors: China, India, and Russia. China and India's shares of world GDP will increase to 26 and 16 percent by 2050, exceeding those of Europe (15 percent) and North America (12 percent). Russia's share will drop from 3.0 to 2.6 percent. China and Russia's GDP per capita at market prices will be roughly equal in 2050 at about USD60,000, above that of Europe (USD54,000), but still lower than that of North America (USD81,000). India's GDP per capita lags behind the others at USD28,000, still eight times higher than its GDP per capita in 2011 (USD3,500).

Next, let us consider the implications of the model runs for Kazakhstan. Figure 12.1a shows the growth paths of GDP per capita through 2050 for the four different scenarios. Not surprisingly the two "high" scenarios (Scenarios 1 and 4, which assume "Kazakhstan high" performance) show the highest growth result. But while the uncapped oil production scenario (Scenario 4) outperforms the capped scenario (Scenario 1) for the first two decades, once the oil production limit is reached in the mid-2030s, there is a quick reversal, with Scenario 1 ending up higher than Scenario 4 by 2050. At the other extreme

---

3. A high investment rate will have to be accompanied by high savings rates to assure macroeconomic stability and avoid a debt trap.

of outcomes is Scenario 3, which represents "Kazakhstan low" or "business-as-usual." Here GDP per capita also increases, but significantly less so. If we then assume that Kazakhstan converges but does not go on a high investment rate path, we get a substantial improvement under Scenario 2 but fall short of the results of Scenario 1.

Figure 12.1b shows the associated growth rates for the four scenarios. For the scenarios where Kazakhstan performs well (convergence and high investment rate), the growth rate remains between 4 and 5 percent for much of the next few decades while it drops to 2 percent and less under the low performance scenarios. Scenario 4 shows a dramatic, albeit temporary, drop in the 2030s, when oil production has to be cut back because oil reserves are largely exhausted. As a result of these different growth rates the absolute size of Kazakhstan's economy varies substantially across scenarios: For Scenario 1 it increases from USD182 billion in 2011 to USD1.5 trillion in 2050, while under Scenario 3 it reaches USD556 billion, only about one-third of the Scenario 1 level.

Figure 12.3c decomposes GDP into oil and non-oil economy for Scenario 1. The graph demonstrates how with time the relative weight of the oil economy will significantly decline, as the non-oil economy has to pick up much of the growth momentum that propels the country forward. This pattern holds for both capped and uncapped oil production scenarios, although through the mid-2030s the oil economy's contribution to GDP is of course larger in the uncapped scenario.

Let us then consider how Kazakhstan performs in the international rankings by looking at Figure 12.1d. It shows the trends over time of Kazakhstan's ranking by per capita income under different scenarios. The main conclusion is that with high performance (Scenario 1) Kazakhstan can just move into the group of top 30 countries (its actual rank is 29) from 59 in 2011. Under Kazakhstan's low performance (Scenario 3) its ranking will significantly worsen to the upper 70s. For the medium scenario (convergence, but lower investment rate) the ranking improves, but only to 41 (under Scenario 2).[4]

Finally, we also ran some scenarios for alternative assumptions regarding the rate of growth of US TFP (i.e., the presumed productivity frontier of the world). For the "global high" performance cases, TFP in the US is assumed to grow at 1 percent per annum, equal to the long-term average TFP growth for the US. For the "global low" performance cases, TFP growth in the US is assumed to drop to 0.6% per annum. This more conservative assumption can be justified on the grounds that US productivity in the 2000s has dropped significantly below its long-term trends, partly due to the effects of the financial crisis of 2007/8, but also due to possible long-term declines in growth of the global TFP frontier.[5] Not surprisingly, the results, which are not shown here, show a generally lower GDP trend for all countries (in 2050 world GDP is 16 percent lower as a result of the lower productivity growth), including Kazakhstan, but Kazakhstan's rankings are not substantially affected.

Let us briefly summarize the key implications of these results:

---

4. In Figure 12.1d countries are ranked by per capita income measured at market exchange rates. An alternative ranking would compare countries according to their per capita incomes at purchasing power parity (PPP). In recent years Kazakhstan has ranked lower in terms of PPP exchange rates than in terms of market exchange rates since its non-tradable goods (such as wages) tend to be higher relative to other countries at similar levels of per capita income. This pattern persists into the future under the Centennial model framework. Accordingly, under Scenario 1 using PPP exchange rates, Kazakhstan reaches 36th rank by 2050, somewhat short of the goal of top 30 rank.
5. See *The Economist* "The Great Innovation Debate," January 12, 2013 for a good overview of the issues regarding past and prospective productivity trends.

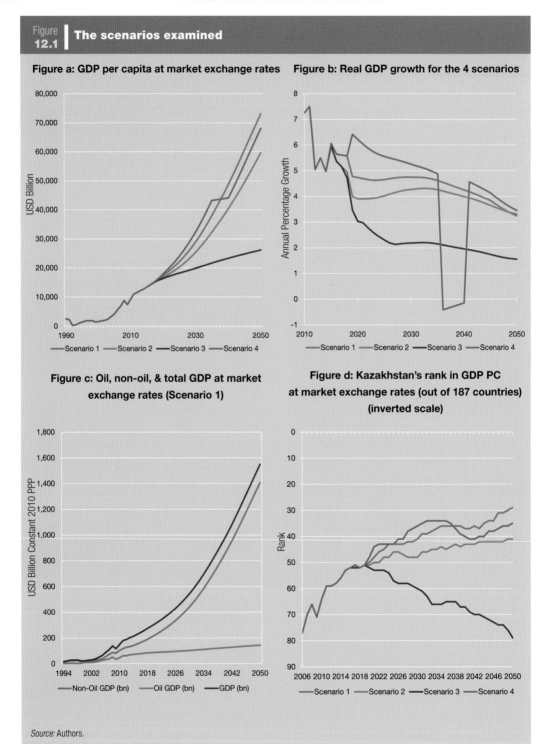

Figure 12.1 | The scenarios examined

Figure a: GDP per capita at market exchange rates

Figure b: Real GDP growth for the 4 scenarios

Figure c: Oil, non-oil, & total GDP at market exchange rates (Scenario 1)

Figure d: Kazakhstan's rank in GDP PC at market exchange rates (out of 187 countries) (inverted scale)

Source: Authors.

- Kazakhstan can achieve a ranking among the top 30 countries, but it requires significant efforts in terms of productivity increase and higher investment rates.
- Productivity growth alone will not suffice to reach the top 30 rank. Investment rates also have to increase.
- If Kazakhstan follows a "business-as-usual" approach in terms of productivity growth and investment rates, it may well fall back significantly in its ranking and will not make great progress in terms of its per capita income.
- Unless there are dramatic new discoveries of energy reserves or sustained rapid increases in energy prices, Kazakhstan's growth will have to come from the non-oil sector, which by 2050 will contribute an overwhelming share of GDP.
- Slow growth in the world's productivity frontier (perhaps due to global warming) will lower Kazakhstan's GDP per capita in the long term but much less so than a low productivity performance by Kazakhstan itself, and it will not affect Kazakhstan's ranking.

Of course, it is important to stress again that the model we are using can only produce indicative results. It does not reflect any possible major external shocks, nor does it link specific policy actions with long-term outcomes. Moreover, the model's simple structure and focus on GDP as the metric of progress is not meant to downplay the very important role that other dimensions of institutional, economic, social, and environmental performance play both as a means to sustained high growth and as a measure of human welfare of the people of Kazakhstan. However, the scenarios confirm what we believe is critical: Kazakhstan controls its own future. With effective action in the seven key priority areas that we have explored in the preceding chapters, Kazakhstan can substantially improve the well-being of its people and create the platform for long-term prosperity. As a result, when the official historian for Kazakhstan looks back in 2050 and contemplates the achievements, she or he might find that the ambitious vision of 2012 was indeed realized.

Kazakhstan 2050 — A Historian Taking Stock of a Vision Achieved

In January 2050 the official historian of the government of Kazakhstan takes stock of the progress achieved in realizing the vision of Kazakhstan 2050:

In December 2012, President Nazarbayev challenged his people and his government to enter the ranks of the world's top 30 developed countries by 2050 not only in per capita income terms, but in the quality of life its citizens enjoyed. As we start the second half of the 21st century, we can proudly say that Kazakhstan has achieved that goal. In four short decades, Kazakhstan has evolved from a country with an average income level of USD11,000 and institutions very much in transition to today's regional and global leader with an income level that puts us among the top 30 countries worldwide.

Looking back, Kazakhstan faced enormous challenges on almost every front in arriving at where we are today. Even though the country made remarkable progress in its first two decades as an independent nation, in 2012 its economy was still highly dependent on natural resource income, especially oil revenues, its people were still adapting to a world in which entrepreneurship and innovation, not state planning, were the keys to success and global competitiveness, and its institutions, both public and private, were still transitioning from an inherited system of state ownership and top-down management that stifled personal initiative and risk taking. Today, Kazakhstan is a very different country.

As Kazakhstan set off on the road that would bring us to the country we are today, it faced the overarching challenge of giving its citizens not only a level of per capita income that places them among the top 30 developed countries but also providing them with a quality of life that ranks among the best of the world. This meant (1) building institutions that Kazakhstan's people, whether as managers, scientists, engineers, and entrepreneurs, or merely ordinary citizens, needed to compete and prosper and that the country needed to remain economically and politically stable and secure; (2) managing its natural resource wealth and environment to support rather than handicap growth in other parts of the economy; (3) creating the human resources needed to drive its economy; (4) shaping a harmonious and stable urban and regional society; (5) constructing the foundations for a modern knowledge-based economy; and (6) forging alliances that would ensure regional stability and help promote global peace. Throughout our approach was one of pragmatism, of building on our successes and learning from our mistakes, scaling up what works, and focusing on the essentials.

Effective institutions

The central challenge has been to create institutions that support civic participation and private initiative, help grow our economy, and provide an effective safety net for our less fortunate citizens. This has meant not just adopting the best institutional structures from around the world but also creating the culture and incentives needed to make those structures deliver for our citizens. We now have laws and regulations that were developed with open and diverse public input, demonstrably achieve the policies they espouse, reward private initiative, and operate in the public interest. We have a judicial system and judges that are respected everywhere as speedy, fair, transparent, and impartial. We have a responsive civil service that has a well-deserved reputation for competence, delivery, and honesty. We have free, independent, and vibrant media and press that connect us with the world and help our citizens shape their own future with reliable information and diverse opinions.

In promoting our economic institutions we have not neglected our political institutions. Ours is now a mature democracy with effective representation of our citizens' interests, appropriate checks and balances for the parties and individuals in power, and sensible delegation of responsibilities to each level of government. Our decentralization process began by strengthening the governance and delivery capacities of oblast and rayon governments. We then increased local accountability by moving to a system of elected local officials, coupled with open and fair national elections initially confirmed by independent international observers. Corruption, once an impediment to our development and our reputation, is now kept at bay by the openness, transparency, and oversight that characterizes our processes and procedures at all levels of government.

A modern human resource base

Kazakhstan's greatest success in the past 40 years has been in developing its human resource base. Kazakhstan now has a population that rivals the world's best at every level of education and training. Its scientists and researchers are acknowledged as world leaders in chemical technologies, genetics, materials, engineering, and physics. Its entrepreneurs are leaders in the application of new technologies. Our arts and culture are flourishing. Our primary and secondary school systems are studied as models for other countries. Kazakhstan's high school graduates are fluent in three languages, regularly top international assessments in mathematics and science, and gain admission to the world's best universities. Our vocational and technical training system is considered a model for other countries. Our universities have evolved into a coherent system that produces graduates in demand not only by Kazakhstan companies but also by the world's top global companies.

Our flagship higher education institution, Nazarbayev University, is the best in the region and ranks among the top universities worldwide, attracting students and researchers from many countries. Our entrepreneurs, scientists, business people, and citizens have made us one of most competitive nations in the world. All this has been driven by a dramatic shift in the mindset of our citizens during last 40 years — from a focus on survival and the short term to a confidence in the present and a belief the future.

Kazakhstan also leads the way in serving its citizens' health needs. Our most significant gains have come through an unprecedented change in the lifestyle of most Kazakhstanis. From a country in which too many citizens lived lives that invited health problems, we have become a nation of health conscious citizens, fully understanding the responsibility for the lifestyle we lead. We rank among the world's best in terms of low incidence of heart- and stress-related diseases, cancer, and maternal and child diseases, not least by avoiding one of today's key global health challenge: pervasive obesity. Our progress in the health arena is a tribute to both our state-of-the-art medical technologies and the availability of preventive medicine programs throughout the country. When our citizens do need medical attention, they have access to universal health care delivered through one of the world' most efficient, cost-effective, and patient oriented health care systems. Kazakhstan's successful medical research program means that our doctors are sought after as collaborators on major international health research programs.

In 2012 the world was in the midst of a heated debate about how best to protect vulnerable citizens. On one side were those who advocated a minimal role for government, stressing the disincentive effects of public welfare systems and their often unsustainable fiscal consequences; on the other side were those who supported strong European-style inclusive and generous welfare systems. Kazakhstan has managed to develop a hybrid system that combines the best of both models, a system that is cost-effective, fiscally sustainable, with the right balance between support and incentives to move off of welfare and unemployment. Our program of retraining for the unemployed has become a model for others. No citizen, no matter how poor, goes without food, shelter, or health services.

Managing our natural resources for long-term national transformation and benefit

None of this would have been possible had we not managed our natural resource wealth and environment in a way that supported rather than distorted our development. When we began this journey, we were the students; now we can also teach. In 2011 nearly a quarter of our economy and three quarters of our exports depended on non-renewable natural resources. We decided in 2014 to cap oil production at two million barrels a day, at the time seen as a radical decision, but one that has turned out much to our advantage. As a result of this decision, and with our conservative management of oil revenues in a transparent National Fund, we were able to avoid the macroeconomic distortions and political disruptions that have plagued other countries with such large natural resource revenues and could deal with the inevitable fluctuations in world prices. Alongside Australia and Canada, we are a model for those struggling to manage their natural resource wealth, and like those nations we have at the same time achieved ambitious goals for combating pollution and protecting natural areas.

Because we have used our wealth wisely, our economy now reflects the attributes President Nazarbayev outlined for it in 2012: More than 50 percent of our energy consumption consists of alternative and renewable energy sources; our non-oil sectors create sufficient numbers of good jobs to give our citizens the opportunities they need to live full, productive, and satisfying lives; our economic base is diverse, with exports including the likes of biotechnology, engineering, materials, IT, nanotechnology, business and financial services, and tourism drawn to our natural and cultural assets. This shields us from global shocks; our banking and financial systems are stable and are seen as safe havens for financial assets in an all-too-volatile world; we have developed a macroeconomic management system that allows us to participate in the global economy but protects us from global economic downturns. We have achieved all this and yet avoided the sharp increases in inequality among our citizens that have often accompanied rapid economic growth in other countries.

Much of our economic success came from our rapid industrialization and the development of our globally competitive services industries. Investments in R&D created smart and innovative urban centers in Astana and Almaty that are now the locus for technological innovation and green growth initiatives. We have created efficient and cost-effective alternative energy sources and transitioned to a green economy that dramatically reduced our country's energy and carbon intensiveness, cleared polluted skies, water, and lands, and preserved our natural heritage.

A harmonious and stable urban and regional society

Along with the rest of the world, Kazakhstan has by now become a predominantly urban society. The deliberate decision of President Nazarbayev to found a new national capital, Astana, in 1997, together with our efforts to assure a balanced urban structure and the growth of "smart," "green," "fun," and "safe" cities and towns and to create well-integrated regions that shared broadly equal access to infrastructure and social services, have made significant contributions to the creation of an efficient, equitable, and integrated national space. We are proud that all of our citizens share opportunities to follow their individual aspirations, without fear of discrimination for their ethnicity, religion, or gender.

A modern knowledge economy

Based on strong, inclusive, and business-friendly institutions, an effective and sustainable management of out natural resources and environment, highly competitive human capital, and smart cities, we have built a modern knowledge economy that has created the basis for rapid productivity growth in catching up with the most advanced countries in the world and has provided us with an innovation system in selected areas of advanced technology and knowledge management that is admired around the globe. We achieved this outcome by stressing cooperation between business and government but always matched with selectivity and competition, meritocracy and a search for excellence, and openness to investment and ideas from abroad.

Kazakhstan as leader on the regional and global stage

We are also now seen as the architect of a system of regional alliances that has contributed to stability and prosperity not only in greater Central Asia but in the world. One key idea has been the "Green Bridge" advanced by President Nazarbayev, which has blossomed with environmental initiatives across Eurasia and the Pacific. In 2012 Kazakhstan was seen as an island of stability in a sea of instability and conflict driven by drugs and fanaticism. Competition for our scarcest regional resource, water, had the potential to worsen already difficult relationships among Central Asian republics, but we solved that problem with more efficient delivery, recycling, reuse, and most of all cooperation. Kazakhstan's leadership in promoting religious tolerance and regional cooperation has been critical. We have proven to be effective partners of our neighboring countries, especially the four other Central Asian republics. The Central Asia Economic Union, which we founded, has created a viable Central Asian market space that has improved not only our economic prospects but also those of our neighbors.

The world recognizes Kazakhstan's role in achieving peace and prosperity in greater Central Asia. Our work with Iran and Afghanistan has reduced world tensions by giving these countries a regional base for development and political dialogue. As a result of all these efforts, Kazakhstan is now the hub of a rapid Eurasian-wide economic integration process, which is transforming our shared super-continent into one great economic powerhouse. Kazakhstan is a respected member of and provides leadership on key global issues in the international organizations and forums, including the United Nations, the international financial institutions, OECD, and the G-Global, the inclusive successor to the G20, which Kazakhstan has helped to create.

Ready for the future

By meeting these five great challenges President Nazarbayev saw for Kazakhstan in 2012, we are now well positioned to face the great opportunities and challenges of the second half of the 21st century, including the continued rapid technological progress and changing competitive pressures we face, the likely stagnation and eventual decline in our population, the potential decline of our natural resource export earnings, and the growing impacts, both positive and negative, of climate change on our country. Moreover, we are now seen around the world as a voice of reason and responsibility. In today's multipolar world, Kazakhstan's unique economic and political history has thrust it into the role of "senior statesman" in the arena of world affairs. A threat to no country, a friend to all, with development credentials that few can match, Kazakhstan has now taken its place among the world's leading nations. Our task now at 2050 is to continue leading, and we embrace that challenge with enthusiasm and confidence in success.

Source: Visioned by Dennis de Tray, with inputs from staff of NAC of Nazarbayev University

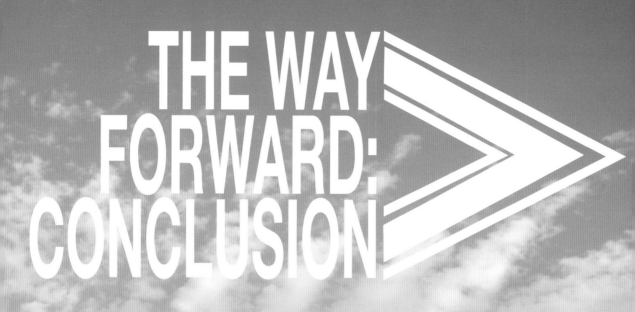

THE WAY FORWARD: CONCLUSION

The Way Forward: Conclusion

Chapter
13

Aktoty Aitzhanova, Shigeo Katsu,
Johannes F. Linn, and Vladislav Yezhov

The Vision of Kazakhstan 2050

In December 2012, Kazakhstan's president laid out an ambitious vision for the country to achieve by 2050: join the top 30 developed nations. We interpreted this vision in a multi-dimensional way and by identifying seven key priority areas, in each of which, we believe, Kazakhstan will need to move forward to achieve its overarching goal of creating a modern society that provides prosperity, stability, and quality of life for all its people at a level comparable to the most advanced countries in the world at that time. We also interpret the vision for Kazakhstan 2050 not as an endpoint, but as a platform on which future generations can sustain and further build a promising future for the second half of the 21st century.

Implementing the Vision

We believe that to realize the vision for 2050 not only in terms of per capita income and the overall quality of life, progress in these seven priority areas will be necessary: human development (education, health, employment, and social protection); efficiency and sustainability of energy development and use; environmental resilience; efficient and livable cities, a balanced regional economy, and a decentralized governmental structure accountable to the people; a diversified knowledge-based economy; a country open toward and economically integrated with its neighbors and the rest of the world, acting as a responsible global citizen; and, underlying it all, the development of effective, accountable, and transparent institutions.

Measuring Progress

When we assess Kazakhstan's current global ranking in these seven priority areas according to the many indexes of comparative country performance that are now available, Kazakhstan ranks mostly close to its current peers in terms of per capita income, rather than among the top 30. In some areas, and especially in regard to its governance, Kazakhstan lags even further behind. Looking ahead, we recommend that Kazakhstan select from among the available global performance indexes those that it feels most relevant to its vision and then track the country's progress toward the top ranks in each of them; when moving away from the top ranks at any given time, it should explore the reasons and justification for such a trend and seek to achieve a prompt turnaround.

Alternative Outcomes

We believe that the vision of Kazakhstan 2050, while very ambitious, is plausible but by no means assured. The history of development tells us that alternative outcomes are perhaps more likely, judging from the many countries that have become mired in the "middle-income trap." Indeed, our scenarios show that with business-as-usual, Kazakhstan might easily slip in the global rankings. Recent reversals of trends in economic and political institutional indicators provide signals that are best not ignored.

Urgency in Action

The year 2050 may seem like a long time in the future. But looking back, time passes quickly, and 35-40 years are but a sliver of history. Three reasons argue for urgency in Kazakhstan's pursuit of its ambitious goal for the middle of the 21st century: First, building the institutional, natural resource, human, and infrastructure capacity needed for a sustainable, diversified, modern knowledge economy takes time. It's like growing trees: If you want a forest in 30 years, you should start planting today. Second, while one cannot be sure, the next 15-20 years are expected to provide a more favorable global environment than the following decades, so it behooves Kazakhstan to move quickly in establishing a resilient, flexible economic and political institutional platform on which it can with confidence face more uncertain global prospects toward the middle of the century and beyond. Third, and perhaps most importantly, showing early resolve and commitment to take the hard actions needed to achieve the ultimate vision would create confidence and trust among citizens and investors alike and help unleash the virtuous cycle seen in the most successful emerging market economies.

Crosscutting Principles for Action

As we look across our analysis in the preceding chapters of how Kazakhstan can achieve its Vision 2050, we note a number of important crosscutting principles that should guide — and be promoted by — a committed, accountable leadership with a sense of urgency. These principles can be summarized best with a list of eight adjectives that portray the essential characteristics of the society that we think Kazakhstan can and should become: **open, resilient, competitive, cooperative, inclusive, sustainable, effective, and accountable**. These key principles interact and reinforce each other and would play a significant role in each of the seven priority areas that discussed in this report. Figure 13.1 projects this idea graphically. The seven principles are by no means exhaustive, but they help crystallize core lessons from global experience that Kazakhstan may wish to reflect in its efforts to realize the vision of Kazakhstan 2050.

Open

As we look across the top 30 developed countries of today, as well as Kazakhstan's competitors for this distinction in future years, we note that all of them are open to the rest of the world in terms of trade, investment, and attraction of people with skills and ideas; in terms of transport and electronic connectivity; and in terms of linkages among individuals, firms, and cities. For each of the seven priority areas discussed in this report we stressed aspects of openness: in the human development area, we noted the need to seek out ideas, lessons, and partnerships for modern education and health delivery; in the energy area, a welcome mat for foreign investors and technology; for green growth, a readiness to learn from and with others about new green technologies; for urbanization, to have cities that can compete internationally and attract the best firms and minds; in the knowledge economy, the readiness to bring in ideas embodied in firms and people and a welcoming business climate; for global and regional integration, openness towards neighbors and the rest of the world; and in the institutional area openness in the sense of transparency and readiness for institutional innovations tried and tested with success elsewhere.

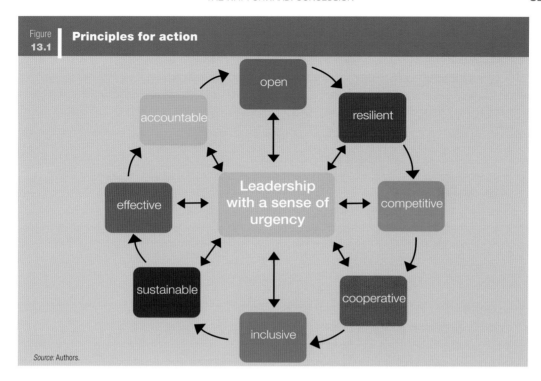

Figure 13.1 | Principles for action

Source: Authors.

Resilient (and flexible)

With openness comes inevitably exposure to external shocks — just as Kazakhstan experienced in the past — whether from fluctuating commodity prices, financial crises, conflicts in neighboring countries, domestic political debate, or in the longer term the headwinds of global warming. The financial crisis of 2007-9 showed that resilience matters: Many developing countries, including Kazakhstan, were relatively well-prepared to deal with the shock of this deep global crisis. Lessons from this experience are valuable, including: the need to ensure that the fundamental macroeconomic policies remain prudent, the financial sector is not overextended, and the country has ample fiscal and foreign exchange space so as to employ a fiscal stimulus to ward off a recession. For Kazakhstan the lesson was to continue its prudent fiscal management, including the National Fund, and to shore up its financial system.

Beyond this, however, in the long term other aspects of resilience will matter even more: (1) an educational system that shapes creative, flexible minds for people who solve problems rather than be cowed by them; (2) the health system and social safety net that protects people in the case of sickness and the vulnerable in the event of an unavoidable downturn; (3) a focus on the key elements of green growth that will help to adapt to climate change; (4) an intergovernmental fiscal system and responsive local governments that work with communities most affected by any negative shocks; (5) a knowledge system that picks up on opportunities created by technological innovation abroad or at home; (6) participation in a regional and international network of support that helps Kazakhstan should it be hit by natural disasters or waves of refugees but also allows Kazakhstan to help its neighbors when they are in need; and (7) governmental institutions that react quickly and flexibly to shocks and a political system that can absorb temporary economic setbacks without the risk of social strife because people feel they have a stake and a voice in what happens to them.

13

Competitive

To reap the opportunities that openness brings, Kazakhstan needs to attain a high degree of competitiveness, whether it is in education and health to create a competitive human capital base, or among the cities, which will need to be smart to provide the support for competitive firms as well as fun and safe to attract the best and the brightest, or in the institutional arena to attract and keep highly qualified firms and individuals. The creation of the modern knowledge economy will be critical to allow Kazakhstan to compete internationally, but only if Kazakhstan is easily accessible to the rest of the world and offers excellent transport and logistical facilities will it be able to successfully become the hub of transit and connectivity of the newly integrated Eurasian super-continental economy. And in the institutional arena Kazakhstan will need to move forward expeditiously to be seen to be able to compete with its international peers.

Competitiveness builds on competition — competition among the many actors in the domestic economy and with the rest of the world. Only if domestic firms, workers, students, teachers, health care providers, civil servants, and politicians face competition that rewards performance, values results, promotes on merit, and provides for accountability to clients and the electorate is the country likely to achieve the kind of competitiveness that will propel it to excellence in terms of international standards of economic, social, environmental, and political performance.

Cooperative

Openness also brings with it responsibilities as a global and regional player, and competitiveness needs to be matched by cooperation and partnerships. For example, Kazakhstan may not have an overriding national need to contribute to the mitigation of climate change, but if it wants to take on the position of a top-30 country, it will be expected, and will expect of itself, to contribute to the global commons, even if this is not necessarily dictated by narrowly defined national interests. Similarly, joining the international community as an aid donor, both through multilateral and bilateral channels, as Kazakhstan has started to do, will become more important. Or as a major exporter of grains, Kazakhstan may want to desist in future from imposing export controls during periods of high food prices since this inevitably hurts its poorer neighbors dependent on grain imports. And in the difficult arena of Central Asian regional relations, Kazakhstan should see itself increasingly as a leader who brings together other actors to find win-win solutions for key challenges, such as the water-energy issues, or cooperative ventures under the Green Bridge initiative, such as a regional bank for seeds and other viable plant and animal tissues.

Inclusive

A cooperative spirit and sense of responsibility should extend not only to neighbors and the international community, but as much and with even greater strength toward all fellow citizens in the country. For that reason, inclusiveness plays a pervasive role in many of the seven priorities that we discussed in the preceding lines, either in an instrumental sense by contributing to an economic and political system that more effectively achieves the goals of the Vision 2050 or as an intrinsic and central element of the vision itself as reflected in title of this report: "Towards a Modern Society for All."[1] Inclusiveness is perhaps most obviously a concern in the institutional arena, especially when it comes to the political dimensions, but also in terms of the economic institutions such as an inclusive public administration, jurisprudence, rule of law, and regulatory systems, which should give all citizens fair and transparent access to information, equal treatment, and opportunity. But it also plays a key role in human development, where access for

---

1. The concept of an "inclusive" society (in contradistinction an "extractive" society) in its instrumental sense plays a key role in the seminal analysis of "Why Nations Fail" by Acemoglu and Robinson (2012), which we discussed in Chapter 11.

all to education, health, employment, and social protection is a critical component of long-term policy. More generally, better and wider access to quality urban services and a balanced effort to assure rural households adequate services are key elements of urban and regional development policy, while greater inclusiveness and empowerment are essential aspects of decentralization.

Sustainable

Sustainability is another integral element of the vision — it underpins the long-term perspective of Kazakhstan 2050, and it is embodied in the notion that 2050 is not merely seen as an endpoint, but as a threshold point by which Kazakhstan should have built a platform that can sustain a prosperous and stable society well into the second half of the 21st century. Beyond this, however, sustainability is a key element of the energy and green growth discussions and also plays a role in the way we saw the need for maintaining urban and regional infrastructure, social protection systems, knowledge networks, and international and regional relationships. In all these areas, sustainability of natural, physical, human, and institutional assets and the services they provide for the people of Kazakhstan is a critical attribute of a successful long-term strategy.

Effective (in implementation)

Through it all, there is a need to focus on the effectiveness of implementation. Positing an ambitious vision and identifying key policies and programs that will contribute to achieving the vision are essential steps. But it is as important to focus on the actual implementation of the policies and programs. In this report we came across examples where Kazakhstan's policies and programs were well designed but where follow-through had failed to take place with the effectiveness necessary to achieve lofty goals, whether in education and health, areas of urban and regional development, building a modern knowledge economy, or the institutional arena (say, in anti-corruption programs). Kazakhstan is of course not alone in this. A lack of follow-through is a pervasive shortcoming in many countries and institutions. The reasons may be found in the pursuit of too many initiatives at a time, i.e., lack of selectivity; in counter-productive incentives and a preoccupation with short-term payoff; and in failure to monitor progress, evaluate results, and adapt and scale-up the program in light of the evidence collected. Therefore we stressed in many of the actions areas the need for selectivity, monitoring, evaluation, adaptation, and scaling-up (see Box 13.1).

Accountable

A key element for effective policy design and implementation is accountability of the actors involved for the results their actions produce. Without accountability it will be difficult to create the incentives necessary to assure effective action. Accountability can take many forms, including the traditional top-down accountability from senior officials or managers to their subordinates. But this has to be complemented by bottom-up accountability of politicians to their electorates, officials to the public, and entrepreneurs to their clients. In addition, horizontal accountability to peers (e.g., in the form of professional associations, etc.) can play a key role. Of course, for accountability effective measurement and monitoring of results is critical, as already mentioned in connection with effective implementation. Openness in turn provides ability to compare oneself with others in a transparent and well-informed way, closing the circle shown in Figure 13.1.

13

Box
13.1   **Effective implementation through a systematic focus on scaling-up**

In many instances, implementation of a program or policy starts (or should start) as an innovation piloted on a small or local scale. It is then helpful to approach the implementation challenge as an iterative process of innovation, learning, and scaling-up as shown in Figure 13.2.[2] The key to the process is to have a clear vision of the scale objective to develop pathways from the initial interventions or pilots to a sustained implementation process where monitoring, evaluating, and adapting throughout are integral elements of the process.

Figure 13.2: The Pathway from Innovation to Learning and Scaling Up

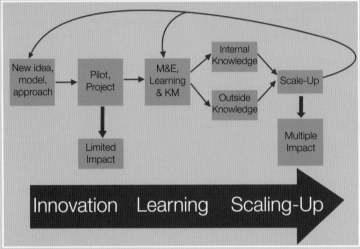

Source: Linn et al. (2010).

Kazakhstan has some excellent examples of a systematic approach to implementation that follows this simple innovation-learning-scaling-up framework. One of them is the approach to the development of Nazarbayev University and its role in reforming the university system of Kazakhstan. The challenge for the future will be to apply a similar approach to other areas of public policy, as we have indicated in our report for many of the actions recommended. Effective monitoring, evaluation, and adaptation are critical aspects of this process and clearly have to be strengthened throughout the policy making and implementation process. The fact that the Kazakhstan 2030 Strategy, and its corresponding 10-year plans, include provisions for monitoring of progress is an excellent start, but more attention needs to be paid to be monitoring outcomes, rather than delivery of inputs, and adjusting targets and programs in light of evolving circumstances and lessons from experience. In short, in striving for effective implementation Kazakhstan can build on some important strengths and experiences. The challenge will be to apply a systematic approach to implementation. The government may wish to explore the experience of the Colombian government with the development over the last 20 years of a national monitoring and evaluation system – SINERGIA – which is reputed to be one of the strongest in Latin America and has been used by at least one of the recent presidents of Colombia to monitor progress with national program implementation on a regular basis.

Source: Authors.

---

2. This framework was developed by Linn et al. (2010), based in part on the experience with of the introduction of Mexico's nation-wide conditional cash transfer program as analyzed by Levy (2006). This framework also includes a systematic consideration of what are the drivers of scaling-up (including incentives) and what obstacles may have to be removed (or what "spaces" have to be created) for the scaling-up process to succeed.

Concluding Comments

In this report we have aimed to provide a comprehensive perspective on the long-term goals and possible pathways that Kazakhstan may wish to explore in achieving its ambitious vision of Kazakhstan 2050. The choices the country faces are neither obvious nor free of tension in terms of economic and political trade-offs. In the end, the people of Kazakhstan have to decide for themselves what works for them and what does not. We have offered recommendations for action based on objective analysis and international experience. From our perspective the policy and programmatic choices matter, but the urgency with which they are tackled and the effectiveness with which they are implemented matter at least as much. And throughout it is important to keep in mind the ultimate goal of the whole effort: to offer all citizens of Kazakhstan an opportunity to participate in a successful modern economy.

Postscript: Summary of a Discussion of Kazakhstan 2050 at the Second Eurasia Emerging Markets Forum in Astana, September 10-11, 2013

Aktoty Aitzhanova, Shigeo Katsu, Johannes F. Linn, and Vladislav Yezhov

On September 10-11, the Second Eurasia Emerging Markets Forum met in Astana, co-sponsored by Nazarbayev University, the National Analytical Center, and the Emerging Markets Forum.[1] On the first day of this event, President Nursultan Nazarbayev addressed a group of about 800 participants in a public meeting on his vision for Kazakhstan 2050, complemented by comments by leading international political figures. This session was attended by members of the Kazakhstani government, representatives of the diplomatic corps, national and international experts and private sector representatives, and students of Nazarbayev University. On the second day of this event, a group of about 100 participants met in closed session to discuss the preliminary findings of the study "Kazakhstan 2050: Toward a Modern Society for All." The participants of this session included high-level representatives of the authorities of Kazakhstan, as well as national and international experts and private sector representatives. Participants in this two-day forum came from 87 countries.

This postscript summarizes the main points of the address of President Nazarbayev and of the leading international figures on the first day, as well as the main conclusions of the discussions during the second day.

Day 1 of the Second Eurasia Emerging Markets Forum (September 10, 2013)

Address by President Nursultan Nazarbayev

President Nazarbayev opened his address by noting that he had just represented Kazakhstan at the G20 summit in Saint Petersburg, which showed that the country could take a seat in the club of the leaders of the world.

He then turned to the great progress the country had made since independence, including the rise of Astana since its creation as the new capital 15 years ago and as a symbol of the new and resurrected country; the fact that Kazakhstan was leading the economic recovery among former Soviet republics, with much improved indicators of the quality of life; the recent achievement of top-50 status in the ranking of the most competitive nations in the world; and the progress made on the seven major tasks identified in Kazakhstan's 2030 Strategy after only 15 years of implementation.

With reference to his speech on December 14, 2012 on the topic of Kazakhstan 2050, the President reiterated the vision of Kazakhstan entering the group of top 30 developed countries by 2050. He emphasized that this was not a utopian dream, but a clear strategy and implementation plan, not only to achieve an ambitious goal by 2050, but also to assure a stable and prosperous future for the citizens of Kazakhstan beyond 2050. For this purpose, he expects the government of Kazakhstan to complete its work on laying out a specific action plan by the end of 2013.

---

1. For more information see http://www.emergingmarketsforum.org/upcoming-meetings/2013-eurasia-emerging-markets-forum/

President Nazarbayev noted that the future of global development is highly uncertain: today's top 30 developed countries may not be those of 2050, new and unforeseen international economic developments may take place, just as they did over the last decades, and the criteria for development may change.

In his view seven aspects will be key features of developed country status:

- a high level of socio-economic development, maintained over decades;
- a strong resilience and flexibility in responding to unforeseen events;
- a high level of technological development, scientific capacity, labor productivity, and energy efficiency;
- full integration into the global information network;
- high quality of education, health and social protection, with full employment;
- a rich cultural life; and
- an intense engagement in global and regional affairs.

Kazakhstan enjoys some strong advantages in aiming for top-30 developed country status: it is a large country with ample natural resources, including wind and solar energy; it is a respected country and a threat to no one; it commands a high level of financial resources in the form of currency reserves and National Fund assets; it has favorable business conditions; and it is home to world-class schools and universities.

But, as the President noted, Kazakhstan also faces a number of challenges: it is still in the process of diversification beyond natural resources; it faces high energy intensity; its community infrastructure is in need of modernization; and the population needs better access to education, health, and jobs.

Against a history of good planning and implementation of programs, the country now needs to focus on two key priorities:

- *Human resource development:* Here a new level of quality needs to be reached in education, with life-long learning, strong technical and vocational education, and a close linkage between higher education, science, and business. In addition, quality health care, early child development, and an improved life style practices will be introduced to Kazakhstan.
- *Effective institutions:* The increased engagement by the state in business during the recent economic crisis needs to be reversed; improved business conditions will be created, with lower trade barriers, protection of intellectual property rights, transparent and effective dispute settlement, and anti-corruption efforts; local governments will be made more accountable to the local electorate, including through the recently introduced elections of mayors in 90 percent of local governments.

In addition to these two key priority areas, President Nazarbayev identified seven areas of action in pursuit of the vision of Kazakhstan 2050:

1. *Effective management of hydrocarbon resources:* Here the authorities will aim for sustainable levels of oil production, with a cap of two million barrels of oil per day, rather than targeting a more rapid depletion of resources.

2. *Energy efficiency:* Alternative sources of energy are to make up half of power produced in 2050, and the government will create an agency for clean energy, which will fund the development of alternative energy sources, support the setting up of energy service companies, and

stimulate industries to become leaders in energy saving technologies, linked to the preparation and follow up of Expo 2017 in Astana.

3. *Optimal industrial policy:* The government will not prop up dying industries; it will be selective in choosing priority areas for support; it will focus on key niche areas such as clean energy, aerospace, genetic engineering, and the high-technology services industries.

4. *Agriculture:* This being an area of great potential for Kazakhstan, the authorities will explore greater utilization of ground water for pasture and crop development, development of new land and technologies, and attraction of foreign investment.

5. *Territorial development:* Here Kazakhstan will focus on developing smart and green cities, serving as innovation clusters, with up to four world-class metropolitan centers, including Astana and Almaty.

6. *Cultural development:* The country will make decisive breakthroughs in the areas of tourism, information management and entertainment. These are modern service industries that will create many exciting jobs.

7. *Economic integration:* The country will seek to use its unique geographic location at the center of Eurasia to establish balanced relations with its neighbors, increase transport access with the completion of the new East-West Highway and a second railway link, and thus support the rebuilding of the Silk Road. In addition, Kazakhstan will pursue openness and pragmatism in its trade relation, including in the Customs Union, and aim to strengthen its regional leadership, since the integration of its economy with the world economy is of paramount importance for the achievement of the vision of Kazakhstan 2050.

In conclusion the President noted that 2050 seems like a long time in the distance, but time will pass very quickly. So there is a need for effective and urgent action so that an official historian in 2050 can write about the progress achieved in attaining the goals set out in 2012.

Comments by Leading International Figures

Alfred Gusenbauer, Former Federal Chancellor of Austria: Mr. Gusenbauer congratulated President Nazarbayev on his robust agenda in response to ambitious vision. He noted that in today's rapidly changing world politicians need to understand underlying trends and respond quickly. While progress had been made in fighting world poverty, now the challenge of reducing rising inequality is paramount. This puts a premium on fostering an educational revolution at all levels of education (including vocational training), so that the potential of all young people is fully realized. In the future, Kazakhstan will not be able to rely on its natural resources alone, but will have to draw increasingly on its ability to innovate, on sharing in intellectual and technological progress. This ability will be critical to manage in an environment of increasing complexity that will characterize the world in 2050. In conclusion Mr. Gusenbauer contrasted historian Hobsbawn's pessimism about society's future with the optimism of President Nazarbayev who sees the future as a positive challenge.

Aleksander Kwasniewski, Former President of Poland: Mr. Kwasniewski considered the goal set by President Nazarbayev as realistic and endorsed his focus on the two key priorities of human resource development and effective institutions. Indeed, sound institutions are essential, if human resources are to be effectively utilized. He identified three institutional aspects for priority attention: (a) decentralization, critical to get people engaged and in particular the younger generation (decentralization early in the 1990s was a main factor behind the Polish success); (b) a modern judicial system; and (c) effective business institutions, including an independent central bank, a sound banking system, a well-functioning stock market, etc.

Romano Prodi, Former Prime Minister of Italy, and Former President, European Commission: Mr. Prodi identified various elements of energy sector reform as critical for the long-term success of former socialist countries, including Kazakhstan. The high levels of energy intensity and reliance on the energy sector for development raises major challenges, including raising domestic energy prices to more efficient levels as well as structural reforms for improved energy efficiency and diversification. Exclusive reliance on the market is not appropriate, but effective government engagement will be needed, including effective regulation, monitoring of progress, and improved social safety nets as energy prices increase.

Ehud Olmert, Former Prime Minister of Israel: Mr. Olmert noted that in the current turmoil in the Middle East a peace between Israel and the Palestine could serve as an axis of moderation, a source of stability, and a force for prosperity in the region. Over the long haul this could benefit countries like Kazakhstan, even though some distance away. He also indicated that Israel, as an example of an innovation-driven society, could provide Kazakhstan with useful ideas and lessons.

Day 2 of the Second Eurasia Emerging Markets Forum (September 11, 2013)

Johannes F. Linn presented the preliminary results of the Kazakhstan 2050 study. This was followed by a vigorous discussion during which the participants welcomed the candor of study and broadly endorsed the directions proposed. The main points addressed can be summarized as follows:

1. There was agreement that the vision of Kazakhstan 2050 was unique, bold, inspirational, worthwhile, and reachable. A focus on reaching top-30 country status in terms of broad measures of quality of life, and not only in terms of economic prosperity, was strongly endorsed.

2. However, participants agreed that the achievement of the vision of Kazakhstan 2050 could not be taken for granted, let alone as preordained. In its pursuit, numerous challenges, known and unknown, would have to be addressed and overcome.

3. A key challenge for Kazakhstan is the avoidance of the "middle-income trap" and the "natural resource curse." These have stifled the long-term growth of so many middle-income countries in the past, especially those well-endowed with natural resources. Participants noted the importance of assuring investment and productivity increases in Kazakhstan's non-oil sector.

4. Regarding the global environment, various speakers stressed concerns about the prospects for world commodity prices. The history of global commodity cycles and the potential for major changes in the supply and demand for oil and gas, make it possible, if not likely, that Kazakhstan could face substantial periods of low prices for its principal commodity exports. Assuring resilience to this and other global risks will therefore have to be of high priority for Kazakhstan.

5. There was broad acceptance that two priorities — human resource development and modern institutions — were at the heart of the strategy to achieve the vision of Kazakhstan 2050.

6. On human resource development, various speakers urged a broad-gauged approach to strengthening the education system, including especially a focus on early child development, on a modern technical and vocational education system, and on developing not only cognitive skills, but also non-cognitive skills, such as team work, creativity, etc. Effective links between the educational system and the needs of the labor market, in particular business, were seen as critical.

7. On institutional development a number of aspects were stressed:
   - The need for an effective business climate will be central for achieving high investment levels and productivity increases in the private sector, which would have to be the engine of growth. Here the importance of an effective financial system, of access to credit, and of logistical capacity, as well as the rule of law and property rights, were stressed particularly by private sector participants.
   - Continuity, predictability, and consistency in decision making by government was critical. Frequent changes in vision and implementation plans, too prevalent elsewhere, would put the achievement of Kazakhstan 2050 into doubt.
   - Trust in governmental and non-governmental institutions is a critical requirement. Key elements for the establishment of trust would be the completion of civil service reform, with a focus on meritocracy, accountability not only to the political leadership but also to the public that it serves, and minimizing the bureaucracy that stifles initiative and creativity.
   - Effective decentralization is another element of a trusted and accountable institutional framework.

8. Speakers endorsed key elements of the energy and green growth strategy, such as establishing a cap on oil extraction, switching from a cap-and-trade to a carbon tax approach, and assuring a productive and environmentally sound agricultural sector.

9. Many speakers stressed the importance of Kazakhstan's economic integration with the rest of the world and the region if it was to achieve the rapid productivity gains and high investment levels postulated under the Kazakhstan 2050 vision. The country's location at the core of the Eurasian continental economic space, surrounded by major world economic powers, could be turned to its advantage through a strategy of transport and ICT connectivity and a consistent openness to trade with all partners. Instead of being "land-locked," Kazakhstan would become "land linked."

10. The process of implementation of the strategy of Kazakhstan 2050 — how to move from vision to action — will be critical. This encompasses the effective timing and sequencing of reforms, the rigorous monitoring, evaluation, and adaptation as needed, and an effective consultative process with a wide range of stakeholders in society — business, civil society, government civil servants, etc.

11. Finally, there was wide agreement that Kazakhstan needed to resist falling into the common trap of complacency at a time when it could look back with considerable pride on two decades of successful economic management and political stability. Leadership that retains a sense of urgency in pursuing the key priorities of its Kazakhstan 2050 strategy and in applying the key principles identified in the Kazakhstan 2050 study will therefore be critical going forward.

Kazakhstan's Standing in International Country Performance Indexes

In recent years the development of international country performance indexes has become an intellectual growth industry. A review carried out by NAC of Nazarbayev University (2012) staff for this report unearthed 24 such indexes for which comparative country rankings are available, including for Kazakhstan, but there are surely more.

International country performance indexes are useful for benchmarking a country's economic, social, and governance performance against other relevant countries or country groups. But they come in a bewildering variety, they have many different ideological, analytical, and informational foundations, and they at times provide conflicting results. Indexes can be very broad or narrow in terms of the performance dimensions they cover: They can be based on original expert assessment of country conditions, they may be based on surveys or on published statistical information, or they may be "meta"-indexes, i.e., aggregates of other indexes. Some indexes are a mixture of some or all of the above.

Many issues plague the interpretation of these indexes, including data reliability, comparability of expert judgment and survey results across countries, and comparability over time of results for the same index (since the country universe and the definition and measurement of sub-indicators will often change over time for the same index). Since most indexes require aggregation of sub-indicators, how to weight the sub-indicators is a thorny question. And country coverage is not uniform across indexes, so comparing rankings of a country can be treacherous. Finally, little work has been done to systematically test the relationship between indicators measuring "input" performance (e.g., business climate or governance indicators) and "output" performance (e.g., economic growth), and those tests that have been reported generally do not yield strong relationships, let alone proof of causation.[1]

Nonetheless, considering the relative position of a particular country for a specific index and across various indexes may be useful for four reasons: First, a well-designed index can convey useful information both in aggregate and in its specific sub-components regarding the relative standing of countries on important policy and institutional parameters, and it can indicate the scope of improvement that is possible in principle. Second, while each individual index and sub-indicator may be subject to questions, when multiple indexes and indicators yield comparable results for the same performance area, this provides prima facie evidence about a country's relative performance.[2] Third, investors, the press, and the public may pay attention to the relative standing of countries in some of the better-known indexes. Fourth, and linked to the first three reasons, governments show interest in — and have been known to act on — the results of the indexes, even if they may feel that some indexes or sub-indicators misrepresent reality.

Annex Table 1.1 summarizes the results of 19 indexes relevant to key economic, social, and environmental issues. Annex Table 1.2 summarizes results for nine indexes that contain rankings on selected

---

1. The World Bank's well-known Doing Business index was recently subjected to a thorough review by an independent panel. The panel's report represents a telling example of the kinds of criticisms that can be leveled against comparative country indexes. See http://www.dbrpanel.org/ .
2. One needs to be aware, however, that indexes frequently are based on the same primary information sources for sub-indicators. Hence the additional information value from multiple indexes may be limited.

A1

governance issues.[3] The main overall implications are summarized in Chapter 2. The results for selected indexes can briefly highlighted as follows:

- Centennial's *Resilience Index*, which rates countries' resilience to international financial and economic crisis, ranks Kazakhstan 88th overall (out of 133), but more highly on fiscal policy (13th), external robustness (41st), private debt (40th) and reserves (56th), and lower on government effectiveness (96th), and external independence and robustness (102nd).

- The *Bertelsmann Transformation Index* ranked Kazakhstan 48th out of 128 countries for the state of the market economy in 2012 but 79th on the state of democracy. Kazakhstan ranks 66th on the Human Development Index, which combines per capita income, education, and health indicators.

- In the World Economic Forum's *Global Competitiveness Report* for 2012-13 Kazakhstan ranked 51st, which was a substantial improvement over the previous year's 72nd, reversing a declining ranking since 2005 when Kazakhstan was also 51st. The improvement was mainly due to increased scores for technological readiness and institutional factors such as the efficacy of corporate boards and investor protection. The main barriers to doing business as reported in the *Global Competitiveness Report* are the low qualifications of the workforce, the tax regime, and access to financing.

- In the World Bank's *Doing Business* index Kazakhstan's overall ranking for 2013 was 49th, up from 56th in 2012. Kazakhstan ranked especially highly on the sub-categories of starting a business, registering property, protecting investors, paying taxes, and enforcing contracts, but poorly (182nd) on trading across borders.

- Kazakhstan performs less well on the World Bank's *Logistics Performance Index*; having improved to 62nd in the latest (2010) *Logistics Performance Index* from 133rd in the previous (2007), it dropped back to 86th rank in 2012.

- The Fraser Institute's *Economic Freedom of the World* index aims to rely on objective components rather than surveys or value judgments, although the choice of components is itself a value judgment. In the 2012 Annual Report Kazakhstan ranked 70th out of 144 countries covered. By components, Kazakhstan ranked higher by size of government and by credit market, labor market, and business regulations. However, the overall ranking was pulled down by a low score (111th ranking) on freedom to trade internationally.

- On the Heritage Foundation *Index of Economic Freedom* Kazakhstan ranks slightly better: 68th in 2013, down from 65th in 2012.

- Kazakhstan ranks less impressively in indicators of governance. In the Freedom House *Nations in Transit 2013* report, Kazakhstan's democracy score of 6.57, on a 1-7 scale, was slightly better than Azerbaijan's (6.64), but trailed all other transition economies except Belarus (6.71), Uzbekistan (6.93), and Turkmenistan (6.93).

- On the Reporters sans Frontières *Index of Press Freedom*, Kazakhstan had a low rank of 160th in 2013. This was a deterioration over 154th in 2012.

- Kazakhstan performs remarkably well on the e-government and e-participation indexes compiled by the United Nations. For the e-government index (which measures the extent to which governments provide access to the population through the Internet), Kazakhstan ranked 38th out of 190 countries; for e-participation (which measures the extent to which the population uses the Internet to access relevant public sector information) Kazakhstan ranks an amazing 2nd out of 193 countries.

---

3. Since there is some overlap of indexes across the two tables, the number of indexes covered totals 24.

Annex Table 1.1 | **Rankings of Kazakhstan in economic, social, and environmental indexes**   A1

index	Business climate					Economic integration		Human development			Environment	General well-being
	general	macro mangm	corruption	innovation	infrastructure	barriers to trade	credit rating	education	health	labor market		
S&P							BBB+ Stable					
Fitch							BBB+ Positive					
Resilience Index	88 (of 133)	13-94 (of 133)				102 (of 133)						
Doing Business	49↑ (of 185)					182 (of 185)						
Global Competitiveness (WEF)	51↑ (of 144)	16 (of 144)		103 (of 144)	67 (of 144)					19 (of 144)		
Logistics Performance Index						86 (of 155)						
Economic Complexity Index	92↓ (of 128)											
Index of Economic Freedom	68↓ (of 179)					78 (of 179)				8 (of 179)		
Legatum Prosperity Index	59 (of 142)							43 (of 142)	60 (of 142)			46↑ (of 142)
BCG Index												79 (of 150)

(contd...)

(Annex Table 1.1 contd...)

Annex Table 1.1 | Rankings of Kazakhstan in economic, social, and environmental indexes (continued)

index	general	macro mangm	corruption	innovation	infrastruc-true	barriers to trade	credit rating	education	health	labor mar-ket	Environment	General well-being
			Business climate			Economic integration		Human development				
Bertels-mann Transfor-mation Index	48 (of 128)											
Worldwide Gover-nance Index		180 (of 215)										
Corruption Perception Index		133↓ (of 176)										
Weakness of State Index		Top 20% (of 141)										
Failed State Index												107 (of 177)
Happy Planet Index												119 (of 151)
GAIN Index											67↑ (of 192)	
Environ-mental Perfor-mance Index											129↓ (of 132)	
Human De-velopment Index								35 (of 187)	132 (of 187)			

(contd...)

(Annex Table 1.1 contd...)

A1

Annex Table 1.1 | **Rankings of Kazakhstan in economic, social, and environmental indexes (continued)**

index	general	macro mangm	corruption	innovation	infrastruc-true	barriers to trade	credit rating	education	health	labor mar-ket		
		Business climate				Economic integration		Human development			Environment	General well-being
Early Childhood Index (ECCE)								24 (of 68)				
Where to Be born Index	74 (of 80)											
Overall Range	50-100	Top 30	130-180	100	50-100	75-185	Bottom Inv. Gr.	Top 50	50-150	Top 30	60-130	40-120

Note: The symbols ↑ and ↓ show improving and deteriorating trends in ranking.

A1

Annex Table 1.2 | **Rankings of Kazakhstan in governance indexes**

Index	Voice and accountability	Government effectiveness mangement	Regulatory quality	Rule of law	Property rights	Overall governance	Overall political	Freedom of press	E-Participation/ Government
Worldwide Governance Indicators	186 (of 215)	116 (of 215)	122 (of 215)	147 (of 215)					
International Property Rights Index					107 (of 130)				
Legatum Prosperity Index						95 (of 142)			
Resilience Index		96 (out of 133)				84 (of 142)			
Weakness of State Index							Bottom 40% (of 141		
Press Freedom Index (RSF)								160 (of 179)	
Freedom of Press (Freedom House)								175 (of 197)	
E-Government Development Index									38 (of 190)
E-Participation Index									2 (of 193)
Overall	186	116	122	147	107	95	Bottom 40%	Bottom 20%	2-38

References for Annex 1

BCG Index

http://odpowiedzialnybiznes.pl/public/files/Introducing%20the%20BCG%20Sustainable%20Economic%20Development%20Assessment_BCG_2012.pdf

Bertelsmann Transformation Index

http://www.bertelsmann-stiftung.de/cps/rde/xchg/SID-7416E337-45920379/bst_engl/hs.xsl/307.htm

Corruption Perception Index

http://www.transparency.org/research/cpi/overview

Doing Business

http://www.doingbusiness.org/rankings

E-Participation Index

http://unpan3.un.org/egovkb/ProfileCountry.aspx?ID=87

Early Childhood Index (ECCE)

http://www.unicef.org/rosa/217145e.pdf

Economic Complexity Index

http://atlas.media.mit.edu/media/atlas/pdf/HarvardMIT_AtlasOfEconomicComplexity_Part_I.pdf

E-Government Development Index

http://unpan3.un.org/egovkb/ProfileCountry.aspx?ID=87

Environmental Performance Index

http://epi.yale.edu/

Failed State Index

http://ffp.statesindex.org/rankings-2013-sortable

Fitch

www.fitchratings.com/web_content/ratings/sovereign_ratings_history.xls

Freedom of Press (Freedom House)

http://www.freedomhouse.org/report/freedom-press/freedom-press-2013

GAIN Index

http://index.gain.org/ranking

Global Competitiveness (WEF)

http://www.weforum.org/issues/global-competitiveness

A1

Happy Planet Index
http://www.happyplanetindex.org/data/

Human Development Index
http://hdr.undp.org/en/statistics/

Index of Economic Freedom
http://www.heritage.org/index/country/kazakhstan

International Property Rights Index
http://www.internationalpropertyrightsindex.org/

Legatum Prosperity Index
http://www.prosperity.com/

Logistics Performance Index
http://web.worldbank.org/WBSITE/EXTERNAL/TOPICS/EXTTRANSPORT/EXTTLF/0,,contentMD-K:21514122~menuPK:3875957~pagePK:210058~piPK:210062~theSitePK:515434,00.html

Press Freedom Index (RSF)
http://en.rsf.org/press-freedom-index-2013,1054.html

Resilience Index
http://www.emergingmarketsforum.org/downloads/Resilience%20Index%20FINAL.pdf

S&P
http://www.standardandpoors.com/ratings/sovereigns/ratings-list/en/us?sectorName=null&subSectorCode=&filter=K

Weakness of State Index
http://www.brookings.edu/research/reports/2008/02/weak-states-index

Where to Be Born Index
http://www.economist.com/news/21566430-where-be-born-2013-lottery-life

Worldwide Governance Indicators
http://data.worldbank.org/data-catalog/worldwide-governance-indicators

Model for Developing Long-Term Growth Scenarios

Annex
2

Harpaul Alberto Kohli

The scenarios presented in Chapter 12 for Kazakhstan's development through 2050 are based on a model that projects GDP as a function of labor force, capital stock, and total factor productivity for 187 countries between 2013–2050 under alternative assumptions. This annex offers an abbreviated description of the model, which for Kazakhstan consists of two sectors: an oil sector and a non-oil sector. A more detailed exposition of the non-oil sector model approach can be found in Kohli, Szyf, and Arnold (2012).

GDP figures are generated for three different measures, all expressed in constant US dollar terms: real GDP (constant 2010 prices), GDP PPP (constant 2010 PPP prices), and GDP at expected market exchange rates, which incorporates expected exchange rate movements and serves as this book's best proxy for nominal GDP.

For Kazakhstan, GDP is defined as follows:

$$GDP = NonOilSectorGDP + OilSectorGDP \qquad (1)$$

For other countries, the entire economy is modeled using the methodology described below for just the non-oil sector.

Kazakhstan's oil sector is defined as follows, with values for both variables given exogenously; that is, they are assumptions and scenario specifications given by the user and not calculated by the model itself:

$$OilSectorGDP = OilPrice \times OilProduction \qquad (2)$$

where *OilPrice* is measured in constant 2010 US dollars per barrel and *OilProduction* in barrels per year.

For the non-oil sector, a Cobb-Douglas function with constant returns to scale is assumed, with α equal to two-thirds, as seen in Equation 3:

$$NonOilSectorGDP = NonOilTFP \times NonOilL^{\alpha} \times NonOilK^{1-\alpha} \qquad (3)$$

The anchor of the estimates for the non-oil sector is historical data for non-oil GDP, non-oil total factor productivity (TFP), non-oil labor force, and non-oil capital stock (which is based on historical investment rates, as described later in this annex). We treat the non-oil labor force as negligible, and thus use the total labor force as the non-oil labor force. We calculate historical TFP as a residual of actual values for the other variables, and so it is derived from historical values of non-oil labor force, non-oil GDP, and non-oil capital stock. But the actual historical data we have for GDP and investment rates includes both oil and non-oil. Therefore, to allow us to use Equation 3 to project the non-oil sector, we must subtract the oil GDP and oil investment from the total GDP and total investment before we start the calculations.

For the oil GDP (Equation 2), we just use the historical oil production and price. Because we do not have exact figures for historical yearly oil capital investment, we use oil FDI as a proxy.

Once we have made these adjustments, the overall strategy to calculate GDP for the non-oil sector is to estimate annual real GDP growth (of the non-oil sector) for each country between 2013 and 2050. These estimates are applied to the previous values of real GDP, GDP PPP, and a measure equal to nominal GDP deflated by US inflation (on which GDP at market exchange rates is based) to derive the full series.

Labor force growth stems from population growth and from changes in labor force participation rates. Population growth is based on the 2010 Revision of the UN's World Population Prospects, while labor force participation rates are projected separately, by gender, for seven age cohorts (15–19, 20–24, 25–29, 30–49, 50–59, 60–64, and 65+) to better capture cohort-specific trends. Male rates are projected directly; female rates are derived by projecting the difference between male and female rates for each age group. Labor force participation rates from 1980 through 2013 are taken from the International Labor Organization.

The cross-country, cohort-specific equations to forecast male rates are simple autoregressions of the following form:

$$(4) \qquad \ln(M_{age,t}) = m_{age} \times \ln(M_{age,t-1})$$

where M_{age} is the percentage of males in age group *age* who are active in the labor force and m_{age} is a constant that varies by age group.

The cross-country, cohort-specific equations to forecast the differentials between male and female participation rates are:

$$(5) \qquad \ln(D_{age,t}) = d_{age} \times \ln(D_{age,t-1})$$

where D_{age} equals the difference between the percentage of males in age group *age* in the labor force and the percentage of females in age group *age* in the labor force, and d_{age} is a constant that varies by age group. In both male and female models, for certain cohorts, rough upper or lower bounds are incorporated to address outliers. Observations that begin in 2013 beyond these bounds are not governed by the regressions but instead gradually converge over time towards the bounds.

Capital stock growth, based on an initial non-oil capital stock and yearly non-oil investment rates and depreciation, is defined as:

$$(6) \qquad (1 + K\ Growth_t) = \frac{K_t}{K_{t-1}} = \left(\frac{I_{t-1}}{K_{t-1}} \right) - 0.06$$

where K is the non-oil capital stock, 0.06 represents the yearly depreciation of 6 percent, and I_{t-1} is the non-oil capital investment from the previous year, which is defined as the previous year's GDP (measured in constant 2010 PPP dollars) multiplied by the non-oil investment rate as a share of GDP.

The initial non-oil capital stock is calculated using the Caselli method, with the following equation:

$$K_0 = \frac{I_0}{g + 0.06} \tag{7}$$

where K_0 is the initial non-oil capital stock, g is the average GDP growth over the subsequent ten years, 0.06 is the depreciation rate, and I_0 is the initial year's non-oil investment. For I_0, for each country, the earliest year for which there exists capital investment data (year y) is identified. The average of the non-oil investment rate values for year y and the two subsequent years is computed and treated as the initial non-oil investment rate. This smoothing out of fluctuations in the initial investment rate is necessary to yield better estimates for certain countries in which there is much volatility in the earliest investment rate values. This rate is then multiplied by the GDP in year y to determine I_0. The earliest year possible is chosen for this estimate because the longer the time frame before the projections commence the more the yearly depreciations will reduce the effects on the model of any initial imprecision in capital estimates.

The model is calibrated by calculating non-oil total factor productivity (TFP) for an initial year (2013)[1] based on labor force, non-oil capital stock, and non-oil GDP, with GDP and capital stock measured in purchasing-power-parity dollars at constant 2010 PPP prices. For subsequent years, TFP is projected. (To simplify the following discussion, we use the term "TFP" in place of "non-oil TFP.")

For the TFP projections, we differentiate four tiers of countries: rich or developed, converging, non-converging, and fragile. The model treats non-converging middle-income countries the same as non-converging low-income countries.

All countries begin with a default TFP growth rate of 1 percent, which, to a strong level of statistical significance, equals the average US rate over the past 40, 30, 25, and 20 years and which, also to a strong level of statistical significance, equals the average rate of all non-converging countries over the same four periods. In our model, this is the fixed rate of productivity growth for non-converging, non-fragile countries. (For the pessimistic world scenarios mentioned in Chapter 12, we use a default TFP growth rate of 0.6 percent, consistent with the most recent US experience.)

Research shows that some growth differences between developing countries can be successfully modeled by separating them into two groups: converging (Tier 2) and non-converging (Tier 3) countries (Gill and Kharas 2007).

A country is deemed to be converging if its per capita income has rapidly converged over a 20-year period to that of best practice economies or if its 2001–2011 TFP growth is closer to what the model would predict for a converger (see below) than to what it would predict for a non-converger; the lower its productivity relative to the global best practice, the more quickly it converges. This convergence reflects technology transfers from richer innovating countries, technology leapfrogging, the diffusion of management and operational research from more developed countries, shifting underemployed agricultural workers to efficient manufacturing, building roads to connect the unconnected to markets, transferring child laborers into schools, and other ways that a country can shortcut productivity-improvement processes by learning from economies that are already at the productivity frontier.

---

1. IMF WEO GDP growth projections are used for 2013.

In the model, the lower the country's productivity relative to that of the US, the larger the boost and the quicker the catch-up.[2] The productivity growth of 14 of the 36 rich (Tier 1) countries is treated the same as that of Tier 2 countries. On the other hand, non-converging (Tier 3) countries and 11of the 36 rich countries have only a 1 percent yearly productivity growth and no boost. The remaining Tier 1 countries are treated as partial convergers, benefitting from half the convergence boost.

The general equation for TFP growth is:

$$(8) \qquad\qquad TFPGrowth = 1.0\% + CB - FP$$

where CB is the convergence boost benefiting "converging" countries and FP is the productivity growth penalty suffered by failing or fragile states.

The convergence boost is defined as follows:

$$(9) \qquad\qquad CB = c \times 2.69\% \times \ln\left(\frac{TFP_{USA,t-1}}{TFP_{i,t-1}} \right)$$

where i is the country, 2.69 percent is the convergence coefficient (derived from historical data), TFP is the total factor productivity, and c takes a value between 0 and 1 and identifies whether a country is treated as a converger ($c=1$) or as a non-converger or fragile state ($c=0$), or in an intermediate state of transition between being a converger and non-converger ($0 < c < 1$).

The failed-state penalty FP is defined as:

$$(10) \qquad\qquad FP = f \times 1.5\%$$

where f plays a role analogous to that of c in Equation 9. For each fragile (Tier 4) nation, f is set equal to 1, corresponding to a penalty in productivity growth of 1.5 percent, so that its yearly productivity is assumed to fall by 0.5 percent a year. The coefficient of negative 1.5 percent and the list of such fragile states is derived by identifying state failures and debilitating wars prior to the global financial crisis that lasted at least two consecutive years in 44 nations.

The projections of non-oil GDP growth are derived by applying the labor growth, non-oil capital deepening, and non-oil productivity changes to each country over the period 2014–2050.

With the non-oil GDP estimates concluded, we then add back in the oil GDP, using Equation 1, based on the exogenous assumptions of real oil price and oil production specified by the user for the scenario of interest. For all seven scenarios in Chapter 12, we begin with the historical 2011 oil price measured in 2010 dollars and assume a 0.5 percent real increase in the oil price each year after that. This concludes the GDP calculations for total real GDP, constant PPP GDP, and the measure equal to nominal GDP deflated by inflation, which we use to generate GDP at market exchange rates by multiplying it by exchange rate appreciation.

---

2. TFP is used in the convergence term instead of the per-capita income used by others for three reasons: First, if the equation were to use GDP per capita, over time the TFP of a converging country would not converge to that of the US but instead to other values. Also, since the convergence equation represents convergence of TFP, we use TFP in order to make the equation consistent with its purpose. Third, using the convergence coefficient from past research in tandem with an income-based convergence term yields large discrepancies with the recent historical data for TFP growth for many countries; using TFP yields a better fit.

A2

The measure of GDP at expected market exchange rates adjusts the GDP estimate by expected changes in the real exchange rate. First, an equation is derived to establish a theoretical relationship between a country's real exchange rate and its PPP income relative to that of the US. Then, the country's modeled exchange rate converges toward the value that corresponds to its income in this theoretical equation. These relationships are not linear, and the countries for which increases in GDP PPP per capita most appreciate their real exchange rates are the countries whose incomes are between a third and two-thirds that of the United States and not the poorest or richest countries.

The model also projects the sizes of the low-, middle-, and high-income populations, again following Kharas (2010), by measuring the number of people in each country with living standards—in PPP terms—within a certain absolute range. An income distribution for each country is derived from the World Bank's PovcalNet and International Comparison Program.

The model calculates what share of the nation's income is available for consumption, and it distributes this consumption income over the population according to the income distribution. As the country's overall consumption income increases, the purchasing power of those at the bottom of the distribution increases, raising more to middle-income status.

For purposes of computing consumption income classes, the model projects changes in what share of the country's income is used for consumption using the following equation:

$$\ln(C_{i,t}) = \alpha_1 \times \ln(C_{i,t-1}) + \alpha_2 \times \ln(GDPPCCap_{i,t}) + \alpha_0 \qquad (11)$$

where t is the year, i is the country, C is the ratio of consumption to GDP, $GDPPCCap$ is the minimum of each country's GDP PPP per capita and USD50,000 PPP (in 2010 PPP international dollars), and α_0, α_1, and α_2 are constants.

The scenarios used in the book are described in Chapter 12. For all scenarios, the starting point is each country's status in 2013: 36 countries are rich (14 convergers, 11 partial convergers, and 11 non-converging), 34 converging, 110 non-converging, and 11 failed.[3]

In all uses of the model, individual countries' transitions between converging and non-converging or from failed to non-converging is gradual. That is, countries are made to adopt an intermediate state between failed and not-failed, or between converging and non-converging, by varying the values of f and c in Equations 9 and 10.

---

3. This adds up to more than 187 countries because it includes some countries for which projections are not made. The classification is taken from Kohli, Szyf, and Arnold (2012), which explains how it is derived, with the exception that the following 11 rich countries that Kohli, Szyf, and Arnold treat as non-convergers are instead treated as partial convergers with $C=0.5$ in Equation 9: Austria, Belgium, Canada, Denmark, France, Germany, Japan, the Netherlands, New Zealand, Slovenia, and Switzerland.

References

Acemoglu, Daron, and James A. Robinson. *Why Nations Fail*. New York: Crown Publishers, 2012.

Acemoglu, Daron, and Pierre Yared. "Trade and Militarism: The Political Limits to Globalisation." VoxEU.org. Published March 7, 2010. http://www.voxeu.org/article/political-limits-globalisation.

Acemoglu, Daron, James A. Robinson, and Thierry Verdier. "Choosing Your Own Capitalism in a Globalised World?" VoxEU.org. Published November 21, 2012. http://www.voxeu.org/article/cuddly-or-cut-throat-capitalism-choosing-models-globalised-world.

Acemoglu, Daron, Philippe Aghion, and Fabrizio Zilibotti. "Distance to Frontier, Selection, and Economic Growth." NBER Working Paper 9066, National Bureau of Economic Research, Cambridge, MA, July 2002.

ADB. *An Infrastructure Road Map for Kazakhstan*. Manila: Asian Development Bank, July 2012.

ADB. *Central Asia: Increasing Gains from Trade through Regional Cooperation in Trade Policy, Transport, and Customs Transit.* Manila: Asian Development Bank, 2006.

ADB. *Energy Outlook for Asia and the Pacific*. Mandaluyong City, Philippines: Asian Development Bank, 2009.

ADB. "Kazakhstan: A Private Sector Assessment – Developing A Strategy to Promote Faster Growth." Contract A72809, RSC-C13088 (KAZ), Asian Development Bank, Manila 2011.

ADB. *Managing Asian Cities: Sustainable and Inclusive Urban Solutions.* Manila: Asian Development Bank, June 2008.

ADB. *Sector Assessment (Summary): Multisector (Urban Transport, Water Supply and Sanitation, and Other Municipal Services).* Manila: Asian Development Bank, 2012.

Agency for Natural Resources and Energy. *Top Runner Program: Developing the World's Best Energy-Efficient Appliances*, revised edition. Tokyo: Ministry of Economy, Trade, and Industry, March 2010.

Agency of Statistics of the Republic of Kazakhstan. "Kazakhstan in Figures." Agency of Statistics of the Republic of Kazakhstan. Last updated July 11, 2013. http://www.eng.stat.kz/Pages/default.aspx.

Aggarwal, Vinod K., and Simon J. Evenett. "Industrial Policy Choice During the Crisis Era." *Oxford Review of Economic Policy* 28, no. 2 (Summer 2012): 261-283.

Alderman, Harold, ed. *No Small Matter: The Impact of Poverty, Shocks, and Human Capital Investment in Early Child Development*. Washington, DC: World Bank, 2011.

Alesina, Alberto, and Eliana La Ferrara. "Ethnic Diversity and Economic Performance." NBER Working Paper No. 10313. National Bureau of Economic Research, Cambridge, MA, February 2004.

Alfaro, Laura, and Maggie Xiaoyang Chen. "The Global Agglomeration of Multinational Firms." Working Paper 10-043, Harvard Business School, Harvard University, Cambridge, MA, October 22, 2012.

Altbach, Philip, and Jamil Salmi. *The Making of World Class Research Universities*. Washington, DC: World Bank, 2012.

Angel, Shlomo. *Planet of Cities*. Cambridge, MA: Lincoln Institute of Land Policy, September 2012.

Annez, Patricia Clarke, Gwenaelle Huet, and George E. Peterson. *Lessons for the Urban Century: Decentralized Infrastructure Finance in the World Bank.* Washington, DC: World Bank, 2008.

Archibugi, Daniele, Mario Denni, and Andrea Filippetti. "The Global Innovation Scoreboard 2008: The Dynamics of the Innovative Performances of Countries." Measuring Innovation Thematic Paper, Inno Metrics, Pro Inno Europe, Brussels, March 2009.

Armytage, Livingstone. *Searching for Success in Judicial Reform.* New Delhi: Oxford University Press, 2009.

Arvis, Jean-François, and Ben Shepherd. "The Air Connectivity Index: Measuring Integration in the Global Air Transport Network." Policy Research Working Paper 5722, International Trade Department, Poverty Reduction and Economic Management Network, World Bank, Washington, DC, June 2011.

Asian Productivity Organization. *Total Factor Productivity Growth: Survey Report.* Tokyo: Asian Productivity Organization, 2004.

Aslund, Anders. "Putin is Shocked by Falling Economic Growth, but We Should Not Be." Real Time Economic Issues Watch, Peterson Institute for International Economics. Published April 26, 2013. http://www.piie.com/blogs/realtime/?p=3547.

Bahl, Roy W., and Johannes F. Linn. *Urban Finance in Developing Countries.* New York: Oxford University Press, 1992.

Bahl, Roy W., Johannes F. Linn, and Deborah L. Wetzel, eds. *Financing Metropolitan Governments in Developing Countries.* Cambridge, MA: Lincoln Institute of Land Policy, 2013.

Baker and McKenzie. "Doing Business in Kazakhstan." Baker and McKenzie. Accessed July 22, 2012. www.bakermckenzie.com/uploads. 2009.

Baldwin, Richard. "Trade and Industrialisation after Globalisation's 2nd Unbundling: How Building and Joining a Supply Chain are Different and Why It Matters." NBER Working Paper No. 17,716, National Bureau of Economic Research, Cambridge, MA, December 2011.

Behar, Alberto. "Neighborhood Growth Effects: An Annual Panel Data Approach." Reshaping Economic Geography Background Paper, Centre for the Study of African Economies, Oxford University, Oxford, February 2008.

Berglof, Erik. *Transition without an Outside Anchor: The Experience of Caucasus and Central Asia*. Bishkek: European Bank for Reconstruction and Development, May 20, 2013.

Berlyne, Colin. "Astana: City with a Future." Edge Kazakhstan. Accessed July 19, 2013. http://www.edgekz.com/astana-city-with-a-future.html.

Berry, Albert, and John Serieux. "Riding the Elephants: The Evolution of World Economic Growth and Income Distribution at the End of the Twentieth Century (1980-2000)." DESA Working Paper No. 27, Department of Economic and Social Affairs, United Nations, New York, September 2006.

Bertaud, Alain. "Land Markets, Government Interventions, and Housing Affordability." Working Paper 18, Wolfensohn Center for Development, Brookings Institution, Washington, DC, May 2010.

Bertelsmann Foundation. "Measuring the Modern Social Market Economy." Policy Brief # 2012/04, Future Social Market Economy, Bertelsmann Stiftung, Gutersloh, Germany, 2012.

Bertelsmann Foundation. *Bertelsmann Transformation Index 2012: Kazakhstan Country Report*. Gutersloh, Germany: Bertelsmann Stiftung, 2012.

Betcherman, Gordon, Karina Olivas, and Amit Dar. "Impacts of Active Labor Market Programs: New Evidence from Evaluations with Particular Attention to Developing and Transition Countries." Social Protection Discussion Paper Series No. 0402, Social Protection Unit, Human Development Network, World Bank, Washington, DC, January 2004.

Bhattacharyya, Sambit, and Paul Collier. "Public Capital in Resource Rich Economies: Is There a Curse?" CSAE Working Paper 2011-14, Centre for the Study of African Economies, Department of Economics, University of Oxford, Oxford, August 10, 2011.

Bhuiyan, Shahjahan H. "Decentralization and Local Governance in Kazakhstan." *International Journal of Public Administration* 33, nos. 12-13 (2010): 658–672. doi: 10.1080/01900692.2010.514445.

Blank, Stephen. "Toward a New Chinese Order in Asia: Russia's Failure." NBR Special Report No. 26, National Bureau of Asian Research, Seattle, March 2011.

Bloom, Nicholas, Helena Schweiger, and John Van Reenen. "The Land That Lean Manufacturing Forgot? Management Practices in Transition Countries." CEP Discussion Papers dp 1065, Centre for Economic Performance, London School of Economics, London, July 2011.

BP. *BP Statistical Review of World Energy: June 2012*. London: British Petroleum, June 2012.

Breznitz, Dan. *Innovation and the State*. New Haven, CT: Yale University Press, 2011.

Brzezinski, Zbigniew. "The Cyber Age Demands New Rules of War." *Financial Times*. Published February 24 2013. http://www.ft.com/intl/cms/s/170b2a62-7c5a-11e2-99f0-00144feabdc0,Authorised=false.html?_i_location=http%3A%2F%2Fwww.ft.com%2Fcms%2Fs%2F0%2F170b2a62-7c5a-11e2-99f0-00144feabdc0.html%3Fsiteedition%3Duk&siteedition=uk&_i_referer=#axzz2o3T7WdLW.

Brockman, John. *The Next Fifty Years: Science in the First Half of the Twenty-First Century*. New York: Vintage Books, 2002.

Brockman, Max. *What's Next? Dispatches on the Future of Science: Original Essays from a New Generation of Scientists*. New York: Vintage Books, 2009.

Brookes, Graham, and Yaroslav Blume. "The Potential Economic and Environmental Impact of Using Current GM Traits in Russia's Arable Crop Production." Briefing Document, May 2012. Provided by Craig Rickard, Crop Life International.

Brown, William Y. "Conserving Biological Diversity." Policy Paper 2011-07, Global Economy and Development, Brookings Institution, Washington, DC, July 2011.

Brown, William Y. "Cultural Heritage and Development." Brookings Institution. Published September 14, 2011. http://www.brookings.edu/research/opinions/2011/09/14-cultural-heritage-development-brown.

Brown, William Y. "DNA Net Earth." Policy Paper 2013-01, Global Economy and Development, Brookings Institution, Washington, DC, March 2013.

Brown, William Y. "It's Time for a New Biotechnology Law." Brookings Institution. Published July 27, 2011. http://www.brookings.edu/research/opinions/2011/07/27-biotechnology-law-brown.

Brown, William Y. "Limits to Climate Change Mitigation and the Adaptation Imperative." Brookings Institution. Published February 7, 2012. www.brookings.edu/research/opinions/2012/02/07-climate-change-reality-brown.

Buiter, Willem, and Ebrahim Rahbari. "Global Growth Generators: Moving Beyond 'Emerging Markets' and 'BRIC'." VoxEU.org. Published April 22, 2011. http://www.voxeu.org/article/global-growth-generators-moving-beyond-emerging-markets-and-brics.

Bush, Robin. "Lessons from Indonesia's Democratic Transition." In Asia. Published May 4, 2011. http://asiafoundation.org/in-asia/2011/05/04/lessons-from-indonesia's-democratic-transition/.

Campos, Nauro F., Vitaliy Kuzeyev, and Ahmad Saleh. "Dynamic Ethnic Fractionalization and Economic Growth in the Transition Economies from 1989 to 2007." CEPR Discussion Papers No. 7586, Center for Economic and Policy Research, Washington, DC, December 2009.

Canadian, American, and Australia Wheat Organizations. "Wheat Biotechnoloy Commercialization: Statement of Canadian, American, and Australian Wheat Organizations." National Association of Wheat Growers. Accessed July 18, 2013. http://www.wheatworld.org/wp-content/uploads/biotech-updated-trilateral-statement-20101206.pdf.

Carbon Tax Center. "What's a Carbon Tax?" Carbon Tax Center. Last modified September 17, 2013. http://www.carbontax.org/introduction/#why.

Carbon Tax Center. "Vs. Cap-Trade." Carbon Tax Center. Last modified March 22, 2011. http://www.carbontax.org/issues/carbon-taxes-vs-cap-and-trade/.

CAREC. "Draft 10-Year Commemorative Study Part 1 (Stock-Take): Appendices." Reference Document for the Working Dinner, 9th Ministerial Conference on Central Asia Regional Economic Cooperation, Cebu, Philippines, October 30, 2010.

Carlin, Wendy, Mark Schaffer, and Paul Seabright. "Soviet Power Plus Electrification: What is the Long-Run Legacy of Communism?" Working Paper No. 43, Dipartimento di Studi sullo Sviluppo Economico, Università degli Studi di Macerata, Macerata, Italy, June 2012.

Castells, Manuel, and Peter Hall. *Technopoles of the World: The Making of 21st Century Industrial Complexes*. London: Routledge, 1994.

Castro, Manuel Fernando. "Insider Insights: Building a Results-Based Management and Evaluation System in Colombia." ECD Working Paper No. 18, Independent Evaluation Group, World Bank, Washington, DC, September 2009.

Chaibong, Hahm. "South Korea's Miraculous Democracy." *Journal of Democracy* 19, no. 3 (July 2008): 128-142.

Cisco. "Broadband and the Opportunity to Accelerate Economic and Social Development in Kazakhstan." Global Technology Policy Country Note Series, Cisco, March 2013.

Cline, William R. *Global Warming and Agriculture: Impact Estimates by Country.* Washington, DC: Center for Global Development and the Peterson Institute for International Economics, 2007.

Cockcroft, Laurence. *Global Corruption: Money, Power and Ethics in the Modern World.* Philadelphia: University of Pennsylvania Press, 2012.

Cohen, Ariel. *Kazakhstan: The Road to Independence*. Washington: Central Asia-Caucasus Institute and Silk Road Studies Program Joint Center, 2008.

Collins, Kathleen. *Clan Politics and Regime Transition in Central Asia*. New York: Cambridge University Press, 2006.

Comin, Diego, and Bart Hobijn. "An Exploration of Technology Diffusion." NBER Working Papers No. 12314, National Bureau of Economic Research, Cambridge, MA, June 2006.

Comin, Diego, and Bart Hobijn. "Technology Diffusion and Postwar Growth." In *NBER Macroeconomics Annual 2010*, vol. 25, edited by Daron Acemoglu and Michael Woodford. Cambridge, MA: NBER Books, 2011.

Commander, Simon, and Zlatko Nikoloski. "Institutions and Economic Performance: What Can Be Explained?" Working Paper No. 121, European Bank for Reconstruction and Development, London, 2010.

Conference Board. *2013 Productivity Brief: Key Findings*. New York: Conference Board, 2013.

Conti, John, and Paul Holtberg. *International Energy Outlook 2011*. Washington, DC: US Energy Information Administration, 2011.

Convention on Biological Diversity. "Aichi Biodiversity Targets." Convention on Biological Diversity. Accessed July 18, 2013. http://www.cbd.int/sp/targets/.

Core Writing Team, Rajendra K. Pachauri, and Andy Reisinger, eds. *Climate Change 2007: Synthesis Report.* Geneva: Intergovernmental Panel on Climate Change, 2007.

Corrado, Carol A., Charles R. Hulten, and Daniel E. Sichel. "Intangible Economic Growth." NBER Working Paper No. 11948, National Bureau of Economic Research, Cambridge, MA, January 2006.

Coulibaly, Souleymane et al. *Eurasian Cities: New Realities along the Silk Road.* Washington, DC: World Bank, 2012.

Cowen, Tyler. *The Great Stagnation*. New York: Dutton, 2011.

Cullen, Heidi. *The Weather of the Future: Heat Waves, Extreme Storms, and Other Scenes from a Climate-Changed Planet.* New York: HarperCollins, 2010.

Dabla-Norris, Era. "The Challenge of Fiscal Decentralisation in Transition." *Comparative Economic Studies* 48, no.1 (March 2006): 100-131.

Das, Mitali, and Papa N'Diaye. "Chronicle of a Decline Foretold: Has China Reached the Lewis Turning Point?" IMF Working Paper 13/26, Research Department and Asia and Pacific Department, International Monetary Fund, Washington, DC, January 2013.

Davé, Bhavna. "Kazakhstan." In *Nations in Transit 2012*, 259-78. Washington, DC: Freedom House, 2012.

Davis, Kevin E. "Institutions and Economic Performance: An Introduction to the Literature." Working Paper No. 09-51, Law & Economics Research Paper Series, Center for Law, Economics and Organization, New York University, New York, December 2009.

DeLong, Bradford J. "Let It Bleed?" Project Syndicated. Published March 28, 2013. http://www.project-syndicate.org/commentary/the-great-depression-redux-by-j--bradford-delong.

de Mooji, Ruud A., Michael Keen, and Ian W. H. Parry, eds. *Fiscal Policy to Mitigate Climate Change: A Guide for Policymakers.* Washington, DC: International Monetary Fund, 2012.

Di Tella, Rafael. "Kazakhstan: Institutions." In "Growth and Competitiveness in Kazakhstan: Issues and Priorities in the Areas of Macroeconomic, Industrial, Trade, and Institutional Development Policies," Ricardo Hausmann, Akash Deep, Rafael Di Tella, et al. Working Paper, Center for International Development, Harvard University, Cambridge, MA, 2011.

Djamankulov, Nuritdin. *SPS Regulations and Access of Kyrgyz Goods to the Customs Union*. Bishkek: USAID Regional Trade Liberalization and Customs Project, April 2011.

Dopazo, Cesar et al. "An Infrastructure Road Map for Kazakhstan." Technical Assistance Consultant's Report, Asian Development Bank, Manila, November 2012.

Earth System Research Laboratory. "Trends in Atmospheric Carbon Dioxide." Global Monitoring Division, Earth System Research Laboratory, National Oceanic and Atmospheric Administration, US Department of Commerce. Accessed July 18, 2013. http://www.esrl.noaa.gov/gmd/ ccgg/trends/weekly.html.

Easterly, William, and Ross Levine. "Africa's Growth Tragedy: Policies and Ethnic Divisions." *Quarterly Journal of Economics* 112, no. 4 (November 1997): 1203-1250. doi: 10.1162/003355300555466.

EBRD. "Forecasts, Macro Data, Transition Indicators." European Bank for Reconstruction and Development. Last modified June 7, 2013. http://www.ebrd.com/pages/research/economics/data/macro.shtml.

EBRD. "Governance and Public Service Delivery." In *Life in Transition: After the Crisis*. London: European Bank for Reconstruction and Development, June 2012.

EBRD. *Transition Report 2012: Integration across Borders*. London: European Bank for Reconstruction and Development, 2012.

Economist.com. "The Cost of Driving." Economist.com. Published April 4, 2013. http://www.economist.com/blogs/graphicdetail/2013/04/daily-chart-2.

Edwards, Sebastian. *Left Behind: Latin America and the False Promise of Populism*. Chicago: University of Chicago Press, 2012.

EIA. "International Energy Statistics." US Energy Information Administration. Accessed July 18, 2013. http://www.eia.gov/countries/data.cfm#undefined.

EITI. *Secretariat Review: Kazakhstan*. Oslo: Extractive Industries Transparency Initiative International Secretariat, 2012.

Ekstrom, Vicki. "China's Pollution Puts a Dent in Its Economy." MITnews. Published February 13, 2012. http://web.mit.edu/newsoffice/2012/global-change-china-air-economy-0213.html.

Esserkepova, Irina, ed. *Kazakhstan's Second National Communication to the Conference of the Parties of the United Nations Framework Convention on Climate Change*. Astana: Ministry of Environment Protection, 2009.

Etzkowitz, Henry. *MIT and the Rise of Entrepreneurial Science.* London: Routledge, 2002

Euromonitor International. "Kazakhstan's Urbanisation Trends Shape Business Opportunities." Published July 27, 2010. http://www.1-property.ru/e-news/3094.

European Forum for Democracy and Solidarity. "Kazakhstan." European Forum for Democracy and Solidarity. Last updated September 26, 2012. http://www.europeanforum.net/country/kazakhstan.

European Observatory on Health Systems and Policies. "Kazakhstan Health System Review." In *Health Systems in Transition* 14, no. 4 (2012).

Evans, Stephen. *Apprenticeships in London: Boosting Skills in a City Economy*. Paris: OECD and LEED, 2012.

Evenson, R.E., Denisard C.O. Alves, and Tatiane de Menezes. "Agricultural Technology Change and Climate Change Impacts." Center for Business and the Environment, Yale University. Published September 1, 2004. http://cbey.yale.edu/uploads/File/evenson_1.pdf.

FAO. *Greening the Economy with Agriculture*. Rome: Food and Agriculture Organization, 2012.

Fay, Marianne, Rachel I. Block, and Jane Ebinger, eds. "Adapting to Climate Change in Eastern Europe and Central Asia." No. 52862, World Bank, Washington, DC, 2010.

Fernández-Arias, Eduardo, Ugo Panizza, and Ernesto Stein. "Trade Agreements, Exchange Rate Disagreements." In *Monetary Unions and Hard Pegs: Effects on Trade, Financial Development, and Stability*, edited by Volbert Alexander, Jacques Mélitz , and George von Furstenburg. Oxford: Oxford University Press, 2004.

Ferré, Céline, Francisco H.G. Ferreira, and Peter Lanjouw. "Is There a Metropolitan Bias? The Inverse Relationship between Poverty and City Size in Selected Developing Countries." Policy Research Working Paper 5508, Poverty and Inequality Team, Development Research Group, World Bank, Washington, DC, December 2010.

Flannery, Tim, Roger Beale, and Gerry Hueston. *The Critical Decade: International Action on Climate Change.* Canberra: Climate Commission Secretariat, Department of Climate Change and Energy Efficiency, Commonwealth of Australia, 2012.

Florida, Richard. *The Creative Class (Revisited)*. New York: Basic Books, 2012.

Fontes, Nuno. "Swiss Economy Grows More Than Expected in Q1." Trading Economics. Published May 30, 2013. http://www.tradingeconomics.com/switzerland/gdp-growth.

Foreign Agricultural Service. *Commodity Intelligence Report: Kazakhstan Agricultural Overview*. Washington, DC: United States Department of Agriculture, January 2010.

Frankel, Jeffrey A. "The Natural Resource Curse: A Survey." NBER Working Paper 15836, National Bureau of Economic Research, Cambridge, MA, March 2010.

Freedom House. *Nations in Transit 2011.* Washington: Freedom House, 2011.

Freedom House. *Nations in Transit 2012.* Washington: Freedom House, 2012.

Freeman, Chris. "The 'National System of Innovation' in Historical Perspective." *Cambridge Journal of Economics* 19, no. 1 (1995): 5-24.

Freinkman, Lev, Evgeny Polyakov, and Carolina Revenco. *Trade Performance and Regional Integration of the CIS Countries*. Washington, DC: World Bank, 2004.

Frey, Miriam, and Carmen Wieslhuber. "Do Kazakh Regions Converge?" Kurzanalysen und Informationen no. 52, Arbeitsbereich Wirtschaft, Migration Und Integration, Osteuropa-Institut, Regensburg, Germany, August 2011.

Frost and Sullivan. "Frost and Sullivan: Recycling and Recovery Drive the Industrial Waste Management Services Market in Europe." Frost and Sullivan. Published September 22, 2011. http://www.frost.com/prod/servlet/press-release.pag?docid=242671976.

Gallup, John Luke, and Jeffrey D. Sachs. "Geography and Economic Development." CID Working Paper No. 1, Center for International Development, Harvard University, March 1999.

Gill, Indermit, and Homi Kharas. *An East Asian Renaissance: Ideas for Economic Growth*. Washington, DC: World Bank, 2007.

Glaeser, Edward. *Triumph of the City.* New York: Penguin, 2011.

Glewwe, Paul, and Michael Kremer. "Schools, Teachers, and Education Outcomes in Developing Countries." In Vol. 1 of *Handbook of the Economics of Education*, edited by Eric Hanushek and Finis Welch. Amsterdam: North-Holland, 2006.

GMO Safety. "Field Trials in Australia." Research Grain, GMO Safety. Published August 12, 2008. http://www.gmo-safety.eu/science/grain/583.drought-tolerant-wheat-promising.html.

Goldberg, Itzhak, and John Nellis. "Methods and Institutions: How do they Matter? Lessons from Privatization and Restructuring in the Post-Soviet Transition." In *Privatization in Transition Economies: The Ongoing Story*, vol. 90, edited by Ira W. Lieberman and Daniel J. Kopf. Oxford: JAI Press, 2007.

Goldstone, Jack. "Rise of the TIMBIs." Foreign Policy. Published December 2, 2011. http://www.foreignpolicy.com/articles/2011/12/02/rise_of_the_timbis.

Gordon, Robert J. "Is US Economic Growth Over? Faltering Innovation Confronts the Six Headwinds." NBER Working Paper No. 18315. National Bureau of Economic Research, Cambridge, MA, August 2012.

Gough, Myles. "Greenpeace Destroys CSIRO Wheat GM Trial.*"* Cosmos Online. Published July 14, 2011. http://www.cosmosmagazine.com/news/greenpeace-targets-csiro-crops/.

Graham, Carol. *The Pursuit of Happiness: An Economy of Well-Being*. Washington, DC: Brookings Institution Press, 2011.

Greif, Avner. *Institutions and the Path to the Modern Economy,* Cambridge: Cambridge University Press, 2006.

Gupta, Nandini."Partial Privatization and Firm Performance." *The Journal of Finance* 60, no. 2 (2005): 987-1015.

Gupta, Sanjeev, Alvar Kangur, Chris Papageorgiou, and Abdoul Wane. "Efficiency-Adjusted Public Capital and Growth." IMF Working Paper 11/217, Fiscal Affairs Department and Strategy, Policy, and Review Department, International Monetary Fund, Washington, DC, September 2011.

Gurenko, Eugene, and Denis Dumitru. *Mitigating the Adverse Financial Effects of Natural Hazards on the Economies of Central Asia.* Washington, DC: World Bank, ISDR, and CAREC, 2009.

Hanna, Rema et al. "The Effectiveness of Anti-Corruption Policy: What Has Worked, What Hasn't, and What We Don't Know." Technical Report, EPPI Centre, Social Science Research Institute, Institute of Education, University of London, London, 2011.

Hanushek Eric, and Steven G. Rivkin. "Teacher Quality." In Vol. 2 of *Handbook of the Economics of Education*, edited by Eric Hanushek and Finis Welch. Amsterdam: North-Holland, 2006.

Hausmann, Ricardo, Laura D. Tyson, and Saadia Zahidi. *The Global Gender Gap Report 2012*. Geneva: World Economic Forum, 2012.

Heckman, James, and Carmen Pagés-Serra. "The Cost of Job Security Regulation: Evidence from Latin American Labor Markets." *Economia: The Journal of the Latin American and Caribbean Economic Association* 1, no. 1 (2000): 109-54.

Heckman, James, Rodrigo Pinto, and Peter A. Savelyev. "Understanding the Mechanisms through Which an Influential Early Childhood Program Boosted Adult Outcomes." NBER Working Paper No. 18581, National Bureau of Economic Research, Cambridge, MA, November 2012.

Heckman, James. "The Case for Investing in Disadvantaged Young Children." In *Big Ideas for Children: Investing in Our Nation's Future*, 49-58. Washington, DC: First Focus, 2008.

Heinemann, Alessandra, and Dorte Verner. "Crime and Violence in Development: A Literature Review of Latin America and the Caribbean." World Bank Policy Research Working Paper 4041, World Bank, Washington, DC, October 2006.

Henderson, Rebecca M., and Richard G. Newell. *Accelerating Energy Innovation: Insights from Multiple Sectors*. Chicago: University of Chicago Press, 2011.

Henderson, Vernon. "Urbanization in Developing Countries." *The World Bank Research Observer* 17, no. 1 (Spring 2002): 89-112.

Her Majesty's Government. *Building a Stronger Civil Society: A Strategy for Voluntary and Community Groups, Charities, and Social Enterprises.* London: Office for Civil Society, 2010.

Hickman, Silke. "Conservation Agriculture in Northern Kazakhstan and Mongolia." Agricultural and Food Engineering Working Document 4, FAO, Rome, 2006.

Howitt, Peter. "Schumpeterian Growth Theory." *Economic Dynamics Newsletters* 3, no. 2 (April 2002).

Huebner, Jonathan. "A Possible Declining Trend for Worldwide Innovation." *Technological Forecasting and Social Change* 72 (2005): 980-986. doi:10.1016/j.techfore.2005.01.003.

Hulten, Charles R. "Total Factor Productivity: A Short Biography." In *New Developments in Productivity Analysis*, edited by Charles R. Hulten, Edwin R. Dean, and Michael J. Harper, 1-54. Chicago: University of Chicago Press, 2001.

Humphreys, Macartan, Joffrey D. Sachs, and Joseph E. Stiglitz. *Escaping the Resource Curse*. New York: Columbia University Press, 2007.

ICG. "China's Central Asia Problem." Asia Report No. 244, International Crisis Group, Brussels, February 27, 2013.

IEA. *Environmental and Health Impacts of Electricity Generation*. Paris: International Energy Agency, June 2002.

IEA. *World Energy Outlook 2012*. Paris: Organization for Economic Co-operation and Development/International Energy Agency, 2012.

IMF. "Globalization: A Brief Overview." *International Monetary Fund Issues Brief* 2, no. 8 (May 2008): 1-8. www.imf.org/external/np/exr/ib/2008/053008.htm.

IMF. "Republic of Kazakhstan, 2012 Article 4 Consultation." IMF Country Report No. 12/164, International Monetary Fund, Washington, DC, June 2012.

"Innovation in Energy 2013." Financial Times. Published Jan. 28, 2013. http://www.ft.com/intl/reports/innova-tions-energy-2013.

International Association for the Evaluation of Educational Achievement. "TIMSS 2011." TIMSS and PIRLS International Study Center, Lynch School of Education, Boston College. Published December 11, 2012. http://timss.bc.edu/timss2011/index.html.

International Service for the Acquisition of Agri-biotech Applications. "Drought Tolerant GM Wheat Makes Great Progress in China." *Crop Biotech Update* (June 17, 2011).

Isakova, Asel, Zsoka Koczan, and Alexander Plekhanov. "How Much Do Tariffs Matter? Evidence from the Customs Union of Belarus, Kazakhstan, and Russia." Working Paper No. 154, European Bank for Reconstruction and Development, London, January 2013.

Islamov, Bakhtior. *The Central Asian States Ten Years After: How to Overcome Traps of Development, Transformation, and Globalisation?* Tokyo: Maruzen, 2001.

James, Clive. "Global Status of Commercialized/Biotech GM Crops: 2012." ISAA Brief No. 4, International Service for the Acquisition of Agri-biotech Applications, Ithaca, NY, 2012.

Jandosov, Oraz, and Lyaziza Sabyrova. "Indicative Tariff Protection Level in Kazakhstan: Before and After the Customs Union (Part 1)." RAKURS Discussion Paper 5.3, Almaty, March 6, 2011.

Jorgenson, Dale W., and Khuong Vu. "The Rise of Developing Asia and the New Economic Order." *Journal of Policy Modeling* 33, no. 5 (2011): 698-751.

Jorgenson, Dale W., Mun S. Ho, and Kevin J. Stiroh. "A Retrospective Look at the US Productivity Growth Resurgence." *Journal of Economics Perspectives* 22, no. 1 (2008): 3-24. doi: 10.1257/jep.22.1.3.

Jovanovic, Boyan, and Peter L. Rousseau. "General Purpose Technologies." NBER Working Paper 11093. National Bureau of Economic Research, Cambridge, MA, January 2005.

Junussova, Madina. "Key Impacts of Economic Integration of Kazakhstan on Spatial Development of Its Settlements." REAL CORP 2012, 17th International Conference on Urban Planning, Regional Development, and Information Society, Vienna, May 2012.

Kadyrzhanov, Rustem. "Decentralization and Local Self-governance in Kazakhstan: An Institutional Analysis." Workshop in Political Theory and Policy Analysis, Indiana University, Spring 2005.

Kaiser, David. *Becoming MIT: Moments of Decision*. Cambridge, MA: MIT Press, 2010.

Kalyuzhnova, Yelena. "The National Fund of the Republic of Kazakhstan (NFRK): From Accumulation to Stress-Test to Global Future." *Energy Policy* 39, no. 10 (October 2011): 6650-6657. doi: 10.1016/j.enpol.2011.08.026.

Kassenova, Nargis, Alexander Libman, and Jeremy Smith. "Discussing the Eurasian Customs Union and Its Impact on Central Asia." Central Asia Policy Forum no. 4, Elliot School of International Affairs, George Washington University, Washington, DC, February 2013.

Katsaga, Alexander, Maksut Kluzhanov, Marina Karanikolos, and Bernd Rechel. "Kazakhstan: Health System in Review." *Health Systems in Transition* 14, no. 4 (2012): 1-154.

Kaufmann, Daniel, Aart Kraay, and Massimo Mastruzzi. "The Worldwide Governance Indicators: Methodology and Analytical Issues." Policy Research Working Paper 5430, Development Research Group, The World Bank, Washington, DC, September, 2010.

Kemme, David M. "Sovereign Wealth Fund Issues and the National Fund of Kazakhstan." US State Department Title VIII Grant Report, Department of Economics, University of Memphis, Memphis, TN, December 15, 2011.

Kharas, Homi. "Latin America: Is Average Good Enough?" In *Latin America 2040: Breaking Away from Complacency: An Agenda for Resurgence*, edited by Drew Arnold, Jose Fajgenbaum, Vonid K. Goel, Tamara Ortega Goodspeed, Homi Kharas, Harinder S. Kohli, Harpaul Alberto Kohli, Claudio M. Loser, Nora Lustig, Jeffrey M. Puryear, Michael Shifter, Anil Sood, Y. Aaron Szyf. New Dehli: SAGE, 2010.

Kharas, Homi, and Harinder Kohli. "What Is the Middle Income Trap, Why do Countries Fall into It, and How Can It Be Avoided?" *Global Journal of Emerging Market Economies* 3, no. 3 (September 2011): 281-289. doi: 10.1177/097491011100300302.

Kharas, Homi, and Johannes F. Linn. "External Assistance for Urban Finance Development: Needs, Strategies and Implementation." In *Financing Metropolitan Governments in Developing Countries*, edited by Roy W. Bahl, Johannes F. Linn, and Deborah L. Wetzel. Cambridge, MA: Lincoln Institute of Land Policy, 2013.

Kimura, Osamu. "Japanese Top Runner Approach for Energy Efficiency Standards." SERC Discussion Paper SERC09035, Socio-economic Research Center, Central Research Institute of Electric Power Industry, Tokyo, 2010.

Klitgaard, Robert. "Toward Results-Based Government in Colombia." Claremont Graduate University, Claremont, CA, March 2012.

Kohli, Atul. "Where Do High Growth Political Economies Come From? The Japanese Lineage of Korea's 'Developmental State'." *World Development* 22, no. 9 (1994): 1269-1293.

Kohli, Harpaul Alberto, Y. Aaron Szyf, and Drew Arnold. "Construction and Analysis of a Global GDP Growth Model for 185 Countries through 2050." *Global Journal of Emerging Market Economies* 4, no. 2 (May 2012): 91–153. doi: 10.1177/09749101120040020.

Kosolapova, Trend E. "Crime Rate Increases in Kazakhstan." Trend. Published October 8, 2012. http://en.trend.az/regions/casia/kazakhstan/2074382.html.

Kuijs, Louis. "Economic Growth Patterns and Strategies in China and India: Past and Future." Working Paper FGI-2012-2, Fung Global Institute, Hong Kong, September 2012.

Lamy, Pascal. "Speech of June 26, 2012." WTO News, World Trade Organization. Published June 26, 2012. http://www.wto.org/english/news_e/sppl_e/sppl239_e.htm.

Laruelle, Marlene, and Sebastien Peyrouse. *Globalizing Central Asia: Geopolitics and the Challenges of Economic Development.* Armonk, NY: M.E. Sharpe, 2013.

Laruelle, Marlene, and Sebastien Peyrouse. "Regional Organisations in Central Asia: Patterns of Interaction, Dilemmas of Efficiency." Working Paper No. 10, Graduate School of Development, Institute of Public Policy and Administration, University of Central Asia, Bishkek, 2012.

Lederman, Daniel, and William F. Maloney. *Natural Resources: Neither Curse nor Destiny*. Palo Alto, CA: Stanford University Press, 2007.

Lee, Il Houng, Murtaza Syed, and Liu Xueyan. "Is China Over-Investing and Does It Matter?" IMF Working Paper 12/277, Asia and Pacific Department, International Monetary Fund, Washington, DC, November 2012.

Lenoir, Timothy. "Revolution from Above: The Role of the State in Creating the German Research System, 1810-1910." *American Economic Review* 88, no. 22 (May 1998): 22-27.

Levy, Santiago. *Good Intentions, Bad Outcomes: Social Policy, Informality, and Economic Growth in Mexico*. Washington, DC: Brookings Institution Press, 2008.

Levy, Santiago. *Progress against Poverty: Sustaining Mexico's Progresa-Oportunidades Program*. Washington, DC: Brookings Press, 2006.

Lewis, Joanna. *Green Innovation in China*. New York: Columbia University Press, 2012.

Leydesdorff, Loet, and Grima Zawdie. "The Triple Helix Perspective of Innovation Systems." *Technology Analysis and Strategic Management* 22, no. 7 (2010): 789-804. doi: 10.1080/09537325.2010.511142.

Libman, Alexander, and Daria Ushkalova. "Post-Soviet Countries in Global and Regional Institutional Competition: The Case of Kazakhstan." MPRA Paper No. 12595, Munich Personal RePEc Archive, January 2009.

Libman, Alexander, and Evgeny Vinokurov. *Holding-Together Regionalism: Twenty Years of Post-Soviet Integration.* Basingstoke, UK: Palgrave Macmillan, 2012.

Limaye Dilip R., and Emily S. Limaye. "Scaling Up Energy Efficiency: The Case for a Super ESCO." *Energy Efficiency* 4 (2011): 133-144. doi: 10.1007/s12053-011-9119-5.

Linn, Johannes F. "Central Asia Regional Integration and Cooperation: Reality or Mirage?" In *Eurasian Integration Yearbook 2012*, edited by Evgeny Vinokurov. Almaty: Eurasian Development Bank, 2012.

Linn, Johannes F. *Cities in the Developing World: Policies for Their Equitable and Efficient Growth.* New York: Oxford University Press, 1983.

Linn, Johannes F. *Economic (Dis)Integration Matters: The Soviet Collapse Revisited*. Washington, DC: Brookings Institution, 2004.

Linn, Johannes F. "The Impending Water Crisis in Central Asia: An Immediate Threat." Brookings Institution. Published June 19, 2008. http://www.brookings.edu/opinions/2008/0619_central_asia_linn.aspx.

Linn, Johannes F. "Managing Compound Risks in Central Asia: A Regional Overview." Overview Paper, Conference on "Improving Regional Coordination in Managing Compound Risks in Central Asia," Almaty, April 2011.

Linn, Johannes F. "Water-Energy Links in Central Asia: A Long-Term Opportunity and Challenge." Brookings Institution. Published June 30, 2008. http://www.brookings.edu/opinions/2008/0630_central_asia_linn.aspx.

Linn, Johannes F., Arntraud Hartmann, Homi Kharas, Richard Kohl, Johannes F. Linn, and Barbara Massler. "Scaling Up the Fight Against Rural Poverty: An Institutional Review of IFAD's Approach." Global Working Paper No. 39., Brookings, Washington, DC, October 26, 2010.

Linn, Johannes F., and David Tiomkin. "The New Impetus towards Economic Integration between Europe and Asia." *Asia Europe Journal* 4, no. 1 (April 2006): 31-41. doi: 10.1007/s10308-006-0046-6.

Loser, Claudio, and Harinder Kohli, eds. *Mexico: A New Vision for Mexico 2042.* Washington, DC: Centennial Group, 2012.

Lundvall, Bengt-Ake. "Innovation System Research and Policy: Where It Came From and Where It Might Go." CAS Seminar, Oslo, December 4, 2007.

Mahbubani, Kishore. *The Great Convergence: Asia, the West, and the Logic of One World*. New York: Public Affairs, 2013.

Makhmutova, Meruert. "Urbanization in Kazakhstan: Issues and Perspectives." Public Policy Research Center, Almaty, October 2012.

Makhmutova, Meruert, and Aitzhan Akhmetova (2011). "Civil Society Index in Kazakhstan: Strengthening Civil Society." CIVICUS Civil Society Index 2008-2010, Analytical Country Report, Public Policy Research Center, CIVICUS, and European Union, Almaty, March 2011.

Maliranta, Mika, Niku Maattanen, and Vesa Vihriala. (2012). "Are the Nordic Countries Really Less Innovative Than the US?" VoxEU.org. Published December 19, 2012. www.voxeu.org/article/nordic-innovation-cuddly-capitalism-really-less-innovative.

Mauro, Paolo. "Corruption and Growth." *The Quarterly Journal of Economics* 110, no. 3 (August 1995): 681-712.

McKibbin, Warwick, Adele Morris, Peter Wilcoxen, and Yiyong Cai. "The Potential Role of a Carbon Tax in US Fiscal Reform." Climate and Energy Economics Discussion Paper, The Climate and Energy Economics Project, Brookings Institution, Washington, DC, July 24, 2012.

Meadows, Donella, Jorgen Randers, and Dennis Meadows. *Limits to Growth: The 30-Year Update.* White River Junction, VT: Chelsea Green, 2004.

Meisenzahl, Ralf R. and Joel Mokyr. "Is Education Policy Innovation Policy?" VoxEU.org. Published June 13, 2001. http://www.voxeu.org/article/education-policy-innovation-policy.

Ministry of Agriculture of Kazakhstan Republic. *Country Report on the State of Plant Genetic Resources for Food and Agriculture in the Kazakhstan Republic*. Rome: FAO, 2007.

Ministry of Finance of the Republic of Kazakhstan. "Official Web Site of the Ministry of Finance of the Republic of Kazakhstan." Accessed July 4, 2013. http://www.minfin.gov.kz/irj/portal/anonymous.

Ministry of Health, Republic of Kazakhstan, and Oxford Policy Management (2010 and 2011). "Phase II: Twinning Arrangements for Health Capacity Building and Strengthening Strategic Purchasing," Kazakhstan Health Technology Transfers and Institutional Reform project, Report Activity B3, C2, C4, C7 and C9.

Ministry of Labor and Social Protection of the Population of the Republic of Kazakhstan. "Ministry of Labor and Social Protection of the Population of the Republic of Kazakhstan." Ministry of Labor and Social Protection of the Population of the Republic of Kazakhstan. Accessed July 25, 2013. http://www.enbek.gov.kz/en/frontpage.

Mogilevskii, Roman. "Re-export Activities in Kyrgyzstan: Issues and Prospects." Working Paper No. 9, Graduate School of Development, Institute of Public Policy and Administration, University of Central Asia, 2012.

Mogilevskii, Roman. "Trends and Patterns in Foreign Trade of Central Asian Countries." Working Paper No. 1, Institute of Public Policy and Administration, Graduate School of Development, University of Central Asia, Bishkek, 2012.

Morris, Adele C. "Proposal 11: The Many Benefits of a Carbon Tax." The Hamilton Project, Brookings Institution, Washington, DC, February 2013.

Morris, Ian. *Why the West Rules—for Now.* New York: Farrar, Straus and Giroux, 2010.

Mowery, David C. "Federal Policy and the Development of Seminconductors, Computer Hardware, and Computer Software: A Policy Model for Climate Change R&D?" In *Accelerating Energy Innovation: Insights from Multiple Sectors*, edited by Rebecca M. Henderson and Richard G. Newell, 159-188. Chicago: University of Chicago Press, 2011.

Mueser, Oliver, and Carsten Giersch. "Preparing for Leadership Succession – Political Risk Scenarios in Central Asia." Global Risk Affair. Published March 31, 2012. http://www.globalriskaffairs.com/?s=preparing+for+leadership+succession.

Muralidharan, Karthik, and Venkatesh Sundararaman. "Teacher Performance Pay: Experimental Evidence from India." *Journal of Political Economy* 119, no. 1 (February 2011): 39-77. doi: 10.1086/659655.

Muralidharan, Karthik, and Venkatesh Sundararaman. "Teacher Performance Pay: Experimental Evidence from India." NBER Working Paper No. 15323, National Bureau of Economic Research, Cambridge, MA, September 2009.

Muzalevsky, Roman. "Turkey Looks Forward, Talks SCO." *Eurasia Daily Monitor* 10, no. 27 (February 13, 2013).

MVV decon. *Energy Efficiency Law in the Republic of Kazakhstan*. Mannheim, Germany: MVV decon, March 2010.

NAC of Nazarbayev University. *Determinants of the Strategic Course of Kazakhstan's Modernization till 2050: Stage 1.* Astana: NAC of Nazarbayev University, 2013.

NAC of Nazarbayev University. *General Transfers (Budgetary Subventions and Budgetary Withdrawals).* Astana: NAC of Nazarbayev University, 2013.

NAC of Nazarbayev University. *Government's Participation in the Economy and Barriers for Foreign Investors*. Astana: NAC of Nazarbayev University, January 2013.

NAC of Nazarbayev University. *Kazakhstan's Development Strategies: Monitoring and Assessment*. Astana: NAC of Nazarbayev University, January 2013.

NAC of Nazarbayev University. *Place of Kazakhstan in the Socio-economic, Political, and Ecological Rankings.* Astana: NAC of Nazarbayev University, 2012.

NAC of Nazarbayev University. *Policy Brief on the Course of Decentralization Reform and Inter-budget Relations in the Republic of Kazakhstan in 2001-2012*. Astana: NAC of Nazarbayev University, 2012.

NAC of Nazarbayev University. *Review of Administrative Reforms and Perspective Directions of Public Administration System in the Republic of Kazakhstan*. Astana: NAC of Nazarbayev University, November 2012.

National Center for the Education Quality Assessment. *National Report on Education System State and Development*. Astana: National Center for the Education Quality Assessment, 2011.

Naudeau, Sophie, Sebastian Martinez, Patrick Premand, and Deon Filmer. "Cognitive Development among Young Children in Low-Income Countries." In *No Small Matter: The Interaction of Poverty, Shocks, and Human Capital Investment*, edited by Harold Alderman, 9-50. Washington, DC: World Bank, 2011.

Nazarbayev, Nursultan. "Address by the President of the Republic, Leader of the Nation, N. A. Nazarbayev: Strategy Kazakhstan 2050, New Political Course of the Established State." Astana, 2012.

NERA Economic Consulting and Bloomberg New Energy Finance. *The Demand for Greenhouse Gas Emissions Reduction Investments: An Investor's Marginal Abatement Cost Curve for Kazakhstan.* London: NERA Economic Consulting, October 2011.

Nickell, Stephen, and Richard Layard. "Labor Market Institutions and Economic Performance." In Vol. 3 of *Handbook of Labor Economics,* edited by Orley C. Ashenfelter and David Card, 3029-84. Amsterdam: North-Holland 1999.

Nolan, Peter. *Is China Buying the World*. London, Polity, 2012.

North, Douglass C. *Institutions, Institutional Change, and Economic Performance*. New York: Cambridge University Press, 1990.

NRC. *Climate Stabilization Targets: Emissions, Concentrations, and Impacts over Decades to Millennia*. Washington, DC: The National Academies Press, 2011.

NRC. *The Impact of Genetically Engineered Crops on Farm Sustainability in the United States*. Washington, DC: The National Academies Press, 2010.

NRC. *Transgenic Plants and World Agriculture*. Washington, DC: The National Academies Press, 2000.

OECD. "2012 Kazakhstan Private Sector Survey Results." Regulations for Competiveness Project and Regional Competitiveness Project, Eurasia Competitiveness Project, Organisation for Economic Co-operation and Development, Paris, October 2012.

OECD. *The Bioeconomy to 2030, Designing a Policy Agenda; Main Findings, and Policy Conclusions*. Paris: Organisation for Economic Co-operation and Development, 2009.

OECD. "Foreign Direct Investment in Kazakhstan." In *OECD Investment Policy Reviews: Kazakhstan 2012*. Paris: OECD Publishing, 2012.

OECD. *The Impact of the Newly Industrializing Countries on Production and Trade in Manufactures*. Paris: Organisation for Economic Co-operation and Development, Paris, 1979.

OECD. *The Jobs Study*. Paris: OECD Publishing, 1999.

OECD. "Kazakhstan Regional Competitiveness Report: Atyrau Oblast." Third Working Group Report on Atyrau, Central Asia Initiative, Organisation for Economic Co-operation and Development, Astana, December 11, 2012.

OECD. *OECD Investment Policy Reviews: Kazakhstan 2012*. Paris: OECD Publishing, 2012.

OECD. "OECD Programme for International Student Assessment (PISA)." OECD. Accessed July 25, 2013. http://www.oecd.org/pisa/.

OECD. *OECD Review of Agricultural Policies: Kazakhstan 2013*. Paris: OECD Publishing, 2013.

OECD. *Recommendation of the Council on Regulatory Policy and Governance.* Paris: Organisation for Economic Co-operation and Development, 2012.

OECD. "Second Round of Monitoring: Kazakhstan." Monitoring Report, Istanbul Anti-Corruption Action Plan, Anti-Corruption Network for Europe and Central Asia, Anti-Corruption Division, Directorate for Financial and Enterprise Affairs, Organisation for Economic Co-operation and Development, Paris, September 29, 2011.

OECD. *Ten Years of Water Sector Reform in Eastern Europe, Caucasus, and Central Asia*. Paris: OECD Publishing, 2011.

OECD. *Tools for Delivering on Green Growth*. Paris: Organisation for Economic Co-operation and Development, 2011.

OECD. *Towards Green Growth: A Summary for Policymakers*. Paris: Organisation for Economic Co-operation and Development, 2011.

OECD. *Trends Shaping Education.* Paris: OECD Publishing, 2008.

OECD. "Working Party on State Ownership and Privatisation Practices: The Size and Composition of the SOE Sector in OECD Countries." Corporate Governance Committee, Directorate for Financial and Enterprise Affairs, Organisation for Economic Co-operation and Development, Paris, May 13, 2011.

OECD and FAO. *OECD – FAO Agricultural Outlook 2012-2021*. Paris: OECD Publishing, 2012.

OECD and World Bank. *Review of National Policies for Education: Higher Education in Kazakhstan*. Paris: OECD and World Bank, 2007.

Office of Management and Budget. *Draft 20112 Report to Congress on the Benefits and Cost of Federal Regulation and Unfunded Mandates on State, Local, and Tribal Entities*. Washington, DC: Executive Office of the President, March 2012.

Office of the Gene Technology Regulator. "Fact Sheet—GM Wheat Field Trial Approvals." Department of Health and Ageing, Australian Government. Published September 2012. http://www.ogtr.gov.au/internet/ogtr/publishing.nsf/content/gmwheatfactsheetSep2012-htm.

Pettis, Michael. *The Great Rebalancing: Trade, Conflict, and the Perilous Road Ahead for the World Economy.* Princeton: Princeton University Press, 2013.

Peyrouse, Sebastien. "The Kazakh Neopatrimonial Regime: Balancing Uncertainties among the 'Family', Oligarchs, and Technocrats." *Demokratizatsiya: The Journal of Post-Soviet Democratization* 20, no. 4 (2012): 345-370.

Peyrouse, Sebastien. "Military Cooperation between China and Central Asia: Breakthrough, Limits and Prospects." *China Brief* 10, no. 5 (March 5, 2010): 10-14.

Piermartini, Roberta, and Linda Rousova (2008). "Liberalization of Air Transport Services and Passenger Traffic." Staff Working Paper ERSD-2008-06, Economic Research and Statistics Division, World Trade Organization. Geneva: December 2008.

Pinker, Steven. *The Better Angels of Our Nature: Why Violence Has Declined.* New York: Viking, 2011.

Plekhanov, Alexander, and Asel Isakova. "Region-Specific Constraints to Doing Business: Evidence from Russia." EBRD Working Paper 125, European Bank for Reconstruction, London, March 2011.

Pomfret, Richard. *The Central Asian Economies since Independence.* Princeton, NJ: Princeton University Press, 2006.

Pomfret, Richard. *East Asian Regionalism: Why Has It Flourished since 2000 and How Far Will It Go?* Singapore: World Scientific, 2011.

Pomfret, Richard. *The Economies of Central Asia.* Princeton, NJ: Princeton University Press, 1995.

Pomfret, Richard. *The Economics of Regional Trading Arrangements*. Oxford: Oxford University Press, 1997.

Pomfret, Richard. "Kazakhstan's Agriculture after Two Decades of Independence." Central Asia Economic Paper. No. 6, Central Asia Program, Elliot School of International Affairs, George Washington University, Washington, DC, January 2013.

Pomfret, Richard. "Regional Integration in Central Asia." *Economic Change and Restructuring* 42, nos. 1-2 (May 2009): 47-68.

Pomfret, Richard. "The Secret of the EMS's Longevity." *Journal of Common Market Studies* 29, no. 6 (December 1991): 623-33.

Pomfret, Richard, and Patricia Sourdin. "Why Do Trade Costs Vary?" *Review of World Economics* 146, no. 4 (December 2010): 709-30.

Posner, Daniel N. "Measuring Ethnic Fractionalization in Africa." *American Journal of Political Science* 48, no. 4 (October 2004): 849-63.

Potsdam Institute for Climate Impact Research and Climate Analytics. *Turn Down the Heat: Why a 4 °C Warmer World Must be Avoided*. Washington, DC: World Bank, 2012.

Property Rights Alliance. "2012 Report: International Property Rights Index." Property Rights Alliance. Published 2012. http://www.internationalpropertyrightsindex.org/ranking.

PRWeb. "Lucintel Estimates Waste Management and Remediations Services Market to Reach US $263 Billion in 2017." PRWeb. Published August 19, 2012. http://www.prweb.com/releases/prweb2012/prweb9794278.htm.

Quammen, David. *Spillover: Animal Infections and the Next Human Pandemic.* New York: Norton, 2012.

Raballand, Gaël. "Determinants of the Negative Impact of Being Landlocked on Trade: An Empirical Investigation through the Central Asian Case." *Comparative Economic Studies* 45, no. 4 (December 2003): 520-36.

Ramajo, Julian, Miguel Marquez, Geoffrey J.D. Hewings, and Maria M. Salinas (2008). "Spatial Heterogeneity and Interregional Spillovers in the European Union: Do Cohesion Policies Encourage Convergence across Regions?" *European Economic Review* 52 (2008): 551–567. doi: 10.1016/j.euroecorev.2007.05.006.

Randers, Jorgen. *2052: A Global Forecast for the Next 40 Years*. White River Junction, VT: Chelsea Green, 2012.

Razavi, Hossein. "Effect of Uncertainty on Oil Extraction Decisions." *Journal of Economic Dynamics and Control* 5 (February 1983): 359-370. doi: 10.1016/0165-1889(83)90030-1.

Reporters without Borders. *Press Freedom Index 2011-2012*. Paris: Reporters without Borders, 2012.

Republic of Kazakhstan. "National Program for Health Care Reform and Development 'Salmatty Kazakhstan'." Government Decree 1113. 2010.

Republic of Kazakhstan. "Program of the Development of Mono Cities for the Period 2012-2020." Government Decree. May 25, 2012.

Riboud, Michelle. "A Taxonomy of Youth Employment Interventions." IEG, World Bank, Washinton, DC, 2012.

Rifkin, Jeremy. *The Third Industrial Revolution*. New York: Palgrave Macmillan, 2011.

Roberts, Dexter, Henry Meyer, and Dorothee Tschampa. "The Silk Railroad of China-Europe Trade." Bloomberg Business Week. Published December 20, 2012. http://www.businessweek.com/articles/2012-12-20/the-silk-railroad-of-china-europe-trade.

Rockstrom, Jack, Will Steffen, Kevin Noone, et al. "A Safe Operating Space for Humanity." Nature 461 (September 24, 2009): 472-475. doi: 10.1038/461472a.

Rodrik, Dani, Arvind Subramaniam, and Francesco Trebbi (2002). "Institutions Rule: The Primacy of Institutions over Geography and Integration in Economic Development." NBER Working Paper 9305, National Bureau of Economic Research, Cambridge, MA, 2002.

Romer, Paul M. "Should the Government Subsidize Supply or Demand in the Market for Scientists and Engineers?" In *Innovation Policy and the Economy*, Volume 1, 221-252. Cambridge: MIT Press, 2001.

Roxburgh, Charles, Susan Lund, and John Piotrowski. *Mapping Global Capital Markets 2011.* McKinsey Global Institute, August 2011.

Ruby, Alan. "Design and Implementation of Education Reform in Post Soviet Kazakhstan: A Beta Testing Strategy?" October, 2012.

Rumelt, Richard P. *Good Strategy, Bad Strategy: The Difference and Why It Matters.* New York: Crown Business, 2011.

Rutkowski, Jan. "The Size and Profile of Informal Employment in Kazakhstan." In *Promoting Formal Employment in Kazakhstan*, 3-11. Washington, DC: World Bank, May 2011.

Sachs, Jeffrey D. and Andrew M. Warner. "Sources of Slow Growth in African Economies." *Journal of African Economies* 6, no. 3 (1997): 335-376.

Salmi, Jamil. "Attracting Talent in a Global Academic World: How Emerging Research Universities Can Benefit From Brain Circulation." *The Academic Executive Brief* 2, no. 1 (2012): 2-5.

Saxena, Naresh C., and Dipa Singh Bagai. "The Singapore Success Story." Capacity is Development, Global Event Working Paper, United Nations Development Program, New York, 2010.

Schultz, Theodore W. "The Value of the Ability to Deal with Disequilibria." *The Journal of Economic Literature* 13, no. 3 (September 1975): 827-46.

Schwab, Klaus. *The Global Competitiveness Report: 2012-2013.* Geneva: World Economic Forum, 2012.

Shepotylo, Oleksandr, and David Tarr. "Impact of WTO Accession and the Customs Union on the Bound and Applied Tariff Rates of the Russian Federation." Policy Research Working Paper 6161, Poverty Reduction and Economic Management Unit, Europe and Central Asia Region, and Trade and Integration Team, Development Research Group, World Bank, Washington, DC, August 2012.

Shirley, Mary M. *Institutions and Development*. Northampton, MA: Edward Elgar, 2008.

Shleifer, Andrei. "Discussion of Institutions." Nobel Symposium on Growth and Development, Stockholm, September 4, 2012.

Silitski, Vitali. "The 2010 Russia-Belarus-Kazakhstan Customs Union A Classic Case of *Prinuzhdenie k Druzhbe* (Friendship Enforcement)." PONARS Eurasia Policy Memo No. 110, PONARS Eurasia, 2010.

Simon, Hermann. *Hidden Champions*. Berlin: Springer-Verlag, 2009.

Singh, Jas, Dilip R. Limaye, Brian Henderson, and Xiaoyu Shi. *Public Procurement of Energy Efficiency Services: Lessons from International Experience*. Washington, DC: World Bank, 2010.

Slater, Helen, Neil Davies, and Simon Burgess. "Do Teachers Matter? Measuring Teacher Effectiveness in England." CMPO Working Paper No. 09/212, Centre for Market and Public Organisation, Bristol Institute of Public Affairs, University of Bristol, Bristol, January 2009.

Smolka, Martim O. "Implementing Land Value Capture in Latin America: Policies and Tools for Urban Development." Cambridge, MA: Lincoln Institute of Land Policy, 2013.

Socor, Vladimir. "At Present, We Can Assess Kazakhstan as a Success Story in the Making." Third Panel, Kazakhstan – USA: 20 Years of Partnership for Security and Development Conference, Astana, May 18, 2012.

Sourdin, Patricia, and Richard Pomfret. *Trade Facilitation: Defining, Measuring, Explaining, and Reducing the Cost of International Trade.* Cheltenham, UK: Edward Elgar, 2012.

Subramanian, Arvind. *Eclipse: Living in the Shadow of China's Economic Dominance*. Washington DC: Peterson Institute of International Economics, 2011.

Suzuki, Hiroaki, Robert Cervero, and Kanako luchi. *Transforming Cities with Transit: Transit and Land-Use Integration for Sustainable Urban Development*. Washington, DC: World Bank, 2012.

Tan, Jee-Peng, and Yoo-Jeung Joy Nam. "Pre-Employment Technical and Vocational Education and Training: Fostering Relevance, Effectiveness, and Efficiency." In *The Right Skills for the Job? Rethinking Effective Training Policies for Workers*, edited by Rita Almeida, Jere Behrman, and David Robalino, 67-103. Washington, DC: World Bank, 2011.

Tay, Janet. Public Service Reforms in Singapore. New York: United Nations Development Programme, 1999.

Taylor, Timothy. "Next Stage for China's Economy." Conversable Economist. Published March 6, 2013. http://conversableeconomist.blogspot.com/2013/03/next-stage-for-chinas-economy.html.

Tengri News. "Samruk-Kazyna to Exit BTA Bank, Alliance Bank and Temirbank: Nazarbayev." Tengri News. February 4, 2013. http://en.tengrinews.kz/politics_sub/Samruk-Kazyna-to-exit-BTA-Bank-Alliance-Bank-and-Temirbank-Nazarbayev-16656.

Thurmond, Michael. *Natural Disaster Risks in Central Asia: A Synthesis*. New York: Bureau for Crisis Prevention and Recovery, United Nations Development Programme, 2011.

Truman, Edwin M. "A Blueprint for Sovereign Wealth Fund Best Practices." Policy Brief 08-3, Peterson Institute for International Economics, Washington, DC, April 2008.

Truman, Edwin M. *Sovereign Wealth Funds: Threat or Salvation?* Washington, DC: Peterson Institute for International Economics, 2010.

Tumbarello, Patrizia. "Regional Trade Integration and WTO Accession: Which Is the Right Sequencing? An Application to the CIS." IMF Working Paper WP/05/94, International Monetary Fund, Washington, DC, February 2005.

UN. "UNcomtrade." United Nations Commodity Trade Statistics Division. Last updated 2010. http://comtrade.un.org/db/.

UN. *United Nations Framework Convention on Climate Change*. New York: United Nations, 1992.

UN. *World Economic and Social Survey 2011: The Great Green Technological Transformation*. New York: United Nations, 2011.

UN. *World Urbanization Prospects: The 2011 Revision Highlights*. New York: United Nations, 2012.

UN Conference on Sustainable Development. *The Future We Want*. Rio de Janeiro: United Nations, June 2012.

UNCTAD. *World Investment Report 2011*. Geneva: United Nations, 2011.

UNCTAD. *World Investment Report 2012: Towards a New Generation of Investment Policies*. New York: United Nations, 2012.

UN Country Team in Kazakhstan. *Post 2015: The Future We Want; National Consultations in Kazakhstan*. New York: United States, 2013.

UNDP. "Decentralization in the Europe and CIS Region." Discussion Paper, Democratic Governance Practice, United Nations Development Programme Bratislava Regional Centre, Bratislava, April 2008.

UNDP. *Millennium Development Goals in Kazakhstan*. New York: United Nations Development Programme, 2010.

UNDP. *National Human Development Report: Climate Change and Its Impact on Kazakhstan's Human Development*. New York: United Nations Development Programme, 2008.

UNDP and CIS. *Central Asia Human Development Report: Bringing Down Barriers; Regional Cooperation for Human Development and Human Security.* Bratislava: UNDP Regional Bureau for Europe and the Commonwealth of Independent States, 2005.

UNDP and ECHO. *Assessment of Disaster Risk Reduction Capacities in Kazakhstan, Kyrgyzstan, and Tajikistan.* Almaty: United Nations Development Programme in Kazakhstan and Humanitarian Aid Department of the European Commission, 2011.

UNDP in Kazakhstan. "Kazakhstan's Judicial System of was Assessed." United Nations Development Programme in Kazakhstan. July 13, 2012. http://www.undp.kz/en/articles/1/194.jsp.

UNECE. "Environmental Performance Reviews: Kazakhstan; Second Review." Environmental Performance Reviews Series No. 27 ECE/CEP/142, Committee on Environmental Policy, Economic Commission for Europe, United Nations, New York and Geneva, 2008.

UNECE. *Innovation Performance Review of Kazakhstan.* New York and Geneva: United Nations, 2012.

UNEP. *Towards a Green Economy: Pathways to Sustainable Development and Poverty Eradication.* Nairobi: United Nations Environment Programme, 2011.

UN Global Compact and IUCN. *A Framework for Corporate Action on Biodiversity and Ecosystem Services.* UN Global Compact and the International Union for Conservation of Nature, 2012.

UNODC. *Global Study on Homicide 2011.* Vienna: United Nations Office on Drugs and Crime, 2011.

USAID. *Kazakhstan Regional Disparities: Economic Performance by Oblast.* Washington, DC: United States Agency for International Development, May 2006.

van Ark, Bart, and Charles Hulten. "Innovation, Intangibles, and Economic Growth: Towards a Comprehensive Account of the Knowledge Economy." Conference on "Productivity and Innovation," Statistics Sweden, Saltsjobaden, Sweden, October 24-25, 2007.

van der Ploeg, Frederick. "Natural Resources: Curse or Blessing?" *Journal of Economic Literature* 49, no. 2 (May 2011): 366-420. doi: 10.1257/jel.49.2.366.

Vandenbussche, Jérôme, Philippe Aghion, and Costas Meghir. "Growth, Distance to Frontier and Composition of Human Capital." *Journal of Economic Growth* 11, no. 2 (2006): 97-127.

Vassilieva, Yelena. "Program on Development of Biotechnology in Russia through 2020." GAIN Report R1239, Global Agricultural Information Network, Foreign Agricultural Services, US Department of Agriculture, Moscow, June 8, 2012.

Vegas, Emiliana, and Ilana Umansky. *Improving Teaching and Learning through Effective Incentives: What Can We Learn from Education Reforms in Latin America?* Washington, DC: World Bank, 2005.

Veugelers, Reinhilde. "The World Innovation Landscape: Asia Rising?" Bruegel Policy Contribution No. 02, Brussels, February 2013.

Viner, Jacob. *The Customs Union Issue.* New York: Carnegie Endowment for International Peace, 1950.

Vinokurov, Evgeny, and Alexander Libman. *Eurasian Integration: Challenges of Transcontinental Regionalism.* London: Palgrave MacMillan, 2012.

Vitaliy, G. Salnikov, and Marat A. Karatayev. "The Impact of Air Pollution on Human Health: Focusing on the Rudnyi Altay Industrial Area." *American Journal of Environmental Sciences* 7, no. 3 (2011): 286-294. doi: 10.3844/ajessp.2011.286.294.

Voloshin, Georgiy. "Kazakhstani Authorities Issue Worrying Macroeconomic Statistics." CACI Analyst. Published May 15, 2013. http://www.cacianalyst.org/publications/field-reports/item/12734-kazakhstani-authorities-issue-worrying-macroeconomic-authorities.html.

Waldrop, Mitchell M. "Online Learning: Campus 2.0." *Nature* 495 (March 2013): 160-163.

Waste Management Inc. "Waste Management Inc. Environmental Policy." Waste Management Inc. Published March 7, 1990. http://actrav.itcilo.org/actrav-english/telearn/global/ilo/code/waste.htm.

Webber, Mark. *CIS Integration Trends: Russia and the Former Soviet South.* London and Washington, DC: The Royal Institute of International Affairs and Brookings Institution, 1997.

WHO. *The European Health Report: Where We Are.* Geneva: World Health Organization. 2012.

WHO. *The World Health Report*. Geneva: World Health Organization. 2010.

WHO Regional Office for Europe. "European Health for All Database." World Health Organization. Updated January 2013. http://data.euro.who.int/hfadb/.

Wike, Richard, and Kathleen Holzwart. "Where Trust is High, Crime and Corruption Are Low: Since Communism's Fall, Social Trust has Fallen in Eastern Europe." Pew Global Attitudes Project. Published April 15, 2008. http://www.pewglobal.org/2008/04/15/where-trust-is-high-crime-and-corruption-are-low/.

Wind Energy. "Wind Data." Published in 2013. http://www.windenergy.kz/vetrovye_dannye.html.

Wolf, Martin. "Why China's Economy Might Topple." Financial Times. Published April 2, 2013. http://www.ft.com/intl/cms/s/0/e854f8a8-9aed-11e2-97ad-00144feabdc0.html#axzz2PQbey2i7.

World Bank. "Assessment of the Costs and Benefits of the Customs Union for Kazakhstan." World Bank Report 65977-KZ, World Bank, Washington, DC, January 2012.

World Bank. "A Diagnosis of Colombia's National M&E System, SINERGIA." ECD Working Paper No. 17, Independent Evaluation Group, World Bank, Washington, DC, February 2007.

World Bank. *Cost of Pollution in China: Economic Estimates of Physical Damages*. Washington, DC: World Bank, 2007.

World Bank. "Country Partnership Strategy for the Republic of Kazakhstan for the Period FY12-FY17." Report No. 67876-KZ, World Bank and International Finance Corporation, Washington, DC, March 30, 2012.

World Bank. "Development of Clean Energy." Draft Report, World Bank, Washington, DC, 2013.

World Bank. *Doing Business 2013: Smarter Regulations for Small and Medium-Size Enterprises.* Washington, DC: World Bank 2012.

World Bank. "Dimensions of Poverty in Kazakhstan." 2 vols. Report No. 30294–KZ. Poverty Reduction and Economic Management Unit, Europe and Central Asia Region, World Bank, November 9, 2004.

World Bank. "Education Quality and Equity in Kazakhstan: Analysis of the PISA 2009 Data." Human Development Sector Unit, Europe and Central Asia Region, World Bank, Washington, DC, 2012.

World Bank. *Fighting Corruption in Public Services: Chronicling Georgia's Reforms*. Washington, DC: World Bank 2012.

World Bank. "Improving the Quality of Life for All Kazakhstani People Through Skills and Good Jobs for Development." Interim Report under the JERP, Human Development Sector Unit, Europe and Central Asia Region, World Bank, Washington, DC, 2013.

World Bank. "Kazakhstan, Country Economic Memorandum." Report No. 10976-KK, World Bank, Washington, DC, November 1992.

World Bank. "Kazakhstan: Reforming the Last Resort Safety Net Program in an Upper-Middle Income Country." Report No. 62551-KZ. Human Development Sector Unit, Europe and Central Asia Region, World Bank, Washington, DC, 2011.

World Bank. "Kazakhstan: Taking Advantage of Trade and Openness for Development." No. 76339, Poverty Reduction and Economic Management Unit, Europe and Central Asia Region, World Bank Washington, DC. July 10, 2012.

World Bank. *Kazakhstan: Targeting Development Transfers*. Washington, DC: World Bank, October 9, 2012.

World Bank. "Modern Companies, Healthy Environment: Improving Industrial Competitiveness through Potential of Cleaner and Greener Production." No. 70471, World Bank, Washington, DC, July 2012.

World Bank. "Pension System and Options for Reform." JERP Technical Note, Human Development Sector Unit, Europe and Central Asia Region, World Bank, Washington, DC, 2012.

World Bank. "Republic of Kazakhstan Regional Development Fund: Options and Alternatives." Presentation to JERP, World Bank, Washington, DC.

World Bank. "Student Assessment System Policy Note: Kazakhstan 2012." SABER Policy Note, Human Development Network, World Bank, Washington, DC, 2012.

World Bank. "Technical and Vocational Education Modernization Project." Project Appraisal Document. Report No. 50768-KZ, World Bank, Washington, DC, 2010.

World Bank. "World DataBank." World Bank. Last modified April 16, 2013. http://databank.worldbank.org/data / home.aspx.

World Bank. *World Development Report 2012*. Washington, DC: World Bank, 2011.

World Bank. *World Development Report 2013: Jobs*. Washington, DC: World Bank, 2013.

World Bank. *World Development Report: Reshaping Economic Geography*. Washington, DC: World Bank, 2008.

World Bank. "Worldwide Governance Indicators Project." World Bank. Accessed July 22, 2013. http://info.world-bank.org/governance/wgi/index.asp. 2012.

World Bank and Development Research Center of the State Council, People's Republic of China. *China 2030*. Washington, DC: World Bank, 2013.

World Bank and EBRD. "Business Environment and Enterprise Performance Survey (BEEPS)." World Bank. Accessed July 22, 2013. http://web.worldbank.org/WBSITE/EXTERNAL/COUNTRIES/ECAEXT/0,,contentMDK:22587588~pagePK:146736~piPK:146830~theSitePK:258599,00.html#reports. 2009.

World Coal Association. "Underground Coal Gasification." World Coal Association. Accessed July 18, 2013. http://www.worldcoal.org/coal/uses-of-coal/underground-coal-gasification/.

Yusuf, Shahid, and Kaoru Nabeshima. *Post-Industrial East Asian Cities*. Washington, DC: Stanford University Press, 2006.

Yusuf, Shahid and Kaoru Nabeshima. *Some Small Countries Do It Better: Rapid Growth and Its Causes in Singapore, Finland, and Ireland*. Washington D.C.: World Bank, 2012.

Ziesing, Hans-Joachim. "Scenarios of Power Demand and Supply for Kazakhstan: A View from Outside." Presentation at the 13th Annual Meeting of the Reform Group "Energy and Climate Policy—Towards a Low Carbon Future," Salzburg, Austria, September 18, 2008.

Zinnes, Clifford. *Tournament Approaches to Policy Reform: Making Development Assistance More Effective*. Washington, DC: Brookings Institution Press, 2009.

About the Editors and Authors

Editors

Aktoty Aitzhanova

Aktoty Aitzhanova is a deputy chairperson at the JSC National Analytical Centre of the Nazarbayev University, coordinating the departments of economic strategies and strategic and corporate development. She worked as the adviser to the Deputy Prime Minister of Republic of Kazakhstan. She also worked at the Statistical Agency of the Republic of Kazakhstan, the Institute for Geopolitical Studies and International Relations, as well as in other private consulting companies. She holds an MSc in innovation and enterpreneurship from the University of Exeter (UK). For the undergraduate degrees, she studied at Milan Catholic University of Sacro Cuore (Italy) and the Gumilyev Eurasian National University (Kazakhstan).

Shigeo Katsu

Shigeo Katsu is President of Nazarbayev University. He joined the World Bank as a Young Professional in 1979. In 1985, he was appointed the Bank's Resident Representative in Benin until fall 1989. Between fall 1989 and the end of 1991, Mr. Katsu was seconded to the Export-Import Bank of Japan as Deputy Director, Country Economic Policy Analysis Department. Between 1992 and 1995, Mr. Katsu served as Principal Operations Officer for the Industry & Energy Operations Division, China Department, East Asia & Pacific Region, and subsequently was appointed Chief, and then Country Director, of the Bank's Regional Mission in Abidjan, Côte d'Ivoire. Mr. Katsu assumed the position of Regional Director, Operations in 1999 where his responsibilities broadly consisted of assisting in the management of the ECA Region's operations and serving as the Regional Liaison with the corporate center. In August 2003 he became Vice President of the ECA Region, where he served in this capacity for six years. He subsequently took on an assignment as Special Advisor to the Managing Directors of the World Bank and retired from the World Bank in December 2009.

Johannes F. Linn

Johannes F. Linn is a Senior Resident Scholar at the Emerging Markets Forum and a nonresident Senior Fellow at the Brookings Institution in Washington, DC. During his 30-year career at the World Bank, he held senior positions, including Vice President for Financial Policy and Resource Mobilization and Vice President for Europe and Central Asia. A collection of his speeches were published under the title *Transition Years—Reflections on Economic Reform and Social Change in Europe and Central Asia* (World Bank, 2004). In 2004/5, he was the lead author of the United Nations Development Program's *Central Asia Human Development Report*. He recently edited (with Werner Hermann) the volume *Central Asia and the Caucasus: At the Crossroads of Eurasia in the 21st Century*.

373

Vladislav Yezhov

Vladislav Yezhov is Chairman of the Executive Board of the National Analytical Center, JSC, of Nazarbayev University. He started his career at the Ministry of Finance, where he worked for 7 years, and went on to serve as deputy head of the Social and Economic Analysis Division of the Presidential Administration, head of the Macroeconomic Analysis and Program Monitoring Division in the Prime Minister's Office, and Adviser to the Chairman of the Executive Council of Nazarbayev University. He graduated as an economist from the Kazakh State Academy of Management in Almaty and later attended several executive training courses at a number of universities abroad.

Authors

William Y. Brown

Bill Brown is a scientist and lawyer with a distinguished career in government, non-profit institutions, and the private sector where he has provided leadership for environmental issues and scientific and cultural institutions. He is currently a nonresident Senior Fellow at the Brookings Institution, where he is writing on environment and culture and pursuing projects including development assistance for Kazakhstan and Libya, global strategy for DNA banking, and the interaction of small hydropower and migratory fish. He previously served as the Science Advisor to Bill Clinton's Secretary of the Interior Bruce Babbitt, Assistant Professor of Biological Sciences at Mount Holyoke College, and as President and CEO of numerous research and scientific organizations, ranging from the Woods Hole Research Center to the Bishop Museum of Hawaii. He holds a PhD in zoology from the University of Hawaii and a JD from Harvard Law School.

Dennis de Tray

Following a 12-year stint at the RAND Corporation, Dennis de Tray joined the World Bank's Research Department in 1983. He was appointed the Bank's Research Administrator in 1987 and moved to the Bank's operations complex in 1992. His last assignments at the Bank were as Country Director for Indonesia and then Central Asia. He is now a principal with the Results for Development Institute and Adviser to the President, Nazarbayev University, Kazakhstan. His recent work has included advising the US military, the governments of Kazakhstan and East Timor, and the Aga Khan Development Network. In 2008 he was a member of an Iraq Governance Assessment Team set up by General Petraeus, and in 2010 he worked with the 173rd Airborne Brigade to develop a governance and development program in Afghanistan's Logar and Wardak Provinces. Dr. de Tray has lived in Pakistan, Indonesia, Vietnam, and Kazakhstan. He holds a PhD in economics from the University of Chicago.

Harpaul Alberto Kohli

Harpaul Alberto Kohli is the Manager of Information Analytics at Centennial Group International and the Emerging Markets Forum, where he is responsible for all modeling, statistics, databases, and technology management. He earned a degree with honors in mathematics and philosophy from Harvard University, where he served as co-president of both the Society of Physics Students and the Math Club and was elected a class vice president for life. He earned his MBA at Georgetown University, with emphases on psychology and on financial markets and public policy. He is also a Microsoft Certified Technology Specialist. Prior to joining Centennial, he served as a teacher in prisons in Ecuador and Massachusetts, a researcher at UBS and in the US Congress, a field organizer for the 2004 American general election, and a communications staffer for the Wesley Clark Presidential primary campaign.

John Nellis

John Nellis is a Senior Adviser to the Development Portfolio Management Group (DPMG) at the University of Southern California. Over a long career as an analyst and consultant with the World Bank, the Ford Foundation, numerous national governments, and several universities, research institutes, and think-tanks in the United States, Canada, Tunisia, and Kenya, he has conceived, implemented, managed, and evaluated socio-economic development operations in more than 50 countries in Africa (including North Africa), Asia, Latin America, and the formerly socialist states in Europe and Central Asia, specializing in monitoring and evaluation of projects in public sector economics and management, privatization, and private sector development. He is the author of more than 60 articles and books on development issues. He holds a PhD in political economy from the Maxwell School of Syracuse University.

Richard Pomfret

Richard Pomfret is Professor of Economics at Adelaide University and Visiting Professor at the Johns Hopkins Bologna Centre. Previously, he has worked at Johns Hopkins' campuses in Nanjing, China and Washington, DC, along with universities in Canada and Germany. He is also currently working as a consultant to the OECD and World Bank on projects related to agriculture in Kazakhstan. His research interests center on economic development and international economics, and he has published more than 100 papers and 21 books in these fields. His most recent book, *The Age of Equality: The Twentieth Century in Economic Perspective*, was published by Harvard University Press.

Hossein Razavi

Hossein Razavi is the former Director of the Infrastructure Department of the World Bank. During his 23-year tenure at the World Bank he held a number of professional and managerial positions including the Director of Infrastructure and Energy Department, Director of Private Sector Development Department, and the Chief of Oil and Gas Division. A long-time consultant and author on infrastructure, environmental issues, and private sector development, Dr. Razavi is well-known in the international financial community for his pioneering work on structuring financial vehicles suitable to the energy and infrastructure operations. Dr. Razavi holds an MS in engineering and a PhD in economics. He serves on the editorial boards of the *Energy Journal* and *Energy Economics*.

Michelle Riboud

Michelle Riboud is an economist who started her professional career working in academia, serving at the University of Abidjan, a Spanish research institute, the University of Orleans, and the Institute d'Etudes Politiques in Paris, along with a visiting role at the University of Chicago. In late 1988, she joined the World Bank, working on education, labor market, and social protection issues, first in Latin America and then the former Soviet Union and South Asia. In her last assignment, she was responsible for analytical work and lending portfolio in education in Afghanistan, Pakistan, Bangladesh, India, Nepal, Bhutan, and Sri Lanka. She holds a bachelor's degree and a doctorate degree in economics from the University of Paris I, as well as a master's degree and a PhD in economics from the University of Chicago.

Shahid Yusuf

Shahid Yusuf is currently Chief Economist of The Growth Dialogue at the George Washington University School of Business in Washington, DC. Prior to joining the Growth Dialogue, Dr. Yusuf was on the staff of the World Bank, leading the World Bank-Japan project on East Asia's Future Economy from 2000-2009 and directing numerous other East Asia-oriented projects. Dr. Yusuf has written extensively on development issues, with a special focus on East Asia and has also published widely in various academic journals. He has authored or edited 27 books on industrial and urban development, innovation systems, and tertiary education. He holds a PhD in economics from Harvard University and a BA in economics from Cambridge University.

Index

Photo Credits